The Cultural Context of Aging

The Cultural Context of Aging

Worldwide Perspectives

Fourth Edition

Jay Sokolovsky, Editor

An Imprint of ABC-CLIO, LLC

Santa Barbara, California • Denver, Colorado

Library of Congress Cataloging-in-Publication Data

Names: Sokolovsky, Jay, editor.
Title: The cultural context of aging : worldwide perspectives / Jay Sokolovsky, editor.
Description: Fourth edition. | Santa Barbara, California : Praeger, [2020] |
    Includes bibliographical references and index.
Identifiers: LCCN 2019057357 (print) | LCCN 2019057358 (ebook) |
    ISBN 9781440852015 (cloth) | ISBN 9781440858260 (paperback) |
    ISBN 9781440852022 (ebook)
Subjects: LCSH: Older people—Cross-cultural studies. | Aging—Cross-cultural studies.
Classification: LCC HQ1061 .C79 2020 (print) | LCC HQ1061 (ebook) |
    DDC 305.26—dc23
LC record available at https://lccn.loc.gov/2019057357
LC ebook record available at https://lccn.loc.gov/2019057358

ISBN: 978-1-4408-5201-5 (hardcover)
        978-1-4408-5826-0 (paperback)
        978-1-4408-5202-2 (ebook)

24 23 22 21 20   1 2 3 4 5

This book is also available as an eBook.

Praeger
An Imprint of ABC-CLIO, LLC

ABC-CLIO, LLC
147 Castilian Drive
Santa Barbara, California 93117
www.abc-clio.com

This book is printed on acid-free paper ∞

Manufactured in the United States of America

To my newly born great-granddaughter Jamie and the wonderful grandchildren Josephine, Alex, Natalie, and Zemanel who have enriched my life and taught me so much.

Contents

Preface

As I move into my seventies and retirement from my academic position looms, it has been both a time of introspection mixed with "OK, what comes next?" It is amazing to think that it is 30 years since the first edition of the *Cultural Context of Aging* was published. Over this time there has been an emergence of a truly expansive anthropology of aging. Over these three decades there has been a monumental growth of interest in global aging as it has begun to impact all parts of our planet and has drawn the attention of the United Nations, the World Health Organization, and increasingly the national bureaucracies of nations including Mexico, Ghana, Thailand, and China. Previously, in those countries government officials and citizens would have been insulted by outsiders questioning if their family systems were up to dealing with older persons in their borders. As seen in the chapters dealing with these countries, this has radically changed through the imperative of globalization, increased longevity, and reductions in fertility rates.

New to the Fourth Edition

Increasingly, the subject of aging and late life has appropriately been coupled with broad concerns of globalization, transnational migration, the life course, gender diversity, ethnicity, community organization, and new understandings of disability. All of these topics are reflected in this volume. I have continued a focus on three themes of culture spaces, cultural scripts, and elderscapes, and more than ever these ideas resonate in the book's chapters. More than half the chapters represent new, original research and touch on more varied places than previously, such as Ghana, Thailand, Romania, Denmark, and Tanzania. Also included are new topics such as successful aging, robotics, gender diversity, ethnic resistance to toxic environments, and new perspectives on disability, eldersourcing, cemeteries as ancestral landscapes of culture, and technologies for "aging in place." Throughout the book readers will find "Web Specials" and the highlighting of new research via "Programs to Follow."

These print chapters are supplemented by a greatly expanded Web Book, which contains not only key articles from previous editions but new pieces on intergenerational sites for care, urban workers in Peru, China's senior companion program, female mutual support in Uganda and Japan, several perspectives on eldercare in Italy, and an exciting new chapter on working across generations to redesign an urban environment. This is all supplemented by a substantial Web site providing links to all these resources and new ones as they emerge: https://www.culturalcontextofaging.com/.

This work would not have been possible without the constant support of my wife, anthropologist Maria Vesperi, who not only provided her professional level of editing skill but just as importantly was always there to cheer me on when I questioned why I was doing another edition of this large book. I would also like to thank Lukas Desjardins who gave vital editorial assistance and helped me track down many of the digital resources referenced in this volume. Thanks must also be sent to Dan Coffman, a former student who became a professional Web designer and has continued to guide the extensive book Web site. Of course special thanks to all the authors of this volume who have made this book a reality. Finally I would like to deeply thank two editors at ABC-CLIO, Debbie Carvalko and Robin Tutt, who have guided this book through its long passage to publication.

Introduction: A 21st-Century Global Perspective on Aging and Human Maturity in Cultural Context

Jay Sokolovsky

Working with elders around the world has taught me that those living in grass huts in Africa with children at their feet are often happier than people in assisted-living homes with a chandelier over their heads.

—Kiyota (2018)

Photo 01.1   An IPal Robot entertains Chinese nursing home residents. (Siyi Chen. "The Companion: Inside China's Experiment to Find Friends for 230 Million Old People." *Quartz*, https://www.youtube.com/watch?v=GerHcmvGM4E)

The picture preceding depicts a big experiment going on in China, but also in Japan, Britain, Denmark, and the United States. These nations are responding to our planet's new age of aging by seeing if robots of various sorts can provide both physical and emotional support to the exploding population of older adults who are rapidly outpacing the capacity of family- and community-based support systems to care for them. This singing, dancing, and chatting robot, called IPal, is a type of caregiving machine that focuses on companionship. Authors in Part II (David Prendergast), Part III (Iza Kavedžija), and Part VI (James Wright) will consider the implications of such technology in attempting to address some of the challenges societies face as their nations age rapidly and kin support networks decrease in size and geographical proximity. We will also consider the reality of the statement by Emi Kiyota, cocreator of Ibasho Cafes, in relation to technology, perceptions of aging well, and global transformations (Part V, Box V.1).

As our planet edges toward the 21st century's third decade, its people are confronted with an unprecedented transformation, the global aging of human populations. Across nations and regions we see the emergence of dynamic new *elderscapes* in the most unlikely places. Within China, India, Mexico, Italy, and especially Japan, with rapid fertility declines and large population cohorts surviving into late adulthood, a whole new matrix of generational relations, scripting of the life course, and emergent late life possibilities has blossomed (Lynch and Danley 2013; Silin 2018, Part II Kao and Albert). The photo on the previous page, set in China, is from a Web site and video titled "Inside China's Experiment to Find Friends for 230 Million Old People." It visually connects to salient issues of China's adaptation to rapid demographic aging (Part III Zhang), that nation's new Senior Companions Program (Part III Shea), the role of emergent technology in elder lives (Part II Prendergast), and the controversial use of senior care robots (Part VI Wright).

Such nations as China and Japan, with extraordinary levels of population aging, are also being forced to innovate new *cultural spaces* for its oldest citizens and to rethink how families and communities can be responsive along the span of life. For example, Iza Kavedžija in Part III shows how the

---

WEB SPECIAL:

Siyi Chen, "Inside China's Experiment to Find Friends for 230 Million Old People," https://www.youtube.com/watch?v=GerHcmvGM4E.

neighborhood she studied in urban Japan has seen the closing of kindergartens, while senior day-care centers, several chiropractic clinics, and an activist café run by senior volunteers have emerged. These developments were
part of creating a new narrative space for aging. Here and elsewhere in the
world, older adults are shaping different ways to think and talk about late
life, even within traditional societies. We will see this clearly in Part II where
Cati Coe uses her long-term work in Ghana to employ the idea of "age-
inscriptions" to explore newly imagined spaces beyond "normative" cultural
ideas about places to age. This idea of aging imaginaries in traditional societies is also taken up in Part III by Felicity Aulino as she explores the future
face of elderhood in Thailand. Clearly, in this era of a new longevity, people
are trying to "reimagine tomorrow" as Barnet and Rivers propose (2016), or
to imagine how ongoing, massive global migration is upending expected
scripts of the life course (Oxlund 2018).

Perceptions of aging itself seem to be maturing in many places with the
creation of a new life stage of late adulthood, identified not so much with
closeness to death but with productive and creative engagement with life
(Gurian 2013). The early manifestation of this shift came in the 1990s
when Western Europe realized the need to mount a public campaign to
promote "Active Aging" (Ney 2005). The rapid aging of its workforce has
added a new focus on remaining economically competitive by opening up
high-tech educational opportunities to older adults and discouraging early
retirement (see Part II Lynch). In 2007 the European Union initiated an
action plan called "Ageing Well in the Information Society," targeted at
improving the life of older people at home, in the workplace, and in society
in general.[1]

It is little wonder that many European news outlets have done major
reports about anthropologist Caitrin Lynch's research on "elder sourcing"
of employees in a medical needle facility in Massachusetts (2012; Part II).
Such ideas about extending the expected practices of adulthood in late life
have reverberated in some unlikely places, such as China, where the collapse of the communal system and reduced availability of filial support has
pushed elders to promote self-care as the key to healthy aging. When
anthropologist Hong Zhang returned to her homeland in 2018 (Part III),
she did not find elders waiting to be cared for by doting relatives. Instead
she encountered mass groups of aged people, flocking to urban parks where
they did tai chi, the waltz, and various other forms of exercise to help avoid
what they saw as a newly problematic dependence on family and state.
More recently, this has developed into a conflicted cultural movement as
older adult public performers blare their music while neighborhood residents assert their need for quiet by throwing water bottles down on the
dancers.

It's Not *Even* Your Mother's Old Age Anymore!

In the last edition of this book I emphasized that it is no longer your grandma's old age. Now, pushing deeper into the 21st century, it may no longer be your mother's *or even your own* expectation of old age. Serious global efforts, such as by Calico, Google's longevity research company, or Human Longevity Inc., seek to push the known boundaries of life by hacking the human genome to effectively achieve immortality (see Introduction, Part VI).

Some dramatic implications of this new millennium of aging are to be noted in the altered chances of persons in a given age cohort reaching 90 years of age. In the United States at the midpoint of the 20th century, a middle-aged woman had less than a 1 in 10 chance of living to age 90. But, as noted in Table 01.1, by the second decade of the 21st century the odds of 20-year-old females living into their ninth decade almost quadrupled, to near 40 percent. Consider the demographic changes expected in the coming decades. For example, according to Social Security Administration data, two-thirds of the children born in 2014 will live past 80 and one-third past 90, and almost 10 percent will live past the 100-year mark (Kiersz 2014). Andrew Scott helps us understand the changing perception of late life in another way: "In the US, a 75-year-old today has the same mortality rate as a 65-year-old in 1952. Similarly, in Japan, 80 is the 'new 65.' As an actuarial matter, then, today's 75-year-olds are not any older than the 65-year-olds of the 1950s" (2018).

Scientists now have a pretty good idea of how humans can live longer, healthier lives, and this is clearly more related to diet, lifestyle, and the environments people age into, rather than genetics (Li et al. 2018; Part VI Willcox et al.). A careful reading of the chapter by Craig Willcox et al. in Part VI of this book can reveal ways to improve your odds of living a longer, healthy life. The authors detail the research of the Okinawa Centenarian Project and the Blue Zones Project, documenting the lives of elders who live the longest on average and also enjoy the planet's highest healthy longevity. More immediately, you can go to https://www.livingto100.com/calculator and get a better sense of whether you will live to 100.

WEB SPECIAL:

Ester Bloom, "Google's Co-founders and Other Silicon Valley Billionaires Are Trying to Live Forever," https://www.cnbc.com/2017/03/31/google-co-founders-and-silicon-valley-billionaires-try-to-live-forever.html.

Table 01.1   Chances of a 20-year-old reaching various ages

Age	Probability of reaching this age (%)	
	Men	Women
30	98.9	99.6
40	97.5	98.7
50	94.9	97.1
60	90.3	93.9
70	80.1	86.3
80	60.3	70.4
90	27.3	39.6
100	3.4	7.5
110	0.1	0.3

Source: Andy Kiersz, "This Is When You're Going to Die," March 21, 2014, *Business Insider,* http://www.businessinsider.com/social-security-life-table-charts-2014-3.

Goals of This Book

A handful of nations including Japan and Italy lead the global aging pack, having grandly ushered in the new millennium with more elders than youths. As will be seen through new original research in this volume, such countries are struggling to both understand their unique situation and to find culturally appropriate answers to their all-too-rapidly maturing societies. We see in Figure 01.1 below that in the United States, this demographic reversal of youth and older adults will not occur even in the next decade, and so we have roughly 15 years to adapt to this reality (US Census 2018).

The Cultural Context of Aging will take readers into the heart of emerging new cultural spaces and provide an entrée point into your likely futures. Importantly, it is *not really about old age*, but the cultural context of later adulthood, its multiple pathways, and the connections with other parts of the life course. More than ever, people can explore how different nations are responding to the challenge with such resources as Helpage International's "The Global AgeWatch Index," which ranks countries by how well their older populations are faring on factors such as income security, health status, and enabling environments (http://www.helpage.org/global-agewatch).

It is the goal of this volume to pull together research addressing such concerns from a global, cross-cultural perspective. The following chapters explore three broad, interrelated facets of late adulthood: (1) how older adults

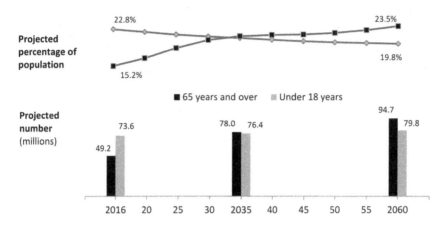

Note: 2016 data are estimates not projections

Figure 01.1   An Aging Nation: Projected Number of Children and Older Adults (U.S. Census 2018).

function as social actors in the settings of diverse societies; (2) how the intersection of culture and globalizing contexts creates increasingly varied ways of experiencing late adulthood; and (3) how we can take knowledge generated from answering the first two questions to find solutions for enhancing life across the life course, not just for those in late adulthood. In every corner of the world these questions are becoming connected to a new reality of what elderhood means and how it connects to the broader society. This global age of aging is catching the world's attention with, for example, the World Health Organization's Decade of Healthy Ageing Plan 2020–2030 (https://www.who .int/ageing/decade-of-healthy-ageing).

This edition of *The Cultural Context of Aging* includes enhanced digital materials, including innovative image-based and video-centered chapters and Web resources. These allow readers to see how anthropology and designers transform urban environments to meet multigenerational needs (Part V Martinez and Ozer); compare community engagement of elders in Papua New Guinea villages with North American RV encampments (Part V Counts and Counts); learn about the struggles of Peruvian elder workers (Part II Bonilla and Ratto); engage via multimedia the reality of elder life in urban Nepal and India (Part V Web Special Mandoki and Mayer); and examine in a video lecture the forefront of socially assistive robots (Part VI Web Special Nejat). With so many new Internet-based resources appearing almost daily, this book's support Web page will try to keep readers up-to-date on such developments at www.culturalcontextofaging.com.

Reimagining Tomorrow . . . Today

We can see in many places around the world not only a dissatisfaction with "aging as usual" but also efforts to craft new environments and social arrangements that address key issues along the life course. Within North American communities, innovative responses include Toronto's "8 to 80" Cities Plan (www.880cities.org) and New Life Village in Tampa, Florida (http://newlifevillage.org/), where foster children, adoptive families, and seniors acting as grandparents live together. Japan's Ibasho intergenerational cafés (Box V.1) and the European Union's TOY Project—Together, Old and Young—also seek to create intergenerational contact zones for the very young and old (http://www.toyproject.net/; see especially Part II Web Book Butts). Engaging the latter part of the life course, we can encounter the Time Slips, Penelope, and Pinocchio projects developed in the United States, which draw upon untapped memories of persons with dementia (see Box VI.2); Dementiaville, a pioneering dementia care village in the Netherlands; or the rapid emergence of "death doulas"[2] who manage the last stages of life.

The emerging perspective on late life as it connects to the rest of the life course includes cocreative spaces exemplified by the Ibasho cafes in Japan (Box V.1), the Senior Living Lab developed in the Alpine region of western Switzerland (Riva-Mossman 2018) and the U.S. National Center for Creative Aging (https://www.govserv.org/US/Washington-D.C./122074914521351/National -Center-for-Creative-Aging). At an innovative, expressive level, we can encounter England's elder rock groups such as the Zimmers, Young@heart in the United States, and Okinawa's "girl" band KBG84 with an average age of 84 (Part II Introduction).

With Box 01.1 describing the Global ASSA Project and also in Sandra Staudacher and Kaiser-Grolimund's chapter (Part VI) centered in Tanzania, we will encounter emergent *cultural spaces* of social interaction and care. These are often transnational, transcending continents through creative and often multimedia means of connection. With social media and virtual worlds coming to saturate people's lives, even among older adults, we are witnessing in certain nations the emergence of a digital and technologically immersive life course (Prendergast and Garattini 2015; Part II Prendergast). As detailed in chapters by David Prendergast (Part II) and James Wright (Part VI), this has ranged from simple call buttons for isolated elders to neurobic software for cognitive stimulation (Part VI Introduction) and now includes the use of companion and socially assistive robots. Jennifer Robertson has called this "Cyborg Able-ism," referencing the cute seal robot called Paro being used as an adjunct to overwhelmed nursing home care systems in Japan, Denmark, Germany, and the United Kingdom (2017). By the time you read this, the use of socially assistive robots will have become a more pervasive element of eldercare and sociality than was imagined a few years ago, with agile performing machines like Pepper who can sing and dance and encourage a group to participate. At the same time, after reading Wright's chapter (Part VI), you will learn how culture and context have slowed the use of eldercare robots in places like Japan, and how Denmark's experience with similar technology has lessons for both Japan and the United States. Moreover, after viewing some of the Web Special links in Part II about fusing preschools with eldercare environments, I hope readers will think about some the missing premises of robotic care.

Global Aging Becomes Topic "A"

From Problem to Catastrophe to Hero

At the top of the 21st century global thinking about elders and aging was transforming from images of dependent frailty and impending disaster. It now includes second "encore" life options, thousands of Elder Universities in China, and new opportunities such as Senior Corp in the United States giving mature minds and hands opportunities for mending breaches in society (Katz 2017). Almost every week I encounter an article about late life in our local newspaper—I live in Florida after all—but also in regular columns in the *New York Times*, the *Guardian* in England, magazines like the *Atlantic*, or public media outlets such as NPR in the United States. The *New York Times*, in particular, runs frequent articles on the subject from many different angles. Such information goes well beyond the usual profiles of "look what an old person can do" and can include long-term personal stories such as the "85 and Up" series highlighted in the Web Special below. Throughout this book I will draw upon many of these sources to provide readers with resources capturing innovative ideas and up-to-date data.

The last two decades have seen a rush of audaciously titled books, including *This Chair Rocks: A Manifesto Against Ageism* (2016), *Disrupt Aging: A Bold New Path to Living Your Best Life at Every Age* (2016), *The 100-Year Life: Living and Working in an Age of Longevity* (2016); *B(older): Making the Most of Our Longer Lives* (2018), or my favorite title, *How to Live Forever* (2018). It is also intriguing to consider the body of psychological research, such as from the

---

WEB SPECIAL:

John Leland, "The Best of '85 and Up': Life Lessons from the Oldest Old," https://www.nytimes.com/2019/01/04/nyregion/the-best-of-85-and-up-life-lessons-from-nyc-elders.html.

Irish Longitudinal Study on Ageing, indicating that negative attitudes by individuals over the life course can lead to deleterious health consequences, both physically and cognitively (Robertson 2016). When set in a global frame, these suggestive titles and studies provide a forward-looking imaginary perspective, which in some cases is materializing into realities that go against traditional ideas about aging and late life. In this regard, noted doctor and activist Bill Thomas is seeking to upend our ideas about aging. He has the audacity to declare in a powerful TEDx presentation, "What we need is a radical reinterpretation of longevity that makes elders and their needs central to our collective pursuit of happiness and well-being" (https://youtu.be/ijbgc X3vIWs). In Part I, Sarah Lamb examines this issue through the related construct of "Successful Aging" with her comparative research in the United States and India (see also Lamb 2017).

Surfing the "Silver Economy"

The maturing of our planet's citizens has become a subject generating heated discussion and "action plans" from Washington, DC, to Mexico City and especially throughout Asia, where the largest number of elders now live. Suddenly the phrase "Global Aging" is topic "A." We see this in new university centers such as Harvard's Global Generations Policy Institute (www.gen policy.com); NGOs such as the United Nation's NGO Committee on Ageing (http://www.ngocoa-ny.org/) or Help Age International (www.helpage.org); international research networks such as NICE, National Initiative for the Care of the Elderly (www.nicenet.ca); and venture capital companies selling advice on making a killing by catching the "Age Wave" (www.agewave.com). Some of this has been stimulated by a "Silver" or "Longevity" economy: "In the US, for example, the 106 million people aged 50 and over comprise a Longevity Economy that accounts for over $7.6 trillion in annual economic activity. . . . This Longevity Economy is now larger than that of any country except the United States and China" (Jenkins 2019).

Over the past two decades the United Nations and other major global organizations including the World Health Organization (WHO) have begun to seriously address key issues and look at the range of global responses to issues like long-term care, age-friendly and dementia-friendly communities, or innovative health care options with the Study on Global AGEing and Adult Health (SAGE) in six countries and across four different world regions (https://www.who.int/healthinfo/sage/en/). And, tired of just hearing recommendations, localities have begun to implement some of these plans (see especially McFadden and McFadden 2014; Sivaramakrishnan 2018; Zaidi 2018).

Large corporations including insurance giants HSBC (2011, 2017), along with technology focused Intel, view global aging as the millennium's golden business opportunity. Each of these companies has begun to invest in substantial international research on retirement planning, creating healthy "livable" communities, and the role of technology in allowing older adults to age well in their own neighborhoods. Intel also initiated the "Global Aging Experience Project" in 2006 to look at how older adults in various parts of the world use their local environments to experience a positive old age. Much of this work is being done by anthropologists applying the kind of qualitative focus elaborated on in this volume (Bailey and Sheehan 2009). For example, David Prendergast in Part II integrates the results of the Intel project into a future-looking exploration of the role of new technology in helping elders "age in place." As of this writing, many nations around the world are seeking the right fit of human capital and all types of tech, from software-based support to robotic conveyers of emotional, recreational, and physical care. This focus has been enhanced over the past decade with the creation of the International Society for Gerontechnology and its associated journal (http://www.gerontechnology.org/).

The Cultural Context of Aging

As explored by Gurven and Kaplan in Part I (Web Book), the evolutionary legacy of aging involves both a substantial postreproductive survival and a powerful biological dimension of senescence. Yet a global perspective on aging also yields a wondrous array of social responses to the physical imperatives of growing old. The chapters in this volume will explore the fabric of values, perceptions, human relationships, and socially engineered behavior that clothes people as they pass through the older adult years. Such varied patterns of created ideology, social organization, and the ways people produce and distribute valued objects constitute the cultural systems into which all humans grow. Each cultural system creates a perceptual lens composed of potent symbols and meanings through which a particular version of reality is developed. A powerful example is provided in the study of East Asian Indian transplants to America who appreciate the availability of high-tech health care but find unbearable, end-of-life norms in hospitals or nursing homes. Likewise, in such settings, well-meaning and compassionate caregiving professionals reject as irrational and unhealthy the behavior of Indian families toward a relative in the last moments of life. This transcultural misunderstanding flows from the Hindu cultural practice of placing dying persons on the floor to sever their link to material things and thereby make it easier for the soul to leave at the moment of death (Lamb 2006; see also Part V Lamb).

People are not just passive recipients of culture, however. We will see examples of this at every turn and in far-flung cultural venues. In globalizing urban India, as Sarah Lamb shows in Part V, new social inventions such as "Laughing Clubs" mark an age-peer alternative to traditional paths to contentment and health in old age. This idea has reverberated powerfully in the United States (see Box V.1; Kontos 2016). More than 40 years ago, J. Scott Francher suggested that the symbolic themes represented in the U.S. glorification of the youthful, competitively self-reliant, and action-oriented "Pepsi Generation" presented a set of core values contradictory and harmful to the self-esteem of the old (1973). Today's elders have a different response. For example, key elements of American culture reflected in the Nike Corporation's "Just Do It" campaign with pro-football player Colin Kaepernick have not been ignored (see Part II Web Book Featherstone and Hepworth). During the past decade, older adults in the United States have been busy harnessing elements of cultural ideals such as independence, personal initiative, and civic responsibility as they reshape the very meaning of mid- and late life in successful aging (Part I Lamb).

As will be further discussed in Parts I, II, and V, this involves a powerful ethos of community engagement through groups and organizations such as the Raging Grannies, Civic Ventures, and the Gray Panthers (Sanjek 2008), or the Elder Action Network (www.eldersaction.org/). At the same time there has been a more introspective turn toward what has come to be called "conscious aging" (see Part I Web Book Moody) and "gerotranscendence" (Tornstam 2005). In recognizing the various kinds of diversity that impact the life course, it will be important to consider studies of transgender and gender-diverse populations, as do Bishop and Westwood in Part I. This helps us challenge the assumptions of heteronormativity that are used to shape most parameters of what is considered "normal" (see also Sandberg and Marshall 2017). In a similar way, Joel Reynolds (Part VI) uses the metaphor of the "extended body" to challenge notions of disability in the context of citizenship and social justice.

Culture exists in relation to the contextual framework in which human actors find themselves Fry 2008. Such "background" factors can be relevant at various levels of analysis. On the personal level, this might involve looking at how childlessness or poor health affects the chances for aging well or the nature of support in one's later years (Kreager and Schröder-Butterfill 2005). For instance, on a societal scale one could examine how differential access to wealth and status through kinship or even structural differences between communities in the same society alter culturally based premises about how one grows old. This will be seen dramatically in Part V (Web Book) with a study of aging among the women-centered Mingakabau of Indonesia where older females control land wealth, homes, and the marriage system, reversing many Western assumptions about gender and the life course. Likewise Zhang's work in China shows that there are dire consequences for elders depending on whether late life is experienced in rural or urban communities especially in terms of access to health care (Part III; see Ford et al. 2018 for the rural United States).

Situational factors can be strong enough to completely reverse patterns of respect and support linked to cultural traditions. As we will see below in the case of the Tiwi of Australia and in Anthony Glascock's chapter in Part I (Web Book), "death hastening" of the aged can take place in societies that, in general, claim to revere old people. Various intermediate cultural responses to significant frailty can be found, such as among the nomadic Tuareg who create spatial, ritual-symbolic, and social patterns that move such elders "a little to one side" as they edge close to an anticipated death (Rasmussen 2012). The decision to quicken the demise of an elderly person is vitally connected to situational conditions, such as very low levels of functioning by an elder or a lack of close kin. Similarly, in Part IV, my own chapter examines how the clash of ethnic cultures and contextual realities in the United States can dramatically transform the traditional meaning of "filial devotion" toward the elderly in some Asian groups (See Part III Zhang for the case of China).

Cultural systems are in fact highly adaptable, although they tend to craft lifestyles within broad patterns of values and ideal behavior. This will be encountered in the day-to-day realities of Iranian immigrants living in the Silicon Valley area of Northern California who strive to retain a sense of Iranian identity without the densely kin-enmeshed neighborhoods of Iran (Part IV Web Book Hegland), or African Americans using their cultural heritage to cope with environmental degradation in Detroit, Michigan (Part IV Luborsky). Here the ethnic mix of the U.S. social landscape greatly complicates any simple analysis of "American" culture. Everywhere we look at the ways people grow old, we encounter increasingly varied *scripts* for the life course, new *cultural spaces* and emergent *elderscapes*.

Cultural Scripts, Cultural Spaces, and Elderscapes

My use of the term *cultural scripts* comes from work in Asia by Kalyani Mehta (1997) and Susan Long (2005). Studying ethnic Chinese, Malays, and Indians in the multiethnic city state of Singapore, Mehta shows that enactment of broadly similar scripts for the life course and late adulthood are impacted by both situational contexts and specific cultural dictates. For instance, late-life migration to the city places kinship ties in a new cultural space and usually means that while one might have a married son and perhaps grandchildren in the local environment, one might not have siblings or many other age-peer relatives around for support. Within a seemingly similar cultural perspective there are different implications among Hindu Indians and Islamic Malaysians in the script of late-life women who experienced the death of a spouse. In the first instance, widowhood was stigmatized and such women were strongly discouraged from remarrying, while the widows practicing Islam were not stigmatized and strongly encouraged to remarry (see also Part II Web Book Cattell). Here the comingling of the situational and the cultural can be particularly powerful for older women, especially in an urban immigrant situation where supportive, homegrown institutions and networks may not be in full flower or even exist.

Susan Long's research in Japan focuses on how people navigate the changing cultural landscape of death and end-of-life decision-making through the use of varied *cultural scripts* (Long 2005; Kawano, Roberts, and Long 2014.) Part of the difficulty for many Japanese is adjusting to a dramatic shift from dying at home versus the cultural space in which death almost always takes place, now, in hospitals. In Part III Iza Kavedžija also looks at Japan and examines the broader new cultural spaces and emergent cultural scripts by which eldercare is being transformed. Such developments as the Ibasho café (Box V.1) pioneered in Japan have the capacity to increase the resilience of communities and families to cope with dramatic changes impacting their lives. This resilience is often magnified when elders themselves take the lead in developing new community-based organizations to fulfill needs that cannot be adequately addressed by family members and traditional community structures.

In both urban China (Part III Zhang) and India (Part V Lamb), cultural scripts focused on filial devotion enacted in multigenerational households are being short-circuited by "outsourced" sons and the competing demands of educating children. Expanding the space for experiencing older life has meant seeking age-peer communion in urban parks with dance groups and laughing clubs and in seeking residential refuge in Hindu temples and new kinds of elder residences.

A dramatic connection of emergent scripts for aging with new interconnected sets of cultural spaces for experiencing late adulthood has developed in certain countries. One of the best places to observe this is Charlotte County, Florida, home to the nation's highest proportion of older adults, with 35 percent of its residents over age 65. In this setting sociologist Stephen Katz (Part V Web Book) uses innovative methods to take readers into the heart of what he calls the "elderscapes" of this elderly dense area. The notions of cultural spaces and elderscapes overlap with a construct Gene Cohen calls "landscapes for aging" to describe the growing number of sites where older persons reside, create active social lives and receive care (2006). This will be seen quite clearly in Caitrin Lynch's chapter (Part II), which takes us into a small medical needle factory in Massachusetts where "eldersourcing" of post-retirement workers provides a new model of work and care across generations that has drawn serious attention from other countries.

These new landscapes for aging include the growing diversity of retirement, life-care, continuing-care, and "active-living" communities, congregate housing, assisted living facilities, senior hotels, foster care, group homes, day care, respite care, and nomadic mobile-home communities. What is particularly important about the elderscapes and new cultural spaces created within them is the continuing engagement of older adults in shaping the very context of their lives (see especially Counts and Counts 1996, Part V Web Book).

Anthropology and the Qualitative Search for Meaning

Typically, cultural anthropologists have chosen to study such human variation by establishing themselves for long-term stays in locales where people carry out their everyday lives. Called "ethnography," this prolonged, personal encounter of an anthropologist with individuals in a community can provide special insight into how people confront and deal with the cultural contexts life has dealt them (Keith 1988; Sokolovsky 2001: Perkinson and Solimeo 2013; Danley 2017). The aim of this approach is to acquire a holistic understanding of cultural systems through "participant observation" enabled by engaging in daily life and recording in the native language the meanings of things, persons, and actions.

Participant observation is critical in understanding the cultural context of late life, and even in learning appropriate questions to ask (Sokolovsky 2006). This applies as much to studying aging in small villages in the South Pacific as it does to research in American nursing homes, ethnic enclaves, rural Japan, or neighborhoods in "world cities." In the introduction to Part IV, (Box IV.3) I discuss how I used the ethnographic approach as part of a team, which trained doctors in geriatric medicine within a large public hospital serving a diverse ethnic population.

In her research with Seattle's black aged, Jane Peterson entered into the midst of their cultural world by working as a nurse for a church group that provided important services to the elderly (Part IV Web Book). In my own work with older homeless populations, I found that asking seemingly straightforward questions without a clear understanding of the lifestyle of long-term homelessness resulted in almost worthless data and frequent hostility. It was necessary not only to learn the colorful argot of the streets— such as "carrying the banner" (sleeping outdoors)—and to travel with people on their daily rounds, but also to work in soup kitchens and drop-in centers, which sustained many of the older homeless adults I worked with (Cohen and Sokolovsky 1988). This understanding was critical to my continuing research in a Mexican indigenous community, in that I while I was accepted as a godparent to children, I could not fully become a "real" member of the community but, rather, an accepted translator of their culture (Part III).

Several of the authors in this volume have had long-term research connections—upwards of four decades—to the people they write about. We shall see the advantages of this approach in the Web Book articles by Harriet

Rosenberg (Part I) and Maria Cattell (Part II) and later on with my work in Mexico (Part III). Such temporal perspectives provide a unique opportunity to scrutinize how well the implications of gerontological theory stand up to longitudinal testing within whole communities. This is an indispensable way to examine the roles of aged citizens and the support directed toward elderly people within the context of sweeping global changes.

The Rise of "Ethnogerontology"

Despite the early seminal book by Leo Simmons, *The Role of the Aged in Primitive Society* (1945), concern for a worldwide, cross-cultural analysis of aging has developed slowly.[3] In the 1950s and 1960s a serious ethnographic gaze was first directed, not within the non-Western world, but at frail elders interacting with the U.S. medical system. In the late 1950s Otto von Mering conducted fieldwork in the geriatric wards of psychiatric hospitals, illustrating how cultural devaluing of old age led to a withdrawal of psychosocial care for older patients (1957). This was followed by Jules Henry's *Culture Against Man* (1963), a searing ethnographic account of life in three American nursing homes and Clark and Anderson's *Culture and Aging* (1967) exploring the dynamics of San Francisco's community-based care of mentally impaired older citizens.[4] The serious issues explored in these pioneering works are far from resolved in the 21st century. They will be explored in this book's final section where the modern quest for what Bill Thomas calls "Gerontopia" is being sought, in part, through the powerful "Culture Change Movement" that seeks to radically reform eldercare via a Pioneer Network (see especially Web Book Part VI McLean; Part VI Web Book Polivka; Gonzalez 2018).

From a global perspective it was not until the publication of the volume *Aging and Modernization*, edited by Donald Cowgill and Lowell Holmes in 1972, that knowledge from modern ethnographic studies was employed to test gerontological theory. Here, detailed studies of 14 different societies were compared to examine the impact of industrialization, urbanization, and Westernization on the status of the aged. Although now superseded by the framework of globalization, the theoretical propositions developed by Cowgill and Holmes in *Aging and Modernization* and their later works have served as a stimulus to subsequent work examining globalization and aging around the world (Cowgill 1986; Rhoads and Holmes 1995; Hyde and Higgs 2017; Part III Introduction).

The maturing of an anthropological specialty in aging has unfolded through gerontologically focused ethnographies and edited books, texts, and special issues of journals (see this volume's Web site). Over time, the distinct realm of anthropological methods and theory has been brought to bear on questions of aging and the life course with books such as *Age and Anthropological Theory* (Kertzer and Keith 1984), *New Methods for Old Age Research* (Fry

---

WEB SPECIAL:

Anthropology resources to follow: www.culturalcontextofaging.com
/anthroresources/.

---

and Keith 1986), *Old Age in Global Perspective* (Albert and Cattell 1994), *The Aging Experience* (Keith et al. 1994), *Other Cultures, Elder Years* (Rhoads and Holmes 1995) and *Ageing Societies* (Harper 2006), *Transitions and Transformations* (Lynch and Danley 2013), *Elusive Adulthoods* (Durham and Solway 2017), *Care across Distance* (Hromadžić and Palmberger 2018). An important new specialty has emerged out of this scholarship over the past two decades; it is variously referred to as "comparative sociocultural gerontology," "ethnogerontology," or "anthropology of aging and the life course." You can keep up-to-date on this subject by following the link to the Web Special link listed above.

The importance of this perspective has spilled over into other disciplines, often focused on developing cultural competence among social workers, psychologists, and physicians who serve ethnically varied communities (Tanabe 2007; Forond 2018.). For example some medical schools, including Stanford and Florida State University, are developing what they call "ethnogeriatrics" as a specialty that explores the interface of late-life health with culture and ethnicity.[5] From a broader perspective, a multidisciplinary movement sometimes referred to as "qualitative gerontology" or "narrative gerontology" has also sought to establish in-depth modes of analysis as an equal partner to more quantitative methods (Rowles and Schoenberg 2002; De Medeiros 2013; Burholt, Stephens, and Keating 2018.) While many of this volume's authors come from my own discipline of anthropology, there are also contributions from social work, psychology, medicine, philosophy, sociology, and public health. Nevertheless, these contributions are framed by a 21st-century paradigm of cultural anthropology that gathers data on cultural systems via community-based, long-term, qualitatively oriented research and then tries to understand this information within broader regional and global settings (Perkinson and Solimeo 2014). In Part IV Box IV.1, I discuss the use of this approach in a training program for physicians in geriatric medicine (Royal Society for Public Health 2018).

Outside of anthropology one of the strongest advocates of this approach is sociologist Jaber Gubrium, who, in an editorial in *Gerontologist*, argues that qualitative approaches should not be viewed solely as a second-class precursor to more "powerful" statistical analysis (1992). According to Gubrium, good qualitative research is scientific in striving to generate theoretically informed findings. Over the past decade there has been an expansion of such work and attempts to represent the "native complexity" of behavior and how that complexity is organized within an existing community (Twigg and Martin 2014; Baars et al. 2015; Danley 2017).

Most of the articles in this volume follow a qualitative approach and seek to deeply enter the world of meaning by viewing how the lives of real people intersect with the reality of cultural systems and community settings. We will see the importance of this approach in Part I where Harriet Rosenberg (Web Book) shows how narratives of elder complaints can be part of a positive system of care, and a Part VI Web Book chapter where Athena McLean shows that much disruptive behavior of cognitively impaired seniors lies outside the disease process and is better explained by how the care system interacts with personhood.

Anthropological Encounters with Aging and Late Life

While gerontological research as an anthropological specialty spans the past four decades, studies conducted earlier in the 20th century can provide revealing, yet tantalizingly incomplete, glimpses of the elderly in non-Western cultural settings (see especially Warner 1937; Arensberg and Kimball 1940; Spencer 1965). For example, in 1928 anthropologist C. W. Hart encountered the cultural context of frail old age among a preliterate people called the Tiwi, who generally accorded the healthy elderly high levels of support. As seen in these diary passages from his early fieldwork, the severe physical and cognitive decline of a particular Tiwi woman set in motion a dramatic ritual for dealing with this situation:

> After a few weeks on the islands I also became aware that [the Tiwi] were often uneasy with me because I had no kinship linkage to them. This was shown in many ways, among others in their dissatisfaction with the negative reply they always got to their question, "What clan does he belong to?" Around the Mission, to answer it by saying, "White men have no clans," was at least a possible answer, but among the pagan bands like the Malauila and Munupula such an answer was incomprehensible—to them everybody must have a clan, just as everybody must have an age. If I had a clan I would be inside the kinship system, everybody would know how to act toward me, I would know how to act toward everybody else, and life would be easier and smoother for all.
>
> How to get myself into the clan and kinship system was quite a problem. Even Mariano [Hart's native guide], while admitting the desirability, saw no way of getting me in. There did not seem much hope and then suddenly the problem was solved entirely by a lucky accident. I was in a camp where there was an old woman who had been making herself a terrible

nuisance. Toothless, almost blind, withered, and stumbling around, she was physically quite revolting and mentally rather senile. She kept hanging round me asking for tobacco, whining, wheedling, snivelling, until I got thoroughly fed up with her. As I had by now learned the Tiwi equivalents of "Go to hell" and "Get lost," I rather enjoyed being rude to her and telling her where she ought to go. Listening to my swearing in Tiwi, the rest of the camp thought it a great joke and no doubt egged her on so that they could listen to my attempts to get rid of her. This had been going on for some time when one day the old hag used a new approach. "Oh, my son," she said, "please give me tobacco." Unthinkingly I replied, "Oh, my mother, go jump in the ocean." Immediately a howl of delight arose from everybody within earshot and they all gathered round me patting me on the shoulder and calling me by a kinship term. She was my mother and I was her son. This gave a handle to everybody else to address me by a kinship term. Her other sons from then on called me brother, her brothers called me "sister's son"; and so on. I was now in the kinship system; my clan was Jabijabui (a bird) because my mother was Jabijabui.

From then on the change in the atmosphere between me and the tribe at large was remarkable. Strangers were now told that I was Jabijabui and that my mother was the old so-and-so and when told this, stern old men would relax, smile and say "then you are my brother" (or my son, or my sister's son, or whatever category was appropriate) and I would struggle to respond properly by addressing them by the proper term.

How seriously they took my presence in their kinship system is something I never will be sure about. However, toward the end of my time on the islands an incident occurred that surprised me because it suggested that some of them had been taking my presence in the kinship system much more seriously than I had thought. I was approached by a group of about eight or nine senior men all of whom I knew. They were all senior members of the Jabijabui clan and they had decided among themselves that the time had come to get rid of the decrepit old woman who had first called me son and whom I now called mother. As I knew, they said, it was Tiwi custom, when an old woman became too feeble to look after herself, to "cover her up." This could only be done by her sons and her brothers and all of them had to agree beforehand, since once it was done they did not want any dissension among the brothers or clansmen, as that might lead to a feud. My "mother" was now completely blind, she was constantly falling over logs or into fires, and they, her senior clansmen, were in agreement that she would be better out of the way. Did I agree? I already knew about "covering up." The Tiwi, like many other hunting and gathering peoples, sometimes got rid of their ancient and decrepit females. The method was to dig a hole in the ground in some lonely place, put the old woman in the hole and fill it in with earth until only her head was showing. Everybody went away for a day or two and then went back to the hole to discover to their surprise, that the old woman was dead, having been too feeble to raise her arms from the earth. Nobody had "killed" her, her death in Tiwi eyes was a natural one. She had been alive when her relatives last saw her. I had never seen it done, though I knew it was the custom, so I asked my brothers if it was necessary for me to attend the "covering up." They said no and they would do it, but only after they had my agreement. Of course I agreed, and a week or two later we heard in our camp that my "mother" was dead, and we all wailed and put on the trimmings of mourning. (Hart 1970: 149–54; Used by permission of South-Western College Publishing, a division of Cengage Learning.)

Aging and the Anthropological Paradigm

This brief encounter with aging among the Tiwi can help introduce students to the ways an anthropological approach can help us understand the late phases of adulthood in cross-cultural context. Such an anthropological paradigm has a dual lens: an internal focus (called an *emic* perspective), which seeks to comprehend the "native's" view of why certain behaviors are performed or images about the world are held; and an external, comparative focus (called an *etic* perspective), which uses the world's societies as a natural laboratory to separate the universal from the particular.

The "Native" View of Aging

The emic component of the anthropological paradigm seeks to understand how the people being studied see the world. Hart's research on the Tiwi was a classic example of ethnographic fieldwork. The Tiwi incorporated Hart into their kinship system and made use of him in a difficult decision, just as he used his designation as "son" and clan member to study their society on an intimate basis. When Hart first lived with the Tiwi, they were a foraging, seminomadic, small-scale society where kin-based groups (clans) named after mythological ancestors controlled key elements of the life cycle. How one entered adulthood, whom one married, and the consequences of frailty in old age were largely determined by the cluster of elder males who have membership in a given clan. The Tiwi represent one of the few actual cases of gerontocracy—rule by the eldest group of males—and an exaggerated case of what has been called "gerontogamy." This latter term denotes a case in which a society not only practices polygyny (men can have more than one spouse at the same time) but where the older adult males have greater access than the younger men to the youngest women. Typically, Tiwi men above middle age already have several wives, including very young teenagers, while a man marrying for the first time after age 25 might be wed to a 45-year-old widow.

While not controlling material wealth as might be the case in an agrarian tribal society, groups of elder males cautiously dole out esoteric wisdom to younger persons. Without this knowledge they cannot relate to spiritual forces or function as culturally competent adults. Regarded with a mixture of fear and reverence, the oldest males sit at the top of a generational pyramid, authoritatively dominating society by the exclusive possession of key cultural knowledge. These elders, as a group, also dominate the dramatic life-cycle rituals that mark the transition from status to status as one goes from birth to death. Unlike the Western linear view of the life cycle, which sees death as a discontinuity from life, the Tiwi have a cyclical, mythologically linked notion of time and the passage of life forms through it. From this perspective, ancestors can have a powerful influence on the fate of the living and can be reborn in a future generation. As Judith Barker shows in her article dealing with another Pacific Island people (Part VI Web Book), an emic understanding of belief systems is necessary to comprehend the radical change in behavior that can accompany the shift from healthy old age to severe senescence. More recent studies among Australian aboriginal peoples have shown how elder knowledge continues to be used, not only to preserve traditional knowledge, but to deal with 21st-century reality by helping tackle broader community issues involving unemployment, racism, and oppression (Busija et al. 2018).

Although females among the Tiwi had fewer formal bases of power, one must not assume from the very limited segment of Hart's research that women in old age are a totally repressed lot. Subsequent work among the Tiwi by Jane Goodale (1971) shows the impressive amount of de facto power women could accumulate by middle age, especially through their ability to control conflict in the community. In another example, Brenda Child notes in her book on the Red Lake Ojibwe peoples that as a women becomes recognized as an elder she comes to be called *mindimooyenh*, or "one who holds things together" (2013). Other classic ethnographic studies have demonstrated how older women can acquire an importance and power far beyond the normative societal constraints placed on females, even in quite "male chauvinistic" cultural contexts (see especially Kerns and Brown 1992; Putnam-Dickerson and Brown 1998).

The Comparative View of Aging

How are we to apply the second, transcultural part of the anthropological paradigm? The treatment of the frail and possibly demented older woman in Hart's narrative must not only be examined through an emic understanding of the process of "covering up" but also by applying an etic comparative perspective. One way of doing this is to translate the insider's "folk" view into comparable categories, such as "abandoning" or "forsaking," that can be used to construct theories and test hypotheses. The broadest such research design, called "holocultural analysis," makes use of the major anthropological data bank, the Human Relations Area Files (HRAF), which houses ethnographic data representing over 1,000 societies. The intent of this approach is to statistically measure "the relationship between two or more theoretically defined and operationalized variables in a world sample of human societies" (Rohner et al. 1978: 128). In this way it is hoped that we may eventually comprehend what aspects of aging are universal, as opposed to those factors that are largely shaped by a specific sociocultural system.

As demonstrated by Anthony Glascock (Part I Web Book), carefully defining types of "death hastening" behaviors allows us to make powerful use of the holocultural method. Using this approach, Glascock's research demonstrates that, counter to what one might expect, about half of his worldwide sample act out variants of behavior that lead to the death of older citizens. As the case of Hart's Tiwi "mother" exemplifies, this is seldom a simple matter and is usually predicated on severe physical and cognitive decline and the redefinition of the person from a functional to a nonfunctional individual (see also Part VI Web Book Barker).[6]

Cross-National Versus Cross-Cultural

Cross-National Research

It is important to distinguish *cross-national* from *cross-cultural* studies in gerontological research (Fry 1988).[7] The first type of study takes as the unit of analysis the nation-state or a major portion of that entity and compares whole countries by measuring, through survey questionnaires, a large array of primarily demographic, interactional, and health-related variables (Chen 2018). In recent decades there has been a dramatic growth of cross-national studies spanning most regions of the globe (Kunkel, Brown, and Wittington 2014). Early projects such as a seven-nation study within Asia, Africa, and the Middle East (Kendig, Hashimoto, and Coppard 1992) and the United Nations Fertility Survey among Six Latin American Nations (De Vos 1990) have provided important demographic sources of information, although their mass survey approach often obscured crucial cultural differences within and between the nations sampled (Sokolovsky 2002). Subsequently, a number of more sophisticated cross-national projects have emerged that integrate more qualitative case materials into the research design. We see this in Part V Web Book where Michael Gusmano pulls together the results of the ongoing World Cities Project. Here he examines the national contexts of four major urban places and the roles played by environment, neighborhood, and city support systems in sustaining older citizens (Rodwin and Gusmano 2006). Other key examples include a study of "Rapid Demographic

Change and the Welfare of the Elderly" in East Asia (Hermalin 2002); the SABE Project in Latin America and the Caribbean (Palloni, Peláez, and Wong 2006); the OASIS project (Daatland 2006); and the still running SHARE studies throughout Europe (Dykstra 2018; http://www.share-project.org).[8]

Cross-Cultural Studies

In contrast to cross-national studies, *cross-cultural* studies of aging tend to focus on small-scale societies or individual communities of industrial states. The chapter by Indrizal, Kreager, and Schröder-Butterfill in Part V (Web Book) reports on research from the *Ageing in Indonesia 1999–2007 Project*, which is a longitudinal anthropological and demographic study of three Indonesian communities. Here the authors focus on a West Sumatra village of the Minangkabau people, who live in one of the world's largest matrilineal societies. The benefit of in-depth cultural analysis comes sharply into focus by contrasting the impact on the life course and aging of this "women-centered" society with impacts in the more male-dominated cultural settings of China (Part III Zhang), Mexico (Part III Sokolovsky), or India (Part V Lamb).

One approach centers on highly controlled comparisons, where the social units under study are similar except for one or two features. A classic example is S. F. Nadel's (1952) study of two African tribal societies, the Korongo and the Mesakin. While alike in terms of environment and economic, political, and kinship organization, each society differed in the degree of intergenerational conflict and the attitude of males toward aging. The key difference seemed to lie in the greater number of age distinctions recognized by the Korongo and the smoother transition into old age characteristic of this society. As a consequence, there was not only a greater congruence between social and physical aging among the Korongo but also an easier and more cheerful acceptance of old age itself. A very different use of this approach is seen in McLean's powerful documentation of how contrasting care philosophies in otherwise identical dementia units result in different outcomes for elder residents (Part VI Web Book).

Alternatively, the more typical approach to cross-cultural studies has been to highlight the differences between the societies or ethnic communities being contrasted. Researchers have either searched the available literature or conducted original research in different places to see what could be learned about a specific aspect of aging such as intergenerational relations, age as a basis of social organization, widowhood, and general aspects of female aging.[9] Most parts of this volume have examples of this kind of approach, such as Beyene's bicultural comparison of menopause in Greece and Mexico (Part I Web Book); or the contrast by Counts and Counts of community engagement of older adults in mobile home parks and a village in Papua New Guinea (Part V Web Book).

One of the significant problems with cross-cultural research, however, is the difficulty of gaining consistency in methods used to qualitatively study the intricate cultural phenomena observed in the societies being contrasted (Lessenich 2018). An attempt at confronting this issue directly was Project AGE (Age, Generation and Experience), the first extensive cross-cultural study of aging by anthropologists doing long-term research focused on aging and the life course. Here a team of anthropologists carried out a comparison of aging in Hong Kong, Botswana, rural Ireland, and two American communities, combining long-term fieldwork with a precise and consistent research protocol (see Keith et al. 1994; Part I Web Book Fry et al.). This project has been especially important in detailing how intercommunity variation interacts with cultural systems to influence how people define successful aging (see Part I Lamb). Such work will be important to consider in connection to Stafford's discussion of factors promoting elder-friendly communities in Part V.

Ongoing Global Projects

Two important new global anthropological projects have continued the momentum of Project AGE. One is "Aging as a Human Condition," which seeks to provide nuanced portraits of aging in all its varieties. Centered in Aarhus University in Denmark and running from 2017 to 2020, this project is being undertaken through ethnographic studies conducted in Denmark, Kyrgyzstan, Uganda, and the United States as well as among Tibetan exiles in India and Nepal. An important component of these anthropological efforts is exciting parallel projects in philosophy and art (http://projects.au.dk /thegoodoldlife/).

A more internationally expansively and applied project is ASSA—Anthropology of Smart Phones and Smart Aging. This five-year study began in 2017 and reflects a growing interest in digital anthropology (Horst and Miller 2012). It investigates fundamental changes in people's relationship to age and health in association with the global rise of smartphones and related technologies. Similar to Project AGE, the team of 10 anthropologists is conducting sustained (16-month) ethnographies, but they are also working in a collaborative, social-media-enabled framework. As noted in Box 01.1 below, an unusual aspect of this project is that the researchers will be making available frequent blogs about their experiences at http://blogs.ucl.ac.uk/assa/. I also include two of these blogs in the Web Book, Part II Walton and Part VI Hawkins and Haapio-Kirk. This global project is highlighted below by the ASSA team, and will connect in a number of ways with David Prendergast's (Part II) broad exploration of technology's role in the lives of older adults and the chapter by Andrea Kaiser-Grolimund and Sandra Staudacher (Part VI) showing how communication technology among families in Tanzania facilitates care among transnational families. It is also connected to initiatives

Box 01.1 The ASSA Team, "Mid-Life, Smartphones and Health: ASSA, a Global Comparison," https://www.ucl.ac.uk /anthropology/assa/

Studies of aging typically emphasize either youth or the elderly—periods in which we are routinely defined by age. The ASSA project (Anthropology of Smartphones and Smart Ageing), however, specifically focuses upon midlife, defined as people who consider themselves neither young nor elderly. With the marked increase in life expectancy, this represents an ever-growing population that could make a considerable contribution to how we understand the contemporary experience of ageing and the life course. In pursuit of this goal, the ASSA project consists of simultaneous 16-month field-based ethnographies being conducted in 10 sites across the globe, from February 2018 to June 2019. Central to the carrying out of our project, as a collaborative endeavor, are digital technologies themselves. Rather than comparing results at the end, this team is in constant communication, daily by WhatsApp, monthly by Skype, rethinking our goals, topics, and methods and appreciating the diversity of our findings. The project also posts a blog about our current research every few days. You can sign up to follow the blog posts at: https://blogs.ucl.ac.uk/assa/.

The ASSA field sites include migrants in Santiago, Chile, and Milan, Italy; low-income settlements in Cameroon and Uganda, but also the middle class in Cameroon; politically marginalized Palestinians in East Jerusalem; a working-class urban population in Sao Paulo, Brazil; as well as relatively affluent populations in Ireland; Shanghai, China; and Kyoto, Japan. The populations that could be considered midlife may vary from 40-year-olds in Cameroon and Uganda to 80-year-olds in Japan, so any attempt to define them as a specific age group was quickly demolished by this evidence for global diversity in the understanding of age.

Few generalizations work for all 10 research sites. In most cases, however, the study reflects the growth in life expectancy. So in our Chinese, Italian, and Irish field sites the 70-year-olds who might once have been considered elderly are often encountered as adult children, who are looking after their own elderly parents in their nineties. In this role they often need to learn entirely new skills, such as how to understand and take care of their parent's dementia. In those same field sites, people retiring in their fifties or sixties may expect to live for decades. They may find themselves relatively free of family obligations, no longer tied to work, in some cases possessing secure pensions representing what has turned out to be quite a privileged generation. Here we find team members studying a process of how "life becomes craft," as this population creates a new combination of activities and social engagements and may become the core of community building. It is possible that there is no real historical precedent for a population that has secured such a position, largely outside of most of the structures of kinship and labor that normally define people. As such, they may represent an important challenge to basic social science assumptions that stem from Durkheim, about the relationship between life and social structure.

Apart from studying the experience of age itself, we are approaching the experience of aging through exploring two topics in particular. The increasing use of smartphones within this age group can be understood in some cases as a potential increase in social and other capacities, while intersecting with health issues that in some cases represent a decrease in such capacities.

One of our main methods is to offer to help teach people to use smartphones. This gives us many insights, first into the "stupidity" of the so-called smartphone, where contrary to the claims of youth, very little is actually intuitive. Moreover, we are learning about the struggles of older people, who face both the impatience of youth and various forms of exclusion, if they fail to keep up with new technologies. As in all anthropological research, we look for unexpected consequences. For example, Charlotte Hawkins arrived in Kampala, the capital of Uganda, thinking that the smartphone-orientated youth living in Kampala would be neglecting older people left behind in villages. Actually, she is finding that the smartphone has become instrumental as a means by which young people can send money back to help pay for health care for older relatives in villages and demonstrate their respect for seniority. Other team members working in high-income areas intended to concentrate upon smartphone health apps, which are currently being produced in profusion, but soon found these to be of very limited consequence compared to the impact of, for example, Google or WhatsApp.

Our approach to health is broad, in that we examine the infrastructures of medical resources, hospitals, community health workers, and doctors, but also the range of complementary health resources, which may include traditional and folk treatments as well as yoga and mindfulness. We are particularly interested in health issues that pertain to midlife, which can include prostate cancer, diabetes, and in general comorbidity—older people tend to experience clusters of health problems rather than isolated instances of ill health. We also focus on the wider experience. For example, menopause includes both physiological issues such as loss of bone density but also social and emotional consequences. It may be celebrated or mourned, depending upon whether you are still trying to have children, or have suffered from decades of period pains. It can also represent a critical moment in experiencing aging, as women no longer define themselves in terms of reproductive capacities (see Part I Web Book Beyene).

The ASSA project aims not just to observe but also to consider how anthropologists might contribute to welfare, especially through trying to imbue a greater cultural and social sensitivity to these new digital technologies. When the acronym ASSA refers to "smart" aging, we are thinking of what Katrien Pype calls "smart from below," that is, the creativity of ordinary people. In many of our research sites we have observed the relative paucity of usage of a vast array of smartphone health apps that already represent huge investments from health and technology companies. So instead we focus more on the myriad ways in which ordinary people in, say, São Paulo or Ireland at midlife have adapted WhatsApp for health concerns, such as the coordination of family care, or their ambivalence about researching health issues. The most important "designers" in our study are not medics, IT experts, or professional designers, but the inventiveness of ordinary families in all our field sites. The advantage of this approach is that instead of relying on speculation about what people might one day do with digital health technologies, we learn from things that people are already engaged in and seem comfortable with. This can include how people in developing countries use short instructive videos from YouTube as an alternative to more formal education.

In conclusion, we represent a holistic tradition within anthropology. On the one hand we are exploring fundamental questions concerning how people craft meaning and purpose in life, acknowledging the opportunities and challenges for those who have markedly increased life expectancy, compared to previous generations. At the same time, we examine quite practical and engaged issues of how to improve people's health and welfare through the employment of new digital technologies, such as smartphones. Anthropology is the discipline that can work with this spectrum of goals, and indeed should do so, simply because that is the true condition of the people we work with and learn from. Every day, people deal with practical concerns of social communication with friends and family, and increasingly at midlife with issues of health, but at the same time they are reflective and challenged by wider questions that concern the changing meaning and experience of age and aging.

being developed by new startups such as Aging2.0 (www.aging2.com) and the AgeWell Global (www.agewellglobal.com; see Part VI).

Using the Global Perspective

Whichever approach is taken, cross-cultural research on aging is important in at least three ways. First, it may suggest general hypotheses about the aging experience that can be tested by employing larger samples or conducting longitudinal studies. By using a relatively small number of cases, it is possible to retain a picture of the qualitative nature of sociocultural variables and thereby hopefully avoid overly simple theoretical models. A good example of this is found in Part I (Web Book), where Yewoubdar Beyene undertakes a classic cross-cultural comparison of menopause. She shows how the complex biocultural interplay of the life course, nutrition, and reproductive histories result in very different bodily responses to this universal experience for midlife females. Her research clarifies the factors that either promote or inhibit what many North Americans mistakenly believe are universal physical symptoms associated with the end of a woman's reproductive capacity. Beyene's work is clearly connected to a wealth of research showing the synergy of a biocultural approach to a woman's midlife (Sievert 2006; Melby and Lampl 2011; Shea 2015).

Second, intercultural comparisons can help us to understand in a detailed fashion how the response to aging in the United States varies from that experienced in other places. Such analysis can suggest alternative strategies for developing diverse environments in which to grow old. This is brought home clearly by the examination of Denmark's innovative eldercare system by Amy Clotworthy, who found that their supposedly "socialist" system actually is based on promoting individual autonomy and freedom (Part VI). It is important to note that a decade after this nation implemented its integrated home- and community-based services system, there is wide access to services and the growth of some eldercare expenditures actually *decreased*, even for the over-80 population. In the United States, opposite trends mark the long-term care system for elders noted by Larry Polivka in Part VI Web Book.

In a related manner, a third use of global information is to create an interactive cultural laboratory where innovations are absorbed, transformed, and sometimes improved as they pass into different societal settings. The last several decades have, in fact, seen a flowering of numerous cultural transplants in areas such as long-term care, service delivery, and residential design. For example, the "Day Hospital" model developed within the British health system as an alternative to traditional nursing homes was used as the archetype for the creation of the very successful "On Lok" community-based long-term care system in the United States. (See https://www.common wealthfund.org/publications/case-study/2016/aug/aging-gracefully-pace -approach-caring-frail-elders-community). In another part of the world,

Japan in 2002 initiated a national long-term care insurance system based on German and British models (see Part III Kavedžija).

Another good example of intercultural exchange comes from a residential and community design model called "cohousing," developed in Scandinavia but inspired by American utopian communities of the 19th century and the mid-1960s. These innovative, resident-run "intentional" communities not only facilitate autonomous aging in place but promote small scale, age-integrated, and sustainable/energy-efficient neighborhoods. Pioneered in Denmark by a young architect named Jan Gudmand-Hoyer during the 1970s, they have been emulated elsewhere in Europe and developed with distinct local slants in the United States since the 1990s (Durrett 2005: Ruiu 2015). By 2018 there were 165 US cohousing communities and another 140 in the planning stages across North America. Their innovations involve radically revamping older urban neighborhoods to the cohousing, multigenerational model (Hammond 2018). You can follow the progress of the cohousing movement at https://www.cohousing.org/. In other chapters we will see other important examples of cultural transfer, involving senior companions in the United States (Part III Web Book Shea) to dementia villages and memory cafes in the Netherlands (Part VI Introduction).

Your Global Aging Future Is *Now!*

Global Gerontology as Frog Candy

In a recent blog post, Frank Whittington states:

> Frog candy is anything new and exotic and slightly strange that has taken on the aura of "cool" and desirable. At least that's what I've decided. And a quick Google search will confirm that frog candy has become ubiquitous. In that sense global gerontology is the frog candy of the second decade of 21st century aging. If you aren't "global" in today's gerontology, you aren't on the cutting edge. (www.springerpub.com/w/gerontology/global-geron tology-the-frog-candy-of-the-future/)

I hope there is plenty of frog candy for readers of this book to consume as you explore challenges in virtually all societies to deal with the viability of cultural scripts, cultural spaces, and elderscapes being created and experienced. In this era of globalization and increasing inequality, such issues interact with movement across all sorts of boundaries: national, generational, ethnic/class, cognitive, work/retirement, life itself, and even the mediation of humans and technology. The following pages will explore the varied ways societies and cultural systems are transforming to meet these challenges, creating new elderscapes through innovative habitats, places, and means of care; changing the boundaries of marriage and gender; building intergenerational community gardens; highlighting civic ecology; and crafting strategies for coping with family networks moving across national boundaries.

Follow along with the laughing clubs of India, waltzing elders and senior companions of urban China, elderscapes of Florida and East Asia, Japan's robotic granny-minders and Ibasho cafés, the Okinawan Centenarian diet plan, elder-friendly communities emerging everywhere, Denmark's "Flexsecurity" system, and Dutch dementia villages. Welcome to your future!

Special Note on This Book's Web Site and the Integration with Web Chapters

There is now an amazing array of serious academic information available on the World Wide Web, including whole books, video and audio documentation, the latest statistical data, and reports from governments, universities, and research centers. Some of these key links are provided in the printed text or in endnotes for each part of this book. I have included in the text e-chapters that use digital media to elaborate through photo essays or video discussion of innovative materials going beyond the printed work. Throughout the book you will see boxed areas that can include Web Special items or Projects to Follow; both connect readers to innovative research that takes readers into the near future. At "The Cultural Context of Aging" Web site, www.culturalcontextofaging.com, click on the Resources menu—keyed to each section of the book—and you will have access to more extensive supplemental resources expanding the text readings. Within the print book there are also links to a number of digital chapters drawn from previous editions or added in the new volume. At the book's Web page, clicking on the Web Book menu will bring you to digital chapters that are listed in the print Table of Contents but only available electronically.

Notes

1. The details of this plan can be seen at: https://joinup.ec.europa.eu/collection /ehealth/document/eu-ageing-well-information-society. It should be noted, however, that the idea of promoting active aging is not the only answer to population aging, and in Europe to date the push to get people to work longer has not been particularly effective. See the following for a report on this situation: https://www .euractiv.com/section/social-europe-jobs/news/workers-unenthusiastic-about -active-ageing/.

2. See also the International End of Life Doula Association, INELDA: https:// www.inelda.org/.

3. There were also short articles by such luminaries as Gregory Bateson (1950) and Margaret Mead (1951, 1967), but this did little to stimulate much interest in global aging.

4. In that same year an article by Margaret Clark (1967) laid out a model for developing an anthropology of aging.

5. For information about these programs see http://sgec.stanford.edu/ and https://med.fsu.edu/geriatrics/home.

6. For a another kind of study on aging using the HRAF files see Winn and Newton 1982.

7. Some of this research I have labelled "cross-national" (e.g., Arnhoff, Leon, and Lorge 1964; Seefeldt 1984) is described by the authors as cross-cultural. However, the survey questionnaire approach of these studies places them in the methodological camp of what I call cross-national studies and perhaps explains why they find so little differences in the samples they examine. A good resource for this issue is: Preparing for an Aging World: The Case for Cross-National Research, www.nap.edu/catalog.php?record_id=10120#toc.

8. A recent example from psychology is Löckenhoff et al. 2009.

9. For comparative analysis of intergenerational relations see Levine 1965; Rubinstein and Johnsen 1982; Simic 1990; Hashimoto 1996. For age as a basis of social organization see Eisenstadt 1956; Stewart 1977; Foner and Kertzer 1978; Bernardi 1985. For widowhood see Lopata 1972, 1987a, 1987b, 1988; Cattell this volume. For general aspects of female aging see Bart 1969; Dowty et al. 1970; Dougherty 1978; Cool and McCabe 1987; Kerns and Brown 1992.

Bibliography

Albert, S., and M. Cattell. 1994. *Old Age in Global Perspective: Cross-Cultural and Cross-National Views.* New York: G. K. Hall.

Arensberg, C., and C. T. Kimball. 1940. *Family and Community in Ireland.* Cambridge, MA: Harvard University Press.

Arnhoff, F., H. Leon, and I. Lorge. 1964. "Cross-Cultural Acceptance of Stereotypes Toward Aging." *Journal of Social Psychology* 63: 41–58.

Baars, J., J. Dohmen, A. Grenier, and C. Phillipson, eds. 2015. *Ageing, Meaning and Social Structure: Connecting Critical and Humanistic Gerontology.* Bristol, UK: Policy Press.

Bailey, C., and C. Sheehan. 2009. "Technology, Older Persons' Perspectives and the Anthropological Ethnographic." *Alter* 3(2): 96–109.

Barnett, R., and C. Rivers. 2016. *The Age of Longevity: Re-Imagining Tomorrow for Our New Long Lives.* New York: Rowman & Littlefield.

Bart, P. 1969. "Why Women's Status Changes in Middle Age: The Turn of the Social Ferris Wheel." *Sociological Symposium* 3: 1–18.

Bateson, G. 1950. "Cultural Ideas About Aging." In *Research on Aging*, edited by E. P. Jones. Berkeley, CA: University of California Press.

Bernardi, B. 1985. *Age Class Systems.* London: Cambridge.

Burholt, V., C. Stephens, and Norah Keating. 2018. "Collecting Qualitative Data with Older People." In *The SAGE Handbook of Qualitative Data*, edited by Uwe Flick. Thousand Oaks, CA: Sage.

Busija, L., R. Cinelli, M. R. Toombs, C. Easton, R. Hampton, K. Holdsworth, A. Macleod, G. C. Nicholson, B. F. Nasir, K. M. Sanders, and M. P. McCabe. 2018. "The Role of Elders in the Wellbeing of a Contemporary Australian Indigenous Community." *Gerontologist*, gny140. https://doi.org/10.1093/geront/gny140.

Chen, Y.-C. 2018. "A Research Note on Challenges of Cross-National Aging Research: An Example of Productive Activities Across Three Countries." *Research on Aging* 40(1): 54–71.

Child, B. 2013. *Holding Our World Together: Ojibwe Women and the Survival of Community*. New York: Random House.

Clark, M. 1967. "The Anthropology of Aging: A New Area of Studies for Culture and Personality." *Gerontologist* 7: 55–64.

Clark, M., and B. Anderson. 1967. *Culture and Aging: An Anthropological Study of Older Americans*. Springfield, IL: Charles Thomas.

Cohen, C., and J. Sokolovsky. 1988. *Old Men of the Bowery: Strategies for Survival Among the Homeless*. New York: Guilford.

Cohen, G. 2006. "Research on Creativity and Aging: The Positive Impact of the Arts on Health and Illness." *Generations* 30(1): 7–15. https://www.agingkingcounty.org/wp-content/uploads/sites/185/2016/07/RESEARCH-ON-CREATIVITY-AND-AGING.pdf.

Cool, L. and J. McCabe. 1987. "The 'Scheming Hag' and the 'Dear Old Thing': The Anthropology of Aging Women." In *Growing Old in Different Societies: Cross-Cultural Perspectives*, edited by J. Sokolovsky. Acton, MA: Copley.

Counts, D. A., and D. R. Counts. 1996. *Over the Next Hill: An Ethnography of RVing Seniors in North America*. Petersborough, ON: Broadview.

Cowgill, D. 1986. *Aging Around the World*. Belmont, CA: Wadsworth.

Cowgill, D., and L. Holmes, eds. 1972. *Aging and Modernization*. New York: Appleton-Century-Crofts.

Daatland, S. 2006. "Filial Norms and Family Support in a Comparative Cross-National Context: Evidence from the OASIS Study." *Ageing and Society* 26(2): 203–23.

Danley, J. 2017. "Aging and Subjectivity: Ethnography, Experience and Cultural Context." In *Cross-Cultural and Cross-Disciplinary Perspectives in Social Gerontology*, edited by T. Samanta. New York: Springer.

De Medeiros, K. 2013. *Narrative Gerontology in Research and Practice*. New York: Springer.

De Vos, S. 1990. "Extended Family Living Among Older People in Six Latin American Countries." *Journal of Gerontology* 45(3): S87–94.

Dougherty, M. 1978. "An Anthropological Perspective on Aging and Women in the Middle Years." In *The Anthropology of Health*, edited by E. Bauwens. St. Louis, MO: C. V. Mosby.

Dowty, N., B. Maoz, A. Antonovsky, and H. Wijsenbeek. 1970. "Climacterium in Three Culture Contexts." *Tropical and Geographical Medicine* 22: 77–86.

Durham, D., and J. Solway, eds. 2017. *Elusive Adulthoods: The Anthropology of New Maturities*. Bloomington: Indiana University Press.

Durrett, C. 2005. *Senior Cohousing: A Community Approach to Independent Living.* Berkeley, CA: Habitat.

Dykstra, A. 2018. "Cross-National Differences in Intergenerational Family Relations: The Influence of Public Policy Arrangements." *Innovation in Aging* 2(1): 1–8.

Eisenstadt, S. N. 1956. *From Generation to Generation.* New York: Free Press.

Foner, A., and D. I. Kertzer. 1978. "Transitions over the Life Course: Lessons from Age-Set Societies." *American Journal of Sociology* 83(5): 1081–104.

Ford, J. A., R. Turley, T. Porter, T. Shakespeare, G. Wong, A. P. Jones, and N. Steel. 2018. "Access to Primary Care for Socio-economically Disadvantaged Older People in Rural Areas: A Qualitative Study." *PLoS ONE* 13(3): e0193952. https://doi.org/10.1371/journal.pone.0193952.

Forond, C. 2018. "Cultural Competency and Cultural Humility in Simulation-Based Education: An Integrative Review." *Clinical Simulation in Nursing* 15: 42–60.

Francher, J. 1973. "It's the Pepsi Generation: Accelerated Aging and the Television Commercial." *International Journal of Aging and Human Development* 4(3): 245–55.

Fry, C. 1988. "Comparative Research in Aging." In *Gerontology: Perspectives and Issues*, edited by K. Ferraro. New York: Springer.

Fry, C. 2008. "Out of the Armchair and Off the Verandah: Anthropological Theories and the Experiences of Aging." In *The Handbook of Theories of Aging*, 3rd ed., edited by V. Bengtson, M. Silverstein, N. Putney, and D. Gans. New York: Springer.

Fry, C., and J. Keith. 1986. *New Methods for Old Age Research.* South Hadley, MA: Bergin & Garvey.

Gonzalez, L. 2018. "Empowering Elders: How Residents Fought for and Won Person-Directed Care." *Pioneer Network.* https://www.pioneernetwork.net /empowering-elders-how-residents-fought-for-and-won-person -directed-care/.

Goodale, J. 1971. *Tiwi Women.* Seattle: University of Washington Press.

Gubrium, J. 1992. "Qualitative Research Comes of Age in Gerontology." *Gerontologist* 32(5): 581–82.

Gurian, M. 2013. *The Wonder of Aging: A New Approach to Embracing Life after Fifty.* New York: Simon and Schuster.

Hammond, M. 2018. "Spatial Agency: Creating New Opportunities for Sharing and Collaboration in Older People's Cohousing." *Urban Science* 2(3): 64.

Harper, S. 2006. *Ageing Societies.* London: Hodder.

Hart, C. W. 1970. "Fieldwork among the Tiwi 1928–29." In *Being an Anthropologist: Fieldwork in Eleven Cultures*, edited by G. Spindler. New York: Holt, Rinehart & Winston.

Hashimoto, A. 1996. *The Gift of Generations: Japanese and American Perspectives on Aging and the Social Contract.* New York: Cambridge University Press.

Heikkinen, E., W. E. Waters, and Z. J. Brzezinski. 1983. *The Elderly in Eleven Countries.* Copenhagen: World Health Organization, Regional Office for Europe.

Henry, J. 1963. *Culture Against Man*. New York: McGraw-Hill.

Hermalin, A. 2002. *The Well Being of the Elderly in Asia: A Four Country Compara-tive Study*. Ann Arbor: University of Michigan Press.

Horst, H., and D. Miller. 2012. *Digital Anthropology*. London: Berg.

Hromadžić, A., and M. Palmberger, eds. 2018. *Care across Distance: Ethnographic Explorations of Aging and Migration*. New York: Berghahn.

HSBC. 2011. "The Future of Retirement: Why Family Matters." https://www .canarahsbclife.com/pdf/Global_Report_Family.pdf.

HSBC. 2017. "The Future of Retirement: Shifting Sands." https://www.hsbc.com /-/files/hsbc/news-and-insight/2017/pdfs/170426-the-future-of-retire ment-shifting-sands.pdf?download=1.

Hyde, M., and P. Higgs. 2017. *Ageing and Globalization*. Bristol, UK: Policy.

Jenkins, J. 2019. "An Ageing Workforce Isn't a Burden. It's an Opportunity." https://www.weforum.org/agenda/2019/01/an-aging-workforce-isnt-a -burden-its-an-opportunity.

Katz, S., ed. 2017. "New Perspectives on Aging Futures." Special issue, *Societies* 7(2).

Kawano, S., G. Roberts, and S. Long. 2014. *Capturing Contemporary Japan: Dif-ferentiation and Uncertainty*. Honolulu: University of Hawai'i Press.

Keith, J. 1988. "A Modest Little Method Whose Presumptions May Amuse You." In *Methodological Issues in Aging*, edited by W. Schaie, R. Cambell, W. Meredith, and J. Nesselroade. New York: Springer.

Keith, J., C. Fry, A. Glascock, C. Ikels, J. Dickerson-Putnam, H. Harpending, and P. Draper, eds. 1994. *The Aging Experience: Diversity and Commonality Across Cultures*. Thousand Oaks, CA: Sage.

Kendig, H., A. Hashimoto, and L. Coppard, eds. 1992. *Family Support for the Elderly: An International Experience*. New York: Oxford University Press.

Kerns, V., and J. K. Brown, eds. 1992. *In Her Prime: New Views of Middle-Aged Women*, 2nd ed. Urbana: University of Illinois Press.

Kertzer, D., and J. Keith. eds. 1984. *Age and Anthropological Theory*. Ithaca, NY: Cornell University Press.

Kiersz, A. 2014. "This Is When You're Going To Die." *Business Insider*, March 21. http://www.businessinsider.com/social-security-life-table-charts-2014-3.

Kiyota, E. 2018. "Co-creating Environments: Empowering Elders and Strength-ening Communities through Design." *Hastings Center Report* 48(S3). https://onlinelibrary.wiley.com/doi/10.1002/hast.913.

Kontos, P. 2016. "Send in the Clowns: Changing the Face of Dementia Care." Inter-national Network For Critical Gerontology. https://criticalgerontology.com /elder-clowns/

Kreager, P., and E. Schröder-Butterfill, eds. 2005. *Ageing without Children: Euro-pean and Asian Perspectives on Elderly Access to Support Networks*. Oxford: Berghahn.

Kunkel, S., J. Brown, and F. Wittington. 2014. *Global Aging: Comparative Perspec-tives on Aging and the Life Course*. New York: Springer.

Lamb, S. 2006. "Aging across Worlds: Modern Seniors in an Indian Diaspora." In *Generations and Globalization: Youth, Age and Family in the New World*

Economy, edited by J. Cole and D. Durham. Bloomington: Indiana University Press.

Lamb, S., ed. 2017. *Successful Aging as a Contemporary Obsession*. New Brunswick, NJ: Rutgers University Press.

Lessenich, S. 2018. "The Dog That Didn't Bark: The Challenge of Cross-Cultural Qualitative Research on Aging." *Journal of Aging Studies* 47: 66–71.

Levine, R. 1965. "Intergenerational Tensions and Extended Family Structures in Africa." In *Social Structure and the Family*, edited by E. Shanas and G. Strieb. Englewood Cliffs, NJ: Prentice-Hall.

Li, Y., A. Pan, D. D. Wang, X. Liu, K. Dhana, O. H. Franco, S. Kaptoge, E. Di Angelantonio, M. Stampfer, W. C. Willett, and F. B. Hu. 2018. "Impact of Healthy Lifestyle Factors on Life Expectancies in the US Population." *Circulation* 138(4): 345–55.

Löckenhoff, C. E., F. De Fruyt, A. Terracciano, R. R. McCrae, M. De Bolle, P. T. Costa Jr., M. R. Aguilar-Vafaie, et al. 2009. "Perceptions of Aging across 26 Cultures and Their Culture-Level Associates." *Psychology of Aging* 24(4): 941–54.

Long, S. O. 2005. *Final Days: Japanese Culture and Choice at the End of Life*. Honolulu: University of Hawai'i Press.

Lopata, H. 1972. "Role Changes in Widowhood: A World Perspective." In *Aging and Modernization*, edited by D. Cowgill and L. Holmes. New York: Appleton-Century-Crofts.

Lopata, H., ed. 1987a. *Widows, Volume 1: The Middle East, Asia and the Pacific*. Durham, NC: Duke University Press.

Lopata, H., ed. 1987b. *Widows: North America*. Durham, NC: Duke University Press.

Lopata, H., ed. 1988. *Widows: Other Countries, Other Places*. Durham, NC: Duke University Press.

Lynch, C. 2012. *Retirement on the Line: Age, Work, and Value in an American Factory*. Ithaca, NY: Cornell University Press.

Lynch, C., and J. Danley. 2013. *Transitions and Transformations: Cultural Perspectives on Aging and the Life Course*. New York: Berghahn.

McFadden, S., and J. McFadden. 2014. *Aging Together: Dementia, Friendship, and Flourishing Communities*. Baltimore, MD: Johns Hopkins University Press.

Mead, M. 1951. "Cultural Contexts of Aging." In *No Time to Grow Old*. New York State Legislative Committee on Problems of Aging, Legislative Document No. 12.

Mead, M. 1967. "Ethnological Aspects of Aging." *Psychosomatics* 8(4): 33–37.

Mehta, K. 1997. "Cultural Scripts and the Social Integration of Older People." *Ageing and Society* 17: 253–75.

Melby, M. K., and M. Lampl. 2011. "Menopause: A Biocultural Perspective." *Annual Review of Anthropology* 40: 53–70.

Nadel, S. F. 1952. "Witchcraft in Four African Societies." *American Anthropologist* 54: 18–29.

Ney, S. 2005. "Active Aging Policy in Europe: Between Path Dependency and Path Departure." *Ageing International* 30(4): 325–42.

Nusberg, C., and J. Sokolovsky, eds. 1994. *The International Directory of Research and Researchers in Comparative Gerontology.* Washington, DC: American Association of Retired Persons.

Oxlund, B. 2018. "The Life Course in a Migrating World: Hybrid Scripts of Ageing and Imaginaries of Care." *Advances in Life Course Research* 38: 72–79.

Palloni, A., M. Pelaez, and R. Wong. 2006. "Introduction: Aging among Latin American and Caribbean Populations." *Journal of Aging and Health* 18(2): 149–56.

Perkinson, M., and Samantha L. Solimeo. 2014. "Aging in Cultural Context and as Narrative Process: Conceptual Foundations of the Anthropology of Aging as Reflected in the Works of Margaret Clark and Sharon Kaufman." *Gerontologist* 54(1): 101–7.

Prendergast, D., and C. Garattini. 2017. *Aging and the Digital Life Course.* New York: Berghahn.

Putnam-Dickerson, J., and J. Brown, eds. 1998. *Women among Women: Anthropological Perspectives on Female Age Hierarchies.* Champaign: University of Illinois Press.

Rasmussen, S. 2012. "A Little to One Side: Caregiving, Spatial Seclusion, and Spiritual Border-Crossing in Frail Old Age among the Tuareg (Kel Tamajaq)." *Anthropology & Aging Quarterly* 33(4): 130–41.

Rhoads, E., and L. Holmes. 1995. *Other Cultures, Elder Years.* 2nd ed. Thousand Oaks, CA: Sage.

Riva-Mossman, S. 2018. "Aging in Resilient Communities—An Alpine Case Study: The Senior Living Lab Experience in Western Switzerland." *Journal of Aging Science* 6(2).

Robertson, D. 2016. "How Negative Attitudes Towards Ageing Affect Health in Later Life." https://tilda.tcd.ie/publications/research-briefs/pdf/2016_Research%20Brief_Ageing%20Perceptions.pdf.

Robertson, J. 2017. *Robo sapiens japanicus: Robots, Gender, Family, and the Japanese Nation.* Berkeley: University of California Press.

Rodwin, V. G., and M. K. Gusmano. 2006. *Growing Older in World Cities: New York, London, Paris and Tokyo.* Nashville, TN: Vanderbilt University Press.

Rohner, R., R. Naroll, H. Barry III, W. T. Divale, E. E. Erickson, J. M. Schaefer, and R. G. Sipes. 1978. "Guidelines for Holocultural Research." *Current Anthropology* 19(1): 128–29.

Rowles, G., and N. Schoenberg, eds. 2002. *Qualitative Gerontology: Contemporary Perspectives.* New York: Springer.

Royal Society for Public Health. 2018. "That Age Old Question." London: Royal Society for Public Health. https://www.rsph.org.uk/uploads/assets/uploaded/010d3159-0d36-4707-aee54e29047c8e3a.pdf.

Rubinstein, R., and P. T. Johnsen. 1982. "Toward a Comparative Perspective on Filial Response to Aging Populations." In *Aging and the Aged in the Third*

World: Part I, Studies in Third World Societies (No. 22), edited by J. Sokolovsky. Williamsburg, VA: College of William and Mary.

Ruiu, M. 2015. "The Social Capital of Cohousing Communities." *Sociology* 50(2):
400–415.

Sandberg, L., and B. Marshall. 2017. "Queering Aging Futures." *Societies* 7(3): 21.
https://www.mdpi.com/2075-4698/7/3/21.

Sanjek, R. 2008. *The Gray Panthers: Age, Youth and Activism.* Philadelphia: University of Pennsylvania Press.

Scott, A. 2018. "The Myth of an "Ageing Society." *World Economic Forum.* https://
www.weforum.org/agenda/2018/05/the-myth-of-the-aging-society.

Seefeldt, C. 1984. "Children's Attitudes toward the Elderly: A Cross Cultural
Comparison." *International Journal of Aging and Human Development* 19(4):
321–30.

Shea, J. 2015. "Venting Anger from the Body at Gengnianqi: Meanings of Midlife
Transition among Chinese Women in Reform Era Beijing." In *Transitions
and Transformations: Cultural Perspectives on Aging and the Life Course,*
edited by C. Lynch and J. Danely. Oxford: Berghahn.

Sievert, L. L. 2006. *Menopause: A Biocultural Perspective.* New Brunswick, NJ:
Rutgers University Press.

Silin, J. 2018. *Early Childhood, Aging, and the Life Cycle: Mapping Common Ground.*
New York: Springer.

Simic, A. 1990. "Aging, World View, and Intergenerational Relationships in
America and Yugoslavia." In *The Cultural Context of Aging,* edited by
J. Sokolovsky. New York: Bergin and Garvey.

Simmons, L. 1945. *The Role of the Aged in Primitive Society.* New Haven, CT: Archon.

Sivaramakrishnan, K. 2018. *As the World Ages: Rethinking a Demographic Crisis.*
Cambridge, MA: Harvard University Press.

Sokolovsky, J. 2001. "Ethnographic Research." In *Encyclopedia of Aging,* 2nd ed.,
edited by G. Maddox. New York: Springer.

Sokolovsky, J. 2002. "Living Arrangements of Older Persons and Family Support
in Less Developed Countries." *Population Bulletin of the United Nations*
42/43: 162–92.

Sokolovsky, J. 2006. "If Not Why Not: Synchronizing Qualitative and Quantitative Research in Studying the Elderly." In *Qualitative and Mixed Methods
Research: Improving the Quality of Science and Addressing Health Disparities,*
edited by L. Curry, R. Shield, and T. Wetle. Washington, DC: American
Public Health Association.

Spencer, P. 1965. *The Samburu: A Study of Gerontocracy in a Nomadic Tribe.* Berkeley: University of California Press.

Stewart, F. 1977. *Fundamentals of Age-Group Systems.* New York: Academic Press.

Tanabe, M. 2007. "Culture Competence in the Training of Geriatric Medicine
Fellows." *Educational Gerontology* 33(5): 421–28.

Tornstam, L. 2005. *Gerotranscendence: A Developmental Theory of Positive Aging.*
New York: Springer.

Twigg, J., and W. Martin. 2014. "The Challenge of Cultural Gerontology." *Gerontologist* 55(3): 1–7.

U.S. Census. 2018. "An Aging Nation: Projected Number of Children and Older Adults." https://www.census.gov/library/visualizations/2018/comm/historic-first.html.

Von Mering, O. 1957. "A Family of Elders." In *Remotivating the Mental Patient*, edited by O. von Mering and S. King. New York: Russel Sage Foundation.

Warner, L. 1937. *A Black Civilization*. New York: Harper & Brothers.

Winn, R., and N. Newton. 1982. "Sexuality in Aging: A Study of 106 Cultures." *Journal Archives of Sexual Behavior* 11(4): 283–98.

Zaidi, A. 2018. "Implementing the Madrid Plan of Action on Ageing: What Have We Learned? And, Where Do We Go from Here?" United Nations Development Programme Human Development Report. http://hdr.undp.org/en/content/implementing-madrid-plan-action-ageing-what-have-we-learned-and-where-do-we-go-here.

PART I

A Global Vision of Aging, Culture, and Context

From the fall of the Roman and the Mayan empires to the Black Death to the colonization of the New World and the youth-driven revolutions of the twentieth century, demographic trends have played a decisive role in many of the great invasions, political upheavals, migrations, and environmental catastrophes of history. By the 2020s, an ominous new conjuncture of demographic trends may once again threaten widespread disruption. We are talking about global aging, which is likely to have a profound effect on economic growth, living standards, and the shape of the world order.

—Neil Howe and Richard Jackson ("Global Aging and the Crisis of the 2020s," *Current History*, 2011)

A Global Vision of Aging

Culture, and Context

Introduction

Jay Sokolovsky

The New Millennium of Global Aging

The Howe and Jackson quote which opens this section sets out the need to pay attention to the unfolding global age of aging, over the next decade and beyond. In the near future most industrializing world regions will still not have reached the level of serious societal aging now faced by North America, much of Europe, and Japan, but currently "maturing" nations such as South Korea, China, and Mexico are starting to catch up. On the demographic surface, numbers can sometime impress. By 2050, the latest global data indicate that the population aged 65 and older is projected to double to 2.3 billion, more than the current population today of China (Population Reference Bureau 2018). The number of Americans in this age category is expected to more than double—from 46 million today to over 98 million by 2060. Already, by 2020, over two-thirds of the globe's population past their sixth decade lives in the industrializing world. Through the first half of this century it is the East Asian region, fueled by dramatic drops in fertility levels and rapid urban industrialization, that will demographically age fastest (see Figure I.1). This trend began in the 1980s and has accelerated dramatically ever since. By 2017 there were already more persons over age 65 in Asia than there are people in the United States (Voice of Asia 2017).

Measuring Global Aging

The National Institute on Aging and the U.S. Bureau of the Census, in 1985, established an International Data Base and later an Aging Studies Branch to address the issue of global population *greying*. In this section's first article, Census Bureau unit chief Wan He and former chief Kevin Kinsella discuss some of the key parameters that have caught the attention of those

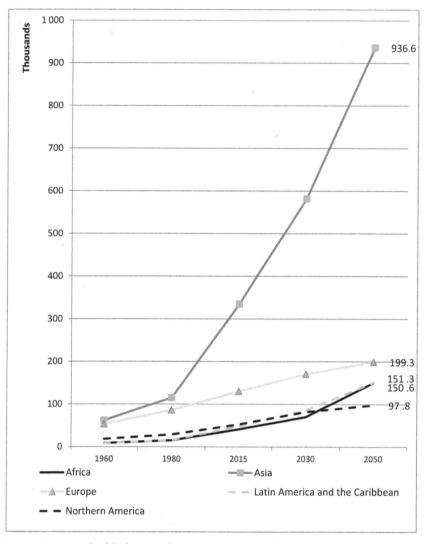

Figure I.1   Total Elderly Population, 65 Years and Above (millions) (United Nations, Department of Economic and Social Affairs, Population Division [2017]. World Population Prospects: The 2017 Revision, custom data acquired via Web site.).

who study the demography of aging. In a global survey, they lay out the critical social, medical, and policy consequences of the numbers flowing from demographic reports. Importantly, they place this information in the broad constructs of gender, in the global burden of disease, and also in how early life course advantages or disadvantages impact late life disability.

WEB SPECIAL:

1. A good place to check out the latest global data on aging is the United Nations Aging Theme Data: https://www.un.org/en/development/desa/population/theme/ageing/index.asp.

The 21st century began with warnings that global aging spelled future societal doom with predictions of slower economic growth, lower labor force participation, looming pension crises, exploding health care costs, and reduced productivity. More recent analysis has produced a more balanced analysis of how to understand and even take advantage of the coming demographic changes (Bloom, Canning, and Lubet 2017). There are also different ways of quantifying aging that have an impact on policy planning, and one of the biggest challenges to traditional methods is found in the blog post: "It's Time to Measure 21st Century Aging with 21st Century Tools" (Sanderson and Scherbov 2016). This article about alternative demographic measures argues that the idea of dire consequences from global aging may be much less significant than some researchers predict. (See also Scherbov and Andruchowitz 2019.)

There Is Societal Aging . . . and Then There Is "Super Aging"

Most Western countries and Japan already contain a sizable portion of older citizens within their boundaries. As of 2020, 10 major nations such as Germany, Italy, and Sweden had more than 20 percent of their population age 65 or older, while the world leader in this regard, Japan, was closing in on a third of its citizens being in this category. In contrast, with just under 15 percent in this older age category, the comparative youth of the United States

---

PROJECT TO FOLLOW:

The Reassessing Aging from a Population Perspective (Re-Aging) project. It seeks to develop new approaches to the study of age and aging that are appropriate for 21st-century conditions. www.iiasa.ac.at/web/home/research/researchPrograms/WorldPopulation/Reaging/Re-Aging.html.

will continue for at least the next two decades. This provides a comparative framework for the ongoing debate in that country around such issues as generational equity and eldercare, topics to be explored later on in this volume. Over the past decade there has emerged a new term in demographics, *super aging*, which designates a nation as having at least a quarter of its population age 65 or older.

Aging and Disruptive Demographics

Director of MIT's Age Lab Joseph Coughlin refers to the flow of 21st-century population changes as "disruptive demographics" breaking patterns that have persisted in the prior century. He notes in various blogs and a video talk on the subject that by midcentury Japan's population may reduce by half and nearly 40 percent of its people will be over 65; in 2018 China there were expected to be sold more adult diapers than baby diapers; almost half of young adults aged 18–34 in the EU and about one-third in the United States were living with parents; and in the United States every hour 500 baby boomers will be turning age 72—my age when this book is expected to be published (Coughlin 2018).

Importantly, in terms of how nations will have to adjust to demographic change, South Korea tops the list of the globe's most rapidly aging population. For example while in 2010 the United States and South Korea had roughly the same median age (37/38 respectively), by 2050 the United States will have bumped up this value by a mere four years while South Korea is expected to match Japan with a figure over age 50! It is little wonder that over the past decade South Korea declared a national emergency concerning the rise of dementia and is actively training the young to deal with these disruptive demographics. Similarly the results of an international survey asking if the growing number of older people in your nation is a major problem show that it is in the most rapidly aging countries (Japan, South Korea, and China) that have the highest level of concern—almost three times higher than in the United States (Pew Global 2014)! Such coming "disruptive demographics" in a rapidly aging planet are impacting all aspects of social life from career paths, family formation, the makeup of households and community, symbolic representations of midlife and old age, attitudes toward disability, and who will care for you in late life.

Demographic Imaginaries and Shortgevity

While some nations in Africa will retain a youthful population well into midcentury, the patterns of change through globalization and migration are beginning to greatly alter culturally based systems of support and provoke significant concern about the ability of family networks to sustain their

---

WEB SPECIAL:

"South Korea Prepares the Young for a Rapidly Aging Population," Anthony Kuhn, https://www.npr.org/2013/01/04/168615553/south-korea -prepares-the-young-for-a-rapidly-aging-population.

WEB SPECIAL:

See the implications for aging in the United States in Jonathan Vespa, "The Graying of America: More Older Adults Than Kids by 2035," https://www.census.gov/library/stories/2018/03/graying-america.html.

---

oldest members. This will clearly be seen in Coe's study in Ghana (Part II) and research on Thailand's "demographic imaginary" by Aulino (Part III). Although in some areas, especially sub-Saharan Africa and Russia, populations have experienced recent "shortgevity," an overall drop in life expectancy, global trends are massively progressing in the opposite direction.[1] It is important to note that a drop in average longevity has also recently happened in the United States, as life expectancy has decreased for three consecutive years since 2015. This is the first time such a sustained drop occurred since the 1915–1918 period, marked by World War I and a global flu epidemic. Now the big drivers in 2017 were drug overdoses, taking 70,237 lives, and suicides, exceeding 47,000 deaths (Solly 2018).

A Global Framework for Culturally Constructing Aging and Old Age

Cultural perceptions of older adulthood or old age link changes in the person's physical being (e.g., reduction of work capacity, beginning of menopause) with social changes (such as the birth of grandchildren) to create a culturally defined sense of oldness (Ikels and Beall 2000; Part I Web Book Fry et al.). As will be elaborated upon in Part II, human cultural systems usually recognize the importance of this part of the life cycle by linguistically creating labels delineating a stage of late adulthood (Part II Kao and Albert). The conception of being "old" is a *near* human universal and is differentially entered by a variety of measures.

As Kao and Albert show in Part II, the socially constructed boundaries of oldness can have various gradations that even extend beyond the point of death into a category of ancestors (Kopytoff 1971). Many societies also recognize, as a different category of old, those truly ancient living adults who show sharp declines in functioning. For example, to the Ju/'hoansi people of Botswana, old age is perceived to begin relatively early and can start in a person's mid-40s when and if changes in physical capabilities begin to diminish functional ability. Here there are three levels of "old," a beginning early stage, a frail but functional stage, and a physically disabled designation. Counterbalancing the Ju/'hoansi linkage of older adults with physical decline is a powerful association with greater spiritual and emotional strength often put to use by the aged in healing rituals or in settling disputes (Part I Web Book Rosenberg).

Only one study to date has systematically used worldwide data to examine the passage into old age. Anthropologists Anthony Glascock and Susan Feinman found that in a random sample of 60 societies, there were three basic means of identifying a category of "old": change of social/economic role, chronology, and change in physical characteristics (1981; see Table I.1). Their study produced the following conclusions:

1. A shift in social/economic roles was the common marker of being designated as old. Typical examples are one's children having their own kids, changes in a person's productive activities, or beginning to receive more goods and services than one gives.

2. A change in physical capabilities is the least common marker. Severe frailty or dementia is quite rare as an initial indicator of being called old. This has happened because sampled societies typically create a category of old starting before many people encounter much radical signs of physical decline.

3. About half of the societies use multiple definitions of being aged. Such varied markers of aging are commonly applied to distinct categories of "old" itself, which can include a phase of oldness linked to images associated with a movement toward death and the loss of normal functioning.

This last item seems to add a component of both complexity and ambiguity to how societies fully articulate their images of aging. As we will see later on in this section, confronting an image of the old, tilted toward the dimensions of death and incapacity, can initiate drastic changes in the attitudes and behavior toward those so labeled (see also Part VI Barker).

Global Perspectives on Status and Support of the Aged

One of the promises of a truly cross-cultural comparative gerontology is to gain an understanding of aging, divorced from the narrow boundary of a single case such as the Ju/'hoansi. In fact, it is among such types of

Table I.1   Percent distribution of old age definitional classifications: From the Human Relations Area Files

(Absolute Numbers in Parentheses)

How the beginning of old age is defined	Single definition of aging	Multiple definitions of aging
Change in social role	71% (30)	46% (27)
Chronology	19% (8)	34% (20)
Change in capabilities	10% (4)	20% (12)
Total	100% (42)	100% (59)

Source: Glascock and Feinman 1981: 20.

society—nomadic, nonagricultural, lacking economic stratification, with bilateral descent—that one is statistically most likely to find the very frail elderly having their lives "hastened." The first serious attempt to deal with such issues on a worldwide basis was the massive study by Leo Simmons, *The Role of the Aged in Primitive Society* (1945). However, despite methodological problems with his very early use of the Human Relations Area Files (HRAF), this book has many insights that have served as a guidepost to more recent, controlled comparisons and holocultural studies.[2] He shows the variety of ways elderly function in society, including knowledge bearing, child care, and ritual, judicial, and political decision-making. Numerous ethnographies have validated how a combination of deep knowledge held by older adults and their nurturing actions toward younger generations sustains human societies. Collins, for example, found that among contemporary Inuit in Canada, ideological rather than material contributions were central to their positive evaluation by younger community members. That is, successful elders were those who were willing to transmit their accumulated knowledge to junior members of their community (2001).

Working independently with small, cross-cultural samples, Cowgill and Holmes (1974) and Press and McKool (1972) proposed similar variables that account for high status in traditional peasant societies. These involve four interrelated clusters of cultural phenomena: (1) an available role set emphasizing continuity and important responsibilities in community organization and public life, (2) integration into a residentially viable extended family organization, (3) control of some important material and informational resources, and (4) a value system praising a group-oriented ideology while deemphasizing individual ego development.

In applying these variables to the Ju/'hoansi people studied by Rosenberg (Part I Web Book), we can see that their cultural context does not fulfill all of the criteria listed above. This is especially the case in terms of their lack of a residentially stable extended-family organization, such as with the families Sokolovsky studied in rural Mexico (Part III). Yet, Rosenberg found that there is a powerful cumulative effect of the important roles the elderly play in kinship relations, control of knowledge, and mastery of the dangerous spiritual force called *num*. When combined with the Ju/'hoansi's communal ideological orientation, what is created is a cultural context in which the elderly are well supported.

A series of holocultural studies have corroborated, in many respects, the association of status and deference with the control of informational and administrative roles (Sheehan 1976; Silverman and Maxwell 1987) as well as valued activities and extended family integration (McArdle and Yeracaris 1981). In terms of resource and information control, Silverman and Maxwell have demonstrated that only certain types of control, particularly administrative and consultative, correlate with beneficent treatment of the elderly. Some forms of supernatural information control, especially transformational powers, were in fact a potential threat to the elderly.

The Dilemma of Older Women in Contexts of Change

The role of older women is highly relevant to some historically known situations of massive societal change, such as in 13th- to 16th-century Europe, colonial North America, and contemporary Ghana. In Europe, the typical person burned at the stake for their "transformational knowledge" (witchcraft) was an older female between the ages of 55 and 65 (Bever 1982; Banner 1992). Similar demographics of witch accusations were found when John Demos studied those most likely to be condemned in 17th-century Puritan Massachusetts. Such female suspects were likely to be old and poor, either single or widowed and known as being unusual or irritating to neighbors (Demos 1982; Haber 1997). As seen in Box I.1 below, similar dynamics appear to be driving accusations of sorcery in northern Ghana over the past two decades (see also Crampton 2013; Richter, Flowers, and Bongmba 2017; Part II Coe).

"First Peoples" and Aging—Lessons for the 21st Century

Anthropologists have long been interested in examining life in societies that, in their traditional way of life, resemble the earliest forms of human cultural systems. While many tribal societies such as the Amazonian Yanomamo remain on the brink of extinction, the last decade has witnessed an unexpected resilience among indigenous, "first" peoples. These groups, which constitute about 4 percent of the earth's population, have sometimes managed to maintain their core cultural values in the face of ferocious onslaughts by industrial nations. Groups such as the Ju/'hoansi and Hadza in Africa and the

---

Box I.1   Older Women as Witches in Ghana

Although both men and women can practice witchcraft, in rural Ghana, it is only the women, especially the older ones, who are branded as witches and banished from the village, while their male counterparts are treated with the greatest caution and are feared. As will be pointed out by Coe in Part II, with a decline in reliance on the extended family for social and financial support, elderly women have become increasingly vulnerable to poverty and physical and emotional abuse (see also Sossou and Yogtiba 2015). A state-based social security system only effectively operates for urban wage workers and has little impact on older persons in rural peasant communities.

It is in Northern Ghana that exiled women in camps for witches are most likely to be found. Some have been in these camps for three decades and the vast majority, about 80 percent, are from 45 to 90 years of age. Upwards of 8,000 female outcasts are estimated to now live in this region. Issah Wumbla has done a recent study of witch accusations, banishing, and movement to the northern camps (2019). Of the women surveyed, a majority were poor widows with dependency on other family members lacking economic resources. This left them relatively defenseless if they were accused of witchcraft. It is important to note that the communities in which these supposed witches originally lived and where they were claimed to cause death had poor sanitary conditions and overcrowding, which promoted high levels of mortality from diseases such as meningitis, malaria, and cholera.

Adapted from Samuel Wiafe, "Witch's Curse: Poor Living Standards Banish Older Women from Their Communities," *New Internationalist*, March 2001. (See also Van der Geest 2002 and Adinkrah 2015 for broader perspectives on aging and witchcraft.)

Tsimane in Bolivia have provided critical models for understanding an evolutionary context of aging with lessons for 21st-century societies.

Among the best studied examples that fit this description are the Ju/'hoansi, described in this section by Harriet Rosenberg (Web Book). They are also part of the Project AGE sample discussed in this section's last Web article. The Ju/'hoansi, also known variously as the Bushmen, !Kung, or San peoples, are a formerly nomadic gathering and hunting group in Botswana. Despite the erroneous image created in the feature film *The Gods Must Be Crazy*, they are not an unchanged people, lacking contact with the outside world.[3] Instead, over the last three decades they at times have been a captive group, restricted to a reservation and forced to significantly alter their quite successful foraging lifestyle. Nonetheless, this harsh political context has not yet destroyed core cultural features of Ju/'hoansi family, community, and ritual life, forums in which the elderly still perform valued roles. These cultural niches for the elderly include being a knowledge repository about kin ties and natural resource management, transcendental curing and performance, entertainment through clowning and dancing, and being an emotional focus for community integration.

Here we clearly see the benefits of long-term ethnographic research combined with discourse and narrative analysis in understanding the cultural mechanisms of caring for the elderly (Perkinson and Solimeo 2013; Buch 2015).[4] Without having lived with the group for an extended period or having had access to her husband's 30 years of experience with the Ju/'hoansi, Rosenberg might have mistaken the constant "kvetching" (sharp complaining) of most elderly as proof that this is a society that habitually abandons its older citizens in need of care. Instead, her nuanced analysis linking the narrative of complaint discourse to the egalitarian and communal roots of Ju/'hoansi society shows that outspoken nagging is a part of their package of cultural devices that reinforce values of caring and extreme compassion for even the very frail elderly. Importantly, caregiving is carried out evenly by persons of both sexes, avoiding the overdependence on female caregivers typical for industrialized countries. A special aspect of this chapter is a 2018 update with discussion of both the continuation of traditional behavior along with cell phones, pensions, and production of fair-trade, globally sold crafts. It will be important to compare this cultural crafting and use of a negative narrative about younger kin with Annette Leibing's chapter (Part VI Web Book). This work set in Brazil looks at an emerging "hero" metaphor directed at grandchildren caring for their older relatives with dementia.

Are We Human Because We Have Elders?

Humans are the primate species with not only the longest life span but also the greatest proportion of those years spent in social and biological maturity (Crews 2003). Clinical psychologist David Gutmann suggests that this evolved, not because of the developing capacities and moral imperative to keep the weak alive, but rather we are in fact human *because we have elders* (1987). This "strong face of aging," as Gutmann terms it, derives from the function of elders in our species' early history, as a vital link in the transmission of our socially learned systems of belief and behavior, which imbue children with the essence of humanity.[5] In other words, we attained our humanity through the very existence of elders and their enactment of postparental roles. More recent work in life-span psychology research in a wide range of cultures also suggests that an adaptive advantage of long life to group survival is the greater integration of knowledge and socio-emotional regulation observed in later years, despite decrements in some aspects of memory and other cognitive processes (Carstensen and Löckenhoff 2003; Carstensen 2019).

One of the interesting issues emerging from both evolutionary anthropology and psychology is whether our species' long, postreproductive life span is a modern artifact or an evolutionary mechanism long adapted through natural selection of our premodern ancestors (Caspari and Lee 2004).[6] The limited age-estimated data on our Paleolithic ancestors did not initially indicate very significant survival past the third decade of life, with life expectancy at birth hovering around the mid-20s. However, as Harper summarizes the current available data, "Even in Stone Age populations, the life expectancy of females at age 45 was more than 10 years, and probably in the range of 12–25 years; and up to 30 percent of the female population was post-reproductive" (2006: 86; Gurven and Kaplan 2007 for discussion of this data).

Since the mid-1990s a very lively debate has emerged around the selective advantage of elder citizens to early human communities. Much of this was stimulated by the work of Kristen Hawkes and colleagues based on her work in East Africa with the hunter-forager Hadza peoples (Chan, Hawkes, and Kim 2016). They have focused on what has come to be known as the "grandmother hypothesis"—the notion that aging women gain an inclusive fitness advantage from investing in their grandchildren. This hypothesis has evolved from an explanation for menopause into an explanation for the exceptionally long postreproductive lifespan in human females. As discussed in the Web Special, while the men were out hunting and mothers out gathering, grandmothers and babies were developing the successful behaviors marking our species' adaptation cultural niche: through sharing food, cooperating on more and more complex levels, and developing new social relationships. In later chapters we will further explore the importance of grandmothers in adapting to change and dealing with the stresses of minority ethnic families.

Beyond the Grandmother Hypothesis

As detailed in the Part I Web Chapter by Gurven and Kaplan, other models of late-life importance to early human selective advantage have developed and are currently being explored through the Tsimane Health and Life History Project (Gurven et al. 2018). Set in the Bolivian Amazon, this project examines over time the economic, demographic, and developmental aspects of aging in 18 communities of forager-horticultural peoples. In doing so they

---

WEB SPECIAL:

John Poole, "Why Grandmothers May Hold the Key to Human Evolution," NPR, https://www.npr.org/sections/goatsandsoda/2018/06/07/617 097908/why-grandmothers-may-hold-the-key-to-human-evolution.

are testing out their "Embodied Capital Model" linking human skill acquisition over long maturation with lowered mortality rates and greater longevity. Their model proposes that cross-generational contributions from both genders were critical to the evolution of longevity in our species. Importantly, continuing study of the traditional dietary complex of the Tsimane have shown that their population has the lowest rates of cardiovascular disease ever measured in a human population (Kraft et al. 2018).

Successful Aging, Conscious Aging, and the "Postmodern" Elder

As upward transformations in longevity and healthy functioning of older adults are exceeding predictions made barely a decade ago (see Part VI), so too is the societally constructed image of aging being altered. One element here is the constructed reality of late life through language, popular culture, and various forms of media. We will address this in the Part II Web Book, especially in the Web chapter by Featherstone and Hepworth exploring the cultural representations of late life. One of the challenges for social sciences has been to tackle the issue of how different societies think about "successful aging." Since the work of Rowe and Kahn (1998)—proposing that "better than average" aging as a combination of three components: avoiding disease and disability, high cognitive and physical function, and engagement with life—there has been a great deal written seeking to frame this subject from a diverse and critical perspective (see especially Stowe and Cooney 2015; Lamb 2017). We have already noted the efforts of Project AGE as well as the ongoing global ASSA and Aging as a Human Condition projects (see book Introduction) to explore this issue and the need for a cross-cultural framework. In this section anthropologist Sarah Lamb draws upon research in the United States and India to explore how different cultures and varied class segments in the United States alter how successful aging is understood. It will be instructive to relate here ethnic and class-based variation and inequality to discussion in Parts IV and VI about how cultural and economic privilege provides greater comparative longevity and freedom from late-life disability (see especially Berridge and Martinson 2018).

"Wellderly" versus "Illderly" and a Postmodern Late Life

Another perspective is the self-conscious effort to transform how individuals think about and seek to experience the aging process. Connected to Lamb's chapter, Harry Moody (Web Book) in this section suggests the shift from perceiving older adults as "wellderly" rather than "illderly" has stimulated the promotion of a construct of "successful aging," keyed to active vitality and "productive aging" linked to redefining retired life (Martinson and Minkler 2006; Bowling 2007).

WEB SPECIAL:

See this article that discusses an emerging shift in India toward a more Western construct of successful aging: Tannistha Samanta, "The 'Good Life': Third Age, Brand Modi and the Cultural Demise of Old Age in Urban India," *Anthropology & Aging* 39, no. 1 (2018), http://anthro-age.pitt.edu/ojs/index.php/anthro-age/article/view/208/236.

Moody argues that both successful and productive aging are a postmodern strategy for turning old age into a "second middle age," in effect a strategy for an age-less old age (Katz 2005). In effect his chapter does two things: (1) it notes how the success and productive aging models narrowly and ethnocentrically enshrine Western ideology concerning success in adulthood; and (2) it shows how understanding cultural variation offers other inner-looking alternatives that many people in North America are embracing (McFadden 2008). This latter focus seeks to move beyond loss and decline and has sparked a "conscious" aging movement nurtured by spirituality and transcendence but also connected to a broad issue of global survival such as global warming (https://www.sage-ing.org/links-2/conscious-aging-alliance/). Moody suggests, in effect, adding a spiritual element of what Tornstam calls "gerotranscendence," to the developmental psychologies of Jung, Erickson, and Maslow (Moody and Carroll 1998; Tornstam 2005; Hughes-Rinker 2019). In the introduction to Part II, I will further discuss the "conscious aging" movement and the new language and discourse about late life it is trying to provoke.

Assisted Suicide and the Darker Side of Aging

A special concern within the growing comparative perspective on being old is confronting the darker side of aging—various types of nonsupportive and even "death-hastening" behaviors directed toward the elderly. In the United States and other countries this has created a legal, ethical, and medical battleground concerning euthanasia as an option for terminally ill aged (Norwood 2007). In 2007, "Dr. Death," Jack Kevorkian, was released after eight years in prison for assisting in over 100 assisted suicides. This event reignited a powerful debate that impacts people of all ages. The judicial dilemmas stemming from this issue are worthy of King Solomon. For example, in January 1996, a man from Petoskey, Michigan, won custody of his Alzheimer's-disease-stricken father in a court case against his own mother. The son had maintained that the mother and his siblings were conspiring to seek the help of Dr. Kevorkian to end the father's life. In Part VI we will say more about what Norwood (2018) calls the new normal: mediated death and assisted dying in the 21st-century United States.

As we have already seen in the discussion of the Tiwi, "high-tech" societies are not the only ones to grapple with this dilemma. Anthony Glascock in this section (Web Book) throws the question into historical and global relief and finds some disquieting results. A majority of the societies in his sample exhibited some form of "death-hastening" behavior, with less than one-third providing unconditional support. However, few societies enforce a single treatment of their elderly, and it was commonly found that both supportive as well as death-hastening behavior coexist in the same social setting.

The important and related issue of elder abuse is beginning to be investigated in diverse settings, such as among Native American tribes (Jervis 2014), North American families (Fisher and Regan 2006), and in varied international settings (Pillemer et al. 2016).[7] In the book's final section, varied cultural responses to the oldest old will be more fully explored.

The Feminization of Old Age

As noted by Kinsella in this section, women constitute more than a majority of the older population in virtually all parts of the world. At birth, females in the United States have a life expectancy almost six years greater than males, and when they reach age 65 they can expect to survive three more years than their male counterparts. For third world nations, there is typically about half this difference in life expectancies and past the sixth decade there is a more even gender ratio than found in the postindustrial world. However, it is in the former type of societies that the worlds of males and females are found to be most socially and culturally divergent (Dickerson-Putnam and Brown 1998). As Ellickson notes for rural Bangladesh, this is especially the case in patrilineal societies with a good deal of social and gendered stratification, where distinct separate male and female subcultures emerge and men try to strongly control the sexuality and reproductive history of women in their family (1988; see also Dickerson-Putman 1996). It is here that one sees a clear divergence of cultural scripts in late life. In Bangladesh there may be rewards for an older woman if she manages to become the head of the domestic realm of an extended family, but this is typically brief, as she loses that role when her husband dies. The elder man, however, only relinquishes authority and economic control upon his own death.

The typical dominance of males in public arenas is linked to the divergent imagery of aging created on the basis of gender. Predominant in this difference is the common hydra-headed perception of older women in the same society, from the positive, nurturing matriarch/granny to the mystical shamaness, and finally to the feared, evil witch. The ethnographic literature now abounds with this type of dramatic alternation between "Dear Old Thing" and "Scheming

Hag" metaphors (Cool and McCabe 1987). In the United States Carole Haber has documented the varied historical image of older women as witch, widow, wife, and worker constructed through the agency of men (1997). It is notewor-thy that in "woman-centered" societies, such as the Indonesian Minangkabu discussed in Part V Web Book, while aging women are seen as the virtual pil-lars of society, they seldom use their cultural dominance to replicate a negative and subordinate image of men that is promulgated toward the opposite sex in strongly male-dominated societies.

In this regard it is crucial to note the impact of colonial domination in Latin America and Africa and the imposition of forms of Christianity and Islam that have altered power relationships in communities as well as within family life, often reducing both the domestic and public roles of adult women. One recently discovered example comes from highland Ethiopia among the Gamo people, where the imposition of Christianity allowed the continuation of a powerful male community leadership role but eliminated a parallel female position, of the *gimuwa* held by postmenopausal women. Such indi-viduals had crucial roles in fertility rituals for crops and families, held feasts to help redistribute resources among households, and settled disputes between men and women in the community (Arthur 2013).

It is unfortunate that until the 1990s the analysis of aging in such societies has largely portrayed the male perspective, despite the importance of older women to the functioning of society. Many authors have begun to document a common pattern in nonindustrial societies of dramatic positive changes in role, power, and status by women as they pass into the middle and latter adult years (Foner 1994; Kerns and Brown 1992; Brown, Subbaiah, and Therese 1994).[8]

The past two decades, however, has seen the publication of important ethnographic studies, especially in Africa, India, Mexico, the Caribbean, and New York City showing the complex interaction of culture, gender, and aging. These include: *Contingent Lives: Fertility, Time and Aging in West Africa* (Bledsoe 2002); *Aging, Gender and Famine in Rural Africa* (Cliggett 2005); *The Poetics and Politics of Tuareg Aging* (Rasmussen 1997); *No Aging in India* (Cohen 1998); *White Saris and Sweet Mangoes* (Lamb 2000); *Midlife and Older Women* (Rawlins 2006); *Maturing Masculinities* (Wentzel 2013); *Unforgotten: Love and the Culture of Dementia Care in India* (Brijnath 2014).

Menopause: A Key Bio-Culture Nexus

One of the universal imperatives of a woman's midlife biological transition is the eventual cessation of reproductive capacity. Various writers have noted that for women, the fourth and fifth decades of life, in their association with menopause, often provide a key turning point.[9] Beginning with Marsha Flint's research in India during the 1970s, it was shown that the biological and social responses to a female's reproductive capacity were quite variable in different cultural settings and responsive to cultural scripts for mid and late life. As Kaufert and Lock note:

> Most women know the script laid out in their particular society for the woman in midlife, including what symptoms she should expect from her body. . . . Women in California are told that a loss in libido is a medical problem to be treated by hormone therapy, whereas a Bengali woman in India knows very well that sexual activity is inappropriate for the postmenopausal woman. . . . Both the denial and the affirmation of sexuality are social phenomena, but for the California woman the responses of her body have been transformed into a medical problem to be medically managed. . . . Just as obstetricians and pediatricians would define how women should feel and behave when becoming mothers, gynecologists and psychiatrists tell women what it is to be menopausal. (1992: 203)

How the complex interplay of biology, nutrition, and culture shapes women's experience of menopause is nicely analyzed by Yewoubdar Beyene in *From Menarche to Menopause: Reproductive Lives of Peasant Women in Two Cultures* (1989). Beyene's Web Book chapter in this section is taken from her book and provides a comparison of rural Mayan and Greek women. She shows that, despite similar values and behaviors regarding menstruation and childbearing, their experience of menopause differed. She found that Greek women typically had a pattern of symptoms and a negative perception of menopause and aging not unlike those reported by many females in North America. In contrast, the Mayan women not only systematically lacked these same responses to menopause but welcomed its new freedoms and saw it as a social passage to higher status in old age.

With the stimulation of such research, cross-cultural studies of menopause and aging have exploded in recent years. It includes both long-term focused comparisons (Sievert 2014; Shea 2015; Kirchengast 2017) and massive cross-national works such as the Decisions at Menopause Study (DAMES) and the largest and most exhaustive comparative investigation of menopause across populations, the SWAN Study of Women Across the Nation (Obermeyer and Sievert 2007; Colvin et al. 2017; https://www.swanstudy.org/).

WEB SPECIAL:

The Woman and Ageing Research Network, www.facebook.com /womenandageing/

Life Course Embodiment, Bodies, and Gender Fluidity

There has also emerged a growing literature, seeking to understand gender fluidity beyond a simplistic male-female dichotomy (Hegarty 2017). This work is intertwined with a "somatic turn" and concern for corporeality and embodiment over the life course (Gilleard and Higgs 2018). Much of this new research argues against traditional cultural scripts inscribing gender privilege for younger adulthood and the reproductive years. These authors suggest that feminist, civil rights, and disability activism movements of the 20th century were primarily oriented toward the young and suggest for example, that gay identity was implicitly imagined as *young* gay identity (Gilleard and Higgs 2013). This approach is developed in the chapter by Bishop and Westwood who take on the issue of trans(gender)/gender-diverse aging as a social justice issue. Their chapter expands on the idea of successful aging by challenging the assumptions of "heteronormativity," and joins a growing critical literature recognizing diversity in our aging futures (Sandberg and Marshall 2017).

"Project AGE" Looks at a Good Old Age

The focus of this section's concluding Web Chapter, Project AGE, represents the most sophisticated cross-cultural approach to questions surrounding aging ever undertaken. Integrating both qualitative and quantitative

---

PROJECTS TO FOLLOW:

With the growing focus on global aging, there have emerged various indexes to measure how well societies promote the well-being of their older citizens.

1. Global AgeWatch Index from HelpAge: http://www.helpage.org/global-agewatch/reports/global-agewatch-index-2013-insight-report-summary-and-methodology/.

2. Columbia University's Mailman School of Public Health, the University of Southern California Schaeffer Center for Health Policy & Economics, with the support of the John A. Hartford Foundation, have developed a new barometer that estimates how countries are adapting to the dramatic increases in the number and proportion of older persons. The Index is composed of specific measures across five social and economic indicators that reflect the status and well-being of older persons in a country and that can be followed over time and used to compare across nations. https://www.mailman.columbia.edu/public-health-now/news/new-global-aging-index-gauges-health-and-well being-aging-populations.

approaches within a common methodology, complex ethnographies of age and aging were conducted at seven sites around the world between 1982 and 1990. The research shows how both "system-wide" community features (such as social inequality) and "internal mechanisms" (such as values) create distinct contexts for conceptualizing the life cycle, establishing age norms, and influencing the perception of well-being in old age (Keith et al. 1994). In their article presented here, the authors of Project AGE address this last vexing issue. Their focus is on how cultures create a sense of a "good old age" and the factors that shape this perception. It is particularly interesting to note that in one of the sites, Hong Kong, despite continuing ideals of filial concern and actual intergenerational co-residence, old age receives the lowest status compared to other parts of the life course.

Notes

1. In sub-Saharan Africa a major culprit in Shortgevity is the AIDS epidemic, while in Russia it is a failed health care system combined with rampant alcoholism and other lifestyle-related unhealthy behavior pattern, especially for men.

2. The methodological flaws included a poorly drawn sample, inadequate statistical controls, and imprecise definition of some key variables.

3. While quite popular with the general public, the 1982 film *The Gods Must Be Crazy* has evoked a storm of protest from scholars. They have criticized the film for depicting an erroneous, benign view of a South African political structure that protects the childlike Ju/'hoansi living in a pristine state of Stone Age existence. In reality the Ju/'hoansi have been placed on a fenced-in reservation, their traditional lifestyle has been prohibited and the men are often conscripted by the South African military to fight guerilla forces in rural areas.

4. For connections to the emerging literature on narrative analysis see Sagner 2002; McKim and Randall 2007.

5. For a discussion of the broad biological implications of aging see Crews 2003.

6. For new research on biological aspects of aging see Ice 2005.

7. An increasing concern and awareness of elder abuse has developed in the past decade. Access to key information can be obtained from the International Network for the Prevention of Elder Abuse (www.inpea.net), the World Health Organization (www.who.int/ageing/projects/elder_abuse/en/), and the Elder Justice Coalitions (www.elderjusticecoalition.com), which is fighting to have the US Congress pass an Elder Justice Act. There is also a relatively new journal dealing with this subject, the *Journal of Elder Abuse & Neglect*.

8. While some theorists have stressed the cultural turning points linked to procreative and family cycles, others have suggested that universal intrapsychic personality development best explains the frequent reversals observed among older adults (Gutmann 1987). For other cross-cultural discussion of this issue

see especially Bart 1969; Brown 1982; Kerns 1983; Cool and McCabe 1987; Teitelbaum 1987.

9. For other classic works on midlife women and menopause in various cultures see: du Toit 1990; Flint and Samil 1990; Kaufert and Lock 1992; Lock 1993; and Callahan 1995.

Bibliography

Adinkrah, M. 2015. *Witchcraft, Witches and Violence in Ghana*. New York: Berghahn.

Arthur, K. W. 2013. "Material Entanglements; Gender, Ritual, and Politics among the Boreda of southern Ethiopia." *African Study Monographs* (CAAS, Kyoto Japan) Supplement 46: 53–80.

Banner, L. 1992. *In Full Flower: Aging Women, Power and Sexuality*. New York: Knopf.

Bart, P. 1969. "Why Women's Status Changes in Middle Age: The Turn of the Social Ferris Wheel." *Sociological Symposium* 3: 1–18.

Berridge, C., and M. Martinson. 2018. "Valuing Old Age Without Leveraging Ableism." *Generations* 41(4): 83–91.

Bever, E. 1982. "Old Age and Witchcraft in Early Modern Europe." In *Old Age in Preindustrial Society*, edited by P. Sterns. New York: Holmes and Meier.

Beyene, Y. 1989. *From Menarche to Menopause: Reproductive Lives of Peasant Women in Two Cultures*. Albany: State University of New York Press.

Bledsoe, C. 2002. *Contingent Lives: Fertility, Time and Aging in West Africa*. Chicago: University of Chicago Press.

Bloom, D., D. Canning, and A. Lubet. 2017. "Economic Perspectives on Global Population Aging: Demography Is Not Destiny." PGDA Working Paper No. 148. https://cdn1.sph.harvard.edu/wp-content/uploads/sites/1288 /2018/03/PGDA_WP_148_Economic-Perspectives-on-Global-Population -Aging_Demography-is-Not-Destiny.pdf (accessed 1/25/19).

Bowling, A. 2007. "Aspirations for Older Age in the 21st Century: What is Successful Aging?" *International Journal of Aging and Human Development* 64(3): 2007.

Brijnath, B. 2014. *Unforgotten: Love and the Culture of Dementia Care in India*. New York: Berghahn.

Brown, J. 1982. "Cross-Cultural Perspectives on Middle-Aged Women." *Current Anthropology* 23(2): 143–48.

Brown, J., P. Subbaiah, and S. Therese. 1994. "Being in Charge: Older Women and Their Younger Female Kin." *Journal of Cross-Cultural Gerontology* 9: 231–54.

Buch, E. 2015. "Anthropology of Aging and Care." *Annual Review of Anthropology* 44: 277–93. https://www.annualreviews.org/doi/pdf/10.1146/annurev-anthro -102214-014254.

Callahan, J. 1995. *Menopause: A Midlife Passage*. Bloomington: Indiana University Press.

Carstensen, L. 2019. "Integrating Cognitive and Emotion Paradigms to Address the Paradox of Aging." *Cognition and Emotion* 33(1): 119–25, DOI: 10.1080/02699931.2018.1543181.

Carstensen, L., and C. E. Löckenhoff. 2003. "Aging, Emotion and Evolution: The Bigger Picture." *Annals of the New York Academy of Science* 1000: 152–79.

Caspari, R., and S.-H. Lee. 2004. "Older Age Becomes Common Late in Human Evolution." *Proceedings of the National Academy of Science* 101(30): 10895–900.

Chan, M., K. Hawkes, and P. S. Kim. 2016. "Evolution of Longevity, Age at Last Birth and Sexual Conflict with Grandmothering." *Journal of Theoretical Biology* 393: 145–57.

Cliggett, L. 2005. *Grains from Grass: Aging, Gender and Famine in Rural Africa.* Ithaca, NY: Cornell University Press.

Cohen, L. 1998. *No Aging in India: Alzheimer's, the Bad Family and Other Modern Things.* Berkeley: University of California Press.

Collins, P. 2001. "'If You Got Everything, It's Good Enough': Perspectives on Successful Aging in a Canadian Inuit Community." *Journal of Cross-Cultural Gerontology* 16(2): 127–55.

Colvin, A., G. A. Richardson, J. M. Cyranowski, A. Youk, and J. T. Bromberger. 2017. "The Role of Family History of Depression and the Menopausal Transition in the Development of Major Depression in Midlife Women: Study of Women's Health Across the Nation Mental Health Study (SWAN MHS)." *Depression and Anxiety* 34(9): 826–35.

Cool, L., and J. McCabe. 1987. "The 'Scheming Hag' and the 'Dear Old Thing': The Anthropology of Aging Women." In *Growing Old in Different Societies: Cross-Cultural Perspectives*, edited by J. Sokolovsky. Acton, MA: Copley.

Coughlin, J. F. 2018. "Disruptive Demographics." Presentation at World.Minds Mobility. www.youtube.com/watch?v=aJbCsS9-9Hk.

Cowgill, D., and L. Holmes, eds. 1974. *Aging and Modernization.* New York: Appleton-Century-Crofts.

Crampton, A. 2013. "No Peace in the House: Witchcraft Accusations as an 'Old Woman's Problem' in Ghana." *Anthropology & Aging Quarterly* 34(2): 199–212.

Crews, D. 2003. *Human Senescence: Evolutionary and Biocultural Perspectives.* Cambridge: Cambridge University Press.

Demos, J. 1982. *Entertaining Satan: Witchcraft and Culture of Early New England.* New York: Oxford University Press.

Dickerson-Putnam, J. 1996. "Women, Age, and Power: The Politics of Age Difference Among Women in Papua New Guinea and Australia." Special issue, *Pacific Studies* 19(4).

Dickerson-Putnam, J., and J. Brown. 1998. *Women Among Women: Anthropological Perspectives on Female Age-Hierarchies.* Champaign: University of Illinois Press.

Du Toit, B. 1990. *Aging and Menopause Among Indian South African Women.* Albany: State University of New York Press.

Ellickson, J. 1988. "Never The Twain Shall Meet: Aging Men and Women in Bangladesh." *Journal of Cross-Cultural Gerontology* 3(1): 53–70.

Fisher, B., and S. Regan. 2006. "The Extent and Frequency of Abuse in the Lives of Older Women and Their Relationship with Health Outcomes." *Gerontologist* 46(2): 200–209.

Flint, M., and R. Samil. 1990. "Cultural and Subcultural Meanings of the Menopause." *Annals of the New York Academy of Sciences* 592: 134–48.

Foner, N. 1994. *The Caregiving Dilemma.* Berkeley: University of California Press.

Gilleard, C., and P. Higgs. 2013. *Aging, Corporeality and Embodiment.* London: Anthem.

Glascock, A., and S. Feinman. 1981. "Social Asset or Social Burden: Treatment of the Aged in Non-Industrial Societies." In *Dimensions: Aging, Culture, and Health*, edited by C. Fry. Hadley, MA: Bergin and Garvey.

Gurven, M., and H. Kaplan. 2007. "Longevity Among Hunter-Gatherers: A Cross-Cultural Comparison." *Population and Development Review* 33: 321–65.

Gurven, M., J. Stieglitz, B. Trumble, A. D. Blackwell, B. Beheim, H. Davis, P. Hooper, and H. Kaplan. 2018. "The Tsimane Health and Life History Project: Integrating Anthropology and Biomedicine." *Evolutionary Anthropology: Issues, News, and Reviews* 26(2): 54. https://doi.org/10.1002/evan.21515.

Gutmann, D. 1987. *Reclaimed Powers: Toward a New Psychology of Men and Women in Later Life.* New York: Basic Books.

Haber, C. 1997. "Witches, Widows, Wives, and Workers: The Historiography of Elderly Women in America." In *Handbook on Women and Aging*, edited by J. M. Coyle. Westport, CT: Greenwood.

Harper, S. 2006. *Aging Societies.* New York: Oxford University Press.

Hegarty, B. 2017. "'When I Was Transgender': Visibility, Subjectivity, and Queer Aging in Indonesia." *Medical Anthropology Theory*, January. http://medanthrotheory.org/read/7092/when-i-was-transgender.

Hughes-Rinker, C., ed. 2019. "Religion, Spirituality and Aging." Special Issue, *Anthropology & Aging* 40(1).

Ice, G. 2005. "Biological Anthropology and Aging." Special Issue, *Journal of Cross-Cultural Gerontology* 20(2).

Ikels, C., and C. Beall. 2000. "Age, Aging and Anthropology." In *The Handbook of Aging and the Social Sciences*, 5th ed., edited by R. Binstock and L. George. San Diego, CA: Academic Press.

Jervis, L. L. 2014. "Native Elder Mistreatment." Forum on Global Violence Prevention; Board on Global Health; Institute of Medicine; National Research Council. Washington, DC: National Academies Press.

Katz, S. 2005. *Cultural Aging: Life Course, Life Style and Senior Worlds.* Peterborough, ON: Broadview.

Kaufert, P., and M. Lock. 1992. "What Are Women For? Cultural Construction of Menopausal Women in Japan and Canada." In *In Her Prime: New Views of Middle-Aged Women*, 2nd ed., edited by V. Kerns and J. Brown. Urbana: University of Illinois Press.

Kerns, V. 1983. *Woman and the Ancestors*. Urbana: University of Illinois Press.

Kerns, V., and J. Brown, eds. 1992. *In Her Prime: New Views of Middle-Aged Women*, 2nd ed. Urbana: University of Illinois Press.

Keith, J., C. L. Fry, A. P. Glascock, C. Ikels, J. Dickerson-Putnam, H. C. Harpending, and P. Draper. 1994. *The Aging Experience: Diversity and Commonality Across Cultures*. Thousand Oaks, CA: Sage.

Kirchengast, S. 2017. *Menopause Female Reproductive Senescence from the Viewpoint of Evolutionary Anthropology*. doi: 10.5772/intechopen.68682.

Kopytoff, I. 1971. "Ancestors as Elders." *Africa* 41: 129–42.

Kraft, T. S., J. Stieglitz, B. C. Trumble, M. Martin, H. Kaplan, and M. Gurven. 2018. "Nutrition Transition in 2 Lowland Bolivian Subsistence Populations." *American Journal of Clinical Nutrition* 108(6): 1183–95. https://doi.org/10.1093/ajcn/nqy250.

Lamb, S. 2000. *White Saris and Sweet Mangoes: Aging, Gender and the Body in North India*. Berkeley: University of California Press.

Lamb, S., ed. 2017. *Successful Aging as a Contemporary Obsession: Global Perspectives*. New Brunswick, NJ: Rutgers University Press.

Lock, M. 1993. *Encounters with Aging: Mythologies of Menopause in Japan and North America*. Berkeley: University of California Press.

Martinson, M., and M. Minkler. 2006. "Civic Engagement and Older Adults: A Critical Perspective." *Gerontologist* 46(3): 318–24.

McArdle, J., and C. Yeracaris. 1981. "Respect for the Elderly in Preindustrial Societies as Related to Their Activity." *Behavior Science Research* 16(3/4): 307–39.

McFadden, S. 2008. "Mindfulness, Vulnerability, and Love: Spiritual Lessons from Frail Elders, Earnest Young Pilgrims, and Middle Aged Rockers." *Journal of Aging Studies* 22(2): 132–39.

McKim, E., and W. Randall. 2007. "From Psychology to Poetics: Aging as a Literary Process." *Journal of Aging, Humanities, and the Arts* 1(3/4): 147–58.

Moody, H., and D. Carroll. 1998. *The Five Stages of the Soul: Charting the Spiritual Passages That Shape Our Lives*. New York: Anchor.

Norwood, F. 2007. "Nothing More to Do: Euthanasia, General Practice, and End-of-Life Discourse in the Netherlands." *Medical Anthropology* 26(2): 139–74.

Norwood, F. 2018. "The New Normal: Mediated Death and Assisted Dying in the United States. In *A Companion to the Anthropology of Death*, edited by A. C. G. Robben. New York: John Wiley & Sons.

Obermeyer, C., and L. Sievert. 2007 "Cross-Cultural Comparisons: Midlife, Aging, and Menopause." *Menopause* 14(4): 663–67.

Perkinson, M., and S. Solimeo. 2013. "Aging in Cultural Context and as Narrative Process: Conceptual Foundations of the Anthropology of Aging as Reflected in the Works of Margaret Clark and Sharon Kaufman." *Gerontologist* 54(1): 101–7.

Pew Global. 2014. *Attitudes about Aging: A Global Perspective*. Pew Research Global attitudes project. http://www.pewglobal.org/2014/01/30/attitudes-about-aging-a-global-perspective/.

Pillemer, K., D. Burnes, C. Riffin, and M. S. Lachs. "Elder Abuse: Global Situation, Risk Factors, and Prevention Strategies." *Gerontologist* 56(Suppl 2): S194–S205.

Population Reference Bureau. 2018. World Population Data. http://www.world popdata.org/.

Press, I., and M. McKool. 1972. "Social Structure and Status of the Aged toward Some Valid Cross-Cultural Generalizations." *Aging and Human Development* 3(4): 297–306.

Rasmussen, S. 1997. *The Poetics and Politics of Tuareg Aging: Life Course and Personal Destiny in Niger.* DeKalb: Northern Illinois University Press.

Rawlins, J. 2006. *Midlife and Older Women: Family Life, Work and Health in Jamaica.* Kingston: University of West Indies Press.

Richter, R., T. Flowers, and E. Bongmba. 2017. *Witchcraft as a Social Diagnosis: Traditional Ghanaian Beliefs and Global Health.* Lanham MD: Lexington.

Rowe, W., and R. Kahn. 1998. *Successful Aging.* New York: Dell.

Sagner, A. 2002. "Identity Management and Old Age Construction among Xhosa-speakers in Urban South Africa: Complaint Discourse Revisited." In *Ageing in Africa: Sociolinguistic and Anthropological Approaches,* edited by S. Makoni and K. Stroeken. Burlington, VT: Ashgate.

Sandberg, L., and B. Marshall. 2017, "Queering Aging Futures." *Societies* 7(3): 21.

Sanderson, W., and S. Scherbov. 2016. "It's Time to Measure 21st Century Aging with 21st Century Tools." *The Conversation.* https://theconversation.com /its-time-to-measure-21st-century-aging-with-21st-century-tools-53033.

Scherbov, S., and S. Andruchowitz. 2019. "Reassessing Aging from a Population Perspective." http://www.iiasa.ac.at/web/home/research/researchPrograms /WorldPopulation/Reaging/Re-Aging.html.

Shea, J. L. 2015. "Venting Anger from the Body at Gengnianqi: Meanings of Midlife Transition among Chinese Women in Reform Era Beijing." In *Transitions and Transformations: Cultural Perspectives on Aging and the Life Course,* edited by C. Lynch and J. Danely. Oxford: Berghahn.

Sheehan, T. 1976. "Senior Esteem as a Factor of Societal Economic Complexity." *Gerontologist* 16: 433–40.

Sievert, L. L. 2014. "Invited Review: Anthropology and the Study of Menopause: Evolutionary, Developmental, and Comparative Perspectives." *Menopause: The Journal of The North American Menopause Society* 21(10): 1151–59.

Silverman, P., and R. Maxwell. 1987. "The Significance of Information and Power in the Comparative Study of the Aged." In *Growing Old in Different Societies: Cross-Cultural Perspectives,* edited by J. Sokolovsky. Acton, MA: Copley.

Simmons, L. 1945. *The Role of the Aged in Primitive Society.* New Haven, CT: Archon [1970].

Solly, M. 2018. "U.S. Life Expectancy Drops for Third Year in a Row, Reflecting Rising Drug Overdoses, Suicides." *Smithsonian,* December 3. https:// www.smithsonianmag.com/smart-news/us-life-expectancy-drops-third -year-row-reflecting-rising-drug-overdose-suicide-rates-180970942 /#Mw3ILd4pwlKJbP1E.99.

Sossou, M., and J. Yogtiba. 2015. "Abuse, Neglect, and Violence Against Elderly Women in Ghana: Implications for Social Justice and Human Rights." *Journal of Elder Abuse & Neglect* 27(4–5): 422–27.

Stowe, J., and T. Cooney. 2015. "Examining Rowe and Kahn's Concept of Successful Aging: Importance of Taking a Life Course Perspective." *Gerontologist* 55(1): 43–50.

Teitelbaum, M. 1987. "Old Age, Midwifery and Good Talk: Paths to Power in a West African Gerontocracy." In *Aging and Cultural Diversity: New Directions and Annotated Bibliography*, edited by H. Strange and M. Teitelbaum. South Hadley, MA: Bergin and Garvey.

Tornstam, L. 2005. *Gerotranscendence: A Developmental Theory of Positive Aging.* New York: Springer.

Uys, J., dir. 1982. *The Gods Must Be Crazy.* Los Angeles: Twentieth Century-Fox.

Van Der Geest, S. 2002. "Wisdom to Witchcraft: Ambivalence towards Old Age in Rural Ghana." *Africa* 72: 437–63.

Van Der Geest, S. 2004. "'They Don't Come to Listen': The Experience of Loneliness Among Older People in Kwahu, Ghana." *Journal of Cross-Cultural Gerontology* 19: 77–96.

Voice of Asia. 2017. "Deloitte Report: Asia Will Be Home to 60% of World's Over 65s by 2030, Creating Growth Opportunities for Business." https://www2.deloitte.com/my/en/pages/about-deloitte/articles/voice-of-asia-demographics.html.

Wentzel, E. 2013. *Maturing Masculinities: Aging, Chronic Illness, and Viagra in Mexico.* Durham, NC: Duke University Press.

Wumbla, I., 2019. "Bewitched, Bothered and Bewildered: A Study of Witchcraft Accusation in Northern Ghana." The ISS Blog on Global Development and Social Justice. January 14. https://issblog.nl/2019/01/14/bewitched-bothered-and-bewildered-a-study-of-witchcraft-accusation-in-northern-ghana-by-issah-wumbla/

CHAPTER ONE

Global Aging in the New Millennium

Wan He and Kevin Kinsella

It is no news that the world population is aging and the older population is growing rapidly.[1] When the global population reached 7 billion in 2012, 562 million were aged 65 and over.[2] Three years later, another 55 million had been added to the older ranks, and the older share of the world's population reached 8 percent. The number of older people is projected to increase more than 60 percent between 2015 and 2030, and by 2050 there will be 1.6 billion older people worldwide, representing 16.7 percent of the total world population of 9.4 billion. This is equivalent to an average annual increase of 27.1 million older people from 2015 to 2050.

However, the world is not homogeneous, and world regions and countries age with a different pace and pattern. With the post–World War II baby boomer generation in the United States and Europe becoming 65 and older in recent years, the next 10 years will witness a rapid increase in proportion older of the total population in these already old countries. Meanwhile, the remarkably swift fertility reduction that had taken place in Asia and Latin America in recent decades resulted in accelerated population aging throughout most of these two regions (with the exception of southern Asian countries). At the other end of the spectrum, Africa remains exceptionally young in 2015, with the vast majority of African countries having less than 5 percent of their total population aged 65 and older.

This chapter discusses ways of measuring population aging and explores similarities and differences among world regions in past, present, and future population aging. It considers the factors that lead to demographic aging and examines the intersection of demographic and epidemiologic changes that will help determine the health profile of older populations. It also highlights the importance of health and socioeconomic conditions in childhood for health in later life.

Measuring Population Aging

The size of the older population is growing everywhere, but this does not automatically mean that a given society is getting older. It is the disproportionate growth of the older population that signifies aging of a population. The three main indicators measuring population aging are proportion of older population among the total population, median age, and dependency ratio.

Increasing Proportion of the Older Population Continues

The most telling illustration of population aging is the growth trajectories of the global older and younger populations from 1950 to 2050—converging, crossing, and then diverging percentages of population aged 65 and older and children under age 5. As Figure 1.1 shows, older people will outnumber children under age 5 by 2020 and increasing from there. This demographic phenomenon is unprecedented in human history. By 2050, the proportion of the population aged 65 and older (15.6 percent) will be more than double that of children under age 5 (7.2 percent).

Among world regions, for many decades Europe has been and will remain the oldest region, even though the pace of aging will slow drastically. In 2015, 17.4 percent of Europeans were aged 65 or older. By 2050, more than a quarter of Europeans will be aged 65 and over, and in the vast majority of European countries, the older population will represent at least 20 percent of the total population.

Meanwhile, Asia leads world regions in the speed of aging and size of older population (Figure 1.2). Today 341 million older people live in Asia, equivalent to more than half (55.3 percent) of the world total older population. By 2050, older Asians will about triple in number and become almost 1 billion. By then, more than 6 out of 10 of the world's older people will be Asian. In comparison, today's older population of 130 million in Europe is projected to grow to only 197 million by 2050.

Even though less than 8 percent of Asians were aged 65 and older in 2015, this regional average masked the sharp variations within Asia. East Asia is currently one of the oldest sub-regions globally, including the oldest major

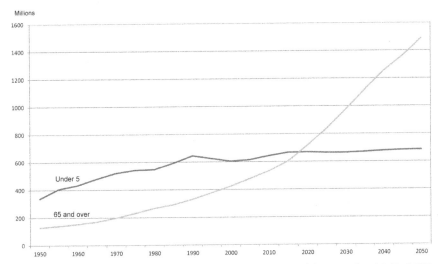

Figure 1.1   Global Number of Young Children and Older People: 1950–2050
(United Nations, 2013).

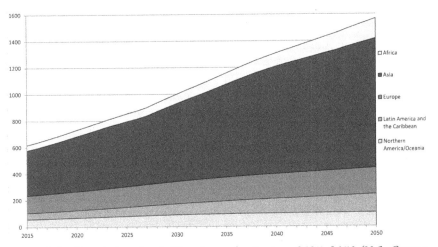

Figure 1.2   Population Aged 65 and over by Region: 2015–2050 (U.S. Census
Bureau, International Database).

country in the world—Japan (26.6 percent of total population are 65 and
older in 2015). Some of the youngest countries in the world are located in
southern and western Asia, with extremely low percentages being older (e.g.,
Afghanistan, 2.5 percent; Laos, 3.8 percent; and Saudi Arabia, 3.2 percent).

One would be remiss to neglect discussing China and India when examining population aging in Asia (see Part III Zhang; Part V Lamb). In 2015, the

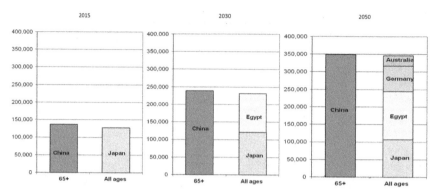

Figure 1.3   China's Older Population vs. Total Populations of Other Countries: 2015, 2030, and 2050 (number in thousands) (U.S. Census Bureau, International Database).

total Chinese population of all ages stood at 1.4 billion, with India close behind at 1.3 billion, and the two countries combined represented more than one-third of the total world population. But being a population billionaire is where the similarity ends. These two countries are on considerably different paths of population aging, thanks largely to different historical fertility trends. Although India introduced family planning programs decades ago, its fertility level has remained well above the level in China since the 1970s. The well-known one-child policy in China drastically and swiftly reduced China's fertility level (more than 5 births per woman in 1972 to fewer than 3 by 1977, and fewer than 2 by the mid-1990s), and resulted in rapid growth in the proportion of older population. It is projected that by 2025, India will surpass China in total population and become the most populous country in the world, but with a much younger age structure (7.7 percent older population in India vs. 14.2 percent in China). Moreover, the sheer size of China's older population (Figure 1.3) is and will be a social force to be reckoned with.

At the other end of the spectrum is Africa, which was exceptionally young in 2015 and will remain so in the foreseeable future. Much of the region is still largely in the early stages of fertility transition with high fertility rates and a young age structure, and the vast majority of African countries had less than 5 percent of their total population aged 65 and over in 2015, with many projected to continue below 7 percent by 2050.

It warrants attention that while Africa is a young region, some African countries already have a large number of older people. In 2015, the older population exceeded 1 million in 11 African countries, including Nigeria, 5.6 million; Egypt, 4.6 million; and South Africa, 3.1 million. By 2050, more than half of African countries are projected to have more than 1 million older people, including 3 countries (Nigeria, Egypt, and Ethiopia) that will exceed 10 million and another 6 countries with more than 5 million.

BOX 1.1   DOUBLING AND TRIPLING OF OLDER POPULATION PROPORTIONS

A commonly used indicator for the speed of population aging is the number of years for a country's population aged 65 and over to double from 7 percent of the total population to 14 percent. It is often noted that it took France 115 years for its share of older population to achieve this doubling, and many European and Northern American countries experienced a span of more than half a century for this doubling to complete (Figure 1.4). Japan is the only exception among more developed countries. Japan's share of older population doubled in a short 25 years.

Many European countries have progressed from doubling to tripling (from 7 percent to 21 percent) of their share of older population. And generally, it will take a much shorter period of time for their percent older to grow from 14 percent to 21 percent. For example, it took 69 years for the share of U.S. older population to double, but in just 20 more years, tripling is likely. Projections show that by 2030, the majority of European countries (32 out of 42) will have completed tripling.

Less developed countries have started the doubling process only recently but are moving at a much faster speed. South Korea, for example, is projected to take just 18 years for its older population to double and half that time (9 years) to reach 21 percent. Chile's doubling will take 26 years and just another 16 years to complete tripling.

That doubling may take only a couple of decades and then a decade or so for tripling to complete in China and many other Asian and Latin American countries raises serious concerns in these countries regarding their readiness to deal with a rapidly aging society. As the director-general of the World Health Organization pointed out at the United Nation's Second World Assembly on Ageing in 2002, "We must be aware that the developed countries became rich before they became old, the developing countries will become old before they become rich" (Butler 2002).

Median Ages Range from 15 to Near 50

Another way to measure population aging is to consider a country's median age, the age that divides a population into numerically equal shares of younger and older people. Africa had the youngest median age in 2015, at 19.7 years, which is projected to rise to 26.0 years by 2050 (Table 1.1). In some African countries such as Niger, Uganda, and Mali, the current median age is 15 or 16—half of the population in these countries are children.

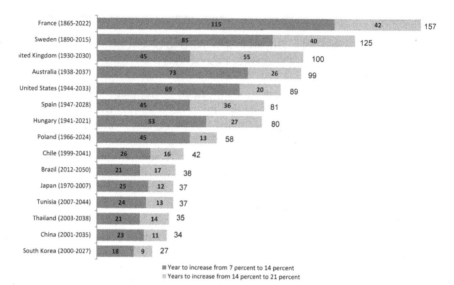

Figure 1.4   Number of Years for Percentage Aged 65 and Older to Double and Triple: Selected Countries (Kinsella and Gist 1995; U.S. Census Bureau, International Database).

At 47, Japan and Germany have the oldest current median ages. It is projected that Japan's median age will reach 53 by 2030 and 56 by 2050. Obviously the allocation of resources in countries with very different median ages will diverge significantly.

While women in all regions have older median ages than men, the female-male gap is currently and projected to be largest in the oldest region, Europe (3.7 in 2015 and 4.8 in 2050). The higher proportion of women among the older population combined with a larger number of older people results in European societies with many more older women than men. In contrast, in the youngest region of Africa, males and females are almost equally young, with a differential of less than one year in median age for 2015, 2030, and 2050.

Composition of Dependency Ratio Varies and Will Continue to Shift toward Older Dependency

Dependency ratios provide a gross estimate of the pressure on the productive population and offer an indication of a society's caregiving burden by estimating the potential supply of caregivers and the potential demand for care (number of care recipients). However, it must be noted that not all individuals who fall in a certain age category are actually "dependents" or

Table 1.1   Median age by sex and region: 2015, 2030, and 2050 (in years)

Region	Both Sexes			Male			Female		
	2015	2030	2050	2015	2030	2050	2015	2030	2050
Africa	19.7	22.0	26.0	19.4	21.7	25.6	19.9	22.3	26.4
Asia	30.6	35.7	40.5	29.9	34.9	39.6	31.3	36.6	41.5
Europe	41.6	45.3	47.1	39.7	43.4	44.8	43.4	47.2	49.6
Latin America and the Caribbean	29.1	34.4	40.6	28.2	33.3	39.2	30.0	35.5	42.1
Northern America	38.1	40.0	41.1	36.8	38.8	39.8	39.5	41.3	42.4
Oceania	34.0	36.8	40.0	33.5	36.1	39.1	34.6	37.5	41.0

Source: U.S. Census Bureau, International Database.

"providers"—some older (or younger) people work or have the financial resources to be independent and some in the "working ages" do not work. The total dependency ratio is the combination of the older dependency ratio (defined here as the number of people aged 65 and over per 100 people of working ages 20 to 64) and the youth dependency ratio (the number of people aged 0 to 19 per 100 people aged 20 to 64).

The aggregate global dependency ratio in 2015 was 73, indicating that every 100 people aged 20 to 64 are supporting 73 youth and older people combined. The world's total dependency ratio is not expected to rise much in the next few decades, reaching 78 in 2050, but the composition will change considerably, illustrated by the examples of Indonesia and Zambia (Figure 1.5). Indonesia's total dependency ratio experienced a nearly 50 percent reduction from 1980 (121) to 2015 (70), due in large measure to a sharp fertility decline and corresponding decrease in the youth dependency ratio, providing an ideal opportunity to reap a demographic dividend.[3] Looking ahead, by 2050, the youth dependency ratio will decrease further to 41 and the older dependency ratio will rise sharply to 33, indicative of a society facing the potential burden of population aging.

The trend in Zambia's dependency ratio combination presents a very different picture. Zambia's total dependency ratio was at a high level in 1980 (165) and is projected to high (116) in 2050. This is a society in which the dependent population of youth and older people will continue to exceed the size of the working age population, offering limited opportunities for the demographic dividend. Even by the middle of the 21st century, population aging will not have materialized in Zambia, and societal support needs will continue to be focused on the care of its young.

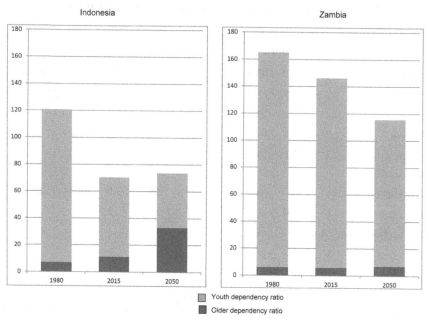

Figure 1.5   Dependency Ratios for Indonesia and Zambia: 1980, 2015, and 2050 (Note: The older dependency ratio is the number of people aged 65 and over per 100 people aged 20 to 64. The youth dependency ratio is the number of people aged 0 to 19 per 100 people aged 20 to 64. Source: U.S. Census Bureau, International Database.).

Determinants of Population Aging

Population aging often reflects a human success story of increased longevity. Today, living to age 70 or age 80 is no longer a rarity in many parts of the world. While the mortality reduction has been an achievement to celebrate, it is the fertility reduction that is the propeller of population aging. Another determinant of aging is international migration, but migration generally plays a limited role in changing a society's age structure (with the exception of a number of Middle Eastern countries where the influx of labor-force-age migrants has had a significant impact on the age distribution of their population).

Total Fertility Rates Have Dropped to or under Replacement Level in All World Regions But Africa

The main demographic force behind population aging is declining fertility rates. Populations with low fertility tend to have an old age distribution with a low proportion of children and a high proportion of older people, resulting in an older society.

Box 1.2   Demographic Transition and Population Aging

The classical model of demographic transition refers to the process where a society starts with extremely high levels of both fertility and mortality and transitions to a point where both rates are low and stable. The demographic transition impacts both the population growth rate and the age structure of a country.

The demographic transition consists of four stages. At the start in Stage 1, both birth rates and death rates are high. A country's age structure is young and pyramidal in shape, with a large number of children at the base and very few older people at the top. In Stage 2, mortality, especially infant and child mortality, declines rapidly while fertility lags and remains high. In this stage, the total population increases rapidly, and the proportion of the older population starts to grow as mortality rates decrease and people live longer. In Stage 3, a fertility transition occurs as fertility declines rapidly, accompanied by continued albeit slower declines in infant and child mortality but accelerated mortality decline at older ages. The population continues to grow; however, the age structure becomes even older as life expectancy continues to improve. In Stage 4, both mortality and fertility are low and remain relatively stable, population growth flattens, and the age structure becomes old. No longer is there a pyramid-shaped age structure; the shape becomes almost rectangular.

Many factors contribute to this process, but it is generally agreed that the initial momentum starts with improvement in public health, including basic sanitation and advancements in medicine. The increased child survival rates, along with general improvements in socioeconomic conditions, then affect fertility behavior through a reduction in the desired number of children. Economic explanations for a lower desired number of children include mechanization of agriculture and expansion of the nonagrarian economy; the quantity-quality tradeoff whereby parents switch their resources from raising many offspring to a smaller number of "quality" children; and the opportunity cost for women to have children versus their own labor force participation.

In many countries today, the total fertility rate (TFR) has fallen below the 2.1 children that a couple needs to replace themselves.[4] In 2015, the TFR is near or below replacement level in all world regions but Africa (Figure 1.6). The more developed countries in Europe, where fertility reduction started more than 100 years ago, have had TFR levels below replacement since the 1970s. Many less developed countries in Asia and Latin America, on the other hand, have experienced more recent and rapid fertility declines than

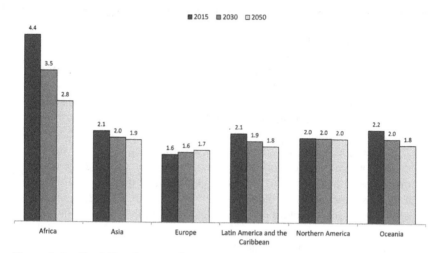

Figure 1.6   Total Fertility Rate by Region: 2015, 2030, and 2050 (U.S. Census Bureau, International Database).

Europe. Overall TFR levels in Asia and Latin America decreased by about 50 percent (from 6 to 3 children per woman) during the period 1965 to 1995, then in the ensuing two decades, the TFR for both regions continued to drop to the replacement level of 2.1 in 2015.

Asia's current low regional TFR is particularly impressive, considering that there are still some Asian countries with quite high 2015 fertility levels, such as Afghanistan (5.3) and Yemen (3.9). These high fertility rates are offset by exceptionally low fertility in regions such as Taiwan (1.1), Hong Kong (1.2), and South Korea (1.3). By 2050, all but four of the 52 Asian countries are projected to have below-replacement fertility rates.

Among the lowest TFRs in Latin America are Cuba (1.5) and Brazil (1.8). By 2050, all Latin American countries are projected to have fertility rates at or below 2.1. This would be a significant achievement in Latin America's fertility transition, regardless of each country's development level today.

Africa's current regional TFR stands at 4.4, more than twice the replacement level. Nevertheless, many countries in Africa have experienced fertility decline in the last 15 years. At the turn of the 21st century, two-thirds (34) of African countries had a TFR at or above 5, with the TFR exceeding 7 in a few of these countries (Uganda, 7.1, and Niger, 8.0). In 2015, 15 years later, the fertility decline has reduced the number of countries with above-5 TFR to 13, and by 2030, it is projected that only Burundi will maintain a fertility level above 5 and the number of countries with a TFR between 4 and 5 will decline to 14.

Despite progress in reducing of Africa's fertility level, it is projected that by 2050, two-thirds of African countries will still have a TFR higher than

2.1. The slow fertility decline in Africa may be the result of a relatively high ideal family size stemming from the distinctive pronatalist cultural norms of African societies, fertility control regimes that focus more on the postponement rather than the stopping of births, and a sizable unmet need for family planning.[5] Furthermore, several African countries that are projected to have the highest future TFRs are also among the most populous African countries. The 11th-highest TFR in the world in 2015 is in Africa's most populous country, Nigeria, which has a total population of 182 million in 2015 and a projected 391 million in 2050. Obviously, the slow fertility transition and above-replacement level fertility in Africa will bring about sustained population growth and a corresponding slow pace of population aging in most of the region, especially in sub-Saharan Africa.

It is worth noting that the current relatively high fertility levels in many African countries could also produce sizable working age populations in 2050 (see the example of Kenya in Figure 1.7). If the fertility decline accelerates, then the proportion of the population in the working ages could rise relative to 2015 and result in lower dependency ratios, potentially enabling demographic dividends in the next few decades for many African countries.

Life Expectancy Increases Not Only at Birth But Also at Older Ages

Increasing longevity around the globe is indeed remarkable, with global life expectancy at birth reaching 68.6 years in 2015. Today life expectancy at birth exceeds 80 years in 24 countries. The global life expectancy at birth is projected to increase almost eight years, reaching 76.2 years in 2050.

But regions and countries have experienced uneven progress in population health. The same factors correlated with the dramatic drops in mortality in more developed countries at the beginning of the 1900s, namely, water, sanitation, and diet, still contribute to mortality rates across many other regions in spite of considerable and ongoing progress. North America currently has the highest regional life expectancy at 79.9 years, while the current life expectancy for Africa is only 59.2 years. In 2015, 27 African countries had a life expectancy at birth below 60 years. However, with likely improvements in health and AIDS-related mortality in the next few decades, aggregate life expectancy in Africa is projected to increase to 71.0 years in 2050, narrowing the gap with North America (84.1 years).

The gender gap in life expectancy has been a prominent example of the differences and persistent inequality in the aging process for men and women. A female born today is expected to live 70.7 years on average and a male 66.6 years. As of 2015, women born in Japan and Singapore are expected on average to live to about age 88, compared with about age 82 for men. The female advantage generally is narrower (about 2 to 3 years) among countries with the lowest life expectancies at birth.

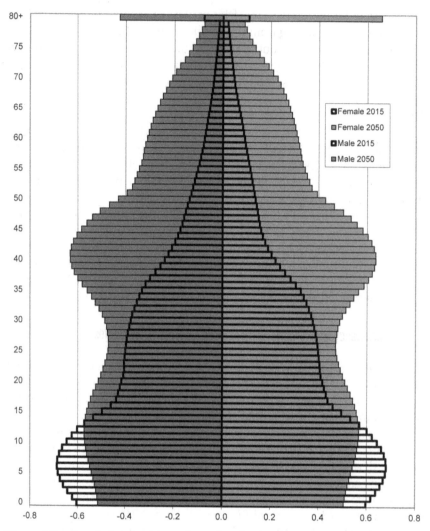

Figure 1.7   Population by Age and Sex for Kenya: 2015 and 2050 (in millions) (U.S. Census Bureau, 2013; International Database).

Extension of life expectancy has also occurred at older ages. In the United States, life expectancy at age 65 increased from 11.9 years in 1900–1902 to 19.1 years in 2009. Life expectancy at age 80 increased more than 70 percent over the same time period, 5.3 years to 9.1 years (Arias 2014).

The female advantage in life expectancy is also demonstrated at older ages. In 2015, older men at age 65 in Singapore and Japan would live on average for about another 20 years, but older women in these countries live on

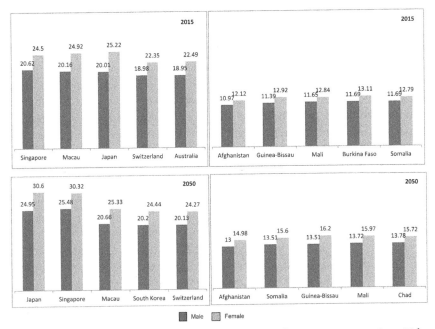

Figure 1.8 Countries with Highest and Lowest Life Expectancy at Age 65 by Sex: 2015 and 2050 (U.S. Census Bureau, unpublished lifetables).

average about another 25 years (Figure 1.8). By 2050, life expectancy for Japanese and Singaporean older men is projected to be about 25 years and for older women about 30 years. One analysis of high-income countries (Mathers et al. 2015) attributes about half of the gains in life expectancy at older ages to improvements in the effectiveness and coverage of health care and half to lower exposure to risk factors, notably tobacco and high blood pressure.

The Changing Composition of Older Populations

Increasing life expectancy at older ages leads to an important feature of population aging, namely, the progressive aging of the older population itself. A nation's older population often grows older, on average, as a larger proportion survives to 80 years and beyond. A nation's oldest-old population, defined here as people aged 80 and over,[6] consumes resources disproportionately to its overall population size. The numerical growth of the oldest old means, among other things, that pensions and retirement income will need to cover more people living into their 80s and beyond, health care costs will likely rise even if disability rates decline, and intergenerational relationships may take on an added dimension if young children know their great-grandparents.

As recently as the mid-1990s, the aggregate global growth rate of the oldest old was somewhat lower than that of the world's older population as a whole, a result of low fertility that prevailed in some countries around the time of World War I and the effects of the influenza pandemic of 1918–1919. Just a few years later, however, the low-fertility effects of World War I had dissipated; from 1999 to 2000, the growth rate of the world's 80-and-over population jumped to 3.5 percent, higher than that of the world's older population as a whole (2.3 percent). Today, the oldest old are the fastest-growing portion of the total population in many countries. On a global level, the 80-and-over population is projected to increase more than 250 percent between 2015 and 2050, compared with 155 percent for the population aged 65 and over.

The oldest old constituted 20 percent of the world's older population in 2015—27 percent in developed countries and 17 percent in developing countries. More than half (52 percent) of the world's oldest old in 2015 lived in six countries: China, the United States, India, Japan, Germany, and Russia. The future percentage of oldest old will vary considerably from country to country. In the United States, for example, the 80-and-over population accounted for 25 percent of all older people in 2015. This percentage is expected to grow modestly to 31 percent over the next 20 years, because the aging baby boomer generation will continue to enter the ranks of the 65-and-over population. In contrast, a striking increase will occur in Japan: today's 30 percent is likely to reach 46 percent by 2035.

Demographers expect a large numerical growth of centenarians, whose experiences may yield empirical clues about the process of aging on both an individual and a population level. While people of extreme old age (age 100 and over) constitute a tiny portion of total population in the world, their numbers are growing rapidly, especially in developed nations. Researchers in Europe found that the number of centenarians in industrialized countries doubled each decade between 1950 and 1990. Using reliable statistics from 10 Western European countries and Japan, Vaupel and Jeune (1995) estimated that some 8,800 centenarians lived in these countries as of 1990, and that the number of centenarians grew at an average annual rate of approximately 7 percent between the early 1950s and the late 1980s. They also estimate that, over the course of human history, the odds of living from birth to age 100 may have risen from 1 in 20 million to 1 in 50 for females in low-mortality nations such as Japan and Sweden. Estimates from the United Nations Population Division put the number of centenarians at close to half a million as of 2015, and projections suggest that the number will swell to 26 million by the end of this century. Approximately 30 individuals in history have attained the status of "longevity millionaire," someone who has lived at least one million hours, or slightly more than 114 years (Chamie 2015).

Scientists are now studying data on centenarians for clues about factors that contribute to longevity. Studies of U.S. centenarians born in the 1880s, which incorporate the use of nonbiological relatives as controls, within-family analysis, and a sampling of control subjects from the same population universe as centenarians, suggest that factors such as parental longevity, lean body mass, and avoidance of early exposure to infections are associated with extreme longevity (Gavrilov and Gavrilova 2013; Gavrilova and Gavrilov 2010). Numerous detailed centenarian studies are now underway throughout the world (e.g., in Sardinia, Denmark, Okinawa, and several sites within the United States), including at least one with a focus on whole-genome sequencing (Gierman et al. 2014; see Part VI Wilcox et al.).

Health and Demographic Change

The broad demographic transition described in Box 1.2 typically is associated with a changing epidemiologic profile, both of which contribute to the changing characteristics of older populations. The transition from high to low mortality and fertility that accompanies socioeconomic development also means a shift in the leading causes of disease and death. Demographers and epidemiologists describe this shift as an "epidemiologic transition" characterized by the lessening prevalence of infectious and acute diseases and the emerging importance of chronic and degenerative diseases. High death rates from infectious diseases are commonly associated with the poverty, poor diets, and limited infrastructure found in developing countries, while high death rates from chronic, degenerative diseases are associated with the affluence and older populations more often found in developed countries. Although many developing countries still experience high child mortality from infectious and parasitic diseases, one of the major epidemiologic trends of the current century is the rise of chronic and degenerative diseases in countries throughout the world—regardless of income level.

Evidence from the ongoing Global Burden of Disease (GBD) project[7] and other international epidemiologic research shows that health problems associated with wealthy and aged populations now affect a wide and expanding swath of world population. Over the coming decades, people in every world region will suffer more death and disability from such noncommunicable diseases as heart disease, cancer, and diabetes than from infectious and parasitic diseases. The myth that noncommunicable diseases affect mainly affluent and aged populations was dispelled by the GBD project, which combines information about mortality and morbidity from every world region to assess the total health burden from specific diseases. The burden is measured by estimating the loss of healthy years of life due to a specific cause based on detailed epidemiological information. In 2008, noncommunicable diseases accounted for an estimated 86 percent of the total burden of disease in high-income countries, 65 percent in middle-income countries, and a surprising 37 percent in low-income countries.

By 2030, noncommunicable diseases are projected to account for more than one-half of the total disease burden in low-income countries and more than three-fourths in middle-income countries. Infectious and parasitic diseases will account for 30 percent and 10 percent, respectively, in low- and middle-income countries. Among the 60-and-over population, noncommunicable diseases already account for more than 87 percent of the burden in low-, middle-, and high-income countries. The increase in chronic, noncommunicable diseases in lower- and middle-income countries requires new public health efforts and interventions on both the population and individual level. Population-level programs typically target smoking rates, the intake of salt and trans-fatty acids, and greater physical activity in sedentary populations. Individual-level programs emphasize the control and treatment of risk factors for chronic diseases and the expanded use of secondary-prevention medications such as aspirin, beta-blockers, angiotensin-converting enzyme inhibitors, and lipid-lowering drugs (Gaziano and Pagidipati 2013).

The Importance of Childhood Health in Older Age

The last two decades have seen a growing body of research that examines adult health from a life-course perspective. This research suggests that many negative health conditions in adulthood stem from risks established early in life. Some (notably, Barker et al. 2002) argue that adult health has a fetal origin whereby nourishment in utero and during infancy has a direct bearing on the development of risk factors for adulthood diseases, particularly cardiovascular diseases. Studies in Latin America have shown that early malnutrition is highly correlated with self-reported diabetes and that childhood rheumatic heart fever is a strong predictor of heart disease (Palloni et al. 2006). Childhood infections may have long-term effect on adult mortality, and slow growth and lack of emotional support in prenatal life and early childhood reduce physical, cognitive, and emotional functioning in later years. Data on China's oldest old show that people who rarely or never suffered from serious childhood illnesses, or who received adequate medical care during sickness in childhood, had a greatly reduced risk of cognitive impairment and disability-related impairment at ages 80 and over (Zeng, Gu, and Land 2007).

A clear demonstration that childhood conditions affect adult development and health is complicated by the fact that it is empirically difficult to separate cohort effects from period effects such as changing living conditions. The improvements in life expectancy at birth described earlier are period effects of public health and medical advances. One study looked at reduced lifetime exposure to infectious diseases and other sources of inflammation in a nation with excellent historical data—Sweden—and concluded that reductions in early morbidity do have an impact on observed increases in life expectancy (Finch and Crimmins 2004). Cross-national data from Puerto Rico and seven urban centers in Latin America and the Caribbean also found links between early conditions and later disability. The older people studied had been born and grew up during times of generally poor nutrition and exposure to infectious diseases such as typhus, polio, malaria, and tuberculosis. In Puerto Rico, the probability of being disabled among those growing up in poor conditions was more than 60 percent greater than among people with better childhood socioeconomic levels. The corresponding probability in the seven urban centers was 43 percent (Monteverde, Norohna, and Palloni 2009).

More recent research is enhancing the understanding of causal early-life conditions. Currie and Vogl have examined the adult correlates of early-life health and the long-term effects of shocks resulting from disease, famine, malnutrition, pollution, and war (2013). McEniry's systematic review of studies in developing countries revealed strong associations between numerous early-life conditions and older adult health (2013). Bhalotra and Rawlings merged survey data on more than 2 million children in developing countries with national-level macroeconomic data and found that poor maternal health disproportionately penalizes children born in adverse socioeconomic conditions (2013).

Final Thoughts

The implications of the demographic and health trends mentioned in the preceding pages are numerous, and many are explored elsewhere in this volume (see Part III and VI). The bottom line is that we now have a reasonably good handle on what the future of population aging will look like. But in spite of the weight of scientific evidence, the significance of population aging and its global implications are still not well appreciated. There is a need to stimulate policy dialogue that will help societies address needed institutional and behavioral changes (National Research Council 2012; Bloom, Canning, and Lubet 2015). Preparing financially for longer lives and finding ways to reduce aging-related disability should become national and global priorities. Experience shows that for nations, as for individuals, it is critical to address problems sooner rather than later; delay increases the costs and difficulties of addressing challenges.

Toward this end, it is important that research be able to put demographic and epidemiologic changes into better context for policy making. Several notable endeavors are underway: the Global Burden of Disease project discussed earlier, the Health and Retirement family of national surveys,[8] the National Transfer Accounts project,[9] and the Study on Global Aging and Adult Health.[10] Results from these and other projects show that the key to insightful understanding of global aging processes rests with cross-national, multidisciplinary, and longitudinal research designs. We must rely on cross-national data to understand the broader implications and consequences of aging, help establish best practices, and guide policies and actions. A multi-disciplinary approach is essential because physical and cognitive health, aging, and economic status are inextricably intertwined. Better scientific information about the interrelationships among these domains will facilitate the crafting of appropriate policies, especially in the developing world. And, increasingly, countries realize the importance of ongoing, longitudinal surveys that can incorporate different life domains and afford continuous feedback in the face of changing circumstances.

Notes

1. Older population is defined as people aged 65 or over.

2. In this chapter, population data come from U.S. Census Bureau's International Data Base (https://www.census.gov/data-tools/demo/idb/informationGateway .php, accessed January 2016) unless otherwise noted.

3. A society's demographic dividend often refers to a period of time when more rapid economic growth might be achieved due to a higher proportion of the population at working ages and increased labor force participation of women, relative to lower proportions of children and older adults.

4. The total fertility rate (TFR) is defined as the average number of children that would be born per woman if all women lived to the end of their childbearing years and bore children according to a given set of age-specific fertility rates.

5. For more information on what has been termed the "stalled fertility decline" in sub-Saharan Africa, see Bongaarts and Casterline 2013; Searchinger et al. 2013; and Ezeh, Mberu, and Emina 2009.

6. The definition of "oldest old" is arbitrary and is used primarily for comparative purposes. It is common in more-developed countries to use an age 85-and-over grouping, and some have considered a redefinition of oldest old to refer to those aged 90 and over (see, e.g., He and Muenchrath 2011).

7. Information about and current estimates from this multifaceted study may be found at http://www.healthdata.org/gbd/about and http://www.who.int/healthinfo /global_burden_disease/estimates/en/index2.html.

8. http://hrsonline.isr.umich.edu/.

9. http://www.ntaccounts.org/web/nta/show/.

10. http://www.who.int/healthinfo/sage/en/.

Bibliography

Arias, E. 2014. *United States Life Tables, 2009*. National Vital Statistics Reports 62/7. Hyattsville, MD: National Center for Health Statistics.

Barker, D. J. P., J. G. Eriksson, T. Forsen, and C. Osmond. 2002. "Fetal Origins of Adult Disease: Strength of Effects and Biological Basis." *International Journal of Epidemiology* 31: 1235–39.

Bhalotra, S., and S. Rawlings. 2013. "Gradients of the Intergenerational Transmission of Health in Developing Countries." *Review of Economics and Statistics* 95: 660–72.

Bloom, D. E., D. Canning, and A. Lubet. 2015. "Global Population Aging: Facts, Challenges, Solutions & Perspectives." *Daedalus* 144(2): 80–92.

Bongaarts, J., and J. Casterline. 2013. "Fertility Transition: Is Sub-Saharan Africa Different?" *Population and Development Review* 38(Suppl 1): 153–68.

Butler, R. N. 2002. "Guest Editorial: Report and Commentary from Madrid: The United Nations World Assembly on Ageing." *Journal of Gerontology: Medical Sciences* 57(12): M770–M771.

Chamie, J. 2015. *Opinion: The Century of the Centenarians.* http://www.ipsnews .net/2015/09/opinion-the-century-of-the-centenarians/.

Currie, J., and T. Vogl. 2013. "Early-Life Health and Adult Circumstance in Developing Countries." *Annual Review of Economics* 5: 1–36.

Ezeh, A. C., B. U. Mberu, and J. O. Emina. 2009. "Stall in Fertility Decline in Eastern African Countries: Regional Analysis of Patterns, Determinants and Implications." *Philosophical Transactions of the Royal Society of London. Series B, Biological Sciences* 364(1532): 2991–3007.

Finch, C. E., and E. M. Crimmins. 2004. "Inflammatory Exposure and Historical Changes in Human Life-Spans." *Science* 305: 1736–39.

Gavrilov, L. A., and N. S. Gavrilova. 2013. "Determinants of Exceptional Human Longevity: New Ideas and Findings. *Vienna Yearbook of Population Research* 11: 295–323.

Gavrilova, N. S., and L. A. Gavrilov. 2010. "Search for Mechanisms of Exceptional Human Longevity." *Rejuvenation Research* 13(2–3): 262–64.

Gaziano, T. A., and N. Pagidipati. 2013. "Scaling Up Chronic Disease Prevention Interventions in Lower- and Middle-Income Countries." *Annual Review of Public Health* 34: 317–35.

Gierman, H. J., K. Fortney, J. C. Roach, N.S. Coles, H. Li, G. Glusman, G. J. Markov, J. D. Smith, L. Hood, L. S. Coles, and S. K. Kim. 2014. "Whole-Genome Sequencing of the World's Oldest People." *PLoS One* 9(11): e112430. http:// www.ncbi.nlm.nih.gov/pmc/articles/PMC4229186/.

He, W., and M. N. Muenchrath. 2011. *90+ in the United States: 2006–2008.* Washington, DC: U.S. Government Printing Office.

Mathers, C. D., G. A. Stevens, T. Boerma, R. A. White, and M. I. Tobias. 2015. "Causes of International Increases in Older Age Life Expectancy." *Lancet* 385: 540–48.

McEniry, M. 2013. "Early-Life Conditions and Older Adult Health in Low- and Middle-Income Countries: A Review." *Journal of Developmental Origins of Health and Disease* 4(1): 10–29.

Monteverde, M., K. Norohna, and A. Palloni. 2009. "Effect of Early Conditions on Disability among the Elderly in Latin America and the Caribbean." *Population Studies* 63(1): 21–35.

National Research Council. 2012. *Aging and the Macroeconomy. Long-Term Implications of an Older Population.* Report of the Committee on the Long-Run

Macroeconomic Effects of the Aging U.S. Population. Washington, DC: National Academies Press.

Palloni, A., M. McEniry, R. Wong, and M. Pelaez. 2006. "The Tide to Come: Elderly Health in Latin America and the Caribbean." *Journal of Aging and Health* 18: 180–206.

Searchinger, T., C. Hanson, R. Waite, S. Harper, G. Leeson, and B. Lipinski. 2013. "Achieving Replacement Level Fertility." *World Resources Institute Working Paper.* https://scholar.princeton.edu/tsearchi/files/Searchinger%20et%20al%2C%20Achieving%20Replacement%20Level%20Fertility%20%28WRI%202013%29.pdf.

Vaupel, J. W., and B. Jeune. 1995. "The Emergence and Proliferation of Centenarians." In *Exceptional Longevity: From Prehistory to the Present*, edited by B. Jeune and J. W. Vaupel. Odense: Odense University Press.

Zeng, Y., D. Gu, and K. C. Land. 2007. "The Association of Childhood Socioeconomic Conditions with Healthy Longevity at the Oldest Old Ages in China." *Demography* 44(3): 497–518.

CHAPTER TWO

Web Book: Complaint Discourse, Aging, and Caregiving among the Ju'hoansi of Botswana—with 2018 Update

Harriet G. Rosenberg

Available at the Web Book: http://www.culturalcontextofaging.com/webbook -rosenberg

Rosenberg's classic chapter about complaint discourse and support of elders among a former hunter forager people is updated here to cover changes over the past decade.

CHAPTER THREE

Web Book: Beyond the Grandmother Hypothesis

Evolutionary Models of Human Longevity

Mike Gurven and Hillard Kaplan

Available at the Web Book: http://www.culturalcontextofaging.com/webbook
-gurven

This chapter goes beyond the "grandmother hypothesis" through the Tsimane Health and Life History Project. The latest data from the project are found in M. Gurven et al., "The Tsimane Health and Life History Project: Integrating Anthropology and Biomedicine," *Evolutionary Anthropology: Issues, News, and Reviews* 26, no. 2 (2017): 54–73. doi: 10.1002/evan.21515.

CHAPTER FOUR

"You Don't Have to Act or Feel Old"

Successful Aging as a U.S. Cultural Project

Sarah Lamb

I took the title for this chapter from Chris Crowley and Henry Lodge's best-selling *Younger Next Year: Live Strong, Fit, and Sexy—Until You're 80 and Beyond.* In a section boldly titled "Decay Is Optional," Crowley and Lodge declare, "You do not have to *act* or *feel* old" (2007: 33). Unfortunately, despite the immense popularity of his health-advice books, physician Henry Lodge died at the early age of 58, succumbing to prostate cancer just two days after his father passed on.[1] This makes one pause: How much is the achievement of healthy longevity until age 80 and beyond within our individual personal control? (See Part IV Wilcox et al.)

Even so, the healthy–active–successful aging movement is thriving, and perhaps for good reason. The key premise of successful aging is that individuals have the responsibility and capability to keep themselves fit, active, and healthy as they age. "Find out how the way you live—not the genes you were born with—determines health and vitality," John Rowe and Robert Kahn announce in their landmark *Successful Aging* text (1998: front cover). The ideology that health and aging are within one's own control can feel inspiring and may be leading to some actual health benefits. Science is not always certain about this—the extent that lifestyle practices such as diet and exercise can ward off old age—but the ideology rests on hope and gives many a comforting sense of control.[2]

This chapter explores the healthy–active–successful aging movement as it is playing out in public discourse and in the everyday lives of older Americans. How do older people themselves internalize, take up, critique, complicate, and/or move beyond the ebullient successful aging messaging? I use the perspectives of older people, and a brief comparison to competing ideologies in India, to help us recognize the fascinating, even peculiar, cultural elements built into what has come to be called "healthy," "active," and "successful" aging (Lamb 2014; Lamb, Robbins-Ruszkowski, and Corwin 2017). This anthropological lens helps us see that "successful aging" is not entirely as productive as it may seem, despite its inspirational elements: It promotes an overconfident sense of control and obscures socioeconomic inequalities, just as it denies aging as a normal and even potentially meaningful part of the human life course.

The Healthy–Active–Successful Aging Movement

Anyone who has paid even scant attention to the media and public health messaging over the past few decades in the United States has encountered visions of a new old age, enabling people in their seventies, eighties, nineties, and beyond to live vibrant, active, fit, healthy, sexy, "younger" lives. Today's emphasis on youthful, healthy aging emerged out of the wider personal health movement of the late 20th century and has been fueled by the baby boomer generation contemplating its own aging, longevity-inducing advances in biomedicine, an antiaging consumer industry, and the demands of population aging, as well as core cultural values (Crawford 2006; Lamb 2014; Ehrenreich 2018).

Emphasizing individual effort as the means to not become "old," public health initiatives target aging individuals. The National Institute on Aging (NIA) Go4Life campaign, launched in 2011, encourages older adults to make healthy "lifestyle choices," promising that "healthy diet and exercise can help control or delay age-related health problems,"[3] sending out daily motivational tweets: "Healthy looks good at every age! You're never too young or too old to take steps to be as healthy as possible"; "Get inspired! These success stories feature real people age 50 years or older doing physical activities they enjoy"; and "No more excuses! It's never too late to be physically active."[4] In academic gerontology for several decades, successful aging has remained the leading paradigm, just as we have witnessed the flourishing of research centers, funding initiatives, and self-help books on the topic (Katz and Calasanti 2015).

One can scrutinize successful-aging popular texts as rich cultural documents, exploring what they reveal about U.S. ideologies of individual control, values surrounding aging and personhood, and visions of the ideal life course. The driving theme of individual control over one's own body and destiny is a central concern in the profusion of popular books on successful and healthy aging: "I want to empower you to take control over your body and the future of your health," Doctor David Agus writes in *A Short Guide to a Long Life* (2014: 7). Offering a clear set of "things you can do that will make you the architect of your health kingdom" (8), he cheers, "You are in charge of you" (10). Steven Schuster, in *Age in Reverse*, promises: "I guarantee that you can scrub some decades off with dedication and commitment" (2017: 25). Ilchi Lee, in *I Have Decided to Live 120 Years*, recounts his process of coming to realize that longevity and health are a matter of personal choice and individual control:

> I realized that I had been thinking passively about my lifespan—in other words, about my time. I had thought only that time had been given to me; I hadn't thought that I could extend my time by my will. I thought that long life was an external thing brought to me by the development of medicine or social and cultural changes; it hadn't really occurred to me that I could direct this process myself. . . . After this series of reflections, I made a choice that would greatly change my thinking. I decided to live 120 years. (2017: 22–23)

A related theme here is that to be "old," as in different from a younger self and specifically to experience decline, is not a natural or inevitable or meaningful part of the life course but is actually an outrage that can be eliminated. "Agelessness" is promoted as an ideal within reach. "For a long period of time, age was considered to be an inevitable, natural part of life," Schuster comments, but no more (2017: 26). "Ailments and deteriorations"—like heart attacks, strokes, common cancers, fractures, serious injuries, and many illnesses—that we have long considered a normal part of aging are "*not* a normal part of growing old. They are an outrage," Crowley and Lodge exclaim (2007: 29).

A third theme running through successful aging public discourse is that by choosing the right lifestyle and taking control of one's body and health, the successful ager benefits not only oneself but also society. As Agus urges: "When we start living strong, robust lives, we'll lessen our need for health care, causing the demand to decrease and costs to go down. Simple as that" (2014: 6). *The Economist*, a British monthly magazine, prods employers and policy makers to foster ongoing productivity among the "young old," thereby keeping health care and pension costs down and tax paying up, preventing today's longevity from becoming "one of society's great headaches."[5] In fact, in lieu of "successful" aging nomenclature, European policy discourse emphasizes "active" and "healthy" aging and is dominated by an economic or productivist perspective prioritizing the extension of working life for a healthy society and economy (Foster and Walker 2015).

It can be illuminating to compare this healthy–active–successful aging project to the U.S. antiobesity movement. Both discourses emphasize personal responsibility for one's own health and well-being, the social-moral imperative to maintain a fit body-self, the economic costs and dangers to self and society of "letting oneself go," and a sense of moral stigma and shame at not being able to maintain a certain healthy, fit body ideal.[6] To be sure, aging is a bit more nuanced than fat, as aging is generally not regarded as *all* bad, especially for those who remain fit as the years advance.

To achieve successful aging is to fend off the sense of moral failure and embarrassment associated with incapacity, dependence, and loss of control in U.S. society. The end result, if all goes well, is the elimination of oldness from the life course itself—as one goes straight from vibrant, good health to a swift and painless death, what public health experts label the "compression of morbidity," that is, reducing the period of disabling illness toward the end of life.

This vision of successful aging can seem positive and uplifting. However, it is also in some respects ageist at its core—in that old age is positioned as so bad ("an outrage") that it should be eradicated. If one actually does become "old," one has failed. On all the age-denying talk in everyday U.S. sociocultural life ("Oh, you're not old!" "You're only as old as you think you are!"), author Ursula Le Guin reflects in an essay written at age 83: "To tell me my old age doesn't exist is to tell me that I don't exist. Erase my age, you erase my life—me" (2017: 14).

Self-Care, Pride, and Blame among Older Americans

How does the public health and popular cultural successful-aging project play out in the lives of older Americans? This is the question I explored through fieldwork from 2013 to 2018 in the Boston and San Francisco areas, with 69 participants, mostly white, from the ages of 62 to 106 and a variety of socioeconomic statuses, health conditions, religious backgrounds, and living situations. The group of 69 formal participants included one black, one Asian American, and three Latino and Latina participants; about equal numbers of men and women; just over 50 percent identifying as Jewish and the rest as Christian, no religion, and (a few) Buddhist; and one-third from working-class and low-income backgrounds, most of these living in state-subsidized housing for the elderly. I formally interviewed participants and engaged in participant observation fieldwork in two upscale suburban retirement communities, a lifelong learning institute, three low-income apartment buildings for the elderly, and one senior center in an urban working-class neighborhood. Since the number of nonwhite participants is small, participants portrayed are white unless otherwise noted.

To a strong degree, I found successful-aging messaging to be widespread and internalized among the older Americans I came to know through this project. Although not always familiar with the label "successful aging," most in my study described at least some and often a great deal of commitment to maintaining lifestyles that would promote health as they age. Many also were inspired by the notion that through executing the right lifestyle, they could be in control of their own good health. Those who felt they were eating well, engaging in daily physical and mental exercise, keeping active, and maintaining a youthful sense of self often expressed pride and pleasure in their successes.

Phyllis Halpern, in her late seventies, noted: "I think there's a big push in our generation to focus on health. We are all trying to be healthier, going to the gym, taking exercise classes. We get a lot of information on the Internet about health, and there's a desire to survive." Commenting on the upscale retirement community she had moved into a decade earlier when it opened with the motto "Take a Healthier, More Active Approach to Life," Phyllis articulated: "This is our last address, and we want to live for as long as possible here."

Jerry, who exercises avidly each morning at the gym on the treadmill, enjoying the competition of racing those next to him, commented: "At 91, it's more a matter of life or death. Either you keep it up or you lose it."

"Is it important to you to maintain physical health?" I asked one married couple. "Yes!" "Oh, yes, absolutely!" Cecil, 83, and his wife Sally, 71, affirmed, describing their avid commitment to nutrition and exercise. Sally added, "We still like to feel like we are controlling our destiny, and I think that's strong."

Connie Brauner described the elaborate, fastidious diet she follows: low-glycemic, only grass-fed beef and wild-caught fish, nuts and whole grains that she sprouts first, seeds high in Omega-3s, and so on. She expressed with pleasure: "What I'm finding is that as I age, it's wonderful being on this diet! I have basically no arthritis at 80! I couldn't *do* all kinds of the things I do now if I weren't so healthy." She walks, practices yoga, meditates, paints, and takes lifelong-learning classes. "Normally I go to the gym three times a week," she said proudly. "I'm an avid exerciser. My son says, 'Walk, walk, walk!' I like to say that when he comes over, he puts me on a leash!" She laughed. Expressing her committed sense of agency, Connie related proudly: "Because of my rigid diet, I'm also one of the rare few—I've been diabetic for 35 years and have never been on insulin! . . . I don't want to go on insulin. It makes me think I'm giving up on myself."

Such successful-aging attitudes and practices among those in my study included a widespread refusal to think of oneself as "old." "I don't really feel a day older than I was in my early adulthood," Sally commented at age 71. When I asked Samuel Sampson, age 76, to tell me a little about what aging means to him, he replied with a smile, "Well, I don't see myself as aging, so in a sense I'm not a participant observer." Frances Brooks commented: "I've never felt old, I guess. I still can't believe I'm 86, almost 87."

Pursuing healthy aging might seem easier for the more elite, like most of those in the examples above, who were all white and (other than Esther) from a middle or higher socioeconomic class. Money enables one to join expensive gyms, shop for pricey nutritious foods, and move into upscale retirement communities offering a plethora of activities. However, I was struck by how healthy aging messaging cut across class lines and was prevalent also, to varying degrees, among low-income participants.

Vincent Gonzalez migrated to the United States from Chile as a young adult, worked for years as a welder, and at 67 now lives with his wife in a subsidized apartment for the elderly. A stroke four years earlier left him in a wheelchair, and he also has diabetes, yet he is upbeat and inspired by all the information he receives from the Internet and doctors about what individuals can do to promote their own health. "People don't focus much on eating healthy in order to prolong living," Vincent commented, speaking of those in his social setting including his eight siblings who suffer from heart disease, high blood pressure, obesity, and diabetes. "But I haven't ordered a pizza in years! I never go to McDonald's. I don't eat junk food. . . . I don't eat meat. No beef. I get fish and a little bit of chicken." He also told enthusiastically of eating lots of fruits and vegetables, beans, whole grains like quinoa, and cold salads in the summers—all delicious!—while keeping his diabetes under control. "But people want to get a big beef sandwich. I'm not that kind of person," suggesting an equation between moral identity and food or diet. He told of becoming especially inspired to pursue healthy living after his stroke, "because I wanted to live longer." "Yes, of course!" Vincent replied when I asked if people can control their own health.

Integral to such an ideology of personal responsibility is not only the potential for success but also for failure. Moral overtones of success and failure, virtue and blame, pride and shame, ran through many conversations. By age 88, several years after our first interview, Cecil had developed an unsteady gait that was beginning to interfere with his active lifestyle, but he utterly rejected the suggestion that he might use a cane, responding with a determined smile that a cane would be "highly embarrassing!" People also blame themselves and feel guilty for not eating as well or exercising as much as they "should," implicitly or explicitly equating good and bad diet and exercise habits with moral character. Polly Nickerson, age 73 and living in state-subsidized housing, told of "sort of falling off the wagon" recently in terms of exercise; Stick Fergus, 69 and also in low-income housing, divulged, "I'm embarrassed about what I've done to myself—physically—and my complete inactivity right now."

At one upscale retirement community where I spent time with elder residents as they dined and chatted, the conversations often turned to health. On one evening, Phyllis was describing their community's many programs for physical therapy, occupational therapy, movement, exercise, nutrition— "Whatever one needs. People partake in these! People want to be as strong and healthy as they can be. There are many, many people in their nineties living here—actively and independently and comfortably—really amazing!"

I asked, "Are there some people who think, 'Well, I've lived this long, and worked this hard, and so now—'"

"Yes, there are!" several answered at once.

"They say, you know, I'm such and such an age—I'm going to eat whatever I want," 88-year-old Steve Rubin related. "My neighbor was like that. She was a physician even, and she would say that, at this stage of her life, she was going to eat whatever she wanted! But—she died shortly after!" Steve smiled; the cause and effect relationship seemed plain: No exercise plus bad diet leads to ill health and death.

"You see, we have both halves here," Phyllis explained. "One, there are those who say, 'What the hell? I've lived this long—I may as well enjoy myself; otherwise, I'll be depriving myself.' And then there's the other half, who say, "This is not deprivation!' I want to be healthy! I want to enjoy life!" The group at my dinner table that evening regarded themselves as proudly among the responsibly healthy, while frankly suggesting that some of their peers were to blame for their own demise through careless health practices.

Sally and Cecil had a similar moralizing conversation: "We had a neighbor in Atlanta," Sally recalled. "She was exactly my age, except she seemed [and] lived like she was 20 years older. And, um, her health was very poor. And she never did anything her entire life to help her health. And she could have!" Cecil broke in, "She just doesn't care." Sally added, "And she doesn't believe in it." Chuck Dowling, 79, remarked, after describing several unsuccessful dieting attempts, "I'm sure that if I didn't make it through tomorrow [i.e., died], people would mumble, 'Chuck never was a—he always had a roll around his belly.'"

Critiquing the broad doctrine of personal responsibility for one's health that has become what she calls a "craze" in U.S. society since the late twentieth century, Barbara Ehrenreich comments on how we subject persons who die (or, I could add, show signs of "old" age) to a kind of bio-moral autopsy: "Did she smoke? Drink excessively? Eat too much fat and not enough fiber? Can she, in other words, be blamed for her own death?" (2018: 93). Such blame discourse charges others for "letting themselves go" while fostering a sense of control among its speakers: We can be safe because we don't do all that.

"But It's a Crap Shoot!" Luck, Genes, and the Human Condition

Despite widespread buy-in to notions of healthy, successful aging, most people in my study were not as confident as the self-help books and public health discourse suggest, that good health is reliably an extension of individual responsibility. Genes, luck, and acceptance of bodily change as an inevitable part of aging were common alternative ideologies—leading me to realize that older Americans' own perspectives on life, health, and aging tend to be more complex and nuanced than the public successful-aging discourse might steer one to believe.

I asked Stanley Goodman, age 82 and a retired physician, if health is something that's in a person's own control. Although appearing to be in excellent health, he had just warned me that I would be "aghast" by his diet, comprising red meat five times per week, sugary pastries for breakfast, three spoons of sugar in his coffee, and four or five flavors of ice cream before bed. (He, by the way, nonetheless appeared to be in quite good physical health and maintains a very active intellectual and social life.) Stanley replied:

> Well, I think a lot of it is genetic. I really think your genes count for an enormous amount. . . . There's *some* control people have [sounding doubtful]; but I think they've been given a sense that they have more control than they do by the media. . . . And I ask myself, to what extent is the deprivation that is caused by adhering to all the good advice preventing you from all the enjoyment that you could be having?

Even those who seemed most committed to healthy aging as a personal project frequently brought up luck and genes as formidable forces beyond personal control. Connie Brauner, for instance, whom I described above as highly dedicated to both exercise and a fastidious diet, peppered her conversations with comments like: "But it's a crap shoot! You don't know!" and, "Who knows? You can get cancer, and boom! All that health stuff you've been doing goes down the drain," and, "Sure, you can do all the right things, all the healthy things, and then can step off the curb, and, boom! You're hit by a car."

Those older than around 90 or 95 who grew into maturity before the doctrine of personal responsibility for health really took hold in U.S. society quite commonly also expressed puzzlement as to why they were living in good health for so long. Agnes Martell, at 105, denied ever having done anything to promote her own health (her family concurred), and she delighted in replying when people asked her secret to longevity: "God doesn't want me, and the devil won't take me!"

Challenging the premise that we each have the capacity to fend off old age, the theme of accepting and adapting to aging as part of the human condition was also common in my interview materials.[7] Maurice Kleinman, 84, described how his health challenges have led him to understand the benefits of realizing that one cannot always be in control. He remarked:

> I've felt the loss of control physically, because I have a very bad back and I can't move around like I used to. It bothers me, but I've tried to put it

outside of myself, because I don't have any control of it. I take shots and I do this and that, but in the end, when the bones are all beat up, there's nothing you can do about it. . . . I have to accept it, and I think that it's not so bad that I understand that I need to give up some control.

His wife Elaine, 82, added: "I think one of the features of successful aging is the capacity to accept your limitations, and not to be in struggle with that. The world changes; you change. . . . I guess I'd say this is what I've learned the most in my later years and what I've found the most reassuring."

Lily Whitefield, now serving as the resident chaplain in her retirement community, reflects on her work as she turns 76: "If we still want to be what we were at 50, we're defeated right out of the box. We can't be. I can't be 50 again. Frankly, I don't want to be 50 again if you want the honest truth."

Accepting changes of aging for Lily also means accepting the inevitability of dying. She told of one of her congregants who at 98 was wishing to stop medical treatment, while her kids were pushing her to be readmitted to the hospital, pleading, "Mama, you're not dying; you're going to live!" Lily recalls, "And [the mother] says, and this is what really struck me; she said, 'How did I raise such dumb kids?' She said, 'I'm 98. Don't they know there's a span?'" As an alternative to successful-aging ideologies, Lily and other older people themselves offered more nuanced, complex, and accepting perspectives—on the changes of age, the finiteness of human life, the impossibility and even undesirability of perpetual youthfulness, and the limits of individual control.

Successful Aging and Its Blind Spots: Unequal Access to Personal Control

Another challenge to the doctrine of individual responsibility at the heart of successful-aging ideology is posed by social inequality. We know that socioeconomic status and race play a large role in determining a person's health status in the United States, although health disparities tied to structural inequalities get scant attention in the successful-aging literature (Katz and Calasanti 2015: 29–30). Several scholars have called for more research into how race and income impact older adults' health conditions as well as their subjective experiences of successful aging (e.g., Baker et al. 2015; Chard et al. 2017; Woody 2017). Tamara Baker et al., for example, suggest that the Strong Black Woman archetype—a cultural ideal highlighting selfless self-reliance and strength—may offer older black women a steadfast sense of perseverance as they face the intersecting oppressions of racism, sexism, and ageism. Yet at the same time, such an archetype can potentially lead women to internalize a sense of disappointment and failure if they cannot maintain the self-reliant ideal (2015; see also Woody 2017). Sarah Chard et al., researching older African Americans with type 2 diabetes, find that although most study participants embraced successful aging's doctrine of agency and personal control, structural factors including a lifetime of accumulated financial stressors made it difficult for most to achieve the state of freedom from disease central to successful-aging models (2017).

My field research also found striking differences by socioeconomic status among the mostly white people in the study, especially regarding the extent people perceived they did or did not have access to personal control over health and aging. Lower-income participants frequently conveyed a sense of powerlessness to achieve ideals of healthy aging due to external obstacles beyond their control, ranging from lack of access to healthy foods and good medical care, to having worked in toxic environments, to living in bedbug-infested buildings hindering one's ability to socialize and go out and do things. Unable to pay for dental work, a few low-income participants had lost their teeth. Tammy Yazbeck, age 63, commented, "So now you can't eat things that you should be eating, like salads." Formerly homeless and now living in subsidized housing, Robert at age 68 tries to practice healthy eating following recommendations he gleans from the news and classes at the local senior center. He carries around packets of honey to use in place of sugar in his coffee, for instance, and aims to minimize intake of red meat, but said there's only so much he can do: "If they give you hot dogs [at the soup kitchen], you gotta eat hot dogs." Tammy reflected: "So it shouldn't be a class issue, but it ultimately is. How well you successfully age is a class issue. . . . If you're at the bottom end of the scale, then you are at the mercy of the system, the health care system, and whatever system is out there."

Connected to this, I was struck by how many lower-income people felt they qualified for my study at relatively young chronological ages like the sixties. This contrasted to the elite who tended to be so engrossed in the culturally normative project of warding off old age that they did not see themselves as qualifying for an "aging" study until at least their seventies or eighties. It was also not uncommon for low-income participants to envision dying by around 70, while most elite participants expressed aspiring to live in good health into their nineties or 100.

Charlie Allen, age 64 and a retired mail-room clerk who now works as a daytime shuttle driver for the Hilton Garden Inn, recounted: "My doctor told me that when I'm 70 years old, I will be blind." "Oh no. Wow," I remarked. "So that's OK," Charlie went on matter-of-factly. "When I'm 70 years old, that will be what happens. I have two kidneys, but unfortunately, they work only as one—60 and 40. They told me that when I'm 70 years old, I will need dialysis." He later mentioned that he would refuse dialysis, though.

And, um, my philosophy is, and [my wife] agrees with the philosophy: You live today. Enjoy today. Because you don't know what's going to happen tomorrow morning. . . . Who knows? I mean, between my kidneys, my heart, my eyes. Who knows? I'm not going to worry about it. I can't.

Everyone seems to think—all my health people seem to think that when I'm 70 years old, I'm in trouble. So! I got six more years. That's all [as in, not a big deal]. I'm not going to worry about it.

Stick Fergus, age 69 and living in low-income housing for the elderly, also envisioned dying around age 70, but this apprehension troubled him greatly. He told of being "massively unhappy" about aging, explaining: "Actually it wasn't until I realized that I don't have the time to do all the things I'd like to do that I started to be as unhappy about it as I am. . . . It's old, it's old. 70. For some reason I was thinking, you know, I'm gonna be dead by the time I'm 70, but 70's right around the corner."

Tammy Yazbeck, drawing on insights she has gleaned from living for the past 13 years in public housing, perceptively articulated the connection between hope and a sense of agency: "I think it would be wonderful if people had more hope. Hope enough to be responsible for themselves. Because that's one thing I see in public housing." She described witnessing so many people without hope. "It would be good for people to have more hope; and not feel like it's all over, and that they have nothing to live for, and you know, what's the point." Tammy herself commented rather grimly when asked how long she might like to live: "To be honest with you, this is my prayer: If I am going to live to old age, please give me the strength, Lord, to endure it."

The sense of motivation that one can, should, and must take control of aging, working as hard as one can to stay healthy, not become old, live with pleasure to 100 or 120, and not die—a sense of inspiration and entitlement I had come to recognize as prevalent among the more elite—was indeed infrequent among the low income in my study. Yet it should not be surprising that those who have faced forms of impotence due to structural inequalities throughout life could feel unable to take on successful aging as a personal project of individual control. The narratives of low-income older adults also resonate with public health studies exposing how low income can accelerate biological aging, not merely due to the lifestyle "choices" (diet, exercise, attitude) emphasized by the successful-aging paradigm but also due to the accumulated bodily harms stemming from years of financial stress (Levine and Crimmins 2014; Simons et al. 2016; Greene et al. 2018).

Cultural Contexts of "Successful Aging": Alternative Views from India and North America

We see how the lives of older Americans—differently situated by socioeconomic status, life circumstances, and personal inclinations—reveal a variety of perspectives on successful aging and how possible it is to achieve ideals of health, agelessness, and longevity as a personal undertaking. Aspirations of successful aging of course take place as well in broader cultural contexts, where assumptions and values surrounding aging, personhood, families, and the human life course are at play.

It can be difficult to recognize as cultural, rather than as simply natural or obvious or scientific, one's own taken-for-granted assumptions, such as the idea—prevailing in the United States perhaps especially among white people—that being old is bad. Recognizing cultural values is what the anthropological project strives to help us do, by making the familiar strange and the strange familiar through cross-cultural comparison. So before closing, I would like to consider a few alternative perspectives from India, the other nation where I have conducted fieldwork related to aging for many years (e.g., Lamb 2000, 2009, Part V).

In fact, models of aging well in India can look quite different from those in the United States. Accepting aging, dying, dependence, and the ephemerality of the human condition are ideals commonly held up as appropriate to older age. According to Hindu philosophies, just as rice plants grow, drop their seeds, and then wither away, so does the human body. To both Hindus and Muslims in India, just as children need help when young, so do elder parents and grandparents need help when old (Part V Lamb).

Purnima Banerjee, a retired English professor and a practicing Hindu in her early seventies, spoke often of her readiness for dying and acceptance of decay. She expressed: "I am not afraid of death, because it is inevitable. Because I am born, I know I have to die. No one born can escape death." And: "A machine also has retirement. When clothes are worn out, you just take them off and wear new ones. The body is also like that." Once after Purnima-di[8] mentioned that she would likely die soon, I commented, in perhaps an American style, that she looked great and healthy to me and might live a good 10 years more. Purnima-di exclaimed, "No, don't say that! I don't want to keep living. I am ready to die."

Such ready-to-die remarks are not generally uttered in a depressed fashion, but rather as expected cultural discourse among older persons who are often in excellent physical and mental health. These remarks express a commonly held cultural perspective that it is inappropriate in one's later years to cling unduly to life, that no body can last forever, and that the person (at least in this body and life—as most Hindus in India believe in an everlasting soul) is transient (Part V Lamb). Purnima-di commented: "The body will die, but the soul will not die. Wherever I go, I will go *somewhere* else. Those dear ones who have died, why should I cry for them? There is no use crying for a departed soul. God is a giver and a taker." It may not be surprising, then, that in contrast to the United States, where "most of us want [and expect] the miracles of medicine to extend our lives" (Kaufman 2015: 2), little medical intervention in India is spent to keep a very old person alive, and the ideal death takes place at home—as the older dying person is consciously aware of and accepting her passing.

People across India also speak of interdependence and dependence as normal and valued parts of human life. Interdependence within an intimate family setting and *seva*—respectful care for and service to elders—are central to prevailing visions of aging well. Though many talk of wishing to die while the "hands and feet are still working" rather than being completely bedridden, most regard it entirely appropriate to receive a lot of help in one's later years, just as it is entirely appropriate for parents to care for their dependent young children. The most common living situation for those over 60 in India remains the intergenerational family (Sathyanarayana, Kumar, and James 2012). In fact, too much independence is commonly regarded as the worst thing that can befall one in old age, rather than the ideal celebrated in U.S. successful-aging discourse.

In the United States, cultural values prominent in the successful-aging movement include individualism (with a strong sense of individual control over bodies and selves), independence, and an aspired-for permanence of the adult self. Rowe and Kahn, in fact, highlight the goal of independence as central to the whole successful-aging project: "Older people, like younger ones, want to be independent. This is the principal goal of many elders, and few issues strike greater fear than the prospect of depending on others" (1998: 42). These values make conditions that we might normally expect to accompany a very long life, like bodily change, frailty, and needing help, seem particularly threatening. In fact, to many in my study, an imagined state of debility in old age was worse—more shattering to a sense of self, more humiliating—than death. Stella commented, for instance, "You know, I don't want to die; but I would rather die than be disabled." Her friend Sadie jumped in, "Right! With dignity! I don't want to live without dignity!" Historian Thomas Cole examines how, as far back as the Victorian era of the 1800s United States, we find evidence in church sermons and other public discourse that "the declining body in old age, a constant reminder of the limits of physical self-control, came to signify dependence, disease, failure, and sin" (1992: 91).

Yet also in North America we witness competing cultural perspectives on aging, the life course, and independence. Rocío Calvo, for instance, finds that "Hispanics, particularly immigrants, are more satisfied with their lives than any other group of older Americans, including Whites," despite worse health and fewer social and economic resources than white elders (2018; see also Calvo, Carr, and Matz-Costa 2017). Why? Calvo suggests that greater satisfaction in later life for Latinos may be tied to cultural emphases within Latinx communities on family support instead of individual self-reliance. Calvo reports: "Hispanic immigrants in our study co-resided with their adult children more often than any other group. Interestingly, while living with their children made older Hispanics happy, it had the opposite effect among older Whites" (2018). It seems untrue that, for all Americans, "few issues strike greater fear than the prospect of depending on others" (Rowe and Kahn

1998: 42). Research on the subjective perceptions of older Indigenous peoples in North America also reports positive feelings about old age, tied to the distinguished role of the "elder" in Indigenous communities, humor, and cyclical versus linear images of the life course with continuities after death—all providing sources of resilience in old age, despite serious health disparities stemming from socioeconomic inequalities (Lewis 2011; Pace and Grenier 2017; Part II Web Book Weibel-Orlando).

Concluding Note

I have found successful aging to be a fascinating contemporary cultural project to examine as an anthropologist exploring meanings of life in the later years. The U.S. successful aging project is particularly intriguing in the way it seems to strive to eradicate old age itself and offer an individualist illusion of control over our own bodies and minds. Yet fieldwork in a variety of contexts shows that diverse older people themselves tend to have more complex, realistic, and even positive understandings of old age than what we find in the public health and popular discourse.

As we look forward, we also see new forms of public thinking evolving: Popular books like *Being Mortal* (Gawande 2017), *No Time to Spare* (Le Guin 2017), and *Natural Causes* (Ehrenreich 2018) all promote the message that aging (if one is fortunate to live long enough) and dying (inevitably for us all) are normal, okay parts of being human. No matter how much effort we exert, not everything is within our control, not even our own bodies.

For myself, I like the idea of striving to be as healthy as I can through whatever lifestyle projects I wish to engage in, while accepting—if I'm fortunate to live that long —the fact that I will indeed be old. This old age should be not an embarrassment, nor an outrage, nor a tragedy, nor a failure. But okay. Part of life. With hope, something I look forward to achieving.

Notes

1. https://www.nytimes.com/2017/03/14/books/henry-lodge-dead-co-author-younger-next-year.html.

2. See, for instance, the *Boston Globe*'s "Wary of Alzheimer's, They're On the Move: With New Drugs Still Elusive, Some Turn to Lifestyle Changes to Try to Head Off the Disease" (Weisman 2018: A1): "Medical researchers say there's no evidence fitness, healthy eating, or mental exercises can halt the progression of Alzheimer's once it has begun. But they express cautious hope such behaviors can at least postpone its onset" (A7).

3. https://go4life.nia.nih.gov/.

4. These Go4Life tweets were sent out respectively on May 16, 2018 (https://t.co/5FoFHoJmmH); June 20, 2018 (https://t.co/ysi0SGH8GI); and July 28, 2018 (https://t.co/dEJZVKSQ1P).

5. *The Economist*, "What to Call the Time of Life between Work and Old Age?" July 7, 2017: https://www.economist.com/news/leaders/21724814-get-most-out -longer-lives-new-age-category-needed-what-call-time-life.

6. For a revealing account of the U.S. anti-obesity movement, see Greenhalgh 2015.

7. My participants' ideas about accepting and adapting to the changes of age resonate with Harry Moody's notion of "decrement with compensation" in his "From Successful Aging to Conscious Aging" (Part I Web Book).

8. "Di" short for "didi" (older sister) and "da" for "dada" (older brother) are common epithets Bengalis use to signal respect for a person senior to the speaker in age. Terms for aunt, uncle, grandmother, and grandfather can also be used.

Bibliography

Agus, D. B. 2014. *A Short Guide to a Long Life*. New York: Simon & Schuster.

Baker, T. A., N. T. Buchanan, C. A. Mingo, R. Roker, and C. S. Brown. 2015. "Reconceptualizing Successful Aging among Black Women and the Relevance of the Strong Black Woman Archetype." *Gerontologist* 55(1): 51–57.

Calvo, R. 2018. "Rethinking Successful Aging: The Happiness of Older Hispanics." *Public Health Post*, July 2. https://www.publichealthpost.org/research /rethinking-successful-aging-the-happiness-of-older-hispanics/.

Calvo, R, D. C. Carr, and C. Matz-Costa. 2017. "Another Paradox? The Life Satisfaction of Older Hispanic Immigrants in the United States." *Journal of Aging and Health* 29(1): 3–24.

Chard, S., B. Harris-Wallace, E. G. Roth, L. M. Girling, R. Rubinstein, A. M. Reese, C. C. Quinn, and J. K. Eckert. 2017. "Successful Aging among African American Older Adults with Type 2 Diabetes." *Journals of Gerontology Series B: Psychological Sciences and Social Sciences* 72(2): 319–27.

Cole, T. R. 1992. *The Journey of Life: A Cultural History of Aging in America*. New York: Cambridge University Press.

Crawford, R. 2006. "Health as a Meaningful Social Practice." *Health: An Interdisciplinary Journal for the Social Study of Health, Illness, and Medicine* 20(4): 401–20.

Crowley, C., and H. S. Lodge. 2007. *Younger Next Year: Live Strong, Fit and Sexy until You're 80 and Beyond*. New York: Workman.

Ehrenreich, B. 2018. *Natural Causes: An Epidemic of Wellness, the Certainty of Dying, and Killing Ourselves to Live Longer*. New York: Hachette.

Foster, L., and A. Walker. 2015. "Active and Successful Aging: A European Policy Perspective." *Gerontologist* 55(1): 83–90.

Gawande, A. 2017 *Being Mortal: Medicine and What Matters in the End*. New York: Metropolitan.

Greene, M., C. Ahalt, I. Stijacic-Cenzer, L. Metzger, and B. Williams. 2018. "Older Adults in Jail: High Rates and Early Onset of Geriatric Conditions." *Health and Justice* 6(1): 1–9.

Greenhalgh, S. 2015. *Fat-Talk Nation: The Human Costs of America's War on Fat.* Ithaca, NY: Cornell University Press.

Katz, S., and T. Calasanti. 2015. "Critical Perspectives on Successful Aging: Does It Appeal More Than It Illuminates?" *Gerontologist* 55(1): 26–33.

Kaufman, S. R. 2015. *Ordinary Medicine: Extraordinary Treatments, Longer Lives, and Where to Draw the Line.* Durham, NC: Duke University Press.

Lamb, S. 2000. *White Saris and Sweet Mangoes: Aging, Gender, and Body in North India.* Berkeley: University of California Press.

Lamb, S. 2009. *Aging and the Indian Diaspora: Cosmopolitan Families in India and Abroad.* Bloomington: Indiana University Press.

Lamb, S. 2014. "Permanent Personhood or Meaningful Decline? Toward a Critical Anthropology of Successful Aging." *Journal of Aging Studies* 29: 41–52.

Lamb, S., J. Robbins-Ruszkowski, and A. Corwin. 2017. "Introduction: Successful Aging as a Twenty-First-Century Obsession." In *Successful Aging as a Contemporary Obsession: Global Perspectives*, edited by S. Lamb, 1–23. New Brunswick, NJ: Rutgers University Press.

Le Guin, U. K. 2017. *No Time to Spare: Thinking about What Matters.* New York: Houghton Mifflin Harcourt.

Lee, I. 2017. *I've Decided to Live 120 Years: The Ancient Secret to Longevity, Vitality, and Life Transformation.* Gilbert, AZ: Best Life Media.

Levine, M. E., and E .M. Crimmins. 2014. "Evidence of Accelerated Aging among African Americans and Its Implications for Mortality." *Social Science & Medicine* 118: 27–32.

Lewis, J. P. 2011. "Successful Aging through the Eyes of Alaska Native Elders: What It Means to Be an Elder in Bristol Bay, AK." *Gerontologist* 51(4): 540–49.

Pace, J. E., and A. Grenier. 2017. "Expanding the Circle of Knowledge: Reconceptualizing Successful Aging among North American Older Indigenous Peoples." *Journals of Gerontology: Series B* 72(2): 248–58.

Rowe, J. W., and R. L. Kahn. 1998. *Successful Aging.* New York: Pantheon.

Sathyanarayana, K. M., S. Kumar, and K. S. James. 2012. "Living Arrangements of Elderly in India: Policy and Programmatic Implications." BKPAI Working Paper, United Nations Population Fund, India 7.

Schuster, S. 2017. *Age in Reverse: Look and Feel Younger, Be More Energetic and Have Better Memory: Live a Long and Healthy Life.* CreateSpace Independent Publishing.

Simons, R. L., M. K. Lei, S. R. H. Beach, R. A. Philibert, C. E. Cutrona, F. X. Gibbons, and A. Barr. 2016. "Economic Hardship and Biological Weathering: The Epigenetics of Aging in a U.S. Sample of Black Women." *Social Science & Medicine* 150: 192–200.

Weisman, R. 2018. "Wary of Alzheimer's, They're On the Move." *Boston Globe*, June 25: A1, A7.

Woody, I. 2017. "Aging Out: Ageism, Heterosexism, and Racism among Aging African American Lesbians and Gay Men." In *Successful Aging as a Contemporary Obsession: Global Perspectives*, edited by S. Lamb, 55–67. New Brunswick, NJ: Rutgers University Press.

CHAPTER FIVE

Web Book: Culture and the Meaning of a Good Old Age

Christine L. Fry, Jeanette Dickerson-Putman,
Patricia Draper, Charlotte Ikels, Jennie Keith,
Anthony P. Glascock, and Henry C. Harpending

Available at the Web Book: http://www.culturalcontextofaging.com/webbook
-fry

This chapter details the work of Project AGE (Age, Generation, and Experience). Here a team of anthropologists carried out a comparison of aging in Hong Kong, Botswana, rural Ireland, and two American communities. Readers can also relate this chapter to the Lamb's chapter in Part I and two newer global projects: "Aging as a Human Condition," https://projects.au.dk/thegood oldlife/, and ASSA—Anthropology of Smart Phones and Smart Aging, https:// www.ucl.ac.uk/anthropology/assa/.

CHAPTER SIX

Web Book: From Successful Aging to Conscious Aging

Harry Moody

Available at: http://www.culturalcontextofaging.com/webbook-moody

Harry Moody suggests that both successful and productive aging are a postmodern tactic for turning old age into a "second middle age," in effect a strategy for an ageless old age. See Sarah Lamb's chapter in Part I for a comparative update on the notion of successful aging.

CHAPTER SEVEN

Web Book: Menopause

A BioCultural Event

Yewoubdar Beyene

Available at: http://www.culturalcontextofaging.com/webbook-beyene

Beyene's ethnographic report provides a comparison of rural Mayan and Greek women. She shows that, despite similar values and behaviors regarding menstruation and childbearing, their experience of menopause differed.

For a discussion of this issue in Brazil from the ASSA Blog see "Woman, Interrupted," by Marilia Duque E S Pereira: https://blogs.ucl.ac.uk/assa/20 20/01/09/woman-interrupted/.

CHAPTER EIGHT

Trans(gender)/Gender-Diverse Aging

Jenny-Anne Bishop and Sue Westwood

Introduction

In this chapter we will examine the equality and social justice issues relating to trans(gender)/gender-diverse (trans/g-d) people and ageing. As Persson has observed, "transgender elders are both underserved and understudied. Neither the etiology nor prevalence of transgender is well understood" (Persson 2009: 633). It has been estimated that 1 percent to 2 percent of the population are trans/g-d (GIRES 2011), although this is generally considered to be a conservative estimate. With growing legal and social recognition of trans/g-d people (Hines 2007), it is likely that their visibility, and this estimate, will increase. In this chapter we argue that increased recognition and representation of older trans/g-d people has significant emancipatory potential for not only older trans/g-d people themselves but also for a broader understanding of embodied, gendered ageing.

We use the term *trans(gender)/gender-diverse* (trans/g-d) as a broad umbrella collective to describe individuals who are transgender, and including all those who are transsexual, transvestite, gender queer, gender fluid, nonbinary, genderless, agender, nongendered, third gender, and bigender people. The term *transgender/trans* has had different meanings in different times and societies, and in some contexts, is used to include all of these gender diversities.[1] However, not everyone is comfortable being described as transgender/

trans, and so here we are using the broader category trans/g-d in order to be more inclusive.

We shall use the term *transgender* to describe individuals who have transitioned in any way from the gender they were assigned at birth to the gender they identify as: Transmen have transitioned from being assigned female to self-identifying as male. Transwomen have transitioned from being assigned male to self-identifying as female. Some will have had chemical and/or surgical interventions to support their transitioning, some will not. Some will have legally changed their gender, in those countries in which they are able to do so, some will not. Some will be living in countries where their rights are recognized, some will not (Human Rights Watch 2018). We explore the issues affecting older trans/g-d people from a social justice perspective, drawing upon Nancy Fraser's (1997) model of social justice. Fraser has argued that inequality includes but also goes beyond resources, to also include recognition (social and cultural value, status, and worth) and representation (political voice). All three mutually inform each other, and combine to produce greater inequalities. All three must be addressed, Fraser argues, for inequalities to be remedied. While Fraser understood resources in terms of the material and financial, we consider other resources to also be of significance, particularly in older age. These include access to housing, health and social care, and support (Westwood 2016). We believe Fraser's model is extremely helpful in understanding the intersecting domains of inequality, and we have previously used it to consider the inequalities associated with dementia experienced by trans(gender)/gender-diverse people (Hunter, Bishop, and Westwood, 2016).

In this chapter we consider how older trans/g-d people are affected by the intersection (Hines 2010) of resources, recognition, and representation to produce later life disadvantage, and how these are informed by cumulative disadvantage, nuanced by their trans/g-d identities across the life span. We identify ways in which such disadvantages need to be addressed by policy makers, service providers, and advocacy organizations. Through identifying the key issues for trans/g-d individuals, this chapter also offers insights into how normative and nonnormative gender identification and attribution informs the ageing process and associated (in)equality issues.

Resources

Material Resources

It might not seem at first glance that there is any reason why trans/g-d individuals should be differently positioned in terms of access to material resources, compared with cisgender[2] women and men. However, this is to not understand the impact of being gender nonconforming on a person's in/

exclusion and positioning in the world of work and social networking, and in turn, a trans/g-d person's accrual of resources, such as pensions, property, and savings (Whittle et al. 2007; Auldridge et al. 2012). Some transwomen and transmen have concealed their identities for many years, with only some eventually transitioning.[3] For many of these individuals the consequences for their mental health and well-being have been harsh, with many suffering from mental health problems, particularly depression (Hoy-Ellis and Fredriksen-Goldsen 2017). Many have also been affected by substance use issues and have been at increased risk of ending their lives (Fredriksen-Goldsen et al. 2013).

Some trans/g-d people have been gender nonconforming all their lives, that is, their gender identity and presentation has never aligned with the gender others perceive them to be. This nonnormativity has resulted in bullying at school, prejudice and discrimination in the workplace, and being subject to transphobic[4] attacks in everyday life (Whittle et al. 2007; Grant et al. 2011). Some trans/g-d people have also been subject to domestic abuse related to being trans/g-d (Cook-Daniels and Munson 2010). Many trans/g-d people have also experienced profound workplace prejudice and discrimination (McFadden and Crowley-Henry 2016). These risks are partially mediated by the extent to which a trans/g-d person can "pass" (which is known as "passing privilege"), i.e., comply with culturally acceptable binary gender norms. This includes both transsexual people who have not yet transitioned and those who have (Bailey 2012).

These challenges and exclusions impact upon a trans/g-d individual's employment—whether they are able to work, the kind of work they choose to do, their increased risk of workplace discrimination, and associated reduced job security promotion prospects (Grant et al. 2011). This in turn has implications for their associated relatively diminished accrual of financial capital, pensions, and property: trans/g-d people are more likely than cisgender people to be living below the poverty level (Crissman et al. 2017).

These material disadvantages are further compounded by ageing, in several ways. The relative economic disadvantage of gender-nonconforming people means that in older age, they are more likely to be on lower incomes and more reliant on state welfare and/or charitable support to sustain their daily living needs. At the same time, they may be more reluctant to seek such support because of ongoing fears about transphobic and cisnormative[5] prejudice and discrimination (Fredriksen-Goldsen et al. 2014). Further, this minority population is more likely to be living in housing that is inappropriate for their needs (Johnston and Meyer 2017; Wathern and Green 2017) in two main ways. First, they may be living in housing that is not age appropriate, where they may or may not be subject to transphobia and/or cisnormativity. Second, they may be living in housing that is age appropriate but where they are subject to such prejudice and discrimination, too often from their peers as well as their care providers.

These associated and accumulated material disadvantages also have profound implications for older trans/g-d individuals' health and well-being and their ability to maintain themselves.

Health and Well-Being

Health issues affecting older trans/g-d people in general and older transwomen and transmen in particular is an emerging area of study. As Age UK has observed:

> Knowledge is improving as trans(gender)/gender diverse people age but there are still unanswered questions about what later life and health will be like for trans(gender)/gender diverse people We are only now seeing the first generation of trans(gender)/gender diverse people in their 60s and over who have taken hormone therapy for 30 years or more, many of whom are living with gender reassignment[6] surgeries performed using the very different techniques of the 1960s and 70s. (2017: 11)

We do already know, however, that trans/g-d people of all ages experience significant physical and mental health inequalities that are compounded in/by older age (Auldridge et al. 2012; Cook-Daniels 2015). Trans/g-d people experience high levels of victimization and discrimination (see Whittle et al. 2007; Grant et al. 2011) as well as reduced levels of social support from social networks, including family, friends, neighbors, work colleagues, and mainstream religious organizations. This in turn leads to being at increased risk of associated mental health problems, especially depression, with trans/g-d people being at increased risk of ending their lives (Fredriksen-Goldsen et al. 2013; McNeil et al. 2012).

These health inequalities are further compounded by ageing. Older trans/g-d people are more likely to suffer from a range of mental health problems associated with a lifetime of discrimination, marginalization, and social exclusion (Auldridge et al. 2012; Fredriksen-Goldsen et al. 2013; Hoy-Ellis and Fredriksen-Goldsen 2017). Older trans/g-d people who are able to create supportive networks and/or construct positive self-images may experience greater resilience in ageing (Witten 2014a). Transwomen and transmen who transition in later life may find their levels of depression become lower post-transitioning (Bailey 2012). However, transitioning itself can be associated with significant family losses, even in older age (Witten 2009; Riggs and Kentlyn 2014). For those transwomen and transmen who do not have compensatory social support networks (see the following section), depression and the risk of ending their lives is a major concern.

Trans/g-d people may be particularly vulnerable to domestic abuse, due at least in part to their social marginalization (Barrett and Sheridan 2017). This can be heightened for older trans/g-d people (Cook-Daniels and Munson 2010) whose vulnerability to such abuse may be compounded by physical and/or mental frailties and/or heightened dependence upon others for care and support. This, in turn, may be even further compounded by unequal access to and provision of services by domestic violence programs, which are rarely set up to include trans/g-d and/or LGB[7] people (Harvey, Mitchell, and Keeble 2014; Seelman 2015; Rogers 2016).

Older trans/g-d individuals also face unique and/or specific physical health challenges (Fredriksen-Goldsen et al. 2013). Particular issues can affect older transwomen and older transmen respectively. For older transwomen, these issues may include the long-term effects of estrogen replacement therapy; estrogen, testosterone, and prolactin (hormone) levels; prostate health (the prostate is not removed even with lower surgery); abdominal aortic aneurysm (AAA) screening; breast screening; dilation and douching advice if a transwoman has had plastic surgery to create a neo-vagina (vaginoplasty); and the state of silicone breast implants (Age UK 2017: 11–12).

For older transmen, the particular issues that may concern them include osteoporosis risk; side effects associated with testosterone therapy; vaginal health (if the transman still has a vagina); whether or not to undergo a hysterectomy; the need for cervical smear tests if he has not had a full hysterectomy; risk of urethral stones if he has had genital reconstruction; breast screening (even when breasts are removed, not all potentially cancerous glands are removed); and the state of silicone testicular implants and/or penile prosthetics (Age UK 2017: 11).

Care and Support

Informal Care and Support

While some older trans/g-d people enjoy supportive family and friendship networks (Witten 2014a), many do not:

> For many trans(gender)/gender diverse and gender-nonconforming older adults, family and social support relationships are either fraught with difficulty or non-existent. (Finkenauer et al. 2012: 318)

Many older trans/g-d people have experienced a lifetime of transphobic rejection from family and friends, and in the workplace. Transwomen and transmen often encounter further rejection when they transition. Riggs and Kentlyn describe the narrative of KrysAnne, featured in the USA Gen Silent documentary,[8] a 59-year-old transwoman who transitioned in her fifties— "cured the depression," she said, laughing, in the film—and who was subsequently diagnosed with lung cancer. A war veteran, previously heterosexually married with children and grandchildren, she was rejected by her entire family post-transitioning:

> Most people that transition expect losses, sometimes a great many losses, but I didn't expect [to lose] everyone. I haven't heard from them since. For two years I desperately tried to connect with my family. And some of [the letters] weren't even opened. [The letters were returned saying] "this person is dead" [images of letters with name struck out saying "no such person!" and "deceased"]. It was horrible. It was vile. (KrysAnne, quoted in Riggs and Kentlyn 2014: 224)

When she became ill and was, eventually, dying, KrysAnne had no informal social support. As Riggs and Kentlyn observed,

> Not only has her family's reaction to her transition left her at a loss for social contact and caring relationships, but it has also left her at risk in terms of her physical health and wellbeing. (2014: 225)

Although KrysAnne was eventually supported by an older LGBT*[9] support network, as Riggs and Kentlyn describe,

> KrysAnne, talking in the form of a video diary, shares the absolute loneliness of her illness, left with a body that no longer functions in ways that allow her to live a full life, and with no one in her life with whom she has established connections. . . . [she spent] her final days at home alone and in distress. (2014: 228)

Formal Care and Support

Access to formal health care is severely constrained, especially in those countries where trans/g-d rights are not respected:

> Many transgender people live on the margins of society, facing stigma, discrimination, exclusion, violence, and poor health. They often experience difficulties accessing appropriate health care, whether specific to their gender needs or more general in nature. Some governments are taking steps to address human rights issues and provide better legal protection for transgender people, but this action is by no means universal. (Winter et al. 2016: 390)

This is then further compounded in older age. Many trans/g-d people, especially older trans/g-d people, will have experienced a lifetime of unhelpful and/or transphobic responses from the health care system, which has pathologized their gender identity issues. In many countries this still endures. As the UK Equality and Human Rights Commission (EHRC) has observed:

> Experiences of discrimination in the health sector include inappropriate diagnoses, denial of treatment, humiliation, and trans(gender)/gender diverse status being raised when seeking treatment for entirely unrelated health concerns. The latter has been described as "trans(gender)/gender diverse cold syndrome," where a clinician views gender history as more important than the presenting medical complaint. (EHRC 2015: 1)

This is often compounded at its intersection with other social divisions, for example trans/g-d people who identify as lesbian, gay, and bisexual; people from black, Asian, and minority ethnic (BAME) backgrounds; people living with HIV/AIDS; sex workers; and those from other marginalized social positions.

Moreover, medical practitioners may be uneasy, underprepared, and uncomfortable in responding to trans/g-d patients (Snelgrove et al. 2012). Many trans/g-d people, especially older trans/g-d people, are extremely wary of engaging with health care providers because of their negative experiences. This can result in a lack of health screening and/or delayed diagnosis of and treatment for illnesses, particularly for those transwomen and transmen with parts of the body they have not assimilated and that may not be associated with their acquired gender:

> It seems than many transgender persons simply live with untreated or under-treated chronic conditions such as hypertension or diabetes. Furthermore, fear of revealing their transgender status may prevent adequate health screenings, such as for breast or prostate cancers. Treatable health conditions may increase in severity unnecessarily, due to the reluctance of transgender people, young and old, to either put themselves in further abusive situations or be forced to confront prejudice in the health care system. This may be particularly true for transgender elders who were part of a generation that was raised to passively accept the authority of medical professionals. (Williams and Freeman 2007: 97)

Even in those countries that are more trans(gender)/gender-diverse-inclusive, specific gender identity health care is often limited (Auldridge et al. 2012) or not available at all. Many gender-diverse people face barriers to accessing gender-confirming health care, particularly genital reconstruction/confirmation surgery. This can be, in part, due to unresponsive and/or unhelpful (medical practitioner) gatekeepers as well as very long waiting lists and/or lack of funding (White Hughto et al. 2017). Although difficulties/delays in accessing gender-confirming treatments are deeply painful and pose significant challenges to many gender-diverse people, such barriers are particularly stressful for those who are older and have only a limited amount of time available for them to realize and fully express their true gender identities.

Formal social care is also problematic. There are significant concerns that social care providers (of home care, day care, and residential care) are at best underprepared to meet the needs of older trans/g-d people and at worst sites of prejudice and discrimination toward them (Ansara 2015; Fredriksen-Goldsen et al. 2014; Siverskog 2014; Jones and Willis 2016; Porter et al. 2016). Writing in Canada, for example, Marshall, Cooper, and Rudnick (2015) have described how a nursing home struggled to care for Jamie, a transwoman with dementia. The staff were unable to deal with her gender confusion (after the home stopped her hormone treatment), the other residents' transphobia, and her daughter's refusal to accept her gender identity. As a result, Jamie died "confused, frightened, and alone" (Westwood 2016: 28). Many trans/g-d people are fearful of needing care and support in later life and of being vulnerable to such inadequate and/or inappropriate care (Witten 2014b, 2016).

There is now a growing number of policy initiatives and good practice guidance in some parts of the world, including Australia, Canada, the United States, and the United Kingdom (Fredriksen-Goldsen et al. 2014; Westwood et al. 2015; Jones and Willis 2016; Porter et al. 2016). However, there would appear to be a long way to go before practice and service provision reaches appropriate standards even in these more enlightened parts of the world. Moreover, in the other parts of the world where gender-nonconforming people's rights are even less well respected and/or protected, such aspirations are even further away.

Recognition

Trans/g-d People and Recognition

Recognition is a central issue for trans/g-d people of all ages, but especially in later life (Kennedy 2012). Many campaigners are arguing for increased visibility for older trans/g-d people who share with all older people the embodied politics of social exclusion, further complicated by gender variance/diversity (Siverskog 2015; Miller et al. 2017). However, not all older trans/g-d people identify as such. For them being associated with the trans /g-d movement—even with a well-meaning emancipatory agenda—would be another form of misrecognition. By contrast, for some older trans/g-d people, positive recognition—that is, recognition that is respectful, validating, and supportive—is important in achieving trans/g-d rights, particularly in relation to health and social care provision and issues relating to death and dying. Some trans/g-d people fear that family members may not respect their true gender at their funerals and will insist on using their birth assigned gender. Some trans/g-d people seek to ensure that this is prevented through legal means, via advance planning. However, more need to be encouraged to do so (Kcomt and Gorey 2017).

Many gender-diverse people have felt misrecognized pretransitioning, that is, recognized for the gender that they were assigned at birth and not for the gender they identify as. For those who have transitioned, a central concern is being able to present themselves according to their true gender identity and being recognized and/or accepted as such. For those who have transitioned but have not had surgical and/or hormone treatment—and some trans/g-d people cannot for a variety of health reasons, especially in older age—their bodies may not be congruent with their gender identities and presentation. This can pose particular challenges in terms of receiving care, especially close personal care, in later life.

My partner and I are both male-to-female trannies [transsexuals]. Neither of us could afford the genital realignment surgery we both so desperately desire. My deepest fear is how the world will see us when we come to a point where we need assisted living care or when one of us dies. God forbid they put together that our lesbian relationship is between two women who have penises. (quoted in Witten 2016: 1157)

Dementia is another particular concern for older trans/g-d people:

I worry that I will become incapacitated and not be able to communicate my history as a trans* person (medical, surgical history) before requiring care. I worry that caregivers will not be experienced in dealing with trans* bodies and health issues and I will at best not get the care I need and at worst be ridiculed, mocked or ignored because of the state of my body. (Witten 2016: 115)
Will I be treated with dignity? Will I be respected? Will I be in a defenceless situation at the mercy of those that do not or are unwilling to understand me being trans? (Witten 2016: 116)

In each of the preceding quotes, these trans/g-d individuals are concerned about how their bodies will be recognized, about issues of misunderstanding and misrepresentation, about stigma, prejudice, and mistreatment. Some trans/g-d people may seek to mask their noncongruent bodies, but in terms of personal care this may not be possible:

How and when people express their gender identity is an extremely personal choice. . . . transgender people may not have complete control over who knows their gender identity. If they choose to live as their preferred gender, some people may have physical features they cannot change (or afford to change). So when a transgender person needs a physical exam from a physician, or needs help with bathing or dressing in an acute care or residential care setting, there is a risk of being found out, with the potential for subsequent discrimination or outright abuse. Transgender older adults may delay or avoid seeking assistance or services because they are concerned about detection and its consequences. (Witten and Carpenter 2015: 1)

There is an urgent need to address stigma in the misrecognition of trans/g-d people in general and older trans/g-d people in particular, especially in relation to health and social care. As Fredriksen-Goldsen et al. have observed from their research:

[There are] important modifiable factors (stigma, victimization, health-related behaviors, and social support) associated with health among transgender older adults. Reducing stigma and victimization and including gender identity in nondiscrimination and hate crime statutes are important steps to reduce health risks. Attention to bolstering individual and community-level social support must be considered when developing tailored interventions to address transgender older adults' distinct health and aging needs. (2013: 488)

Ageing Bodies

Trans/g-d ageing is not all doom and gloom (Witten 2014a), however. It also offers significant emancipatory potential, not only for older trans/g-d people specifically, but for all older people. Trans/g-d politics, and ageing trans/g-d politics in particular, make a unique and significant contribution to the understandings of embodied ageing. The growing number of trans/g-d individuals who consider gender transitioning in later life, having reached a place of freedom to transition, throws new light on the concept of "successful ageing" (Fabbre 2014) and on (hetero-)normative constructs of the life course (Bailey 2012):

Perspectives on ageing trans bodies destabilize previous notions of failure in relation to timing during the life-course. This could be a flaccid penis, softened muscles, menopause, etc. However, for transgender-identified people, these expected bodily changes can actually mean that one's previous failure becomes something more normalized. To have a flaccid penis or to lack menstruation can be a failure when it is "off time" earlier in the life-course, but could actually be perceived as being "on time" if it occurs in later life, even though it may be surrounded by ageist discourses. (Siverskog 2015: 16)

Although there is currently a "striking lack" (Kellaway 2015) of visual representations of older trans/g-d people, with increasing legal and social recognition of trans/g-d people this is changing. Such changes pose interesting challenges to the norms and normativities of successful ageing (Fabbre 2014). One of the key criticisms of successful ageing is that it privileges those who are able to remain fit and active and fully engaged in society, while further marginalizing those who—due to physical and/or cognitive disabilities—are unable to do so. These individuals are then seen as having "failed" to age successfully. Stigmatized (ageing) bodies play a significant part in this so-called failure and associated social exclusion (this is also explored in the subsequent section on representation). Trans/g-d people and trans politics challenge the notions of "normal" bodies and offer a vehicle to conceptualize and validate diversity and worth in nonnormative ageing bodies (Sandberg 2008). Increasing the recognition of trans/g-d people in general, and trans/g-d older people in particular—reducing stigma, increasing acceptance and validation, and indeed making them more visible—will be of significant benefit to their health and well-being. It will also be an important step in achieving social justice for trans/g-d people. Most importantly, it opens up avenues to reconsider what we mean when investigating successful ageing and how we need to take into account the diversity and changeability of ageing (gendered) bodies when we do so. Achieving improved recognition for older trans/g-d people is interimplicated in achieving increased representation of and by them as well, as the next section demonstrates.

Representation

Citizenship

Representation involves, in Fraser's model, being actively engaged in society and having a political voice at both the local and national level. Many gender-diverse people of all ages "remain on the margins of citizenship" (Hines 2007: 8.1). This is further compounded by the exclusions and marginalizations associated with ageing. With the notable exception of some specialist organizations,[10] trans/g-d ageing issues and the voices of older trans/g-d people are underrepresented in ageing services (Age UK 2017). Furthermore, the voices of trans/g-d people are often conflated with those of lesbian, gay, and bisexual people (only some of whom may also be trans/g-d) while the voices of older people are generally already underrepresented in LGBT advocacy. Thus, the voices of older trans/g-d people are marginalized because of both their age and their trans/g-d status. Additionally, diversity within and among the (older) gender-nonconforming community is also underrepresented:

Rather than thinking of a unified trans* community, it is more useful to understand different groups of trans* people as constituting a collection of sub-communities, with some shared characteristics but with many and significant differences, including a variety of different socio-political and medical aims. (Hunter, Bishop, and Westwood 2016: 125)

Because many older trans/g-d people are marginalized and socially excluded, they may be unable and/or unwilling to fully participate in society, one of the prerequisites of successful ageing. As Riggs and Kentlyn have observed,

> There are significant social and personal factors that impact upon transgender women's capacity to live a life that adheres to the norm of "successful ageing." This is not to say that many transgender women do not age extremely well, despite the negative social and personal contexts they live in. Rather, it is to say, well-founded critiques of the neo-liberalism of the concept of "successful ageing" aside . . . transgender women continue to face significant barriers to active participation in the world around them. (2014: 231)

This marginalization—linked to both trans/g-d status and to ageing—also applies not only to transwomen but also transmen and gender-nonconforming individuals. Breaking down barriers to participation is key to improving representation of older gender-diverse people and moving towards increased social justice for them.

Research

Representation also involves—and this is particularly important for people from minority groups—inclusion in research. For without a presence in knowledge production, the needs, issues, and concerns of individuals remain invisible and unheard. This in turn informs their misrecognition and/or non-recognition, which also informs the lack of tailored policies and provision (resources) to meet their needs. While there are emerging specialist research projects,[11] older trans/g-d people are, as yet, underrepresented in research:

> Little is known about transgender elders. The need to make broad assumptions about the size of this population underscores one of the major problems in understanding the needs of this group. Transgender elders are not only underserved, they are also understudied. There is a need for continued efforts in the areas of research, education, service, and advocacy. Trans-sexuals, cross-dressers, intersex, and other persons whose gender expression or identification is other than traditional represent an invisible minority within the worldwide elderly population. (Persson 2009: 642)

Without sufficient research, the needs, issues and concerns of older trans/ g-d people are underrepresented, underrecognized, and underresourced. Only increased knowledge production can remedy this.

> A lack of knowledge regarding the needs and experiences of trans and gender-nonconforming older adults contributes to and perpetuates the experiences of marginalization associated with being trans. Mitigating the conditions of marginalization—including those that are compounded by age—requires the production of trans aging knowledge. (Finkenauer et al. 2012: 311)

Addressing the marginalization of older trans/g-d people in relation to knowledge production is best tackled by increasing their presence in both mainstream and specialist research and is key to improving their representation and increasing social justice for them.

Conclusion

In this chapter we have highlighted some of the inequalities, particularly those associated with resources, recognition, and representation, in the lives of older trans/g-d people. As Fraser herself acknowledged, these three dimensions of social justice do not stand alone but intersect and mutually inform each other. For example, increased representation will lead to increased (positive) recognition and social inclusion, which will in turn lead to improved resources. In this way the social justice model has much to offer both in terms of understanding sites of inequality experienced by (older) trans/g-d people and pathways to remedy them.

Increased recognition and representation of older trans/g-d people, particularly through research and awareness raising, has the potential to reframe conceptualizations of embodied, gendered ageing. In particular, gender diversity inclusion and acceptance has the potential to create new avenues for all older people whose bodies do not comply with the stereotypical cultural expectations associated with successful ageing. Trans/g-d inclusion thus offers a pathway to increased social justice not only for older trans/g-d people but for all people, as we age in embodied ways.

Acknowledgment

We wish to thank Kathy Dear and Elen Heart for their feedback and advice on an earlier draft of this chapter.

Reprinted from Jenny-Anne Bishop and Sue Westwood, "Trans(gender)/ Gender-Diverse Ageing." In *Ageing, Diversity and Equality: Social Justice Perspectives*, edited by Sue Westwood, 82–97. London: Routledge, 2018. Used by permission of Taylor & Francis.

Notes

1. In some contexts, the term *transgender/trans* includes all these gender diversities. See, for example: www.gires.org.uk/resources/terminology/ and www.apa.org/topics/lgbt/transgender.aspx.

2. *Cisgender* describes someone who identifies with the (sole) gender they were assigned at birth.

3. *Transitioning* describes the process whereby an individual moves from the gender they were assigned at birth—with which they did not identify—to the gender with which they do identify.

4. *Transphobia* describes negative attitudes, feelings, and/or actions toward trans(gender)/gender-diverse people.

5. *Cisnormativity* refers to the assumption that a cisgender identity is the norm, and also involves the privileging of cisgender people.

6. We prefer the terms *genital reconstruction surgery* (GRS) or *gender confirmation surgery* (GCS).

7. Lesbian, gay, and bisexual.

8. https://www.theclowdergroup.com/gensilent.

9. This acronym uses another variant of the term *trans*.

10. E.g., the Transgender Aging Network (USA), http://forge-forward.org/aging/; and SAGE USA, www.sageusa.org/issues/transgender.cfm.

11. E.g., the Trans Ageing and Care (TrAC) project, http://trans-ageing.swan.ac.uk/.

References

Age UK. 2017. *Transgender Issues and Later Life*. London: Age UK. www.ageuk.org.uk/globalassets/age-uk/documents/factsheets/fs16_transgender_issues_and_later_life_fcs.pdf.

Ansara, Y. G.. 2015. "Challenging Cisgenderism in the Ageing and Aged Care Sector: Meeting the Needs of Older People of Trans and/or Non-binary Experience." *Australasian Journal on Ageing* 34(S2): 14–18. doi: 10.1111/ajag.12278.

Auldridge, A., A. Tamar-Mattis, S. Kennedy, E. Ames, and H. J. Tobi. 2012. *Improving the Lives of Transgender Older Adults: Recommendations for Policy and Practice*. New York: Services and Advocacy for Gay, Lesbian, Bisexual & Transgender Elders (SAGE). www.lgbtagingcenter.org/resources/resource.cfm?r=520.

Bailey, L. 2012. "Trans Ageing." In *Lesbian, Gay, Bisexual and Transgender Ageing: Biographical Approaches for Inclusive Care and Support*, edited by R. Ward, I. Rivers, and M. Sutherland, 51–66. London: Jessica Kingsley.

Barrett, B. J., and D. V. Sheridan. 2017. "Partner Violence in Transgender Communities: What Helping Professionals Need to Know." *Journal of GLBT Family Studies* 13(2): 137–62. doi: 10.1080/1550428X.2016.1187104

Cook-Daniels, L. 2015. "Transgender Aging: What Practitioners Should Know." In *The Lives of LGBT Older Adults: Understanding Challenges and Resilience*, edited by N. A. Orel and C. A. Fruhauf, 193–215. Washington, DC: American Psychological Association.

Cook-Daniels, L., and M. Munson. 2010. "Sexual Violence, Elder Abuse, and Sexuality of Transgender Adults, Age 50+: Results of Three Surveys." Journal of GLBT Family Studies 6(2): 142–77.

Crissman, H. P., M. B. Berger, L. F. Graham, and V. K. Dalton. 2017. "Transgender Demographics: A Household Probability Sample of US Adults, 2014." *American Journal of Public Health* 107(2): 213–15.

Equality and Human Rights Commission (EHRC). 2015. "Is Britain Fairer?': Key Facts and Findings on Transgender People." www.equalityhumanrights .com/sites/default/files/ key_facts_and_findings-_transgender_0.pdf.

Fabbre, V. D. 2014. "Gender Transitions in Later Life: A Queer Perspective on Successful Aging." *Gerontologist* 55(1): 144–53. doi: 10.1093/geront/gnu079.

Finkenauer, S., J. Sherratt, J. Marlow, and A. Brodey. 2012."When Injustice Gets Old: A Systematic Review of Trans Aging." *Journal of Gay & Lesbian Social Services* 24(4): 311–30. doi: 10.1080/10538720.2012.722497.

Fraser, N. 1997. *Justice Interruptus.* New York: Routledge.

Fredriksen-Goldsen, K. I., C. P. Hoy-Ellis, J. Goldsen, C. A. Emlet, and N. R. Hooyman. 2014. "Creating a Vision for the Futures: Key Competencies and Strategies for Culturally Competent Practice with Lesbian, Gay, Bisexual, and Transgender (LGBT) Older Adults in the Health and Human Services." *Journal of Gerontological Social Work* 57(2–4): 80–107. doi: 10.1080/01634372.2014.890690.

Fredriksen-Goldsen, K. I., L. Cook-Daniels, H.-J. Kim, E. A. Erosheva, C. A. Emlet, C. P. Hoy-Ellis, J. Goldsen, and A. Muraco. 2013. "Physical and Mental Health of Transgender Older Adults: An At-Risk and Underserved Population." *Gerontologist* 54(3): 488–500. doi: 10.1093/geront/gnt021.

Gender Identity Research and Education Society (GIRES). 2011. The Number of Gender Variant People in the UK—Update 2011. http://www.gires .org.uk/assets/Research-Assets/Prevalence2011.pdf,

Grant, J. M., L. Mottet, J. E. Tanis, J. Harrison., J. Herman, and M. Keisling. 2011. *Injustice at Every Turn: A Report of the National Transgender Discrimination Survey.* Washington, DC: National Center for Transgender Equality.

Harvey, S., M. Mitchell, and J. Keeble. 2014. "Barriers Faced by Lesbian, Gay, Bisexual and Transgender people in accessing domestic abuse, stalking, harassment and sexual violence services." https://www.bl.uk/collection -items/barriers-faced-by-lesbian-gay-bisexual-and-transgender-people -in-accessing-domestic-abuse-stalking-harassment-and-sexual-violence -services.

Hines, S. 2007. *Transforming Gender: Transgender Practices of Identity, Intimacy and Care.* Bristol: Policy.

Hines, S. 2010. "Sexing Gender; Gendering Sex: Towards an Intersectional Analysis of Transgender." In *Theorizing Intersectionality and Sexuality*, edited by Y. Taylor, S. Hines, and M. Casey, 140–62. London: Palgrave Macmillan.

Hoy-Ellis, C. P., and K. I. Fredriksen-Goldsen. 2017. "Depression among Transgender Older Adults: General and Minority Stress." *American Journal of Community Psychology* 59(3–4): 295–305. doi: 10.1002/ajcp.12138.

Human Rights Watch. 2018. *Human Rights: World Report.* Washington, DC: Human Rights Watch. www.hrw.org/world-report/2018.

Hunter, C., J.-A. Bishop, and S. Westwood. 2016. "The Complexity of Trans*/ Gender Identities." In *Lesbian, Gay, Bisexual and Trans* Individuals Living with Dementia: Concepts, Practice and Rights*, edited by S. Westwood and E. Price, 124–37. Abingdon: Routledge.

Johnston, T. R., and H. Meyer. 2017. "LGBT-Specific Housing in the USA." *Housing, Care and Support* 20(3): 121–27. doi: 10.1108/HCS-07-2017-0016.

Jones, S. M., and P. Willis. 2016. "Are You Delivering Trans Positive Care." *Quality in Ageing and Older Adults* 17(1): 50–59. doi: 10.1108/QAOA-05-2015 -0025.

Kcomt, L., and K. M. Gorey. 2017. "End-of-Life Preparations among Lesbian, Gay, Bisexual, and Transgender People: Integrative Review of Prevalent Behaviors." *Journal of Social Work in End-of-Life & Palliative Care* 13(4): 284–301. doi: 10.1080/15524256.2017.1387214.

Kellaway, M. 2015. "Photos: Transgender Elders Show Us the Meaning of Survival." *The Advocate*, February 24. www.advocate.com/politics/transgen der/2015/02/24/photos-transgender-elders-show-us-meaning-survival.

Kennedy, S. 2012. "Gaining Visibility: The Challenges Facing Transgender Elders." In *Improving the Lives of Transgender Older Adults: Recommendations for Policy and Practice*, edited by A. Auldridge, A. Tamar-Mattis, S. Kennedy, E. Ames, and H. J. Tobin, 23–28. New York: Services and Advocacy for Gay, Lesbian, Bisexual & Transgender Elders (SAGE).

Marshall, J., M. Cooper, and A. Rudnick. 2015. "Gender Dysphoria and Dementia: A Case Report." *Journal of Gay & Lesbian Mental Health* 19(1): 112–17. doi: 10.1080/19359705.2014.974475.

McFadden, C., and M. Crowley-Henry. 2016. "A Systematic Literature Review on Trans* Careers and Workplace Experiences." In *Sexual Orientation and Transgender Issues in Organizations: Global Perspectives on LGBT Workforce Diversity*, edited by T. Köllen, 63–81. New York: Springer.

McNeil, J., L. Bailey, S. Ellis, J. Morton, and M. Regan. 2012. *Trans Mental Health & Emotional Wellbeing Study 2012.* Edinburgh: Scottish Transgender Alliance. www.scottishtrans.org/wp-content/uploads/2013/03/trans_mh _study.pdf.

Miller, P. R., A. R. Flores, D. P. Haider-Markel, D. C. Lewis, B. L. Tadlock, and J. K. Taylor. 2017. "Transgender Politics as Body Politics: Effects of Disgust Sensitivity and Authoritarianism on Transgender Rights Attitudes." *Politics, Groups, and Identities* 5(1): 4–24. doi: 10.1080/21565503.2016.1260482.

Persson, D. I. 2009. "Unique Challenges of Transgender Aging: Implications from the literature." *Journal of Gerontological Social Work* 52(6): 633–46. doi: 10.1080/01634370802609056.

Porter, K. E., M. Brennan-Ing, S. C. Chang, L. M. Dickey, A. A. Singh, K. L. Bower, and T. M. Witten. 2016. "Providing Competent and Affirming Services for Transgender and Gender Nonconforming Older Adults." *Clinical Gerontologist* 39(5): 366–88. doi: 10.1080/07317115.2016.1203383.

Riggs, D. W., and S. Kentlyn. 2014. "Transgender Women, Parenting, and Experiences of Ageing." In *Queering Motherhood: Narrative and Theoretical Perspectives*, edited by M. F. Gibson, 219–30. Toronto: Demeter.

Rogers, M. 2016. "Breaking Down Barriers: Exploring the Potential for Social Care Practice with Trans Survivors of Domestic Abuse." *Health & Social Care in the Community* 24(1): 68–76. doi: 10.1111/hsc.12193.

Sandberg, L. 2008. "The Old, the Ugly and the Queer: Thinking Old Age in Relation to Queer Theory." *Graduate Journal of Social Science* 5(2): 117–39. www.gjss.org/sites/default/files/issues/chapters/papers/Journal-05-02 -06-Sandberg.pdf.h.

Seelman, K. L. 2015. "Unequal Treatment of Transgender Individuals in Domestic Violence and Rape Crisis Programs." *Journal of Social Service Research* 41(3): 307–25. doi: 10.1080/01488376.2014.987943.

Siverskog, A. 2014. "'They Just Don't Have a Clue': Transgender Aging and Implications for Social Work." *Journal of Gerontological Social Work* 57(2–4): 386–406. doi: 10.1080/01634372.2014.895472.

Siverskog, A. 2015. "Ageing Bodies That Matter: Age, Gender and Embodiment in Older Transgender People's Life Stories." *NORA-Nordic Journal of Feminist and Gender Research* 23(1): 4–19. doi: 10.1080/08038740.2014.979869.

Snelgrove, J. W., A. M. Jasudavisius, B. W. Rowe, E. M. Head, and G. R. Bauer. 2012. "'Completely Out-at-Sea' with 'Two-Gender Medicine': A Qualitative Analysis of Physician-Side Barriers to Providing Healthcare for Transgender Patients." *BMC Health Services Research* 12(1): 110. doi: 10.1186 /1472-6963-12-110.

Wathern, T., and R. W. Green. 2017. "Older LGB&T Housing in the UK: Challenges and Solutions." *Housing, Care and Support* 20(3): 128–36. doi: 10.1108/HCS-08-2017-0019.

Westwood, S. 2016. "Gender, Sexuality, Gender Identity and Dementia." In *Lesbian, Gay, Bisexual and Trans* Individuals Living with Dementia: Concepts, Practice and Rights*, edited by S. Westwood and E. Price, 41–54. Abingdon, UK: Routledge.

Westwood, S., A. King, K. Almack, S. Yiu-Tung, and L. Bailey. 2015. "Good Practice in Health and Social Care Provision for LGBT Older People in the UK." In *Lesbian, Gay, Bisexual and Trans Health Inequalities: International Perspectives in Social Work*, edited by J. Fish and K. Karban, 145–58. Bristol: Policy.

White Hughto, J. M., A. J. Rose, J. E. Pachankis, and S. L. Reisner. 2017. "Barriers to Gender Transition-Related Healthcare." *Transgender Health* 2(1): 107–18. doi: 10.1089/trgh.2017.0014.

Whittle, S., L. Turner, M. Al-Alami, E. Rundall, and B. Thom. 2007. *Engendered Penalties: Transgender and Transsexual People's Experiences of Inequality and Discrimination*. Wetherby: Communities and Local Government Publications.

Williams, M. E., and P. A. Freeman. 2007. "Transgender Health: Implications for Aging and Caregiving." *Journal of Gay & Lesbian Social Services* 18(3–4): 93–108. doi: 10.1300/ J04lv18n03.

Winter, S., E. Settle, K. Wylie, S. Reisner, M. Cabral, G. Knudson, and S. Baral. 2016. "Synergies in Health and Human Rights: A Call to Action to Improve Transgender Health." *Lancet* 388(10042): 318. doi: 10.1016/S0140-6736 (16)30653-5.

Witten, T. M. 2009. "Graceful Exits: Intersection of Aging, Transgender Identities, and the Family/Community." *Journal of GLBT Family Studies* 5(1–2): 35–61. doi: 10.1080/15504280802595378.

Witten, T. M. 2014a. "End of Life, Chronic Illness, and Trans-identities." *Journal of Social Work in End-of-Life & Palliative Care* 10(1): 34–58. doi: 10.1080 /15524256.2013.877864.

Witten, T. M. 2014b. "It's Not All Darkness: Robustness, Resilience, and Successful Transgender Aging." *LGBT Health* 1(1): 24–33. doi: 10.1089/lgbt.2013 .0017.

Witten, T. M. 2016."Trans* People Anticipating Dementia Care." In *Lesbian, Gay, Bisexual and Trans* Individuals Living with Dementia: Concepts, Practice and Rights*, edited by S. Westwood and E. Price, 110–23. Abingdon, UK: Routledge.

Witten, T. M., and B. Carpenter. 2015. "Invisibility Squared: The Challenges of Living as a Transgender Older Adult." Psychology Benefits Society (Online blog) March 9. https://psychologybenefits.org/2015/03/09/invisibility -squared-the-challenges-of-living-as-a-transgender-older-adult/.

CHAPTER NINE

Web Book: Is Killing Necessarily Murder?

Moral Questions Surrounding Assisted Suicide and Death

Anthony Glascock

Available at: http://www.culturalcontextofaging.com/webbook-glascock

Anthony Glascock uses the global ethnographic HRAF database to examine "death-hastening" behavior. This chapter has connections to·Judith Barker's chapter in Part VI.

PART II

The Life Course and Intergenerational Ties in Cultural and Global Context

It is utterly false and cruelly arbitrary to put all the play and learning into childhood, all the work into middle age, and all the regrets into old age.

—Margaret Mead

Introduction

Jay Sokolovsky

From Elderscape to Technoscape: Music to Transcend Generations

Recently a relative in his thirties asked what I remember from being at the 1969 Woodstock rock festival, the summer I graduated from college. My stock answer is, "You know what they say. . . . If you remember anything, you weren't there." In reality I do not remember much except the sheer joy of hearing in person some of my favorite music makers of the time such as Jimi Hendrix, Crosby Stills Nash and Young, Janis Joplin, and the Who. In thinking about this time and how it defined in some ways my boomer generation, I came to listen to the 1969 recording at Woodstock of the song "My Generation" by the Who. I found it ironic to think of that song's refrain "Hope I die before I grow old," even though some of these performers managed to do just that. My boomer generation is famously making every effort to counter that song lyric—and seeming to do that in the context of seeking to engage with the healthy–active–successful aging movement that Sarah Lamb analyzed in Part I. This irony is amplified in listening to how the elder singing group, the Zimmers, composed largely of persons past age 90, some over 100—perform the same song. You can hear them literally challenging, with gusto, the angel of death as part of a BBC documentary (see https://www.youtube.com/watch?v=zqfFrCUrEbY).

WEB SPECIAL:

Watch the Zimmers audition on *Britain's Got Talent*: https://www.youtube.com/watch?v=-m0EZO5O2dM.

The Zimmers, along with the North American elder singing group Young@ heart and their counterpart Japanese granny band KBG84, are all part of the broader redefinition of both age categories and how group performance may enhance physical, mental, and emotional health. We will see this again in Zhang's chapter on China where in cities like Beijing older adults have taken over large parts of urban parks for a wide range of singing, dancing, or exercising (Part III). Such public performances have not been without considerable generational tension and sometimes provoke the ire of younger generation city dwellers and even an attempt by the government to control these performances.

The Zimmers are in fact collective heroes of mine. I had the opportunity to be interviewed on a public radio broadcast along with the husband and wife who started the group. They made me understand how forming the group and taking it public was a determined challenge to the invisibility persons of their generation were facing in urban England. There has also been a growing recognition that such social exclusion and potential isolation can have serious negative health impacts (Miller 2011; Mikkelsen 2016; Cudjoe 2018). This has made an impression on former Prime Minister Theresa May, who in 2018 appointed the United Kingdom's first minister for loneliness, with various surveys showing high levels of perceived isolation among the elderly and their carers (Cotterell, Buffel, and Phillipson 2018). We will see in Parts II and III that this can be a problem even in so-called traditional societies such as Ghana in West Africa and rural Mexico.

Generations Unbound and Reconnected: "OK Boomer"

In *Boomsday*, Christopher Buckley's 2007 comedic best-seller novel set in the "not too distant future," angry mobs of youths storm gated senior communities and deface golf courses. They are egged on by Ms. Cassandra Devine, a 29-year-old blogger and central character in the book. She is perplexed and agitated about why someone her age should spend their entire life paying unfair taxes, just so the boomers can hit the golf course at age 62 and drink gin and tonics until their nineties. Certain that this grave social injustice is due to the coming mass retirement of 77 million baby boomers set to reach age 65 in 2011, she offers a neat solution to the national costs of aging. Ms. Devine proposes a national "transitioning ceremony," where volunteers at age 70 receive a wonderful vacation paid by the federal government and then are required to commit suicide; in return, their heirs pay no inheritance tax.[1]

Buckley's book captures in exaggerated and dramatic terms one of the generational narratives that emerged in the last decade of the 20th century— the tyranny of the greedy geezer, or what market analysts call WHOOPIES, "well-off older people" (see Pew Research Center 2018). At the beginning of the 21st century, associations such as Americans for Generational Equity

---

WEB SPECIAL:

The BBC's new Generation Project, https://www.bbc.com/worklife /generation-project.

(www.nndb.com/org/319/000168812/) or the Concord Coalition (www.con cordcoalition.org) have echoed these sentiments and premises underlying *Boomsday*. It is also connected to the meme "O.K. Boomer," which began in 2015 and flourished on social media as a generational rebuttal to complaints by baby boomers about the bad behavior of "kids these days" (Romano 2019). In 2020, an age discrimination case at the Supreme Court is considering whether use of "O.K. Boomer" as a dismissive retort directed at an older employee by her boss is part of why she was denied a promotion based on her age.

However, another narrative slant emerging in the United States is captured by the words on the jacket of another book, *The Boomer Century: 1942–2046*:

> They didn't just date, they reinvented Western sexuality. They didn't just go to the doctor; they reinvented Health Care and are now reinventing retirement and aging. They are pioneers in a new stage spanning the decades between middle and late life. Neither young nor old, they represent an extraordinary pool of social and human capital. And in large numbers, they want to do work that serves a greater good. (Croker 2007)[2]

A decade later these two seemingly irreconcilable perspectives frame the outer edges of the dynamics of a changing life course and the multiplying cultural spaces in which generations interact and new models of late life are being enacted (Vanderbeck and Worth 2015). This will be seen especially in organizations such as Generations United, which seeks to replace the generational tribalism of *Boomsday* with models of meaningful intergenerational contact zones (see Part II Web Book Butts).

Derailing the Narrative of Decline—Rebranding Aging

With the development of ideas such as "Conscious Aging" and "Gerotranscendence" (see Part I), the rapidly changing global landscape of late life is being altered through popular culture, language, discourse, and imagery. As noted by Featherstone and Hepworth (Part II Web Book), some gerontological writers see the postmodern life course as characterized by a blurring of traditional age divisions and the integration of formerly segregated periods of life (Vesperi 2008). New images of aging are being created where "elderhood has been constructed as a marketable lifestyle that connects the commodified values of youth with bodycare techniques for masking the appearance of age" (Katz 1995: 70).

This began in earnest during the 1990s with attempts to recast the life span in fantasy images of timelessness drawn from fountain-of-youth movies such as *Cocoon* (Howard 1985) and *Cocoon: The Return* (Petrie 1988) and self-help books such as Dr. Deepak Chopra's *Ageless Body, Timeless Mind* (1993). In this new millennium with a seeming obsession of bodily make overs, there are also books like *Don't Retire, Rewire* (Sedlar and Miners 2002). There are even Web sites to help preserve yourself after death (see https://cdt.org/insight/digital-legacy/ and http://www.thedigitalbeyond.com/online-services-list/).

A more serious re-visioning of aging has arisen, creating new vocabularies, turning aging into "saging" and "eldering," proffering a positive, active embrace of nonmaterial gains from human maturity, especially in the creative and spiritual realms (Lifshitz, Nimrod, and Bachner 2018; Nelson-Becker 2018). This seems more than just another kind of "rebranding" that readers might have noticed when their local "retirement community" became an "active living adult community." There has opened up an astonishing range of largely new cultural spaces involving social activism, electronic blogs and social networking, third age niche magazines, senior-oriented cable TV networks, and performance groups.[3]

All this is set in new constructions of the latter part of the life course that are being shaped by Catherin Bateson's notion of Adulthood 2.0 (2010) or the related idea of an "Encore Adulthood" by Phyllis Moen (2016). Both authors see the unravelling of our linear life passage of education, work, and retirement into a host of reengaging possibilities. Conventional aging cultural scripts are indeed unraveling around the edges especially with millennials

---

WEB SPECIALS:

1. A podcast interviewing Marc Freedman: https://shows.acast.com/workandlifepodcast/episodes/ep-106-marc-freedman-the-power-and-beauty-of-intergeneration.
2. Listen to the keynote presentation by Mary Catherine Bateson, author of *Composing a Further Life: The Age of Active Wisdom*, TEDxCapeMay, 2015: https://www.youtube.com/watch?v=AVXEGM4Z5Qc.

born 1981–1996—sometimes referred to as an emerging and sometimes elusive adulthood, a time between adolescence and standard adult responsibilities, job, and partnering (Durham and Solway 2017). At another level, social entrepreneur Marc Freedman, president and CEO of encore.org, in a 2018 book suggests *How to Live Forever*, not by Silicon's Valley's quest for immortality, but by creating a legacy in forging enduring bonds between generations.[4] Of course many traditional societies have long realized this.

The articles in this section address both the universal and culturally particularistic features of how societies think about and operationalize ideas about generation and the very construction of values and expected actions associated with different phases of the life course.

It's Not Even Your Parents' Life Course Anymore

As we grow older, many of us are recalling memories of our parents and grandparents at our current ages, but we are seldom experiencing our elder relatives' life courses. We can often expect to live longer, reach the boundaries of late adulthood in better health, and have taken different passages through youth and adulthood. As Kao and Albert tell us in Part II's first chapter, the cultural reshaping of late life is part of a potent rethinking of aged-based social passages and the broad cross-cultural contexts of being aged, "ancient," and sometimes attaining ancestorhood. They examine the place of elderhood in the broader life course as emerging global patterns transform notions of childhood, maturity, and generation. This includes a discussion of the cultural shaping of links to ancestors, which can also be seen in Sokolovsky's participation in the Day of the Dead (Part III) in a globalizing Mexican village. In another context, by linking to the Web Special below, readers can see how citizens in urban China are beginning to use digital spaces to connect with their ancestors.

Kao and Albert's chapter will help readers understand not only the kinds of dramatic changes taking place in North American society but also the variations emerging globally (Danley and Lynch 2013; Durham and Solway 2017; Silin 2018). In essence, they lead readers in a quest to rediscovering the

---

WEB SPECIAL:

Xinyuan Wang, "Scan the QR Code to Connect with the Deities," ASSA Global Aging Project, https://blogs.ucl.ac.uk/assa/2018/11/12/scan-the-qr-code-to-connect-with-the-deities/.

WEB SPECIALS:

1. Chief Oscar Mokeme talks about how the creation of Ikenga wood sculptures marks the life course of Igbo males in the West African nation of Nigeria: https://www.youtube.com/watch?v=W YAwTt396aE.
2. The Newar People of Nepal honor elders who reach age 77 with the Bura Janko ritual where elders can be worshipped as "living gods." Read about the basics of the Newar life course rituals at https://www.hinduismtoday.com/modules/smartsection/item .php?itemid=5100.

---

life course in how it is perceived from different disciplines and coming to be reconfigured within new cultural spaces and scripts.

Old School Meets the Digital Life Course

The 2013 movie *Her* is set in the unspecified near future of Los Angeles and focuses on a lonely, soon to be divorced, 30ish male, Theodore Twombly (played by Joaquin Phoenix). He becomes enamored with the new artificial intelligence operating system he installs on his computer. In the initial software setup, Theodore designates the new brain of his computer as "female" and this new OS names herself Samantha. She proceeds to quickly learn all about his likes, desires, and preferences by asking questions and mapping a digital template of him from the hard drive and social media links. Theodore's relationship with Samantha proceeds to serious dates mediated by his smartphone and even an attempted sexual encounter with a digitally hired human female surrogate. To make this more real (or perhaps surreal) and relate to the idea of a digital life course, read the Web Special below, which details contemporary attempts to socially and emotionally connect with robotic and even virtual partners, in the case of a 35-year-old Japanese man

---

WEB SPECIAL:

Love, Android Style: Alex Williams, "Do You Take This Robot . . ." *New York Times*, January 19, 2019, https://www.nytimes.com/2019 /01/19/style/sex-robots.html.

---

who married a holographic female singer that only exists in holographic and doll personas.

The film *Her* poignantly maps out some of the dramatic changes in store for the millennial generation as they might encounter, as digital natives, the second half of the 21st century. At the later end of the life course, David Prendergast in his chapter takes readers into the cultural spaces engendered by new technologies that heavily impact late adulthood (Biniok and Menke 2015; Kania-Lundholm and Torres 2018). He has worked as an applied anthropologist for the Intel corporation and had a vital role in their Global Aging Project, which examined how technology could be used by older citizens to maintain autonomy and help them stay in their homes if they so desired. His comprehensive chapter takes some key principles from the Intel project and updates their implications based on the amazing array of technology and digital mechanisms connecting elders to family, community, and the world.

The focus here is to look at the role of technology in shaping the interaction of older citizens, especially for remaining in their communities and residences (Cahill 2018). This is a massive, relatively new area of research. It examines how use of a wide range of technology from simple e-mail to a multitude of visual communication apps, and even interaction with robotic devices and social entities, is impacting all generations. His work can be connected to chapters by Kavedžija on Japan (Part III) and Wright (Part VI) who compares social robot use in Japan and Denmark.

WEB SPECIAL:

Intel Global Aging Booklet, http://ideasbazaar.typepad.com/GAEBrochureFinal.pdf.

PROJECTS TO FOLLOW:

For the last few years Aging2.0 (www.aging2.com) has been connecting, educating, and convening innovators from around the world who are working to improve the lives of older adults. Some of these are detailed in the 2017 report, *A Snapshot of Global Innovation in Aging and Senior Care*: https://www.dropbox.com/s/i6b5o0r2wkl56wf/A2_RWJ_report_FINAL_may.pdf?dl=0.

Language and the Persistence of Ageism

A universal feature of human cultural systems is having language categories that describe certain boundaries of the life course. This will vary considerably, but most languages have, at a minimum, words designating infant, child, adult, and elder. Importantly, existing words marking life cycle periods can show radical changes in meaning over time. For example, the word *hag* derives from the Greek root *hagia* or "holy one" and prior to the 13th century referred to a woman with positive supernatural capabilities. During the Middle Ages, the Catholic Church felt competition from literally hundreds of new religious movements. Independent older women, especially those working as midwives, came to be seen as a threat. In this context, the term *hag* became synonymous with evil, ugliness, and witchcraft (Rhoads and Holmes 1995).

In Western society, how key points along the life span are evaluated, perceived, and represented within a society and the study of negative stereotypes of ageism have received a good deal of attention (Chasteen and Cary 2015; Ayalon and Tesch-Römer 2018). The word *ageism* was coined by noted gerontologist Robert Butler, founding director of the National Institute on Aging, in 1969, a fateful year for my baby boomer generation (Achenbaum 2015). Like with the uptick since 2017 of public expression of racism, the reemergence of concern about ageism has been discussed in new books such as *This Chair Rocks* (Applewhite 2016) and *Ending Ageism* (Gullette 2017), an article seeking to explain "Why Ageism Never Gets Old (Friend 2017), and even an essay suggesting how to "Talk about Growing Older"—see Web Special below.

One study (see Box II.1 below) found that in the United States, the further along the life course one is, the more negative the associated words are and less congruence is found between older and younger samples. Both young and old adults use mostly positive adjectives to describe youth, while their words for describing mature adults are more disapproving. Additionally, a salient difference between younger and older respondents was that the under-55 crowd used fewer positive words to describe aging itself. At the same time, since 2014 a coalition of organizations has come together to change the way

---

WEB SPECIAL:

M. M. Gullette, "Against 'Aging'—How to Talk about Growing Older," *Theory, Culture and Society*, December 21, 2017. https://www.theoryculturesociety.org/margaret-morganroth-gullette-aging-talk-growing-older/.

Americans think about aging through the Reframing Aging Initiative (http://www.frameworksinstitute.org/reframing-aging.html). You might ask, why is this important? One answer is indicated through data collected in the Baltimore longitudinal study. Tracking people over long periods of time, researchers found that those with the strongest ageist views as early adults have a heightened cardiovascular response to stress and a greater chance of early Alzheimer's Disease, thus becoming their own worst fears (Levy et al. 2016).

Box II.1 Do You Know the Dirty Words for Old Age?

PHILADELPHIA—Adriane Berg recently wrote a financial planning book she wanted to call *How to Have a Great Old Age*. The publisher wouldn't hear of it, the 53-year-old New Jersey author said this week. The title would contain no hint of "old." The book came out as *How Not to Go Broke at 102*.

What makes the concept of "old" or "old age" so radioactive? In a National Council on Aging study three years ago, half the people between 65 and 74 thought of themselves as middle-aged, as did a third of people over 75.

What's wrong with "old age"? Janice Wassel, gerontologist at the University of North Carolina at Greensboro, has no ready answer. But her linguistic research suggests that society's frequent avoidance of the word "old" leads to something worse: a contorted language that can anger the very people it is intended to soothe. Wassel, 54, looked up in a thesaurus all the words that apply to different age groups. Then she surveyed people, both young and old, about the images and emotions those words evoke.

Infants nearly got a free ride. Fifteen of 16 words describing them were deemed positive. Everyone liked "cherubs," "babies," and "bambinos." Only "preemie" fared poorly. Toddlers evoked more neutral images, though the six positive words, including "peewee" and "tyke," outdistanced the one negative, "brat." Even teenagers overcame "punk" and "teenaged juvenile" to score more positive words than negative.

But something changes in middle age. Only one of 10 phrases, "prime of life," was considered positive, versus seven negative phrases, including "middle life." "I don't know what happens to us at middle age," Wassel said, speaking at a joint meeting of the National Council on Aging and American Society on Aging in Philadelphia. "But it's a sad statement of how we perceive people as they grow older." Words that applied to the oldest group took a different twist. With all other age groups, survey respondents generally agreed whether a term was positive, negative, or neutral. When assessing the older group, though, opinions about words often split along generational lines.

People age 54 or younger apparently saw "old" as a pejorative, Wassel said. Fourteen of 16 phrases containing the word "old" were deemed negative. Only "old gentleman" and "old person" evoked a neutral image. But respondents 55 and older liked many of the images, such as "old chap," "old dog," "old granny," and "older generation." The only negatives containing the word "old" were "dirty old man," "old maid," "old woman," and "the old."

OLD DOGS AND SPRING CHICKENS

Younger people, perhaps straining not to call older people "old," sometimes use surrogate words that older people can find offensive. Professor Janice Wassel of the University of North Carolina at Greensboro measured how two different age groups reacted to images of aging represented by different words. Here are some examples:

NEGATIVE	55 OR OLDER	54 OR YOUNGER	
Battleaxe		Battleaxe	Old man
Dirty Old Man		Codger	Old Maid
Elderly		Dirty Old Man	Old Timer
Geriatric		Geezer	Old Wife
Old Maid		Geriatric	Older Generation
Retiree		No spring chicken	Oldest
Senior citizen		Old Dog	Oldster
The Old		Old Duffer	Over the Hill Gang
		Old Granny	The Old

POSITIVE			
Eldest	Old Granny	Elderly	Golden-ager
Gramps	Old Timer	Eldest	Grandfather
Grandfather	Old Wife		Matron
Granny	Older Generation		Old chap
No spring chicken	Over the Hill Gang		Retiree
Old chap	Veteran		Senior
Old Dog			Veteran

NEUTRAL			
Codger	Old man		
Geezer	Oldest		Gramps
Golden-ager	Oldster		Granny
Matron	Senior		Senior citizen
Old Duffer			

Times art – TERESANNE COSSETTA

What older people really didn't like were the words society has created while trying not to call them old. Retiree? Nope. Elderly? Nope. Senior citizen? Not a chance. Meanwhile, younger people saw these surrogate words as either positive or neutral. Older and younger respondents could agree on only a third of the words describing older people. Younger people thought "no spring chicken" and "over-the-hill gang" were insults. Older people liked those phrases. "Young people and older people aren't speaking the same language. That's a problem," Wassel said. "This is important because of social changes that are coming. We will have people in their 70s in the work force, working with people in their 20s and 30s. "We have to come up with a language that works and is respectful to all of us."

AARP figured it out five years ago when it dropped "retired" from its name and became just AARP. What used to be senior citizen centers in Nebraska are now active adult centers. The Barnstable Senior Center in Massachusetts is about to become the Barnstable Center: A Center for Lifelong Learning. Language depends on the context, said Phyllis Rule, 76, who works for the National Council on Aging in Michigan. "When we go to breakfast, you see us sitting there with gray hair, we can call each other old and crack jokes. That doesn't mean I would appreciate someone many years younger than me saying I'm old. I prefer to be called mature or a work in progress."

Worse than words themselves, conference goers said, are the ways some younger people treat older people in misguided, condescending attempts to be sympathetic. A waitress calls someone "sweetie" or "honey" but doesn't use those terms to customers in their thirties or forties. Or they refer to an older person as "young man" or "young lady." Or they dole out exuberant praise in response to a mundane task, like parents do when a picky-eating child cleans his or her plate.

To the extent that society sometimes needs labels, Wassel suggested "older adult" to describe someone in the later stages of life. As a role model, she recalled a telephone conversation a few years ago with her mother, who had just turned 77. Hearing her mother refer to herself as old, Wassel said she hemmed and hawed, trying to politely deflect the issue. Finally, her mother interrupted. "She said, 'Janice, it's okay that I'm old. I never thought I would be this old. I never thought that I would be this healthy. I never thought I would have this much fun. It's okay that I'm old. I wish it for you.'"

Adapted from Stephen Nohlgren, "Do You Know the Dirty Words for Old Age?" *St. Petersburg Times*, March 12, 2005. Reprinted with the permission of the *St. Petersburg Times*.

Families and Genealogical Generations

A basic structural difference between kin-based, small-scale societies such as the Tiwi or the Ju/'hoansi and the United States is that elderly in the first type of society have continuous access over the life span to essential resources derived from membership in kinship groupings. In such cultural settings, the wide embrace of family frequently provides what Simic (1978) calls a "life term arena"—a stable setting for the engagement of an entire life. Even in the age-set societies discussed by Kao and Albert (Part II), the intense ties among age-mates or the ritual bonds across "social" generations do not destroy the links between "genealogical" generations—forged from the developmental cycle of family formation.

In capitalist, postindustrial societies, it is more typical that access to resources and status over the life span requires productive participation outside of one's kin group and the transition through numerous "short-term arenas." Careful historical research has shown that this pattern is not new in North America or Western Europe (Ruggles 2002). Various studies have decried any easy assumption that the elderly are socially divorced from their younger kin but emphasize instead that family networks in the United States have not been destroyed but rather transformed along the following lines: (1) family support systems are becoming more "vertical," with more relationships that cross generational lines and fewer links to siblings and cousins; (2) a shift toward "top-heavy" family caregiving roles, with middle-generation women now likely to spend more time dealing with dependent parents over age 65 than with children under 18; (3) the development of "reconstructed" or stepfamilies emerging out of increased divorce and single-parent families; (4) changing patterns in the timing of childbearing; and (5) extended potential ties across multiple generations as those in the oldest generation live longer (Lowenstein 2005). With the inclusion of the grandparental generation increasingly taking on serious and sometimes total care responsibility for grandchildren, these changes have major implications for policy in the United States (see the Web Special below).

WEB SPECIAL:

J. L. Angel and R. A. Settersten Jr., "What Changing American Families Mean for Aging Policies," *Public Policy & Aging Report* 25, no. 3 (2015): 78–82, https://doi.org/10.1093/ppar/prv011.

Age Inscriptions and Agency in Late Life

One of the issues to be encountered in the next section is the impact of globalization on the frameworks that were once thought to bind generations together and the anticipated place of elders in their families and community. Here Cati Coe uses the construct of "age inscriptions" to explore in the West African nation of Ghana the dynamics of both domestic care of elders and the national dialogue on aging. This nation has experienced lower birth rates, significant urban and international migration, and longer life spans. The state is seen as using a stereotype of the horrors of Western treatment of the elderly to forestall any significant mechanisms of care beyond the family. Yet this chapter highlights the agency of older adults in imagining their futures, criticizing the status quo, and pragmatically adjusting their strategies (see Hoffman and Pype 2016; Alber and Coe 2018; Sadruddin 2019 for a broad discussion of Africa and eldercare).

Is Necessity the Grandmother of Invention?

In *The New American Grandparent*, Cherlin and Furstenberg noted that in the 1950s, psychologists were talking about the appropriate distancing of grandparents from younger generations and some even elaborated on a negative "grandparent syndrome," implying potential harm from meddlesome behavior to grandkids and adult children (1992: 3). This perspective has certainly changed in a more positive direction, prompted by powerful changes in American family structures over the last three decades (Bengtson 2001; see Harper 2005 for a discussion of Europe and Ando 2005 for Japanese grandparents).

Grandparents increasingly occupy an "expanding position" in North American and European families and society at large as many people are now grandparents for approximately a third of their life span, or about 25 years. This importance of grandparenthood within families is due not only to demographic changes but also to the development of welfare states, resulting in greater resources for the elderly (in time and money), which in turn increased capacities of financial intergenerational transfers (Harper 2005).

Within many non-Western cultures the fostering of children by the grandparental generation is a well-established cultural mechanism and even a normative right that many older adults invoke. In fact, in some societies, such as among certain South Pacific Islanders, upwards of 40 percent of children get fostered by older adults who are not their biological parents (Dickerson-Putnam 2007). For certain American ethnic groups a parenting role for grandparents has always been a normative, anticipated option (Part IV Web Book Peterson). One such example is seen in Joan Weibel-Orlando's Web Chapter, which focuses on Native American grandparents in urban California and at a reservation in South Dakota.

Compared to Euro-American background families, less-restricted boundaries between genealogical generations often provided the possibility for grandparents to have crucial roles as "cultural conservators" and even to request that they bring up as their own one or more of their offspring's children (Mooradian, Cross, and Stutzky 2007). However, in her sensitive portrayal of contemporary Native American life, Weibel-Orlando shows that there are a diverse variety of grandparenting models among the peoples she studied (Schweitzer 1999; Kepple and Brewer 2017). These different ways of being an Indian grandparent reflect not only ancient, indigenous patterns but also the needs generated by poverty-imposed stresses placed on the parenting generation.[5] The lessons from her study can profitably be connected to discussion in Part IV on the growing custodial nature of grandparenthood when Marta Rodríguez-Galán looks at the Puerto Rican American community.

Widowhood and Cultural Context

As will be noticed in many of the case studies presented within this book's chapters, loss of a spouse in late life, especially for women, provides important guideposts to how cultural systems provide options for surviving into old age. While not exclusively a late-life or female experience, widowhood does disproportionately relate to the lives of older women (Martin-Matthews 2015). Globally, there is usually at least a three-to-one differential in the number of females versus males past age 65 who are widowed. As well, the consequences of becoming widowed can have dramatically varied economic and social impacts depending on culture and the broad context of community life (Irudaya Rajan and Sunitha 2018). In Part II, Maria Cattell (Web Book) combines a global examination of widowhood with her long-term research in rural Kenya to draw readers into the experience of older widows in Africa, Guatemala, India, and the United States. From this perspective she explores how the different vulnerabilities among widows intersect with the new cultural spaces in which widowhood is being experienced. Cattell shows how postmenopausal Samia women often see widowhood as a way of consolidating social and economic power and independence, which they have accrued slowly over a lifetime. This chapter shows that older women not only are crucial to the functioning of households and larger kin groupings but also can act as initiators of changes that have broad importance to the community. In this regard, as we will see in Part III, while large proportions of older adults in industrializing nations live with or quite near to family, globalization and urbanization are rapidly altering the framework of kin support (see for example Eeuwijk 2006).

Retirement, Eldersourcing, and Workplaces as Sites of Care across Generations

With the rapid aging of postindustrial nations in Europe and North American there has developed new patterns of retirement and a significant rise of persons working past typical retirement ages in people's mid-60s or early 70s. There has also emerged in nations like Japan a new kind of transnational retirement in places like Malaysia, which connects to similar patterns of retirees from Britain in Spain or Americans in Mexico and Costa Rica (see especially Shakuto 2018 for Japan). This interest has sparked special columns in both Britain's *Guardian* newspaper, called "The New Retirement" (www.theguardian.com/membership/ng-interactive/2017/jan/16/the-new-retirement-catch-up-with-this-series) and the *New York Times*, called "Retiring" (https://www.nytimes.com/column/retiring).

Yet, as Joseph Coughlin notes in an essay dealing with what he calls the Retirement Economy, longer life is not simply a story of retirement or more older workers (2018). It is about more generations at work and that some employers today are dealing with five-generation workplaces: Generation Z workers born after 2000, millennials, Gen Xers, and the young and older boomer set (Malburg 2018). According to the U.S. Bureau of Labor Statistics, labor force participation rate for those past age 65 went from 12.12 percent in 1996 to 19.3 percent in 2016 and is expected to exceed 20 percent in 2026 (Johnson and Smith 2016). By that future date just over 10 percent of persons age 75 and older are expected to still be employed (U.S. Bureau of Labor Statistics 2018). For the past several decades there has been a lively debate over the effects of retirement versus some kind of employment on issues like depression and cognitive decline (see especially Celidoni, Bianco, and Weber 2017). In the United States this is often interconnected with the discussion of a postmodern life course, where especially in adulthood, chronological age loses much of its prior relevance. Here the sequence of education–employment–leisure becomes intertwined as workers adjust to new demands of changing labor markets. In some national contexts such as Singapore, the state has come to depend on its elderly work force (see Web Special above). In Peru, as noted in Part II's Web Photo Essay by Gabriela Bonilla and Erika Ratto, work experiences in old age are framed as a product of accumulated social inequalities throughout the life course.

Eldersourcing and Care in a Work Environment

A different spin on work and the life course in Part II is provided by anthropologist Caitrin Lynch, author of *Retirement on the Line* (2012). She draws from her study of an unusual medical needle factory in Massachusetts to explore what she terms "eldersourcing." Here a family-owned business, along with employing younger adults, sought to purposefully hire formerly retired individuals such as Rosa who worked there until she was 100 years of age. A crucial point Lynch makes is that workplaces can also be a place for care. She calls for a reframing of the meaning work has for older adults, especially in the context of the model of postretirement flex work. Soon after her 2012 book was published, enormous interest developed for this study in the United States, Europe, and Japan. One example is the PBS report noted in the Web Special below.

Intergenerational Contact Zone and the Quest for Intergenerational Engagement

I live in St. Petersburg, Florida, which was once demographically the "oldest" city in North America and nicknamed "God's waiting room." I have been here long enough (25 years) to observe the rapid youthing of the city. This is apparent, not only in the young families who have moved into my downtown neighborhood, but also in the proliferation of sleek coffee houses and numerous local beer breweries that have opened within the past decade. It has also been intriguing to observe the intermingling of generations as incoming millennial citizens of the town have flocked to one the nation's oldest and largest shuffleboard clubs.

In the center of all this are more directive, global efforts often situated in university centers, nonprofit organizations, and governmental agencies promoting intergenerational cooperation and interdependence as a mechanism of finding solutions for common problems faced by society. There is an assumption that one aspect of promoting collective generational spaces is a mechanism to combat ageism. One of the most interesting early efforts in this direction is documented by Leng Leng Thang in her ethnographic study of Kotoen, a facility in Tokyo that combines housing and services for older people with a nursery for children under five years old (2001). A key goal at Kotoen is to produce a feeling of *fureai*, which means not only a coming together but also seeking to promote spontaneous interaction involving feelings and emotions. Thang's work became a framework for many other studies in Asia, Europe, and the United States thinking about cultural spaces involving what has come to be called intergenerational contact zones or sites of interaction (Kaplan et al. 2015). This has given rise to more serious constructs of intergenerational care, with the first intergenerational care facility in the United Kingdom opening in 2017. A related but broader effort is the European Union TOY Project—Together Old and Young—which promotes development of spaces and context for young children and older adults to learn together (Cortellesi and Kernan 2016).

Such efforts have also spread to Italy, France, and the United States and have come to be called *intergenerational education*. For example, the Little Havana section of Miami, Florida, is the site of the Rainbow International Learning Center & Child Care Program. Here elders from local senior centers provide needed day care for low-income families and improve the emotional and mental health of elders in the process of child care (http://www.lhanc.org/child-care.html). As well, in Seattle, Washington, a new documentary *The Growing Season* depicts a preschool housed within a home for the elderly, showing especially the emotional benefits for both young children and very elderly adults (see trailer at: https://www.youtube.com/watch?v=6K3H2VqQKcc).

WEB SPECIAL:

M. Senthilingam, "Intergenerational Care: Where Kids Help the Elderly Live Longer," CNN Health, October 15, 2018, https://edition.cnn .com/2018/02/16/health/longevity-intergenerational-care-elderly -children-intl/index.html.

PROJECT TO FOLLOW:

The TOY Project, http://www.toyproject.net/blog/, with examples from Pakistan, Japan, Nicaragua, and around the globe.

Generations United

In the United States various organizations, especially Generations United, have flourished with a mission to "improve the lives of children, youth, and older people through intergenerational collaboration, public policies, and programs for the enduring benefit of all" (www.gu.org). The director of the organization, Donna Butts, contributes in Part II a focused chapter (Web Book) written for the United Nations. It provides a global perspective on the development of, importance of, and policy recommendations for intergenerational sites of connection and engagement. Her chapter provides the framework for understanding a 2018 report detailing a multitude of such efforts including an innovative intergenerational LGBT Center in Los Angeles providing support for youth and seniors (Generations United 2018). We will learn from Stafford's chapter in Part V, on the elder-friendly community movement, about more expansive efforts to embed the lives of older citizens into the fabric of city life (see also Generations United 2019).

Notes

1. At the end of the 1980s, ex-Governor Richard Lamm of Colorado raised the sensitive issue of the costs associated with the medical care of the terminally ill elderly and even suggested that terminally ill people may have the "duty to die."
2. To see the reaction to this book by a member of the younger generation see Harrison 2007.

3. Blogs for electronic elders include "2young2retire," http://2young2retire .com; new third-age niche magazines include *Grand—The Magazine of Grandparents*; and senior-oriented cable TV can be found at *Retirement TV* (http://rl.tv/).

4. A contribution to the qualitative discussion of legacy and intergenerational ties is found in Savishinsky 2006.

5. It should be noted that a transition is currently going on between the elder generation of respondents studied by Weibel-Orlando who refer to themselves as Indians and their children and grandchildren who are more apt to use the term *Native Americans*.

Bibliography

Achenbaum, A. 2015. "A History of Ageism since 1969." *Generations* 39(3): 10–16(7).

Alber, E., and C. Coe, eds. 2018. "Age-Inscriptions and Social Change." Special Issue of *Anthropology and Aging* 39: 1.

Ando, K. 2005. "Grandparenthood: Crossroads between Gender and Aging." *International Journal of Japanese Sociology* 14(1)1: 32–51.

Applewhite, A. 2016. *This Chair Rocks: A Manifesto Against Ageism*. New York: Macmillan.

Ayalon, L., and C. Tesch-Römer, eds. 2018. *Contemporary Perspectives on Ageism*. Cham, Switzerland: Springer Open.

Bateson, M. C. 2010. *Composing a Further Life: The Age of Active Wisdom*. New York: Vintage.

Bengtson, V. 2001. "Beyond the Nuclear Family: The Increasing Importance of Multigenerational Relationships in American Society." *Journal of Marriage and the Family* 63(1):1–16.

Biniok, P., and I. Menke. 2015. "Societal Participation of the Elderly Information and Communication Technologies as a 'Social Junction,'" *American Anthropology Quarterly* 36(2): 164–81.

Buckley, C. 2007. *Boomsday*. New York: Twelve.

Cahill, J. 2018. "The Design of New Technology Supporting Wellbeing, Independence and Social Participation, for Older Adults Domiciled in Residential Homes and/or Assisted Living Communities." *Technologies* 6(1): 18. doi: 10.3390/technologies6010018.

Celidoni, M., C. Bianco, and G. Weber, 2017. "Retirement and Cognitive Decline. A Longitudinal Analysis Using SHARE Data." *Journal of Health Economics* 56: 113–25.

Chasteen, A., and L. Cary. 2015. "Age Stereotypes and Age Stigma: Connections to Research on Subjective Aging." *Annual Review of Gerontology and Geriatrics* 35(1): 99–119.

Cherlin, A., and F. Furstenberg. 1992. *The New American Grandparent: A Place in the Family a Life Apart*. Cambridge, MA: Harvard University Press.

Chopra, D. 1993. *Ageless Body, Timeless Mind: The Quantum Alternative to Growing Old*. New York: Three Rivers.

Cortellesi, G., and M. Kernan. 2016. "Together Old and Young: How Informal Contact between Young Children and Older People Can Lead to Inter-generational Solidarity." *Studia paedagogica* 21(2): 2016. http://www.phil.muni.cz/journals/index.php/studia-paedagogica/article/view/1379/1657.

Cotterell, N., T. Buffel, and C. Phillipson. 2018. "Preventing Social Isolation in Older People." *Maturitas* 113: 80–84.

Coughlin, J. 2018. "Commentary: Rethinking Investment, Work Life and Retirement." Pensions & Investments, http://www.pionline.com/article/20180319/PRINT/180319898/commentary-rethinking-investment-work-life-and-retirement.

Croker, R. 2007. *The Boomer Century: 1942–2046.* New York: Springboard.

Cudjoe, T. K. M., D. L. Roth, S. L. Szanton, J. L. Wolff, C. M. Boyd, and R. J. Thorpe. 2018. "The Epidemiology of Social Isolation: National Health & Aging Trends Study." *Journal of Gerontol B Psycholology* 75(1): 107–13. doi: 10.1093/geronb/gby037

Danley, J., and C. Lynch. 2013. *Transitions and Transformations: Cultural Perspectives on Aging and the Life Course.* New York: Berghahn.

Dickerson-Putnam, J. 2007. "Cultural Contexts for Grandparent Adoption on Raivavae." *Pacific Studies* 30(3&4): 118–34.Durham, D., and J. Solway. 2017. *Elusive Adulthoods: The Anthropology of New Maturities.* Bloomington: Indiana University Press.

Eeuwijk, P. van. 2006. "Old Age Vulnerability, Ill-Health and Care Support in Urban Areas of Indonesia." *Ageing and Society* 26: 61–80.

Freedman, M. 2018. *How to Live Forever.* New York: Public Affairs.

Friend, F. 2017. "Getting On: Why Ageism Never Gets Old." *New Yorker*, November 20, 46–51. https://www.newyorker.com/magazine/2017/11/20/why-ageism-never-gets-old.

Generations United. 2018. "All In Together: Creating Places Where Young and Old Thrive." https://dl2.pushbulletusercontent.com/Moj5hxfxqtBGfGfXb2O0qeQvIeie9vmi/18-Report-AllInTogether.pdf.

Generations United. 2019. "The Best of Both Worlds: A Closer Look at Creating Spaces that Connect Young and Old." https://www.gu.org/app/uploads/2019/06/Intergenerational-Report-BestofBothWorlds.pdf.

Gullette, M. 2017. *Ending Ageism, or How Not to Shoot Old People.* New Brunswick, NJ: Rutgers University Press.

Harper, S. 2005. "Grandparenthood." In *Cambridge Handbook of Age and Ageing*, edited by M. Johnson. Cambridge: Cambridge University Press.

Harrison, F. 2007. *Why Baby Boomers Suck!: (No Offense Mom).* Seattle, WA: Codec.

Hashimoto, A. 1996. *The Gift of Generation.* New York: Cambridge University Press.

Hoffman, J., and K. Pype. 2016. *Ageing in Sub-Saharan Africa: Spaces and Practices of Care.* Chicago: University of Chicago Press.

Howard, R., dir. 1985. *Cocoon.* Los Angeles: Twentieth Century-Fox.

Irudaya, Rajan S., and S. Sunitha. 2018. "Impact of Widowhood and Disability Among Elderly." In *Handbook of Research on Multicultural Perspectives on*

Gender and Aging, edited by R. Pande and T. van der Weide. Hershey, PA: IGI Global.

Johnson, R. W., and K. E. Smith. 2016. "How Retirement Is Changing in America." Urban Institute, https://www.urban.org/features/how-retirement -changing-america.

Kania-Lundholm, M., and S. Torres. 2018. "Ideology, Power and Inclusion: Using the Critical Perspective to Study How Older ICT Users Make Sense of Digitisation." *Media, Culture & Society* 40(8): 1167–85.

Kaplan, M., et al. 2015. "Intergenerational Contact Zones: A Compendium of Applications." https://aese.psu.edu/extension/intergenerational/articles /intergenerational-contact-zones.

Katz, S. 1995. "Imaging the Life-Span: From Premodern Miracles to Postmodern Fantasies." In *Images of Aging: Cultural Representations of Later Life*, edited by M. Featherstone and A. Wernick. London: Routledge.

Kepple, D., and N. Brewer. 2017. "Grandparents of the Community: Lakota Elders' View of Intergenerational Care." *GrandFamilies* 4(1). https://scholar works.wmich.edu/grandfamilies/vol4/iss1/9.

Levy, B. R., L. Ferrucci, A. B. Zonderman, M. D. Slade, J. Troncoso, and S. M. Resnick. 2016. "A Culture-Brain Link: Negative Age Stereotypes Predict Alzheimer's Disease Biomarkers." *Psychology and Aging* 31(1): 82–88.

Lifshitz, R., G. Nimrod, and Y. Bachner. 2018. "Spirituality and Wellbeing in Later Life: A Multidimensional Approach." *Aging & Mental Health*. doi: 10.1080/13607863.2018.1460743.

Lowenstein, A. 2005. "Global Ageing and Challenges to Families." In *Cambridge Handbook of Age and Ageing*, edited by M. Johnson. Cambridge: Cambridge University Press.

Lynch, C. 2012. *Retirement on the Line: Age, Work, and Value in an American Factory*. Ithaca, NY: Cornell University Press.

Malburg, M. 2018. "Designing Spaces That Work for a Multigenerational Workforce." Progressive AE. https://www.progressiveae.com/creating-multi generational-spaces/.

Martin-Matthews, A. 2015. "Experiencing Widowhood." In *Routledge Handbook of Cultural Gerontology*, edited by J. Twigg and W. Martin. New York: Routledge.

Mikkelsen, H. 2016. "Unthinkable Solitude: Successful Aging in Denmark Through the Lacanian Real." *Ethos* 44(4): 448–63.

Miller, G. 2011. "Social Neuroscience. Why Loneliness Is Hazardous to Your Health." *Science* 331(6014): 138–40.

Moen, P. 2016. *Adulthood: Boomers on the Edge of Risk, Renewal and Purpose*. Oxford: Oxford University Press.

Mooradian, J., S. Cross, and G. Stutzky. 2007. "Across Generations: Culture, History, and Policy in the Social Ecology of American Indian Grandparents Parenting Their Grandchildren." *Journal of Family Social Work* 10(4): 81–101.

Nelson-Becker, H. 2018. *Spirituality, Religion, and Aging: Illuminations for Therapeutic Practice*. Thousand Oaks, CA: Sage.

Petrie, D., dir. 1988. *Cocoon: The Return*. Los Angeles: Twentieth Century-Fox.

Pew Research Center. 2018. *The Generation Gap in American Politics*. http://www.people-press.org/2018/03/01/the-generation-gap-in-american-politics.

Polivka, L. 2000. "Postmodern Aging and the Loss of Meaning." *Journal of Aging and Identity* 5(4): 225–35.

Rasmussen, S. 1997. *The Poetics and Politics of Tuareg Aging Life Course and Personal Destiny in Niger*. Dekalb: Northern Illinois University Press.

Rhoads, E., and L. Holmes. 1995. *Other Cultures, Elder Years*, 2nd ed. Thousand Oaks, CA: Sage.

Romano, A. 2019. "'OK Boomer' Isn't Just about the Past. It's about our Apocalyptic Future." *Vox*, November 19. https://www.vox.com/2019/11/19/20963757/what-is-ok-boomer-meme-about-meaning-gen-z-millennials.

Ruggles, S. 2002. "Living Arrangements and Well-Being of Older Persons in the Past." *Population Bulletin of the United Nations*, nos. 42/43: 111–61.

Sadruddin, A. 2019. "The Care of 'Small Things': Aging and Dignity in Rwanda." *Medical Anthropology*. doi: 10.1080/01459740.2019.1643852.

Savishinsky, J. 2006. "The Quest for Legacy in Later Life." *Journal of Intergenerational Relationships* 4(4): 75–90.

Schweitzer, M. 1999. *American Indian Grandmothers: Traditions and Transition*. Albuquerque: University of New Mexico Press.

Sedlar, J., and R. Miners. 2002. *Don't Retire, Rewire*. New York: Alpha.

Shakuto, S. 2018. "An Independent and Mutually Supportive Retirement as a Moral Ideal in Contemporary Japan." *Australian Journal of Anthropology* 29(2). https://onlinelibrary.wiley.com/doi/abs/10.1111/taja.12277.

Silin, J. G. 2018. *Early Childhood, Aging, and the Life Cycle: Mapping Common Ground*. Cham, Switzerland: Palgrave Macmillan.

Simic, A. 1978. "Introduction: Aging and the Aged in Cultural Perspective." In *Life's Career Aging: Cultural Variations on Growing Old*, edited by B. Myerhoff and A. Simic. Beverly Hills, CA: Sage.

Thang, L. 2001. *Generations in Touch: Linking the Old and Young in a Tokyo Neighborhood*. Ithaca, NY: Cornell University Press.

U.S. Bureau of Labor Statistics. 2018. Employment Projections. https://www.bls.gov/emp/tables/civilian-labor-force-participation-rate.htm.

Vanderbeck, R., and N. Worth. 2015. *Intergenerational Space*. London: Routledge.

Vesperi, M. 2008. "Evaluating Images of Aging in Print and Broadcast Media." In *Boomer Bust? Economic and Political Dynamics of the Graying Society*, edited by R. Hudson. Westport, CT: Praeger.

CHAPTER TEN

Aging and Society in the New Life Course

Philip Y. Kao and Steven M. Albert

Introduction: Redefining the Life Course

The life course perspective in aging research considers human lives in terms of personhood, place, and time and how the interactions among these features shape and structure experiences of aging from birth to death—and even beyond, reaching into memory and the ancestral realm. During the final quarter of the 20th century, life course studies expanded from a narrow focus on the temporal patterning of life stages (and their associated qualities/behaviors) to highlight more complex relationships between human development, cultural systems, demography, and history. This shift was a welcome move; it allowed the life course and its cultural variations to be cast in a new light within the larger context of society, encapsulating political economy and sociocultural history. In other words, there was value in wrestling the life course framework away from a narrow gerontological emphasis on developmental psychology and personality. This perspective responds to Funder's call for a more complex understanding of personality in context: "Personality refers to an individual's characteristic patterns of thought, emotion, and behavior, together with the psychological mechanisms—hidden or not—behind those patterns" (Funder 2013: 5). Notwithstanding the problems associated with the ideology of an attainable coherent and "stable" self, approaching personhood from a life course perspective thickens the social constructive nature of the self.

Today, life course research faces additional challenges brought on by aging populations, increases in human longevity and life expectancies, new geographies of inequality, emergent communities of care, advances in information and communications technology and artificial intelligence, and even climate change and worsening environmental destruction. In addition to studying how persons in society age, and the resources and meanings they wrestle with while doing so, anthropologists working in the field of aging and life course have an opportunity to create new analytical and methodological opportunities in reimagining the life course. The time is ripe for turning critical gerontological theories into real world praxis. For instance, S. Jay Olshansky argues for a Longevity Dividend framework that targets delaying the biological aging process instead of targeted disease/pathology management (Olshansky 2013). The framework acts as a public health strategy, delivering positive health and economic outcomes. Because people live longer and healthier under this regime, older people could contribute substantially to economic growth and future generations. Along these transformational lines, writers such as Joseph Coughlin, founder and director of the MIT AgeLab, argue that businesses and innovators continue to misunderstand the process of aging and how late life affects the economy in fundamental ways, offering opportunities for those who can grasp the new paradigm shift from the ageism of yesteryear (Coughlin 2017).

For a few anthropologists, however, the turn to the life course provides for new contextual and theoretical opportunities. For example, Jennifer Johnson-Hanks argues that conventional life stages, such as motherhood, are in fact fluid. They are stages that are loosely bounded for educated Berti women in southern Cameroon. The author proposes the need to view the life course not as a series of rites of passages but rather as vital conjectures that showcase agency and practice in emergent ways (Johnson-Hanks 2002). *Age-inscriptions* is a term Cati Coe and Erdmute Alber employ to take account "for the ways that transitions, expectations and markers around age and life-course stages are modified in interplay with social change" (Coe and Alber 2018; see also Part II Coe).

With the recent establishment of the American Anthropological Association's Interest Group on the Anthropology of Aging and the Life Course, the life course has gained a certain amount of analytic urgency. According to the Interest Group's mission, the stakes are quite high for anthropologists: "The consequences of global aging will influence virtually every topic studied by anthropologists, including the biological limits of the human life span, generational exchange and kinship, household and community formations, symbolic representations of the life course, and attitudes toward disability and death." This chapter aims to frame the discussion of aging and the life course within new social contexts that require challenging our conceptualizations (and discourses) of normative aging (e.g., "successful," "experiential," "unhealthy" aging). By doing so, the reader will get a glimpse at how future ethnographic accounts can capture new configurations of intimacy, care, interdependence, and the role of technology in digital personhood and the life course.

Aspects of the life course are biologically based to the extent that psycho-biological development (the "life cycle" or "life span") occurs from birth to death and is variably linked to chronologic age. However, our focus is not how biology constrains culture, but rather how life course practices illuminate the ways aging affects social institutions amid changes in economy, living arrangements, and technology, and how these institutions in turn affect aging. Chronologic age does not explain the life course. Elements of the life course have been conventionally and oftentimes "chronologized" in the sense that transitions, such as movement from "youth" to "adulthood," are based on the number of years since birth (Settersten 1999). In many cultures, chronological age is important for assuming or vacating roles and statuses. In other contexts, however, certain roles and relations, such as the birth of a grandchild or hosting key ritual events, define life course transitions. Among the Lak of New Ireland, Papua New Guinea, for example, hosting a mortuary ritual for a deceased lineage member defines seniority and leadership capacity, eschewing simple chronological age calculations.

We will thus be updating our treatment of the life course, moving beyond Christine L. Fry's original conceptualization of the life course as a methodological and cognitive domain (Fry 1990), in order to study the connection between individual lives and the historical and socioeconomic context in which these lives unfold. This chapter begins by outlining some of the diverse perspectives on the life course from many disciplines. We then consider cultural distinctions in definitions of the life course, stressing cross-cultural variation in the stages of life and in particular, old age, which may have its own divisions such as young-old, old-old, or even ancestors. This is followed by an examination of explicit and implicit cultural models of the life course and their stages and transitions, followed by questions regarding how old age and wisdom highlight challenges to conventional readings of work, sociality, and life experiences. Following on from that, the next section tackles the issue of locating the shifting contours of the life course by considering the notion of elderscapes and the nature of intergenerational exchanges that see the life course not only as a product of an individual (like the wake or track of waves left behind by a boat) but as a collective and temporally fluid expression. The final section in this chapter addresses emerging cultural spaces and cultural scripts that showcase how this new understanding of the life course interacts with emerging structures of care support, citizenship, and practices of the body.

What will emerge in the end is the realization that contemporary anthropology is more than well suited to rediscovering the life course. To track changes in the now booming field of life course research, we begin with a brief review of the growing interest in the field and identify emerging principles that link different disciplines in their approach to the life course.

The Life Course as a Multidisciplinary Field of Investigation

The life course perspective has been embraced by scholars in many disciplines, including anthropology, history, developmental psychology, sociology, demography, and epidemiology. Life course perspectives guide research on a wide range of topics, such as cognitive function, crime, disability, divorce, friendship, gender, health, identity and agency, intergenerational relations, migration, risk perception, spirituality, time use, violence, and work. The life course has been the focus of chapters in all eight editions of the *Handbook of Aging and the Social Sciences*, spanning 40 years, from 1976 to 2015 (George and Ferraro 2016). The study of the life course has its own handbook (Mortimer and Shanahan 2003), updated in 2016 (Shanahan, Mortimer, and Johnson, 2016), and methodologies for life course research continue to evolve, covering such new areas as three-generational longitudinal research designs, growth curve modeling, lifespan epidemiology, and multilevel geospatial models.

Investigations of generational processes in the United States and other postindustrial nations have shown that the life course is more flexible, less standardized, and more open to the possibility of change than earlier research had indicated (Hareven 1982; Elder 1999; Elder and Conger 2000; O'Rand and Campbell 1999: 61). A key illustration of this greater flexibility is evident in changes in labor force participation. Under pressure from increasingly older populations, Canada and the European OECD nations now seek policies that decouple age from work experience, or at least provide flexibility in work across the life span. The goal for this effort is "to develop a set of incentives that would allow parents to take extended leave during their 'prime' working years, while allowing older adults to work into their 70s" (Policy Research Initiative, Canada 2004; see Part V Lynch). Thus, policy initiatives often recognize changes in life course patterning. Newer research showing links between early age at retirement and lower cognitive performance ("cognitive or mental retirement") in cross-national studies may also lead to changes in pensions and other retirement incentives, or may spur new opportunities for cognitive investment at work for older employees (Rohwedder and Willis 2010; Nishimura and Oikawa 2017).

The power and challenges of life course research are well illustrated in ongoing cohorts that have been followed since high school graduation, as in the Wisconsin Longitudinal Survey (WLS), begun in 1957, or since birth, in the British Medical Research Council (MRC) National Survey of Health and Development, which used a random sample of children born in 1946.[1] The WLS enrolled over 10,000 people, and the MRC cohort includes over 16,000. Each cohort has been followed for nearly 60 years through periodic surveys, which in some cases include performance assessments of physical ability and cognition, biomarker studies, and merged records from school assessments and medical contacts. The challenges of maintaining participation in these efforts over half a century are legion. People move; they change names and statuses. Likewise, investigator teams change. Researchers retire, and funding comes and goes. For all these reasons, true life course studies, in which people are followed over their entire lifetimes, are extremely difficult, and to this day there is no study that has followed a large cohort from birth to death. Thus, the half century of follow-up available in the WLS and MRC studies is an extraordinary resource.

The WLS, for example, seeks to answer a wide array of questions relevant to aging and life course processes, including:

> Which women and men will be "healthy, wealthy, and wise," and which will be less fortunate in their later years? . . . How does the quality of life among the elderly depend on conditions and experiences in childhood, youth, and midlife? . . . What vocational or social activities lead to better cognitive and psychological functioning among the aging? . . . When and how do the near elderly begin to prepare for their own deaths? How—and for how long—are the lives of parents disrupted by disability or death among their own children? How do family structure and history affect the transition to retirement? (Hauser and Rowan 2006: 12)

Other longitudinal studies such as the Harvard Second Generation study[2] track down participants from childhood cohort studies and pick them up again for follow-up, sometimes decades later.

These studies of the life course have mostly stressed microlevel phenomena, occurrences related to individuals and families, as evident in life course patterns. Increased attention has also been paid to macrolevel phenomena—social structure and economic and political contexts—and the linkages between micro- and macrolevel phenomena (Hagestad and Dannefer 2001). Still lacking, in our view, are cultural accounts of the life course that take into account the temporal perspective made possible by long-term fieldwork. Few anthropological investigations carry fieldwork forward over 60 or more years, because such efforts are plagued by the same challenges facing the WLS and MRC long-term follow-up of birth cohorts.

Approaching the Life Course and Aging

Life Course Stages and Individual Agency

Most Americans would likely view the life course as a progression from childhood and youth, marked by schooling; through adulthood, which is characterized by college or technical training, employment, parenthood, and citizenship; to retirement and leisure-filled "golden years" followed by a decline into frailty. To this they might also add a "finding myself" period, a decade or so of wandering between adolescence and adulthood that has been called the "odyssey years" (Brooks 2007). As a formula for life course development, most Americans expect individual agency to play a central role in this shaping of a person's life.

But in many places, poverty, war, and other forces limit individual agency. For example, among poor communities in South Asia, where child bondage and family migration for work are common, childhood has a different meaning, and formal education is unlikely to be part of this stage of life (Dannefer 2001). Separation from family may be a normal part of early and mid-career as workers leave South Asia for the Gulf states, for example, or Philippine nurses or home attendants move to Israel to care for frail older adults. This can also include East Asian children sent to live with distant relatives in the United States to increase the odds of a college admission and citizenship, or children who are separated from parents who have crossed into the United States from Mexico as part of government campaigns against "open" borders. Currently, in some African nations, children as young as 10 or 12 are forced to become soldiers, surely a violation of our understanding of the separate spheres of childhood and adulthood, as it enforces a violent end to childhood and initiates adulthood at developmentally problematic ages. Even in the United States, a group's behavioral rules can limit individual agency, as among urban gangs, which have their own markers for transitions from lowest to highest rank and the expectation of not living much past age 30 (Dannefer 2003).

Old Age: Powerful Seniors, Declining Elders, Ambiguous Ancestors

A few examples (only a few among many possibilities) of cultural models of old age in the life course follow. The Elizabethan and Thai models illustrate elaboration in the cultural organization of old age, with powerful seniors at the peak of their lives who then decline into "ancients" or frail elders. In some models, old age is not the final stage of the life course, as in many African societies where powerful seniors may decline into frailty and death but then become spiritually powerful as ancestors. Also, the boundary between very old person and ancestor may be porous, as in the case of Sukuma

Figure 10.1 Nicola D'Asc-enzo, *Seven Ages of Man*, from *As You Like It*, 1932 (Folger Shakespeare Library. FSL Interior: Seven Ages of Man Stained Glass Window 1985. Copyright Julie Ainsworth. https://luna.folger.edu/luna/servlet/s/5ue2mf. Used by permission of the Folger Shakespeare Library.).

agropastoralists in Tanzania, among whom the very old live in an ambiguous zone between life and death, elderhood and ancestorhood. In this situation, death is not a sharp dividing line, and elders enter an ancestral state in a gradual process that imbues those still living with the qualities and powers of ancestral spirits (Stroeken 2002).

Turning to Shakespeare's "seven ages of man" (*As You Like It*, II.7), we can see another archetypal framing of life as a series of roles. By comparing the world to a stage and life to a play, Shakespeare offers an Elizabethan model of the life course as roles in a theatrical performance (Figure 10.1). "One man in his time plays many parts, his acts being seven ages." The seven stages include infancy, "whining schoolboy . . . creeping unwillingly to school," lover, soldier ("seeking the bubble reputation even in the cannon's mouth"), judge or administrator, retirement based on frailty ("his big manly voice, turning again towards childish treble"), and finally "second childishness and mere oblivion . . . sans teeth, sans eyes, sans taste, sans everything." In this seven-stage model, the pinnacle is reached in middle age as the individual moves from the family to the civic sphere, and old age is a time of decline into childishness—a decline perhaps long accepted as inevitable but that America's baby boomers are now currently resisting.

Figure 10.2 Shinobu Kitayama, *The Aging Mind: Opportunities in Cognitive Research* (Shinobu Kitayama, *The Aging Mind: Opportunities in Cognitive Research*. National Research Council. Washington, DC: National Academy Press, 2000, p. 222. Copyright 2019, National Academy of Sciences. Reprinted with permission from the National Academies Press.).

Compare the Elizabethan model to the nine-stage life course pictured in a Thai temple engraving (Figure 10.2). The same curvilinear shape appears, with the pinnacle again reached in middle age. The left side shows ascension through infancy, courtship, parenthood, and career, culminating in civic responsibility and statesmanship. The right side shows decline, indexed by use of a cane, increasingly stooped posture, and the shrinking of the body typical of old age frailty. A major difference between the Elizabethan and Buddhist models is the recycling of lives implied in the Thai conception, in which the infant emerges from, and the elder returns to, the same place (see Part III Aulino). Asian systems stress decline but also recycling of lives into newborns (Albert and Cattell 1994; Lamb 2000; Langford 2013).

Yet another model occurs in many African societies, where lives reach fullest potential not in middle age but in ancestorhood. In the worldview of many sub-Saharan African societies, the passage through death opens the door to a new life stage, that of ancestors, who—as the most senior members of their lineages—play an active role in the lives of their descendants. For example, among mid-20th-century Tallensi in Ghana, dead lineage elders were transformed into ancestor spirits with great power and authority, both mystical and worldly (Fortes 1961). Ancestors were fed at gravesites and crossroads and regularly consulted by their descendants. They were petitioned when crops failed or someone was sick, or when a lineage's fortunes declined. Ancestors' responses could be to curse or to bless, to bring further disaster or good fortune. Junior lineage members were linked to clan ancestors through living elders who represented the ancestors. The living elders communicated with ancestors, spoke for them, and drew on ancestors' authority to enhance their own.

While Meyer Fortes was working with the Tallensi, a man named Teezien gave him a vivid account of the immediate, direct connection Tallensi saw between themselves and their ancestors:

> We provide for them . . . and beg crops. . . . If we deny him [ancestor], he will not provide for us, he will not give to us, neither wife nor child. It is he who rules over us so that we may live. . . . If you gave him nothing, will he give you anything? He is the master of everything. We brew beer for him and sacrifice fowls so that he may eat to satisfaction and then he will secure guinea corn and millet for us. (1961: 186)

Fortes challenged Teezien: "Ancestors . . . are dead; how can they eat and do such material things as making crops thrive?" Imperturbable, Teezien responded: "It is exactly as with living people."

In her research in western Kenya in the mid-1980s, Cattell found that for Samia, as for Tallensi, Zulus, and many other Africans, death marked the end of life but not the end of a person's role in the family (Cattell 1992, 1996). Old women and men were closely associated with the ancestors and shared in the mystical powers of the spirits, especially in the power to curse. As spirits (*emisambwa* or *emisebe* in Samia), the dead used their spiritual powers to continue to affect their kin in various ways, for good or ill. This was true of women as well as men, for in this very patriarchal society where females were subordinated throughout life, ancestorhood brought equality. Ancestor spirits expected descendants to be named after them and appeared in dreams to their descendants. Such dreams could be interpreted by diviners, who advised their clients on sacrifices or other actions to be taken when an angry spirit was causing problems, and spirit mediums could communicate with the ancestors.

This brief review of cultural models of the life course suggests that the biological imperative of maturation and decline lends itself to a variety of cultural emphases. People everywhere age and die, but within African and other cultural systems personhood and agency are viewed as extending beyond death. Aging brings decrements in physical strength and cognitive capacity but also continuing accumulation of experience and cultural expertise. Societies differ in whether they emphasize progressive loss or accumulated wisdom and power. Some consider middle age as the pinnacle of life and old age as a period of declining abilities and powers. Others focus on new, socially valued statuses in old age, such as Australian aboriginal elders who gain power from their close connection to the ancestral dreamtime and the degendered powerful elders of Papua New Guinea. Senescence and death put limits on conceptions of the life course, but cultures may place old age in a domain outside chronologic time.

Locating the New Life Course

Elderscapes

Rethinking the life course means moving away from explanatory models that fix the world (and human experience) into neat containers of normative values, capacities, and social relations. When people speak of aging, they usually consider a life course that begins with growth and addition and ends with senescence and loss. Seen from a wider lens, however, cultural variation and the context of aging is much more complex, made so by changes in livelihoods and shifting global economic networks. In order to reassess the life course as an emergent field of opportunities, and a source of social and ontological imaginings, the term *elderscapes* comes to mind.

Before turning to the notion of -scapes as postulated by anthropologist Arjun Appadurai (1996), it is useful to situate "landscape" etymologically. A *landscape* refers to the artistic rendering of a scenery with all its distinguishing components. In viewing the land, the -scape is more than just the backdrop, it is the shifting and oftentimes heterogeneous forms (natural and human made) that help to explain particular phenomenon lodged within a geographic area or a visual/virtual frame. A landscape can be frozen in time, dynamic, or momentary. Moreover, various -scapes (soundscapes, financescapes, etc.), according to Appadurai, are fluid and shifting dimensions that counteract hegemonic institutions and ideologies. They can be practices and imaginings that contribute to the global exchange and flow of ideas, information, and ways of being. More radically, -scapes resist eclipsed readings of grand narratives and the nature of the phenomenon under view. An idea within the scape changes according to the context and the positionality of the spectator.

The elderscape defines a geography of possibilities, relationships, and imaginings. It illuminates how older people live and make sense of their lives simultaneously, along with the relations of care and support they find or don't find in their respective environments. Elderscapes stress that aging is a social process contingent upon context (e.g., location, culture) and thus is a process of becoming, not ossifying according to some deterministic model of the life course. Elderscapes allow us to see variations in the life course as unique landscapes onto themselves. They force us to ask just what kind of course aging follows and the agency and role of individual perspectives. By locating aging and the life course within particular elderscapes, we can analyze the interaction between resources/services devoted to the elderly and the social experience of these resources within a particular environment, given the diverse set of heterogeneous experiences and perceptions.

Anthropologists Annika Mayer and Roberta Mandoki, along with filmmaker Jakob Gross, capture the various insights and experiences of aging in Delhi, India, and the Kathmandu Valley, Nepal. In an open access and interactive transmedia project entitled "Elderscapes: Ageing in Urban South Asia,"[3] they offer an interconnected meditation on the everyday lives of older people from the middle class in urban South Asia, how people perceive, experience, and experiment with aging and show increasing longevity. Rather than a mash-up of various media, their project synthesizes stories, representations, anthropological theory, and audiovisual material. By situating their research within the realm of elderscapes, the project leaders were able to create new combinations and interconnections. These creative moments capture the fluid ethnographic reality of elderscapes because of the transmedia format and the global cultural flows that inform contemporary life and aging in particular South Asian cities.

The ethnographic focus on elderscapes challenges the linear teleology of the conventional life course by bringing into focus the changing needs, bonds, and commitments of the elderly, with gestures toward new potentialities and configurations of time, space, and memory. All in all, "What is particularly important about the elderscapes and new cultural spaces created within them is the continuing engagement of old adults in shaping the very context of their lives" (Sokolovsky 2009: xxiv). Moreover, as we continue to embrace new technologies and the further digitization of our "selves," anthropologists must continue to examine interconnections between technology, artificial intelligence, advances in cognitive psychology, and cultural spaces and their repertoires that will shape emergent and varied life course pathways.

Evolving Age Sets

The stages of the life course may be explicitly articulated, as in East African age-set systems, or largely implicit, as in American ideas about the life course. Americans will tick off "childhood," "adulthood," and "old age" as stages of life but will be hard pressed to say when these stages begin or end. For example, a National Council on Aging (NCOA) survey in 2000 determined that people dated the start of old age to vastly different ages and that these ages depended most critically on the age of the interviewee. People in their teens thought old age began at age 40; people in their 60s thought it began in the 70s (Albert 2006). The implicit model of the life course in American culture is also evident in language: people speak about the elderly in terms similar to those used for children (Albert and Brody 1996).

Insight on the staging of life course transitions is best seen in African age-set systems, where elaborate rituals mark transitions (Spencer 2018). Age-sets are lifelong identities that cut across kinship and residence and allow a group to assume statuses as a whole. Age-mates marry at the same time, are initiated into religious ritual as a group, and generally take on social responsibilities collectively. Age grading, by contrast, is simply use of age (or indicators of plausible age) to assign both a social status and most critically, senior or junior status. Thinking again of the American system, what does it take to be considered an adult? For some purposes, such as buying alcohol, voting, or obtaining a driver's license, chronologic age is enough to establish "adulthood." But in other contexts, age 21 may not confer adult identity. Adults are expected to work to support themselves, buckle down and accept the responsibilities of marriage and parenthood, or serve in the military. Any of these social indicators may be used to assign status as an adult and serve an age grading function. Violators pay a heavy social price. We may be ashamed of the adult who stays home to play video games on the computer; this person refuses to "grow up." Until recently, the same was true for the college graduate who returned to the parental nest, though this has now become both common and acceptable.

What social indicators assign status as an older adult? Sixty-somethings bristle when younger people want to give them a seat on the bus. Eighty-somethings enjoy surprising younger people with their computer literacy. These are a far cry from Sri Lankan age-based deference, in which younger people about to depart bow and touch the feet of seniors while receiving a blessing on the head. Still, age remains a key element of the dynamics of senior-junior status, along with assumptions about competence, abilities, and preferences. With life course changes of the types described earlier, we can expect these social indicators of old age to change. For example, the proportion of people aged 65+ in the U.S. labor force will double, from 12.1 percent to 21.8 percent, between 1996 and 2026 (Bureau of Labor Statistics 2017). How will this greater social involvement in old age affect definitions of old age? Similarly, nearly a third of Americans born in 2011 may reach age 100 (Anzilotti 2017). If a whole society shifts to older ages, what happens to definitions of "old" and "aging"?

Globalization and the Life Course

Emerging Cultural Spaces: Community Living and Care

Changes in the new life course also relate in interconnected ways to the types of communities of living and care that pockmark the various elderscapes in societies around the world. Rather than rely on models that partition and map health outcomes onto particular chronological stages, anthropologists in working partnerships with architects, policy makers, and gerontologists are exploring new models and communities of care for the elderly and their family members. Diving deeper into concerns surrounding well-being and life narratives, and regardless of where and what life course people actually constitute historically over time, issues regarding quality have become front and center. According to a 2011 poll carried out by the Cambia Health Foundation, American respondents indicated that in the context of palliative care and serious illness, people did not favor life extension if particular interventions brought about a reduction in quality of life. Therefore, investigating various community models of living that address (or fail to address) the quality and tenor of the everyday in the context of the new life course will become more and more important.

As "Western" long-term care models continue being built and replicated in places around the world, some communities are exploring new and creative ways to meet the needs of the elderly, especially in societies where ageism is literally in the built environment. There is the issue of making cities more age friendly and ensuring that the elderly, especially those in remote areas, have access to services both at home and in nearby medical centers (see Part V Stafford).

More transformatively, "nursing home abolitionist" movements have been challenging not only the way aging is medicalized but also what conventional approaches to assisted and independent living have to say about the life course and how these approaches can be rethought and challenged. For example, the continuing care retirement community (CCRC) model of long-term care recognizes that aging is part of life's journey. By focusing on aging-in-place marketing and care delivery, CCRC or "life care" models are at least able to recognize particular narratives and attitudes regarding the life course. The CCRC does not, however, go far enough in rethinking how their residents are pulled away from their home context and the memories and activities they associate with for most of their lives. Only a few residents, and those who can more or less live independently, have access to kitchens, where cooking plays a central role in not only gift exchange but socialization throughout the life course.

The philosophy of the Green House Model takes another tack, demoting health and eldercare as the number one priority. Rather, this model engages older adults by reintroducing valued roles throughout all aspects of the life course, where stages, relationships, and activities are not segregated by a utility function of care needs. According to the Green House Model mission, "We envision homes in every community where elders and others enjoy excellent quality of life and quality of care; where they, their families, and the staff engage in meaningful relationships built on equality, empowerment, and mutual respect; where people want to live and work; and where all are protected, sustained, and nurtured without regard to the ability to pay" (Green House Project n.d.; Part VI Web Book McLean).

Another set of factors contributing to the changing elderscapes, and also what we see as "aging societies," stems from the reduction of morbidity around the world. Increases in wealth and decreases in fertility are enabling societies to invest in old age, with the dividend of longer and healthier lives. As described earlier, longevity is reorganizing the ways people work, retire, and play, thus driving vast changes in our understanding of the life course. Nevertheless, emerging communities that work towards enabling people throughout the entire life course to live and interact more meaningfully and interdependently will be welcomed by baby boomers and their future generations. By linking the life course to social context, that is, the role of family and kinship, individuals will begin to change the nature of their communities and the kinds of relations, responsibilities, and roles that people will enact throughout a diverse set of life journey and pathways, no matter their social/chronological/psychological age. Continuities and discontinuities throughout one's life mean that a new life course perspective is in dialogue with the material world and evolving communities. Emerging communes, including cohousing, green house models, and even the CCRC are looking way beyond just addressing the health care needs of the elderly to consider how people are valued and participate in society and ultimately redefine the life course.

The "Longevity Economy"

Increasing numbers of people are reaching traditional retirement ages with potentially many years of life remaining as well as high levels of function (see Part II Lynch). This favorable "health expectancy" allows older people an "encore adulthood," with additional work years and a promise of high economic productivity that societies are only slowly learning to harness (Moen 2016). Increasingly, we find people aged 65+ retiring multiple times; in one survey, 40 percent of people aged 65+ who were currently working had retired earlier (see Part V Lynch). Their turnover is lower and in some cases their occupational productivity is higher because of expertise and absence of competing demands. Older adults aged 50+ are also the greatest donors to charitable causes. They contribute disproportionately to tax revenue, consumer spending, volunteering, and family caregiving. This is part of what Coughlin calls the "longevity economy," the contribution to economic activity generated by people aged 50+ (2017). As a proportion of total GDP, the longevity economy could very well top 50 percent of the total US economy by 2032. Older adults have thus become highly desirable to local economies. They bring wealth and higher salaries, do not have school-age children, and have most of their medical and social service needs covered through state and national programs outside local jurisdictions, such as Medicare, Medicaid, and Social Security.

This new conjunction of age and productivity may be shifting a fundamental life course expectation up by a decade or two. Older Americans today are not only viewing their seventies or eighties as productive and financially rewarding years, but also ripe for making some of their greatest contributions (Cappelli and Novelli 2010; Fried 2014). Thus, 7 of 10 Americans planning to retire expect to work in some capacity postretirement. Success in business startups is more likely if the entrepreneurs are in their fifties and sixties (so-called olderpreneurs) than in their twenties (Cox, Henderson, and Baker 2014). Leisure patterns have changed as well. The public health consequences of these changes are often surprising. For example, the incidence of severe fall injuries at older ages continues to increase, not because of greater frailty at later ages but most likely because older people participate in active leisure, such as sports, at higher rates (Burns and Kakara 2018).

The upshot of this conjunction of greater life expectancy, better health, and accumulation of cultural expertise with age may mean not just a better old age but also increased decoupling of chronologic age from life course transitions and expectations. Vast social experiments will allow us to see how understanding of the life course changes with the growing dominance of the longevity economy.

Conclusion

In a 2018 *Wall Street Journal Healthcare Report* entitled "Is There a Limit to the Human Lifespan?" debaters squared off over whether the human life span has a set cap.[4] In any case, biomedical science continues to seek out ways to slow down the aging process, but also and more importantly to achieve a kind of "bio-resilience" that keeps people biologically healthy and younger over longer stretches of the life course—and ultimately throughout old age (see Part VI). Take for example, the work of biomedical gerontologist and mathematician Aubrey de Grey. This research focuses on regenerative medicine, targeting cellular damage and repair before larger systems of pathology set in. Instead of offering a solution to the retardation of aging, Dr. de Grey prefers reversing cellular aging altogether. His foundation, Strategies for Engineered Negligible Senescence (SENS), is named after the techniques and therapies in current development to rejuvenate the body. By identifying the types of molecular and cellular damage caused by particular metabolic processes, SENS is betting on engineering the end of senescence as we know it today.

Similar to our rethinking of the life course, the discourse of longevity may also come to signify different and emergent practices for different people. For some, engineering longevity might mean changes in health attitudes and behaviors throughout the life course. If medical technologies are able to deliver healthier and younger bodies for longer, then humans will most likely coevolve with these possibilities. Humans may take on more risks, such as having and raising children during two periods of the life course, one before the height of their careers and one after work retirement. Along with changes in life choices and the timing of particular activities and commitments, people will continue to explore and conceive of human reproduction and kinship in new domains and aspects. If people are living longer, how does the increased collection of memories interact with the life course and even phenomenologically with their future selves and life goals?

Extended healthy longevity also carries with it new debates and cultural attitudes. For example, Aubrey de Grey describes "the pro-aging trance . . . as the impulsion to leap to embarrassingly unjustified conclusions in order to put the horror of aging out of one's mind" (de Grey 2008: 713). In a personal communication e-mail with de Grey from November 2012, one of us wrote (PK):

> I thought of another reason why people are so against this defeat of aging. If SENS finds a workable intervention, this means that you might actually undermine how people have approached life up to this point. People were living with the assumption that tomorrow is not given, and so they were more short-sighted in their life goals and plans. If they knew they could be healthy and for longer, they certainly would have lived out their relational/ emotional life differently. So, discovering a "cure" undermines their life choices and rationalizations up to now. It doesn't change the future, but rewrites the past as a kind of wasted opportunity—so to speak.

Aubrey de Grey replied:

> Interesting point you raise, which is indeed often mentioned, and which I think is probably at least a little bit true. The question is whether we can learn about that, and about how to address it, by examining existing examples of abrupt and dramatic changes to people's expectations for their future. We can consider the discovery that one has a terminal disease, or that what one thought was a terminal disease is actually survivable (in whatever state of health) for a long time.

In the future, longevity studies may very well emerge as a new subfield within medical anthropology and science and technology studies in order to address our understanding and experience of the life course, kinship, the moral economy, evolution, and the shelf life of particular societal institutions and ideologies. Rethinking the life course along with qualitative changes in capturing various kinds of longevity will inevitably lead to the extinction of old myths and the creation of new ones.

Notes

1. https://www.ssc.wisc.edu/wlsresearch/ and www.nshd.mrc.ac.uk/.
2. http://www.adultdevelopmentstudy.org/.
3. http://kjc-sv013.kjc.uni-heidelberg.de/elderscapes/klynt/.
4. https://www.wsj.com/articles/is-there-a-limit-to-the-human-lifespan-1529 892420.

Bibliography

Albert, S. M. 2006. "Cultural and Ethnic Influences on Aging." In *Encyclopedia of Gerontology*, 2nd ed., edited by J. E. Birren. San Diego: Academic.

Albert, S. M., and E. M. Brody. 1996. "When Elder Care Is Viewed as Child Care: Significance of Elder Cognitive Impairment and Caregiver Burden." *American Journal of Geriatric Psychiatry* 4: 121–30.

Albert, S. M., and M. G. Cattell. 1994. *Old Age in Global Perspective: Cross-Cultural and Cross-National Views.* New York: G. K. Hall.

Anzilotti, E. 2017. "Our Aging Population Can Be an Economic Powerhouse—If We Let It." Fast Company, March 13. https://www.fastcompany.com/306 8543/our-aging-population-can-be-an-economic-powerhouse-if-we-let-it.

Appadurai, A. 1996 *Modernity At Large: Cultural Dimensions of Globalization.* Minneapolis: University of Minnesota Press.

Brooks, D. 2007. "The Odyssey Years." *New York Times*, October 9.

Bureau of Labor Statistics, U.S. Department of Labor (2017). Occupational Outlook Handbook, 2016–17 edition.

Burns, E., and R. Kakara. 2018. "Deaths from Falls among Persons Aged ≥65 Years—United States, 2007–2016." *Morbidity and Mortality Weekly Report* 67(18): 509–14.

Cambia Health Foundation. 2011. "New Poll: Americans Choose Quality over Quantity at the End of Life, Crave Deeper Public Discussion of Care Options." http://www.cambiahealthfoundation.org/media/release/07062 011njeol.html.

Cappelli, P., and W. D. Novelli. 2010. *Managing the Older Worker: How to Prepare for the New Organizational Order.* Boston: Harvard Business Review Press.

Cattell, M. G. 1992. "Praise the Lord and Say No to Men: Older Women Empowering Themselves in Samia, Kenya." *Journal of Cross-Cultural Gerontology* 7: 307–30.

Cattell, M. G. 1996. "Gender, Aging and Health: A Comparative Approach." In *Gender and Health: An International Perspective*, edited by C. F. Sargent and C. B. Brettell. Englewood Cliffs, NJ: Prentice Hall.

Coe, C., and E. Alber. 2018. "Age Inscriptions and Social Change." *Anthropology and Aging* 39(1).

Coughlin, J. 2017. *The Longevity Economy: Unlocking the World's Fastest-Growing, Most Misunderstood Market.* New York: Public Affairs.

Cox, E., G. Henderson, and R. Baker. 2014. *Silver Cities: Realising the Potential of Our Growing Older Population*. IPPR North. http://www.ippr.org/publications /silver-cities-realising-the-potential-of-our-growing-older-population.

Dannefer, D. 2001. "Whose Life Course Is It, Anyway? Diversity and Linked Lives in Global Perspective." In *Invitation to the Life Course: New Understandings of Later Life*, edited by R. A. Settersten. Amityville, NY: Baywood.

Dannefer, D. 2003. "Toward a Global Geography of the Life Course." In *Handbook of the Life Course*, edited by J. T. Mortimer and M. J. Shanahan. New York: Kluwer Academic/Plenum.

De Grey, A. 2008. "Editorial: Combating the Tithonus Error: What Works?" *Rejuvenation Research* 11(4).

Elder, G. H., Jr. 1999. *Children of the Great Depression: Social Change in Life Experience*, 25th anniversary ed. Boulder, CO: Westview.

Elder, G. H., Jr., and R. D. Conger. 2000. *Children of the Land: Adversity and Success in Rural America*. Chicago: University of Chicago Press.

Fortes, M. 1961. "Pietas and Ancestor Worship." *Journal of the Royal Anthropological Institute* 91: 166–91.

Fried, L. 2014. "Making Aging Positive." *The Atlantic*. https://www.theatlantic .com/health/archive/2014/06/valuing-the-elderly-improving-public -health/371245/.

Fry, C. L. 1990. "The Life Course in Context: Implications of Research." In *Anthropology and Aging: Comprehensive Reviews*, edited by R. L. Rubinstein. Norwell, MA: Kluwer.

Funder, D. C. 2007. *The Personality Puzzle*. New York: W. W. Norton.

George, L., and K. F. Ferraro, eds. 2016. *Handbook of Aging and the Social Sciences*, 8th ed. San Diego: CA: Academic Press/Elsevier.

Green House Project. n.d. Vision/Mission. http://www.thegreenhouseproject.org /about/visionmission.

Hagestad, G. O., and D. Dannefer. 2001. "Concepts and Theories of Aging: Beyond Microfication in Social Science Approaches." In *Handbook of Aging and the Social Sciences*, 5th ed., edited by R. H. Binstock and L. K. George. San Diego: CA: Academic.

Hareven, T. K. 1982. *Family Time and Industrial Time: The Relationship between the Family and Work in a New England Industrial Community*. Cambridge: Cambridge University Press.

Hauser, R. M., and C. L. Rowan. 2006. *The Class of 1957 in Their Mid-Sixties: A First Look*. CDE Working Paper 2006-03. University of Wisconsin, Center for Demography and Ecology.

Johnson-Hanks, J. 2002. "On the Limits of Life Stages in Ethnography: Toward a Theory of Vital Conjunctures." *American Anthropologist* 104: 865–80.

Lamb, S. 2000. *White Saris and Sweet Mangoes: Aging, Gender, and Body in North India*. Berkeley: University of California Press.

Langford, J. 2013. *Consoling Ghosts. Stories of Medicine and Mourning from Southeast Asians in Exile*. Minneapolis: University of Minnesota Press.

Moen, P.. 2016. *Encore Adulthood: Boomers on the Edge of Risk, Renewal, and Purpose.* New York: Oxford University Press.

Mortimer, J. T. and M. J. Shanahan, eds. 2003. *Handbook of the Life Course.* New York: Kluwer Academic/Plenum.

Nishimura, Y., and M. Oikawa. 2017. "Mental Retirement: Evidence from Global Aging Data." MPRA Paper No. 84555. https://mpra.ub.uni-muenchen.de/84555.

Olshansky, S. 2013. "Reinventing Aging: An Update on the Longevity Dividend." *American Society on Aging*, March 19, 2013. https://www.asaging.org/blog/reinventing-aging-update-longevity-dividend.

O'Rand, A. M., and R. T. Campbell. 1999. "On Reestablishing the Phenomenon and Specifying Ignorance: Theory Development and Research Design in Aging." In *Handbook of Theories of Aging*, edited by V. L. Bengtson and K. W. Schaie. New York: Springer.

Policy Research Initiative, Canada. 2004. *Views on Life-Course Flexibility and Canada's Aging Population.* https://recherchepolitique.gc.ca/doclib/Life-Course_E.pdf.

Rohwedder, S., and R. J. Willis. 2010. "Mental Retirement." *Journal of Economic Perspectives* 24(1): 119–38.h

Settersten, R. A. 1999. *Lives in Time and Place: Problems and Promises of Developmental Science.* Amityville, NY: Baywood.

Shanahan, M., J. T. Mortimer, and M. K. Johnson, eds. 2016. *Handbook of the Life Course*, Vol. 2. New York: Springer.

Sokolovsky, J., ed. 2009. *The Cultural Context of Aging: Worldwide Perspectives*, 3rd ed. Santa Barbara, CA: Praeger.

Spencer, P. 2018. "Age Systems and Kinship." *The International Encyclopedia of Anthropology*, edited by H. Callan. New York: Wiley.

Stroeken, K. 2002. "From Shrub to Log: The Ancestral Dimension of Elderhood among Sukuma in Tanzania." In *Ageing in Africa: Sociolinguistic and Anthropological Approaches*, edited by S. Makoni and K. Stroeken. Burlington, VT: Ashgate.

CHAPTER ELEVEN

Ethnography, Technology Design, and the Future of "Aging in Place"

David Prendergast

Across all stages of the life course, technological developments are greatly reframing how we engage with our physical and digital landscapes. Notions of community, ways of working, shopping, using health care, and interacting with friends, family, and colleagues are being transformed by innovations in online social media, mobile communications, cyber-physical platforms, and autonomous machines. In-home sensing and monitoring devices cover everything from medical needs such as falls detection and medication adherence to personal or "quantified self" measurements focused on calorie and step counting, sleep quality, and air quality. New branches of knowledge such as data science and digital service design are emerging in response to the sociotechnical changes rapidly affecting our societies. Anthropologists in particular are often sought out for the nuanced, qualitative insights that ethnographic theory and methods can provide.

This chapter attempts to provide some insight into how ethnographers, often working in academic-industrial-public collaborations, have approached the question of culturally sensitive technology design in the context of one such issue: independent living and enabling older adults to "age in place." While focused on such work in Europe, it explores related developments around the world. By midcentury, 28.5 percent of the European population will be aged 65 or over. According to Eurostat, by 2050, there will be more than a doubling in the proportion of the "very old" or those aged 85+ from 13.5 million in 2018 to 31.8 million in 2050. The number of centenarians in the EU will increase from 106,000 to more than half a million within the same time period. (Eurostat 2019). What should older people and their children, both today and in future years, expect to experience as they move out of the routines and responsibilities of work into the rhythms and transitions of the later digital life course?

Joseph Coughlin, director of the MIT AgeLab and author of the *Longevity Economy* (2017), reminds us that because Americans can expect two decades of healthy life after the age of 60, planning for retirement needs to be taken seriously as it "demands something more than an occasional cruise or family visit" (Coughlin 2018a). He argues that city planners and developers should consider four key factors—activities, diversity, density, and accessibility—when considering if communities will meet both the needs and wants of older people. In terms of caregiving in the future, Coughlin suggests that Gen X and millennial cohorts will be the first to experience the full implications of what he terms "the Caregiver Crunch" as a result of pressures such as high levels of student debt, permanent migration away from hometowns, and fewer numbers relative to older generations (Coughlin 2018b). In an article in *Forbes* magazine, he is optimistic that the familiarity of these cohorts with a suite of technologies and sociotechnical services may position them to adopt and accept new caring practices that will lessen the "friction" of aging (2018b). These range across the digital life course and include new forms of transportation and ridesharing options such as Uber and Lyft, "sharing economy" apps and services such as Honor founded in 2015 for locating care professionals, Task Rabbit and Hello Alfred for household maintenance, Instacart for grocery shopping, not to mention a plethora of solutions to monitor the home and facilitate increased social connectivity.

It has been clear for some time that as the technological architectures and socioeconomic assemblages underlying these apps and services stabilize and proliferate, there will be new opportunities to rethink late 20th-century models of care. Equally it will be important to critically investigate unintended consequences for all involved as these technologies and practices mature. To address this, I spent several years working with colleagues at Intel's Digital Health Group on ethnographic projects, exploring how to utilize social research to sensitively design, develop, and evaluate culturally appropriate technologies to help enable older people to live independently. As Social Science Research Lead and a Principal Investigator in the Technology Research for Independent Living Centre (TRIL) in Ireland, I had the opportunity to participate in a diverse range of multidisciplinary research initiatives focused on improving health and social care for older adults (Prendergast and Roberts 2009; Prendergast and Garattini 2015).

The evolution of our thinking was significantly influenced by a multiyear ethnographic research project we carried out to develop a global, comparative understanding of the practices and meanings associated with growing older (Plowman, Prendergast, and Roberts 2010). During the first major leg of the Global Aging Experience study, the team conducted ethnographic research in 75 older households in seven European countries on the experiences and expectations of aging. The sample included older people with physical and cognitive conditions, those living with lifelong or chronic disease, "healthy" older people, as well as many additional interviews with informal caregivers and domain experts. The qualitative data was supplemented by detailed institutional and policy-oriented research reports focused on aging in each region. This research was designed to help frame the questions being asked to imagine new technologies of independent living for the future. It aimed to analyze the multiple meanings of "home" for older people and the implications for those seeking to deliver service, technology, or other interventions. Over the course of the ethnographic encounters we explored multiple domains including care networks, technology in everyday life, health and housing histories, as well as access to health information for informed decision-making.

The older adults and caregivers we met during this research helped generate a wide range of insights, principles, and warnings that can guide planning and design of services both today and into the future (Photo 11.1). One illuminating example was Erik, a retired farmer in Sweden who reminded us of the practical and emotional importance of embracing a holistic bio-psycho-social approach to care.

Erik's Story

At the age of 83, Erik still lived in the farmhouse where he had spent most of his life. The house sits in its own acreage at the end of a long, rough gravel track in the flat rural landscape of central Sweden. Barns, overgrown lawns, a root cellar, and old sheds surround it. An abandoned tractor rusts in a nearby field, poignantly symbolizing the freezing of Erik's work and life. In late October the atmosphere seemed very still, with the scent of wood smoke hanging in the air and just the odd rumble of a car from the highway in the distance.

At the time of interview, Erik had lived alone since he was widowed in the mid-1990s. He has one daughter who lives in a village about 15 kilometers away. This wheelchair-bound daughter has multiple sclerosis and is married to her caregiver. Erik meets with her only rarely as he can no longer drive a car. He handed in his driving license as his vision deteriorated and, in his opinion, as road users got faster and more reckless. Like many retired farmers, Erik underwent a phased retirement, gradually selling off outlying fields when his knees became arthritic; choosing instead to focus on his market garden near to the house. Unfortunately, Erik's ability to walk decreased over the years. He became prone to losing his balance and has now accumulated a long history of serious falls. Erik has also had a heart attack and often has small spells or mini attacks where he gets dizzy or almost blacks out. His method of coping is to tightly hold onto the nearest stable object and wait for it to pass. He recalls how only a month previously, he went down his driveway to get his newspaper but slipped and collapsed with his walker. Erik was shaking so much he couldn't get up. He recalls "it was very cold in the morning air. I pressed my alarm watch panic button and 20 minutes later, two angels appeared." As a result, by the time he participated in the Global Aging study, Erik's world had narrowed down to a bench in his kitchen, his bedroom, and his bathroom. The rest of the large house was covered in a layer of dust and went unheated. A calendar on the wall is used for important dates as Erik thinks his memory is decaying. The kitchen countertops are crowded with old devices that he has not used since his wife died. He does very little cooking as he says he has no appetite, though he makes porridge in the mornings. He used to bake his own bread but says he can't stand up long enough to do this anymore. He never uses anything that he has on his top shelves but satisfies himself with two shelves within easy reach.

Erik is an example of an older man living alone who receives what many in Europe and America would consider excellent home care services and supports. Beyond the effective emergency response system mentioned above, he has a small pension that is adequate for his needs, a home help care worker paid for by the city council who visits him three times a day to put drops in his eyes, and a district nurse who comes by twice a week to dress his feet. His son-in-law occasionally collects him and drives around, mows the lawns, and does the basic maintenance to keep the outside of his place tidy. Erik himself is very proud of keeping the inside clean. Since his fall, Erik's newspaper is brought in for him at 5:30 a.m. by a neighbor, Matthias, a carpenter, before he goes to work. "He pops in to make sure I am alive." Everything functionally necessary to help Erik "age-in-place" is being done. He would doubtless score highly on a quantitative survey of services. However, what emerges over the course of the two-day ethnographic encounter is overwhelming despair and loneliness. Erik has lots of small microinteractions with people who pass through his life every day. They dress his wounds and see to his meals, but there is seldom opportunity for a good conversation, or for opportunities to feel useful. Little is offered in the form of companionship care, and since losing his driving license he has no longer been able to attend the choir at a local Lutheran church that once comprised much of his social life. There is a limited rural transport scheme that he sometimes uses, but he notes that "it can sometimes be difficult to get a lift from them."

Erik rises from his bed at 4 a.m. As a farmer he always had an early start, but nowadays he gets woken by leg cramps. An early breakfast leads to a day sitting on his kitchen bench, his body an object to be tended by fleeting visitors, just as he tends the few plants on the windowsill next to his seat. Momentary bustles of activity punctuate great long silences in his kitchen, which he attempts to dispel with the chatter of the radio. Poor eyesight makes watching the TV uncomfortable. Since losing much of his sight, Erik has no interest in hobbies or finding new things to do. Two important things keep him sane. One is his cat and the other is the telephone. Whenever possible, Erik loves to call his daughter and his friends. He restricts the length and number of his calls, however, because he can't afford large bills. He has never heard of Skype or free calls through the Internet. He has no plans for the future. Lacking purpose and energy in recent months, he reflects: "To work is important for a good life. Not just have leisure. There is nothing better than work for good health. . . . I am just hanging on as long as I can."

Erik's experience of aging is not uncommon and holds many lessons for designers, gerontologists, and health and social work practitioners. Although it is important to get the basics of care provision right, it is imperative that we broaden our definitions of independent living or aging-in-place. This should include the ability to feel useful, to remain socially and mentally active through affordable flexible transport options, and to maintain physical and digital connections to friends, family, and the wider community life that lies beyond the physical walls of hospital and the home.

Designing for Independent Living

Many case studies similar to Erik's were collected during the Global Aging Experience fieldwork. These were discussed and analyzed by a team of anthropologists and designers. A number of key principles were identified as common to many accounts (Plowman, Prendergast, and Roberts 2009). For the purpose of this chapter, these insights will form a framework to reflect on existing and emergent technologies and services for older people and the social practices in which they are embedded across the digital life course.

(1) People Want to Focus on What They CAN Do, Not What They Can't.

Many people are reluctant to accept a perception of themselves as being or feeling sick or old regardless of their chronological age. Many seek out physical and mental challenges within the parameters of what they can do, pushing boundaries and shunning assistive devices.

In Italy, one of our participants, 77-year-old Giuseppe, lives with his sister in a small house facing a village square in Tuscany. Behind his house is a beautiful garden. He has had two hip replacements and uses walking sticks

Photo 11.1   Co-designing technologies with older people in Ireland. (Photo by David Prendergast)

to get around. Despite his mobility challenges, Giuseppe makes a daily round of the village square as a form of physical and mental practice, explaining that "to keep going is the important thing." During bad weather, he walks laps around his dining room and he frequently looks forward to a time when he will be sufficiently able to negotiate the steep, crooked staircase to his back garden, which he hasn't seen in two years. In the meantime, he prefers to think in terms of purpose and aspirations rather limitations, often lying in bed planning every step and resting place on the route down.

Many older adults refuse to use walking sticks or other assistive devices such as mobility scooters in public for fear of being stigmatized as old or incapable. As Graham Scrambler explains in his work on stigma, an assigned label that pushes individuality into the background can quickly become a "master status" (Scrambler 2008). Many consequently defer use until absolutely necessary. We frequently heard complaints about assistive technologies being designed purely for function with no appreciation of style or aesthetics. Such technologies are often encased in chrome and androgynous "beige plastics" to be sold in bulk to hospitals and health services. One research participant in Ireland suffering from Parkinson's disease noted that she felt so stigmatized by her unattractive, clunky "health service" walking cane that she usually attempts to negotiate the streets without support or on icy days with a more stylish but far less sturdy alternative bought by her children. Designers should challenge themselves to develop solutions that people wish to display or alternatively blend seamlessly into what Paul Dourish and Genevieve Bell (2011) call the "everyday messiness of lived experience" of those using and purchasing them.

In terms of the approach of emphasizing *what can be done*, there is a small but growing literature that suggests self-identified challenges are an essential component of sustainable behavioral change programs where the goal is to maintain or improve levels of activity or capabilities. McCabe et al. (2014) explored this with a study of both clinician-led and patient-initiated goals and educational activities for people diagnosed with chronic obstructive pulmonary disease (COPD). Participants were encouraged to work with a videographer to develop peer support materials, sharing experiences about how they had overcome challenges and the strategies they were adopting to maintain their lifestyles. One inspiring example, a woman named Betty Sutton, whose aim was to get and keep fit enough to continue to indulge her love of line dancing, became an icon to many in the Irish COPD community due to the videos she made to mentor and help others recently diagnosed with the condition.[1]

A systematic review of the mobile health (mHealth) literature indicates that the majority of studies to date have focused on aspects such as the remote monitoring and measuring of vital signs, most unfortunately neglecting the motivational, psychological, and social factors underlying ongoing use and engagement with assistive and chronic disease management health care technologies (Free et al. 2013). The health psychologist John Dinsmore notes that current studies show a lack of patient adherence to learned practices after the completion of a healthy lifestyle intervention and calls for longer-term, interactive programs designed to sustain change and engagement (Dinsmore 2015). He argues that most apps claiming to facilitate the self-management of chronic diseases "not only have poor content but also lack a strong user centric design to target the condition they are developed for. As we move forward, one to one self-management coaching of patients is unlikely to be feasible or cost effective for health service providers, therefore the use of mobile, home-based video education and rehabilitation will be of increasing importance in enhancing patient outcomes" (Dinsmore 2015: 143).

(2) People Often Mark the Progression of Aging by Watershed Events such as Falls, Change of Residence, or Loss of a Loved One.

Monitoring, assessment, and early intervention are useful, but people often are in a state of healthy denial about aging and thus may not be willing to adopt technologies that are not aligned with their desired ways of living.

Erik was one of a number of participants who described a series of critical health or personal events leading to a period of extended frailty and a dangerous loss of resiliency and self-efficacy. He suggested that this moment first came to him after a fall when he realized he could no longer work and had to sell his few remaining livestock. At the other extreme of resiliency is 90-year-old Mary, from Cork in Ireland, who when asked why the television in her bedroom was unplugged, explained that she was saving it for when she got old and had to spend more time in bed. In this she was part of a minority among our sample in that she was actively planning ahead for a time when she becomes less capable. At the time of interview Mary lived with her daughter's family in a city on the southern coast of Ireland 168 miles from Dublin, where she spent most of her life. Mary married at the age of 25 and lost her husband when she was 53. To pay the mortgage she had to continue working as a civil service administrator until retirement at 65. She was delighted to stop working and enjoyed her retirement with the exception of occasional illness, a broken hip, and losing her driving license at 80. This began to place limits on her activity, and at 87 as her health began to fail she decided to take action and finally leave her home as it would make it easier for her daughter to look after her. Mary established a regular routine upon arriving in Cork and plays bridge several times a week in a local club, visits the hairdresser weekly "to keep up the beauty," and helps her daughter with the grocery shopping. Every morning she sets herself the goal of walking two blocks to the local newsagent to purchase a paper. On the way home she visits a friend for a rest and chat. Mary sees her future in terms of events she wants to see. "I hope I last until after my granddaughter's wedding. That's a milestone I set for myself, but that's only September." Seeing great-grandchildren is her current stretch goal. For now she tries to keep active and retain her mobility. Many older people measure themselves by personal indexes of aging—whether they can shower unaided, go shopping, or indeed continue gardening or line dancing. Occasionally Mary is reminded of her growing frailty, such as the time she visited a self-service restaurant and struggled with a tray she had to carry herself while walking.

There are important design insights to be gained here. Since 2007, lifelogging, biohacking, and the Quantified Self Movement have become routine activities with the proliferation of Fitbit watches, calorie-counting apps, and sleep-monitoring actigraphy devices. As Amy Farnbach Pearson reminds us, the current pursuit of wellness through "technologies of the self" hearkens back to the Victorian pursuit of the virtues of a well-regulated self. She notes, "the wearable technology of fitness trackers and pen and ink monitoring, with their promises to 'hack' our biology toward better health and to return power to the consumer through self-knowledge, is only an extension of the medical gaze. Rather than consult ourselves—do I feel good?—we turn to the authority of our data and our devices" (Farnbach Pearson 2018: 17).

It is common for older adults to use step counters or zealously monitor glucose levels, but drawing on the accounts of Mary and others, it is possible to see hints of a future where technologies will move beyond reflecting generic, decontextualized data back to their human generators. This needs to incorporate meaningful self-identified goals that are valued and achievable by sometimes deteriorating users—without destroying self-confidence. This latter caveat is important. There are some incredible technologies emerging such as qTUG[2] from the company Kinesis—a small sensor that can be placed in a patient's socks to measure walking patterns that rivals very expensive gait analysis sensing platforms used by Falls and Blackout Units in hospitals. New algorithms and methods of measurements and sensing have allowed a very complex and specialist process to be simplified and used by community-based practitioners to quantify and predict an impending falls risk. The current implementation and business model has been carefully developed over a decade and is still gaining cautious support. The ability to do this has potential to save many lives—but only if coupled with an effective intervention. Should it move to a consumer device without sufficient supports and context, accurate or not, an ongoing awareness of potentially heightened risk and monitoring of decline may run the risk of damaging self-efficacy.

Rebuilding shattered self-confidence is an important goal in itself and is a core component of many stroke rehabilitation and cognitive function programs. As Astell points out, sometimes the easiest solution to a problem facing someone with dementia, such as providing meals for them as they lose the ability to keep track of the myriad steps of food preparation, can also be most harmful. She notes this "would deprive them of the opportunity to keep exercising many important and meaningful skills, such as shopping, cooking, etc., which in turn will undermine their abilities further. Disabling people in excess of the difficulties produced by their current level of impairment is already a major burden for people with dementia" (Astell 2015: 152). Instead Astell advocates finding ways to use technology to supplement retained cognitive processes and replace impaired functions. To demonstrate this, she helped develop CIRCA (Computer Interactive Reminiscence and Conversation), a touchscreen system designed to facilitate conversation and communication between caregivers and adults with dementia (Alm et al. 2004; Purves et al. 2015). With the proliferation of tablets and smartphones and telecommunications enabling easy transfer of visual media, we will see the development of increasingly sophisticated platforms such as CIRCA that will help augment function. The technology, however, will not always be obvious.

A project called Engineering Alertness led by neuroscientist Ian Robertson at Trinity College Dublin uses galvanic skin response sensors attached a participant's fingers to measure levels of cognitive alertness. Through a home-based course delivered remotely over several weeks, older adults with mild cognitive impairment were able to train themselves to first recognize their attention level and self-alert for a short period through the use of a command word allowing themselves to concentrate on achieving a set task such as climbing the stairs and remembering a sequence (Milewski-Lopez et al. 2014). There is little doubt that well-publicized emergent technologies such as artificial intelligence, robots, the Internet of Things, and autonomous vehicles will play an essential role for aging populations in coming decades. Yet, it is the careful development and sensitive application of quiet break-throughs following on the heels of programs such as CIRCA and the Engineering Alertness Project that will make a profound difference in the lives of millions of adults suffering from dementia.

(3) Aging in Place Means More Than Staying at Home.

Independence for many does not refer to merely dwelling in a private residence, but to being able to prepare meals, shop, work in the garden, take part in community life, and remain socially active.

In 1959, the staff of Benjamin Rose Hospital in Cleveland, Ohio, led by Sidney Katz published a landmark article that outlined a new graded index for measuring activities of daily living (ADL). Departing from the medical model, the multidisciplinary team embraced a holistic approach to recording functional dependence and independence across the six key areas of bathing, dressing, toileting and continence, transferring (mobility such as walking and getting out of bed), and eating (Noeklker and Browdie 2014). In many countries these became established as basic criteria for assessing the abilities of an older adult to function independently and eligibility for assisted living supports or long-term residential care. Numerous technology companies have been developing robotic solutions for ADL problems guided by a 2014 standard for service robots known bureaucratically as ISO13482.[3] These guidelines outline the expected international safety standards required for close human-robot interactions for physical assistant robots, mobile servant robots, and person carrier robots. Resyone, a care service robot developed by Panasonic, was the first to meet this standard.[4] This commercially available robot is a bed that can transform itself into an electric wheelchair. Japan's Riken institute has taken a different approach and developed Robear,[5] a robot that can physically lift and transfer an older person from a bed to a chair. Robear creator Toshiharu Mukai is cautious, however, about its usage, stating that it was developed for academic purposes and is still too rough for older patients with delicate skin. It is also too cumbersome for many small Japanese apartments.[6] Other approaches include ongoing work by IBM's Aging in Place Lab in Austin, Texas, that has been developing MERA (Multi-purpose Eldercare Robot Assistant),[7] a robot that can interface with ambient sensors in the instrumented home and help detect falls, when the stove is on, and monitor vital signs. In terms of companionship, perhaps the most famous robot is PARO, the therapeutic robot baby harp seal that was developed to reduce stress and provide the benefits of animal therapy in environments such as hospitals or nursing homes where it is not always feasible to bring live animals. Neven and Leeson observed how successful PARO was at facilitating a feeling of "social togetherness" between the residents of a Japanese nursing home, and that the seal became an "object of desire," partly because of how the staff restricted and controlled access to the robots (Neven and Leeson 2015). Softbank have also launched a companion robot called Pepper, a half-sized humanoid robot with a screen attached to its chest, that can perceive emotion, adapt its behavior, and memorize personality traits.[8] Pepper is currently deployed in many environments, servicing use cases such as welcoming bank customers in Canada, guiding hospital patients in Belgium, and providing community engagement and memory games to older people in the United Kingdom (Purvis 2017; Olsen 2018). James Wright in Part VI of this book details the use of Pepper in a Japanese eldercare center as well as other robots in varied contexts.

However, as Astell warns, even the best services and technologies can sometimes unintentionally create their own problems in terms of further disabling their clients or only focusing on the biological or basic functional needs of older adults (2015). Companionship care especially tends to be underresourced and deprioritized. Replacing human home-care assistants with robots has the potential to create greater social isolation, loneliness, and depression. At best the emerging workforce of care service robots should be designed to augment rather than replace human care services. With both robots and service interactions designed sensitively, however, there may be "a right way to incorporate robotics and AI into how we age," as Coughlin argues. For many older adults having robots help with the most private bodily functions such as toileting may well be preferable in terms of dignity than relying on human caregivers (Coughlin 2014).

Lawton and Brody expanded the original list of basic functional ADLs to include IADLs, more complex instrumental activities of daily living. Originally focused on developing a scale for older women to continue living independently, they defined eight areas: shopping, preparing food, housekeeping, doing laundry, using transportation, using the telephone, handling finances, and taking medication (Lawton and Brody 1969). Hospital discharge planners continue to use the ADL and IADL scales for functional assessments in clinical settings (Noeklker and Browdie 2014). These eight domains are also critical areas for technologists seeking to build independent living solutions. Technologies need to go beyond basic functional needs, as a home can become a prison as well as a refuge. The frequent focus on aging in place should be interpreted as aging in the community as much as aging at home. Finding ways for older adults to continue caring for themselves is an important step beyond simply providing home care supports such as precooked meals or robots that help with showering, but designers of home care systems need also consider how an aging individual or couple are able to travel outside the physical house and make use of retail, entertainment, and social/emotional resources available within their communities.

(4) Healthy Aging Is Inextricably Linked to Social Participation.

Social relationships benefit health. Beyond simple contact and companionship, a sense of belonging to a larger group or community can provide psychosocial security, especially if it is linked to opportunities to be useful, productive, and engaged. Nobody of any age likes to feel they are a burden.

Loneliness and social isolation are among the most pressing problems for aging populations around the world. International studies estimate that between 5 and 16 percent of older people experience loneliness with significant consequences for both mental and physical health (Cacioppo and Cacioppo 2014). A well-cited meta-analytic review found a 26 percent increased likelihood of mortality for lonely people and 32 percent higher risk for adults living alone (Holt-Lunstad et al. 2015). The authors argue that heightened risk for mortality from a lack of social relationships exceeds that from obesity and may be equivalent to smoking 15 cigarettes a day. Loneliness is a subjective state of negative feeling associated with perceived social isolation. According to De Jong Gierveld and Van Tilburg, health practitioners need to differentiate between at least two forms of loneliness: (1) *social* loneliness, which stems from a perceived lack of social contacts or engaging social network; and (2) *emotional* loneliness, which is perceived as arising from the absence of an intimate relationship or close attachment (De Jong Gierveld and Van Tilburg 2006). This distinction is critical for interventions focused on encouraging greater social connectivity, as it can mean the difference between finding ways to help someone who has lost contact with the world due to contracting networks of friendships and kinship supports versus helping someone who may have lots of friends and supports but finds themselves desperately lonely in crowded room filled with friends.

Loneliness is not a steady state. Like grief and depression, it can "bubble," swell, and sweep in waves. Older adults often explain how it can strike out of the blue, sometimes in the middle of the night when they are unable to sleep or over long periods of isolation while caring for a housebound spouse. Jean, a widow from the United Kingdom, described how she had moved in with her daughter's family in the countryside after experiencing some mobility issues but rapidly found herself suffering greatly from loneliness despite a loving family bustling with activity. Jean found herself alone in the house for several hours every day while her family were out at school and work. When they arrived home, she joined them for dinner but then would withdraw to her room for much of the evening to give them privacy. Loneliness can also be particularly acute at certain times of the year or on significant dates, such as the birthday of a spouse, parent, or child who has died, or on Christmas.

A 2017 study by the charity and advocacy agency Age UK found that almost half of the older people they surveyed felt their days were repetitive and around 1.4 million adults aged 65 or older experienced Christmas as just another day, with 873,000 of these not seeing or hearing from another person for whole days over the festive period.[9]

There have been many attempts to help tackle the endemic problem of loneliness. Age UK creates television advertisements to draw attention to the issue and attempts to encourage good neighbor schemes and befriending programs.[10] A systematic literature review of the efficacy of health promotion interventions for alleviating loneliness, mainly carried out in the United States and Canada, concluded that 9 out of 10 of the most effective interventions focused on group activities with an educational or support input (Cattan et al. 2005). In other words, befriending schemes, one-on-one counseling, or providing health advice were not as effective as bringing lonely older adults into group activities with a specific purpose such as learning a new skill. The TRIL Centre Building Bridges Project brought together a research and development team to explore how online technologies can augment social connection among older adults (Wherton and Prendergast 2009). The study incorporated Cattan's findings into the platform and found similar results of heightened engagement during events we scheduled online that were of personal importance to the participants, such as talks on dementia and caregiving. The Building Bridges platform was used most frequently and enthusiastically by study participants classified as socially lonely. From the outset we aimed to create a technological tool that complements or supports rather than replaces human contact, by providing ways for people to have access to our online "tea room" any time day or night (Garattini, Wherton, and Prendergast 2012). Future research projects into loneliness will explore the efficacy of emerging augmented reality technologies. Virtual, augmented, and merged reality is already becoming familiar to us, and although it is still unwieldy, the proliferation of new virtual reality technologies such as the Microsoft Hololens, HTC Vive, and Oculus Go are driving the development of relatively inexpensive and seamless immersive technologies. The possibilities are endless. Imagine living in rural Ireland and going online to wander around Machu Picchu in real time with your adult children and grandchildren who have emigrated to Australia and Florida.

Research around how new forms of communication and online social media can help alleviate loneliness and social isolation is still very much in its infancy, though this will likely expand greatly in future years as a critical area of gerontological investigation. Connection alone is insufficient, however, as Catton explained. Most people want to feel useful, so having a productive reason to meet can frequently motivate engagement. An incredibly successful example of this over the last decade has been the growth of "Men's Sheds" around the world. Originating in Australia, the Men's Sheds project was designed to provide inviting places for men of all ages to meet and share skills and experiences.[11] The early groups focused on collectively pursuing "social good" initiatives such as repairing old bicycles for deprived communities. Today many Sheds offer a range of activities from skills-based development to exercise programs, but the core idea remains of creating an inclusive place for men to gather.

As the ethnographic case study of Erik the farmer demonstrates, a loss of mobility can often lie at the root of loneliness and depression. This may be declining personal capacity to walk and balance without falling. It can also mean loss of ability to travel easily beyond the thresholds of home because of the lack of a driving license, confidence to walk the streets, or inability to walk "the last mile" to use public transport. This is an area where technology will continue to make significant improvements in creating lives of quality for older adults. An early example of a carefully planned and tested sociotechnical system focused on transportation was Independent Transport Network America, founded by Katherine Freund in 1995 to provide an "alternative transportation solution for seniors."[12] Prompted by her three-year-old son's near fatal accident after being run over by an 84-year-old driver, Kathy set up ITNAmerica to provide affordable travel options that would allow older people to give up their driving licenses when they no longer felt comfortable on the road. This is a problem particularly in suburban and rural America where few public transit services exist. ITNAmerica recruits volunteer drivers, many of them older, to provide cheap taxi services to its members. The members get a substantial discount from normal cab services, providing they book 24 hours in advance via the automated system. People wishing to give up their licenses can trade in their cars to the organization and receive mileage credits. These can also be bought for members by relatives or earned through supermarket shopping. Volunteer drivers also receive mileage credits. Local taxi companies sometimes opt into the system during off-peak hours. This system benefits around 11,000 members and has scaled to cities across America. It is enabled technologically by an electronic booking and credit system, an innovative business model, and "humans in the loop," whether service users, drivers, or local businesses.

It is often very difficult to get access to a taxi cab at short notice in parts of America. This is changing rapidly with the growth of services such as Uber that combine seamless, app-based journey planning, booking, payment, and credit rating systems with private drivers hiring out their services. More generally the deployment of a plethora of e-hailing services, ride and bike share initiatives, "pop-up" bus routes, and integrated multimodal transport systems are ushering in a quiet revolution in "mobility as a service," which can create significant opportunities for older people to travel more easily outside their homes. All may be problematic, however, especially for users without smartphones or who are unfamiliar with the idea of just-in-time booking.

Trust of unregulated drivers and automatic payment services are also issues for many users. It was to explore these issues as well as consider how best to design autonomous vehicles to best cater for the needs of older adults that led to the establishment of the AV65+ project between Intel, Maynooth University, and Science Foundation Ireland. This study is interviewing older drivers, nondrivers, and people who are in the process of ceasing to drive in Italy, Germany, Ireland, and the United Kingdom (McGoughlin, Prendergast, and Donnellan 2018).

Multiple layers of skyways filled with flying cars as envisaged in the film *Blade Runner* are unlikely to be with us in the immediate future, though passenger drone taxis are already being evaluated by the city of Dubai.[13] Semiautonomous cars are also becoming the norm, though fully automated driverless ground vehicles cars are unlikely to form the majority of road traffic until midcentury or later. Many car manufacturers are already adding advanced driver assistance systems (ADAS) to their products such as automatic braking and parking, adaptive cruise control, collision avoidance, driver drowsiness detection, blind spot detection, and night vision. Lane assistance and vehicle-to-vehicle/infrastructure communication will also become commonplace. These innovations can significantly extend the driving life of an older driver whose arthritis makes it difficult to look over their shoulder, whose reactions have slowed, or who longer drives in twilight or after dark due to diminished eyesight or confidence. Older and disabled people are often represented as core market for the development of the partial and fully autonomous vehicle, yet surprisingly little research on the potential for adoption of assisted and autonomous vehicles has been done with this important demographic. Older people are seldom early adopters of technology and are also the market segment most skeptical about dependability and surrendering control to a full autonomous system (Abraham et al. 2016). If we want to build trust and encourage older people to become lead users, then we need to properly attempt to understand how the mobility needs, challenges, and behaviors of older adults in different geographies change through the later life course. We must also consider how current and future advanced driver assistance systems (ADAS) and autonomous systems may both assist and hinder mobility of people who require not just door-to-door—but arm-to-arm service.

(5) Health Is Not an Objective Quality.

Health is defined collaboratively through social interaction and personal and cultural history and is often the outcome of complex negotiations between all manner of stakeholders.

As Erving Goffman famously examined in his 1963 book on stigma, people work to manage impressions of themselves, often using concealment, in order to protect their identities, particularly when they feel they are likely to be stigmatized or perceived as departing from an approved or agreed standard or norm. Older adults may conceal financial worries from their children, alcoholics who fall might blame the cat, and a driver might minimize the effect of declining eyesight, memory, or wayfinding abilities in order to retain their driving license. Likewise caregivers, health professionals, and friends in a care network may underestimate or misunderstand complex capabilities and unintentionally infantilize an older adult. Assessments of health and ability can vary from person to person, even within the same family. Issues around decision-making and competencies can become particularly stressful during key stages in the later life course, particularly in relation to discussions about whether someone has lost the ability to live independently and requires long-term care. Actions following this decision to move an older adult out of their own home to live with their children or into sheltered accommodation, a retirement home, or nursing facility can vary widely according to cultural norms and supports available.

One critical element for independent living not mentioned so far is the economic cost of providing assistive and telecare services to enable people to remain at home. There has been considerable experimentation with shifting homecare services from a *direct provision model*, where health services hire and manage nurses and domiciliary care workers going into the home of an older adult, to a *financing model*, where public monies (or an insurer) contributes towards some or all of the costs of home-based supports, often delivered by third-party commercial or nonprofit providers (Timonen, Doyle, and Prendergast 2006). In practice, however, a hybrid model of care is emerging in many countries (see Part VI Clotworthy). In the United Kingdom and Ireland, the national health care systems have been developing financial "homecare packages" that are provided as part of a hospital discharge process. These funds are attached to a patient, depending on their needs, but often with considerable latitude about how, and with whom, the older adult can spend the budget. There has been a subsequent expansion in the number of private companies offering a wide span of home care services. These range from skilled nursing care to domiciliary help with cooking and cleaning, to advanced telehealth systems that help consumers, monitor their conditions, set collectively agreed behavioral change goals, measure sleep and exercise patterns, and have access to personal emergency response systems (PERS) in the event of a critical incident such as a fall, stroke, or heart attack.

Equally important is supporting family caregivers. Frequently the point of hospitalization arrives, not at some well-defined apex of ill health for the patient, but when the primary carer—whether spouse, child, or friend—feels they can no longer cope. Caregiving, especially over a long period of time, can be physically, emotionally, and financially exhausting, often leading to depression, poor health, and social isolation. Finding ways to support caregivers and prevent caregiver burnout will be a major challenge of the future. It was for this reason that the TRIL Centre invested heavily in research into clinical scales that measure psychological distress among caregivers of people with dementia. We embedded this measurement tool into a computer tablet called the Caregiver's Companion that asked caregivers daily questions about their feelings and activities (McHugh et al. 2012; Schnittger et al. 2012). Based on the responses, a series of targeted actions were generated including identifying supports and needs-driven access to professional and peer-driven information in many formats. Just for context about the scale of this issue, in the United States in 2013, 40 million family caregivers provided 37 billion hours of care to older adults (Jenkins 2016).

How will an increasingly complex mixture of services look from the perspective of a 90-year-old woman who has recently lost her husband? Will bots or new "virtual concierge services" following on the heels of Hello Alfred or Honor help her navigate the organizational and bureaucratic pathways of health care? Ensuring that the "digital divide" does not exclude many older people from access to services of all types of course requires more than providing technology hardware. It requires that we pay attention to what Mackey and Jacobsen term "metaliteracy"—not only the multiple forms of information, media, and digital and cyber literacy but also how people learn and communicate, produce and share in "participatory digital environments" (Mackey and Jacobsen 2011). This applies for caregivers as well as care recipients. New ways of mapping services and reliably updating information systems in real time are needed. Intel together with local academic and community partners conducted a survey of every service for older people they could identify in Southampton, England, and Stoneybatter in Dublin, Ireland. Researchers quickly compiled a complex and overlapping directory of resources ranging from health services to energy grants, home repair, information advisories, sport and exercise, and retail venues with discounts and offers for older people. Many of these services were unknown to local residents and officials alike. Some agencies like Age UK attempt to keep lists of services, but these are seldom exhaustive and can rapidly become outdated. In Ireland, numerous cities and communities are striving to become age-friendly environments, revamping facilities and support systems and rethinking spatial and transport access, and some are building directories of services for older people. These are gradually becoming easier to maintain, update, and rate online, but good search tools that can be easily used by older adults will be required for this flood of data. For the immediate future, regularly refreshed hardcopy paper versions will remain important for many older adults. Helping citizens navigate the complex webs of services, options, and activities within the digital life course will be a key task for local authorities. The "smart cities" of the future need to think beyond wireless sensor networks, energy management, and litter collection to these more human-scale issues if they are to become truly intelligent.

Conclusion

As Joseph Coughlin suggests, there is good reason to be cautiously optimistic about the opportunities of technology to lessen the "frictions of aging" (2018b). This chapter has briefly explored a selection of state-of-the-art and emergent technologies across a broad range of use cases, from tackling social loneliness, falls, cognitive decline, transport, and mobility, to navigating complex organizations and patient-centered, holistic approaches to health care. The core message, however, is that for these technologies to work most effectively, we as anthropologists, designers, engineers, and clinicians must consider and understand how they are or will be embedded in social practice and have value within the daily lives of their users. As Elizabeth Shove and Mika Pantzer point out: "Products alone have no value. They do so only when integrated into practice . . . and forms of competence and meaning" (2005).

The case study of Erik poignantly reminds us that aging in place needs to be about more than just smart homes, robots, or providing good home care services. We need to get better at keeping older adults socially connected and engaged, with access to options for meaningful, productive activity. Everybody wants to feel they can be useful. How do we develop reliable and flexible alternative transportation possibilities following the loss of a driver's license, or that cater to challenging needs such as memory loss, incontinence, or arm-to-arm care? We need to get better at predicting and preventing falls and adapting to other health-related life changes, but also at rebuilding shattered confidence and helping individuals regain resilience and self-efficacy, all while avoiding stigmatizing labels. Designers need to think about how older people learn and how needs are not static but unfold over time. We can think holistically about an individual's care ecosystem, engineering systems that give voice and reflect and support the roles of different participants, including caregivers, but this must be done while considering economics, power dynamics, and decision-making hierarchies as well as how to protect privacy and dignity. As we imagine, plan, and navigate across the myriad digital life courses of the future, many research challenges lie ahead if we are to build lives of quality for those wishing to age in place. Technology is simply a tool. It is understanding the complexities of how, what, when, and why we design and apply technology that will determine its success, and for that, ethnography can help.

Notes

1. https://youtu.be/VgXw977SfNA.
2. http://www.qtug.org/.
3. https://www.iso.org/standard/53820.html.

4. https://news.panasonic.com/global/topics/2014/26411.html.

5. http://www.riken.jp/en/pr/press/2015/20150223_2/.

6. https://foreignpolicy.com/2017/03/01/japan-prefers-robot-bears-to-foreign-nurses/.

7. https://www.ibm.com/able/aging/.

8. Initially developed in 2014, 12,000 units have been sold by 2018 at a price of $23,000 each. Softbank plans to scale production dramatically.

9. https://www.ageuk.org.uk/latest-news/articles/2017/december/almost-a-million-older-people-feel-lonelier-at-christmas/.

10. https://youtu.be/inyaBPWdZIM.

11. https://mensshed.org/what-is-a-mens-shed/.

12. https://itnamerica.org/.

13. https://www.youtube.com/watch?v=qArZGwtRINg.

Bibliography

Abraham, H., C. Lee, S. Brady, C. Fitzgerald, B. Mehler, B. Reimer, and J. Coughlin. 2016. *Autonomous Vehicles, Trust and Driving Alternatives: A Survey of Consumer Preferences.* MIT AgeLab White Paper.

Alm, N., A. Astells, M. Ellis, R. Dye, G. Gowans, and J. Campbell, J. 2004. "A Cognitive Prosthesis and Communication Support for People with Dementia," *Neuropsychological Rehabilitation* 14(1–2).

Astell, A. 2015. "Supporting a Good Life with Dementia." In *Aging and the Digital Life Course*, edited by D. Prendergast and C. Garattini. Oxford: Berghahn.

Cacioppo, J. T., and S. Cacioppo. 2014. "Social Relationships and Health: The Toxic Effects of Perceived Social Isolation." *Social and Personality Psychology Compass* 8(2): 58–72.

Cattan, M., M. White, J. Bond, and A. Learmouth. 2005. "Preventing Social Isolation and Loneliness among Older People: A Systematic Review of Health Promotion Interventions." *Aging and Society* 25(1): 41–67.

Coughlin, J. 2014. "Caregiving Takes Two Hands: High Tough & High Tech." https://bigthink.com/disruptive_demographics/caregiving-needs-high-touch-high-tech/.

Coughlin, J. 2017. *The Longevity Economy: Unlocking the World's Fastest Growing, Most Misunderstood Market.* New York: Public Affairs.

Coughlin, J. 2018a. "What Does the Smart City of the Future Look Like?" https://www.bluezones.com/2017/11/city-of-the-future/.

Coughlin, J. 2018b. "Caregiver Crunch? No Problem, This Is How Tech-Savvy Millennials Will Care for Aging Baby Boomers." *Forbes*, May 21.

De Jong Gierveld, J., and T. Van Tilburg. 2006. "A 6-Item Scale for Overall, Emotional and Social Loneliness: Confirmatory Tests on Survey Data." *Research on Aging* 28(5): 582–98.

Dinsmore, J. 2015. "Avoiding the 'Iceberg Effect': Incorporating a Behaviourial Change Approach to Technology Design in Chronic Illness." In *Aging and the Digital Life Course,* edited by D. Prendergast and C. Garattini. Oxford: Berghahn.

Dourish, P., and G. Bell. 2011. *Divining a Digital Future: Mess and Mythology in Ubiquitous Computing.* Cambridge, MA: MIT Press.

Eurostat. 2019. *Ageing Europe: Looking at the Lives of Older People in the EU – 2019 Edition.* Luxembourg: Publications Office of the European Union.

Farnbach Pearson, A. W. 2018. "False Steps: Biohacking and Fitbits Promise Better Health, but Deliver a Very Victorian Mindset." *Anthropology News* 59(1).

Free, C., G. Philips, L. Galli, L. Watson, L. Felix, P. Edward, V. Patel, and A. Haines. 2013. "The Effectiveness of Mobile-Health Technology Based Health Behavior Change or Disease Management Interventions for Health Care Consumers: A Systematic Review." *PLOS Medicine* 10(1).

Garattini, C., J. Wherton, and D. Prendergast. 2012. "Linking the Lonely: An Exploration of a Communication Technology Designed to Support Social Interaction among Older Adults." *Universal Access in the Information Society* 11(2): 211–22.

Goffman, E. 1963. *Stigma: Notes on the Management of Spoiled Identity.* Englewood Cliffs, NJ: Prentice-Hall.

Holt-Lunstad, J., T. B. Smith, M. Baker, T. Harris, and D. Stephenson. 2015. "Loneliness and Social Isolation as Risk Factors for Mortality: A Meta-analytic Review." *Perspectives on Psychological Science* 10: 227–37.

Jenkins, J. 2016. "Caregiving Costly to Caregivers." American Association of Retired Persons. https://www.aarp.org/caregiving/financial-legal/info-2017/family-caregiving-costly-jj.html.

Lawton, M. P., and E. Brody. 1969. "Assessment of Older People: Self-Maintaining and Instrumental Activities of Daily Living." *Gerontologist* 9(3).

Mackey, T., and T. Jacobson. 2011. "Reframing Information Literacy as Metaliteracy." *College & Research Libraries* 70(1).

McCabe, C., J. Dinsmore, A. Brady, and D. Prendergast. 2014. "Using Action Research and Peer Perspectives to Develop Technology That Facilitates Behavioural Change and Self- Management in COPD." *International Journal of Telemedicine and Applications* 15.

McGoughlin, S., D. Prendergast, and B. Donnellan. 2018. "Autonomous Vehicles for Independent Living of Older Adults—Insights and Directions for a Cross-European Qualitative Study." 7th International Conference on Smart Cities and Green ICT Systems (SMARTGREENS).

McHugh, J., J. Wherton, D. Prendergast, and B. Lawlor. 2012. "Identifying Opportunities for Supporting Caregivers of Persons with Dementia through Information and Communication Technology." *Gerontechnology* 10(4): 220–30.

Milewski-Lopez, A., E. Greco, F. van den Berg, L. P. McAvinue, S. McGuire, and I. H. Robertson. 2014. "An Evaluation of Alertness Training for Older Adults." *Frontiers in Aging Neuroscience* 6.

Neven, L., and C. Leeson. 2015. "Beyond Determinism: Understanding Actual Use of Social Robots by Older People." In *Aging and the Digital Life Course*, edited by D. Prendergast and C. Garattini. Oxford: Berghahn.

Noelklker, L., and R. Browdie. 2014. "Sidney Katz, MD: A New Paradigm for Chronic Illness and Long-Term Care." *Gerontologist* 54(1).

Olsen, P. 2018. "Softbank's Robotics Business Prepares to Scale Up." *Forbes*. May 30.

Plowman, T., D. Prendergast, and S. Roberts. 2009. "The Global Aging Experience: From People to Prototypes and Products." *Intel Technology Journal* 13(3).

Plowman, T., D. Prendergast, and S. Roberts. 2010. "The Global Aging Experience Project: Anthropology, Technology and Independent Living." *Gerontechnology* 9(2).

Prendergast, D., and C. Garattini, eds. 2015. *Aging and the Digital Life-Course*. Oxford: Berghahn.

Prendergast, D., and S. Roberts. 2009. "Practice, Systems and Technology for Seniors." *Universal Access in the Information Society* 8(1).

Purves, B. A., A. Phinney, W. Hulko, G. Puurveen, and A. J. Astell. 2015. "Developing CIRCA-BC and Exploring the Role of the Computer as a Third Participant in Conversation." *American Journal of Alzheimers Disease and Other Dementias* 30(1): 101–7.

Purvis, K. 2017. "Meet Pepper the Robot—Southend's Newest Social Care Recruit." *The Guardian*. October 16.

Schnittger, R., J. Wherton, B. Lawlor, and D. Prendergast. 2012. "Risk Factors and Mediating Pathways of Loneliness and Social Support in Community-Dwelling Older Adults." *Aging and Mental Health* 16(3): 335–46.

Scrambler, G. 2008. "Deviance, Sick Role and Stigma." In *Sociology as Applied to Medicine*. 6th ed., edited by G. Scrambler, 205–17. Philadelphia: Saunders Elsevier.

Shove, E., and M. Pantzer. 2005. "Consumers, Producers and Practices: Understanding the Invention and Reinvention of Nordic Walking." *Journal of Consumer Culture* 5(1): 43–64.

Timonen, V., M. Doyle, and D. Prendergast. 2006. *No Place Like Home: Domiciliary Care Services for Older People in Ireland*. Dublin: Liffey.

Wherton, J., and D. Prendergast. 2009. "The Building Bridges Project: Involving Older Adults in the Design of a Communication Technology to Support Peer-to-Peer Social Engagement." In *HCI and Usability for e-Inclusion*, edited by A. Holzinger and K. Miesenberger. Berlin: Springer-Verlag.

CHAPTER TWELVE

Imagining Institutional Care, Practicing Domestic Care

Inscriptions around Aging in Southern Ghana

Cati Coe

In July 2014, an aged fellowship group within the Presbyterian Church of Ghana presented a play about their predicaments. The play told the stories of two exemplary aging couples in a rural town who raised their children to be educated and Christian, to the extent of going into debt to pay their school fees. Although the children of one of these couples remitted to them once they had completed school and migrated to the city, the migrant children of the second couple cut off contact with them and accused them of witchcraft, perhaps as an excuse to stop supporting them.[1] The play revealed older people's concerns about abandonment in small towns in southern Ghana, and the criticisms that older adults are beginning to launch, laments that are meant to incite others to proper action (see Cattell 1999).

As the play illustrated, social norms in Ghana deem adult children particularly responsible for an aged person's care because of the contributions parents have made to their children's biological and social personhood (Coe 2011). Kin care is the orthodox position, in the terminology of Bourdieu, meaning that it is the conventional, formulaic, and normative position (1977). It is the only position articulated and promoted by the state and NGOs that advocate for older adults and with whom the state has written its unenacted aged policy. It coincides with local discourse, which similarly emphasizes the morality of kin care. Isabella Aboderin has noted that this onus on adult children constitutes a shrinking of the network of responsibility for care and is connected to changes in inheritance that increasingly privilege children over other members of extended kin (2006). As Ghana goes through a demographic transition in which people are living longer and increasingly with chronic diseases (de-Graft Aikins et al. 2012), the sense of an old age crisis generates a particular narrative about aging that focuses attention on adult children's failure to meet their caring obligations and older people's risk of neglect and abandonment (Apt 1996; Aboderin 2006; Dsane 2013). It is because the discourse on abandonment is dominant and somewhat standardized that the neglect of older adults can be presented publicly in the form of a play, by a church group. Simultaneous with the strong critique of adult children, however, are various age-inscriptions. As noted by Coe and Alber, age-inscriptions are fragmented, hesitant discourses (2018). They are largely unacknowledged, seldom-discussed practices that do not correspond to existing norms, but may become normative one day. As a result, age-inscriptions are highly significant in understanding social change.

According to Bourdieu (1977), what is articulated as orthodoxy can also be challenged by other ideas and discourses, which he calls *heterodoxies*. These are positions that are not shared by all and not even intended to be legitimized as such, but are nevertheless shared by some. However, not all alternative discourses and practices are heterodox, set up in direct opposition to the orthodoxy. Instead, some of these discourses and practices are simply alternatives, designated with the term *alterodoxies* (Coe and Alber 2018). Those whose children were living up to their obligations were content with the current arrangements. It was those who perceived the reliance on adult children's support to be precarious who were open to exploring alterodoxies. These alterodox age-inscriptions urged acceptance of children's financial and emotional limitations and expressed openness to alternative arrangements, including hiring a domestic servant to care for an aging person and articulating an interest in old age homes as a solution to the problems older adults face.

As discussed by Coe and Alber (2018), knowledge of other societies' aging trajectories can be used to harden national boundaries and cultural identities (Amselle 2002). Even when negatively evaluated through contrasting dichotomies (Sewell 2005), as in "we do things this way and they do it that way" or "this is traditional and that is modern," such dichotomies can introduce heterodoxies that can become incorporated as possible solutions when "the way that we do things" or an orthodoxy no longer seems to be viable or reliable. Arjun Appadurai expresses it this way: "Lives today are as much acts of projection and imagination as they are enactments of known scripts or predictable outcomes" (1996: 205). Cultural resources in the form of ideas and practices are necessary for the acts of projection and imagination that Appadurai discusses. Ideas and institutions travel and are translated. Sarah Lamb discusses how old age homes have traveled to India, despite representing an "alien, Western-inspired institution," and have been adapted to the local context (2016: 183, Part V Lamb). In Ghana, the resources for age-inscriptions include representations from societies constructed as "Other" and different, as illustrated in the interest in institutional facilities for older persons. However, age-inscriptions also come from within, such as through adaptations of familiar practices like child fostering, or substitutions of adjacent relations. These age-inscriptions are less articulated and formulated than standardized discourses about the significance of children's care in old age, although they are shaped by this dominant discourse.

The use of old age homes to think through the problems of aging means that older persons situate themselves—and Ghana—within a "global horizon" of value and orientation, and not simply within a social field of kin (Graw and Schielke 2012). Within this wider horizon of the social fields of nations, Ghana is positioned as failing; other nations are used by older congregants to criticize the inadequate efforts of the Ghana government. The unfamiliar thus becomes an important hook on which older adults can hang their dreams of a good old age. Alongside the discourses of critique of the next generation, there was a willingness to experiment and engage imaginatively with different possible futures, including ones that were perceived as foreign or even antithetical to Ghanaian ways of life. This chapter thus highlights the important role the social imagination plays in generating social change in aging and care practices, and the ways that these coexist and do not always converge with actual practice.

The age-inscriptions being generated in Ghana signal the agency of older persons, which is often neglected and overlooked. As Jennifer Cole has discussed, we in the West have a "synoptic illusion," that is a normative, simplified assumption, which views young people as a source of social change and newness and older adults more engaged in cultural preservation and conservation (2013). Yet, as she notes, "the movement toward old age is a profoundly innovative process" for those who are aging and encountering new circumstances of bodily decline and changing social networks (226). As this stage of life becomes more expansive—lasting a decade or more—new questions about its meaning and practices need to be answered by those who are encountering aging (see Thelen and Coe 2017). This article highlights the agency of older adults in imagining their futures, criticizing the status quo, and pragmatically adjusting their strategies.

Older persons draw on the cultural and social resources available to them, including normative age narratives, in making the personal transitions of aging. They also create new social forms and possibilities as they undergo personal and social transformation and encounter new life problems.

Sometimes, in my research, older people seemed more open to possibilities that differ from the norm of a child's care precisely because they acknowledge that the norm seems unlikely. However in my conversations with younger people, they were often more categorical and judgmental about deviations from the ideal, such as saying, "In Ghana, we do not use old age homes" and "We take care of our elderly." Although I heard laments and complaints in my visits with Ghanaian older adults, I also heard resignation to the existing circumstances that led to pragmatic, solution-oriented approaches and political critique, particularly from older women who sympathized with the economic struggles of their children and tended to be poorer than older men. This line of thinking included age-inscriptions and a desire to explore them further. Despite their variability, these discourses and imaginaries arise from a common ground, the topic of the play: a shared sense that the contemporary situation places older adults at risk of neglect.

There is no standard definition of what it means to be an older adult in Ghana. For many, the marker is physical, with frailty and debility more significant than age per se. Those in the civil service—including teachers, police, and medical personnel—tend to use the compulsory retirement age of 60 as the definition of old age, but very few people are employed in the civil service and have an opportunity to "retire."[2] The Ghana census designates those over the age of 65 to be old, while the Presbyterian Church considers only those over 75 years to be eligible to participate in its aging programs.

In thinking about aging and social change, we need to account for the use of heterodox discourses and alterodox practices that go unremarked, as well as the lack of fit between them. The state's relative silence about and lack of attention to aging creates a weak hegemonic discourse about aging solutions. As a result, older people in Ghana have the space to construct new practices and heterodox discourses, however tentative and disconnected, from which new norms may be generated.

Understanding Age-Inscriptions in Southern Ghana: Methodology and Setting

This chapter draws from my conversations with older people in Akropong, Kwahu, and Akim in the Eastern Region who were involved in the Presbyterian Church, though I situate these discussions within the context of other aging initiatives happening in Ghana. It is based on fieldwork that I conducted sequentially from 2013 to 2015 (about 20 weeks in duration over three years).

My research on changes in old age care was prompted by my visit to the town and district capital of Akropong in the Eastern Region in June 2013, after a four-year absence. During my visit, I learned that the building in progress next to Christchurch, the main Presbyterian church in the town, was intended to be a senior day center.

On Sundays, the congregation of Christchurch is dominated by older women, who are sometimes living with and looking after their grandchildren or great-grandchildren because the middle-aged generation lived and worked in the major cities in Ghana. Another reason for the absence of young people in Presbyterian congregations is that they are more attracted to Pentecostalism or other new churches with a dynamic minister and founder. Thus, it makes sense that the Presbyterian church was trying to meet the needs of its aging congregation.

The church was already organizing quarterly day-long gatherings of congregants aged 75 and over as well as sending a nurse to visit older congregants regularly in their homes, to check their blood pressure and blood sugar and give them health advice. I was able to attend one of their quarterly gatherings in June 2013, including accompanying the driver in the church van to collect and return some of the participants who could not walk to the church on their own. Before and after the program, I interviewed the organizers and a few participants. I also interviewed the nurse in charge of the program, who had just retired from the position, and her assistant, who would take over the program. I read through the nurse's detailed records of her activities over the past several years, and accompanied her assistant as she visited several older congregants' households on three days, one day in June 2013 and two days in July 2014.

The Presbyterian Church of Ghana has organized aged fellowship groups in two other districts, Kwahu and Akim, also in the Eastern Region. These districts contained towns like Akropong with a long history of Presbyterian activity and in which Presbyterianism is the dominant religion of the town (Gilbert 1995). I visited both Kwahu and Akim, spending a week in each one in June 2014, and with the help of the district minister, attended hour-long programs of several aged fellowship groups with 50 to 75 people in attendance: seven meetings in Akim and eight in Kwahu.

In Akim, these meetings were mainly organizational ones, in which the ministers expressed their interest in expanding and institutionalizing the aged program, and I asked the older attendees about their problems and their thoughts about solutions to those problems. Attendees expected me, as a foreign visitor, to give some assistance and often articulated pleas for help, despite the ministers' and my repeated explanations of my actual role as an ethnographer. At the same time, with the encouragement of the ministers, the attendees thought about what the church might do to support them, and what they could do on their own. At one of these meetings, the participants engaged in their regular activities of singing Presbyterian hymns while doing exercises (Photo 12.1).

In Kwahu, where the aged fellowship groups met regularly once a week, organized under the auspices of older congregants rather than ministers, I was less often a participant than an observer to their ongoing programs,

Photo 12.1   Members of the Aged Fellowship Group from New Tafo singing hymns while exercising, July 11, 2014. (Photo by Cati Coe)

which focused on singing and dancing, board games, religious sermons, health information, and competitions and debates. These group discussions and meetings in Akim and Kwahu were more superficial than my discussions with those in Akropong, where I knew many more people and had ongoing relationships. Furthermore, those in attendance were by necessity those older persons who could walk from their homes to the church for the meeting, or had the resources to organize and fund their transportation there. Although they were well and relatively strong, in the discussions they referenced neighbors and friends who were more frail or bed-bound and could not attend these meetings.

I also explored events happening in Accra and its twin city Tema, visiting a senior day center run by the St. Vincent de Paul Society of the Catholic Church several times and three old age homes, talking to the organizers and some of the attendees and residents. I talked to several leaders of HelpAge Ghana, the major advocacy group on aging in Ghana, as well as key members of the Presbyterian Church and the Catholic Church, who seemed among the other churches the most interested in aging issues. I also visited an NGO in the Volta Region that organized support groups for older adults. I attended three gatherings of the NGO accompanied by the founder and head organizer, who was personally affiliated with the Evangelical Presbyterian Church of Ghana: one in which they prepared a porridge to teach participants about nutrition and a potential income-earning activity, a second in which the participants were served a hot meal, and a third in which the participants sang and had their blood pressure monitored.

According to the 2010 population census in Ghana, those over the age of 65 constitute 4.6 percent of the population, or about 1 million people out of a total population of 24.7 million (Ghana Statistical Service 2012). Women are 57 percent of those 1 million; 43 percent are men. After the Volta Region, where 6.4 percent of the population is over the age of 65, the Eastern Region has the next highest proportion of older adults (5.7% of the population). But in the North Akwapim district, where Akropong is located, 8.18 percent of the population is over the age of 65; in Kwahu South and East, the districts of the towns I visited, the proportions were 7.35 percent and 8.14 percent respectively. In the three districts in Akim that I visited (Akim East, Akim West, and Kwaebibirim), the proportions were lower, at 5.51 percent, 6.7 percent, and 4.85 percent respectively, but still included more older people than was true of Ghana as a whole. The towns in the Eastern Region where the Presbyterian Church is dominant thus, in general, have a higher proportion of older adults, probably because of the migration of the middle-aged population to the larger cities. This may account for why there are new initiatives for older adults in these places, prompted by the Presbyterian Church, as well as why older people in these towns are inscribing age in new ways.[3] The history of missionization in these areas means that many older adults are educated, including many literate older women, although there are other areas in southern Ghana with higher rates of education.

From my conversations with ministers and elders within the Presbyterian Church, religious leaders are deeply ambivalent about aging initiatives. Most congregations do not have strong social welfare missions but instead are influenced by the Prosperity Gospel, in which wealth is a sign of God's blessings. To that end, church construction seems a major goal of many congregations. Most of the congregations in these towns have rebuilt their older, modest churches and ministers' residences into spectacular buildings with tiled floors, glass windows, and wooden ceilings. Accompanying ministers in Kwahu, I noticed that when two ministers met one another, they quickly entered into a conversation about construction, discussing the price of cement bags, for example, or commenting on the aesthetic of the tiles in another's church. Within this environment focused on church building, ministers and church elders were concerned that supporting the aged would solely be a drain on church financial resources. The Presbyterian Church is interested in attracting young and middle-aged people into their congregations because they are the income earners who can give money. Older women, on the other hand, are stereotypically portrayed as devout but impoverished, putting only small coins into the collection boxes. In a religious environment in which the mainline churches have lost their younger members to the newer churches, the Presbyterian Church is becoming more like the new churches in its rhetoric and, to some extent, its programming. Thus, while the Presbyterian Church might be a source of new age norms and new programs to support the aged, its voice in this regard is muted by competing demands and goals. There are ministers and elders in the church who are pushing it to support the aged, but there are others who find the focus irrelevant or distracting from the long-term survival and growth of the church.

The State's Role in Shaping Norms About Old Age Care

Government policy documents on aging uphold Ghanaian families as the proper site for the care of senior citizens. Successive governments, since the 1990s, have explicitly advocated against old age homes, as I discuss below. The state constructs its draft Aged Policy around a traditional, idealized Ghanaian family, and highlights the expense, foreignness, and inappropriateness of other countries' approaches. Instead, state resources in Ghana seem to be concentrated on the futures of the young (Doh 2012). As Sjaak van der Geest has argued, this approach seems to ignore the plight of the aged in Ghana and presents the government as needing to do little to support senior citizens (2016). One indication of the government's lack of concern for older adults is that, although it drafted an aged policy almost 10 years ago, Parliament has still not passed this policy (GhanaWeb 2018).

Influential NGOs like HelpAge Ghana have had a major hand in shaping government policy in this area, in which the orthodoxy is a discouragement of old age homes. A founder of HelpAge in Ghana, a psychiatrist, said about old age homes:

> To remove the old people, segregate them and put them into a place: one, you are going to put them in an unnatural environment. Number two, we think that they cannot be looked after very well [in these environments]. Thirdly, they will have to pay a lot of money to do it, unless government supports it, and we are against even government providing such facilities, unless that person is severely ill and infirm and has to be in a facility. Even that one, we would still want the person to manage at home.[4]

Mrs. Ollennu, another founder of HelpAge in Ghana, said more diplomatically: "HelpAge is not keen to establish homes. Rather, they should stay with their families, whatever family is available, because it is not easy."[5] HelpAge emphasizes policies Ghana should avoid, like residential facilities, rather than what Ghana should do.

Photo 12.2 The completed, but mainly unused, senior day center, Akropong, December 29, 2016. (Photo by Cati Coe)

Nana Araba Apt, *the* sociologist of aging in Ghana, also considers old age homes to be antithetical to Ghanaian kinship, as well as too expensive for government budgets (1991, 1996). She was active in shaping government policy and HelpAge's advocacy during the 1990s and early 2000s, including writing a draft aged policy for the government in 2002. In her report to the Department of Finance and Economics, she said that institutionalization of older adults in residential facilities should be the final alternative and that emphasis should be placed on options that support kin care and keep older adults in their households (Apt 1991).[6]

Although HelpAge Ghana was strongly against the establishment of old age homes, it did set up several senior day centers in the capital city Accra in 1992 and 1993 (Ayete-Nyampong 2008).[7] These centers provided a hot meal, activities like games, a nurse on site to conduct medical checks, and occasional excursions for participants. Of these centers, all but one in the Osu neighborhood of Accra are now defunct. I visited the Osu center in June 2014; it is under the management of a young man and a retired nurse. It is these defunct senior day centers in Accra that served as the inspiration for the construction of the senior day center (Photo 12.2) in Akropong. However, while the building was completed in 2017, it is now only used for quarterly gatherings of older people.

Similar to my discussions with older Presbyterians in Akropong, Kwahu, and Akim, van der Geest noted an openness to old age homes in his discussions with older people in Kwahu, where he has long done research (2016). Given government policy and NGO advocacy against institutional facilities, it is surprising that older Ghanaians find them attractive. Yet precisely because the social norm of kin care is perceived as not working and because the government is not implementing alternative solutions, there is some agentive space for older people to develop age-inscriptions, in the forms of alterodox discourses, practices, and solutions. Older adults perceive current government policy as disregarding them and blame their plight on a lack of state care. Thus, in the absence of a strong state policy about what to do, they are free—or perhaps forced—to imagine their own solutions to the difficulties they face.

Why an Interest in Institutional Facilities?

There are four actual old age homes operating in Ghana to my knowledge: three in the capital Accra and one on its far outskirts. They are small by American standards; the largest has 27 residents. They are all heavily subsidized by their owners, who operate the facilities as charitable enterprises, although some of the residents pay fees. HelpAge views these residential facilities as the institutionalization of older adults, an option that it suggests Ghana not pursue, but owners are interested in finding a way to meet a need and hopefully make a profit. Owners report that the cost of care is the biggest barrier to attracting and keeping residents. As a result, the main clientele are return migrants or those whose children are international migrants, both of which can afford such care. Despite the small number of institutional facilities that are operating in Ghana and their difficulties with financial viability, there is considerable discussion of them as an imagined or potential institutional solution among those concerned about older adults. Some owners of home nursing agencies, along with the manager of the St. Vincent de Paul Center in Accra-Tema and the Kwahu Presbytery of the Presbyterian Church of Ghana, expressed their eagerness to build old age homes.

The institutional residences operating in Ghana are not known to the older people I spoke to in Akropong, Kwahu, and Akim, nor have these older adults visited them. Instead, they imagine old age homes operating in other countries, namely, in Europe and North America. They do not seem to be influenced by Ghanaian migrants in the United Kingdom and United States who work in these kinds of facilities and whose representations of these care environments tend to be quite critical and even horrific. Thus, Presbyterian congregants' knowledge of old age homes arises from highly general discourses in Ghana in which, "We take care of our own older people, unlike you [foreigners] who put your older adults in an old age home." Old age homes were discursively set up as the heterodox position to the orthodoxy of kin care, without concrete representations of what they are like. This heterodox position is therefore available for aged persons to promote and reimagine.

The Attractions of Institutional Facilities: A Heterodox Idea, But Not a Practice

What made old age homes attractive in theory to the older people I talked to in Akropong, Kwahu, and Akim in 2013–2015? First, old age homes were seen as places of sociability, where older people could gather to talk to one another. Living alone was common among older people in towns in southern Ghana, because their children had migrated to the cities. "Our children have grown and left us at home," said one old man, and "we are alone." Loneliness was considered a major problem for older adults, causing illness, depression, and ultimately death. A man said, "Sadness . . . kills people." A woman said, "If you get something to amuse yourself, then you won't be thinking [worrying] too much." Another man said, "Staying in one place . . . is bitter, and a person's spirit declines. Maybe all his classmates have died, all of his contemporaries." Being alone at home is associated with worrying over one's current finances and previous losses. Sociability, amusements, and moving around are the cures for this worried and worrisome kind of thinking, in distracting the aged from their problems. Being with others "enlivens" you, as one man said.

Second, institutional spaces are associated with a cooked meal. Food is taken as the sine qua non of good care more broadly in Ghana, as we see in Togo also (Häberlein, 2018). Its discussion in my interviews and the public meetings I attended signaled that many older people were seen as going hungry, a sign that they were badly cared for (see also de Jong et al. 2005). A man said, "Hunger is always there and it makes you worry, and these things also make you sick." A woman described another man who lives alone without anyone looking after him, and therefore has difficulty getting food. The nurse's assistant at Christchurch in Akropong said she had met some older adults who did not receive good care. What she meant was that they were not given a well-balanced diet, such as eating porridge without bread, or *kenkey* (a fermented, cooked starchy ball) with hot pepper but no fish. Abandoned and neglected older people were viewed as eating plain cooked rice, without stew or gravy. Food is a symbol of good care and attention in general and a way to index other forms of care, like cleanliness and medical attention.

Third, old age homes are associated with free medical attention with a nurse on site, although the imagined medical care was often preventative, like checking blood pressure or fasting blood sugar levels, rather than more intensive nursing care or elaborate physical tests (e.g., x-rays). This type of preventative medicine was similarly provided in the aged programs of the Presbyterian Church. Older adults can spend much of their time and energy seeking health care, waiting in decrepit waiting rooms in hospitals and clinics where they are treated harshly and disrespectfully by arrogant medical authorities, in their opinion. Some people in my conversations proposed that senior citizens should be treated first in hospitals. For example, they should jump the queue like pregnant women and young children. Although older Ghanaians have free health care, the cost and ease of transportation to medical facilities is also an issue for them as they try to seek care.

Fourth, the institutional space of an old age home with its loss of privacy and institutional food seemed familiar. Educated older men made the analogy to schools. Many secondary schools in Ghana are boarding facilities, and while they are associated with physical discomfort, strict teachers, and heavily scheduled days, they also generate deep, lifelong friendships. Social networks formed in boarding schools enable alumni to navigate bureaucratic and business environments in adulthood. One man spoke about old age homes in this way:

> If we had a place where when you grow old and no one lives with you, you could go live there, like a school where they sent you, where there are doctors, and they cook you food; everything! You will meet your classmate, and it makes you happy, and it will make your old age long. That kind of place is not common in Ghana or our region, so it bothers us.

Thus, although I personally had difficulty imagining an institutional space as attractive, previous experiences with institutions like schools, particularly for the educated men, meant that they saw old age homes as having the potential for intense sociality and friendship within a peer group.

Finally, these spaces were taken as a symbol that a society cared for its senior citizens. The foreignness of the institution was taken to critique the Ghanaian state among the nations of the world, rather than to bemoan the fact that their children were not Ghanaian enough by avoiding their care obligations. The presence of old age homes in Western countries was taken as a sign that these societies recognize and have not forgotten their senior citizens. In my conversations, just as Egyptians formed a critique of the state around their failing kidneys and experience of dialysis centers (Hamdy 2008), old age homes functioned as a tool of political critique and advocacy to highlight older people's plight in Ghana. Older persons were concerned about their low status in society that they felt contributed to their neglect and abandonment by their children, by their church to which they had contributed over the years, and by the state. Advocating for institutional facilities was a way to make that complaint stronger by showing that other societies respected their senior citizens by building such facilities. Old age homes were seen as their right given their previous contributions to society. If children were not going to step up, then perhaps the state and the church would.

Thus, old age homes in Ghana became a symbol of dignity and respect, which they felt they lacked in society at large, whereas in the West, nursing home residence often signals a loss of dignity and independence.

Thus, when asked what they would like to have happen, in public fora organized by the church, old age homes were one of the solutions articulated. There was some lack of distinction between old age homes, where they would reside, and senior day centers, where they might go for the day for food, companionship, and medical attention while younger members of their households were off at work or school. Interestingly, they were not concerned about institutional facilities as a response to physical frailty, disability, or serious illness, but rather as a response to social abandonment and neglect by their families and the state. Similar to aged persons in Burkina Faso (Roth 2005), insecurity in aging by these aging Ghanaian Presbyterians was perceived as a social problem, not a physical one. Their openness to institutional forms of care, which did not exist in the communities around them, speaks to their concerns about abandonment, their positive experiences of institutional residence in the past, and their general knowledge that old age homes exist elsewhere but not a specific and informed knowledge of what they are like in practice. Thus, they adapted old age homes in their imaginations to look like secondary schools and to meet their needs for food, sociability, routine medical care, and recognition.

Older Ghanaians express interest in institutions that they see as common in the West where the state, the church, or outside benefactors might make up for their children's failures in caring for them. In other words, they use the foreign figure of an old age home to advocate for their well-being within the local social and political context. And yet, old age homes can only function in this way because they *are* strange and not experienced or known. In India, in contrast, old age institutions have been adapted to allow social norms of aging to be realized: some are conceptualized as a joint kin structure, with the older residents treated as the parents or grandparents of the owner couple, and others as an ashram, supporting the retreat of the aged from the cares of daily life to allow them to focus on their spiritual development (Lamb 2016). In the case of Ghana, where only a few, small, and struggling old age homes in Accra exist, such support for foreign institutions in theory shows that older adults are open to new ideas and may be agents of social change.

Older adults may support heterodox age-inscriptions in the face of changing kin reciprocities. Yet it is not clear that they will become a political force in their critique of their neglect by the state and other significant social groups. Lois McNay, drawing on the work of Susan Gal, argues, "There is a huge difference between recognizing injustice, identifying systemic domination and common interests, devising strategies for action and, finally, feeling able to act. Even when there is substantial misrecognition and subordination,

resistance might not emerge if the symbolic elements with which to formu-
late agency are not present" (2008: 140). In the contemporary moment, older
adults in Ghana have not been able to harness the symbolic element
of neglect and Ghana's position in the world to engage in explicit political
advocacy. Instead, these heterodox discourses simmer within their local
networks.

Home Care through Domestic Service and Fosterage

Although institutional facilities were discussed speculatively in my fieldwork, what families seemed to be actually doing, but not discussing in public
fora, was using fostered adolescents or domestic servants to substitute for
busy adult children and provide home care. Adult children support such care
financially by paying the wages or school fees of the fostered child or domestic servant and manage care crises, but the otherwise day-to-day care is in
the hands of the younger woman living in the household with the older person.[8] This solution was only available to adult children who could and were
willing to send remittances to support a foster child or domestic servant.

Fostering has long been common in Akropong, particularly among adolescents, for the purpose of their education, training, and discipline. Children were often sent to live with an educated professional—a nurse or
teacher—who lived in an urban environment; their school fees were paid for
by the foster parent or they helped their foster parent with their business
(Coe 2013). More recently, it has become more difficult to differentiate a foster child from house help, particularly when a child who is more extended
kin or non-kin is being fostered in a household.[9] Because migrant adult
daughters living in the cities have competing responsibilities, and because
they have access to cash, they may delegate the work of daily eldercare to
more extended kin or house help, whether an adult woman or an adolescent
girl. This practice is thus a fully developed norm, with participants aware of
the "rules of the game," such as knowing to pay adolescents' school fees in
exchange for their labor. What makes it an alterodox age-inscription is its
adaptation to eldercare. Fostering is not articulated as a narrative about how
to age well, but it is enacted in practice as a way to provide care.

I encountered the household of Mama Adelaide in Akropong during a
survey I was doing of fostered children in 2008. Mama Adelaide was a
78-year-old woman who could not walk easily. She was living with Esther,
the 15-year-old great-granddaughter of Mama Adelaide's maternal uncle
(wɔfa). In exchange for her domestic care, Esther's junior secondary school
fees were paid by Mama Adelaide's four adult children who all resided in
Accra with their own children. The children worked in a range of occupations, with varying status, educational levels, and income: one son owned a
beer hall, the second installed car alarms, and the two daughters worked as

a nurse and a trader respectively. Esther had come to live with Mama Adelaide from a village near Suhum, where her father grew cacao and she had gone to primary school. In Akropong, in Mama Adelaide's household, after school each day, Esther went to the market and cooked the main meal. During my interview with Mama Adelaide one morning during the school holidays, Esther was washing clothes in the courtyard.

When Mama Adelaide had been in her fifties, she had returned to Akropong to look after her mother's sister, a former seamstress, for eight years, before the older woman died at the age of 82. While living in Akropong, Mama Adelaide had farmed a small plot of land, but in the last year, she had become too weak to do so. At that point, her children realized that she needed help and recruited Esther. Although Mama Adelaide framed this decision as her children's, indicating her pride in the fact that they took responsibility for her care, I have no doubt that she was involved in the decision, at least to the extent of acquiescing to it.

I was not able to speak to Mama Adelaide's children about why they did not come to live with their mother or send one of their own children to live with her in Akropong. However, other older women in Akropong told me that they did not expect their children or their grandchildren to come to live with them to help run the household and provide daily care. For example, one vigorous woman in her sixties who made money trading in yams anticipated that her children in the capital Accra would not return home to take care of her, but instead would pay for another woman to help her, a situation to which she seemed resigned. Her yam marketing involved hiring a truck with other women and going to farms in northern Ghana to buy yams to sell in the town, so perhaps, given the strength and energy this activity entailed, thoughts of future frailty seemed a bit abstract to her.

The yam trader and others said that it is becoming more difficult to send a child or adolescent to live with an older person because of the longer period of schooling that is considered a young person's right. Because many people in Akropong and elsewhere no longer consider schools in Akropong to be providing high-quality education, those living in urban environments with better schools view sending a child to live with a grandmother in Akropong as a sacrifice of that child's educational future. Fostering one's own children out is becoming increasingly antithetical to the middle class and to those who aspire to be middle class in Ghana, although they are amenable to having a child fostered into their own households as a dependent (Coe 2013). As Erdmute Alber (2010) found in Benin, the rural-urban exchange of children has become unidirectional. Whereas previously children moved in both directions, urban middle-class people tend to no longer give their children to poorer kin, although they continue to accept foster children of poorer kin into their households. The reasons that brought Mama Adelaide back to her hometown did not have the same significance for her migrant daughters, given the changing intergenerational entrustments. Thus, adult children living in the city raise their children in their own households and turn to more extended and poverty-stricken relatives whose children would otherwise not continue their schooling. They offer to pay their school fees in exchange for eldercare, or promise an apprenticeship after some years of service for those who have already completed junior secondary school. They may even pay monthly wages. In a context in which daughters have historically been responsible for the daily care of aging relatives and sons for financially supporting their sisters and mothers, daughters of older people are hiring or substituting more vulnerable young women for themselves; they can be good daughters by being care managers, rather than care providers (Coe 2016). In fact, when I returned to Akropong for a brief visit in January 2017, a retired primary school headmistress, disabled by diabetes, told me that all her friends in Akropong were hiring women to care for them. Nine years after I first suspected that this age-inscription was emerging, she articulated it as a norm.

Conclusions: Age-Inscriptions Articulated, Age-Inscriptions Practiced

Age-inscriptions are happening in practice and discourse in Ghana in part because two major producers of public discourse and shapers of social norms—the state and NGOs—are relatively silent on these issues. Instead, the state, with the support of NGOs closely allied to it and also involved in generating state policy, aims to support a social norm of kin providing eldercare in part to avoid what would probably become a major financial expenditure, as it is in Western state budgets. Thus, the orthodox discourse is about children living up to their responsibilities for eldercare. From the perspective of older Presbyterians in the towns of the Eastern Region I talked to, this "solution" is not reliable, and perhaps not viable. As a result, older people in Ghana are coming up with their own solutions, to some extent in conversation with the leadership of the Presbyterian Church, which also does not articulate a clear, strong discourse because of its own ambivalence about tackling these issues directly. Through its conceptualization of heterodox discourses and alterodox practices, this article has captured the messy and uneven process of social change at a particular moment in time, to help us understand changes in eldercare and in its connection to other social relationships.

In my conversations with older people in the Presbyterian congregations of Kwahu, Akim, and Akropong, they expressed openness to the heterodox possibility of residential facilities, a surprise to me given my extensive exposure to criticism of them by the government and NGOs. Although residential facilities were associated with foreign countries, older people transformed them in their imagination to be like secondary schools in Ghana and to meet their needs for companionship, food, easy access to medical care, and dignity. Furthermore, they did not distinguish strongly between residential facilities and senior day centers, since both were institutional settings, despite the fact that HelpAge Ghana has supported senior day centers in Accra, but not old age homes. The foreignness of institutional residences and the fact that they were not available in their communities was precisely what allowed them to be imagined in this way, rather than as sites of neglect, loneliness, and indignity, as they tend to be viewed in the United States. Old age homes were able to be appropriated in this way because of the discursive orthodox comparisons that were made between Western modes of helping senior citizens and Ghanaian ways within the families, even though these orthodox comparisons evaluated old age homes negatively. Thus, the negative comparison between the West and Ghana produced by the state and HelpAge made old age homes available as a heterodox solution, in the minds of older Ghanaians looking to address their concerns about neglect and loneliness.

However, in many ways residential facilities were discussed speculatively. They served simply as a figure in the social imagination. What was actually emerging in practice as an alterodox age-inscription was the use of fosterage to provide eldercare. In other words, more distant kin or non-kin were substituted for adult children or adolescent grandchildren as an adjacent relation. Care was provided by even poorer, more rural, and more distant relatives or by young women to support older people to live in their own households. These practices were familiar but were not discussed as a formal option. Instead, this alterodox age-inscription emerged in practice and not discursively. This strategy was reliant on the financial support of adult migrant children who could send remittances back to pay for such care, and thus was not available for those adult children who could not afford to send much in the way of remittances to their mother or father. It allowed children of older people to maintain their sense of self-worth in that they could say they were caring for their parents by helping them financially. It also meant that the grandchildren of these older persons did not have to sacrifice their schooling, seen as critical for their own futures, by caring for them. This strategy generated inequalities between differently positioned persons and may contribute to new constructions of social class through eldercare. Although most visible in the cities, where domestic service has been more established and there were greater discrepancies between social and economic status, it was emerging in the rural towns of the Eastern Region also.

In Ghana at the present time, aging seems very much in flux, with a wealth of emergent possibilities and no dominant patterns of care. This chapter has illustrated that older people are anxious about this state of affairs and, given what is at stake, are willing to imagine and explore heterodoxies, even those from abroad, such as institutional facilities, which the literature on aging in Ghana posits is deeply antithetical to "Ghanaian traditions." At the same time, in daily practice, some kin groups are adapting existing practices of domestic service and child fosterage for the purposes of eldercare, in which children pay for care and supervise it but do not provide it directly themselves. This practice is more amenable to social norms that children provide care to reciprocate the care given to them as children by their parents. Based on this, it seems likely that alterodox practices of domestic service and fosterage will become more widespread than the heterodox use of old age homes: one age-inscription may become a social norm and another may wither away or be used only as a mechanism to critique the state for its neglect. Whatever happens in the future, older people are key actors in shaping eldercare in Ghana, as they use their emotional and social responses to aging to imagine unseen possibilities and reinterpret more familiar ones.

Notes

This chapter is adapted with permission from Coe 2018.

1. Adinkrah (2015), in his study of witchcraft in Ghana, notes that older women are at higher risk of being accused of witches, and are particularly accused by their children, grandchildren, and caregivers.

2. See Alber (2018) for the case of Benin.

3. The moderator of the Presbyterian Church of Ghana during this time, Rev. Ayete-Nyampong, was very interested in gerontology, having written his dissertation on how the church might care for the aged. However, his role as moderator seemed to blunt his ability to work on aging initiatives within the church itself.

4. Interview with Prof. J. B. Asare, cofounder of HelpAge Ghana, June 28, 2013, Accra.

5. Interview with Mrs. Alberta Akoley Ollennu, May 30, 2013, Accra.

6. Interview with Nana Araba Apt, July 2, 2013, Accra.

7. Also see interview with Father Campbell, June 27, 2014, Accra.

8. In China, a similar dynamic of using domestic servants is emerging, despite an ideal of kin care by adult children (Wang and Wu 2016).

9. In Accra, the use of house help has been quite common among elite households since the 1960s at least (Ardayfio-Schandorf and Amissah 1996; Oppong 1974).

Bibliography

Aboderin, I. 2006. *Intergenerational Support and Old Age in Africa*. New Brunswick, NJ: Transaction.

Adinkrah, M. 2015. *Witchcraft, Witches, and Violence in Ghana*. New York: Berghahn.

Alber, E. 2010. "No School without Foster Families in Northern Benin: A Social Historical Approach." In *Parenting After the Century of the Child. Travelling Ideals, Institutional Negotiations and Individual Responses*, edited by H. Haukanes and T. Thelen, 57–78. Aldershot, UK: Ashgate.

Alber, E. 2018. "Préparer la Retraite: New Age-Inscriptions in West African Middle Classes." *Anthropology & Aging Quarterly* 39(1): 66–81.

Amselle, J.-L. 2002. "Globalization and the Future of Anthropology." *African Affairs* 101: 213–29.

Appadurai, A. 1996. *Modernity at Large: Cultural Dimensions of Globalization.* Minneapolis: University of Minnesota Press.

Apt, N. A. 1991. *The Aged and Disabled in Ghana: Policy Perspectives.* Prepared for the Ministry of Finance and Economic Planning, Social Sector Division, Accra, June 1991. Report in the Center for Social Policy Research/Social Work Department Library, University of Ghana, Legon.

Apt, N. A. 1996. *Coping with Old Age in a Changing Africa.* Aldershot, UK: Avebury.

Ardayfio-Schandorf, E., and M. Amissah. 1996. "Incidence of Child Fostering among School Children in Ghana." In *The Changing Family in Ghana*, edited by E. Ardayfio-Schandorf, 179–200. Accra: Ghana Universities Press.

Ayete-Nyampong, S. 2008. *Pastoral Care of the Elderly in Africa: A Comparative and Cross-Cultural Study.* Accra North: Step.

Bourdieu, P. 1977. *Outline of a Theory of Practice.* Translated by Richard Nice. New York: Cambridge University Press.

Cattell, M. G. 1999. "Elders' Complaints: Discourses on Old Age and Social Change in Rural Kenya and Urban Philadelphia." In *Language and Communication in Old Age: Multidisciplinary Perspectives*, edited by Heidi E. Hamilton, 295–317. New York: Garland.

Coe, C. 2011. "What Is Love? The Materiality of Care in Ghanaian Transnational Families." *International Migration* 49(6): 7–24.

Coe, C. 2013. *The Scattered Family: Parenting, African Migrants, and Global Inequality.* Chicago: University of Chicago Press.

Coe, C. 2016. "Orchestrating Care in Time: Ghanaian Migrant Women, Family, and Reciprocity." *American Anthropologist* 118(1): 37–48.

Coe, C. 2018. "Imagining Institutional Care, Practicing Domestic Care: Inscriptions around Aging in Southern Ghana." *Anthropology and Aging* 39(1): 18–32.

Coe, C., and E. Alber. 2018. "Age-Inscriptions and Social Change." *Anthropology and Aging* 39(1): 1–16.

Cole, J. 2013. "On Generations and Aging: 'Fresh Contact' of a Different Sort." In *Transitions and Transformations: Cultural Perspectives on Aging and the Life Course*, edited by C. Lynch and J. Danely, 218–30. New York: Berghahn.

de-Graft Aikins, A., J. Addo, F. Ofei, W. Bosu, and C. Agyemang. 2012. "Ghana's Burden of Chronic, Non-Communicable Diseases: Future Directions in Research, Practice, and Policy." *Ghana Medical Journal* 46(2 Supplement): 1–3.

de Jong, W., C. Roth, F. Badini-Kinda, and S. Bhagyanath. 2005. *Ageing in Insecurity: Case Studies on Social Security and Gender in India and Burkina Faso.* Münster: Lit Verlag.

Doh, D. 2012. *Exploring Social Protection Arrangements for Older People: Evidence from Ghana.* Saarbrücken, Germany: Lambert Academic.

Dsane, S. 2013. *Changing Cultures and Care of the Elderly.* Saarbrücken, Germany: Lambert Academic.

Ghana Statistical Service. 2012. *Ghana 2010 Population and Housing Census.* Accra: Ghana Statistical Service.

GhanaWeb. 2018. "Parliament Must Pass Ageing Policy—Prof. Mate Kole." June 15. https://www.ghanaweb.com/GhanaHomePage/NewsArchive/Parliament -must-pass-ageing-policy-Prof-Mate-Kole-660405.

Gilbert, M. 1995. "The Christian Executioner: Christianity and Chieftaincy as Rivals." *Journal of Religion in Africa* 25(4): 347–86.

Graw, K., and S. Schielke, eds. 2012. *The Global Horizon: Expectations of Migration in Africa and the Middle East.* Leuven: Leuven University Press.

Häberlein, T. 2018. "Complexities of Elder Livelihoods: Changing Age-Inscriptions and Stable Norms in Three Villages in Rural West Africa." *Anthropology and Aging* 39(1): 33–47.

Hamdy, S. 2008. "When the State and Your Kidneys Fail: Political Etiologies in an Egyptian Dialysis Ward." *American Ethnologist* 35(4): 553–69.

Lamb, S. 2016. "Traveling Institutions as Transnational Aging: The Old-Age Home in Idea and Practice in India." In *Transnational Aging: Current Insights and Future Challenges*, edited by V. Horn and C. Schweppe, 178–99. New York: Routledge.

McNay, L. 2008. *Against Recognition.* Malden, MA: Polity.

Oppong, C. 1974. *Marriage among a Matrilineal Elite: A Family Study of Ghanaian Senior Civil Servants.* Cambridge: Cambridge University Press.

Roth, C. 2005. "Threatening Dependency: Limits of Social Security, Old Age, and Gender." In *Ageing in Insecurity: Case Studies on Social Security and Gender in India and Burkina Faso*, edited by W. de Jong, C. Roth, F. Badini-Kinda, and S. Bhagyanath, 107–38. Münster: Lit Verlag.

Sewell, W. H. 2005. *Logics of History: Social Theory and Social Transformation.* Chicago: University of Chicago Press.

Thelen, T., and C. Coe. 2017. "Political Belonging through Elder Care: Temporalities, Representations, and Mutuality." *Anthropological Theory* 19(2): 279–99.

Van der Geest, S. 2016. "Will Families in Ghana Continue to Care for Older People? Logic and Contradiction in Policy." In *Ageing in Sub-Saharan Africa: Spaces and Practices of Care*, edited by J. Hoffman and K. Pype, 21–42. Bristol: Policy.

Wang, J., and B. Wu. 2016. "Domestic Helpers as Frontline Workers in China's Home-Based Elder Care: A Systematic Review." *Journal of Aging and Women.* doi: 10.1080/08952841.2016.1187536.

CHAPTER THIRTEEN

Eldersourcing and Reconceiving Work as Care

Lessons from Retirement on the Line

Caitrin Lynch

In September 2017, HBO's Vice News Tonight aired a news segment focusing on a man named Howard Ring who is 83 and works in a needle factory outside Boston, Massachusetts. The show put Howard's work into a wider context when it noted that "Nine million Americans over the age of 65 still work full or part time. That number has more than doubled since 2000." The program followed Howard at work (interacting with peers, getting his job done) and then going home to his empty house at the end of the day. The clip ended with a shot of him watching TV at home alone, with a voiceover from Howard: "I will work at Vita Needle and they will come by and think that I'm asleep in my bed, and I'll be dead in my bed. . . . And they'll say, 'Howard Ring, what dedication'" (Vice News Tonight 2017). This HBO segment is only one of many stories that have aired in the United States and abroad since 1997 featuring Howard and his coworkers (see Web Special).

In an era when people live longer and want to, or need to, work past the traditional retirement age, to people across the world the Vita Needle Company has provided inspiration and important lessons about the value of older workers. Vita Needle is a small family-owned factory that was founded in 1932 and makes needles, stainless steel tubing and pipes, and custom-fabricated

WEB SPECIAL:

Vice News Tonight, "83-Year-Old Engineer Is the Face of America's Aging Workforce," https://www.youtube.com/watch?v=vqbWy3xRNhw &feature=youtu.be.

parts. As part of its unusual business model, the company seeks out older workers; the median age of the employees is 74. Vita Needle's model of "elder-sourcing," sourcing labor from older adults, has been featured in documentary films that have aired in Europe and South America; in news programs in Japan and Korea; in the *New York Times*, PBS *NewsHour*, and more. I wrote a book in 2012, *Retirement on the Line*, about the people in this needle factory, the policy of employing older workers, and the global interest in the model (Lynch 2012). My book has been translated into German and Japanese. I traveled with Howard and a representative from the company's management to Germany in 2013 to participate in a symposium of public and private employers, policy makers, and analysts on "Older Employees in the World of Work," sponsored by the foundation Körber Stiftung (Körber Stiftung 2013). While we were there, Howard became the darling of German talk radio when an interview with him aired that had listeners writing or calling in for days after.

So, why is there so much outside interest in this small workplace where a bunch of old people make needles?

With the dramatic global increases in older populations noted in Part I by He and Kinsella, policy makers and employers in many countries have looked to Vita Needle as a model for how to enable older adults to feel productive and earn a paycheck, well into old age.

An Anthropological Study of Work and Aging

As a cultural anthropologist who studies work and aging, I spent five years doing fieldwork at Vita Needle. This chapter reflects on the central lessons of that research and uses Vita Needle as a springboard to rethink the role of work and retirement in people's lives as they age. The case of Vita Needle gives us the chance to understand the importance of community, purpose, and care to older adults.

I write this chapter as an anthropologist who teaches at a school where all my students are engineering majors. My goal is to help students see engineering as a people-centered effort, where engineers develop products, services, and systems that are appropriately suited to the wider contexts that inform people's lives. One aging-related example: An engineer in the United

States would err in designing new eldercare systems without understanding the meanings of caregiving relationships in the United States. To create innovations in this domain that matter most to people, we first need to understand culturally and historically situated concepts such as independence and individuality, as well as familial notions of obligation, debt, responsibility, and love. "Care" and "care work," after all, carry different meanings among diverse communities in the United States and elsewhere. And one of the biggest mistakes engineers can make in redesigning eldercare systems is to remove from it the parts of it that people (caregivers and receivers) value. Ideally those include the opportunities to provide for others, to have intimate connection to others, and to provide a two-way sense of purpose. A robotic caregiving seal, like PARO, the therapeutic robot, may entirely miss the mark, as anthropologist Sherry Turkle cautions. Referring to "care," Turkle asks, "Why are we, essentially, outsourcing the thing that defines us as people?" (NPR 2013).

I guide my engineering students to be careful not to inadvertently create innovations that remove what matters most for people. For example, what if an engineer decides to improve grocery shopping for older adults by allowing them to have groceries delivered by a drone, or by an online service? With such high-tech innovations applied to shopping, the experiences that were of the most value for the shopper could accidentally be removed: the outing, the choices, the social contact, the sense of continued competency and self-care. An online service could deliver ground turkey, but it could also make someone feel lonely (Lynch 2018; Adler, Lynch, and Martello 2018).

Likewise, as we consider the impending radical population changes that the United States and societies all over the world face as the global population ages, we must consider the meanings of work for people in their conventional retirement years. Vita Needle provides a model of how people can find fulfillment in factory work well past the age when they could collect Social Security benefits. The eldest worker, a woman named Rosa, was 101 when she stopped work a few years ago (Photo 13.1). Rosa passed away a year later, living in a nursing home, lonely and, as she told me, feeling "like a dope" because she had nothing to do with her time other than think about her life. As I write in 2019, the current eldest worker at Vita Needle is a 100-year-old man.

The Meanings of Work for Older Workers

Let's consider the meanings of work for people in their conventional retirement years. Vita Needle provides a model of how older workers can find financial and emotional fulfillment through work. At Vita Needle, the workplace is much more than a place to earn money. It is a site for narrating lives, finding value, and asserting personhood.

Photo 13.1   Rosa at work.
(Photo by Jose Colucci Jr.)

Think for a moment of people in the United States in their seventies and above. I have seen this all over the world: people's roles in life change as they age, and many people (and this varies by gender and other forms of identity) feel the new phase of retirement is a "roleless role." This is a term coined by the sociologist Ernest W. Burgess in 1960, wh-en he described the fate of retirees who find that they "have no vital function to perform" (Burgess 1960: 20). They find it hard to know where to focus their lives when many people expect they don't have much to contribute anymore.

In his 1975 book called *Working*, the journalist Studs Terkel wrote: "[Work] is about a search . . . for daily meaning as well as daily bread, for recognition as well as cash, for astonishment rather than torpor; in short, for a sort of life rather than a Monday through Friday sort of dying" (Terkel 1997 [1975]: xi). When I ask my students in the United States to consider the notion of work as a search for "recognition as well as cash," as Terkel described it, I ask them to imagine their parents. What would they miss if they didn't have work? In an ideal workplace (I know this is often *not* the case), perhaps a sense of accomplishment, regular challenges to meet, social interaction and friends, and a sense of being recognized for who you are and what you can do.

Then I ask students to consider the older adults they work with in projects with me. Older adults may feel profoundly unrecognized and invisible in many aspects of their lives. I've heard this from many people I have interviewed and befriended. In that context, there seems to be a special significance to work and the recognition it may bring. Work might also bring a reason to get up in the morning, the knowledge that people expect you to show up and perform well, and a sense of accomplishment. Productivity means this and so much more to older adults.

All this is complicated culturally for Americans and for many people worldwide. Retirement is a complex ideal, and there's a new twist on that complexity with the financial strain that many older adults now face and that societies now also face.

Top Five Lessons from Vita Needle

My book, *Retirement on the Line*, holds a few central lessons. They lead up to one big insight, which is about *work as a site of care*. Let's turn first to the Top Five Lessons.

1. Work during the Retirement Years Provides a Paycheck . . . and Much More.

We know that the absence of work during retirement has an economic impact on retirees. Less obvious are the social implications that result from the absence of work. Vita Needle's older workers exhibit a range of personalities and backgrounds and have diverse reasons for working. Even those who come out of financial need also seek social engagement and purpose. For people of all ages, work provides more than a paycheck. Work can provide a route to social contact, enable a sense of contribution, and offer relief from domestic troubles.

In U.S. society, paid work is central to identity, and nonworking adults often struggle to feel self-worth when their lives do not live up to the cultural and economic norm. If Americans measure themselves by work, imagine how awkward the social position of retirees can be. Indeed, retirees often ask each other, "What did you do in *real* life?"

In the United States, one can enter any local card shop and find a section of retirement greeting cards. There is a stock set of common images that portray the American retirement ideal, including fishing poles, rocking chairs, and torn-up or empty "to do" lists. Many Americans look forward to and plan for this life stage, and they consider it a phase of life in which one is no longer ruled by clocks, schedules, and bosses. But many people still want to work in the conventional retirement years in part because they believe that a person's value correlates with the ability to earn income. They also want to work for a sense of purpose. The workers at Vita Needle show us what meaningful work can look like in the retirement years.

2. Retirement Work Needs to Feel Different Than Work at Other Life Stages.

Many older adults certainly are capable of working, and many want to work. But because of the different role work plays at this life stage, they want work that feels a lot different than it did at earlier points (when they were paying mortgages, raising children, etc.). Vita Needle's older workers describe their work in this factory as remarkably different from previous work. They value its flexible hours, its easy integration into family life, how they are recognized for their contributions, and that they have coworkers who depend on them. When we pay attention to the meaning of work, we start to understand something new about a situation one might at first glance assume to be exploitative.

The Vita case challenges us to think in new ways about orthodox labor categories such as *retired*, *illegal*, and *immoral*. The workers at Vita Needle have actually created a new stage in a worker's life, and this may well be the first look at a future to come. But there is one limitation: Vita Needle's business model requires state support. The company pays minimum wage to the older workers and assumes that they receive Social Security benefits and Medicare (state-mandated health insurance). The labor arrangement depends largely on the workers' receipt of these state-provisioned pensions and health care coverage. When so many governments worldwide, in part due to the demographic transitions described by He and Kinsella (Part I), are under pressure to rearrange state expenses and pay off debt, this eldersourcing arrangement begs the question: What happens in a world without those guarantees?

3. Rich Connections Are Forged When Old and Young Work Together.

Designers of elder-friendly communities and environments increasingly aim to create intergenerational programming. Employers increasingly try to make the most of multigenerational workforces they may accidentally have in their employ. What does rich intergenerational contact really look like? At Vita Needle, four generations of employees work on tight deadlines in a mixed-gender and multistage assembly where the quality and timing of one person's work affects the next. Vita Needle has employees in every age decade from teens to 100—talk about intergenerational contact!

In interviews, workers in their teens, twenties, and thirties invariably reflect positively on working with older adults. One 19-year-old, who had often visited his grandfather in a nursing home before coming to Vita Needle, noted that Vita Needle allowed for more authentic and comfortable interaction across generations because they were all "in it together." By contrast, he found that "for some reason I just could never talk to the people in the nursing home. I don't know that it was, like, the environment we were in. I felt like I was in their territory. . . . There's something to be said for the fact that you're all kind of doing something together." The older workers, for their part, spoke positively about what they could learn from younger workers, at times overcoming stereotypes they may have had of their younger coworkers. This example challenges our assumptions that there is invariably a "generation gap" in a multigenerational workplace.

4. Under the Right Circumstances, Work Arrangements Can Benefit Employers, and Also Workers.

This example of eldersourcing may offer a model for providing financial and social value for older adults, and for reinvigorating the U.S. economy. Vita Needle's workers and employers claim that eldersourcing is a net positive, economically and socially. In fact, both groups use work to achieve ends other than what is obvious (e.g., for the employers it is not simply profit; for the workers it is not simply a paycheck). Some of the retirees claim to need money; all say they want social contact. Vita Needle's president explains that he employs older workers as a social good—to counter adverse health impacts of isolated old age. Yet he and observers invariably note the success of this business model: this is a company that is nearly 90 years old, as of this writing, and has withstood economic pressures that have closed many U.S. manufacturers since the 1970s. Many U.S. manufacturers have been unable to compete with cheap labor in the global South; Vita Needle found its own solution in eldersourcing.

This case shows that a practice can make both economic and social sense: eldersourcing can be positive for employers and employees, though there is plenty of debate and discussion as both sides make sense of their experiences and their goals. The Vita Needle story challenges us to move analyses of labor and capital beyond the common assumed dichotomy of exploited and exploiters. Questions of exploitation remain important, but the answers are not black-and-white. In the end, the Vita Needle case leads us to think in new ways about work.

5. Membership and Mattering Are Key Values for Today's Older Americans.

Many older Americans value doing something that is meaningful to others and to themselves (mattering). They also value acting in concert with others (membership). *Mattering* refers to the sense of relevance and value that comes from knowing one's life makes a difference to others; it provides an answer to the question "So what?" that people often ask themselves as they grow older. *Membership* refers to social contact, connection to others, a sense of belonging, being able to point to an "us" in opposition to a "them."

While we can analyze membership and mattering for people of any age, by listening to the stories of Vita Needle's workers we learn that there is something distinctive about these sentiments for older adults. Many people want to remain busy and engaged throughout their lives, and they want to be recognized for the contributions they make. *Vita* means "life" in Latin, and indeed it is life (and life with meaning) that is created at Vita Needle, where not only needles but also lives are made on the shop floor. Retirees and older adults simply want to continue to live and to be part of life, where life itself means community engagement and contribution. Vita Needle is a place of life for people who may otherwise be written off as nonproductive, useless, invisible, and no longer human. When Vita Needle's workers (like Howard, from the HBO segment) assert that "working here keeps me alive," they draw a concrete connection between work and life—and in so doing add complexity to the oft-heard expression that gets at questions of work and value in capitalist societies: "Do you 'live to work' or 'work to live'?" We see in Vita Needle one path for engagement and recognition—for life.

The Central Insight: Work as an Opportunity to Give and Receive Care

My take-home message in this study is *not* that we must create more factory jobs for older adults. Nor is it necessarily that we must create more *paid work* for older adults. And it is certainly *not* that the retirement age should be abolished in the United States or any country because older adults can and want to work. My argument is subtler. I use this model, an extreme example, as a prompt for us to think in new ways about *care*. Vita Needle allows us to think creatively about where we can find care, and what benefits care provides to people (care givers and receivers). Ultimately I believe that framing work as care may offer us a way to get beyond the common questions asked about work and aging: whether older workers are taking jobs from younger people (Photo 13.2), whether governments should or should not support older adults, and whether retirement ages should be raised.

I urge us to take this case study and draw wider lessons on the *quality of life* for older adults. At Vita Needle, the experience of work provides both self-care and care for others. Everyone at Vita is simultaneously a care giver and receiver. They are receiving and giving care, in a dynamic of mutuality. Rosa asks her coworkers about their grandchildren, and she seeks advice on medical treatment. Howard escorts Rosa down the steep factory stairs at the end of the day, and Rosa tells him stories about her children, who are close to his age (Photo 13.3). They all join together and help each other out at work. Rosa's macular degeneration prevents her from seeing her work closely, but

Photo 13.2 Rosa at work; collaborating across generations. (Photo by Caitrin Lynch)

Howard and others make sure to set up her workstation so she can find everything she needs. If someone takes a nap on the job, or comes in late because of a doctor's appointment or a grandchild's violin performance, the manager can make adjustments.

Key elements of success in the Vita model have to do with care. The workplace provides a cultural space that enables *mutual caring opportunities*. Everyone is both a carer and someone being cared for; this is not a one-way relationship of care. The workplace also provides its workers *multiple settings for intimate relationships*, and demonstrates the importance of creating a setting of intimate relationships that also extend to a network of outside relationships. Finally, for the workers at Vita Needle, the workplace provides opportunity for *choice*, *control*, and *agency*. It underlines the importance of providing older adults with a sense of obligation and of caring for others by choice, by being in control, and by demonstrating agency.

During my research, I interviewed Dr. Simon Weitzman, a physician in the town where Vita Needle is located. Dr. Weitzman is the care provider for some of Vita Needle's employees and is also the medical director at a local

Photo 13.3   Rosa and Howard (from the HBO special), during break at work. (Photo by Jose Colucci Jr.)

continuing-care retirement community. I had heard many times at Vita Needle that some workers were there on their doctor's recommendations, so I wanted to get a sense from Dr. Weitzman of what work provides to older workers—in addition to a paycheck. In response to a question about how work affects older workers' health, Dr. Weitzman said the following:

> I think that a lot of the older people we see here who are sharpest, are people who remain employed. And it's hard to separate whether you are employed because you're still sharp or vice versa. But definitely . . . the sharpest older people that we have [as patients] are working, are usually doing something and most of the time, [they are] doing something *for* someone. The interaction *with* other people or the work *intended for others* helps.

Dr. Weitzman here emphasized working *with* people and working *for* people. He also added that for older workers, "Work provides an umbrella. It provides a blanket. It provides love. It provides warmth. It provides everything that has nothing to do with money." Dr. Weitzman was careful to say that the work that provides an umbrella, a blanket, love, and warmth does not need to be *paid*. Volunteerism can also provide a sense of purpose, but earning a wage plays a critical role for workers at Vita Needle as they make sense of the value of their skills and time. These workers are making money for themselves. And, more important in some forms of accounting, they are making money for their boss, Fred. A common expression at the factory is that "We're making money for Fred." They have a *cause beyond themselves*. And because of a profit-sharing system, they know that the more money Fred makes, the more money they also make.

I've heard of geriatricians who write prescriptions to older adults to "Get a job." Dr. Weitzman has recommended Vita Needle to patients. He also told me he recommends that lonely elders get a cat so they have something they can do for someone. In my work and travels I often hear stories of mutual care in age-related settings. An anthropologist who works on aging in Sri Lanka told me about woman who regularly feeds the alley cats outside her Sri Lankan "old age home." In so doing she is able to exhibit her moral agency through acting beneficially toward others (see Part VI Web Book Hawkins and Haapio-Kirk).

Dr. Atul Gawande, who is a surgeon, wrote a 2014 book called *Being Mortal*. In this book, Gawande argues for a new perspective on what doctors should prioritize in their work with people with terminal illnesses. Gawande describes how early in his career in the 1990s, Dr. Bill Thomas (who later founded the Eden Alternative eldercare programs) brought plants and birds into nursing homes. The goal "was to attack what he [Thomas] termed the Three Plagues of nursing home existence: boredom, loneliness, and helplessness. To attack the Three Plagues they needed to bring in some life. They'd put green plants in every room. They'd tear up the lawn and create a vegetable and flower garden. And they'd bring in animals" (Gawande 2014: 116). Thomas found that the dogs, cats, birds, and children all had dramatic positive effects on the residents. For example, researchers found a decrease in the need for psychotropic drugs for agitation (Gawande 2014: 123). Drug costs dropped and death rates fell. In short, it was pets, not meds, that led to improvements in quality of life for the nursing home residents.

Rather than pets, Vita Needle solves human problems with humans. At Vita Needle, older adults, and people of all ages, are caring for each other in a workplace where they are mutually dependent to get the work done, make money for their boss, and to take care of each other.

Conclusion: Vita Needle as a Site of Care

I use this Vita Needle model, admittedly an outlier example, as a prompt to think in new ways about care, including care for self and care for others. Vita Needle allows us to think creatively about where we can find care, and what benefits care provides to people (both care givers and receivers). Dr. Atul Gawande, Dr. Bill Thomas, and the people at Vita Needle all provide an important perspective on providing care and a life worth living to older adults. One key to quality of life for anyone, including older adults, is to enable people to feel that they can do something for a cause beyond themselves.

In the United States at least, older adults do not want to think that their life is exclusively oriented toward the satisfaction of basic needs: food, water, and shelter. Yet, it's hard for older adults to feel that there is a cause beyond themselves if their life is subsumed by dependence, or by deference. I heard about deference from Harold, an 86-year-old man who is legally blind as a result of age-related vision loss. Harold told me that because of his vision loss he feels that his life is just "holding my hat in my hand"—using an early 20th-century idiom (from back when many American men wore hats whenever outdoors) that conveys deference and respectful humility.

Many governments worldwide are confronting what policy makers portentously consider a "silver tsunami." In Japan, the recurring English-language term is "the aging society problem." When I went to Australia to speak about this work, I repeatedly heard the term *burden* to describe the challenges of an aging population. Note the negative connotation: *tsunami, problem, burden.* How might we reframe population aging in less negative terms? After all, these are actual people whose lives are being cast as burdensome, problematic, and portending disaster.

As the global population grows, health care improves, and birth rates drop, the world is getting older. Policy makers worldwide anticipate social and economic *crises*—more old people, fewer young people and state resources to support them, and longer periods of "unproductive" retirement. In response, some governments are raising the retirement age. Because my study has policy implications, I find myself often being invited to comment on whether this study provides evidence for the benefits of raising the retirement age in light of the changing "dependency ratio." This term refers to the ratio of people 18–65 (considered the productive, supporting members of society) to those in the under-18 and over-65 "dependent" age groups (see Part I He and Kinsella). If economists can demonstrate the financial benefits of older adults contributing to rather than drawing from state coffers for a few more years, does my work in parallel demonstrate the social benefits of "disburdening" the state?

No. I do not want to be misinterpreted as saying people must, should, and invariably want to work until they die. Instead, I am calling for a reframing of what work means for older adults. Let's reframe work as a form of belonging and as a site for care giving and receiving. If we do that, our task at hand is to enable people to work if they choose to, but without relieving the ethical and political obligation of the state to support its citizens. As I earlier noted, even Vita Needle's model requires state support: the minimum wage income is accompanied by Social Security benefits and subsidized health care (Medicare).

When we think about replicating Vita Needle, a central question is how to create environments where people have control like they do at Vita Needle. One of the remarkable features of the managerial approach at Vita Needle is that the workers on all levels can make decisions about how to do their work—they don't feel like cogs in machinery, like in the Charlie Chaplin movie *Modern Times*.

Some years ago Sue Jameson, a nursing home administrator, contacted me because she saw a German documentary film about Vita Needle, *Pensioners Inc.*, on television in Canada and quickly envisioned an opportunity (Verhaag 2008). Could she perhaps establish light work or industry within retirement home or long-term care settings? She asked me if human beings have a propensity to be industrious throughout their life span, or does the Vita Needle story mostly tell us about economic need?

Sue went on to tell me a moving story about Bob, a resident of the Canadian retirement home she ran who voluntarily took on light maintenance work (sweeping the front patio, greeting guests, shoveling light snow, and gardening). As Sue saw it, the ability to do this work improved Bob's quality of life because it gave him a sense of proprietorship. When Bob moved to a different setting, the new management did not allow him to take on this role. Sue tried to advocate on his behalf and portended that, as she told me, "His life will be short-circuited if he is not allowed to feel purposeful." And indeed, without a job to do, Bob passed away within months of the move. Now Sue wanted to learn from his death and from the Vita Needle story to create appropriate programming in older-adult living settings.

Sue knew that people seek a cause beyond themselves. Bob had it with his role at the nursing home. Rosa died at age 102, living her last year in a nursing home. I met with Rosa many times in her nursing home, and she helped me understand that in light of changing family structures and the emotional and financial need many have for work at all ages, work was much more than a place for earning money for her. It was a place where she offered and received care. Rosa lived in a society that lacks effective formal societal structures to provide care for older adults. In today's neoliberal context in which everyone is expected to be responsible for their own health and care, even older adults need to figure out how to care for themselves.

In this context, work offered Rosa a surprising place of love and care. But she could not stay there, due to family circumstances. Yet, as I and journalist Ari Daniel reported for a feature story on National Public Radio's *All Things Considered*, Rosa then struggled to find the same affective ties in a nursing home (Daniel and Lynch 2014).

Vita Needle is in many ways an outlier. Its success with eldersourcing has to do with its small size, the nature of the product it makes, and the particular personalities and commitments of its owners, managers, and employees. Nevertheless the example raises questions to consider about concrete systems and social frameworks that could support older workers, including part-time work, mentoring systems, retraining and career services, flexibility, and adjustments to workspace and work performance expectations. And it raises questions about emotional as well as financial well-being: How can we create more places like Vita Needle—workplaces or not—for people at all ages where they can perhaps receive a paycheck, and certainly connect with others while also finding an outlet for their continued sense of personhood, participation, purpose, and love? (See Box 5.1 and Part III Web Book Shea.)

Finally, how would this look in different societies throughout the world? Consider Japan, which leads the world in population aging. In 2015, the Japanese think tank NIRA (Nippon Institute for Research Advancement) interviewed me and a group of labor experts for a publication focusing on "Offering the Elderly the Opportunity to Work" (Lynch 2015). The concern was with aging and work in Japan exclusively (see also Suzuki 2012). NIRA's Executive Vice President Noriyuki Yanagawa described the motivation for the publication as follows:

> The negative economic impact of a low birthrate and an aging society [in Japan] has been sufficiently pointed out. However, it is also the case that many seniors possess long years of experience and abundant knowledge. Many seniors are also energetic and motivated. It would be a great waste for our society not to make adequate use of these elderly people, treating their existence rather as a burden. Surely it could be possible to consider the elderly in a positive light? (NIRA 2015: np)

Referring to Japan in particular, Yanagawa categorized the take-home messages of the expert interviews as follows:

> (1) "Modern seniors differ significantly from the vision of the elderly that we have harbored up to the present."
> (2) "Japan's social systems remain unchanged, and we do not possess mechanisms sufficiently able to provide the healthy elderly with opportunities to involve themselves and places in which they can do so." (NIRA 2015: np)

Journalist Joseph Coleman, who specializes in Japan, has written about how national and local governments, nongovernmental organizations, employers, and individuals in Japan and elsewhere are responding to the changing demographics (Coleman 2015; see also Part III Kavedžija). Coleman reminds us to consider whether the policies that governments and employers have are humane and equitable toward older adults, and whether they provide older workers with the freedom to pursue their own goals and exercise their talents and capabilities.

I will end with the words of Rosa, from Vita Needle. Rosa stopped working because her family needed to move away from the town where the factory was located—a fair consideration when a worker is 101 and her children are "older adults" who must make arrangements as they themselves age:

I always felt that I could work forever. Made me feel like I was a worthwhile person. I liked the companionship of people around me and we're all working. I really feel like a dope. I should never have stopped. That was the sorriest day of my life. (Daniel and Lynch 2014)

Note

Some material reprinted from Lynch 2012. Copyright (c) 2012 by Cornell University. Used by permission of the publisher, Cornell University Press.

Bibliography

Adler, J. M., C. Lynch, and R. Martello. 2018. "Want to Solve the World's Problems? Try Working Together across Disciplines." *The Conversation.* September 2. https://theconversation.com/want-to-solve-the-worlds-problems-try -working-together-across-disciplines-102319.

Burgess, E. W. 1960. *Aging in Western Societies.* Chicago: University of Chicago Press.

Coleman, J. 2015. *Unfinished Work: The Struggle to Build an Aging American Workforce.* New York: Oxford University Press.

Daniel, A., and C. Lynch. 2014. "At 102, Reflections on Race and the End of Life." *All Things Considered,* February 12. http://www.npr.org/2014/02/12/275 918145/at-102-reflections-on-race-and-the-end-of-life.

Gawande, A. 2014. *Being Mortal: Medicine and What Matters in the End.* New York: Metropolitan.

Körber Stiftung. 2013. Ältere in der Arbeitswelt. Bericht über das Symposium. [Older Employees in the World of Work. Report on the Symposium]. https://www.koerber-stiftung.de/fileadmin/user_upload/koerber-stif tung/mediathek/pdf/import/Bericht_A__ltere_in_der_Arbeitswelt.pdf.

Lynch, C. 2012. *Retirement on the Line: Age, Work, and Value in an American Factory.* Ithaca, NY: Cornell University Press.

Lynch, C. 2015. "Create Meaningful Jobs for the Elderly," "Expert Opinion" in "Offering the Elderly the Opportunity to Work." *MyVision* no. 9, 2015.5. http://www.nira.or.jp/pdf/e_vision9.pdf (In Japanese and English).

Lynch, C. 2018. "Engineers, Go WILD." TEDx Natick, January 20. https://www .youtube.com/watch?v=OudPLC-N7fc.

NIRA (Nippon Institute for Research Advancement). 2015. "Offering the Elderly the Opportunity to Work." *MyVision* no. 9, 2015.5. http://www.nira.or.jp /pdf/e_vision9.pdf (In Japanese and English).

NPR. 2013. "Are We Plugged-In, Connected, But Alone?" *TED Radio Hour*, "Do We Need Humans?" part 1, February 26. https://www.npr.org/2013/08/16/172988165/are-we-plugged-in-connected-but-alone.

Suzuki, N. 2012. "Creating a Community of Resilience: New Meanings of Technologies for Greater Well-Being in a Depopulated Town." *Anthropology & Aging Quarterly* 33(3): 87–96. https://doi.org/10.5195/aa.2012.58.

Terkel, S. 1997 [1975]. *Working: People Talk about What They Do All Day and How They Feel about What They Do.* New York: New Press.

Verhaag, B., dir. 2008. *Pensioners Inc.* Munich: DENKmal Films.

Vice News Tonight. 2017. "83-Year-Old Engineer Is the Face of America's Aging Workforce." *American Jobs*, September 7. https://youtu.be/vqbWy3xRNhw.

CHAPTER FOURTEEN

Web Book Photo Essay: Curriculum Vitae

A Photographic Essay of Elderly Urban Workers from Peru

Gabriela Ramos Bonilla and
Erika Jaclyn Tirado Ratto

Available at: http://www.culturalcontextofaging.com/webbook-bonillaratto

This Web photo essay by Gabriela Bonilla and Erika Ratto examines, in Peru, how late-life work experiences in old age are framed as a product of accumulated social inequalities throughout the life course.

CHAPTER FIFTEEN

Web Book: Images of Aging
Cultural Representations of Later Life

Mike Featherstone and Mike Hepworth

Available at: http://www.culturalcontextofaging.com/webbook-feathersto nehepworth

Featherstone and Hepworth suggest some gerontological writers see the postmodern life course as characterized by a blurring of traditional age divisions and the integration of formerly segregated periods of life. They explore how new images of aging are connected to marketable lifestyles for elders linked to commodified values of youth masking the appearance of age.

CHAPTER SIXTEEN

Web Book: Intergenerational Sites

New Trends in Urban Planning, Global Trends, and Good Practices from the United States and Beyond

Donna M. Butts

Available at: http://www.culturalcontextofaging.com/webbook-butts

Writing for the United Nations, Executive Director of Generations United Donna Butts provides a global perspective on the development, importance, and policy recommendations for intergenerational sites of connection and engagement.

CHAPTER SEVENTEEN

Web Book: Global Perspectives on Widowhood and Aging

Maria G. Cattell

Available at: http://www.culturalcontextofaging.com/webbook-cattell

This Web Book chapter provides a global examination of widowhood along with her long-term research in rural Kenya and draws readers into the experience of older widows in Africa, Guatemala, India, and the United States.

CHAPTER EIGHTEEN

Web Book: Grandparenting Styles

The Contemporary Native American Experience

Joan Weibel-Orlando

Available at: http://www.culturalcontextofaging.com/webbook-weibel

Joan Weibel-Orlando, focusing in this section on Native Americans she studied in urban California and at a reservation in South Dakota, makes a strong contribution to our knowledge about how cultural context affects the grandparenting role. Here she finds a broad cultural space with fluid boundaries between genealogical generations that provides a context for cross-generational cultural transmission and fostering of grandchildren. The lessons from her study can be profitably added to the articles on the ethnic aged in Part IV.

PART III

Aging, Globalization, and Societal Transformation

The local is not transcended by globalization, but rather that the local is to be understood by global relationships.

—Savage, Bagnall, and Longhurst (2005)

We have moved away from a world in which the nation-state is seen as the dominant spatial form to a world characterized by a series of overlapping global, regional and local spaces. These transformations represent a radical re-ordering of the spatial and social modes of living for older people.

—Hyde (2016)

Introduction

Jay Sokolovsky

A famous Far Side cartoon shows a scene of tribally dressed natives, perhaps living along the Amazon, inside their simple thatched abode. They peer through a window at goofy-looking, pith-helmeted first world scholars arriving by canoe on their river bank. You notice the natives clutching a variety of fancy electronic gadgets in their arms. With panic in their eyes they seek to hide these signs of modernity as someone shouts to his compatriots, "Anthropologists, Anthropologists!"

Such cartoons really hit home to anthropologists who must take into account the local-global nexus implied by the two quotes leading off Part III. This is especially the case with the dramatic increase in access to communication technology in far-flung parts of the world. Periodically over the past months while writing this, I have had repeated Facebook Messenger conversations with my 12-year-old godson about his family in the Indigenous Mexican community I have been connected to for over 45 years and discussed in Part III. This is a big change even in the past few years as most households now have access to at least one smartphone and radically increased their connection to their nation and the world. At the same time this has been but a very tiny aspect of the kinds of social and economic transformation the community has undergone since the dawn of the 21st century.

This is certainly not a laughing matter as globalization has unleashed the kinds of changes that are at the root of massive immigrant and refugee movement now challenging Europe and the United States in the past few years. At the same time wealth production has coincided with increasing robotics and automation to produce a glaring divide between high-skill, high-wage versus low-wage, low-tech work along with dramatically increased inequality sparking angry dystopian movements such as America's red hatted "Make America Great Again" and France's "yellow jacket" rebellion of rural folk who feel left out of the prosperity accorded to select parts of their population.

PROJECT TO FOLLOW:

Ageing in a Time of Mobility Project: Centered in Germany's Max Plank Institute—this is a global and interdisciplinary project investigating the interconnections between aging populations and global migration. https://www.mmg.mpg.de/mprg-amrith.

The quotes at the top of this introduction reflect the complex interweaving of local and global and how that is reshaping the social, environmental and technical spaces in which populations are aging. Consider the implications of these kinds of changes. On the one hand, it jokingly illustrates a key point in Part III's Web Book by Chris Fry: the overly optimistic anticipated benefits for "less developed" peoples of an accelerated movement of consumer goods, people, and capital across once inaccessible boundaries. On the other hand, it also obscures the fact that overall the enduring economic and social benefits from this explosion of "free" trade pacts, privatization of governmental functions, and Internet accessibility end up helping small, affluent sectors of national citizenry—often those who needed it least. Along with DVD players and smartphones in Mexico or Kenya has come "structural adjustment," imposed by the IMF or World Bank to liberalize markets, end government support for basic commodities and services, and stimulate foreign investment. Such imposed reforms have often resulted in loss of jobs to local citizens and resulted in less effective and more expensive goods and services.

Until recently, the primary model for considering how massive worldwide change has impacted the elderly has been "modernization" theory. It tries to predict the impact of change from relatively undifferentiated rural-/traditional-based societies with limited technology to modern urban-based entities. This shift is marked by the use of complex industrial technology, inanimate energy

---

PROJECTS TO FOLLOW:

There are ongoing long-term projects about aging in developing nations such as South Africa (HAALSI—Health and Aging in Africa http://haalsi.org) and India (LASI—Longitudinal Aging Study in India, https://lasi.hsph.harvard.edu/). See also the Program on the Global Demography of Aging at Harvard University, https://www.hsph.harvard.edu/pgda/.

sources, and differentiated institutions to promote efficiency and progress. Third world countries are said to develop or progress as they adopt, through cultural diffusion, the modernized model of rational and efficient societal organization. While such a transformation is often viewed as an overall advance for such countries, a strong inverse relationship is suggested between the elements of modernization as an independent variable and the status of the aged as a dependent variable. Donald Cowgill, first by suggesting a number of discrete postulates and later in developing a more elaborate model, has been the most dominant writer on this subject (1974, 1986). The hypothesized decline in valued roles, resources, and respect available to older persons in modernizing societies is said to stem from four main factors: modern health technology, economies based on scientific technology, urbanization, and mass education and literacy.

Validation of this paradigm has been uneven and has spurred a small industry of gerontological writings, which debate the proposed articulation of modernization and aging (see Rhoads and Holmes 1995: 251–85; and Aboderin 2004 for excellent reviews). Historians have sharply questioned the model, saying not only that it is ahistorical but also that, by idealizing the past, an inappropriate "world we lost syndrome" has been created (Kertzer and Laslett 1994). For example, summing up research on the elderly living in Western Europe several hundred years ago, historian Andrejs Plakans states, "There is something like a consensus that the treatment of the old was harsh and decidedly pragmatic: dislike and suspicion, it is said, characterized the attitudes of both sides" (1989).

A good example of the complexity of this issue is seen in a study of three untouchable communities in India (Vincentnathan and Vincentnathan 1994). The authors show how in the poorest communities, the assumption of respect and high status as a prior condition did not hold. Here the elders had no resources to pass on. Modernization programs that included providing material resources for the elders became a new basis for binding together the young and old. However, increased education of the young led many children and young adults to feel superior to parents, fostering a distinct change in generational relations, closer to the predictions of modernization theory.[1]

Beyond Modernization and toward Globalization

The dramatic upsurge of older citizens remaining alive in third world countries is a legacy of the last three decades. The demographic changes detailed by He and Kinsella (Part I), have been intertwined with alterations in economic production, wealth distribution, and the often violent devolution of large states into smaller successor nations. Properly understood, such changes are but the latest wave of globalism emerging since the 1970s. Called "supercapitalism" by Robert Reich, it features radical expansion of communication technology, multicountry agreements such as NAFTA to promote the unimpeded flow of capital across national borders, unprecedented population movement, and shifts in the location and nature of production of goods and services (2007).

Globalization and the Moral Economy

Within this "Culture of Wealth," despite the rise in numbers of billionaires, global inequality has dramatically accelerated (Crystal 2016; McGill 2016). At the start of this new wave of globalization, in 1970, the difference in GNP wealth between the poorest and wealthiest nations was 88 to 1; by the 21st century this differential had risen to 267. Such growing inequalities have had an impact on the United States. Despite impressive production of wealth from 1970 to 2000, there was a 7 percent *decline* in relative wages and benefits, a dramatic decline in employer-supported pension programs, and a record number of Americans now lacking health insurance (Henrickson 2007). In the United States, a specific impact on the health of the most vulnerable elderly has been share-trading of nursing homes, as is done for entities like Dunkin Donuts, the *Wall Street Journal*, or Wal-Mart. We will see in Polivka's Web Book chapter in Part VI how this has seriously worsened both the care of our impaired elders and the working conditions of those keeping them alive.

Beginning in the 1990s, neoliberal economists began to expand their view of the "aging crisis" to a global arena. The basic argument as put forth by the World Bank in *Averting the Old Age Crisis* (1994) is that informal and public sector programs are incapable of handling the impending demographic imperatives brought about by aging in the developing world (see also Chawla et al. 2007). They stress allowing the private and voluntary sectors to fill the coming needs in social welfare and reducing state provision of support to only the most extreme cases of need. A presumption in such a model is that universal public pensions and other public support programs undercut "informal" family-based systems of support for the elderly. The work of Lloyd-Sherlock in Latin America (2004) and Briller in rural Mongolia (2000) provide a strong critique of this perspective. Briller for example showed that pensions can have a very positive effect on reinforcing the preexisting family-centered sentiments and practical support of the aged, while not "crowding out" traditional systems of filial devotion and assistance.

Others, such as in Fry's Web chapter, focus discussion on the risks globalization imposes on the life of older adults. Her work sets the stage for examining this issue in diverse community- and national-based cultural settings—where, in essence, the globalized rubber hits the demographically aging road (Hyde and Higgs 2017).

Managing Warm Contact in the World's Oldest Society

Japan is one of the best examples for looking at how a society adapts to the extremes of population aging. Its retention of high co-residence rates compared to other major, urban postindustrial societies and a cultural system stressing prerogatives of senior status have collided with their unparalleled success in promoting exceptional longevity and the growing trend of adult women who desire to remain in the workforce. Iza Kavedžija's chapter in Part III is the most central of several chapters that focus on Japan and connects to both Wright's chapter (Part VI) on eldercare robots and unravelling the secrets of Okinawa's many centenarians (Part VI Willcox et al.). Here Kavedžija draws upon her extensive research in Japan to lay out the dimensions of changes in the cultural spaces and scripts for aging which were accelerating in the early 21st century. Within this context she shows that in the emergent Japanese context it is not as a simple relationship between carer and cared-for, but new elderscapes of flowing exchanges involving neighbors, cafés, and initiatives begun by elders themselves. Importantly she also explores zones of abandonment that have emerged with a growing inequality among Japan's older population.

Since the 1980s there has begun a radical rethinking of the place of older citizens in Japanese society, countering the glowingly positive view presented in Erdman Palmore's *The Honorable Elders: A Cross-Cultural Analysis of Aging in Japan* (1975). This work and a revised volume (1985), with Japanese gerontologist Daisaku Maeda, was largely based on statistical patterns of household organization and ideal cultural norms. It was criticized by scholars both in North America and Japan (Plath 1987; Koyano 1989).

Japan's societal response to such problems has been to undertake a succession of ambitious plans of public sector support for the social, economic, and health needs of their oldest citizens. These efforts established widely arrayed, taxpayer-funded eldercare services including adult day care, home visit nurses, and short-term and long-term stays at public nursing homes.

WEB SPECIAL:

Takehito Hayakawa, "Using 'Community Life Support' to Spread Citizen-Driven Health Promotion Activities," *Radiant: Ritsumeikan University Research Report*, May 15, 2017, http://www.ritsumei.ac.jp/research/radiant/eng/aging-society/story4.html.

Web Special:

AARP International, "Kotoen—An Innovative Model for Intergenerational Care," *The Journal*, December 19, 2018, https://vimeo.com/3072 83754.

This has also included some of the first experiments at creating cultural spaces uniting senior centers with nursery schools.

Imaginary Landscapes of a Rapidly Aging Nation

Thailand, another Southeast Asian country, is the subject of the chapter by Felicity Aulino. Her research there began as an intern with a Thai elder-care NGO where she was able to learn not only about the realities of family care but how people imagined and were beginning to narrate the future of leisure activities and supports beyond the local kin group. This is happening as the nation has become the third most rapidly aging country in the world. With the growing public sense of Thailand becoming part of the aging wave that has already overtaken neighbors such as Japan and China, the near future of this "demographic imaginary" is providing a new framework for rethinking age categories and an anticipated late life. Aulino explores this through narrative in which, while it can have a base of multigenerational care set in Buddhism, one of her respondents exclaims "Condos! That is our dream!" Others imagine supportive services in an age-integrated setting with younger kin nearby. Importantly, while the current narrative of old age involves an ensuing abandonment by children, like with the similar complaints by the Ju'hoansi of Botswana (Part I Rosenberg) or in the Mexican village of Amanalco (Part III Sokolovsky), the reality is that care still revolves around the family (Knodel and Teerawichitchainan 2017; Aulino 2019).

Web Special:

Kiyoto Kurokawa, "What Do Thailand and Japan Have in Common, in Terms of Aging Populations?" *Radiant: Ritsumeikan University Research Report*, July 10, 2017, www.ritsumei.ac.jp/research/radiant/eng/aging -society/story9.html/.

Filial Devotion and the God of Wealth

While whole new social landscapes focusing on autonomous older adults are glaringly obvious to the casual visitor to Florida (see Part V Katz), this is also happening in the most unexpected societal contexts such as China, India, Japan, and Italy. Here the plaintive cry of "Family is everything and will take care of the elders" often echoes off of empty rooms in closed elementary schools, especially in rural areas. East Asia is a global epicenter for considering the collision of unprecedented aging populations, unrivaled engagement with capitalism, and three of our planet's most rapidly aging nations: South Korea, China, and Thailand (Cheng et al. 2015; World Bank 2016).[2]

While the West's attention is focused on migration from the poorer South of our planet to Europe and North America, China is undergoing the largest movement of human population that we know of in human history. Here, since the beginning of the 21st century, 200 million rural peasants have migrated to work in urban settings and factory towns.

Zhang's chapter on China in Part III deals with the confluence of the globe's most rapid and massive urbanization meeting the second most rapid rate of population aging. Here we encounter this nation learning the limits of cultural scripts centered on son-dependent filial devotion (see Santos and Harrell 2017). Her work on China undertakes a monumental task, to understand the realities of aging in a nation with a fifth of the planet's citizens, a deeply rooted non-Western cultural heritage, and a profoundly changing economic system. These factors have placed its elders at the leading edge of a globalizing world, challenging the limits of an ancient pattern of filial piety. The changes since the last edition of this volume a decade ago and even the very recent past are breathtaking. These include massive urban building plans for retired citizens, 7,000 senior universities, and high-tech senior expos including major investment in robotic elder entertainment and care. Such changes are examined in the context of filial expectations being modified and redefined.

WEB SPECIAL:

See the videos about a small factory town in southeast China where more than two-thirds of the 60,000 residents are part of this rural–urban migration. University College London, "Industrial China," http://www.ucl.ac.uk/why-we-post/research-sites/industrial-china.

WEB SPECIAL:

Conflict between dancing grannies and younger residents: Channel 4 News, "Meet the Grannies of China Who Won't Stop Dancing," September 7, 2014, https://www.youtube.com/watch?v=QU9AY1r2zaw.

Hong Zhang takes her experience of having grown up in Mao-era China, with her extensive anthropological research in both rural and urban areas, to capture the incredible dynamism of aging in the world's most populous nation. Since the 1980s and the end of the collectivist period, China has embraced what some have called the "God of Wealth" (Ikels 1996), while at the same time its population has begun to age at a pace equal to Japan. Most state efforts to support a rapidly growing older population have been concentrated in urban areas, where nonfamilial social and economic infrastructure supports are concentrated and are invoking new cultural constructions of aging and retirement. With new laws seeking to extend basic health insurance coverage and strengthen family support, the government has a national "90–7–3" goal—that is, to have 90 percent of the elderly cared for at home, 7 percent at community care centers, and the remaining 3 percent at nursing homes (Leong 2018).

The new urban late-life script stresses age-peer mutual support and health, promoting outdoor activities and, with new wealth, the undertaking of leisure activities and travel. This often extends to public spaces by taking over public parks and squares for mass dancing, exercising, and performance, which the government has tried but failed to control. This is in competition with the more traditional late-life pattern of dependence on adult children and confinement to the home. Urban elders especially see public group dancing as maintaining good health while building community relations (Chen 2018).

"One to One" and "Five by One"

Another important change in enhancing the community engagement of older adults is seen in China's most elder-dense city, Shanghai. Here Jeanne Shea (Web Book) documents the operation of a senior companion program in China, which since 2012 has assigned "young-old" neighborhood volunteers to check on vulnerable elders 80 and older living alone. In this case one volunteer is expected to monitor and assist five elders needing assistance. Studies of community-based social engagement of older adults such as this have shown a variety of benefits to the broader society as well as the elders themselves. In China their Health and Retirement Longitudinal Survey showed a significant link of social engagement to improved measures of self-rated health and reduced mental distress of the elderly (Liu et al. 2019). The Chinese program in Shea's chapter is connected to a discussion of more widespread programs in the United States such as the Experience Corps, Foster Grandparents, Senior Companions, and RSVP (Retired and Senior Volunteer Program). These programs together involve 360,000 Americans aged 55 and older in volunteer community service opportunities annually.

Multilocal Familism Meets 21st-Century Reality

Aging in Translocal Communities

Among the most common processes to provoke local-level change in the industrializing world is the delocalization of social and economic resources that sustain and connect families with their natal communities. Viewing this process in Africa, Weisner used a construct of "multilocal" families to think more realistically about kin support (1997). In many of the rural places anthropologists have worked, economic necessity and changed patterns of transportation and communication have created translocal and increasingly transnational communities (see Yaris 2017; Part II Coe; Part VI Staudacher and Kaiser-Grolimund). In some cases, such as is noted in the Web Special below, there are equal numbers of persons in a Mexican village as there are in a neighborhood of Brooklyn, New York.

Unlike Asia, until recently Latin America has received relatively little attention in terms of the social consequences of aging. This has changed with the realization that countries like Mexico will become demographically as old as the United States by midcentury (Montes de Oca, et al. 2014; Angel, Vega, and López-Ortega 2017). The chapter by Jay Sokolovsky, set in a Mexican indigenous village, examines how familial, work, and public spaces in which people age have been transformed as the community has grown from a village to a globally connected town.

Here in Amanalco, a substantial portion of a community's citizens, while still residing in their home community, have almost daily reliance on nearby towns and cities for economic sustenance, social interaction, and cultural

---

WEB SPECIAL:

Deborah Sontag, "A Mexican Town That Transcends All Borders," *New York Times*, July 21, 1998, https://www.nytimes.com/1998/07/21/nyregion/a-mexican-town-that-transcends-all-borders.html.

---

ideas. Returning to Amanalco in 2018 for the Mexican Day of the Dead, he encounters firsthand a powerful negative impact of the globalization of food. He is there to memorialize the death of his 52-year-old compadre from diabetes. Over the past several decades the easy access to soda, fast food, and sugar-/fat-laden snacks even in rural indigenous communities has sparked the rise of diet-related chronic diseases (Aguilar-Navarro et al. 2015; He, Kowal, and Naidoo 2018). In his chapter Sokolovsky tries to understand the factors that have kept elders integrated in the heart of this rural community, despite some forces pushing them to the margins. This has occurred despite the replacement of the agrarian, campesino life course script by a proletarian worker lifestyle surrounded by TVs, DVD players, cell phones, Internet cafés, and a club for the elderly.

One of the threads connecting Zhang's chapter with this work in Mexico is a shift toward a more equal relationship between generations over the past three decades. This has also been noted by Aboderin for urban Ghana (2006) and may represent a pervasive impact of globalization (see Samanta 2019 for India). While shifting ideas about gender in late life are not altering as rapidly as in urban Mexico (Wentzell 2013), an important change in Amanalco was the movement of middle-aged and older women into important positions of community leadership over the past two decades. Similar to the discussion in Box III.1 below, older women play an increasingly important role in familial and public cultural spaces. Overall, Sokolovsky finds that global transformations are not necessarily a horrible thing for the aged, if their locality has some control over key resources and older citizens are included in the process of figuring out what adaptations are best for the community.

Postsocialism East Europe Meets Neoliberal Reality

The final chapter in Part III by Gerard Weber takes readers deep into lives of retirees struggling to get by in the East European nation of Romania. Set within the city of Galați, the chapter traces the radical changes in societal structure following the collapse of the Soviet Union (see Gramshammer-Hhol and Ursulesku 2020 for aging in East Europe). The ensuing transition to a neoliberal capitalist economy has intensified hardships of most older adult in terms of their poverty, isolation, and access to health care. Gerard

Box III.1   The Grandmother Projects

On mornings during farming season, Djina Sabaly cares for her granddaughter, brings food to her husband in the fields, and gathers milk from the family cows. By lunchtime she has already walked eight kilometers. A long-time resident of the south Senegalese village of Darou Idjiratou, she takes great pride in her importance to the family. "We say that a family without a grandmother has no foundation because it has no guardian of traditional values." Sabaly, 68, provides daily childcare for four grandchildren, assists her farmer husband, advises seven children and their spouses, and works in the garden and fields. "In my village," she says, "elders always occupy the foremost position. They are consulted regarding the most important affairs."

The grandmothers of Darou Idjiratou, a rural village of 700 inhabitants, are not unique in the developing world. Throughout Africa, Asia, and Latin America, grandmothers provide primary childcare, do domestic and farm work, act as family advisors, and pass on cultural traditions. In areas without access to schools or health care, in countries where parents have fallen ill due to AIDS or other diseases, grandmothers frequently become the main parent and teacher. Despite grandmothers' importance, Western organizations that work in developing countries have been slow to incorporate elders into their activities. Fearing that grandmothers will be unwilling to accept new ideas, they offer young women training in health and nutrition while ignoring the grandmothers to whom these women turn for help. New mothers have to choose between the advice of a trusted family elder and the modern practices taught by an outside organization. The Grandmother Project, a U.S. nonprofit, is working to redress this oversight (www.grandmotherproject.org). Founder Judi Aubel launched the organization in 2004 in order to strengthen the leadership of grandmothers in improving health for women and children. Since 1997, Aubel has been involved in community activities in Laos, Senegal, Mali, Uzbekistan, and Albania that demonstrated the effectiveness of involving grandmothers in projects. Evaluations have documented greater confidence among grandmothers, increased community respect for elder women, and improvements in advice to young women on pregnancy, infant feeding, and neonatal health. In Senegal, the number of grandmothers advising women to give infants nutritious foods increased from 57 percent to 97 percent as a result of project efforts. Health improvements were greater in communities where grandmothers participated than where only younger women were involved.

The Grandmother Project's approach succeeds at introducing new practices by working with existing social structures and leaders. Using stories and songs, the Grandmother Project celebrates the traditional advisory role of grandmothers. Group training sessions teach health and nutrition to young and old alike—to women of childbearing age and to grandmothers who provide advice and care. Combining traditional practices and modern knowledge strengthens grandmothers' ability to promote good childcare and increases the likelihood of lasting improvements in health.

These efforts enjoy widespread community support in Sabaly's rural village. Residents of Darou Idjiratou have noticed that fewer neighborhood children suffer from malnutrition and related illnesses than in the past. "In order for a development activity to work in the village, elders have to be included," says village leader Tidian Cisse. "We are thrilled that grandmothers are involved in nutrition activities because their role is to transmit knowledge to the younger generation."

Related Resource: J. Henry and I. Landsberg-Lewis, Powered by Love: A Grandmothers' Movement to End AIDS in Africa. Fredericton, NB: Goose Lane Editions, 2017. http://grandmotherscampaign.org/.

Adapted from: Michael Gubser and Kristina Gryboski, "The Role of Grandmothers in Developing Countries," AARP, 2006. http://globalag.igc.org/elderrights/world/2006/grandmarole.htm. Used by permission of Michael Gubser.

details the variety of coping strategies Romanian retirees employ to survive and the growth of activism to improve their conditions. This chapter helps us understand the context of migration out of that country by younger kin to work as family care workers in such places like Italy (see Part VI Web Chapter Nicolescu).

Notes

1. A 1995 nationwide survey in India conducted by HelpAge India showed that almost 30 percent of India's aged have no family to live with or cannot live with the family they have.

2. See Canning 2007 for a broad discussion of aging and development in Asia.

Bibliography

Aboderin, I. 2004. "Modernization and Ageing Theory Revisited." *Ageing and Society* 24: 29–50.

Aboderin, I. 2006. *Intergenerational Support and Old Age in Africa*. New Brunswick, NJ: Transaction.

Aguilar-Navarro, S. G., H. Amieva, L. M. Gutiérrez-Robledo, and J. A. Avila Funes. 2015. "Frailty among Mexican Community-Dwelling Elderly: A Story Told 11 Years Later. The Mexican Health and Aging Study." *Salud Pública de México* 57(Supp. 1): S62–69.

Angel, J. L., W. Vega, and M. López-Ortega. 2017. "Aging in Mexico: Population Trends and Emerging Issues." *Gerontologist* 57(2): 153–62.

Aulino, F. 2019. *Rituals of Care: Karmic Politics in an Aging Thailand*. Ithaca, NY: Cornell University Press.

Briller, S. 2000. "Crowding Out: An Anthropological Examination of an Economic Paradigm." PhD diss., Case Western University.

Canning, D. 2007. "Ageing in Asia: The Impact of Aging on Asian." Harvard School of Public Health Seminar on Aging. http://adb.org/AnnualMeeting/2007/seminars/presentations/dcanning-presentation.pdf

Chawla, M., G. Betcherman, A. Banerji, A. M. Bakilana, C. Feher, M. Mertaugh, M. L. S. Puerta, A. M. Schwartz, and L. Sondergaard. 2007. *From Red to Gray: The Third Transition of Ageing Populations in Eastern Europe and the Former Soviet Union*. Washington, DC: World Bank. http://documents.worldbank.org/curated/en/185581468034762694/pdf/408960From1Red1ew01see0also04053210.pdf.

Chen, C. 2018. "Designing the Danceable City: How Residents in Beijing Cultivate Health and Community Ties Through Urban Dance." *Journal of the American Planning Association* 84(3–4): 237–249.

Cheng, S.-T., I. Chi, H. H. Fung, L. W. Li, and J. Woo, eds. 2015. *Successful Aging: Asian Perspectives*. Dordrecht: Springer.

Cowgill, D. 1974. "The Aging of Populations and Society." *Annals of the American Academy of Political and Social Sciences* 415: 1–18.

Cowgill, D. 1986. *Aging Around the World*. Belmont, CA: Wadsworth.

Crystal, S. 2016. "Late-Life Inequality in the Second Gilded Age: Policy Choices in a New Context." *Public Policy & Aging Report* 26(2): 42–47.

Gramshammer-Hhol, D., and O. Ursulesku, eds. 2020. *Foreign Countries of Old Age: East and Southeast European Perspectives on Aging*. New York: Columbia University Press.

He, W., P. Kowal, and N. Naidoo. 2018. *Trends in Health and Well-Being of the Older Populations in SAGE Countries: 2014–2015*. Washington, DC: U.S. Census Bureau. https://www.census.gov/content/dam/Census/library/publications/2018/demo/p95-18-01.pdf.

Henrickson, C. 2007. "Longevity's Impact on Retirement Security." In *Global Health & Global Aging*, edited by M. Robinson, W. Novelli, C. Pearson, and L. Norris. San Francisco: Jossey-Bass.

Hyde, M. 2016. "Ageing and Globalization." *International Network for Critical Gerontology*. October 20. https://criticalgerontology.com/ageing-globalisation/.

Hyde, M., and P. Higgs. 2017. *Ageing and Globalization*. Bristol, UK: Policy.

Ikels, C. 1996. *The Return of the God of Wealth: The Transition to a Market Economy in Urban China.* Stanford, CA: Stanford University Press.

Kertzer, D., and P. Laslett, eds. 1994. *Demography Society and Old Age.* Berkeley: University of California Press.

Knodel, J., and B. Teerawichitchainan. 2017. "Family Support for Older Persons in Thailand: Challenges and Opportunities." University of Michigan Population Studies Center Research Report 17-879.

Koyano, W. 1989. "Japanese Attitudes Toward the Elderly: A Review of Research Findings." *Journal of Cross-Cultural Gerontology* 4(4): 335–46.

Leong, C. 2018. "'Too Busy, Too Much Pressure': An Ageing China and the Erosion of Filial Piety." *Hong Kong Free Press*, April 15: 21.

Liu, J. 2019. "Social Engagement and Elderly Health in China: Evidence from the China Health and Retirement Longitudinal Survey (CHARLS)." *International Journal of Environmental Research and Public Health* 16(2): 278.

Lloyd-Sherlock, P., ed. 2004. *Living Longer: Aging, Development and Social Protection.* London: Zed.

McGill, K. 2016. *Global Inequality: Anthropological Insights.* Toronto: University of Toronto Press.

Montes de Oca, V., S. Garay, B. Rico, and S. J. García. 2014. "Living Arrangements and Aging in Mexico: Changes in Households, Poverty and Regions, 1992–2009." *International Journal of Social Science Studies* 2(4): 61–74.

Palmore, E., and D. Maeda. 1985. *The Honorable Elders Revisited: A Revised Cross-Cultural Analysis of Aging in Japan.* Durham, NC: Duke University Press (1975).

Plakans, A. 1989. "Stepping Down in Former Times: A Comparative Assessment of Retirement in Traditional Europe." In *Age Structuring in Comparative Perspective*, edited by D. Kertzer and K. W. Schaie. Hillsdale, NJ: Lawrence Erlbaum.

Plath, D. 1987. "Ecstasy Years—Old Age in Japan." In *Growing Old in Different Societies: Cross-Cultural Perspectives*, edited by J. Sokolovsky. Acton, MA: Copley.

Reich, R. 2007. *Supercapitalism: The Transformation of Business, Democracy, and Everyday Life.* New York: Knopf.

Rhoads, E., and L. Holmes. 1995. *Other Cultures, Elder Years*, 2nd ed. Thousand Oaks, CA: Sage.

Samanta, T. 2019. "The Joint Family and Its Discontents: Interrogating Ambivalence in Intergenerational Relationships." *Asian Population Studies* 15(1): 28–46. https://www.tandfonline.com/doi/full/10.1080/17441730.2018.1560659.

Santos, G., and S. Harrell, eds. 2017. *Transforming Patriarchy: Chinese Families in the 21st Century.* Seattle: University of Washington Press.

Savage, M., G. Bagnall, and B. Longhurst. 2005. *Globalization and Belonging.* London: Sage.

Vincentnathan, S., and L. Vincentnathan. 1994. "Equality and Hierarchy in Untouchable Intergenerational Relations and Conflict Resolutions." *Journal of Cross-Cultural Gerontology* 9: 1–19.

Weisner, T. 1997. *African Families and the Crisis of Social Change*. Westport, CT: Greenwood.

Wentzell, E. 2013. *Maturing Masculinities: Aging, Chronic Illness, and Viagra in Mexico*. Durham, NC: Duke University Press.

World Bank. 1994. *Averting the Old Age Crisis*. New York: Oxford University Press.

World Bank. 2016. *Live Long and Prosper: Aging in East Asia and Pacific. World Bank East Asia and Pacific Regional Report*. Washington, DC: World Bank.

Yaris, K. 2017. *Care across Generations: Solidarity and Sacrifice in Transnational Families*. Stanford, CA: Stanford University Press.

CHAPTER NINETEEN

Web Book: Aging and the Age of Globalization

Christine L. Fry

Available at: http://www.culturalcontextofaging.com/webbook-fryglobalization

This chapter focuses discussion on the risks globalization imposes on the life of older adults. Her work sets the stage for examining this issue in diverse community- and nation-based cultural settings—where, in essence, the globalized rubber hits the demographically aging road.

CHAPTER TWENTY

Communities of Care and Zones of Abandonment in "Super-Aged" Japan

Iza Kavedžija

What kind of wish to make? I asked myself as I walked past the school, quiet during teaching hours. It was the first week of July, just before Tanabata, the "star festival" when the two lovers Orihime and Hikoboshi (the stars Vega and Altair) meet briefly after their annual separation. A bamboo tree is always erected, and people hang up wishes and hopes written on colorful strips of paper, so I was wondering what I might write upon arrival in Mitsuba, a local community café run by volunteers (Photo 20.1). It was also Wednesday, so likely to be a busy day there, as each Wednesday Sano san and his other retired friends would offer to sharpen knives for those in the neighborhood.

Happy to escape the stifling heat, I entered the large courtyard and stopped in the bathroom. Small pink sinks hung low and I had to bend to check my sweaty appearance in the mirror at toddler height. Mitsuba was located in a large building that used to be a kindergarten, and the facilities remained unchanged. An L-shaped building with a large enclosed lawn, it must have had 20-odd classrooms across two floors, spreading to the left and right of the entrance. I walked past a room in which 10 older women were practicing the Hawaiian hula dance and slipped in through the sliding door into the air-conditioned space of the community café. I was met by the sound

Photo 20.1   Wishes for Tanabata festival hanging on an
ornamental bamboo in Mit-
suba, a community café. (Photo
by Iza Kavedžija)

of many voices; Mitsuba seemed quite busy despite the heat. Sano san, a
bespectacled quiet man in his early seventies, had set up his space for knife
sharpening on a large table to the right and was chatting with two women
who lived in the apartment block across the road, both in their late sixties. A
group of senior volunteers was arranging some bamboo branches in the back
of the room, a decoration for the upcoming Tanabata. No doubt, later that
day we would start decorating it with our wishes. After greeting the women
encircling the tree, I sat with a group of five older women and men. Some of
them were also café volunteers on other days. Their glasses, set on white
handmade crocheted coasters, were filled with a pale orange drink—cold
yuzu citrus tea, they told me, was the best in hot weather, very refreshing.
We sat, chatting and laughing, looking over the empty playground.

Demographic change in Japan has been so rapid that the face of the neighborhood in the north of Osaka, where Mitsuba was located, changed in front
of its inhabitants' eyes. Two of the three kindergartens in the area had closed
down, and one school was facing closure; meanwhile, several chiropractor's
clinics, two day-care centers for the elderly, and a large shop with mobility
equipment had recently opened. Over 70,000 people in Japan are above the
age of 100, and in 2017, the ratio of people aged 65 years or over to the total
population reached 27.7 percent (Figure 20.1). This ratio is expected to rise

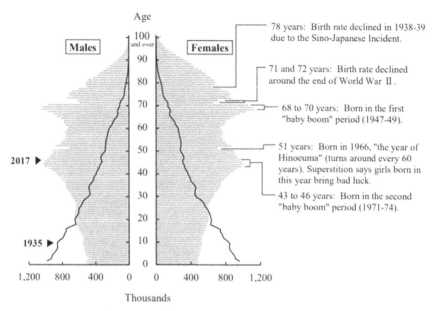

Figure 20.1   Population Pyramid (Statistics Bureau of Japan 2018. Japan Statistical Yearbook 2018, p. 8. Available online at: https://www.stat.go.jp/english /data/handbook/c0117.html).

to about 40 percent by around 2060 (Statistics Bureau of Japan 2017, based on census data in 2015; Statistics Burau of Japan 2018). As a consequence of longevity combined with a very low birth rate, Japan has now for a while been a "super-aged" society.

This is the highest ratio of its kind in the world with wide-ranging ramifications[1] for Japanese society, including the pension system, health care, gender relations, voting, and consumer preferences, to name just a few. The understanding of population aging became entangled with issues of longevity and dependency, leading to an increasingly negative view of aging, manifest in public dilemmas such as the paradox of reserved "silver" seating: How, in a society so well known for its respect for the elders (Photo 20.2), did reserved seating on public transport become necessary (Goodman 2010)?

Changing Roles and Images of the Elderly

Demographic changes have indirectly affected the capacity of families to look after aging relatives once they require support. The ideal of a strong family network was strengthened after World War II, when many siblings survived into adulthood and were able to provide support to their aging parents (Ochiai 1997: 71), forming a base for "Japanese-style" welfare with the

Photo 20.2 Writing prayers for the Keiro no Hi, or Respect for the Aged Day, a national holiday held on the third Monday of September every year. This photograph was taken near Shintennoji in Osaka, where many people go on this day. (Photo by Iza Kavedžija)

family unit at its core (Goodman 1998: 150). Today, not only do older family members live longer but families have fewer siblings to look after their aging parents. Older people themselves now often refuse to move in with their son's family and prefer to continue living on their own, where possible (Figure 20.2). Kondo san, a lady in her late seventies whom I met in another community café and got to know quite well, had simply decided to live on her own and often praised the ease and comfort of doing so: "This is heaven [*gokuraku*]!" she would say, with a smile. After many hardships in her life and a somewhat strained relationship with her husband, she now felt a sense of relief and enjoyed having relatively few responsibilities. She told me she had tried living with both her son and, later, her daughter's family, but found she needed to make so many efforts to adjust to life with their families that she simply decided she was better off on her own in Osaka, in a neighborhood she knew well, a place where her community ties gave her a sense of support. She was proud of her independence and like many others I spoke with— particularly those in relatively good health—enjoyed the ease of living alone (*raku de ii*). But for Kondo san, the community and her ties to the neighborhood were just as important as her independence.

Older people in the area where Mitsuba was located typically became involved in a range of community activities, from organizing events for the

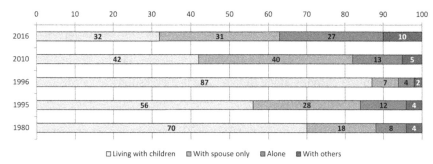

Figure 20.2   Living Arrangements of Older Japanese (Adapted from: Japan National Institute of Population and Social Security Research, "Housing with Seniors: 1975–2010" and Annual Report on the Aging Society 2018, https://www8.cao.go.jp/kourei/whitepaper/w-2018/gaiyou/30pdf_indexg.html).

local children, to staging singing sessions in the local day care for less-mobile elderly, to helping with meal deliveries for housebound elders.[2] Far from being exclusively the recipients of care, many of these elders actively extended care to others. In southern Osaka, where I met Kondo san, some of my older acquaintances volunteered in a community café and cultivated a wide range of community ties, effectively keeping track of each other, recommending services in the area, and sometimes making arrangements through acquaintances—asking a younger neighbor to help with an older man's rubbish when he was feeling unwell, for instance, or giving a phone number of a retired salaryman who was willing to help with small repairs free of charge to an older woman living alone. In both cases, the community café also served as a hub for exchanging information about municipal services and events, as well as the activities of the nonprofit sector. Its clientele cultivated a network of support and multiple dependencies, including the use of available welfare services, in order to live independently. Those very elders who deliberately rejected the ideal of the "three-generation family" can indeed be seen as actively shaping social change.

  This decision, when taken, was facilitated in those places where alternative sources of support were available but was perhaps also made possible by the fact that deciding to live alone was no longer seen as entirely out of the ordinary. In her ethnography of a nursing home a quarter of century ago, Diana Bethel (1992) wrote of the shame associated with lack of family support. Many residents were too ashamed to admit to their friends or neighbors that they had moved to an institution for the elderly, while others believed they had brought shame onto their children, in spite of the latter's disapproval of the move, since they were condemned by the community and by relatives as being insolent and egoistic (Bethel 1992: 131). Today, the number of people over the age of 65 and living in single households surpasses 5.5 million, having nearly doubled since 2000 (Statistics Bureau of Japan 2018: 12). This includes the vast numbers of people whose life alone is not a reflection of choice or preference, but as it becomes an ever more common occurrence, the option of living alone in older age is increasingly recognized. With the three-generation family ideal no longer the only positive option for older Japanese, it is possible to speak of a new narrative space for aging.

This space is no doubt made possible by the many support options available to older people, mostly through the long-term care insurance (*kaigo hoken*, LCTI) effectively introduced in 2000, covering everyone above the age of 65 according to their needs. Unlike previous kinds of welfare and support outside the family, services through the LCTI system are accessed with less hesitation or sense of stigma due to the universal and compulsory character of the scheme. While cash allowances are not possible, it is built around the provision of services in the public, private, and not-for-profit sectors. The possibility of making claims through a variety of providers allows for a wide range of care and support arrangements, including home-helper services, various kinds of nursing homes, day care and assisted living, according to the assessment of individual needs. Care and housing options have diversified, with many market actors offering housing and services to the elderly.

Just like new housing options, some of the spaces for aging in Japan that have opened up are material, physical spaces supporting the elderly and their communities. The cafés or salons (sometimes called *salon-kissa*) are spaces run by volunteer organizations, sometimes registered as nonprofit organizations and sometimes partially supported by the local government. Mitsuba had received both space and a small amount of income from the local government, but other volunteer organizations paid for their space by providing some services as a business and then utilizing their income for the expenses of running a community café and organizing public events. Mitsuba aimed to provide a space for anyone in the neighborhood who might feel somewhat disconnected, and while it was almost entirely run by and for people over the age of 65, Sugawara san—an elegant woman in her mid-sixties and one of the volunteers in charge—explained that its purpose was to advise on neighborhood services and opportunities to young mothers and those who might be new to the area. Such people might not have the community ties or knowledge to take advantage of the local amenities.

Mitsuba's ostensible aim of creating a sense of community for those without links in the area, regardless of their age, was confirmed in the practice of note taking: every time someone entered, the volunteer made a note in one of the following categories: child, elderly person, male or female. This tabulated data was summed up monthly and provided part of the report submitted to the local government. Mitsuba brought together a large body of mostly senior volunteers who took care of the local park and children's playgrounds, cleaned the grassy areas, pruned plants and planted flowers, ran vegetable growing sessions in the school next door, and organized local festivals, to mention just a few activities. A woman whose previous job involved working in an office on a computer took care of the Web site, which listed activities for various community members, including families with children, and a man who prior to retirement worked as a graphic designer helped with the newsletter, quite popular in the neighborhood as a source of information. Mitsuba volunteers told me they hoped to involve both older people and mothers of younger children, who were also seen at risk of social isolation in the early years of childrearing. Furthermore, this was seen as a good way of bringing people of different generations together.

The aim was to re-create a sense of community, without necessarily re-creating the community relationships of the past, which may have been seen as burdensome and ridden with obligations (see Kavedžija 2018). Volunteering was seen as a way of moving away from gift giving and meticulous exchange between families in the neighborhood, toward a new form of local organization and a more distributed reciprocity. This new relationship fit in well with earlier forms of community volunteering, such as organizing summer festivals, but was seen as less constraining since the number of people involved was larger, and the number of options for involvement more diverse.

Spaces of Influence: Silver Democracy and Silver Economy

As the proportion of older voters rises, the media have recently started warning of the dangers of "silver democracy": one in four Japanese is above the age of 65, yet they represent an even larger proportion of the electorate. Children, of course, do not vote, and older people are far more likely to attend elections than their younger counterparts, considering voting as their "civic duty" (Seo 2017). In an attempt to mitigate this imbalance, the voting age was lowered from the age of 20 to 18 in June 2016. This move was discussed for a while, and I recall heated conversations in 2009, including one when I chatted with a group of nine women aged between 45 and 65 who adamantly argued that young people are irresponsible and not mature enough to make serious decisions about politics when they are not even financially independent. In any case, now that the law was passed, it nonetheless seemed that the younger voter turnout would be relatively low. The predominance of older voters is seen to present a danger in terms of favoring policies supporting elderly welfare over measures helping families with children, while increasing the financial burden for the working population (Yoshida and Osaki 2016). Furthermore, older voters have been shown to be more conservative and more loyal in their voting preferences (Uchida and Iwabuchi 1999: 38f; Coulmas 2007: 99). Yet as new spaces for aging open up in Japan and the older population diversifies in terms of lifestyles and values, as the ethnographic data above indicate, perhaps older people need not be seen exclusively as a homogenous conservative group—instead some may take a role as drivers of social and political change.

The media attention given to the "silver market" makes it clear that older Japanese are recognized as a large consumer population with relatively high spending power. One large motor company, for instance, recently launched its most popular car model in a shorter version with older buyers in mind, who according to their studies find longer cars more difficult to turn (Waka-matsu 2012). Many stores and coffee shops target older people, especially those over 65, in a less direct way, as goods or services that are explicitly marketed "for those above the age of 70" do not necessarily appeal to customers (The Economist 2011). Many of the most affluent Japanese are now retiring, and luxury products and services are thoughtfully marketed towards this sizeable group. East Japan Railway Company opened a new super-luxury sleeper train "Twilight Express Mizukaze" in May 2017, offering tours of a kind popular among the older generation (Cooper and Ujikane 2017). Of course, while the resources at the disposal of older people may be considerable—hence the expression "elderly nobility" (*rōjin kizoku*)—not all older people are wealthy, and many fall below the poverty line (Cabinet Office 2007: 18). Recognition of this fact may mitigate the resentment of younger generations toward the older generations "living in wealth," with the prospect of even more older people in the future living with less income in smaller or single households.

Gaps and Spaces of Abandonment

If some older people are well off and have a comfortable existence bolstered by savings and homeownership, increasingly large numbers of people above the age of 65 face poverty. In fact, households headed by the elderly comprise the largest share (45.3 percent) of households receiving public assistance (NIPSSR 2014: 43; see also Sekine 2008: 51). At the same time, reports of families who struggled or even starved as they were unable to receive public assistance indicate that much larger numbers of people are at risk (Sekine 2008: 65). Furthermore, despite the positive effects of assistance in 2004, over half the older women living on their own fell below the poverty line (Shirahase 2010). The disparities in income are increasingly seen as an indication of a much more dramatic rift in the social fabric. Japan has now moved away from a self-perception as a homogenous middle-class society (*chūkan kaisō shakai*) to a designation as a "gap society" or *kakusa shakai* (Sato 2000; Yamada 2004; Hommerich 2012). The sense of disparity extends beyond income alone: sociologist Yamada Masahiro (2004) suggests Japan has now become a society of "disparity of hope" (*kibō kakusa shakai*)—hope

Photo 20.3   People praying in a temple in Tokyo specializing in prayers for *pok-kuri*, a quick, painless death. (Photo by Jay Sokolovsky)

is abandoned by those who cannot envisage a better life (Photo 20.3), thus becoming a privilege reserved for those who are socioeconomically secure (Allison 2013: 34).

The very same mechanisms that have been set in place to provide support can at times generate new zones of neglect. The LCTI, which has provided support for so many, while universal does not guarantee that everyone will be looked after. Nursing homes paid for through the insurance scheme and operated through nonprofit welfare corporations are scarce and in high demand, while the partially funded private homes charging large sums for room and board are expanding and opening, often offering higher standards and luxury, at a higher price (Campbell 1992: 22). Under conditions of budget strain, national debt, and the increasing costs of the pension system, health care, and the LCTI, which is partly funded through taxes, the welfare system again is placing demands on families: "As the cost of a comprehensive welfare policy in an ageing society became apparent, policy-makers quickly reverted to one that sought to place more of the burden back on the family, legitimated by reference to traditional customs" (Neary 2002: 199). More recently, according to my interlocutors in the Osakan volunteer sector, local governments are hoping to shift some of these responsibilities onto the community and community volunteer organizations.

The LCTI offers a choice of service providers, which can include actors across the private, nonprofit, and public sectors, effectively distributing responsibility for eldercare between family, state, and community. Yet, according to Jason Danely, this fragmentation divides the responsibility, and these new configurations of social welfare can lead to exclusion. Danely argues that such distribution opens up spaces for abandonment, as many people fall through the cracks in the system (2015). This "ideology of care through abandonment" produces a particular kind of subjectivity, one "unable to uphold human connections, recognition, and care without producing shame, isolation and estrangement" (Danely 2015: 161). This sounds like a rather strong indictment of the system, and while no doubt many receive sufficient support and the LCTI has many beneficial effects, the problem of abandonment of a growing number of elderly living in poverty and isolation is an issue too serious to be overlooked. In other words, the newly opened-up space of independent living enabled by the insurance and supportive communities, in the absence of strong neighborhood and familial ties and material security, all too easily transforms into a space of abandonment, particularly in those rural areas most affected by depopulation.[3]

Robots and Immigrants—The Carers of Tomorrow?

The demographic changes Japan is undergoing have implications for eldercare in multiple ways: larger numbers of older people living longer, even when they are in relatively good health, still translate into larger numbers of older people requiring help, support, and care. Moreover, the workforce is diminished, which puts a fiscal strain on the budgets for care and limits the number of workers who are able to care for the elderly, particularly when such professions are not well remunerated. Care work in Japan is therefore facing a serious issue of staff shortages. Possible answers to this problem include opening up the sector to skilled migrants and developing robots to assist with eldercare. At the moment, however, neither option looks particularly viable as a solution to the demographic challenge of the worker shortage: the number of foreign care workers is limited by the high immigration requirements they face, and while the incorporation of robots into everyday life is a national project, the use of social robots in institutions and house-holds remains far from commonplace (Kaerlein 2015, cited in Sone 2017; Robertson 2017; Wright Part VI). Nonetheless, the way these carer stories are framed reveals much about contemporary Japanese society.

In recognition of labor shortages, various organizations and groups, including Keidanren (Japan Business Federation, an influential employer organization), have long called for acceptance of higher numbers of skilled foreign workers (Takenaka 2012). The Japanese government indeed intro-duced a policy encouraging skilled migrants under a skill-based points scheme, and the demand for care workers was acknowledged. The 1998 Economic Partnership Programmes with Indonesia (and earlier with the Philippines) made it possible for a select number of qualified workers to train to become care workers or nurses in institutions for the elderly for a period of five years, after which they were eligible to apply for long-term employment. Long-term employment and residence were conditional upon passing a national examination in Japanese—a condition widely considered to be a very high requirement. The early cohorts had a very low success rate: between 2009 and 2011 merely 19 out of the 817 who took the examination passed. Later cohorts did somewhat better (Takenaka 2012: 39). Takenaka's work with skilled immigrants showed that they often considered Japan to be a stepping-stone in their careers, and effectively Japan's immigration pol-icy for skilled workers encouraged a "revolving-door" migration (Takenaka 2012).

Similarly, many Indonesian care workers who arrived in Japan in 2008 (Świtek 2016) faced challenges of working in Japanese organizations, partic-ularly with respect to the interpersonal relationships at work. Many consid-ered that these drawbacks and the discrepancy from their initial expectations as outweighing the benefits of the work arrangement. Despite the possibility of long-term employment, they came to think of their migration as tempo-rary. The case of foreign care workers is particularly interesting and has received a large amount of media attention, mostly due to the proximity and intimacy of care work, which used to be performed by family members. On the one hand, it appears that the management in some institutions was pri-marily concerned with the reactions of the elders and their families and avoided allocating bodily care to foreign trainees. On the other hand, the attitudes of the elderly towards the Indonesians were often warm and posi-tive, even if some were skeptical or reserved to begin with. At least for the elderly, the long-term involvement made a difference, and attitudes changed for the better.

Świtek's ethnography successfully adds layers of complexity to the image of a country opening up to migrants. In fact, this case made me wonder if in fact the presence of migrants was accepted only so long as they were guests: respected and well treated but implicitly expected to leave, rather than settle.

Also, as such, they could not be expected to perform certain menial or intimate body care tasks. At the same time, I wonder if this was a source of positive reports of smiling eldercare facility users: it is nice to have visitors! If this were the case, and the migrant carers were effectively neatly slotted into the preexisting category of visitor or guest, then the encounter becomes less challenging but also hardly transformative of attitudes towards migrant carers or promising for this strategy of staffing long-term care.

In nationwide surveys people express a sense of unease with foreigners as carers, while at the same time many indicate that they would be interested in a robot as a care assistant (Robertson 2014: 578). "When Paro shows up, their expression lights up," announces an early article on the use of social robots in care facilities accompanied by a photograph of an older resident of a care home smiling at the robotic baby seal Paro (Asahi 2005, cited in Coulmas 2007: 82). Over a decade later, a remarkably similar photograph accompanies a recent article on social robots. An older woman in the photo is smiling at Paro, a white furry baby seal robot, in the photograph accompanying the recent newspaper article in the recent major daily, *Mainichi Shinbun* (2017). The title announces a finding of a study confirming that 34 percent of the elderly who used social robots experience an increase in the sense of independence in everyday life. The nationwide study of the elderly in care institutions, conducted by the Japanese Agency for Medical Research and Development, indicates an increase particularly in basic daily activities, such as walking, eating, and maintaining physical appearance. The focus of the study was the effect that the "communication robots" have on everyday life. Informal reports often confirmed that the elderly would smile or brighten up in the presence of social robots, but this was the first study to explore the issue systematically—according to the article, at least, the positive effect is now "proven."

What is perhaps particularly interesting here is that the robots in the study, used in a variety of institutional settings, do not replace human carers but instead function as a kind of social or therapeutic aid. Other robots designed for care have supportive functions (such as exoskeletons that support movement or protect carers from injuries) or monitoring functions. In this context, it does not appear that robots are substituting human care work. In other words, robots are not regarded as ends in themselves, so much as a means (Bender 2012; Sone 2017).

So far so good, but the critics of social robots put forward a different argument of caution towards the robotization of care—the use of social robots promotes normalization and responsiveness to norms (Sone 2017: 204; Part II Prendergast; Part VI Wright). No doubt, the engineers who design robots are themselves embedded in specific cultural contexts and envisage help and care in culturally specific ways. In this sense, the envisaged use of robots in households and society is allowing for the protection and replication of "traditional" or conservative gender norms, where care is considered to be a women's work in the context of a heteronormative family unit (Robertson 2007, 2017). But the normalization is apparently also enforced on a higher level, too, at the level of national strategy. The government supports development and innovation in robotics, considering it a national priority under the conditions of demographic aging. While support for immigration appears to be moderate, support for the robotics industry is more robust as it aligns with the image of a technologically advanced nation—"the state is continuing a postwar trend of pursuing automation over replacement migration" (Robertson 2014: 558). Unlike foreigners, robots are readily naturalized, as they embody Japanese technological virtuosity. Their acceptance is sometimes justified with reference to a special Japanese "affinity" for robots, purportedly based on an animistic sensibility that does not draw a sharp line between animate and inanimate. According to Robertson, robotic help is enlisted to preserve the cultural values of the nation.

Should we therefore conclude that *plus ça change, plus c'est la même chose*—the more things change, the more they stay the same? The immigrants neatly assimilated to the figure of the guest present less of a problem, and blueprints for interacting with them can readily be found among the existing cultural resources. So far some of the foreign care workers indeed decided to return, but perhaps in order to be able to stay, they must resist their quiet designation as visitors. Until this happens, does the future of care work in Japan rest in the steady hands of the robots? Both the migrants and the robots may have an important place in care, but in a different way than one can immediately envisage: migration is often taking the shape of a revolving door, while robotic care assistants need not be very human-like. Meanwhile, much of the responsibility for care falls to the family members, who are themselves sometimes above the age of 65: children in their sixties caring for parents in their nineties, say, or a spouse taking care of their partner at an advanced age.

Vulnerability and Fostering Resilience

On March 11, 2011, an earthquake measuring 9.0 on the Richter scale struck eastern Japan. This great natural disaster triggered a 40-meter tsunami wave that killed 18,580 people, mostly by drowning, and displaced another 390,000. The older population was the most affected, with approximately 65 percent of the victims aged over 60 (Cabinet Office, 2011). Just under half were 70 or older. The older population further suffered in the prolonged aftermath of displacement. This tragic event exposed the vulnerability of the older population, leading to a number of responses, including the improvement of disaster response actions (Tsukasaki et al. 2016) as well as numerous grassroots efforts to create spaces of resilience.

The foundation of Ibasho café in Tohoku, the region most affected by the tsunami, is one such example. Ibasho—the name could be glossed as a place where one feels a sense of belonging—is a volunteer-run endeavor not unlike the community salons discussed above, created with the aim of making a social and a physical space operated by and for the elderly (Aldrich and Kyota 2017; Part V Box V.1). Here, too, the elders are themselves involved in care, but in an active and positive way. For example, some of the older inhabitants of a town in the Tohoku region were enlisted by the local government to visit and support those elders who were housebound. This "positive social participation" was valuable for all parties, as they not only provided support to others, but the community action aided their own identity reconstruction in times of severe crisis (Yotsui, Campbell, and Honma 2016).

Spaces of resilience are most acutely needed in times of disaster, but they have also been opening up in other times and places. The town of Kamikatsu, on the island of Shikoku in the south of Japan, while far removed from the region most affected by the natural disaster of March 2011, has been deeply affected by depopulation and aging. As described in detail by Nanami Suzuki, the recognition of the crisis in this town has led some of its inhabitants to start an enterprise that would both stimulate the local economy and help to get older people, some of whom live in remote locations, involved in a community project (2005, 2012; see also Part V Stafford). The enterprise sells seasonal edible leaves to selected restaurants nationwide that use them as a garnish. The leaves are collected mostly by older people living in forested areas who are notified of the demand of particular leaves centrally. The enterprise creates a network and strengthens and expands their mutual aid networks (Suzuki 2012). While largely operated by the elderly, the enterprise was envisaged with the help of an agricultural specialist, and their systems of communication depend on younger persons.

Suzuki shows how other generations are involved in this community project that, while largely operated by and for the elderly, still relies on the involvement of others. I believe this is a crucial point: there is a difference between belief in resilience and abandonment. From these selected examples, I believe, emerge a few key characteristics[4] of new spaces for aging in Japan that successfully foster resilience without risking abandonment.

Spaces for independence, involvement, and activity are created through support and the fostering of interdependence (Photo 20.4). First, then, we can observe the importance of intergenerational contact and *support*. Such support need not be paternalistic—assuming that all the "elderly" are frail or a burden in some way is highly problematic. Conversely, however, assuming that the elderly are capable of being left to their own devices, that communities will pick up the slack, or that the volunteer sector can make up for the shortcomings of social welfare can nevertheless result in abandonment, as discussed by Danely (2015). The elderly and the communities they live in

Photo 20.4   Shopping in a *shōtengai* or a shopping arcade. These shopping arcades with a large array of small specialized shops serve as a backbone of community and provide a form of sociality for many elders. Many of my interlocutors told me they enjoy chatting with the shopkeepers and the opportunity to meet their neighbors while shopping. (Photo by Harry Walker) ·

may have the capacity for resilience, yet this capacity must be fostered and supported. The balancing act involved is challenging, but makes a significant difference—as large as that between communities of support and zones of abandonment.

The second characteristic of the new spaces for aging is *flow* or movement—the spaces created are not static. In Tohoku, the space created is marked by the comings and goings of older volunteers. In Kamikatsu, the space comes into being though the comings and goings of the leaf producers. Furthermore, control over the money they earned in a way that suited them opened possibilities for new interactions and activities, forming a basis of a "cyclical coexistence" (Suzuki 2005: 355, 366). "In other words, a practice of care that works only when everything moves in cycles in conformity with the setting and situation of the people who are related to a certain place" (Suzuki 2012: 95). As successful spaces for aging are both physical and social, they expand beyond the specific location created.

Finally, most such spaces were created intentionally, upon recognition of specific *vulnerabilities*—those of the elderly, of mothers of young children facing isolation, of carers and communities. Sometimes, it was precisely those who were most intimately aware of these vulnerabilities, either personally or through close contact, who undertook the efforts required to create community networks. In the old merchant downtown neighborhood where I conducted my fieldwork, the women who were most involved in creating a mutual aid system had themselves experienced caring for older family members and remembered well the challenges of child raising in busy urban Japan. Small acts of support or help in the community could make a big difference: older people could keep an eye on the house of someone going away, perhaps water their plants, and they could accompany them on a hospital visit or help with small repairs or shopping. Once such contacts were established, the flow of exchanges could continue and the network of people involved could spontaneously and informally expand. Recognition of the various vulnerabilities of older people, carers, and communities was instrumental in fostering the resilience of these groups.

Conclusion

I cannot remember what I wrote on the colored piece of paper that hot July day, but I remember the steady hum of activity in Mitsuba, where I first arrived several months earlier expecting to find a group of older people socializing and relaxing but instead encountered a colorful crowd of socially engaged people, whose contacts and volunteer activities reached to the farthest corners of the neighborhood. That same day, according to my fieldnotes, Ozaki san, an apt amateur photographer in his early seventies, showed me a series of group photographs he took in a day-care center for the elderly and nursing home nearby, where he also performed regularly with his a capella choir. He had used his home printer to prepare copies for all those who had posed for him. He enjoyed his hobbies, not least because of their sociality and the opportunity to offer entertainment to others. The contacts for both of these hobbies originated in Mitsuba, but extended beyond it and involved numerous others in a lively community, encouraged and supported by volunteer activity and the local government. Ozaki san rejected the possibility of moving in with his son's family in a different city, where he did not know any of his neighbors or know the area. Since the passing of his wife, he lived on his own, but told me that so long as there is a lively community in this area, he is confident everything will work out. Ozaki san's way of living was facilitated not only by his own relative health and the LCTI—it became conceivable as a new narrative space and supported by a network of informal links of mutual aid.

If some of the new spaces of aging are empowering and enabling, other, more sinister places have opened up in the form of social cleavages and income gaps, as well as the rural-urban divide. Under these conditions, many elderly—particularly those in single households—are particularly vulnerable and face poverty and abandonment. Sometimes, this vulnerability is recognized and provides an impetus for the creation of inclusive and supportive social spaces, like community cafés or social enterprises. What many of these have in common is the variety of roles and relationships they open up for older people, facilitating involvement in an active manner. Rather than casting older people as merely recipients of care, these new spaces of care reconfigure care itself: the support offered by the volunteers, and their social involvement, often promotes their own well-being. Care should here be conceptualized, not as a dyadic relationship between carer and cared-for, so much as a new space of flowing exchanges.

Notes

1. The aging of the population is widely considered to have many adverse effects on the state of the Japanese economy. Social security costs have been steadily growing and have reached the highest level until present, and it is predicted that population aging will adversely affect economic growth and raise expenditure on health care and social security (Dekle 2003: 71). This is understood to be the effect of a declining labor force (which can partly be neutralized by the participation of older people in the workforce) and the rising fiscal burden, referring to the transfer of income between generations (Yashiro 1997: 245). The latter has been labeled the "pension burden problem" and is related to the decreasing number of people supporting the social security system (Coulmas 2007: 13). Initially, the Japanese pension system was designed as a fund from which contributors could withdraw what they paid in during their working life. This system has gradually shifted toward a "pay-as-you-go" system, which means that beneficiaries receive benefits from current contributions (Yashiro 1997). This makes it more vulnerable to changes in the demographic structure of the population. The resentment felt by the younger generations, especially young urbanites who work hard and experience financial hardships while feeling that they are ensuring a very comfortable existence for the older generations (Coulmas 2007: 13), has led some to speak of "intergenerational exploitation" (e.g., Kunieda 2002) as replacing intergenerational solidarity.

2. These two tendencies—towards independence and involvement in community activities, or mutual support, can both be seen as increasingly important moral imperatives for aging people in Japan (Shakuto 2018).

3. Zones of social abandonment (Biehl 2013) are spaces characterized by exclusion of some elements of the population in zones of truly inadequate living conditions, spaces where those who were not cared for by the social institutions or families were left, often suffering from disease or mental health problems— yet while outside the system they appeared to be somehow socially sanctioned or generated by the system. Much has been written about the rural depopulation and life in the changing village communities in Japan, particularly by Japanese and other scholars in the fields of sociology and regional studies. A question that

might be worth addressing ethnographically today is whether some of those communities are becoming zones of social abandonment.

4. Characteristics, of course, are not new themselves and have been often present in a variety of spaces seen as supporting living well more generally, yet they have often been intentionally and thoughtfully pursued.

Bibliography

Aldrich, D., and E. Kyota. 2017. "Creating Community Resilience through Elder-Led Physical and Social Infrastructure." *Disaster Medicine and Public Health Preparedness* 11(1): 120–26.

Allison, A. 2013. *Precarious Japan*. Durham, NC: Duke University Press.

Bender, S. 2012. "Robots and the Human Sciences." *Keisokuto Seigyo* 51(7): 644–48.

Bethel, D. 1992. "Life on Obasuteyama, or Inside a Japanese Institution for the Elderly." *Japanese Social Organization*: 109–34.

Biehl, J. 2013. *Vita: Life in a Zone of Social Abandonment*. Berkeley: University of California Press.

Cabinet Office. 2007. *Annual Report on the Aging Society 2007*. http://www8.cao.go.jp/kourei/english/annualreport/2007/2007.pdf.

Cabinet Office. 2011. *Heisei 22-nen kokumin seikatsu ni kan suru yoron chōsa*. Tokyo: Naikakufu Daijin Kanbō Seifu Kōhōshitsu.

Campbell, J. C. 1992. *How Policies Change: The Japanese Government and the Aging Society*. Princeton, NJ: Princeton University Press.

Cooper, C., and K. Ujikane. 2017. "This Is What Elderly Millionaires Spend Their Cash on in Japan." Bloomberg Businessweek, July 17. https://www.bloomberg.com/news/articles/2017-07-17/older-and-a-lot-richer-japan-s-retirees-fuel-luxury-travel-boom.

Coulmas, F. 2007. *Population Decline and Ageing in Japan: The Social Consequences*. London: Routledge.

Danely, J. 2015. *Aging and Loss: Mourning and Maturity in Contemporary Japan*. New Brunswick, NJ: Rutgers University Press.

Dekle, R. 2003. "The Deteriorating Fiscal Situation and an Aging Population." In *Structural Impediments to Growth in Japan*, edited by M. Blomström, J. Corbett, F. Hayashi, and A. Kashyap, 1–88. National Bureau of Economic Research. Chicago: University of Chicago Press.

The Economist. 2011. "Turning Silver into Gold. Stealth Marketing to the Elderly." July 30. http://www.economist.com/node/21524920.

Goodman, R. 1998. "The 'Japanese-Style Welfare State' and the Delivery of Personal Social Services." In *The East Asian Welfare Model: Welfare Orientalism and the State*, edited by R. Goodman, G. White, and H.-J. Kwon, 139–59. London: Routledge.

Goodman, R. 2010. "Silver Haired Society: What Are the Implications?" *Social Anthropology* 18(2): 210–12.

Hommerich, C. 2012. "The Advent of Vulnerability: Japan's Free Fall through Its Porous Safety Net." *Japan Forum* 24(2): 205–32.

Kavedžija, I. 2018. "Of Manners and Hedgehogs: Building Closeness by Maintaining Distance." *Australian Journal of Anthropology* 29(2): 146–57.

Kunieda, S. 2002. "Japanese Pension Reform: Can We Get Out of Intergenerational Exploitation?" *Hitotsubashi Journal of Economics*: 57–71.

Mainichi Shinbun. 2017. "Effectiveness of Robots Confirmed: Increased Independence in Walking and Eating. Provision of Care [*Robotto no yūkōsei kakumin. Hokō ya shokuji jiritsudōkōjō*]," May 30.

Neary, I. 2002. *The State and Politics in Japan*. Medford, MA: Polity.

NIPSSR (National Institute of Population and Social Security Research). 2014. *Social Security in Japan 2014.* http://www.ipss.go.jp/s-info/e/ssj2014/.

Ochiai, E. 1997. *The Japanese Family System in Transition: A Sociological Analysis of Family Change in Postwar Japan*. LTCB International Library Foundation.

Robertson, J. 2007. "Robo Sapiens Japanicus: Humanoid Robots and the Posthuman Family." *Critical Asian Studies* 39(3): 369–98.

Robertson, J. 2014. "Human Rights vs. Robot Rights: Forecasts from Japan." *Critical Asian Studies* 46(4): 571–98.

Robertson, J. 2017. *Robo Sapiens Japanicus: Robots, Gender, Family, and the Japanese Nation*. Berkeley: University of California Press.

Sato, T. 2000. *Fubyōdō shakai Nihon: sayonara sōchūryū* [Unequal Japanese Society: Goodbye Middle Class]. Tokyo: Chuo Koron Shinsha.

Sekine, Y. 2008. "The Rise of Poverty in Japan: The Emergence of the Working Poor." *Japan Labour Review* 5(4): 49–66.

Seo, Y. 2017. "Democracy in the Ageing Society: Quest for Political Equilibrium between Generations." *Futures* 85: 42–57.

Shakuto, S. 2018. "An Independent and Mutually Supportive Retirement as a Moral Ideal in Contemporary Japan." *Australian Journal of Anthropology* 29(2): 184–94.

Shirahase, S. 2010. *Ikikata no Fubyodo: Otagaisama no Shakai ni mukete* [Inequalities in Life Course: Seeking for the Mutually Supportive Society]. Tokyo: Iwanami.

Sone, Y. 2017. *Japanese Robot Culture: Performance, Imagination, and Modernity*. New York: Palgrave Macmillan.

Statistics Bureau of Japan. 2017. *Japan Statistical Yearbook 2017.* http://www.stat.go.jp/english/data/nenkan/66nenkan/index.htm.

Statistics Bureau of Japan. 2018. *Japan Statistical Yearbook 2018.* https://www.stat.go.jp/english/data/handbook/c0117.html.

Suzuki, N. 2005. "Kakinoha wo tsumu kurashi: Nōmalaizeishon wo koete, Bunkajinruigaku [Creating a New Life through Persimmon Leaves: Living More Than a 'Normalized' Life]." *Japanese Journal of Cultural Anthropology* 70(3): 355–78.

Suzuki, N. 2012. "Creating a Community of Resilience: New Meanings of Technologies for Greater Well-Being in a Depopulated Town." *Anthropology & Aging* 33(3): 87–96.

Świtek, B. 2016. *Reluctant Intimacies: Japanese Eldercare in Indonesian Hands.* New York: Berghahn.

Takenaka, A. 2012. "Demographic Challenges for the 21st Century: Population Ageing and the Immigration 'Problem' in Japan." *Anthropology & Aging* 33(2): 38–43.

Tsukasaki, K., H. Kanzaki, K. Kyota, A. Ichimori, S. Omote, R. Okamoto, T. Kido, C. Sakakibara, K. Makimoto, A. Nomura, and Y. Miyamoto. 2016. "Preparedness for Protecting the Health of Community-Dwelling Vulnerable Elderly People in Eastern and Western Japan in the Event of Natural Disasters." *Journal of Community Health Nursing* 33(2): 107–16.

Uchida, M., and Iwabuchi, K. 1999. *Eijingu no seijigaku* [*Political Science of Ageing*]. Tokyo: Waseda Daigaku Shuppanbu.

Wakamatsu, J. 2012. "Toyota Targets Aging Japanese with Smaller Corolla." *Asahi Shimbun*, May 11. http://web.archive.org/web/20120728235413/http://ajw.asahi.com/article/economy/business/AJ201205110083.

Yamada, M. 2004. *Kibō kakusa shakai: "makegumi" no zetsubōkan ga Nihon o hikisaku* [Society of Split Hopes: The Despair of Japan's "Losers" Pulls Japan Apart]. Tokyo: Chikuma Shobō.

Yashiro, N. 1997. "Aging of the Population in Japan and Its Implications to the Other Asian Countries." *Journal of Asian Economics* 8(2): 245–61.

Yoshida, R., and T. Osaki. 2016. "Young Voters Hope to Reform Japan's 'Silver Democracy.'" *Japan Times*, July 8. https://www.japantimes.co.jp/news/2016/07/08/national/politics-diplomacy/young-voters-hope-reform-japans-silver-democracy/#.Wp_f3kx2tZU.

Yotsui, M., C. Campbell, and T. Honma. 2016. "Collective Action by Older People in Natural Disasters: The Great East Japan Earthquake." *Ageing and Society* 36(5): 1052–82.

CHAPTER TWENTY-ONE

Narrating the Future

The Demographic Imaginary in an Aging Thailand

Felicity Aulino

It should have a temple.

It doesn't need a temple. It could just have a lawn, a place to relax, for exercise and walking and so on. And an exercise room. . . . Suppose it just had a yard or field, monks could come and give sermons, maybe there would be a tour bus for outings. That would make people happy, right?

Brapin[1] and her husband went back and forth like this, working out the details of an ideal community for senior citizens in Northern Thailand. A medical clinic here, leisure activities there. It was clear they had discussed these possibilities before. Though Brapin repeatedly steamrolled her husband's suggestions (like the need for a Buddhist temple, for instance), in large part they agreed. "If we were old, 80 years or so, and we lived like this, we'd be ok," Brapin (68 at the time) declared, and her husband nodded his approval.

I heard many such idyllic visions for later life over the course of 16 months of ethnographic fieldwork in urban Thailand (2008–2009). For this research, I worked with people caring at home for bedridden older people and the various organizations that support such endeavors. I interned with a Thai eldercare NGO, shadowing and interviewing caregivers in the northern urban center of Chiangmai. These caregivers included children and other relatives, nurses and home care workers, and the growing legions of volunteers organized by governmental and international aid organizations bracing for anticipated age-related social change. I spent time in people's homes as well as in organizational meeting rooms and community centers, observing and participating as people planned and plodded through the daily affairs of care. I also interviewed key ministry officials, activists, demographers, and scholars engaged in related government policy making, studied policy and intervention trends, and took part in conferences on care reform in Thailand and the greater southeast Asia region. In all these spaces, people shared visions for the future.

The importance of thinking about and narrating one's own future has recently come to the fore in psychological research. Noting, for instance, how people are living longer but not adequately saving for retirement, researchers have proposed a "future-self continuity" hypothesis. Studies in this vein find that when people imagine a closer connection between their current and future selves, they make choices more in line with future needs. In psychological parlance, psychological connectedness affects intertemporal choice. In this chapter, I want to show how an anthropological twist on this insight is illuminating—not only for influencing future directed behavior (of the kind psychology and gerontology research hopes to inspire) but also for understanding care in the present.

The projected scenarios I encountered in the field were by and large personal musings, though some of my interlocutors were professionals in eldercare and working to make their aspirations a reality. The similarities found in their visions speak to nationwide concerns and global discourse that deserve critical attention. The divergence of specific details in their stories is also noteworthy, as these differences highlight personal priorities—the unique ways these themes take hold in individuals' lives and manifest, implicitly and explicitly, in their hopes and dreams. But the mere existence of these stories, their ubiquity and their particularities, points us to a creative space in the social world: an emerging *demographic imaginary* that both marks and guides contemporary understandings of older individuals and their "aging societies." Below, I define what I mean by the term *demographic imaginary* and then illustrate its utility for social analysis through a series of vignettes. As I tack between macro- and microsocial instantiations, I show how demographic categories take hold and shape group identification, in turn underscoring the importance of narratives about the future for the lived experience of today.

Population Aging and the Demographic Imaginary

Global population aging is predicated on epidemiological and demographic transitions, transnational economic forces, and new medical technologies coalescing to increase the long-term care needs of people in many societies. A political discourse of crisis is emerging around the world, as governments fashion trade agreements that include provisions for the migration of care workers, and domestic programs attempt to meet projected demands of citizens. But here I resist taking at face value expected contours of any so-called aging society. Over 20 years ago, Lawrence Cohen (1994) recognized the irony of a would-be critical geroanthropology that simply takes on the parameters of gerontology, operationalizing theory in service of the eldercare industry without scrutinizing the paradoxes of a field that seeks to support the independence of older people while simultaneously relying on the dependencies of old age for its existence. Research and policy platforms are, not surprisingly, justified by aging trends, and popular programming repeatedly drives home risks and needs in the face of demographic change. But more troublingly, in recent years, population aging has been added to the anthropological narrative about the importance of documenting shifts in age cohort dynamics. Scholarly publications on aging generally begin with a requisite statement of global population aging, with attention to care for elderly people cast as analytically crucial at this time in human history.[2] While this phenomenon absolutely merits attention, anthropology can do more. Our theoretical tools need simultaneously to assess how people navigate changing conditions and to take critical account of demographic discourse, in order to trace how such discourse comes to shape people's subjectivity—from social norms and personal narratives to the core of intimate experiences.[3]

As the chapters in this volume and its predecessors attest, anthropologists have long grappled with transformations of social norms with growing elderly populations. People around the world seem to be struggling with what will happen to them and to their societies as they age. Danely (2015) speaks of emergent "elderscapes," Long (2005) writes of new "cultural scripts," Gullette (2004) tracks thwarted expectations and dominating "decline narratives," and Hashimoto and Traphagan (2008) document the growing pressures to "reimagine" possibilities for eldercare. The changes signaled by new idealized visions for older age and long-term care are not superficial. They entail corresponding changes in religious ideology and cultural logics, economic circumstances, and social welfare systems (see Part III Lamb). Ethnographic work cumulatively serves to help mark that which is changing. For instance, Brijnath (2014) notes a move in India in the last decade away from traditional explanations of dementia toward contemporary medical, modern, and technical renderings. Yet here again, Brijnath justifies her study of Alzhiemer's on what is predicated epidemiologically at the population level. Of course, anthropologists like Greenberg and Muehlebach (2006) and Lamb (Part I) vitally point out false claims of universality in transnational discourse, such as found in the "successful aging" movement; as important as such work is, recognizing the values, cultural assumptions, and political motivations built into circulating models of aging and long-term care may not be enough.

If changes predicated by international demographic discourse dominate our analysis, we may miss subtle (and not so subtle) ruptures, continuities, and new formations at a more local level. Still, transnational discourse may reflect (or become) locally meaningful categories, as careful attention to "successful aging" makes clear. So rather than reify a global/local distinction, in this chapter I aim to bring attention to feedback loops between forecasting, analyses, and lived experience. Without recognition of the feedback loop between social analyses and everyday life, anthropological work may inadvertently uphold an old "unquestioned sense of the burdensomeness of old people" (Cohen 1994: 141), even as it seeks to open up to alternate configurations of care and community.

Understandings of the population at large—in particular, characteristics related to birth, migration, gender, ethnicity, and aging and death—play an increasingly major role for individuals and institutions alike. The "demographic imaginary" provides a conceptual framework for exploring how population categories take hold and shape group identification and personal expectations. The term builds on attempts to conceptualize shared understandings in and through which new ideas find shape in a given social world.[4] Age and other demographic factors form the basis of identity and predictions about the future in a confluence of individual experience and social discourse. Group categories emerge in personal actions, values, and idealized futures in a feedback loop with overarching social, religious, economic, and political forces. The demographic imaginary thus reflects emergent ideals for old age and long-term care, as well as the social effects of demographic inquiries themselves. The concept is meant to bring attention to demographic studies, (trans)national discourse, and individual narratives as mutually constitutive and in need of a combined analysis.

The Thai population is reportedly aging rapidly, following a pattern recognizable the world over. Nearly two generations of family planning efforts (beginning in the late 1960s) reduced the total fertility rate in Thailand from six children per woman to less than two, while medical advances increased life expectancy by about a decade during the same time period. Issues of eldercare are prominent in Thailand, as demographers and global health organizations trumpet the country's "aging society" status: "older people" (defined as people over the age of 60) currently make up over 13 percent of the total population, and that percentage is expected to increase steadily in the coming decades.[5] These older people are said to face the prospect of dependency without traditional safety nets, as young people work outside the home to support their families and no longer have a large sibling base with whom to share the responsibilities of providing for their elders. Myriad governmental and nongovernmental programs are springing up with the purpose of supporting long-term care, and international interventions are focusing attention on anticipated age-related social change.[6]

So what would it look like to take this reporting not as a given and clear impetus for study, but as a key ingredient of the social landscape to be scrutinized? Below, I look to personal narratives about the future as a window into the lived experience of shifting social parameters. These narratives show how demographic categories are key variables in people's stories. What's more, generating prospects for the future has become a form of care itself. From a macrosocial perspective, these personal storylines clearly mirror components of demographic analyses and resultant institutional strategies. Thus, as categories of older people are negotiated and planned for, demography becomes an impetus for study: not only for its predictions, but also for its workings in the present.

Imagined Communities: Personal Designs

Brapin's and her husband's comments about their ideal senior citizen community stuck with me, although I heard similar visions from many others. In Chiangmai, this style of contemplation was prominent among a particular subset. For these semiurban, working- and middle-class people, long-held values, economic pressures, and the increasing prevalence of both medical facilities and demographic discourse all contribute to emerging ideas about, and ideals of, old age and long-term care. This group is generally between 50 and 70 years old. They include family caregivers, volunteers for the elderly, professional healthcare providers, and people unconnected to eldercare. They are relatively affluent, not struggling to make ends meet, and they have technological conveniences at their disposal. They tend to be familiar with population aging forecasts and are in a position to make changes to their personal trajectory or to influence planning priorities in local organizations. What emerges from this mix is a style of contemplating the future that has developed alongside parallel trends in business, government, and international development.

High-caliber medical services were paramount in these accounts; family caregiving was not. A Thai cultural logic for generations emphasized the need to take care of one's parents as they age, framed in Buddhist terms as repayment for one's own childhood care. Caregiving in many Thai contexts is still understood to provide a means for transforming karmic debts and accruing spiritual merit (Aulino 2016, 2019). During my research, I repeatedly heard people speak of the "traditional Thai family" and the manner in which children have classically cared for parents, often in multigenerational homes. This was an ideal form, described with pride, often in a way to set Thai culture apart from what many perceived as the neglectful norms of Western families. Yet when it came to individual expectations, people rarely predicted their own children would or should care for them. Instead, they were developing new expectations for long-term care and new narratives to account for the changing economic and social circumstances of an aging population.

These musings were voiced with increased frequency from those who had no children or whose children were professional people with little time to provide care. For instance, senior academic nurses who had never married and were daily immersed in research on aging spoke about a variety of retirement communities. These women generally envisioned either condominium-type dwellings or small private homes close together, somewhere in the foothills of the north's lush mountains. Condominiums were particularly compelling. As one nurse laughed, "Condos! That is our dream!" Therein, disability mapped onto floors: nursing and hospice facilities on the ground level, and decreasing dependency on upper levels. Some imagined their most able and independent years enjoying views from penthouse suites. And whether in high-rise or clustered low-rise dwellings, these nurses imagined that state-of-the-art health facilities and home care aids would be readily available, along with community facilities for public gathering and recreation activities. Like Brapin's and her husband's ideal senior citizen community, these places would have all the perceived benefits of village life alongside urban creature comforts and modern biomedical advances. Nurses were in a position to create such places, "pilot projects" of shared dreams. One senior nurse had the property for such a demonstration village in mind; another had enlisted Chinese collaborators. Early phases of these plans were stalled by the 1997 economic crash, but by 2008 (when people were voicing these dreams to me), many felt the time was ripe to reignite their visionary elder community initiatives. To date, the projects have yet to materialize.

Others preferred to integrate their visions of idyllic eldercare into existing communities, often with children in mind. They wanted citizens to delight in, and impart their knowledge to, the youth. Their ideals were thus described as demarcated places, within existing neighborhoods, designed for older people. These seniors would have access to care as needed, both at home and in care facilities. But instead of re-creating the essentials of village life, these areas would seamlessly integrate with existing institutions, such as the local temple or the community center. Boonsii, an activist who worked with both local and international NGOs for the elderly, spoke of such a vision. She had identified the plot of land within her urban slum on which a community home could be built for elders who could no longer care for themselves. Once built, she said, people in the community would volunteer to help fellow residents as needed. When we last spoke, she had plans of writing grants to secure project funds, and though she had yet to begin, her "imagined community" was certainly in the making.

The term "older person" or "elder" (*phū sūng àyu*) was a key descriptor for Boonsii, the nurses, Brapin and her husband, and many others. Comparable to "senior citizen," this term dominates national programming and strategic planning, as discussed below. At the same time, this category of "older person" is suspect for some. Take Bert, for example. Bert, age 70, is a *song taew* driver, shuttling Chiangmai University students in his pickup truck. The term "older person" was, for him, associated with government-initiated "elder persons' clubs." Although he qualified for membership, Bert was turned off by what he perceived as the political conniving (and perhaps elite status) of such groups and their members. Like most people unaffiliated with eldercare organizations, he was less prone to plotting grand society-wide scenarios and keener to refashion particular elements of the immediate social world: village dynamics, access to care. Even so, he too had ideal scenarios in mind. His dream? A designated area in his urban village for retired people to sit and chat, a special clinic for old folks (*khon kæ*), and home help as needed.

Class dynamics are at work here. Bert is not as well off as Brapin, though neither is Boonsii—and all have idyllic visions at play. In the main, class dynamics emerge in word choice (old folks versus senior citizens, for instance), but much stays constant across working and middle classes, particularly the need for medical care and community improvements.

Casually and without prompting, this cohort articulated visions for the future that drew attention to their dual concerns of medical care and community, parallel to trends I detail below at the national and transnational level. From the nursing faculty's condominium outfitted with ground floor medical care to Brapin's ideal neighborhood for elderly people complete with state-of-the-art health clinic, access to biomedicine was seen as a requisite component of well-being in later years.[7] A change in kinship relations, or some deviation from the standard story of traditional family care, was also prominent. For my interlocutors, children were not expected to provide care. Brapin's eldest son was pursuing a career in Bangkok, while a car accident had robbed her of her youngest; Boonsii's neighbors' children were stretched too thin to provide consistent eldercare; many of the nurses had pursued education rather than marriage, and while some felt supported by nieces and nephews in their middle age, they imagined a future without relying on them. Nonetheless, everyone made a point to include family, peers, children, and the community at large in their declared ideals in some way, reflecting priorities and predictions.

A striking aspect of temporality in contemporary subjectivity is evident in these scenarios. Rather than uniting in age cohorts in the present, I found people imagining their future selves as part of a future community of "senior citizens." Brapin and her husband and others like them were not so much imagining themselves as part of a unified, middle-aged, soon-to-be-old population, nor as part of a community united in the present across difference and space, as Anderson (1991) so powerfully described for the birth of nations and national identity. They were imagining their future selves as part of a future community of senior citizens. The ruptures in current social and familial circumstances dropped away in favor of a utopian time just on the horizon. Boonsii, for instance, imagined a community house without any allowances for the political turmoil that had tensions high in her small neighborhood.[8] Yet even as Boonsii relayed her plans for such a group home, a dispute erupted between her and several of her peers present for our interview. Boonsii presumed people would drop all animosity, just under the surface of placid social relations, to feed and bathe and support one another when the dependencies of old age arose.

Just as modern Thais tend nostalgically to imagine a unified, simple, premodern past, they also here imagine a unified, simplified, utopic future out of the problematic present. What might this mean in terms of future-self continuity? Population aging is heralded as a coming catastrophe for families by global experts and Thai citizens alike. Rutherford (2013) describes similar moments of potential catastrophe in which the "rhetoric of descent" becomes powerful. Global warming, for instance, was (until recently) presented at the transnational level as a crisis for future generations. Interestingly, this tends not to produce in citizens a "sense of continuity," but rather "a sense of potential rupture" (Rutherford 2013: 262). In the case of population aging, the rhetoric of descent is less about worrying about one's children's children (as climate change sometimes suggests), and more about a potential crisis for oneself; and still, a rupture between present and future self can be felt in the ideal scenarios portrayed. Most people with whom I worked had experience providing care for elderly people, whether professionally or personally, and the long hours of such work gave immediacy and shape to their future ideals; nevertheless, their projected futures held their own need for such care at a distance.

Instead of a continuity with a future self, I think we can see here a synchronic future at play in the present in which imagined communities bear the weight of sustaining community today. Imagining the future and narrating its contours becomes a form of care in the present—a way of providing a road map for one's self and society, no matter how unlikely or inconsistent such plans may be. This is different from the instrumental support that substantiates "community care" in transnational and national renderings. It is also different from that which prompts particular choices in the present in service of a future self. One can care for children, neighbors, even oneself through the very designs of a livable tomorrow, stitching together the stakes of the future with what matters most right now.

The Demands of the Age(d): Institutional Plans

"In the old days," begins a common modernist refrain, "family members took care of one another."[9] In Thailand, one hears time and again how children used to care for their parents, but now "throw them away" to be cared for in institutions or by strangers. Such assertions are made in the cramped bedrooms of care providers as readily as in air-conditioned government offices—despite reports of how little has changed in actual caregiving arrangements in recent decades.[10] The moral fabric of society is seen and felt to be eroding, particularly in cities, regardless of conditions that could suggest otherwise.

In my research, mass media programs were repeatedly cited as evidence of changing social conditions. The popular television show *The Circle of Life* was a prime example. Each nightly installment of this public program documented the plight of a poor and abandoned older person, generally eliciting a rush of donations from around the country. Laypeople and policy makers alike referred to *The Circle of Life* as proof that Thai people were increasingly abandoning their elderly, "throwing them away" or leaving them to the substandard care of strangers—again, despite demographic studies to the contrary. Senior citizen communities imagined in national strategic plans, the media, and personal narratives reflected a shared fantasy about how to stave off abandonment. With TVs and radios ubiquitous in their communities, everyone I talked with was, actively or passively, subject to reports of changing conditions for elderly Thai people.

Problems and Solutions

The way people design solutions is an indication of the way they are framing the problem at hand. Whether in individual scenarios or at the policy level, forecasting will address some issues at the exclusion of others. A type of complacency or acceptance of one's stage in the life course, understood as conditioned by karmic debts, has long persisted in Thai contexts, captured by the Buddhist-inflected adage: birth, old age, pain, death (*gerd, gae, jep, dtai*).[11] Thirty years ago, projected futures for the elderly—both individual and collective—revolved primarily around family care and Buddhist merit accrual in accordance with the inevitability of the life course and soteriological goals; and indeed, preparations for aging made by many older people reflect such priorities (Duangduan, Wanapa, and Manderson 2012). But now, an alternate set of coordinates is evident in state-sponsored imagined futures, including emphasis on access to medical services, home-based care, and productive community outlets for elders. International attention has added urgency as well as roadmaps for such national planning. Thailand has strategized about older people since the 1980s, in step with international concerns beginning with the first World Assembly on Ageing in 1982 (see Sutthichai and Suvinee 2009). The UN's touchstone Madrid International Plan of Action on Ageing of 2002 pressed governments to make preparations for aging populations in regard to development, health care, and "age-friendly environments." Thailand's Second National Plan for Older Persons 2002–2012 echoed the global call, with the theme "Productive ageing is a victory of society" (Sutthichai and Napaporn 2002; Knodel, Vipan, and Napaporn 2013). In the Ministry of Social Development and Human Security renderings, institutional nursing homes are downplayed in favor of home, hospital, and clinic-based services, but the availability of a range of medical professionals is taken as a necessary given. Gerontological discourse—from "successful aging" to "aging in place"—is broadcast globally through international bodies and finds purchase in national policy plans created with the aid of these external legitimizing forces.[12]

A community volunteer system is at the center of the Thai government's current plan for addressing long-term eldercare (recall Boonsii's community home).[13] In part, this is because rural communities are imagined as unscathed by modernity's march, and romantic notions of the caring villager underpin policy platforms and public health initiatives. A whole host of homecare services are attributed to volunteers who allegedly do what they would normally (or traditionally) do, just with a bit of government training and modest compensation. The functionality of this volunteer network is somewhat opaque; while implemented nationwide, promotional renderings of the accomplishments of elder volunteers often overstate their actual roles, especially in terms of sustained interpersonal responsibility. (This mirrors evaluations of the nation's public health volunteers, as described by Komatra et al. 2007.) National focus is nonetheless clear in this volunteer system of home-based care and a harmonious Thai society. Tropes regarding traditional Thai social impulses—if not particular relations—are proposed as the means to deal with aging crises. In turn, a classic paradox emerges as elders are depicted as a potential drain on the health care system amid rhetoric to bolster public opinion of elders' social utility, and infrastructure is designed to keep folks locally sustained. But while rhetoric emphasizes keeping people at home, health care professionals increasingly emphasize trustworthiness to rationalize institution-based care.

Policy makers and aging specialists in Thailand also look to Japan and Sweden for national models of social welfare programs for the elderly. Those countries are home to senior citizen compounds that are similar to what so many Thais described to me, livable and self-supporting environments with a mixture of government and private services. But while Thai policy makers and health professionals directly assess circulating program models for adaptation in Thailand, the roots of their strategic plans are not common knowledge. As with Brapin and her husband just "thinking up" an idea for a senior citizen community, the forms seem invented in each instance, whether at personal or national levels.

The schemes that people imagine, and thus the stories they tell, offer a glimpse into something operating at a collective level. Certain influences on narratives may be traced—a media talk show here, a policy report there—though the specific distribution of ideas quickly becomes too diffuse to document with certainty. Technology, politics, economics, and ethics intersect in the realm of collective imagination, as problems arise and present themselves to be solved, and a type of calibration occurs as people craft stories about future possibilities.

If we suppose that concerns with aging emerge only in response to the actual makeup of, and existent changes in, societies (as the stated impetus for so many studies suggest), we miss crucial aspects of the demographic imaginary. For one thing, discussed above, the demographic imaginary provides access to a form of care made possible by identifying with a community, not in the present, but in the future. For another, the demographic imaginary rests on the understanding that social objects, including categories of people, are necessarily constructed. Humans' ability to construct, document, and solve demographic challenges are part of the demographic imaginary. As Cornelius Castoriadis, originator of the umbrella term "social imaginary," explains:

> When it is asserted that the imaginary plays a role with respect to the institution only because there are "real" problems that people are not able to solve, this is to forget, on the one hand, that people manage to solve these real problems, precisely, to the extent that they do solve them, only *because* they are capable of the imaginary; and, on the other hand, that these real problems can be problems, can be constituted as *these* specific problems, presenting themselves to a particular epoch or a particular society as a task to be completed, only in relation to an imaginary central to the given epoch or society. (Castoriadis 1987: 133)

The demographic imaginary, and its specific manifestations in particular places, draws from people's capacity to imagine and to create as much as from any external conditions. Objects in the world—the conditions to which we refer and our reference to them—are made possible by the existence of the imaginary: "The 'object' as reference is always co-constituted by the corresponding social imaginary signification—the individual object as well as objectivity as such" (Castoriadis 1987: 365). Rather than take the object as given, this type of critical distance from demographic studies can help us assess their effects in the social world.

At some level, it remains an open question as to whether any enumerated category of persons represents an actual group or, instead, serves to create one.[14] Could it be that the international community is essentially "making up" older people? Certainly not, if you take literally the statistics based on people's ages and population distribution.[15] But whether or not aging projections come to pass, the *implications* of the age category "older people" are solidifying—in terms of what care people of a certain age need, the burdens they place on society, and even what they have to offer their social worlds.

The malleability of categories and identities is apparent in the work of Thai groups lobbying to win recognition of and welfare benefits for older people. The Older People's Organization (OPO), for example, places great emphasis on countering societal perceptions of older people as dependent. OPO is a local Chiangmai NGO, directed and staffed by Thai nationals and closely affiliated with a major international aging organization. OPO joins its international counterparts in promoting, among other things, "healthy aging" and an engaging life after retirement. OPO deems this necessary pushback on the negative consequences of increased global attention on aging, which has, in the process of seeking resources for the aged, cast them in need of help. Instead of charity, OPO and its allies prefer that society recognize the worth of older people and act in solidarity to support them. This type of "empowering" attention also serves to legitimize "older people" as a standing entity, the meanings and implications of which are still up for grabs.

Collective Futures, Individualized Neoliberal Strategies?

A dynamic interplay exists between individual engagements and (trans) national policies, discourse, and practices. As I now consider, the narratives above in some ways indicate neoliberal entrepreneurial inclinations, though political economy alone proves insufficient for explaining people's proclivities. For instance, family and community care are idealized in both national and personal renderings; but the imagined futures I encountered in Thailand all implied the provision of professional care services or community care that looked a lot like professional services. This included access to state-of-the-art health care facilities and assisted home care. There was an implicit acknowledgment by health care professionals and laypeople that paid care workers would eventually alleviate the care burden. If family care is ideal, why do so many people envision an idyllic future without family assistance? When pressed on such issues, individuals equivocated, with vague twists and turns in their scenarios to include family. "Do you want your sons to take care of you?" I asked Brapin and her husband. Brapin was fast to reply, "Oh, they are so busy. Of course, they would visit. There could even be special houses somewhere. But they have their own lives."

The demographic imaginary reflects a relation between traditional ideals and neoliberal biopolitics, as the elder population is increasingly defined, reified, regulated, and made self-reliant via government plans and practices. In this context, one might predict an increase in paid care, as well as the business sector more generally, in an emerging Thai elderscape. Privatization is a key element in neoliberal reforms, which are once again on the rise in Thailand, and a private sector home care industry has grown in recent years driven in part by population studies. In turn, professional groups—most notably the Thai Nursing Council—jostle, via scant regulations, for control over certain physical tasks and the overall domain of care both inside and outside of facilities.

But how readily do Thai older people and their families imagine themselves as consumers of paid care? As Stephen Collier warns, "the formal rationality of neoliberalism tells us nothing about its relationship to the substantive form of human communities" (2005: 375). In countries like Italy, similarly approaching an inversion of the population pyramid, the state promotion of compassion and volunteerism reflects the shrinking of the welfare state in the wake of neoliberal reforms (Muehlebach 2012; see also Rugolotto, Larotonda, and van der Geest 2017; Part II Weibel-Orlando). In Thailand, volunteer programs do not so much replace a welfare system, but rather create one. Direct pension funds are now available to everyone over the age of 60, with over 80 percent of the eligible population receiving such funds, whereas just five years ago, only 20 percent did so. Thai volunteers for the elderly are state sponsored, forming the cheapest element of the welfare state. This system of care is emerging alongside a push for personal and community responsibility, and the proliferation of training schools and for-profit care facilities indicates that privatized elements will increase in the system. Yet with care emerging through a focus on tomorrow, presumptions about what these Thai neoliberal subjects will demand and the scope of consumerism in this arena could easily miss what is prioritized as providing for others. What may look like a future need for instrumental physical support within communities may instead be a reinstantiation of traditional care of the collective in the form of idealized stories of the future, an expanded temporal scope emergent in contemporary subjectivity. Analysis of the demographic imagination provides a way into both public and private manifestations of the intermingling of political, economic, and social forms.

A Mother's Journal

Buapan was 93 when she died, at home in her bed, with her only daughter Saree, aged 63, by her side. The two had lived together all of Saree's life, in a wooden house close to the banks of the Ping River. After Saree married and had children of her own, they too resided there, in the house where Saree was born, the house her family owned for 100 years, the house Saree thought perhaps she too would live out her days. There they had watched the city of Chiangmai grow up around them. And as Buapan's health declined in the months prior to her death, Saree remained close, sleeping next to her mother at night and providing the physical care needed to keep her comfortable and well attended.

Buapan had the habit of keeping a diary. Not much personal information, Saree thought: just notes about her days, religious sermons, and visits from grandchildren. However, after her death, Saree read an entry that "broke her heart." It was about a dream Buapan had in which she died and went to heaven. It was an important dream, and she awoke convinced she had had an actual vision of the afterlife. But, as Buapan lamented in her journal, no one seemed to care about it—or any of her stories. As Saree explained:

> When Mother described [the dream] the first time, I listened. She was old already though, and so she would often say the same things 5 times, 10 times, 15 times, the same stories. So I was prepared to listen the first couple times, eager in fact to hear. But then the 5th time, the 10th time, the 20th time, I just didn't have the same patience for listening. So while listening, I'd do something else, walk here or there, clean this or that. Oh tears, to know that my mother wanted me to know these things she felt were true. . . . But she would say a story one day, and then forget she said it, and say it 1, 2 . . . 5 . . . 10 more times! She would tell the story every day! So I would listen a little, do this and that a little.

Saree went on to say that, if only she had more money, she would have paid someone to come and listen to her mother's stories. (She had daydreamed about doing so throughout the old woman's decline.) Like so many of the so-called oldest old, Buapan had loved to tell stories of the old days, her youth, the war years. But Saree had heard all her stories before. She had thus angered her mother by filling in details, by guessing punch lines, by not sustaining the interest of a good listener. In the realities of cleaning and cooking and other chores, even a most loving and devoted daughter grew inured to this seemingly simple demand.

While many people's imagined futures stem from their own caregiving experience, Saree's caregiving did not translate directly into imagining who would care for her, who would walk her to the toilet, or who would listen to her stories. Similarly, as noted above, catastrophic renderings of the future in policy rhetoric are transfigured in personal narratives, not only into hopeful possibilities of an imagined future but also into what amounts essentially to a form of coterminous community care with multitemporal valence. I highlight this to make clear that the demographic imaginary is one piece of a complex reckoning with present and future, here including Buapan's imminent death, Saree's imaginary of Buapan and their caregiving relationship, and Saree's imaginary of her own aging.[16] While Saree did not volunteer an ideal vision for the future, she did express what she thought was most important in old age: how to prepare one's heart for the inevitable. Like many other aging caregivers I encountered, she spoke readily of awaiting fate.

The desire for someone to listen to stories raises another problem in need of solution, but not so clearly as the industry of home care might suggest. In the thick of Saree's caregiving, we come to see that patterns arise that are difficult to traverse and that occupy a space quite separate from medical or otherwise physical needs. Paid care here is at present imaginable in some realms and not others. Saree was unwilling to hire out physical tasks of care for her mother, though paying someone to be a good listener was conceivable. Relationships are being negotiated to create the intimacy needed to embody culturally appropriate help in ways we are just beginning to understand. Rather than read only monetary drives, professional protections, and international crises in the demographic imaginary, one must also consider habituated moral logics. In many Thai cases, such moral logics revolve around a felt sense of community, karma (ultimately a theory of cause and effect across lifetimes), and dharma (the Buddhist natural order of things): the more intangible elements of making someone comfortable.[17] While economy and morality are far from opposed here, it can be taboo to emphasize financial payments made for care. "Paid care," and "hired care" are not common terms in Thai, and the care arrangements between people need further study to understand the categories deployed for such relationships. Future ethnographic work primed by the demographic imaginary to listen for narratives of the future in light of practices of the day can help us trace the evolution of such matters, perhaps even give our social analyses more predictive power, while forcing us to confront the boundaries of the foreseen and the foreseeable.

Conclusion: Toward an Anthropology of the Future

Saree told me that she never cried before her mother died: she was too busy providing care to have the time or space to cry. For Saree, the crux of the caregiving role was to give encouragement (*hai kamlang čhai*), to keep playing as if all were well—even if and when the sick person knows otherwise (Stonington 2009). Saree admitted everyone "secretly knows" when the end is nigh, when hope for a better tomorrow is gone. Certain futures are there, but too dangerous or unproductive to admit. Harmony, internal and external, is ideally achieved through appearances, which require certain disavowals.

Nevertheless, the future is often the direct object of contemplation. In fact, imagining the future emerges as a form of care in the present: as if providing a road map for one's future self and future society. Where reliance on existing structures and adherence to norms used to seem enough for preparing for the inevitable unfolding of birth, old age, pain, and death, there is a mounting appreciation of something new that demands a future orientation. And whether the "aging" of Thailand's population would, without preparation, cause a crisis of care or not, the presence and promotion of possible futures affect the present. We have to pay attention to how people describe the future, for it speaks directly to what matters most to people today.

Here I have outlined a modern Thai subjectivity forged in a dynamic interplay between collective and personal visions of population aging. Theories of modernity generally pivot on the notion of change, a break in the way things have traditionally been done. In *Modernity at Large*, Arjun Appadurai goes so far as to say that certain aspects of culture are so destined to become less a matter of habitus and more a matter of "conscious choice," an agency activated by "ordinary people [who] deploy their imaginations in the practice of their everyday lives" (Appadurai 1996: 43–44, 45). The shared dreams voiced by my informants reflect a type of self-consciously created modern community, promoted and extended by shared imaginary practices. Interestingly, these imagined communities (1) are driven by a sense of population characteristics, which (2) are themselves a function of an imaginative capacity, and which (3) invoke a sense of community not so much among actors in the present, but for a demographic category they may inhabit in the future.

The demographic imaginary, as an analytical tool, can help bridge the persistent gap between structural and humanistic approaches in the anthropology of aging. But while it may lend itself to operationalization in service of critical gerontology and related fields, I intend for this framing to caution against a simplistic deployment. Meredith Minkler (1999) has identified the two main strands of critical gerontology as those studies concerned with political economy and structural determinants and those that take a more humanistic approach to individual experience of old age. The demographic imaginary helps acknowledge the importance and indirect relationship of both—allowing room in our analyses for the interplay of structures, discourse, and lived experience, without demanding a logical sequencing from one to the other. Rather than rely on aging trends to justify study, the demographic imaginary invites exploration of the co-construction of aging studies and related social discourse, individual ideals, and collective expectations. In this way, we can capture how biopower and other governing structures of neoliberal development and capitalism manifest in intra- and interpersonal relations, while also remaining sensitive to the social construction of overarching frames and the dynamism that exists between scales of analysis.

Attention to social and personal expectations of old age could prove vital for health promotion. What do people imagine to be ideal circumstances for their later years? Where do they want to live? With whom? And what if they should require assistance in their day-to-day? Imagined futures may very well provide guidance for developing best practices of caregiving. But building from there, beyond linear connections to prefigured care options, imagined expectations are also revealing of identities, values, and social worlds more broadly. Considering health in relation to the demographic imaginary points us to a collective capacity for inventiveness, as well as to how trade in stories of the future affects the well-being of today.[18]

Future narratives can also help mark contradictions and disputes present in social worlds. Take, for example, the timescapes of capitalism. The economic system demands one plan and invest in the future; yet at the same time, markets stymie concern for the future to optimize profits in the present. People's narratives accommodate both extremes, addressing the present and the future at once. One might say that karmic logics too contribute to people's ability to navigate contradictions in Thailand, with an ethos of moderation, social norms of acceptance, and the tracing of cause and effect across lifetimes. Nevertheless, people do confront immediate perils in the social landscape. In turn, the narratives people tell about the future are emerging not only to address problems to come, but as care for that which cannot be otherwise confronted in the present. In particular, the importance of community in the Thai demographic imaginary yields a future in which imagined communities future ruptures present as much as forecasted.

This ideation is a kind of care quite distinct from instrumental aid in moments of physical dependence. International organizations and nation-states propagate an apocalyptic vision of demographic change, yet rely on a sense of hope to plan and adapt to coming population shifts—often with instrumental road maps. The narratives in my study too reflect an ideal, rather than a catastrophic, future. But with these stories, projected selves do not so much firmly establish continuity with current selves as mark out possibilities for future collectives. This is a powerful salve for present problems. Thus the stories about the future I present here provide a means for people to care for one another in the here and now, rather than aid in future-oriented decision-making. Rather than formal adherence to traditional ethical arrangements, the Thai demographic imaginary signals an internalized call for plotting of new forms, which are proving to be powerful moral vehicles indeed.

Notes

A version of this chapter appeared in 2017 as "Narrating the Future: Population Aging and the Demographic Imaginary in Thailand," *Medical Anthropology* 36(4): 319–31. doi: 10.1080/01459740.2017.1287181. Used by permission from Taylor & Francis, www.tandfonline.com.

1. All personal and organizational names are pseudonyms.

2. See, for example, Buch 2015. Her analyses are consistently critical and absolutely vital to the field, and so her nod to the crisis of population aging is all the more telling.

3. For more on subjectivity in the field of anthropology, see Biehl, Good, and Kleinman 2007.

4. Castoriadis (1987) posited the "radical imaginary" as the human capacity to create possibilities in general and the "social imaginary" as that aspect of the radical imaginary that builds upon the symbolic system of a given society. The social imaginary is akin to a shared background, which finds its expression in "images,

stories, and legends," rather than "explicit doctrine" (Taylor 2002: 106–7). Like the "medical imaginary" (Good 2010) and the "pharmaceutical imaginary" (Jenkins 2010), the "demographic imaginary" aims to frame a more targeted analysis than the social imaginary provides.

5. See Knodel and Bussarawan 2017; Knodel, Vipan, and Napaporn 2013. At the time of research (2008–2009), Thailand had not yet achieved "aging society" status nationwide, though older people made up over 7 percent of the Chiang-mai population. At the time of writing (2018), Thailand is ranked the third most rapidly aging population in the world and is on track for the number of older people to surpass the number of children under 15 this year.

6. Sutthichai and Napaporn 2002; World Bank 2012.

7. Traditional Thai medicine was not emphasized, although it may be implied in other aspects of community life.

8. For background on this turmoil, see Aulino, Elinoff, Sopranzetti, and Tausig 2014.

9. For more on such modernist refrains, see Dirks 1990; Mitchell 2000; Tanabe and Keyes 2002.

10. See Knodel and Bussarawan 2017; Knodel and Napaporn 2008; Kamol 2007. Filial support, monetary and nonmonetary, remains high, despite changing family size; decline in coresidence and geographical dispersal of family members raise concerns for future support, though to date 90 percent of older people needing assistance receive it from a child, child-in-law, or spouse (Knodel and Bussarawan 2017).

11. See Hallisey 2010; Eberhardt 2006.

12. Thai public health strategy has a long history of serving as a template for global initiatives (Joe Harris, personal correspondence); future work could help decipher Thailand's influence on WHO aging strategy worldwide.

13. For extended discussion of volunteer schemes and the historical lineage of care at play in their deployment, as well as across the social world, see Aulino 2019.

14. Ian Hacking (1986) argued for the constitutive relationship between phenomenon and human classification in terms of "dynamic nominalism"; in this case, we might note people tending to behave and be in ways consonant with the categories and descriptions of older people continually referenced and reinforced by the social world.

15. For demographic statistics serving as "not merely fact but fodder for a politics of cultural struggle," see Krause 2001: 576; for a social constructivist depiction of demography, see Greenhalgh 1996.

16. Many thanks to an anonymous reviewer for this insight.

17. For more detail on Thai moral logics and phenomenological orientation to care, see Aulino 2014, 2016, and 2019.

18. Much contemporary work seems on the brink of direct engagement with people's contemplation of the future, and I thank Charles Hallisey for the notion of an "anthropology of the future" (personal communication).

Bibliography

Anderson, B. 1991 (1983). *Imagined Communities.* New York: Verso.

Appadurai, A. 1996. *Modernity at Large: Cultural Dimensions of Globalization.* Minneapolis: University of Minnesota Press.

Aulino, F. 2014. "Perceiving the Social Body: A Phenomenological Perspective on Ethical Practice in Buddhist Thailand." *Journal of Religious Ethics* 42(3): 415–41.

Aulino, F. 2016. "Rituals of Care for the Elderly in Northern Thailand: Merit, Morality, and the Everyday of Long-Term Care." *American Ethnologist* 43(1): 91–102.

Aulino, F. 2019. *Rituals of Care for the Elderly: Karmic Politics in an Aging Thailand.* Ithaca, NY: Cornell University Press.

Aulino, F., E. Elinoff, C. Sopranzetti, and B. Tausig. 2014. "The Wheel of Crisis in Thailand." Society for Cultural Anthropology, September 23. https://culanth.org/fieldsights/series/the-wheel-of-crisis-in-thailand.

Biehl, J., B. Good, and A. Kleinman, eds. 2007. *Subjectivity: Ethnographic Investigations.* Berkeley: University of California Press.

Brijnath, B. 2014. *Unforgotten: Love and the Culture of Dementia Care in India.* New York: Berghahn.

Buch, E. 2015. "Anthropology of Aging and Care." *Annual Review of Anthropology* 44(1): 277–93.

Castoriadis, C. 1987 (1975). *The Imaginary Institution of Society.* Trans. K. Blamey. Cambridge: Polity.

Cohen, L. 1994. "Old Age: Cultural and Critical Perspectives." *Annual Review of Anthropology* 23: 137–58.

Collier, S. 2005. "Budgets and Biopolitics." In *Global Assemblages: Technology, Politics, and Ethics as Anthropological Problems*, edited by A. Ong and S. Collier, 373–89. Malden, MA: Blackwell.

Danely, J. 2015. "Of Technoscapes and Elderscapes: Editor's Commentary on the Special Issue 'Aging the Technoscape.'" *Anthropology & Aging* 36(2): 110–11.

Dirks, N. B. 1990. "History as a Sign of the Modern." *Public Culture* 2(2): 25–32.

Duangduan Rattanamongkolgul, Wanapa Sritanyarat, and L. Manderson. 2012. "Preparing for Aging Among Older Villagers in Northeastern Thailand." *Nursing and Health Sciences* 14: 446–51.

Eberhardt, N. 2006. *Imagining the Course of Life: Self-Transformation in a Shan Buddhist Community.* Honolulu: University of Hawaii Press.

Good, M.-J. D. 2010. "The Medical Imaginary and the Biotechnical Embrace: Subjective Experiences of Clinical Scientists and Patients." In *A Reader in Medical Anthropology: Theoretical Trajectories, Emergent Realities*, edited by B. J. Good, M. M. J. Fischer, S. Willen and M.-J. D. Good, 272–83. Malden, MA: Wiley-Blackwell.

Greenberg, J., and A. Muehlebach. 2006. "The Old World and Its New Economy: Notes on the 'Third Age' in Western Europe Today." In *Generations and Globalization: Youth, Age, and Family in the New World Economy*, edited by J. Cole and D. Durham, 190–213. Bloomington: Indiana University Press.

Greenhalgh, S. 1996. "The Social Construction of Population Science: An Intellectual, Institutional, and Political History of Twentieth-Century Demography." *Comparative Studies in Society and History* 38(1): 26–66.

Gullette, M. 2004. *Aged by Culture*. Chicago: University of Chicago Press.

Hacking, I. 1986. "Making Up People." In *Reconstructing Individualism*, edited by T. Heller, M. Sosna, and D. Wellbery, 222–36. Stanford, CA: Stanford University Press.

Hallisey, C. 2010. "Between Intuition and Judgment: Moral Creativity in Theravada Buddhist Ethics." In *Ethical Life in South Asia*, edited by A. Pandian and D. Ali, 141–53. Bloomington: Indiana University Press.

Hashimoto, A., and J. Traphagan. 2008. "Changing Japanese Families." In *Imagined Families, Lived Families*, edited by A. Hashimoto and J. Traphagan, 1–12. New York: SUNY Press.

Jenkins, J. H., ed. 2010. *Pharmaceutical Self*. Santa Fe, NM: School for Advanced Research.

Kamol Sukin. 2007. "What Ails the Thai Family? Social Problems Mount as the Traditional Institution Caves in to Present-Day Pressures." *The Nation*, April 15.

Knodel, J., and Bussarawan Teerawichitchainan. 2017. *Family Support for Older Persons in Thailand: Challenges and Opportunities*. PSC Research Report No. 17-879.

Knodel, J., Vipan Prachuabmoh, and Napaporn Chayovan. 2013. *The Changing Well-Being of the Thai Elderly: An Update from the 2011 Survey of Older Persons in Thailand*. Ann Arbor, MI: Population Studies Center.

Knodel, J., and Napaporn Chayovan. 2008. *Population Ageing and the Well-Being of Older Persons in Thailand: Past Trends, Current Situation and Future Challenges*. UNFPA Papers in Population Ageing No 5.

Komatra Cheungsatiansup et al. 2007 (2550). *Public Health Volunteers: The Spirit of Volunteering and Health in Thailand* (อาสาสมัครสาธารณสุขจิตอาสากับสุขภาวะไทย.). Nonthaburi: Society and Health Institute.

Krause, E. 2001. "'Empty Cradles' and the Quiet Revolution: Demographic Discourse and Cultural Struggles of Gender, Race, and Class in Italy." *Cultural Anthropology* 16(4): 576–611.

Long, S. 2005. *Final Days: Japanese Culture and Choice at the End of Life*. Honolulu: University of Hawai'i Press.

Minkler, M. 1999. "Introduction." In *Critical Gerontology*, edited by M. Minkler and C. Estes, 1–14. Amityville, NY: Baywood.

Mitchell, T., ed. 2000. *Questions of Modernity*. Minneapolis: University of Minnesota Press.

Muehlebach, A. 2012. *The Moral Neoliberal*. Chicago: University of Chicago Press.

Rugolotto, S., A. Larotonda, and S. van der Geest. 2017. "How Migrants Keep Italian Families Italian: Badanti and the Private Care of Older People." *International Journal of Migration, Health and Social Care* 13(2): 185–97.

Rutherford, D. 2013. "Kinship and Catastrophe: Global Warming and the Rhetoric of Descent." In *Vital Relations: Modernity and the Persistent Life of Kinship,* edited by S. McKinnon and F. Cannell, 261–82. Santa Fe, NM: SAR.

Stonington, S. 2009. "The Uses of Dying: Ethics, Politics and End of Life in Buddhist Thailand." PhD diss., Medical Anthropology, University of California, San Francisco, and University of California, Berkeley.

Sutthichai Jitapunkkul and Napaporn Chayovan. 2002. "National Policies on Ageing and Long-Term Care Provision for Older Persons in Thailand." In *Ageing and Long-term Care: National Policies in the Asia-Pacific,* edited by D. Phillips and A. C. M. Chan, 150–80. Ottawa, ON: IDRC.

Sutthichai Jitapunkul and Suvinee Wivatvanit. 2009. "National Policies and Programs for the Aging Population in Thailand." *Aging International* 33: 62–74.

Tanabe, S., and C. Keyes, eds. 2002. *Cultural Crisis and Social Memory: Modernity and Identity in Thailand and Laos.* New York: Routledge.

Taylor, C. 2002. "Modern Social Imaginaries." *Public Culture* 14(1): 91–124.

World Bank. 2012. *Reducing Elderly Poverty in Thailand: The Role of Thailand's Pension and Social Assistance Programs.* Bangkok: World Bank.

CHAPTER TWENTY-TWO

Globalizing Late Life in China and Realigning the State, Family, and Market Interests for Eldercare

Hong Zhang

Images to Frame the Subject

Scene 1

On November 7, 2015, dressed in bright red suits, 18,000 middle-aged women danced to the hit song "Little Apple" in the city of Xianghe, Hebei Province, China, setting a Guinness world record for the largest line dance in one location. A year later, on November 7, 2016, more than 50,000 Chinese retirees simultaneously performed choreographed dance moves to music, in 14 different Chinese cities. This event set another Guinness record as the largest group dance in multiple sites (China News Network 2016). According to both event organizers, the whole society is concerned with the physical and mental health of an ever-rising elderly population. The goal of these two large-scale public dance performances was to further promote a healthy life-style for China's aged (China News Network 2016). Public dancing has

---

Web Special:

See the 2016 record-breaking dance at: https://www.youtube.com
/watch?v=8mBZAkSR15Y.

---

recently become the most popular recreational activity for middle-aged and elderly people to stay fit and enjoy life in China.

Scene 2

In May 2018, a photograph titled "Only Child" won the best prize in China's 26th Photograph Contest. This photograph shows an exhausted and helpless young man in a hospital room with both his parents sick and lifeless on the hospital beds. The image went viral that month in China's social media and led to nationwide discussion on the crushing eldercare burden for millions of China's one-child generation whose parents would soon enter old age and need eldercare. Headlines with such catch phrases as "only child's eldercare anxiety," "fearful future of eldercare," and "aging and dying in loneliness" gripped the public for months since the photo first went viral (Fenghuang Weekly 2018, see image at https://wxn.qq.com/cmsid/20180516A0052C00).

Population aging is accelerating rapidly in China. While in 2010, people over 60 years old accounted for 13.25 percent of that nation's citizens, by 2017, the proportion of people aged 60 and over reached 241 million, representing 17.3 percent of China's total population (Chi 2018; Part I He and Kinsella). In the meantime, due to both the impact of China's decades-long birth control policy and the career-motivated migration since China's market reform in 1978, more and more Chinese elderly are living in empty-nest households. Filial responsibility is understood as adult children's duty to provide eldercare and still remains a core cultural value for Chinese families today. Yet, new demographic and socioeconomic realities have presented challenges to the age-old tradition of family-based eldercare and led to new responses from the state, family, and market in confronting the challenges of rapid populating aging in China.

In this chapter, I draw upon documentation from recent government programs and my ethnographic research in China from 2010 to 2017 to discuss the ongoing transformations of eldercare and aging in China. It will be argued here that the state, family, and market are realigning their shared interests in recalibrating and redefining the filial tradition for eldercare. This is an ongoing process for charting new patterns of late life in contemporary China.

The State Factor: From Pension Overhaul to Promoting Filial Virtues and Lifelong Learning at Universities for Senior Citizens

Mao's socialist revolution (1949–1978) had paradoxical effects on the traditional Chinese family system and old age support. On the one hand, parental authority based on patriarchal power and family resource control was severely weakened by the public ownership system and ideological attacks on ancestor worship and parental arranged marriage. On the other hand, collectivization in the countryside, restriction on rural-to-urban migration, and the pension system that came with state employment in the cities not only provided a measure of socialist safety net for the elderly but also facilitated the delivery of parental care by keeping the adult children physically close to their parents (Davis-Friedmann 1991; Ikels 2006; Whyte 2004).

China's post-Mao market reform, however, has dismantled the collective-based welfare system and pursued a market-based economic policy that loosened restrictions on migration and emphasized individual and family responsibility for old age support. This reversal of the Mao Era's collective and state welfare system has generated enormous uncertainties over old age support for urban and rural families alike, but its impact on the livelihood and filial support of rural elderly in the first two decades of market-driven reform was particularly devastating. In his study of Xiajia village in Helongjiang in the 1990s, Yan noted a rise in parental abuse and abandonment after decollectivization (Yan 2003). In my study of a village in central China in the 1990s, family disputes over parental care flared frequently, with many elderly parents ending up living alone and providing their own care despite old age (Zhang 2004). In urban China, although the government has kept the pension system for urban retirees, downsizing of the state sector and elimination of work-unit welfare benefits have shifted eldercare burden from the work unit to families and individuals.

Rebuilding a National Social Security System

Since the late 1990s and early 2000s, the Chinese government has sought to rebuild a nationwide pension system. In urban China, this new policy direction includes two schemes. One was to set a social pooling combined with individual accounts requiring contributions from both employers and employees. The other was to establish "a minimal income stipend" (*dibao*) for those urban elderly who are unable to participate in the labor force due to illness or disability, or who were previously excluded from the pension plan (PRC White Paper 2006). The pension reform in urban China has enabled retirees and the elderly to have a moderate means of financial security for their old age support. According to a seven-province survey conducted in

2010, 78.88 percent of urban residents 65 and older have their own sources of income, mostly from their pension or spouse's pension, 6.11 percent get the *dibao* from the municipal government, and only 15.01 percent of urban elderly depend on their adult children for financial support (Yuesheng Wang 2012).

Beginning from 2002, the Chinese government began to address the imbalance between urban and rural development and introduced a series of pro-rural polices such as the New Rural Cooperative Medical Scheme (NRCMS) in 2003,[1] removal of agricultural taxes and levies in 2005, and most importantly, the New Rural Old-Age Insurance (NROAI) in 2009.[2] These new measures, although lagging far behind in comparison to the benefits and services available to urban elderly, are beginning to provide some relief for rural families with regard to old age support. During my trip in 2010 to the Hubei village where I had conducted research in the mid-1990s and early 2000s, I witnessed improvement in intergenerational relations and the well-being of rural elderly as the following case exemplifies.

When I first met Mr. Wei in 1993–1994, he was 72 years old and full of bitterness about how old people were discarded by both their children and the state after decollectivization. He had two sons but chose to live separately due to family conflicts. He said he would end his own life if he became too sick to provide his own care. In my subsequent trips to the village between 2000 and 2003, he was still in despair about the deteriorating life of the rural elderly, and told me about several more cases of elderly parents committing suicide in the village. He said that his own days were numbered as he now suffered from prostatitis and did not want to get any treatment for fear of burdening his sons with medical bills. However, when I saw him again in 2010, the 89-year-old was not only reasonably healthy, but in a more relaxed mood. He told me that he almost ended his own life in 2005 when his prostatitis worsened. But his two sons intervened and took him to the county hospital, where he underwent a successful operation and fully recovered. Mr. Wei's younger son told me that initially his father refused treatment for fear of high medical cost, and insisted that he had lived long enough and there was no point wasting money on him. Mr. Wei finally agreed to be treated after learning that his hospital fees would be "mostly" covered by the new rural medical plan. In the end, the new rural medical plan covered 30 percent of Mr. Wei's surgery and hospital charges, and his two sons and one daughter shared the rest of the cost.

My impression of improved intergenerational relations was validated by the village party secretary, who told me that family disputes over parental support had declined in the village in the past few years. He pointed out that

Photo 22.1 Ms. Cao with her grandson in the village. (Photo by Hong Zhang, 2010)

most villagers had seen their income increase due to the removal of the agricultural tax in 2005, and that the new rural medical plan also helped lessen the burden of medical costs for rural families. But the most pivotal change he emphasized was the new rural pension plan, which made every rural elder aged over 60 eligible to receive a monthly pension of 55 yuan (roughly US$8). The party secretary told me that when the new rural pension program was piloted in the village in 2008,[3] many elderly villagers were in disbelief that they too could receive a pension like urban retirees. Mr. Wei, who had only despairing words to say about the misery of rural elderly in the 1990s, now said that the pension plan offered rural elderly a sense of relief and hope for the future.

I encountered the same response in June 2012 when I visited a rural village in Hebei province, about 100 miles from Beijing. When I asked the villagers about the change in old age support in their village, they unanimously pointed to the new rural pension plan implemented at the beginning of 2012. One 75-year-old villager said, "Never in my wildest dream would I imagine myself, a farmer, to receive old age pension from the government." Even though the monthly pension of 55 yuan was meager in comparison to the average monthly pension of 1,000 to 3,000 yuan in urban China, rural elderly felt that at least they began to receive some pension from the government for their old age upkeep.[4]

Legislating Parental Support and Promoting Filial Virtues

Parental support was codified in the 1950 Marriage Law, but in the Mao era there was little need for legal recourse since both the urban work-unit system and the rural collectives could effectively prevent potential negligence of parental support. When China launched market reform in 1978 and shed the welfare benefits associated with the urban work-unit system and rural collectives, the family became responsible for the well-being of the elderly. In 1996, China passed the Law of the PRC on the Protection of the Rights and Interests of the Elderly (hereafter, the Elder Law), which explicitly states, "The elderly shall be provided for mainly by their families," and outlines specific legal obligations of family members for parental upkeep: financial support, housing, and medical expenses.

While the intent of the Elder Law was to protect the well-being and rights of the elderly, in reality the law was marred by problems of enforcement, and even strained intergenerational relations when parents had to sue their children to secure old age support. When the 1996 Elder Law was passed, China was undergoing structural market reform that not only led to large-scale layoffs at state-owned enterprises but also sent health care and education costs skyrocketing. Job competition and life pressures forced many adult children to make difficult choices between paying for their only child's education or providing eldercare and medical costs for their aging parents. As a result, despite the 1996 Elder Law, there were increasing incidences of parental neglect and abandonment—dead parents in empty-nest homes unnoticed for days, sick parents dumped in hospitals, and a sharp rise in elder suicides.[5] Indeed, there was widespread fear that the competitive market economy and rapid urbanization would lead to the final demise of the filial tradition.

It is perhaps in recognition of this rising public fear that in 2004 the Chinese state began to launch a series of high-profile campaigns attempting to revive the Confucian virtues of filial piety. In 2004, seven government branches collaborated to launch a nationwide campaign of selecting "filial exemplars" and publicizing their filial deeds. The filial exemplars campaign would culminate with an award conference every other year in Beijing, where more than 2,000 people selected all over the country would receive such titles as "Chinese Filial Exemplars," "Chinese Filial Exemplars Runners," and "Chinese Filial Stars" at the award conference. These new filial exemplars not only included children (adults or teens) devoted to parental care, but also private citizens who volunteered their time to care for seniors, entrepreneurs who donated money to build eldercare facilities, or government officials who prioritized work on behalf of the senior citizens (Li 2005).

Beginning in 2010, the Chinese government designated every October as "Respecting the Elders Month." During this month, the whole society is urged to show respect for the elderly around five themes: mobilizing all walks of life to visit the elderly, encouraging volunteers to provide companionship or do chores for the elderly, publicizing elder rights protection, organizing recreational events for the elderly, and raising the public awareness of the challenges of population aging (National Committee on Aging 2011).

The New 24 Filial Codes and the Amendment of Elder Law

In August 2012, the All-China Federation of Women and the National Committee on Aging published "New 24 Filial Codes," modeled on the "24 Paragons of Filial Piety" compiled during the Yuan dynasty (1271–1368 CE). Some of the listings in the 2012 version of the Filial Codes are: "Teach parents how to surf the Internet," "Buy old age insurance for parents," "Take parents for regular health check-ups," "Listen to parents telling stories of the past," and "Support widowed parents to remarry." This modern version of filial codes was met with criticism, cynicism, and even amusement from the public, as some argue that the government should put more effort into building a better social safety net for the elderly rather than exhorting families to follow the filial code of conduct. Many also point out that low-income college graduates and millions of young migrant workers who are struggling to make ends meet in cities far away from home may not have the financial means to support their parents, let alone visit them and take them out on holidays (Li 2012a; Yiqing Wang 2012).

Also in 2012, the Chinese state amended the 1994 Elder Law by reaffirming the family's role in parental upkeep and adding a clause requiring adult children to visit parents regularly. This 2012 Elder Law Amendment, dubbed as the "visit-home-often law" by the public, reignited an intense public concern on the rise of elderly parents living in empty-nest households. While many see this amendment as encouraging the whole society to pay more attention to the well-being of the elderly, others argue that job-related migration and work pressures of modern life have made it difficult for adult children to keep close contact with and provide care for their parents (Li 2012b).

On the whole, there is little disagreement among the Chinese public that adult children should provide parental old age support. Recent national surveys show that over 80 percent of the respondents agreed that children should be filial and have an obligation to support parents (Li 2010; Liu 2012; Xu 2017). By reviving filial virtues and emphasizing the legal obligation for eldercare, the state can both ease some public fears about the decline of filial piety and gain legitimacy by officially endorsing the filial tradition.

Implementing Pro-Elder Measures to Encourage Active and Healthy Aging

Since 2010, many Chinese cities have begun to waive subway or bus fees for the elderly to give them incentives to get out of their home and socialize with other retirees (Photo 22.2). In public parks all over China, many senior

Photo 22.2   Chorus singing at a park in Beijing, 2012. (Photo by Hong Zhang)

citizens spend hours in the early morning doing various group recreational and physical activities: chorus singing, ballroom or line dancing, tai chi, playing ball games such as badminton and ping-pong, practicing calligraphy, playing music instruments, and other group activities (Zhang 2009).

In more recent years, it has become very popular for urban retirees to attend universities for senior citizens. These universities are subsidized and funded by municipal governments and offer a wide range of courses geared toward the interests of senior citizens to enrich their retirement life. From the government's point of view, keeping senior citizens engaged and busy with learning new things is the best way to keep them healthy and out of hospital and to fight loneliness. In the summer of 2017, I visited three universities for senior citizens in Wuhan, a city with more than 10 million people in central China. All three universities were filled to capacity, and eager "students" were busy taking lessons on choral singing, modeling, dance, literature and poetry, English, photography, painting and calligraphy, computer and social media apps, and piano and other music instruments (Photo 22.3). According to the director in charge of senior citizen universities in Wuhan, the demand for attending senior universities is so high that the city is unable to meet it. There are often long lines waiting for class registration when the new semester begins, and popular classes are booked within hours. In order to ensure more retirees get a spot, senior universities have to limit students to two classes per semester. Many senior students take classes year after year

Photo 22.3   Electronic piano class at a university for senior citizens in Wuhan, 2017. (Photo by Hong Zhang)

with no intention to ever "graduate."[6] In my conversation with the students at the senior universities, they appreciated the opportunities to go back to college after retirement, and some even said that they finally realized their "college dream" that they missed out on due to the Cultural Revolution. The high demand for attending universities for senior citizens has been reported in all major cities throughout China (Phillips 2017; He 2018).

Changing Family Structure, Rising Care Burden, and Modified Filial Expectations

Both new demographic realities and China's massive labor migration in the market reform era have put strains on the traditional family-based system for eldercare. But there are also new signs that intergenerational relations are being renegotiated and filial practices readjusted to cope with new demographic challenges and changes in the lifestyle trends. In rural northern Guangdong, Santos notices that "surrogate parenting arrangements" have become a widespread practice in which grandparents take care of grandchildren while their grandchildren's parents go to the city to earn money (Santos 2017). My recent ethnographic studies in both rural and urban China have revealed a shift from the son-centered filial relation to gender-neutral relation and from the traditional dependent eldercare to intergenerational independence and interdependence.

Gender Equity and Changing Filial Role of Daughters

Mao's socialist revolution after 1949 weakened the son-centered family system of filial responsibility, as the redistributive and collective economy undermined patriarchal authority and women were able to join the labor force to earn income. But a daughter's filial role was mostly optional and marginal—giving parents spending money, providing emotional support by visiting parents, or offering temporary caregiving when parents were sick (Miller 2004). However, China's birth control policy since the 1980s has made the daughter's filial role essential and obligatory for many families. For urban families with only a daughter and no sons, this change is obvious, but even among multisibling families in rural China, daughters are assuming a greater role and obligation in the current low fertility context (Fong 2002; Shi 2009). In my study of rural parents under China's birth control policy, I noticed that when parents had no more than two children due to the birth control policy, they were keen on cultivating emotional bonds with their daughter and investing in her future too. These parents would emphasize to me that when you had only one son and one daughter, they were equally important to you; some parents even claimed that daughters were more reliable and filial than sons. As a result, a new marriage pattern dubbed as *liangbian dianli* (bilateral marriage), which mandates a daughter's filial obligation to her natal parents, has quickly gained momentum in this local area, rising from 25 percent of such marriages in 2002 to over 80 percent in 2010 (Zhang 2005, 2007, 2009).[7]

In my 2012 research on eldercare in Beijing and Shanghai, I also found that daughters played an active role in providing long-term care for their parents. In the following examples, we see that in some families daughters would be willed an equal or greater share of parents' assets when they contributed to parental caregiving.

Ms. Zhao was born in 1954, and has four brothers and five sisters, all of whom contributed care to her parents when they were alive. Her parents had a courtyard house in Beijing with 10 rooms, and each of the 10 siblings inherited one room. Ms. Zhou in Shanghai was the youngest of three siblings, with an elder sister and an elder brother. She was given the largest share of her parents' property, as she was the main caretaker of her widowed mother who suffered from dementia. In other words, the patriarchal tradition of emphasizing the son's importance for parental support has been revised in contemporary China. Not only do some parents begin to recognize the importance of a daughter's filial role, but they also actively seek to secure their daughter's filial obligation, whether through financing their daughter's marriage or through willing them equal or greater parental assets.

Filial Expectations Modified and Redefined

My interviews with elderly parents in Beijing and Shanghai in 2012 also revealed that even though these parents were living in empty-nest households providing their own care, or had to seek eldercare through institutional care or paid home care, they were reluctant to blame their adult children as "unfilial." The new dominant discourse on eldercare from the parents' point of view is "not to become a burden on their child(ren)." To these parents, "not becoming a burden" on their children is now embraced as a "modern" way of life as it demonstrates both their financial independence and their own autonomy in living their later years on their own terms. The following two case studies collected in 2012 show how some Chinese parents view moving into an elder home for their eldercare needs as an act of securing both the best care for themselves while not becoming a burden to their children.

> Mr. Yang, a Beijing native, was an 85-year-old widower. He had one son and two daughters, all of whom lived in Beijing. He used to live with his son's family, but in 2011 after his wife passed away, he decided to live in a neighborhood-run elder home. He had a monthly pension of ¥3,000, enough to cover the cost of ¥1,800 at this elder home. He told me that his son was busy at work, and he did not want to become a burden on him and his family, so he made the decision himself to live in the elder home. Mr. Yang was in reasonably good health and was very enthusiastic about the various recreational activities offered by this elder home such as tai chi, singing, and chess playing. His three children took turns visiting him once a week, so he still maintained frequent contact with his children. Mr. Yang was very happy with the current arrangement and was even proud of the fact that he used his own pension to pay for his eldercare need and did not burden his children financially or physically.
>
> Ms. Wan and her husband worked and lived in Beijing for more than 55 years, and were 77 and 83 years old respectively. Both were professionals and retired with a combined pension of more than ¥8,000 a month. But the couple had only one son, and he had settled his family in Germany in the mid-1990s. In 2011, the Wan couple decided to move to Shanghai, which was Ms. Wan's hometown and where she still had several siblings. Since the Wan couple did not have housing in Shanghai, they moved into an elder home, not far away from Ms. Wan's elder brother's home. When I asked Ms. Wan why she did not consider moving to Germany to live with her son's family, she said that she and her husband traveled to Germany twice to see their son and his family, but they did not want to live there. She added that her son was a chief engineer for a German auto company and was busy with his career, and that she did not want to burden him with eldercare.

Ms. Wan's case can be seen as a harbinger of a future awaiting China's one-child parents. These parents want the best education and career for their only child, even though it can mean that their only child will study, work, and live far away from them or even in a foreign country. Most middle-aged parents of single children whom I interviewed indicated that emotional connection was more important than financial support or physical care and that children do not have to live with parents in order to be filial. A study in 2007 on the changing perception of institutional care and "filial piety" in urban China also shows that placing elders in institutional care can be considered filial as long as adult children have made efforts to find a good quality facility for their parents and help with paying the cost (Zhan, Feng, and Luo 2008). Clearly many Chinese families still hold dear filial virtue, but its practices are redefined and reconfigured.

From Traditional Dependent Eldercare to Intergenerational Independence and Interdependence

What seems to have emerged in China is a shift from the past traditional dependence on eldercare to the emphasis on intergenerational autonomy and mutual reciprocity. Together with this shift are new attitudes and beliefs about the proper relationship between the generations, one that includes both feasible independence of the older generation and a more balanced reciprocity between them and their children. Several strategies exist for achieving this new interdependence. First, there is a growing belief among parents that the best guarantee for their future old age support is their own financial independence. For urban parents, this is more achievable as they have pensions after retirement. Even in rural China, saving for their future old age support has become a common practice among young and middle-aged parents. In my 2010 research trip to the same village in central China, the enrolment in the rural pension plan already reached 100 percent among the working adults under the age of 60. The party secretary told me that when the government first piloted the pension plan in this local area in 2008, there was already a demand for this pension program and the village cadres did not need to persuade the villagers to participate. Some even chose higher premiums for higher pension returns.

Second, small family size resulting from China's birth control policy also allows parents to better invest in their children's future and maintain a closer intergenerational bond, as there is less competition for parental resources. Beginning from the mid-2000s, the first generation of parents under China's strict birth control policy began to reach middle age and become grandparents. While eager to offer childcare, many of them also want to make sure that their grandparenting is not free and will not compromise their own source of income. Villager Cao's family (Photo 22.1) is a case in point.

> Mr. Cao and Ms. Cao both turned 50 in 2010 and had two daughters, the elder one born in 1982 and the younger one in 1988. In 2010, their younger daughter passed the highly competitive college entrance examination and was attending a college in Wuhan, and their elder daughter was 700 miles away working as a migrant worker in a factory in the coastal Zhejiang province. The main source of income for the Cao couple came from harvesting crops in the field, supplemented by Mr. Cao doing some odd jobs of installing solar panels and satellite cables or selling farm products during the off-seasons. The Cao couple's elder daughter left the village and went to work in Zhejiang in 2002, where she met her future husband who was a coworker in the same factory; the two married in 2006. In 2008, the elder daughter returned to her natal village to give birth to a son, and stayed in the village taking care of her son until he was one year old. Then she returned to Zhejiang to work and rejoin her husband, leaving her one-year-old son in the care of her parents. When her son turned two years old in 2010, he was sent to a local kindergarten from 9:00 a.m. to 4:00 p.m. The monthly kindergarten fee was ¥100, and was paid with the money sent home by the boy's mother. Mr. Cao told me that his daughter and son-in-law were making a good monthly income of ¥1,700–2,000 each, and that while they wanted to support the young couple by taking care of their son, he and his wife did not want grandparenting to consume all their time and energy. Besides, they still needed to generate income to cover their younger daughter's college fees and to pay for their own pension premium. This trend of grandparent outsourcing was a fairly recent phenomenon and started around 2007 when privately run kindergartens in this rural area sprang up to meet the need of two working-age generations.

In urban China, we begin to see the trend of older adult age peers socializing to cope with the consequence of the universal one-child policy in the past three decades. The whole generation of urban parents born in the 1950s and 1960s are under intense pressure to invest heavily in their only child's education and career success since he or she is their "only hope" (Fong 2004). As China's economy has become more market based and more fully integrated with the global economy since 2001 when China joined the World Trade Organization, many singletons born in the 1980s and 1990s are able to pursue higher education and settle down in other Chinese cities or even abroad in Western countries. This means that many of these parents will live their retirement lives in empty-nest households and manage their own elder-care needs. By 2005, these parents began to enter retirement age in large numbers. Between 2011 and 2012, I interviewed 40 such parents in Beijing and Shanghai on their views about aging and eldercare in the future.[8]

Although almost all of them said that they would face an empty-nest future in their old age, none viewed empty-nest living as bleak or lonely. What is more, these parents were busy forging a social network of mutual support among their age-cohort for fun group activities such as dancing, sightseeing, and shopping. Many told me that they were having a more fulfilling life than ever before because they now had the leisure time to do what they like or even pick up new hobbies.

Ms. Hao's story provides a window for us to see how her generation of urban retirees pursue an active retirement life with her age cohorts (Photo 22.4).

A Beijing native, Ms. Hao was born in 1955 and was sent to work in a state farm in Heilongjiang in 1969 during the Cultural Revolution together with her junior high classmates, a fate of millions of urbanites born in the 1950s. She returned to Beijing in 1978 and worked in a state-owned department store until she retired at age 50 in 2005. She had one son born in 1983, who had a job but was not married yet. I first met Ms. Hao in 2009 in a community center where she took lessons on modeling with a group of seven or eight retired women of her age. When I met Ms. Hao again in the summer of 2012, she told me that her retirement life was getting busier and more enriched by the day as more people were joining the ranks of retirement and there were more and more diverse and interesting activities in the parks and community centers to keep her active and happy. She had a packed weekly schedule with new activities since I saw her last time: folk dancing on Monday, square dancing on Tuesday and Wednesday afternoon, modeling on Wednesday and Thursday mornings, and ballroom dancing on Friday. She told me that she reconnected with her junior high classmates and other sent-down youth friends in 2010, and they began meeting with each other every Wednesday for square dancing and organizing group outings to various parks on weekends periodically.

I went with Ms. Hao on a Wednesday afternoon to meet her square dancing pals—six women and four men who have known each other since 1969 as sent-down youth working at the same state farm in Heilongjiang during the Cultural Revolution. I watched them dance for an hour, and we had a group chat over their retirement life and intergenerational relationships. Like Ms. Hao, they all had a busy schedule with various recreational activities throughout the week. Some of them had recently become grandparents, but they emphasized that while they helped their son or daughter with childcare when they could, every Wednesday from 2:30 p.m. to 5:00 p.m. was set aside for them to have a good time with their former sent-down youth friends. They told me that they cherished the time they were together as sent-down youth and were occasionally nostalgic of the collective and idealistic spirit of those years. Now that they were retired and their only children were grown up, reuniting with their sent-down youth

Photo 22.4   Square dancing with friends, Beijing, 2012. (Photo by Hong Zhang)

friends or childhood friends was more than just having fun by reliving their youth; it would also help keep each other company to face old age together.

They emphasized that the traditional filial care model is no longer feasible with so many families having only one child, nor is it desirable as modern life is busy and competitive for young people already. As parents the best they can do is to keep themselves healthy and active as long as possible so that their only child need not worry about them. From talking to these midlife parents, it was clear that Chinese parents still consider intergenerational reciprocity important, but it can be best achieved when older and younger generations have independent lives and do not get in each other's way.

The Market Factor: Commodification of Filial Piety

With the generation of parents under China's one-child policy entering retirement age in large numbers, the public fear about facing a lonely old age and crushing care burden as encapsulated in the photo "Only Child" is palpable and real. In the current mix of macroeconomic and demographic shifts, and with the government's blessing, an entire eldercare industry has emerged, rapidly expanded, and gained more momentum in the past three decades. The main selling point for this new eldercare industry is often the cultural tradition of filial piety.

The Emergence of Paid Household Services for Eldercare

In urban China, market reform has spurred on the emergence of a household service industry for childcare, household chores, and eldercare. The government has encouraged the growth of this service sector, since it provides employment for rural migrants and middle-aged laid-off workers from the state sector, while meeting diverse needs of urban families at the same time. As a result, the household service companies have sprang up in Chinese cities, offering a wide range of fee-based household services, including eldercare. In 2008, a national TV program broadcast the story of a Chinese businessman hiring three high-salaried home aides to care for his aged mother. Although he did not have time to attend to his mother's eldercare need, he was still considered a very filial son as he spent a large sum to provide high-quality care for his mom (S. Chen 2009: 174). While this extreme case of "purchased filial piety" is out of reach for the majority of urban families, hiring a live-in caregiver or an hourly helper for parental care has become a common option for urban families since the 1990s (Chen, Li, and Wang 2011; Ma 2011).

Booming Fee-Based Institutional Care

In Mao-era China, institutional care was limited and reserved for the so-called three without elderly only: without children, without source of income, and without ability for self-care. Thus until the 1980s institutional care had a reputation as a place for the destitute elderly who had no family members nor financial resources for eldercare. Since the 1990s, the government began to allow the public institutions and the private sector to open fee-based elder homes. As a result, fee-based elder homes have grown exponentially in major Chinese cities. A survey on the growth of elder homes in selected cities shows that from 1990 to 2009, the number of elder homes grew from 27 to 140 in Nanjing, from 11 to 136 in Tianjin, and from 105 to 331 in Beijing (Feng et al. 2011).

In February 2017, I visited two elder residences in Beijing. One was located in the heart of Beijing's central business district and marketed itself as a "high-end" eldercare facility (Photo 22.5). This elder home was funded by a private company and opened for business in 2012. The monthly charge for this elder home ranged from 10,000 to 15,000 yuan depending on the care need and the room size. Each room was equipped with a private bathroom and a cable TV set. The facility also provided a common reading room for the residents to read newspapers and magazines, a recreational room for the residents to do arts and crafts, a movie theatre, and a fenced garden for the residents to take a walk and enjoy the outdoor greens. The dining room offered three meals a day in a buffet style. The staff who showed me around proudly

Photo 22.5   A "high-end" elder home in Beijing, 2017. (Photo by Hong Zhang)

claimed the occupancy rate was 100 percent and the majority of the residents were retired professionals and scientists who chose to live in this high-end home because of the high-quality lifestyle and the personalized eldercare it offered.

The other, "lower end," elder home I visited was located within a residential cluster for a former large state-owned enterprise (Photo 22.6). It opened for business in 2016 by a not-for-profit organization in partnership with the neighborhood community. This residence had one open floor room with nylon curtains to separate each bed for privacy for its 19 residents there. In one corner of the room was a long table where the residents would eat their meals or perform simple recreational activities. Most of the residents were wheelchair-bound and incontinent. The monthly fee for this elder home was 4,000 yuan, and most residents were blue-collar retirees. The contrast between the above-mentioned "high-end" elder home and this simple one-room facility is obvious, showing both the stratification in access to the eldercare quality and the market response to the need of the divergent income strata of elderly population (see the photos below).

Considering the average pension for Beijing retirees was 3,633 yuan per month in 2017, even the low fee of 4,000 yuan for institutional care would require family pooling of resources to cover the cost. No matter whether they

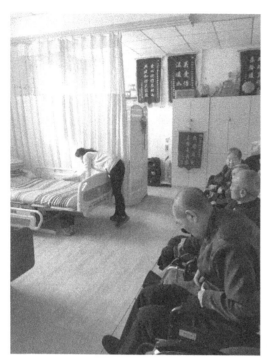

Photo 22.6 A "low-end" elder home in Beijing, 2017. (Photo by Hong Zhang)

are high-end elder homes or low-end ones, they are promoted as helping "fulfill the filial duties for sons and daughters" by providing parental eldercare for them. In other words, institutional care is repackaged as helping parents and families reconcile the moral dilemma of the modern and competitive life by meeting their eldercare needs through purchase.

Buying Eldercare Insurance as Filial Piety

China is still in the early stage of developing a national social security system, and as mentioned earlier, the pension system for the rural population started only in 2010, and its coverage is still very limited. Moreover, the Chinese government has emphasized that China has "become old before getting rich," and the government does not have the resources or the time to build a comprehensive old age social security system for a rapidly aging population. On the other hand, China's market reform and rapid economic growth have given rise to a growing middle class with strong purchasing power. The combination of an underdeveloped social security system and a rising middle class with more disposable income has become an impetus to the fast growth of commercial insurance companies in China. Since eldercare is still considered the responsibility of the family both by law and by the continuing cultural expectation of filial piety, commercial insurance companies see a market niche for eldercare insurance by targeting adults in their thirties and forties, urging them to buy eldercare insurance for their parents as a modern form of filial piety. Eye-catching phrases tapping filial virtues are often seen in TV commercials or in Internet advertisements: "Mother's Day is coming, purchase insurance to express gratitude to your mother." "Do your filial act early, don't forget to buy health insurance for your parents."

Senior Care Expo and Technology Innovation for Eldercare

Since 2012, China began to host large-scale senior care expos frequently to foster business opportunities on eldercare and promote senior care products and services. In 2017 alone, there were at least seven such large expos: the China International Senior Care Expo in Beijing, the Care and Rehabilitation Expo in Beijing, the annual China Aid Trade Show in Shanghai,[9] the Aging Industry Expo in Chengdu, the Sixth China International Senior Services Expo in Beijing, and the Fourth China International Silver Industry Exhibition in Guangzhou. These senior care expos attract participants and companies from abroad and at home to introduce and present their latest products and technology in the senior care and health industry. The sheer size of China's growing elderly population is seen as a huge market for senior care products and technological innovation. I attended the 2017 China International Senior Care Expo in Beijing (Photo 22.7) where more than 200 companies displayed cutting-edge elder-friendly furniture and bathroom facilities, rehabilitation equipment, robots and smart care devices, assisted living technologies, home care products and equipment, and senior housing developments.

Both China's rapid population aging and the market economy further facilitate commodification of filial piety and the eldercare industry. The Chinese government also encourages the development of eldercare industry and technology innovation for eldercare as a new growth engine for the country's economy. However, we must also see a huge social and moral risk in commercialization of filial virtue and parental care. As a consequence of China's market reform in the past 40 years, China has witnessed a rapid spike in income inequality with the Gini coefficient rising from among the lowest income inequality in the world in the early 1980s to over .50, putting China among the world's worst by the 2010s (Hsu 2016). Pitching paid parental care may enable families with good financial resources to receive better eldercare, but for those families who are financially distressed, their inability to purchase paid eldercare products or services could potentially implicate these families as somehow morally lacking in fulfilling their filial obligation.

Photo 22.7 "The Robot as Parents' Companion." The robots on display at the 2017 Senior Care Expo in Beijing. (Photo by Hong Zhang)

Conclusion

In this new realignment of state, family, and market interests, what has emerged is a "modernized filial piety" that not only reinvigorates the filial tradition in a new light but also spawns new practices. Ideologically, the new formulation of filial piety is no longer associated with the traditional notion of "subordination of the young to parental authority" but is reembraced and modified as compatible with the changes of the times. In practice, this new filial piety emphasizes both generational interdependence and independence, underscores a parent-child relation that is reciprocal rather than hierarchical, and demonstrates a more gender-egalitarian stance where both sons and daughters are important. Filial piety in its modern form gains new currency in China as it both solidifies the cultural value of family obligation and at the same time frees family members to pursue and adapt flexible filial forms and practices in accordance with different family situations and inclinations.

This new filial piety is appealing to the state, because it not only carries on the cultural tradition but also helps stabilize the family and society at large. It is also appealing to parents and children alike: parents feel they are able to manage their own care and avoid becoming a burden to their children, while children feel that they can pursue their careers and personal lives without compromising their filial obligation to their parents. The beneficial impact of commercialization of filial piety for the business and eldercare industry is evident and will grow even bigger in the years to come, as population aging accelerates faster in China and the need for diversified and innovative eldercare grows exponentially. However, as pointed out above, China is a developing country with a high level of income inequality, and commercialization of filial obligation may have the danger of further increasing social disparity in access to quality eldercare for those families who are struggling financially already in a highly competitive market economy.

Notes

Fieldwork for this chapter is based on Colby College's Humanities Research Grants (2012, 2013, and 2017), Fulbright Senior Scholar Grant (2009–2010), and ASIANetwork Student-Faculty Fellows Program (2012). The author gratefully acknowledges this support. Much appreciation also goes to Jay Sokolovsky for his encouragement and suggestions for revising this chapter. This chapter is adapted with permission from H. Zhang, "Recalibrating Filial Piety," in *Transforming Patriarchy: Chinese Families in the 21st Century*, ed. G. Santos and S. Harrell, 234–250 (Seattle: University of Washington Press, 2017). Copyright (c) 2016. Reprinted by permission of the University of Washington Press.

1. According to the document issued by Ministry of Health in 2006, the NRCMS first started as a pilot program in 2003 with the goal to reach 40 percent of the rural counties by 2006 and 60 percent by 2007, and all rural areas by 2008. See http://finance.people.com.cn/GB/1037/4045163.html.

2. "Pensions Reach Out to Aging Villagers," *China Daily*, December 31, 2010, http://www.chinadaily.com.cn/china/2010-12/31/content_11779418.htm.

3. The New Rural Old Age Plan was first piloted in 2008 and 2009 in selected counties. Due to its success and popularity, the rural pension plan was promoted and expanded to other rural counties nationwide in 2010. By 2012, the pension coverage reached most rural counties.

4. The 2010 national survey by Wang shows a sharp contrast in sources of income for the rural elderly of 65 years old and over: only 9.27 percent had pensions, 24.6 percent still had to work to support themselves, and over 55.56 percent depend on their children (Yuesheng Wang 2012).

5. Jing et al.'s study (2011) shows the urban elder suicide rate was higher in 2000–2009 than in 1990–1999, with the highest rate in 2005. Chen's study on suicides among rural elderly shows a relative stable rate of suicides among rural elderly from 1980 to 1994 but a sharp spike between 1995 and 2008 (B. Chen 2009).

6. My fieldwork notes in 2017.

7. The marriage data on 2010 was obtained in my fieldwork on the village in 2010.

8. These parents were born between 1950 to 1955 and all had retired by 2011. In China, the retirement age differs along the gender lines and occupation/

education. For women without a college degree and as blue-collar workers, the retirement age is 50. For women with a college degree and working in public institutions or as civil servants, the retirement age is 55. The retirement age for men is 60 regardless of work or educational background.

9. The introduction about China Aid describes its annual trade show as "the leading exhibition for the fast developing senior care market in China." http://www.china-aid.com/en/about-show.

Bibliography

Chen, B. 2009. "Changes in Intergenerational Relations and Elderly Suicides— An Empirical Study in Rural Jingshan of Hubei Province." *Sociological Research* 4. (In Chinese)

Chen, Q., X. Li, and R. Wang. 2011. "The Development of Industry of Domestic Work in Shanghai." *Shanghai Economic Research* 6: 113–18. (In Chinese)

Chen, S. 2009. "Aging with Chinese Characteristics: A Public Policy Perspective." *Ageing International* 34: 172–88.

Chi, D. 2018. "China's Elderly Population Continues to Rise, with 241 Million Now 60 or Over." GBTimes, February 27. https://gbtimes.com/chinas-elderly-population-continues-to-rise.

China News Network. 2016. "50,000 Middle-Aged and Elderly Women Dance Together, Creating Another New Guinness Book of Record." http://www.chinanews.com/sh/2016/11–07/8055541.shtml. (In Chinese)

Davis-Friedmann, D. 1991. *Long Lives: Chinese Elderly and the Communist Revolution.* 2nd ed. Stanford, CA: Stanford University Press.

Feng, Z., H. J. Zhan, X. Feng, C. Liu, M. Sun, and V. Mor. 2011. "An Industry in the Making: The Emergence of Institutional Care in Urban China." *Journal of the American Geriatrics Society* 59: 733–44.

Fenghuang Weekly. 2018. "The Eldercare Anxiety of 176 Million Singleton Children: We Dare Not to Die, Dare Not to Be Poor, and Dare Not to Travel Afar." May. https://wxn.qq.com/cmsid/20180516A0O52C00. (In Chinese)

Fong, V. 2002. "China's One-Child Policy and the Empowerment of Urban Daughters." *American Anthropologist* 104(4): 1098–109.

Fong, V. 2004. *Only Hope: Coming of Age Under China's One-Child Policy.* Stanford, CA: Stanford University Press.

He, Q. 2018. "China's Senior Citizens Flock Back to School." *China Daily*, June 23. http://www.chinadaily.com.cn/a/201806/23/WS5b2d4787a3103349141de584.html.

Hsu, S. 2016. "High Income Inequality Still Festering in China." *Forbes*, November 18. https://www.forbes.com/sites/sarahsu/2016/11/18/high-income-inequality-still-festering-in-china/#4aaa484d1e50.

Ikels, C. 2006. "Economic Reform and Intergenerational Relationships in China." *Oxford Development Studies* 34(4): 387–400.

Jing et al. 2011. "Suicide among the Elderly People in Urban China." *Population Research* 35(3): 84–96. (in Chinese)

Li, S. 2012a. "Are Filial Piety Standards Achievable?" *Beijing Review* 36, September 6. http://www.bjreview.com.cn/forum/txt/2012-09/03/content_4795 83.htm.

Li, S. 2012b. "To Legislate Filial Piety?" *Beijing Review* 30, July 25. http://www .bjreview.com.cn/forum/txt/2012-07/23/content_469869.htm.

Li, W. 2005. "Ten Great Filial Exemplars of China Are Selected." http://mil.news .sina.com.cn/2005–01–09/0700257200.html. (In Chinese).

Li, Y. 2010. "Report on Five-City Survey on Family Structure and Family Relationship." Chinese Academy of Social Science (CASS) Five-City Research Project.

Liu, W. 2012. "Decline of Filial Piety? Concepts, Behaviors and Impact Factors of Adult Children on Parental Support." *Zhongguo Qingnian* 2: 22–32. (In Chinese)

Ma, D. 2011. "A Study about the Domestic Workers in Beijing." *Beijing Social Science* 2: 55–60. (In Chinese)

Miller, E. 2004. "Filial Daughters, Filial Sons: Comparisons from Rural North China." In *Filial Piety: Practice and Discourse in Contemporary East Asia*, edited by C. Ikels, 34–52. Stanford, CA: Stanford University Press.

National Committee on Aging. 2011. "Brief Introduction to National Elder Respect Month." http://www.cncaprc.gov.cn/contents/82/23476.html.

Phillips, T. 2017. "China's Answer to Its Ageing Crisis? A University for 70somethings." The Guardian, February 24. https://www.theguardian.com /world/2017/feb/24/grey-wall-china-rudong-town-frontline-looming -ageing-crisis.

PRC White Paper. 2006. *The Development of China's Undertakings for the Aged.* http://www.chinadaily.com.cn/china/2006-12/12/content_756690.htm.

Santos, G. 2017. "Multiple Mothering and Labor Migration in Rural South China." In *Transforming Patriarchy: Chinese Families in the 21st Century*, edited by G. Santos and S. Harrell, 91–110. Seattle: University of Washington Press.

Shi, L. 2009. "Little Quilted Vests to Warm Parents' Hearts: Redefining the Gendered Practice of Filial Piety in Rural North-eastern China." *China Quarterly* 198: 348–63.

Wang, Y. [Yiqing]. 2012. "Filial Piety Does Not Need a Code." *China Daily*, August 31. http://www.chinadaily.com.cn/opinion/2012-08/31/content_157227 63.htm.

Wang, Y. [Yuesheng]. 2012. "Research on Intergenerational Relations in Urban and Rural China." *Kaifang Shidai*, no. 2: 102–21. (In Chinese)

Whyte, M. 2004. "Filial Obligations in Chinese Families: Paradoxes of Modernization." In *Filial Piety: Practice and Discourse in Contemporary East Asia*, edited by Charlotte Ikels 106–27. Stanford, CA: Stanford University Press.

Xu, A. 2017. "Introduction." In *The Chinese Family Today*, edited by A. Xu, J. Defrain, and W. Liu, 1–13. London: Routledge.

Yan, Y. 2003. *Private Life Under Socialism: Love, Intimacy, and Family Change in a Chinese Village, 1949–1999.* Stanford, CA: Stanford University Press.

Zhan, H., X. Feng, and B. Luo. 2008. "Placing Elderly Parents in Institutions in Urban China." *Research on Aging* 30 (5): 537–71.

Zhang, H. 2004. "'Living Alone' and the Rural Elderly: Strategy and Agency in Post-Mao Rural China." In *Filial Piety: Practice and Discourse in Contemporary East Asia*, edited by Charlotte Ikels, 63–87. Stanford, CA: Stanford University Press.

Zhang, H. 2005. "Bracing for an Uncertain Future: A Case Study of New Coping Strategies of Rural Parents under China's Birth Control Policy." *China Journal* 54: 53–78.

Zhang, H. 2007. "From Resisting to Embracing? the One-Child Policy: Explaining New Fertility Trends in a Chinese Village." *China Quarterly* 192: 855–75.

Zhang, H. 2009. "The New Realities of Aging in Contemporary China: Coping with the Decline of Family Care." In *Cultural Context of Aging: Worldwide Perspectives*, 3rd ed., edited by Jay Sokolovsky, 196–215. Westport, CT: Greenwood.

CHAPTER TWENTY-THREE

Web Book: "One to One" and "Five by One"

The Senior Companions Program in China

Jeanne Shea

Available at: http://www.culturalcontextofaging.com/webbook-shea

This chapter documents the operation of a Senior Companion Program in Shanghai, China, which since 2012 has assigned "young-old" neighborhood volunteers to check on vulnerable elders age 80 and older living alone.

CHAPTER TWENTY-FOUR

Indigenous Mexican Elders Engage the 21st Century

Jay Sokolovsky

Nov. 2, 2018, the Highlands of Central Mexico

I am back in San Jerónimo Amanalco for El Dia del Muertos, the Day of the Dead, with my compadres and our extended family in that indigenous Mexican community. The trip was largely to pay respect to the memory of my compadre, Juan Velazquez, who died almost a year ago at age 52 from untreated complications of diabetes. I was last there in 2015 to present the prepublication draft of *Indigenous Mexico Engages the 21st Century*, my multimedia book about Amanalco's residents (2015). Part of this recent trip was to deliver this book to schools, community leaders, and some families (www .indigenousmexicobook.com).

On this 2018 trip I was eager to feel the warm embrace of the large kinship network living within and connected to the house compound called Buena Vista (beautiful view). I first stayed there from 1972 to 1973 to explore how global change was impacting the community. Driving into Amanalco now I observed numerous trails of bright yellow marigold petals (*cempaspuchitl* in Nahuatl) snaking from the road through household doors up to family altars. It was thought that the scent of the flowers would entice the spirits of dead relatives to visit the house altars, where they would appreciate this intense, colorful conjunction of devotion and memory. Pulling into the Buena Vista house compound, I saw the yellow streak of petals flowing into the

Photo 24.1a   November 2, 2018. Part of the extended family standing in front of the Buena Vista family altar decorated specifically to welcome the spirit of Juan Velazquez back to the house for the Day of the Dead. (Photo by Jay Sokolovsky. See a short video of this event at: https://www.youtube.com/watch?v=ZQ2djw Dn278)

Photo 24.1b   November 2, 2018. Jay Sokolovsky welcoming the spirit of Juan Velazquez back to the cemetery with family associated with the Buena Vista house compound. (Photo by Jay Sokolovsky)

doorway of the main building and up the stairs. They ended in the shape of a cross in front of the transformed family altar, festooned with more of the yellow flowers around mounds of food, chocolate death heads, smoking copal incense, tequila, and even new articles of clothing and photos of the recently departed family member. Sobbing uncontrollably with Juan's widow Anastacia, his 82-year-old mother, Doña Concha, and his married daughters Rosalba and Elizabeth, we all hoped that his spirit would find the way back into Buena Vista that day (see photos 24.1a and 24.1b).

This ritual and its connection to family, generation, and ancestors brought to a head how this indigenous Mexican community has been affected by globalization but has found ways to alter its traditional culture to sometimes transcend the powerful forces of global change. At the local level, a key lynchpin to understanding how people now think about late life versus my residence there in 1972 is that a majority no longer tie their identity to an agriculturally focused campesino lifestyle. This economic and social way of life was centered on growing crops, tending animals, and domestic life around the hearth. Here I will explore the nature of aging and the life course in Amanalco, and how the shift away from this orientation is transforming domestic and public cultural spaces and situating people in new elderscapes and cultural scripts. I begin by detailing changes in the community over the past four decades and then examine how cultural spaces in families and community are adapting to life in a multilocal, globalizing context.

Amanalco in Regional and Cultural Context

Amanalco is nestled in a mountain valley 8,500 feet above sea level and adjacent to the archeological remains of the residents' Aztec forbearers. It is one of 27 pueblos (rural communities) in a municipal unit politically led by the city of Texcoco, about 12 miles away. In 1972, Texcoco was a sleepy municipal capital of 25,000, but by 2018 its population had swelled to about 180,000. This urban center with its banks, supermarkets, appliance stores, movie theaters, medical clinics, Internet cafés, Domino's Pizza delivery, technical schools, and car dealerships serves as a juncture for the diffusion of Mexican national culture and increasingly international ideas and products. Here the inhabitants of Amanalco come to register titles to land, obtain a civil marriage, or complain about an injustice that cannot be handled by their own authorities. Over the past three decades Texoco has become a major site of employment for Amanalco's citizens, especially as bus and taxi drivers, hair stylists, or workers in the stores and small factories located there.

An hour west of Texcoco sits the edge of massive, vibrant Mexico City, with an estimated 21 million inhabitants clinging improbably to a dry, extremely polluted, high altitude valley. Since the early 15th century when Amanalco was founded, its fate was connected to this urban zone. While isolated in a rugged mountain region, its families periodically hauled valuable forest products to the city's ancient urban markets, even before the availability of burros introduced during the 16th-century Spanish conquest.

However, within the past several decades Mexico City has drawn Amanalco deeply into its social and cultural fabric through jobs and expanding markets for its goods. It is the preferred source for machinery, consumer electronics, and ritual items such as my goddaughter Rosalba's wedding dress. The frequent travel from small town to megalopolis has entrenched most of Amanalco's residents, especially the young, in a global cultural network of personal style, work, consumption, and ideas. Yet, we will see that the vibrancy and strength of their culture and economy has so far resisted the worst kinds of potential social dissolution and exclusion that can result from globalization (Part III Web Book Fry).

In the early 1970s residents of Amanalco culturally identified themselves as *indios* (Indians) and were, in fact, thought to be the most ardent followers of indigenous traditions in their region. They were bilingual in Spanish and the classic form of the Aztec language, Nahuatl. This was the first language children learned, often while being carried around wrapped in a shawl by their resident grandmother. Elders resided in house compounds of their lineage surrounded by adult sons and typically multiple generations of their extended families. Kin boundaries and connections were ritually marked every day as close relatives were always greeted by a distinctive bowing and hand-kissing respect gesture. Women used the Aztec sweatbath (*temazcal*) in many of their healing regimens, and while devout Catholics, the populace kept the Aztec deity Nahuake in their spiritual pantheon. Moreover, a regular system of communal labor and a traditional fiesta complex was continued in which families took on time-consuming and costly responsibilities for ritually celebrating the lives of various Roman Catholic saints. Along with four other Nahuatl-speaking villages in the high mountain lands, Amanalco remained culturally distinct from the rural communities in the lower ecological zones stretching down toward Texcoco. Inhabitants of such villages spoke only Spanish and disdained the "backward" *indios del monte* (mountain Indians) while touting themselves as mestizos, agrarian exemplars of a more cosmopolitan, urban style of life. Today while few women regularly use sweatbaths for health and the indigenous language is regularly spoken by only 20 percent of the populace, most of these patterns above still persist, although somewhat transformed.

What originally drew me to study Amanalco was a seeming paradox. How could these traditional cultural features coexist with a series of locally initiated, "modernizing" changes that also made the village the most rapidly transforming of the *indio* communities in its region? Some changes, such as village electrification and the building of a new elementary school, had begun a few years before I arrived. Others were transpiring during and within five years of my initial research stay. These changes included construction of a passable, flat dirt road; the creation of a potable water system; and building a medical clinic and a high school. In the early 1990s Amanalco also became the Catholic parochial center for the other nearby *indio* communities and finally acquired its own resident priest. By the beginning of the 21st century the community had an expanded paved road, very regular bus connections, a technical high school, and two bilingual elementary schools (in Spanish and Nahuatl).

Amanalco was not a passive receptor of these changes. Instead the community has sought through its collective initiative to recast itself in terms of local concepts of a modern "civilized" place. Fortunately for the elderly, Amanalco has resolved this paradox of remaining the most traditional while also being the most changing community by relying upon and eventually transforming its most customary aspects of belief and village organization to pursue the goal of community transformation. However, over the last decade, accelerated levels of community change and the dramatic expansion of Mexico City into the world's largest metropolis have created new challenges which are beginning to test the best of cultural intentions. During this time as the village's population rapidly increased and the urban zones of Texcoco and Mexico City dramatically expanded, young adults sought wage labor outside the community in transportation, service trades (e.g., hair styling), factory work, textile production, and eventually in bilingual education, especially for young women. In the context of such changes the framework for the path through the life cycle is being written from a more diverse and complex script.

Into the Multilocal, Global Village of 2018

Driving through Amanalco in 2018, one sees a former agrarian village grown into a globally connected town of over 8,000 residents. Approaching the central plaza you will see a cell phone tower that sits on the edge of an uncultivated corn field across from the colonial-era church. Now almost every house has a TV antenna on the roof and, inside, video and audio entertainment centers compete with saints' altars for the family's attention. For example, in 2018, sitting in a friend's house, near their family altar, an adjacent flat-screen TV was playing a Teletubbies episode in Spanish.

Every few streets, especially in the central part of town, there are small general merchandise stores, selling everything from Coca-Cola and toilet paper to school supplies and cell phone cards. Previously, these items were only available in cities such as Mexico City or Texcoco. Along the paved central road leading cars and buses into the community's center, one passes an Internet/computer store (one of five now in the village), hair salon, a used CD and DVD store, kids on skateboards, and a little store advertising "Pizza and Hamburger."

Today, if you spend a while in any of Amanalco's house compounds, you will encounter young and middle-aged adults who work in an urban store, perform music, sell flowers in a city market, style hair, teach in a school, drive a bus, or make clothing for sale in regional markets or wholesalers. Although they likely think of their elder parents and grandparents as campesinos, they talk about themselves in relation to their employment as a musician, teacher, market seller, clothing maker, or bus or taxi driver. In 2018 three-quarters of the elder campesino men and women lived in multigenerational extended-family house compounds with their mostly non-agrarian-focused offspring. These older adults are involved with a delicate balancing act of managing their expectations for late life and the potentially difficult handing-down of a cultural legacy in a world few expected to encounter in their lifetimes (Photo 24.2). This is far from a unique situation, as you will learn in other chapters in this volume about Thailand, China, India, and Ghana.

As is happening in Asia, cultural scripts of filial devotion for rural indigenous Mexicans in multigenerational households are being disrupted (see Part III Coe, Part III Hong, and Part V Lamb). Multilocal and transnationally "outsourced" sons and the competing demands of educating children are key factors in moderating elders' authority. In Amanalco to date there has been limited international migration, likely under 5 percent of the population.

Photo 24.2   The generation gap grows, 2000. An elderly grandmother back from gathering herbs in mountain valleys stops to talk to her grandchildren playing ninjas they had seen on TV. (Photo by Maria Vesperi)

This contrasts with other Mexican regions, especially in the state of Puebla or Oaxaca, where one might find equal numbers of villagers in Brooklyn, New York, as in their Mexican hometown (Boehm 2013).

Yet, since the 1990s Amanalco has become a truly multilocal community, with 60 percent of households having one or more persons working or being educated in nearby urban communities or regional market centers. Counterbalancing this, local occupational niches, especially textile production among young adults, have expanded rapidly and fostered a growing equality in generational relations while promoting continued extended family patterns. This is indeed a community that has undergone a profound transformation from

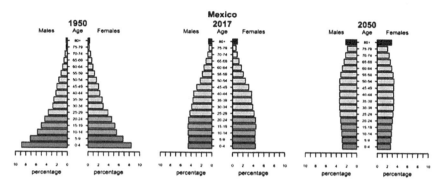

Figure 24.1   Age Pyramids for Mexico, 1950, 2017, 2050 (Adapted from United Nations 2017).

an agrarian peasant village to a proletarian, wage-earning populace stretching the limits of a traditional cultural system to contain its globalizing circumstances.

Demographic Imperatives, New Worlds of Work, Education, and Aging

Early 21st-century Mexico, like some other globalizing nations, is still demographically young, with 7 percent of its populace aged 65 or older. Yet, as noted in Figure 24.1, the shape of the nation's age distribution had already lost the classic pyramid shape by 2017 and by 2050 is expected to resemble the more mature demographics of European societies today. This is led by a reversal of 20th-century patterns; between 1997 and 2010 the population growth in young children (ages birth to five) was actually in decline by -0.4 percent, whereas the elder part of the population grew by 2.5 percent. The major factor here was that the nation, along with improved health care, witnessed a rapid drop in its fertility rate from 6.8 babies born per woman in 1970 to just 2.2 in 2017. At that date Mexico's average life expectancy had risen to 77 years, only two years less than the United States (World Bank 2018).

In Amanalco, by 2005, the community's age structure still had the classic pyramidal, youth-dominated shape (Figure 24.2), although the reduction in childbirths was beginning to be seen at the youngest end of the lifespan. With just 3.4 percent over age 65, this was still a young community, especially compared to other rural pueblos closer to Texcoco where migration and earlier limitations on fertility typically doubled or even tripled this measure of agedness.

Another significant change has occurred in the work pattern of young women. As depicted in the 2018 award-winning movie *Roma*, up to the

Age group

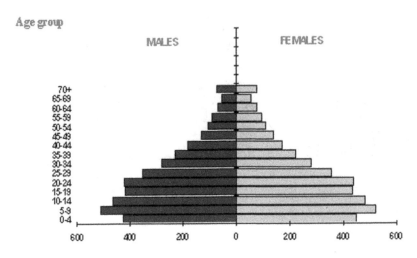

Figure 24.2   Age Pyramid, Amanalco, 2005 (Annual census completed by Amanalco's community nurse, 2006).

1980s the most typical wage work sought by rural indigenous teenage girls was to serve as a live-in servant for middle-class families in Mexico City or Texcoco. However, in the 1980s, the town of Chiconcuac on the outskirts of Texcoco began to abandon its traditional small-scale production of wool products for large-scale production of inexpensive synthetic fiber clothing. For the prior 100 years, Amanalco's sheep had provided much of the wool for Chiconcuac's once famous serapes and sweaters. Now they began to send their teenage daughters and some sons to help produce inexpensive dresses, shirts, and other clothes for markets throughout Mexico and even the United States.

At the beginning of the 21st century about 200 villagers (such as my god-daughter Rosalba) still worked in Chiconcuac; however, global competition began to force these factories to downsize. Eventually, families in Amanalco decided to use their children's accumulated skills and wages to invest in sewing and weaving machines and create clothing in their own homes for sale in regional markets. By 2018 about 150 households engaged in the production of clothing. Home-based textile work had become particularly attractive to young couples who could work side by side while living in the groom's parent's house and contributing monies to extended family coffers on a weekly basis.

It is important to note that for the vast majority of households producing textiles, this work often stabilizes multigenerational households. Typically, the capital outlays for the expensive machines are initially funded by the elder generation, and part of the resulting monies from this work are shared

---

with parents or other older relatives. This happened for my goddaughter Rosalba and her new husband Herardo, who in their case make textiles for Herardo's uncle, who following their wedding gave them land to set up a house next to his family.

A smaller core of young women were also taking advantage of growing educational opportunities, completing high school in the new local facility built in the early 1980s or a technical school completed in 1995. Some were going on to outside technical schools, junior college, and even university in Mexico City. A small core of these women were becoming hair stylists, secretaries, nurses, and teachers in both regular grade schools and bilingual schools opening in the region. One such 21-year-old female, a computer science major at Texcoco's junior college, opened up Amanalco's first computer café in 2003, with the financial backing of her parents. Similarly, young, educated women are beginning to reshape ideas about the life course.

The Demography of Reproduction

When I began my research in the early 1970s, Mexico was undergoing economic expansion, and Amanalco, like many other rural regions, began a population explosion resulting from an extremely high rate of live births, averaging 9.39 per family (Millard 1985). This was initially counterbalanced by an extraordinarily high child mortality rate, where on average one out of three children could not be expected to live past age five. In Buena Vista, for Concha (now age 82) only three of her seven children born made it past childhood. Yet, of these living adult children, none of their own eight kids died in childhood, and all of her grandchildren and great-grandchildren have so far survived past early childhood. This dramatic change occurred largely because in the 1980s the community acquired clean, piped household water from its mountain springs and opened a medical clinic, so that by the next decade child mortality had plummeted to about 5 percent (Mindek 1994).

Of course it should be remembered that one of Concha's adult children, my compadre Juan, died at age 52 from diabetes in 2018. More sedentary lifestyles and diet changes, especially since the 1990s, have contributed to a dramatic rise in obesity (now over 30 percent) and diabetes (16 percent) across Mexico and in communities like Amanalco (OECD 2016). This brought home to me comments by elders who insisted that in prior times many people lived to enjoy long, healthy lives because they only ate "natural food" that they grew in their fields. Unfortunately, the easy access to white bread, Twinkies, and Coca-Cola in Amanalco, beginning in the early 1980s, was coming home to roost in ill health in adulthood (Crónica al Momento 2016).

In Amanalco, fertility rates also began to drop in the 1980s, facilitated by growing educational opportunities for females and the work of a local woman, Hipólita Duran. Despite strong parental opposition, she got support from an aunt and left the village to attend nursing school. Returning with a nursing degree, Hipólita eventually became Amanalco's first permanent public health nurse. She worked in collaboration with a doctor in the new village medical clinic, and together they initiated the first effective family planning program.

In 1973, when I would ask young men and women what the ideal family size was, the standard response was "Only God knows." At that time most couples sought to have as many children as they could, and it was not unusual to record genealogies involving the eventual birth of 10 to 14 children. By the 1990s attitudes were changing dramatically, especially among young women who completed high school. Almost like a Greek chorus, adults in their twenties would repeat the maxim, "Dos hijos es mejor, pero cuatro es el maximo!" (Two kids is ideal, but the maximum is four).

In 2000, when I asked about the changed desire for a limited number of children, young parents noted the great reduction in child mortality but also cited the rapidly rising costs of supporting children, especially in the area of education. Although by 2018 the average completed fertility for women had been reduced to about 3.2 children, the equally dramatic increased child survival and limited permanent migration meant that the population had soared to over 8,000 residents.

The Cultural Construct of Maturity, Aging, and Generation

Individuals will attempt to retain the image of a fully functioning adult as long as possible. However, it was recognized that sometime during the sixth or seventh decade of life, men and women will gradually give up total executive control of the household to one of their married sons and his wife. People would begin to refer to such persons as old by generically using the Nahuatl term *cultzin* (grandparent) or *culi* (old person) for both males and females.[1] They will begin to be talked about as *culi* when several grandchildren have survived childhood.

However, the *culi* label is not consistently applied to a person until their early to mid-sixties when changes in strength and vitality reduce work capacity in some way. Once persons are accepted as *culi*, they will be excused from communal work groups and most public ritual sponsorship. The last stages of agedness are defined by steep declines in functional abilities with the most obvious sign of "real" old age being the need to walk with a cane.[2] If this mobility shift is accompanied by other dramatic declines that might forecast an impending demise, people might refer to a person as *youtla moak* or "all used up."[3] This term is not used often but sums up more precise Nahuatl words that describe the loss of real adult functioning. By the time people are labelled *yotla moak* they have generally restricted their daily activity to their house compound and rely on nearby grandchildren and great-grandchildren to assist with their activities of daily living.

Older men are especially sensitive about being labeled *yotla moak*. For example, Manuel Duran lived in an adjacent house to Buena Vista, so I knew him very well over several decades. When I was back in the village in 2000, he came out of his house to say hello. He was then age 86. Only in the last few years had he become quite hard of hearing, started to wear thick glasses, and sometimes walked slightly bent over with a cane. When I asked him about the phrase *yotla moak*, he gave a nervous laugh, patted himself on the chest, implying but not saying that this described himself. Immediately he said he had some wooden fence posts to cut and left. Over the following week I visited Manuel's house every day, and he made a point to tell me each activity he was about to do such as cutting more wood or walking halfway up the mountain to gather sap from his cactus plants to make fresh *pulque* (cactus beer). When we looked at old pictures I had taken of him working with his son in their cornfield in 1972, he thought back to how strong he had been then and readily said that now he was a *culi*. Reluctantly he admitted that most would call him in Nahuatl *tepikn*, meaning so old he needs a cane. Manuel would never admit to being *yotla moak*, although many people were beginning to say this when he was not around.

Gendered Aging

For menopausal and older women there is a noticeable lessening of social constraints on behavior, and they are allowed greater latitude in social interaction, especially with male age peers. By the time a woman is 60 she may be seen on occasion casually chatting with a group of men or guzzling a beer at a public festival, things culturally taboo for younger females. Similar to Yewoubdar Beyene's findings in a study of older Mayan women in southern Mexico (Part I), midlife females in Amanalco do not report the kinds of hot flashes or painful symptoms mentioned by many females in North America (see also Huicochea-Gómez et al. 2017). The local explanation of older women in Amanalco was that, unlike urban women, they are brought up not to complain, and anyway, females have no time for such symptoms or even illness—they just bear it.

Beginning in midlife, through their forties and fifties, women may cultivate skills in nondomestic arenas. One of these is midwifery and/or some other traditional folk healing specialty such as *tepatike* (general healer), *tlamemelawa* (massage), or *tlapupua* (herbal medicine). Of the most active midwives in 2015, four were in their midforties, one was 55 and the other two were in their midseventies. Each of these women practice at least one of the other healing traditions in addition to assisting with childbirth.[4]

A second area of activity for middle-aged women is in the entrepreneurial realm. After menopause, women have the opportunity to venture to urban markets by themselves to sell. Most typically this will involve hawking flowers, herbs, food, or animals in the crowded satellite urban areas ringing Mexico City. For example, Doña Maria, at age 64, had been a widow for a decade and lived with her married son and his children on a tiny, unproductive plot of land. She began selling sheep and goats about 15 years ago. Later, she used this money to trade in flowers and put a deposit down toward the purchase of a small textile-making machine from the factory where her son was working in Chiconcuac. They started to produce sweaters in their house and eventually used the profits for Doña Maria to set up a paper and notebook store in the late 1980s. This enterprise has done quite well, with the completion of Amanalco's own high school soon after the store opened.

As is typical in the life cycle of rural agrarian communities, women in old age show a greater continuity in the roles they play than men (Cool and McCabe 1987; Bledsoe 2002). Most elderly women, almost to the time of their deaths, continue a familiar domestic regimen centering on food preparation, weaving, nurturance of children, and the care of small livestock. Continuing this work pattern keeps old women deeply embedded in a network of both age peers and younger women from four to six households, who must cooperate to produce the huge quantities of food consumed on ritual occasions. For example, during the 2006 wedding of Rosalba in Buena Vista, Doña Concha (then age 70) and her two resident daughters-in-law coordinated the work of 10 other women from ages 46 to 75 who seemed to work constantly and seamlessly over a three-day period to prepare and serve food to several hundred people. One female relative, age 72, had the specialized task of rapidly dispatching 75 chickens that were cooked for the main celebration (Photo 24.3).

Older men, even after relinquishing control of their farms or other work, will continue to undertake arduous work alongside their sons until their mid-to-late sixties. It is after this point that they switch to more sedentary tasks such as preparing cactus beer, repairing tools, or collecting wild vegetables from nearby cornfields. However, by 2010 with so many men in the

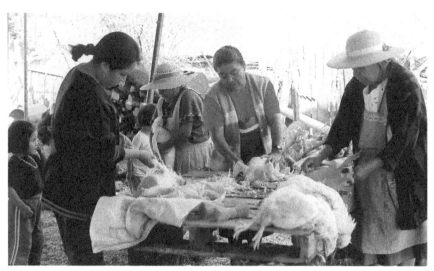

Photo 24.3   Concha (far right) working with one of her two resident daughters-in-law (far left) and two older female relatives. They are preparing chickens to be cooked for Rosalba's wedding feast, 2006. (Photo by Maria Vesperi)

20-to-40 age bracket working out of the village on any given day, it is not unusual to see a male in his seventies planting a field by himself or with a couple of age peers. Their sons will typically help when they can, but only if it does not interfere with a wage-producing job.

Despite this, in Amanalco, extended family organization is the normative form of residence older adults hope to generate over the long run. Ideally, as male offspring get married, at least one is expected to raise children in his parents' house and provide the core basis of support in old age. More often than not these days, resident married sons and their families live in a physically independent house set within a residential compound, a moment's walk from their parents' dwelling—just across a courtyard or down a dirt path. The experience of aged individuals living by themselves is still extremely rare and usually happens following the death of a spouse, where the older couple had been living alone in one of the relatively isolated mountain neighborhoods. In most such instances there will be an attempt, as seen in Photo 24.4, to send adolescent or teenage children to live with and help grandparents who would otherwise be living by themselves.

Elders are in constant contact with children, if not with a resident grandchild then with a wide range of very young kin and godchildren living within a few hundred yards from them. The child-minding aspect of grandparenting has, in fact, increased over the last decade, as in many households at least one of the parents is working in the city during the day. Relations of the very old with their grandchildren are especially important. In extended families,

Photo 24.4   Fifteen-year-old
boy sent to live with his
widowed grandmother, 1993.
(Photo by Jay Sokolovsky)

young children were observed sleeping in the same bed as a grandparent (Photo 24.5). This seldom seemed a matter of space, but rather a case of mutual need. The children help to warm up old bones and the grandparent provides emotional security at night when various spirits and demons are thought to travel through the village.

While archive research has shown that the percent of elders living in extended household contexts has remained at about two-thirds over the past 80 years, important structural changes have taken place (Sokolovsky 2002). From the 1920s to the current time, a major shift has involved the significant reduction of very large extended households, where two or more married sons stayed in the house compound to work with and eventually care for their parents. Such "joint" patrilineal (male-linked) households, containing 12–25 persons, were enclosed within 120-by-70-foot rectangular compounds protected by 15-foot-high adobe walls and at least two dogs. By the early 1970s, reductions in per capita land holdings and the rise of new money-making activities outside the village had stimulated a shift from "joint" to "stem" patrilineal groupings where only one married son would remain with the parents. At that time the proportion of joint, patrilineal households with more than one married son living under the parent's domain had been reduced by about half. Nonetheless, as will be seen with Buena Vista, some households have combined various nonagrarian work by many adult kin to build successful multifamily, multigenerational households.

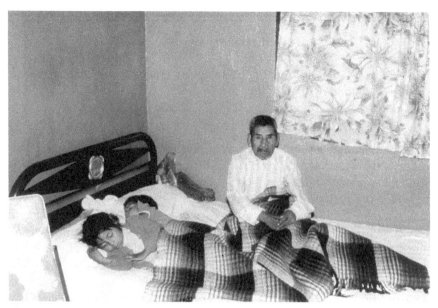

Photo 24.5 Ninety-six-year-old man sleeping with two coresident great-grandchildren, 1978. (Photo by Jay Sokolovsky)

Also of recent vintage is the formation of extended households that incorporate an adult daughter's family into her parents' residence, either by themselves or along with a married son. In most of these cases, the adult daughter has married someone from outside the village from a poor family who had little to offer the young couple. Such marriages are especially unstable and are many times more likely to break up than if the husband and wife both were born in the village. In almost all such cases of marital dissolution, the daughter will remain in her parents' house, especially if she has any young children.

One of the most subtle but profound changes, also found in many other developing world regions, is the gradual social distancing of nuclear family units from the parental generation (Aboderin 2006). I am not talking about the dramatic privatization of living and social space that North American families expect; people in Amanalco, even though they now see such things on TV dramas and soap operas, remain puzzled and even repulsed by the idea that young children can have their own room with a door they can close! Most would consider this child abuse through isolation.

From Authority to Love

In the early 1970s the emotional structure of family systems was quite authoritarian, dominated by the elder couple, especially the male. Following Aztec legal tradition, parents could take disobedient children to the

WEB SPECIAL:

Respeto—a fluid and transforming generational kin marker. See https://youtu.be/vSzPYYlABlA.

community judges for punishment in the form of labor for the community or a fine. I witnessed several such cases during 1973. However, by 2018 this was an exceedingly rare event, and the current community leaders could not recall the last such case in the past decade.

On a more subtle level, during my earliest research in Amanalco I found that the physical gesture of *respeto* (respect) masked an underlying tension and fear that embraced the realm of kinship. Especially for men, access to adult roles and community status was largely predicated on inherited lands. This engendered not only filial conflict but also tension among certain male cousins (the sons of a father's brother). The total acceptance of *respeto* behavior was thought to help avoid angry emotions and envy among relatives. It was such disruptive feelings that were believed to invite sorcery, with its subsequent misfortune.

Over the past two decades there has developed a feeling that young couples require a more "companionate" social and emotional connection to each other, while basing the strong respect still directed toward elder kin more on earned affection and less on unquestioned authority. This is reinforced by some new economic strategies such as household garment manufacture, where couples work as equal partners to form the core of family teams that produce clothing for market sale. In a majority of such cases it is typically the husband's parents who provide the capital for these endeavors. As noted in the Web Special video, this is also reflected in the shift of hand-kissing greetings of elder kin. This behavior is now more often punctuated with an affectionate kiss to the cheek and a smile, altering the totally somber respect gesture I observed in the 1970s.

Maturing in the Nonagrarian *Tochantlaca*

I had first met my recently deceased compadre Juan Velazquez, in 1972, when he was just six years old and I was a 24-year-old graduate student moving into his parent's house for a year of anthropological fieldwork. As children grow, they quickly learn that their social world is centered around their *tochantlaca*. This indigenous Nahuatl word literally translates as either "my house" or "my family." In functional reality this term also applies to the core relatives connected to both parents. Most important, however, are the surrounding homesteads of the father's brothers that form the boundaries of what anthropologists call a patrilineage—that is, a locally generated kin network tied together by brothers, male cousins, uncles, and grandparents often living on contiguous lands. A given surname group such as Duran, Arias, or Velazquez tends to have many of its kin-linked households in the same area on one side of the community's dual administrative division, although they can be found on both sides. The word *tochantlaca* also increasingly encompasses the network of relatives in the mother's natal household and that of one's own spouse when a male marries.

Despite the ideal dominance of patrilineal descent, key kinship ties generated through one's mother are also acknowledged by respect behavior and since my first time in Amanalco have gained in practical importance. As the campesino lifestyle has declined and drawn villagers outside the community for work, maternal relatives have increasingly come to comprise a significant portion of a household's total personal network of support. It is through the exchange of labor, tangible goods, and money with both male and female kin links that families are able to carry out family rituals, which have become more elaborate, costly, and time consuming, especially over the past two decades. For, example my wife and I returned to Amanalco when Juan's daughter (and our goddaughter) Rosalba was married in 2006. In participating in and documenting the wedding rituals that spanned three full days, I calculated that over 30 percent of the labor was provided by people linked to the *tochantlaca* networks centered in the households where the bride's mother and grandmother were born.

Aging beyond the Family

Beyond the family, the most important source of prestige, respect, and power during middle and old age derives from the carrying out of community ritual and civil responsibilities. Known in Latin American scholarship as either the *cargo* (literally, "burden") system or the *fiesta* system, this involves a hierarchy of ranked positions (*cargos*) occupied for short periods of time by specific households (Cancian 1992; Chick 2002).

In Amanalco, community roles are loosely ranked, with the higher ones generally requiring more money and/or time but yielding more prestige and

---

Web Special:

See a video about Rosalba's wedding at: https://youtu.be/oq1WnQ 6Ke70.

Box 24.1   The Case of the Reluctant Campesino and the Educated Daughter-In-Law

As noted in Figure 24.3, in 2018 the Buena Vista house compound contained a multigenerational extended family that early on had moved away from a campesino orientation. The eldest resident is the shy, widowed, very traditional, Nahuatl-speaking Concha Duran Juarez, age 82, whose husband Encarnacion had died at age 63 in 1997. Concha had four children who survived childhood: two adult sons (Juan and Angel), a daughter who wed on the farthest reaches of the other side of the village, and another daughter, Ana, who lives with a man and his parents in a nearby community (note these daughters are not indicated in Figure 24.3).

Although, Concha's husband had been fluent in Nahuatl and enjoyed participating in the traditional fiesta system, he had never liked farming. He would often intersperse tending his small fields with temporary factory jobs, or making change on buses in Texcoco. Encarnacion also made wooden crates for sale with their sons, or bought and sold flowers with Concha in the shanty towns springing up around Mexico City. In 1984, their oldest son Juan brought his village-born wife Anastacia into his parents' house, and over a 15-year period they had four children, the oldest of whom is Rosalba.

With population and urban congestion booming in the Texcoco region by the 1990s, the government encouraged individuals to lease buses or vans to enhance the existing intercity public transport system.

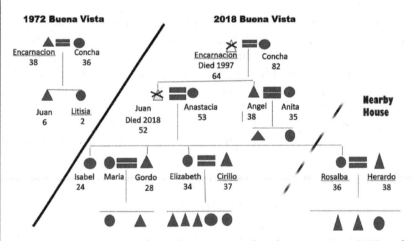

Figure 24.3   Kin Chart of Families Associated with Buena Vista: 1972 and 2018.

By 1994, Encarnation had leased both a large van and a small bus, which he and his two sons would drive in long shifts to support the household. They also used their collective savings to open up a small convenience store in the front of their house, which Concha managed. Following Encarnacion's death in 1997, the family gave up one of the buses, and by the late 1990s Concha's resident teenage granddaughters Rosalba and Elizabeth had both dropped out of school and were commuting daily to make sweaters in a small factory in the nearby town of Chiconcuac.

In 2018, following Juan's death, the kin configuration in Buena Vista found two extended family clusters, with one each residing on either side of an enclosed courtyard. Juan's younger brother, Angel, had brought his longtime girlfriend, Anita, into Buena Vista, eight years prior, and they now had two young children. Angel had just completed a new extension to the oldest building in the compound to provide for his young family and Concha. Bringing Anita into the household had been a tricky business, as her father had invested in her education to be a schoolteacher, and Angel swore everyone—including me—to secrecy about Angel's plans until she had graduated. Things had worked out, and while Concha cheerfully watched Anita's children, the younger woman traveled during the week to a teaching job an hour away near Mexico City.

Interesting enough, women such as Anita as a group tend to remain in the village and are among the most vocal supporters of traditional indigenous culture, especially the retention of the *Nahuatl* language. A dozen of these women have found employment as bilingual Nahuatl/Spanish teachers in Amanalco as well as recently built bilingual schools in the other nearby indigenous communities.

On the other side of the compound a second story completed in 2017 housed Juan's widow Anastacia and the families of her son Gordo, who worked with his uncle Angel selling flowers, and her daughter Elizabeth, who along with her husband made clothing in the house. Elizabeth and her husband had recently (2017) moved back home to her family, as there was too much conflict living with her in-laws. Also living there was Isabel, an unmarried daughter who attended a technical school in Texcoco for nursing. It should be noted that Rosalba and her family, who live in a nearby house, are separated in Figure 24.3 from Buena Vista by a dotted line. For her and her husband Herardo, this is truly their most important *tochantlaca*, born of deep affection for Rosalba's parents and Concha.

In the back of the house, Concha still maintains a garden of greens and chiles and tends a small flock of chickens and turkeys as well as a handful of pigs. When she became a widow in 1997, her quiet, warm personality made relations with her daughter-in-law Anastacia run smoothly. When I visited the next year, Concha admitted she was now, at age 61, *culi* (old) and let Anastacia know that she could take charge of the domestic scene. In fact, returning frequently to their household, one could not really determine who was the boss, as they just did things with and for each other with such unspoken ease that it appeared to occur via telepathy.

authority. The positions are divided between *cargos* of the church and those associated with political office; the former carry out costly folk Catholic rituals (fiestas), while the latter form the local government.

The annual religious cycle of four fiestas was carried out by an annually elected set of 22 ritual sponsors or *mayordomos* (stewards) who are led by a two *fiscals* (literally "prosecutors") who collectively are responsible for a single year of ritual.[5] The *fiscal* is the most prestigious religious position, with election to this post usually predicated on prior service in at least one other major religious *cargo*. For the general male population there is an expectation that over a lifetime an individual will have undertaken at least one important sacred *cargo* and thereby be worthy of public esteem.[6]

At the center of local political authority and administration is the first *delegado* (commissioner), who serves for three years as the combined mayor and head judge. The second and third commissioners serve as secretary and community treasurer respectively. The *delegados* are expected to oversee the community, settle most levels of internal disputes, and protect local interests from any outside forces. They lead all village meetings and must solicit opinions from all present until a general consensus is reached. Other personnel in the political hierarchy distribute irrigation waters, protect community boundaries, and organize the traditional system of unremunerated collective labor that carries out public works projects. It is this civil wing of community service that since the late 1960s has initiated and carried out the series of modernizing projects of which Amanalco is so proud. By the time most males reach age 60, they will have shouldered at least some local political responsibility.[7]

Besides ritual sponsorship and administrative positions, the *cargo* system affords other opportunities to enhance public esteem in old age. Some of the fiestas involve dance troops and elaborate processions. Older men, and to a lesser extent women, can volunteer to take roles as dance leaders, instructors, special musicians, or simply participants. Such activities proclaim not only moral uprightness and continuing prestige but also that one is still actively involved in the life of the community.

Although women participate in the masses, processions, and dancing associated with each fiesta, until 2002 they assumed no overt public leadership position in these activities. That year for the first time single women in their early twenties were elected for minor posts in the fiesta system. Moreover, with the establishment of Amanalco as a parish center, the resident priest has encouraged middle-aged and older women to become leaders of a children's catechism group. Yet, during major public ceremonies, older women generally operate behind the scenes, directing the production and serving huge quantities of the special foods required for successful ritual sponsorship.

Despite the emphasis on age, hierarchy, and formal deference between generations in family formations, this pattern is not totally replicated in the public groupings that carry out ritual. Although the fiesta system performs an implicit age-grading function, it also provides one of the only community-wide arenas where males and females of all ages can theoretically participate as relative equals. This occurs in the large dance groups that perform at most fiestas as part of the community's "folk" version of Roman Catholic pageantry. However, as will be noted below, gradually over the past two decades the number of fiestas has been reduced, especially those in which the elderly were most likely to participate.

From Leaders to Audience

While the decline in campesino identity and its associated work patterns has to some extent fostered the functional importance of elders and multi-generational links in domestic spaces, this has not been the case in public cultural spaces of the civic life and the church. In the civil side of the cargo system there has been a general reduction in roles for elders in favor of younger and better educated leaders. Prior to 1950 it was unheard of for a man to be considered for first *delegado* or senior *fiscal* before the age of 50, and persons chosen were often at least 60. For the last four decades first *delegados*, holders of the most potent political position, have been 41 years of age or younger; the youngest was 31. This change was partly compensated for by sometimes selecting the older men, aged 55 to 65, as third *delegado*. I was told that this facilitated working with other elders who serve as informal judicial go-betweens in difficult cases where parties initially refused to abide by legal decisions.

Similarly, in the religious realm, prior to 2000 one of the two fiscals was designated as "senior" and typically was in his midfifties or older. Since then the senior title has been dropped, and community leaders of the religious hierarchy are likely to be under 50 years of age. Although the new millennium has brought greater engagement by women in these activities, elder males, with some exceptions, have been pushed from active participants to audience members, from center to periphery of this key cultural space.

Mature Women Take Charge . . . and Some Older Men

With the shifts in work drawing younger adults outside of the community, I was frankly shocked and pleasantly surprised to learn in 2010 about the election of two women to core positions in the community's political governance. One was a 45-year-old teacher in the local elementary school, elected to be second commissioner, and the other a 58-year-old woman elected to head the committee of public works. She had recently retired as a secretary at the national agricultural college near Texcoco. Such changes followed upon regional and national changes in women's roles that Amanalco's residents are becoming keenly aware of. For example, in 2009 one of the other nearby indigenous communities elected a woman to lead the community. Importantly, in November 2012 the first female was elected to lead the municipal district of Texcoco, which includes Amanalco.

Several years after that, older men in Amanalco were regaining some of the public positions they could previous expect to hold. In 2015 for the first time in a generation, the community elected four men who were all over age 65 to run the committee that decides on the proper use of public lands. It was recognized that not only were they persons who would constantly be in the community to take care of issues as they arose, but that they had the accumulated knowledge to deal with conflicts that might be beyond younger men.

The *Casa de la Tercera Edad*

Indicative of the gradual recognition by the Mexican government that aging was an issue it should pay more attention to, in 2006 a *Casa de la Tercera Edad* (House of the Third Age) was started in Amanalco. Funded as an initiative by the political party then in power, social workers from Mexico City and Texcoco came to organize the group, which is housed in a small, centrally located public building. A local elder couple was elected president and vice president; there is also a secretary, treasurer, and two assistants. In monthly meetings, such as one I attended in 2010, there might be distribution of inexpensive food staples and talks on various topics; in one case it was a discussion of the health issues involved with diabetes and some assistance in getting glasses from a visiting optometrist from Texcoco (Photo 24.6).

Nationally, Mexico instituted an official "Day of the Elderly" in 1983, and since 2000 state and municipal governments have become more aware that extended families in rural areas are not always capable of caring for the needs of the elderly. For example, in August 2014 Amanalco's elder club took part in a large, municipal-supported elder-day celebration in Texcoco where wheelchairs, walkers, and blankets were distributed (see Angel, Montes-de-Oca Zavala, and Rodríguez-Rodríguez 2019).

Photo 24.6   An optometrist from Texcoco talks about diabetes and its impact on vision and other health problems at a meeting at the House of the Third Age in Amanalco, 2010. (Photo by Jay Sokolovsky)

Most seniors expressed appreciation for even the limited material support provided through their House of the Third Age. Yet, in talking to participants, they were acutely conscious of the social and cultural losses occurring in the public cultural spaces. Some regarded this club as a pale substitute for what was lost and equated it with the withering of the Nahuatl language as the centerpiece of a quickly fading indigenous, campesino-centered identity. Yet others viewed the club as a positive indication of Amanalco entering the 21st century and, along with younger adults, contested the very need for an indigenous identity.

Aging within Altered Cultural Spaces

Unlike the harping seniors of the Ju'hoansi (Part I Rosenberg) who complain about their own mistreatment at the hand of kin, in Amanalco the only time one hears a personal narrative of neglect concerns people who are considered "strange," mentally unbalanced, or who have ignored their duty to others. However, complaints across the generational divide are easy to come by.

Generational Bickering: A Classic Synoptic Illusion

While such cases are still exceedingly rare, since 2000 I have heard an increasing litany of negative comments about young people's attitude toward work and the way older persons are treated. As noted by Coe in Part II, narratives of care and generational issues often produce what Bourdieu calls a "synoptic illusion," in that it condenses a great deal of actual heterogeneity with simple, ideal statements that stand in for a more complex whole.

Ask an older male in Amanalco what has changed the most in his lifetime, and one will likely hear: "The young, they are different now. . . . they see the land we have here and do not see the beauty or the worth in it"; "Ask anyone, the young simply do not know about hard work like we do." More generally, there are increasing accusations of a decrease in respect shown the elderly. From the younger part of the life course I would hear youth disparage elders as clinging to a lost world with little value and that the older generation did not appreciate how they, the young, were the ones who *really* understood the present.

What I encountered and observed "on the ground" was more complex than these common expressions of generational angst that others have recorded under similar kinds of community transformations. Even the hardest-working youth and young adults will complain about the difficulty of matching elders' agrarian lifestyle. Behind such statements is also the realization, by both generations, that to now support a family with the contemporary needs of children, one must produce a constant flow of money. In the Web Special video below, pay attention to the dialog between a father and his son, a young man who works making clothes in the household of his campesino parent. Here the son laments the physical difficulty of working the fields, while the older man calmly notes the monetary benefit of his son's work compared to his own agrarian pursuits.

The Retired Campesino—End of a Cultural Script?

In 2018, on my last day in Amanalco, I had to visit a dear friend who also had lost a loved one to diabetes. He was among those elders who had early on seen the cultural handwriting on the wall and were radically altering the last

---

WEB SPECIAL:

A father and son discuss the new realities of work in Amanalco: https://youtu.be/64SRENT95r4.

phases of their campesino lifestyle. Miguel Duran, now age 78 (also seen in the Web Special above), lives halfway up the mountain from Amanalco's central plaza. When I first entered his house compound in 1972, I found the classic campesino-based lineage. Miguel, although not well off, had just enough land to support his large family, economically supplemented by making crates and growing small amounts of flowers. In his compound was his widowed 62-year-old mother, his wife Anna, five of their children (ages 1 to 9) and his recently married younger brother Juan, age 23, who was building a small new house next door. Most people considered Miguel one of the best farmers in the village, someone who managed to feed his large family through his skill and knowledge of the land. As late as 2003 both he and his wife, then in their late fifties, seemed quite healthy and vigorously maintained the beautiful corn fields growing beyond their home. Miguel's mother had then recently died at age 90. They told me, that of two coresident sons only their married one still had some interest in farming, although he also liked making clothes with his unmarried 19-year-old brother. Together, with two teenage sisters, working in a newly built room, they made children's clothes for sale in regional street markets. Returning to visit in 2006 I saw that the cornfield was gone, replaced by two new houses, a greatly enlarged workshop, and a grazing area for the few horses, goats, and cows they had left.

Noting my surprise at this, Miguel proudly explained that he was *really* retired, and he would just watch the young do the work—words I had never previously heard uttered by a healthy, vigorous man in his early sixties. This was not the only dramatic change in his life. A year earlier his wife had succumbed to diabetes, which, like my compadre Juan, she did her best to ignore. Not long after this, his oldest daughter's husband left her and her two teenage daughters, and they moved in with him. His older married son decided to give up the campesino life and devote full time to home production of clothes in an enlarged family "factory." This work team included his wife, his now married brother and spouse, and the two sisters. Miguel had used all his resources and taken out a loan to buy the sewing and weaving equipment in Mexico City. Miguel explained with a smile: "I know Jay, you must be surprised how easily I gave up being a campesino. Some of my cousins and friends still cling to this path, but with my wife's death and my daughter's coming back home I realized one must adapt to things you never expected to happen."

Now in 2018, I presented him with a copy of my multimedia book on the community and indicated the prominent place he and his family had in this volume. I also admired a small plot of herbs and vegetables growing in front of his house, which he planned to sell in the community's Sunday market. He assured me that while this was no more than a token of his early life and he was certainly now *nada mas campesino* (no longer a campesino), it still burned in his soul.

Before driving my rental car to the airport for a return home, I needed to have some private time with Concha and Anastacia back at Buena Vista. We talked of happy times together over many decades, but most of all we speculated about how long it would take before Juan's spirit would wander from the cemetery to enter our dreams and tell us how to watch over his family.

Notes

1. Sometimes the term *sickn* is used for older women, usually when someone is referring to themselves.

2. This went beyond saying someone was a *culi* (old man) or *sickn* (old woman). The most common specific terms linked to perceptions of extreme old age and frailty were *akmukilnamiki* (cannot comprehend); *yomopaltilw(he)* (is incontinent); *akmunnenemi* (can't walk); or *aqueli itlaayi* (cannot work). A typical conversation about a very old relative considered *yotla moak* might provoke the following statement: "*Noachsitntzn y kipia yosio(wk) aqueli itaayi*" (My revered great-grandmother has more than 100 years, she is very weak and cannot work). Another Nahuatl term, which is rarely used today, for a frail elder who needs a cane is *tepikn* (nasal n).

3. This term could also be applied to sickly looking individuals who were not particularly aged.

4. To date, the local nurse and the doctors annually sent to the village medical clinic have maintained a good relationship with these midwives. Although more of Amanalco's women now give birth in the clinic or even in a hospital in Texcoco, the population growth over the last 25 years has assured these midwives many clients.

5. In 1995 the organization of the fiesta system was simplified with a reduction in the number of major fiestas from six to four, and the fiscal position no longer had a senior and junior member but equal positions, chosen from two men from each side of the community.

6. Since 1988, the community has served as the center of a parish for the other Nahuatl villages in the area and has had its own priest living in the community since then. Over this time the number of fiestas has been cut in half and the financial burden spread more evenly within the community.

7. Wealth will condition, to a certain degree, the extent of public prestige and power men and their families will garner as they age. Nevertheless, virtually all older men from Catholic families had carried out at least once the sacred burden of ritual sponsorship, which gives them lasting honor in the eyes of the community and the saints.

Bibliography

Aboderin, I. 2006. *Intergenerational Support and Old Age in Africa.* New Brunswick, NJ: Transaction.

Angel, R. J., V. Montes-de-Oca Zavala, and V. Rodríguez-Rodríguez. 2019. "Strengthening Solidarity: A Theoretical Inquiry into the Roles of Civil Society Organizations in the Support of Elderly Citizens in Mexico City." In *Contextualizing Health and Aging in the Americas*, edited by W. A. Vega, J. L. Angel, L. M. F. Gutiérrez Robledo, and K. S. Markides. New York: Springer.

Bledsoe, C. 2002. *Contingent Lives. Fertility, Time and Aging in West Africa*. Chicago: University of Chicago Press.

Boehm, D. 2013. *Intimate Migrations Gender, Family, and Illegality among Transnational Mexicans*. New York: New York University Press.

Cancian, F. 1992. *The Decline of Community in Zinacantan*. Stanford, CA: Stanford University Press.

Chick, G. 2002. "Cultural and Behavioral Consonance in a Tlaxcalan Festival System." *Field Methods* 14(1): 26–45.

Cool, L., and L. McCabe. 1987. "The 'Scheming Hag' and the 'Dear Old Thing': The Anthropology of Aging Women." In *Growing Old in Different Societies: Cross-Cultural Perspectives*, edited by J. Sokolovsky. Acton, MA: Copley.

Crónica al Momento. 2016. "Consumo de refrescos perfila estilo de vida de los mexicanos." http://www.cronica.com.mx/notas/2016/942650.html (accessed September 29, 2018).

Huicochea-Gómez, L., L. L. Sievert, D. Cahuich-Campos, and D. E. Brown. 2017. "An Investigation of Life Circumstances Associated with the Experience of Hot Flashes in Campeche, Mexico." *Menopause* 24(1): 52–63.

Millard, A. 1978. "Corn, Cash and Population Genetics: Family Demography in Rural Mexico." PhD diss., University of Texas at Austin.

Mindek, D. 1994. "'No Nos Sobra, Pero Gracias a Dios, Tampoco Nos Falta,' Crecimiento Demographico y Modernizacion en San Jerónimo Amanalco." Master's thesis, Iberoamericana University.

OECD. 2016. *OECD Reviews of Health Systems: Mexico 2016*. Paris: OECD.

Sokolovsky, J. 2002. "Living Arrangements of Older Persons and Family Support in Less Developed Countries." *Population Bulletin of the United Nations* 42/43: 162–92.

Sokolovsky, J. 2015. *Indigenous Mexico Engages the 21st Century*. New York: Routledge.

World Bank. 2018. "Demographic Data." https://data.worldbank.org/indicator/SP.DYN.LE00.IN?locations=MX&view=chart.

CHAPTER TWENTY-FIVE

Aging after Socialism
Global Capitalism, Social Transformation, and Retirement in Romania

Gerard A. Weber

Introduction

Sitting in his yard in a village in eastern Romania on a sunny June morning in 2015, Ciprian[1] complained to me about the lack of plumbing in his small, unfinished house that sat a few feet away from us. No running water forced him to rely on a source outside his house, which was inconvenient and made it difficult to stay clean. The house was also not yet insulated, causing him to go through wood more quickly than he could afford in order to stay warm during the often frigid winters. Added to all this, Ciprian was still single, having not succeeded in fulfilling his desire to find a new companion to share the place with him following a divorce from his first wife.

These concerns were not new to Ciprian, whom I had known by that summer for more than a decade. They had festered over the past decade, during which he had been working on the house on a small plot of land he had purchased with his divorce settlement. The village was located northwest of Galați, a city in the comparatively unprosperous region of Moldavia, where between 2004 and 2015 I have carried out approximately 20 months of anthropological research. At base, Ciprian's circumstances were the result of his standing as a working-class retiree in his sixties with a paltry pension, which, by that summer, was equivalent to approximately US$287 a month or about $3,400 annually. It is true that one could do more with this money in Romania than in the developed world, but it was insufficient for paying for health care services, transportation, electricity, and other necessities, much less covering the expenses of constructing a very modest dwelling like his. Even a bank loan he had taken out had not been enough to finish the house, and he was already repaying on it. Meanwhile, heavy reliance on inexpensive alternative therapies rather than health care consultations and services did not make much of a difference to his budget. This left him with the question of why, despite having worked for 25 years in what he said was a "toxic environment," a comfortable life was so elusive to him.

Although understandably dissatisfied with his state of affairs, Ciprian was in a markedly better position than many of the other retired people I had come to know in Galați. His pension was relatively high, especially in comparison to those of women of the same social class background. Many of them, unlike Ciprian and most men, had not worked outside the domestic sphere, instead raising families, which had earned them no retirement income whatsoever. This left them to depend on husbands' or survivors' pensions in order to get by in a very harsh economic and social climate since the country's revolution from communist rule in 1989 and subsequent construction of a capitalist economy characterized by very conservative conventions. It is true that subsidies such as small packets of food and reductions in the cost of winter heat were available to the most indigent retirees, but they were hardly enough to fully ease the strain under which they lived. Even women who had worked in agriculture or in food processing, textiles, or other light industry fared poorly in comparison to most men since those domains had offered smaller retirement benefits than the heavy industrial sector in which mostly men had labored.[2] Still more disadvantaged in most cases—despite the widely believed myth that they harbor boundless wealth—were retired members of the Roma/Gypsy[3] ethnic minority. Their pensions were low if they had one at all, they were excluded from many of the even marginal benefits into which Romanian retirees could tap, and they unremittingly faced discrimination within society.

This chapter examines the lives of working-class, retired Romanian[4] women and men in Galați following the revolution from socialism in 1989. I offer an explanation for the deep and prolonged privation and social fragmentation suffered by pensioners with the making of a neoliberal capitalist economy. Their overall impoverishment, notwithstanding some variations in its intensity, is underscored, as is their resemblance to working-class retirees in more developed regions of Romania and other Eastern European countries. Described as well are some of the coping strategies that Romanian retirees have devised to mitigate their poverty and social isolation, and the social activism in which some pensioners have engaged in order to entirely alter the course their lives have taken in this era is briefly addressed.

Historical Context

Romania entered the 20th century with the overwhelming majority of its population living in rural areas and working in agriculture. As a result, most of the elderly women and men I met had roots in the countryside, having grown up in villages typically to the north of Galați. Social and economic opportunities were restricted in large part because land reform earlier in the century had failed to bring about the distribution of productive holdings to landless farmers, and the industrial sector of the economy was still too minute to absorb the agrarian population. Life expectancy was low in comparison to other European countries, contagious illnesses were prevalent, people had little to no access to health care services, and few had more than a couple years of schooling.[5]

After World War II, Romania fell under the influence of the Soviet Union. In 1948 the Romanian Workers Party, later renamed the Romanian Communist Party, gained power, a position it held until the revolution in 1989. A Soviet approach to economic development inspired by Joseph Stalin was adopted, paving the way for the construction of industrial facilities in certain parts of the country, a process that continued unabated for many years after Stalin's death in 1953. Galați was selected for this makeover, resulting in the building of a prodigious steel manufacturing plant immediately to the east of the city and numerous other factories. For some years, steel plant and other factory workers mostly commuted between village homes and the city for work. However, once urban infrastructure was put in place, people began to move permanently to Galați. This included nearly every older person I met, including Ciprian.[6]

The industrialization and urbanization of Romania under socialism was accompanied by many other changes. Access to education was expanded, permitting millions to complete a high school degree, greatly reducing illiteracy by the 1960s, and many were trained in technical and scientific fields (Gilberg 1975: 97–118). Thus, it was common for me to hear of experiences such as those of a retiree I got to know well named Mihaela, who left her family home in a village for schooling in a nearby city, later moving to Galați for vocational training that qualified her for a career in the dairy industry. A national health care system was also set up, allowing for an impressive reduction in the incidence of many infectious diseases, helping to increase life expectancy from 42 years in 1932 to nearly 70 by the mid-1970s (Bucur, Dragomir, and Botezat 2004: 61).

Resources were funneled to the training of medical professionals so that by 1974 there was one physician for every 630 people, a steep increase from the ratio of one to 17,000 that had existed between World War I and World War II. Health care facilities also grew in number, making consultations and treatment available to the public free of charge even though providing gifts to medical professionals was common practice.[7] One elderly woman, Victoria, told me about being prescribed medication for her anxiety from all the work she juggled as a young mother living in a village in the 1960s and 1970s. She also availed herself of treatment when she injured herself from a fall on ice one winter. A generation earlier, these health issues would more likely have led to permanent disability or have been treated with home remedies. Victoria also recalled health care professionals visiting village homes in that period to ascertain whether children were being raised according to government mandates. Added to these changes was the creation of social welfare entitlements—maternity leave, illness and accident benefits, disability insurance, pensions, and so on—that provided support to the population for the first time in modern history (Mihăiță 2003). Due to this, older people no longer faced deprivation and dependence on kin when they retired and instead were able to retire in greater comfort.

The politics underlying this economic and social transformation were authoritarian, a chief failing of the socialist systems in Romania and the entire region. This was particularly glaring in the state-sanctioned violence that was enacted against some people and the domestic espionage that infiltrated everyday life. Partly for this reason, it is conventional in the West for the socialist histories of Eastern Europe and the former Soviet Union to be denounced. Romania is particularly susceptible to this because of the misguided policies of Nicolae Ceaușescu, who held power from 1965 to 1989. Widely unpopular was his decision to wipe out all government debt to foreign entities beginning in the early 1980s. It ushered in a period of deep austerity that curtailed many people's access to basics, including health care services, utilities, and even staples, leading to the efflorescence of a robust second economy. Public resentment was further spawned by the squandering of sparse public funds on lavish urban renewal projects, arguably the most profligate being the construction of what is today called the Palace of the Parliament.[8] All of this ultimately proved fatal to the regime, playing a role in generating the December 1989 revolution. Yet an incomplete picture of the socialist period is rendered by focusing only on these elements, blinding one to the achievements that also occurred in that era.[9]

Postsocialist Transformations

"This city is dead," Doina firmly said to me as I sat on a bench near the apartment where I was staying in Galați in summer 2015. Our meeting was by chance; Doina, a retired worker in her sixties, was in a rush possibly to care for a frail aunt or to perform a service for another person. She expressed this opinion not so much in reference to her own, immediate circumstances, however. Instead, they pertained to her nearly 30-year-old son, Adrian. He had a very stressful job in security and despite this earned a meager $225 monthly salary. "His generation is being sacrificed," she went on, because employers paid people so poorly, and workers were expected to contribute to the public pension system. "They've shut everything down," she continued, calling my attention to the loss of factory employment in the city that had caused so many to depart Galați since the revolution. This included Adrian, who had gone for some time to work in Italy because he could not find a gainful job in Galați but returned to the city when working there, too, had become fruitless.

This commentary came from a person who had herself endured considerable adversity since the revolution. I had met Doina several years earlier when, by then in retirement, she was performing miscellaneous services for an older woman who could not fully look after herself. It was work on the informal market that brought her some additional, needed cash but no benefits, no protections from potential abuse, and no assistance in locating further employment when the woman, with whom she fortunately had an affable relationship, passed away. The extra money was vital since her pension from laboring for more than 30 years in a textile factory totaled an amount similar to her son's. The son lived with her and his father because there was no way he could afford an apartment of his own. Even so, their carefully balanced lives were continually prone to immense uncertainty. Her husband had, for instance, sustained a bad fall earlier that year, leaving him bedridden and in a cast in the stifling summer heat. I already knew that his alcoholism cost them dearly, but suspected his medical treatment added to their bills too.

Doina and her family's lives poignantly shed light on several of the transformations that have affected retired working-class people and their kin since the end of socialism in 1989. This period has been characterized by crushing changes that have left a sizeable portion of the population in a seemingly perpetual state of material scarcity and social dislocation. Beginning immediately after the revolution, the economy had tremendous difficulty getting on its feet partly on account of the ruinous economic policies under Ceaușescu and the retreat of Comecon (the Council for Mutual Economic Assistance), an organization that had played an important role in linking the Soviet bloc economies. Worsening matters was the multifaceted shift to neoliberalism (or post-Fordism) that the global capitalist economy was undergoing since the 1970s. The mass, at-home production of standardized goods that had been central to Fordism was being replaced by customized manufacturing carried out in underdeveloped societies with low-cost, compliant labor and lax environmental laws. State regulation of corporations in regards to wage policy and the rights of workers was eroding, and the sway of unions was ebbing, which chipped away at incomes and benefits. Access to affordable health care services, education, and housing was becoming rare, substantially degrading people's lives.[10]

Within this global context, industrial production in Romania in the 1990s was incapable of successfully competing due to its inefficiency and failure to manufacture sought-after goods. Many industries that continued to operate survived on financial support from the state and on debt, and the agricultural and services sectors performed little better. The currency (the *leu*) lost considerable value during the decade, and at times inflation soared to alarming levels. It was very difficult to lure foreign investors both because of economic headwinds and political instability.[11] The economy entered a period of growth in the early 2000s, particularly in the aftermath of the election of the probusiness National Liberal Party–Democratic Party coalition in 2004, but the costs of this expansion were high. Privatization of industries, including, in 2001, the steel plant in Galați, occurred at an increasing rate yet often at considerable financial loss. Mass layoffs ensued as a result of restructuring that followed change of ownership. The tax structure was altered, with a flat tax of 16 percent initiated in 2005. Changes to labor laws favored business over workers. A steep decline in the investment of state revenue in education, health care services, and the public sector more generally transpired, and low-wage, no-benefits work in the production of modest-standard goods proliferated. All told, a particularly conservative approach to the transformation of the Romanian economy unfolded, in other words, the effects of which have continued to be profound.[12]

In 2004, the European Commission concluded that Romania had a "functioning market economy," fortifying its application for accession to the European Union, which followed in 2007. A small middle class began to surface in large, diversified urban settings—particularly Bucharest—and a few people grew extraordinarily wealthy, but poverty persisted among many, and people watched their kin and community ties break apart. The global financial crisis starting in 2008 had a severe impact on economic output, prompting political leaders to call upon the International Monetary Fund and other institutions for loans totaling over $20 billion. However, those were offered only with the stipulation that a series of austerity measures be applied. Recovery from the crisis has been slow although enough improvement has occurred for public sector wages to be raised and the value-added tax (VAT) to be lowered. Still, most people do not feel their lives have become substantially better.[13]

As we have already seen in the case of Adrian, many working-age people have departed the country as a result of these changes, furthering a decline in the country's population from a historic high of 23.2 million in 1990 to 19.8 million in 2015, a drop of 15 percent (Institutul Național de Statistică 2016). Galați has followed this trend even more acutely, the 1992 estimated population of 326,000 falling to 231,000 in the most recent (as of 2018) census in 2011, a 30 percent reduction (Direcția Județeana de Statistică Galați 2011). It was therefore not unusual for some retirees to talk about kin who lived in Western European countries, particularly Spain and Italy. This included Mihaela, the retired woman who had worked in the dairy industry and had raised four children all but singlehandedly because her husband had worked outside Galați for long stretches of time under socialism. She endured the permanent departure from Romania of all four for work after 1989. The separation was stressful to her because of the uncertainty it created about how they were doing on a day-to-day basis, but it also left her feeling disheartened given all the years she had devoted to caring for them while also accomplishing her duties as a midlevel manager in the dairy industry. "I'm used to having them at my table," she dejectedly told me one day. And this was despite her actually being in a better position than many other older people whose daughters and sons had departed. Unlike Mihaela's children, who held occupations that made it possible for them to regularly send her money and gifts and to treat her to vacations in places she had never imagined visiting, their children did not have enough income to send remittances or, if they did, they decided not to do so—or they had completely dropped out of their parents' lives. Still, Mihaela's children were gone, filling her with doubts about their well-being and stranding her in solitude.

Her dread of being left alone was more than an emotional matter, however. It would also mean that those who would most likely have cared for her as she grew older would not be present, obliging her to create a social network that could potentially assist her if it ever became necessary. Many pensioners not only in Romania but throughout Eastern Europe and the former Soviet Union have been in this position since the revolutions, a point I return to later, and it will continue if younger people cannot obtain employment that affords them the opportunity to remain in their home countries. In 2015, Mihaela resolved the issue at least for the time being by leaving Romania and joining her children abroad, but there are many who do not have that option.

Retirement in postrevolutionary Romania has become challenging as well by the diminished purchasing power of pensions. There are several reasons that this has happened, a chief one being the demographic shift that has long been reducing the number of contributors to the pay-as-you-go (PAYG) public pension system on which most retirees today count. This has been caused not only by the emigration of people from the country, but also by a drop in the fertility rate and an increase in life expectancy. In spite of periodic, slight upturns in the number of births, the overall trend since 1970 has been one of decline: while 21.1 births out of 1,000 occurred that year, in 2014 it was 9.2 out of 1,000. Life expectancy was 67.3 years in 1970 (69.5 for females and 65.1 for males), and in 2014 it was 75.5 (78.9 for females and 72.0 for males) (Institutul Național de Statistică 2015).[14] As a result, over the past half-century, the percentage of people who are 65 and over has grown. In 1970, the figure was 11.6 percent, but by 2014 it had reached 16.8 percent, an amount that is estimated to continue rising for the foreseeable future (Institutul Național de Statistică 2016). Amplifying the negative impact of these demographic shifts on the public pension system has been the propagation of a shadow economy and corruption in the postsocialist years.

The reduced value of pensions has been a grievance of working-class retirees in Galați since the onset of my research, and their sentiments have been echoed by retirees around the country. Increases that have been occasionally approved—for example, prior to national elections, arguably to draw the large pensioner population to the polls—have been minimal and have not always kept up with inflation. It is no wonder then that Ciprian, the man who now lives in a village, has made only piecemeal progress on his home. It is likewise not surprising that working-class women and men have interminably spoken of the impossibility of paying for food, electricity, winter heat, hot and cold water, medical expenditures (a problem I specifically take up next), transportation, and other essentials. As a result, many just do without or go into insurmountable debt. In a sign of this dilemma, when I arrived in Galați in June 2015, hot water had been unavailable to residential dwellings since April, and it was still not readily accessible when I departed in August. The major reason for this was that residents who had not been able to withdraw from the municipal heating system and install their own generators had also not had the capacity to pay their monthly hot water bills. Arrears had mushroomed so significantly that the company that heated the water took the extreme step of suspending that activity.

As the economy has staggered in the postsocialist years, public services have also been a victim. For many older people this is perhaps most palpable during encounters with the public health care system. Already severely trimmed by the austerity measures under Ceaușescu, public hospitals and clinics have been all but broken by depressed funding and a lack of needed reform since 1989. Physicians, nurses, and other medical professionals have earned salaries that are far lower than those their counterparts in the West are paid, resulting in many leaving Romania.[15] Even though medical services are officially free, such poor compensation has led to an expectation for gratuities. This has been one of the top sources of stress among working-class retirees and other vulnerable people in Romania (Weber 2015; Stepurko, Pavlova, and Groot 2016). Magnifying the repercussions of this is the need to purchase supplies for treatment, because hospitals and clinics are often bereft of them. Furthermore, pharmaceutical drugs can cost retirees far more than they can afford, causing some to forgo filling prescriptions and instead using teas and other alternative therapies to minister to health problems.

During summer 2015, I was reminded once again of these barriers to health care services. Victoria, the woman who spoke of visiting a clinic in her village during the socialist period, was chronically suffering from undiagnosed discomfort in her abdomen. At that point in her seventies, she had already seen doctors about it a couple of times but said they had prescribed pills that seemed to be doing nothing for her. The treatment perplexed her so much that she even became convinced the physicians were testing drugs on her to measure their efficacy. Learning that what she really needed was an MRI, she set out to amass the funds for it. Once she finally managed to do so by turning to kin, it was difficult to make an appointment with the specialist she needed because of his schedule. Ultimately successful at arranging a date, she still could not see the doctor because he was overbooked on the day she went in. The episode was both frustrating and costly for Victoria because she had to pay out-of-pocket for a taxi to the office, which subtracted from the money she would give to the doctor.[16] Victoria's experience was not out of the ordinary, over the years many people—old and young—often bitterly recounting similar obstacles to cost-free and high-quality health care services. It was one of the clearest signs of how the conservative remaking of the economy in particular was a threat to the lives of many people in Romania.

Retirees in Eastern Europe and the Former Soviet Union

Working-class pensioners in Romania have not been the only retirees to struggle in the years since the end of socialism. Social science research among older people in other Eastern European countries and the former Soviet Union has exposed comparable loss albeit with local and national differences attributable in part to specific histories of economic development and former incorporation into particular empires. One study, for example, concentrates attention on differences between rural and urban areas in Romania and Bulgaria, underscoring that poverty is often far greater among the elderly in the countryside than in cities (Kulcsár and Brădăţan 2014). Notwithstanding such distinctions, several general processes have been under way in most of the other postsocialist countries that have affected retirees in a manner akin to those already described for Romania. One widespread trend has been a decline in births due in large part to foreboding among people about their future economic prospects. The unprecedented emigration primarily because of job loss or employment insecurity has been another. Life expectancy has meanwhile begun to rise in many of the postsocialist countries. An outgrowth of all this is the aging of Eastern Europe and the former Soviet Union, a transformation for which the region is ill-prepared relative to other rapidly aging societies in Western Europe and East Asia. As in Romania, the PAYG pension systems constructed under socialism are incapable of adequately supporting retirees given the decline in contributions to the systems due to the migration, growth of informal markets, and increases in the number of people reliant upon them.[17] This puts unending pressure on migrant kin to give social and financial support to older relatives who remain in the home country (Bauer and Österle 2016). It also has compelled family members of different generations to reside together, particularly in response to the Great Recession of 2008, an arrangement that at least one study shows has had negative mental health implications for people in Eastern Europe (Courtin and Avendano 2016).

State support for long-term care is in short supply across the region, even in relatively prosperous countries such as the Czech Republic, where Andel reports capacity at long-term care facilities is limited and quality is poor (2014). Related to this appears to be the observation that comparatively fewer people in Eastern Europe support the use of state-sponsored care of the elderly than in Western Europe, especially Scandinavia (see especially Part VI Clotworthy). According to one extensive study, the majority of people living in formerly socialist countries believes that primary responsibility for the care of older kin should be borne by the family (Österle, Mittendrein, and Meichenitsch 2011: 28–29). Ethnographic research supports this conclusion although, again, with some degree of variation. In postsocialist Croatia, for instance, eldercare is typically performed by very close kin, in most cases women (Leutloff-Grandits 2012). Fulfilling this expectation can, however, be difficult. This is true especially for those who have moved abroad for work, but it can also be very challenging for people who have only migrated domestically or who live in the same community as their elder kin because their work schedules are tight and they have other family responsibilities.[18]

I learned about such hardship when a woman in her late seventies, Anca, described her dependence on a daughter, who had moved to another city about 100 miles away after being laid off from her job in Galați. Since the daughter was Anca's only living immediate family member, she spent time and money commuting to Galați to look after her mother, who was quite ill, and she also used a large percentage of her salary to pay for medical care and medication for her. "She hasn't so much as bought a pair of nylons in the two years since I had my operation," Anca told me. "She gives all her money to me so I can pay the doctor, [and] I also pay for medication from her salary," she continued. This arrangement was very distressing to Anca, who felt as though she was "troubling" her daughter and worried about what would happen once her daughter retired, which was only a few years away, and would no longer be able to buy medications and pay for treatment. Similarly, I learned about the complications experienced by a middle-aged couple who lived in Galați and worked in the public sector when the parents of the husband became infirm and needed care. Their salaries were too low to afford paying someone informally to help out, an arrangement that would likely not have satisfied them anyway, but it was punishing performing their full-time jobs and looking after them. Such predicaments have become routine across Eastern Europe and the former Soviet Union since the end of socialism, instilling stress into people's lives.[19] The concern is that they will only get worse as the region ages further, the new capitalist economies fail to provide gainful employment, and states do not invest in long-term care services and infrastructure.

Coping Strategies in Romania

Retired people in Galați have devised many innovative strategies for getting by in such an unforgiving environment, an example of which I have already presented in describing Doina's work as an informal caregiver. Indeed, working after retirement, usually off the books, was a common tactic employed by retirees. Ciprian offered his skills as a mechanic to others as a means of gaining assistance in building his house, and he further cultivated his relations in the village with gifts of wine he had made from grapes grown on his property. Even Mihaela, the retiree whose children sent remittances, worked after retirement in order to augment her pension, taking on a position in her building association and running bureaucratic errands for people.[20]

Accepting food, beverages, and occasionally other material items bestowed at cemeteries and churches was another strategy I witnessed on numerous occasions. Called "giving *pomană*," the revered practice of tendering such items is widely viewed as a way of honoring and caring for the deceased. Kin and friends of someone who has passed away assemble at the person's gravesite, or they go to a church in order to recite and sing prayers in remembrance of the person. A priest and another clergy member are invited to lead the ceremony. Food and drink are brought by the deceased's family and given to people, including passersby who have no direct connection to the person to whom tribute is being paid.[21] "I've spent five years at the cemetery," a retired cook named Maria told me one day, explaining that she had been coming to one of the city cemeteries on a regular basis to gather *pomană* for herself and her family, particularly on weekends and during important holidays in the Romanian Orthodox calendar when many people would be present there. We had met by happenstance one afternoon in 2004 when I was visiting the cemetery. Inviting her to tell me more about her life, I learned that she lived in very cramped quarters with a son, his wife, and their two children, and that she had another son and three daughters. None of her children or their spouses could provide support to her financially, however. The son with whom she lived, who worked in construction, was suffering from a serious medical problem. This made it difficult for him to put in much time on the job, which in any event was temporary and did not pay well, and his wife had been laid off from a position at the steel plant. The other son had left for Italy, the only word of him coming from an acquaintance who said he had been jailed for committing a crime, and she said that her daughters were destitute. Maria herself had a pension, but at $34 a month in 2004, it was far too little to cover even essentials for the family. A neighbor occasionally gave them staples, but they were not enough to meet their needs, so she headed to the cemetery. The results could be rewarding, Maria showing me a packet of food she had gathered on one occasion. But in her mind the trips were not without their risks. Warning me about walking by myself in the vast cemetery, she expressed fear that thieves came there to mug people, and she also worried about the police throwing her out of the cemetery and thereby disrupting her procurement of *pomană*. Less real in my estimation than she imagined, these concerns nevertheless reminded me of how pensioners' strategies for improving their lives often came with drawbacks that stoked stress.

I learned about many other methods for addressing material needs and mending the social fabric brought on by the transformation to capitalism. The place in Galați where I launched my research, a foundation serving the elderly, presented examples of this. Not only were minor medical services offered to visitors free of charge there, but it was also where retirees or their kin came on a monthly basis to get the food packets mentioned earlier. In addition, it had a day center where pensioners formed new relationships, learned about political activities (more on this next), played games, celebrated holidays, and engaged in other recreation. Living with a retired couple, Victoria and Costică, during segments of my research afforded me the opportunity to observe yet other strategies, in this case more personal ones. One of the most impressive was field gleaning, which Costică carried out. After the harvest was completed, he rode his worn-out bicycle to farmland where he gathered an assortment of produce, including potatoes, carrots, parsnips, onions, and corn, on which they would subsist for months. He also spent many days at local waterways fishing in order to supplement their diets. It was common for me to find him late into the evening in the kitchen scraping scales off of fish that he then put in plastic bags and placed in the freezer. Furthermore, they participated in masses and religious rituals and leaned on kin who had not left Romania, both for social and emotional support. Needless to say, I was not surprised by the fact that retirees such as Victoria and Costică sought to improve their lives. What did impress me, however, was the intense rigor that at times was involved in some of the efforts they made. It was another reminder that a comprehensive commitment to reducing poverty among older people and to making decent-paying jobs available to the young and middle-aged was in desperate need in Romania.

Political Activism

In addition to, or in place of, engaging in coping strategies, some retired people were determined to reverse the downward trend their lives had taken through political activism. I observed a number of provocative examples of this, my understanding of which was furthered in part by reports in the media of pensioner organizing and demonstrating at local and national levels. On the one hand, they reaffirmed the freedom people felt in Romania after the overthrow of an authoritarian regime. Even if there were a few retirees who told me that they were apprehensive about negative reactions by authorities to political activism, many seemed unhindered by such concern, openly participating in social movements, something that was completely prohibited under the socialist regime. On the other hand, there were people who felt that such effort was in vain since over time they experienced few upgrades to the material conditions of their lives and their social worlds continued to break down as people departed the city. They were convinced leaders were only out for themselves, a judgment that has appeared prescient in view of the deluge of allegations of corruption against a wide range of officials in the last few years. "Today you can say all you want, but nobody will listen to you," was therefore a common refrain voiced by the elderly and their family members.

This has not always been entirely accurate, however. On occasion, pensioner protests have had favorable outcomes or at least have appeared to have them. This was the case in 2010 when thousands of retirees and public sector workers demonstrated in Victory Square in Bucharest and in other cities in Romania against the austerity measures imposed by the government in response to the global financial crisis. Among their plans was a 15 percent reduction in some pensions. Although we may never know with precision the impact the protests had, in the end the cutbacks to pensions were rescinded by the Constitutional Court. In early 2012 retirees and many others rallied against plans to partially privatize emergency health care services. The proposal was directed at the popular emergency ambulance service that was spearheaded in the 1990s by Raed Arafat, a doctor of Palestinian origin. He resigned after learning of the privatization initiative, inciting vehement protests that resulted in cancellation of the plans and Arafat's return to his post (Holt 2012). Then, in early 2017, the largest protests in the country's history—including in comparison to those that transpired during the 1989 revolution—commenced in Bucharest and other parts of the country with the backing of retirees and many other sectors of the population. These protests were in response to decrees proposed by a new government to pardon certain crimes and alter Romania's penal code. Partly because of the outcry, the bills were rescinded, at least for a period.

Conclusion

Many scholars who conducted research in Romania and other countries of the former Soviet bloc in the years immediately following the revolutions expressed uncertainty about the direction those societies were taking politically, economically, and socially (e.g., Verdery 1996). By the time I entered the field in 2004, the pathway was arguably far more evident. The consolidation of democracy was under way, however tenuously, and a sharply conservative variety of capitalism was being widely championed. The possibility for people to enjoy greater political freedom has been one of the laudable outcomes of the commitment by some political leaders to democracy, even if it has by all means been incomplete. At the same time, however, the economic transformation has had devastating effects on many families and communities by forcing working-age people to depart often for the long term and marooning older women and men with scant resources and severed social connections.

In my opinion, none of this has had to be inevitable, nor does it have to continue as it is. Aging in Romania should not entail the descent into penury and the shattering and straining of kin and community relations that I have observed for so many years. Policy directing revenue toward the building and maintenance of infrastructure in Romania—rather than pushing for austerity, which the influential head of the Central Bank has advocated—would be one way to help make this possible. The country is still lacking an adequate highway system that would better enable commerce, and much of the rest of its infrastructure is in need of repair. This would lead not only to the employment of many thousands of people, but it would also increase the tax base, money that could be applied to the social insurance system, including to pensions for retired men and women.

Notes

1. All names used in this text are pseudonyms, and I have slightly altered descriptions of people in order to protect their identities.

2. See Wolfe Jancar 1978: 25–28 for a discussion of this disparity.

3. I use both *Roma* and *Gypsy* in recognition that not all members of this ethnic group accept the increasing use of the word *Roma* to refer to their ethnic background. For example, a woman I know in the capital explicitly said to me "Sunt Țigan," or "I am a Gypsy." Still, the word *Țigan* or *Gypsy* is often used pejoratively and therefore should be avoided by people who are not members of this ethnic group.

4. People who are Roma/Gypsy may also identify themselves as Romanian, as is true of members of other ethnic groups. I use this to make clear that none of the retirees I came to know in Galați openly identified him or herself as Roma/Gypsy.

5. See Hitchins 1994 for a history of this period.

6. See Cole 1981 for anthropological insight into this period.

7. Kaser 1976 describes the development of medicine in Romania and other countries in the Soviet bloc.

8. See Giurescu 1994 for an examination of some of the architectural destruction that took place in this era.

9. Siani-Davies 1996 investigates the revolution in Romania. Ujică's 2010 film presents a captivating history of Ceaușescu's rule.

10. See Collins 2003; Harvey 2005, 2010; Calhoun 2011; Smith 2015; Rothstein 2016; and Salemink and Rasmussen 2016 for general discussions of this history.

11. See Smith 2006 for a brief overview of this history.

12. See Ban 2016 for an examination of the conservative "translation" of capitalism that has taken place in Romania.

13. See Smith 2006 for part of this history. Also instructive are the late Edward Hugh's blog posts on Romania at http://romaniaeconomywatch.blogspot.com/ and reporting available at Balkan Insight, https://balkaninsight.com/.

14. Note, however, that this trend has not been continuous, Romania experiencing the transitional mortality crisis in the 1990s that affected many other countries in the region as well. (See Cornia and Paniccià 2000.)

15. See Vlădescu, Scîntee, and Olsavszky 2008 for an analysis of the system and Holt 2010 for discussion of salaries.

16. See Weber 2016 for a fuller description and analysis of this episode.

17. See Hoff and Perek-Białas 2008 and Kidrič 2009 for more on this.

18. At the same time, it is important to note that even by the 1980s this nation was developing a limited number of senior care facilities, mostly in urban areas, and these places had waiting lists (Sokolovsky, Šošić, and Pavleković 1991).

19. See Pitheckoff 2017 for the particularly dire case of Bulgaria.

20. I have written further about working Romanian retirees in Weber 2014.

21. These ceremonies are also held in people's homes.

Bibliography

Andel, R. 2014. "Aging in the Czech Republic." *Gerontologist* 54(6): 893–900.

Ban, C. 2016. *Ruling Ideas: How Global Capitalism Goes Local.* New York: Oxford University Press.

Bauer, G., and A. Österle. 2016. "Mid and Later Life Care Work Migration: Patterns of Re-Organising Informal Care Obligations in Central and Eastern Europe." *Journal of Aging Studies* 37: 81–93.

Bucur, A., L. Dragomir, and L. Botezat. 2004. *Anuar de statistică sanitară 2003.* Ministerul Sănătății Centrul de Statistică Sanitară și Documentare Medicală.

Calhoun, C. 2011. "Series Introduction: From the Current Crisis to Possible Futures." In *Business as Usual: The Roots of the Global Financial Meltdown,* edited by C. Calhoun and G. Derluguian. New York: New York University Press.

Cole, J. 1981. "Family, Farm, and Factory: Rural Workers in Contemporary Romania." In *Romania in the 1980s,* edited by D. N. Nelson. Boulder, CO: Westview.

Collins, J. 2003. *Threads: Gender, Labor and Power in the Global Apparel Industry.* Chicago: University of Chicago Press.

Cornia, G. A., and R. Paniccià. 2000. "The Transition Mortality Crisis: Evidence, Interpretation and Policy Responses." In *The Mortality Crisis in Transitional Economies*, edited by G. A. Cornia and R. Paniccià. Oxford: Oxford University Press.

Courtin, E., and M. Avendano. 2016. "Under One Roof: The Effect of Co-Residing with Adult Children on Depression in Later Life." *Social Science & Medicine* 168: 140–49.

Direcția Judeţeana de Statistică Galaţi. 2011. *Populaţiei-Demografie.* Galaţi: DJS.

Gilberg, T. 1975. *Modernization in Romania since World War II.* New York: Praeger.

Giurescu, D. C. 1994. *Distrugerea Trecutului României.* Bucharest: Editura Museion.

Harvey, D. 2005. *A Brief History of Neoliberalism.* Oxford: Oxford University Press.

Harvey, D. 2010. *The Enigma of Capital and the Crises of Capitalism.* New York: Oxford University Press.

Hitchins, K. 1994. *Rumania 1866–1947.* Oxford: Clarendon.

Hoff, A., and J. Perek-Białas, eds. 2008 *The Ageing Societies of Central and Eastern Europe: Some Problems—Some Solutions.* Kraków: Jagiellonian University Press.

Holt, E. 2010. "Romania's Health System Lurches into New Crisis." *Lancet* 376(9748): 1211–12.

Holt, E. 2012. "Romania Redrafts Health-Care Law After Violent Protests." *Lancet* 379(9815): 505.

Institutul Naţional de Statistică. 2015. *Anuarul Statistic al României.* Bucharest: INS.

Institutul Naţional de Statistică. 2016. *Populaţia rezidenta la 1 ianuarie.* www .insse.ro/cms.

Kaser, M. 1976. *Health Care in the Soviet Union and Eastern Europe.* Boulder, CO: Westview.

Kidrič, D. 2009. "An Overview of Pension, Labor Market, and Financial Market Reforms in Southeastern Europe." In *Pension Reform in Southeastern Europe: Linking to Labor and Financial Market Reforms*, edited by R. Holzmann, L. MacKellar, and J. Repanšek. Washington, DC: World Bank.

Kulcsár, L., and C. Brădăţan. 2014. "The Greying Periphery: Ageing and Community Development in Rural Romania and Bulgaria." *Europe-Asia Studies* 66(5): 794–810.

Leutloff-Grandits, C. 2012. "Kinship, Community and Care: Rural-Urban Contrasts in Croatia." *Ethnologie Française* 1(42): 67–78.

Mihăiţă, E. 2003. "The Romanian Pension Reform." *Discussion Papers in Applied Economics and Policy* No. 2003/4. Division of Economics, Nottingham Trent University.

Österle, A., L. Mittendrein, and K. Meichenitsch. 2011. "Providing Care for Growing Needs: The Context for Long-Term Care in Central and South Eastern Europe." In *Long-term Care in Central and South Eastern Europe*, edited by A. Österle. New York: Peter Lang.

Pitheckoff, N. 2017. "Aging in the Republic of Bulgaria." *Gerontologist* 57(5): 809–15.

Rothstein, F. A. 2016. *Mexicans on the Move: Migration and Return in Rural Mexico*. New York: Palgrave Macmillan.

Salemink, O., and M. Borg Rasmussen. 2016. "After Dispossession: Ethnographic Approaches to Neoliberalism." *Focaal* 74: 3–12.

Siani-Davies, P. 1996. "Romanian Revolution or Coup d'état? A Theoretical View of the Events of December 1989." *Communist and Post-Communist Studies* 29(4): 453–65.

Smith, A. 2006. "The Romanian Economy since 1989." In *The European Union and Romania: Accession and Beyond*, edited by D. Phinnemore. London: Federal Trust for Education and Research.

Smith, B. E. 2015. "Another Place Is Possible? Labor Geography, Spatial Dispossession and Gendered Resistance in Central Appalachia." *Annals of the Association of American Geographers* 105(3): 567–82.

Sokolovsky, J., Z. Šošić, and G. Pavleković. 1991. "Self-Help Hypertensive Groups and the Elderly in Yugoslavia." *Journal of Cross-Cultural Gerontology* 6(3): 319–30.

Stepurko, T., M. Pavlova, and W. Groot. 2016. "Overall Satisfaction of Health Care Users with the Quality of and Access to Health Care Services: A Cross-Sectional Study of Six Central and Eastern European Countries." *BioMed Central Health Services Research* 16(342): 1–13.

Ujică, A., dir. 2010. *The Autobiography of Nicolae Ceaușescu*. The Film Desk.

Verdery, K. 1996. *What Was Socialism and What Comes Next?* Princeton, NJ: Princeton University Press.

Vlădescu, C., G. Scîntee, and V. Olsavszky. 2008. "Romania: Health System Review." *Health Systems in Transition* 10(3). Copenhagen, Denmark: European Observatory on Health Systems and Policies.

Weber, G. A. 2014. "After a Lifetime of Labor: Informal Work among the Retired in Romania." *Anthropology Now* 6(1): 15–24.

Weber, G. A. 2015. "'Other Than a Thank-You, There's Nothing I Can Give': Managing Health and Illness among Working-Class Pensioners in Post-Socialist Moldovia, Romania." *Human Organization: Journal of the Society for Applied Anthropology* 74(2): 115–24.

Weber, G. A. 2016. "'Please Ask the Priest to Pray for Dana, the Sick One': Health-Seeking, Religion and Decline of the Public Sector in Post-Communist Romania." *Transylvanian Review Supplement: Health Seeking and Caregiving: The Changing Romanian Healthcare Climate* 25(1): 77–90.

Wolfe Jancar, B. 1978. *Women under Communism*. Baltimore, MD: Johns Hopkins University Press.

PART IV

Cultural Diversity and the Ethnic Dimension in Aging: Culture, Context, and Creativity

Introduction

Jay Sokolovsky

One of the most poignant discussions of ethnicity, cultural spaces, and late life is found in Barbara Myerhoff's powerful book, *Number Our Days* (1979). It describes how a very old, ethnically Jewish population, disconnected from their kin and the surrounding ethnic community, established an unusual local variant of *Yiddishkeit* or Jewishness.[1] This did not center their lives around traditional religious behaviors, but unique interpretations of ritual and personal performance. Surrounded by the bikini-clad, roller-blading youth culture of Venice Beach, California, these men and women in their eighties and nineties sought refuge in a senior center. They created within its walls, and outside on boardwalk benches, an ethnic-tinged elderscape with their own transcendent sense of meaning in late life. The early cultural worlds of these elders had been largely spent in small East European shtetls[2] (market towns) drastically different from the large North American cities in which their adulthoods were experienced. A 1977 film about this community, also titled *Number Our Days*, was awarded an Oscar for best short documentary film (see Part V Web Book Tsuji and Part VI Pieta for discussion of other senior centers).

Like many of the newer refugees and migrants who recently came here escaping the specter of death for them or their family members, many of these elders Myerhoff studied had escaped 20th-century ethnic cleansing movements in Europe targeting persons of Jewish descent. In essence they had resituated their ethnic heritage, within in a highly changing urban landscape and lived this legacy in cultural spaces and cultural scripts of their own making.

Such actions exemplify this book's prevailing themes and the emerging realities of 21st-century community life. Like many of the elders discussed in this section, the scripts they anticipated for late life, and the spaces they expected to inhabit once they got there, had largely vanished or been radically transformed. It was up to them to create new possibilities for their old age. Over the past two decades there has been ample documentation of the creation of new cultural spaces and constructed elderscapes from community-wide elder-focused landscapes in Florida (Part V Web Book Katz), Chinese public exercise groups (Part III Zhang) or the Ibasho cafés of Japan and elsewhere (Box V.1).

Ethnic unions, societies, or clubs have long been an adaptive model for first- and second-generation migrants, especially those coming into urban areas. In my own great-grandparental generation when these forbearers migrated to New York City from Romania and Poland, one group formed a small medical association of kin that collectively bought the services of a doctor. Another side of the family formed a burial society to be able to gain access to grave sites for immigrant kin.

The need for forming such groups is exacerbated under conditions of various forms of exclusion and discrimination either legal or informal. For example in St. Petersburg, Florida, where I now live, segregation-era ordinances mandated where African Americans could live. At the same time, custom, enforced by both white police and citizens, prevented blacks, young and old, from sitting on the downtown public green benches that were an icon of the city for white tourists and residents alike (Vesperi 1998). In St. Petersburg, with the end of legal segregation in the early 1970s, misplaced urban renewal exacerbated the dispersal of the black community using eminent domain law to build a highway and baseball stadium, ripping through the oldest part of the black community.

In Box IV.1 we learn about the traditions of an "Affrilachian" community in the region of Western, North Carolina. The term *Affrilachian* was coined in 1990 by poet and scholar Frank X Walker in response to the historical context of marginality directed at people of African descent in the Appalachian region (Barbour-Payne 2014).

What Is Ethnicity?

Ethnicity is the manifestation of a cultural tradition in a heterogeneous societal framework. The expression of ethnic identity and the performance of ethnically rooted behaviors invariably take place under new conditions and in different locales from where the traditions originated. Ethnicity is therefore typically a creative act, meshing ancestral "native" patterns with restraints imposed by the broader society and the demands of the local environment. For example, anthropologists working in urban sub-Saharan Africa in the 1950s and 1960s found that some of the "tribal" groups they were studying in industrial cities were actually new cultural phenomena forged in the crucible of places dramatically different than their rural homelands. The topic of ethnicity opens up the question of diversity to be understood within such contextual variables as gender, economic differentiation, and the migration process (Zubair and Norris 2015; Baker et al. 2018).

Box IV.1 "Staying Close:" Storied Community in an Affrilachian Elder Club

Heidi Kelley and Ken Betsalel

Denied both *de jure* and *de facto* access to public space, Affrilachians (African Americans living in Appalachia) developed and reinforced communal ties of kinship, church, social clubs, and wherever possible, neighborhood and political associations that could pragmatically and imaginatively create an imagined community of cultural wholeness and emplacement (Walker 2000). Our work now focuses on a group of Affrilachian elders in the Burton Street Elite Club who "came up" in the West Ashville neighborhood of Burton Street in the mountains of Western North Carolina (Polanco 2014; Kelley and Betsalel 2017; Waters, Hyde, and Betsalel 2017).

According to neighborhood elder and community activist Ms. Vivian Conley, the club had its origins in the 1940s segregation era as a cooking club that evolved over the years into a saving club. In the early 1960s, Ms. Conley's mother, Mrs. Rosie Lee Conley, and other neighborhood women founded the Silver Star Club that encouraged neighborhood women to save for Christmas shopping. By the 1980s a number of these

Photo IV.1   Members of the Burton Street Elite Club, June 6, 2017, from left to right: Jessie Coleman, Carolyn Johnson, Heidi Kelley, Pearlie May Dixon, Ruth Wells (seated), Henry Anderson, Ross Peterson, Fannie Anderson, Annette Mills, Theresa Bowman, Ann Peterson, and Ernestine Rawls (12 members of the 28 total present for photograph). (Photo by Ken Betsalel)

women helped found the Elite Club, whose goal was to create an association for seniors. Looking back, Mrs. Mattie Wells Douglas, better known among the elders as Mother Wells, explained the creation of the Elite Club as way to maintain the "sharing and caring" that once characterized the neighborhood. Mr. Henry Anderson, the club president at the time, explained at a Black History Month event held at the Burton Recreation Center community room, "We have a lot of history worth telling."

The club meets three days a week, with Tuesday Bible study, seated exercise, crafts, bingo, films, Thursday lunches, and monthly formal club meetings (which accord to Robert's Rules of Order). The group sponsors events that include field trips to civil rights memorials, Thanksgiving dinners, celebrations of Black History Month, and just plain "gathering" time. They connect as a community through phone calls, visiting nursing homes, and going to funerals and birthday parties. This has managed to keep them "right close" despite the social forces of suburbanization and gentrification that have broken apart their one-time geographically cohesive, working-class, urban Affrilachian neighborhood (North Carolina Humanities Council 2010: 7).

Their collective effort fashions what might theoretically be considered liminal "third spaces" between spheres of historically and contemporaneous racialized public order and inside spaces of gendered home and family. This group of Affrilachian elders uses stories as a way to tie their dislocated community together and overcome spatial injustice. Elders tell stories of the Burton Street Agricultural Fair that once brought people from throughout the area into the neighborhood for games, cooking, and baking competitions. Elders also retell stories of their experience in the segregation era when people in the neighborhood maintained their sense of personal dignity in the face of racial discrimination. Mother Wells recalls her father was the only passenger on the bus coming home from work late one evening when the driver invited him to sit up front in the white section. Her father refused, saying "I know where my place is." Mother Wells explained her father's answer as a way to affirm his pride as a person and member of a community. Mr. and Mrs. Ross and Ann Peterson tell stories of how neighborhood elders keep a watchful eye on children's doings. Such stories contribute to the cultural heritage the club members want to pass along, especially to the younger generation, because it expresses the determination and caring values that make for resilient people and strong neighborhoods. Such stories weave time, place, and character together to create what Zora Neal Hurston called "thought pictures" that are not easily forgotten (1937 [1998]: 51).

This historical context is necessary to understand Affrilachian elders today, for in these isolated Affrilachian communities, storytelling and occasions for gathering in third spaces, including "front porch talk," were critical for their survival and sense of intactness as a people. Over the years, while the marginalization and isolation of Affrilachian communities may be lessening due to myriad social factors from television to gentrification, it is older Affrilachians who continue to maintain what they call "closeness." The problematic paradox of this closeness is that it is distant in physical space but mythically close in storied relationships of community (Monterescu and Hazan 2018).

Traditionally a home-owning, working-class community, the Burton Street neighborhood has changed markedly since the oldest members of the Burton Street Elite Club were "coming up" in the 1940s, 1950s, and early 1960s. How do the elder members of the Elite Club maintain this sense of "closeness" when the Burton Street community has been subject to the social disruptions of urban renewal (in the form of three road-widening projects from the 1960s to the present), gentrification, and racial discrimination (gone underground from the days of segregation, but still wounding to the club members)? How do the elders retain this sense of closeness when the Elite Club members are now dispersed all around the community of Asheville and subject to the inevitability of illness and death that comes with living a long life?

We have been addressing those questions ethnographically since the summer of 2016 when we became members of the Burton Street Elite Club, drawing on a 20-year history of doing long-term fieldwork with our students in the Burton Street community (North Carolina Humanities Council 2010: 7). Joining the club—as ethnographers and aging people ourselves—we began to experience for ourselves the historical depth and social complexity of the aging members of the community (Kelley and Betsalel 2017). What we are learning is that for these elders, stories are a survival mechanism that allows the community to stay connected despite all the structural forces aligned against it.

For these elders, wisdom does "sit in places" (Basso 1996), places of memory, like the Recreation Center, formerly the Burton Street Elementary School. For these elders, diverse temporalities—from Scripture time to reminiscing time—have been brought together with place, as the club meets in the Recreation Center, a place rich with remembrances, including a battle with the City of Asheville to reopen the then shuttered school as an all-purpose building in the late 1960s. The members of the Elite Club manifest not only resilience in adapting to change through storied imagination but also resistance as they anchor their everyday experience in remembrances of place. Both resilience and resistance among these elders is contingent on the solidarity only human and place-based continuity of relationship can provide.

WEB SPECIALS:

1. A CDC site on Native Americans with diabetes: https://www.cdc
.gov/vitalsigns/aian-diabetes/index.html.
2. A short video about the dramatic rise of diabetes among the Pima
peoples: https://www.youtube.com/watch?v=SfPdhhXcGRQ.

We will see that these factors play a large role in how ethnic individuals experience late life and the implications those experiences have for aging policy, especially related to health (Ferraro, Kemp, and Williams 2017). Below in Box IV.2 we have a discussion of one such effort—Project REACH—trying to ameliorate the impact of minority health disparity, in this case working to reduce the high incidence of diabetes among Hispanic elders in Texas.[3]

Linda Carson's Web Chapter also focuses on this disease, this time among ethnic elders of Native American communities. This chapter draws on her training in public health and gerontology to explore the devastating impact of soaring diabetes rates among older Native Americans in Oklahoma. Her work shows the complex interaction between a legacy of colonial oppression, indigenous health beliefs, and Western models of health behavior. As was seen in Box IV.2, impacting this matrix to increase positive health outcomes is never a simple matter, but must always be undertaken by first understanding the culture system from the inside. Carson's work shows how important this is for understanding how to provide a better fit between divergent cultural models of disease and the modern health care system, especially among native, indigenous populations (Browne et al. 2017).

McDonaldized Americans or a *Glocalized* Nation?

As the current political discourse toward immigration and ethnic diversity has reached a boiling point with a president demonizing select populations and trying to ban their entrance to the United States, it recalls earlier periods when Asian, Irish, and Slavic European immigrants were considered less human than certain West European heritage peoples and legislation was passed to limit their entrance into the United States. Yet, by 2017 the Census Bureau found that the foreign-born population in the United States reached 13.7 percent, its highest share since 1910 when it stood at about 15 percent of our population. Since the 1965 Immigration and Nationality Act ended the prior system of racially tinted quotas established in the 1920s, numerous ethnic communities have taken advantage of "family reunification" provisions

---

Box IV.2   Project REACH: Attacking Health Disparity among Ethnic Elders

An underlying theme of this report is the growing problem of racial and ethnic health disparities among older adults. Two factors continue to increase the urgency of this problem—the dramatic aging of the U.S. population and the growing proportion of racial and ethnic minority groups. The health status of racial and ethnic minorities of all ages lags far behind that of nonminority populations. For a variety of reasons, older adults may experience the effects of health disparities more dramatically than any other population group. For one, older adults are more likely to have chronic illness and require frequent contact with the health care system. Also, many live in poverty, making access to health care a challenge. The care of older adults who are chronically ill, poor, and members of an ethnic community is an increasingly urgent health priority.

A major effort to help address these health disparities is the Racial and Ethnic Approaches to Community Health (REACH 2010) Program, which supports community-based coalitions in the design, implementation, and evaluation of innovative strategies to reduce or eliminate health disparities among racial and ethnic minorities. These groups include African Americans, Hispanic Americans, American Indians, Alaska Natives, Asian Americans, and Pacific Islanders. One example of a successful REACH 2010 Program is the Latino Education Project (LEP), in the Corpus Christi, Texas, area which targets midlife and older Latinos—a population that suffers disproportionately from diabetes and its complications. The need for assistance in these small, rural, and isolated communities is great. Approximately 80 to 95 percent of the residents are Hispanic, and almost 50 percent are aged 60 or older. The depressed economy and chronic unemployment rates that characterize these communities perpetuate poverty from generation to generation. (Follow the project at: www.facebook.com/LatinoEmpowerment Project/.)

This area has been classified as medically underserved for decades, and the high cost of health care, lack of access to health insurance, and limited community resources contribute significantly to health disparities. LEP Program activities focus on enabling and mobilizing key community institutions and organizations to respond to the diabetes crisis among midlife and older Hispanics. Communitywide health forums bring together health care providers; advocates; elected officials; radio, television, and newspaper representatives; and local leaders to identify the best strategies for the prevention, early diagnosis, and management of diabetes. Small study circles allow for personalized attention, focusing on individual behavioral change through the selection of healthier foods, promoting and facilitating physical activity, and mobilizing informal support networks. Lay health educators (*promotores de salud*) use their leadership skills to assist communities and individual participants to access resources on their own. The educators provide case management that leads to healthier behaviors, better health, and improved management of diabetes.

As a result of these activities, LEP participants have increased their levels of physical activity and consumption of water, fruits, and vegetables, as well as improved communication with their health care providers. REACH 2010 and the multiyear Reach 2014 Followup continue to foster community commitment and active participation of seniors, stakeholders, and state and local officials—two key strategies for improving health and access to health care among older adult communities of color.

The related ongoing Community REACH II project focused on cognitive health and Alzheimer's disease and enhancing the health of Alzheimer's Caregivers Community is analyzed in Czaja et al. 2018 and Reach 2018: https://www.cdc.gov/nccdphp/dnpao/state-local-programs /reach/current_programs/index.html.

Some of this information is adapted from: Centers for Disease Control and Prevention 2007.

See the Resources for Enhancing Alzheimer's Caregiver Health (REACH) trials, funded by NIA and the National Institute for Nursing Research, that tested strategies for helping dementia caregivers manage their stress and emotional burden. The interventions included education on dementia, training in specific caregiving skills, and encouragement and techniques for physical and emotional self-care. The REACH findings are now being put into practice through two federal agencies, the Veterans Administration (VA) and the Administration on Aging (AoA).

that have been a cornerstone of federal immigration law for half a century. As an indication of how dependent the care system for disabled elders is on our immigrant population, "One in four of the direct-care workers in the nation's nursing homes, assisted living facilities and home care agencies are foreign-born" (Span 2018; see also Coe 2019).

Despite a prevailing notion of the United States as a melting pot, effectively homogenizing immigrant cultures into an invariant, "McDonaldized" social soup, a highly contentious cultural plurality remains a powerful element of national life and what Roger Sanjek (1998) calls "the future of us all" (see also Aguirre and Turner 2006). The variation of *Yiddisheit* created by the elders who Myerhoff studied is related to what has been called "glocalization,"

WEB SPECIAL:

The Interned and the Undocumented: The Immigration Spectrum in the US Today: https://aeon.co/videos/the-interned-and-the-undocumented-the-immigration-spectrum-in-the-us-today.

---

transforming a cultural pattern that traveled over global boundaries into a new variant of its original form. Within the bounds of a senior center, they altered Jewish ritual performance and modes of learning scripture to the exigencies of their lives, and when a learned rabbi came to dissuade them from straying from "tradition," *he was asked to leave*. In this section, the Web Chapters on Iranian and Cuban migrants will be instructive in pointing out how they are creating their own glocalized ethnic meaning in senior centers, parks, and other public settings.

In the early 21st century, with vigilante posses guarding borders against Mexican intruders and immigrants from Islamic-centered cultures preemptively assumed to be potential terrorists, the issue of cultural diversity has grown with special intensity. In the field of aging this has been recognized by an explosion of new research, the establishment of national centers to study the issue (www.rcmar.ucla.edu/index.php), and as noted in this book's introduction, the invention of terms such as "ethnogerontology" and "ethnogeriatrics" to designate those with a specialized focus on ethnicity and age, such as the program developed at the Stanford School of Medicine (https://geriatrics.stanford.edu/culturemed/overview/introduction/field.html).

Moreover, the growing diversity in our older population is beginning to impact aging policy around such issues as social security and the delivery of health care and social services (Cummings-Vaughn and Cruz-Oliver 2016; Mehrotra and Wagner 2018). This is also a powerful issue within European nations, and the experience in such places may help us develop alternative models for integrating new immigrant elders and their families into the existing social fabric. In this section's Web Chapter by Shireen Walton, she shows how older Italian women in Milan use the cultural space of a multicultural center to connect Middle Eastern migrants to their new migrant lives.

Ethnic Culture and Aging

It must be noted that only a tiny number of groups in our society have maintained sociocultural systems that are not only highly variant from American cultural norms but also stress factors that foster high status for the aged (Johnson 1995). Among the most distinct are the Amish, Hasidic Jews,

Box IV.3 Anthropology Helps Doctors Go beyond the Standard Clinical Interview with Ethnic Elders

Over the past decade I have used the anthropological ethnographic approach as a team member providing specialized training in geriatric health for physicians and psychiatrists in a memory disorder clinic at a public hospital in Brooklyn, New York. A special challenge was that a majority of the doctors in this program grew up in nations like China, India, Mexico, or Croatia, although all had taken some of their medical training in the United States. Part of my task was to help them effectively evaluate and treat elder patients from a relatively poor and quite diverse cultural patient population, likely different than their own backgrounds. Initially I would give some lectures about ethnicity, health, and culture or dementia in global context, focusing on the first-generation heritage groups they would most likely encounter in the clinic. I stressed the need to think about *process* and learning about the narrative by which their patients discuss health issues in their own communities. In this way I suggested how cultural process could be added to the doctor's clinical interview guideposts. One of my training tasks was being on rounds with these doctors and demonstrating how they sometimes missed key health information with a standard clinical interview or how to best use cultural knowledge to convince the patient and/or their families to follow through with suggested treatment. It might involve how to ask about traditional medicine and how families make use of the nearby *botanicas* (traditional medicine stores). In terms of promoting families and their elders to go along with treatment plans, it was important to realize that women, especially in the local Afro-Caribbean community, would likely be more influenced in following a doctor's orders by their nonfamilial age-peer support groups in churches than by family members who might have accompanied patients to the clinic. This helped physicians understand the need to alter seemingly simple questions like "Have you ever gone to a traditional healer in your neighborhood?" More often than not such questions elicit a quick "No." I found it helped to normalize the behavior with asking "We know many people in this neighborhood go to *botanicas* for various ailments—when was the last time you or a family member did that?" This way of asking a question not only will produce more reliable information but can get at the process of what people seek out in such places. Importantly, it can help us learn which herbal ingredients consumed from a such a store might conflict with medicines a doctor is planning to prescribe to a patient.

For video of some of the lecture and case examples at SUNY Downstate Geriatric Fellowship Program, at the Web site below scroll down to Anthropology of Aging: http://www.downstate.edu/geriatricfellowship/lectures.html.

A good analog to multiethnic medical care is found in this series of cases from the Centre for Biomedical Ethics at the Yong Loo Lin School of Medicine at the National University of Singapore, "Caring for Older People in an Ageing Society: A Singapore Bioethics Casebook." http://www.bioethicscasebook.sg/caring-for-older-people-in-an-ageing-society/.

and Native American groups such as the Navaho and Zuni or relatively recent arrivals such as the Hmong from Vietnam (Goodkind 2006). The long-term positive maintenance of these groups' ethnic divergence has been possible so far as they have remained economically independent of outside groups.

The Amish stand as a strong contradiction to the rule (Crist, Armer and Radina 2002). Most other immigrant groups have not been able to maintain such a close integration of ideology, social organization, and economic tradition. Accordingly, the expression of ethnicity varies tremendously from encompassing communities that can satisfy most material and spiritual needs, to having a select repertoire of subjective identity markers (food, clothes, music) or merely perceiving a vague sense of belonging to a historically felt past.

This can also include how populations from divergent ethno-religious perspectives memorialize their dead relatives. Doris Francis in this section draws upon her dual training in anthropology and landscape design to consider how cultural heritage shapes ancestral landscapes in cemeteries in England. Most importantly, she explores how for elder persons, what happens in these cultural spaces not only helps them cope with loss, continue a relationship with the departed, and transmit to younger kin the value of family ties. What happens here in dirt, stone, and flowers will provide a contrast with the new digital spaces urban Chinese (Part II Intro) have come to use in remaining connected to ancestors.

Context and the Realities of Ethnic Compensation

A major theme in researching the cultural diversity of America's aged has been the examination of ethnicity as a positive resource for the aged—a form of compensation for the problems associated with aging (Chappell 2006). In our own societal context a positive dimension of ethnic attachments can promote a nondenigrating component of identity to balance out potentially difficult transitions in work and family life. In a more general sense it has been suggested that ethnicity carries with it "special resources or ethnically-inflected strategies that may be mobilized to maximize personal well-being . . . in the development of long-term 'careers' for successful elders, and in the management of the inevitable . . . crises that individuals must confront toward the end of the life cycle" (Weibel-Orlando 1987: 102).

In this section's first chapter, Jay Sokolovsky looks at the available data to try to assess the limits of ethnic beliefs and support as a compensator for aging in our urban postindustrial society. The chapter complicates easy assumptions about ethnic family systems being able to deal with all the needs of late-life family members (Diaz et al. 2019). A central point of his argument is to question a false policy dichotomy pitting family caring against state support of the aged. He shows that even among Asian groups, known for their attention to filial piety, certain immigration contexts can result in a very low-perceived quality of life by the elderly. Sokolovsky, in looking at the ethnic family's approach to Alzheimer's disease, also finds that when dealing with difficult mental health problems, the traditional ethnic response can sometimes actually exacerbate the situation. Among the more important points made in this chapter are that (1) the female perspective on family support of the aged can be dramatically different from that of males; (2) elderly with social networks linking them to both kin and the broader community have better mental health profiles than those encapsulated totally in the ethnic family; and (3) formal supports can be effectively used to strengthen the ability of the family to care for its elderly members. He argues that these ideas should be used as policy touchstones to counter ongoing efforts to dismantle the system of nonfamilial supports built up over the last half-century. Important confirmation of the ideas in this article comes from both recent research in North America (Noguchi et al. 2019), Chile (Gallardo-Peralta 2018), Korea (Kim, Park and Antonucci 2016), England (Purewal and Jasani 2017), and longitudinal network studies in rural and urban England and elsewhere in Europe (Wenger 1997; Burholt, Dobbs, and Victor 2018).

The Growing Diversity of Our Older Population

As seen in Figure IV.1, our nation's population of older adults will get dramatically more diverse over the next several decades, essentially producing a "browning" of a graying America. Between 2014 and 2060 the share of the older population that is non-Hispanic white is projected to drop by 24 percentage points, from 78.3 percent to 54.6 percent. This means those past age 65 classified as ethnic minorities—African American, Native American, Asian/Pacific Island American, and Hispanic American—by 2060 this group of elders is projected to represent more than four out of every 10 older

Race and Hispanic or Latino Origin	2014		2060 Projections	
	Number (in Thousands)	Percent	Number (in Thousands)	Percent
Total	46,243	100.0	98,164	100.0
Non-Hispanic or Latino				
White alone	36,208	78.3	53,566	54.6
Black alone	4,017	8.7	11,954	12.2
Asian alone	1,869	4.0	8,491	8.7
All other races alone or in combination	598	1.3	2,644	2.7
Hispanic or Latino (any race)	3,551	7.7	21,508	21.9

Note: Some columns do not sum to total due to rounding error.

Source: Federal Interagency Forum on Aging-Related Statistics.

Figure IV.1   Population Age 65 and over, by Race and Hispanic Origin, 2014, and Projected to 2060.

Americans (Federal Interagency Forum 2016). Asian and Hispanic elders will be the fastest growing sectors of this population, reshaping the social fabric of towns and small cities across the United States. (Schulz and Eden 2016).

The Class Context of Minority Status and Ethnicity

In the United States and other postindustrial societies, the cultural dimension of ethnicity must also be understood within the framework of a class system that has created minority groups (Aguirre and Turner 2006). These are parts of populations singled out for different and inferior treatment based on characteristics such as their ethnic heritage, sex, nationality, or language (Hayes-Bautista et al. 2002). While U.S. minority populations discussed in this book—African Americans, Hispanics, Native Americans, and Southeast Asian refugees—still have a considerably smaller proportion of elderly than Euro-American groups, their income, education, and access to quality housing, safe communities, and health care are far below that of the majority of older Americans (Crystal, Shea, and Reyes 2017; Buch 2018). These inequalities represent a "cumulative disadvantage" predicting that disparities in health and quality of life accrue over a lifetime and amplify differences in late life (OECD 2017).

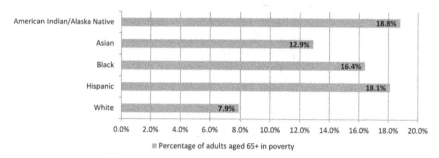

Figure IV.2   Poverty Level of Minority Seniors in the United States Age 65+ (U.S. Census Bureau, American Community Survey, 2016).

The most comprehensive multinational study of cumulative disadvantage took place in 10 European nations. It concludes that while some nations, such as Switzerland, show a relatively low level of accumulated disadvantage in late life, overall there is a continuing negative impact of socioeconomic inequality in comparing older to middle-age samples of people (von Dem Knesebeck et al. 2007; OECD 2017). Certainly, in the United States, as noted in Figure IV.2, we see the long-term consequences of unequal access to education, jobs, and promotions mandated by the U.S. apartheid system that effectively operated up to the 1970s. While the poverty rate for white elderly is now less than 8 percent, as noted in Figure IV.2, it is more than twice that level for African American, Hispanic, and Native American older adults). Despite a substantial decline in rates of poverty for older African Americans over the past three decades, this has not decreased the economic disparity between older whites and ethnic minority populations (Lincoln 2018). A consequence for minority families has been dramatic disruptions in anticipated family structures, especially related to parents' consistent ability to care for children.

Grandfamilies and Ethnicity

Over the past two decades a new vocabulary has emerged in social science and legislative documents talking about "grandfamilies," "skipped generation families," and the general system of "kincare" (Hayslip and Musil 2017). In the United States such terms are connected to the reality that by 2017, 2.6 million children were in custodial care of grandchildren by elders without birth parents in the home, and this was an increase of almost 18 percent over the prior decade (Annie E. Casey Foundation 2014–2016). At some point in their lives more than one in 10 American grandparents will have primary responsibility for raising a grandchild, typically for two or more years. This pattern began to increase significantly in the late 20th century and has continued to accelerate more recently with the dramatic rise of opioid addiction and deaths rampaging through families in North America (Generations

United 2018). One response has been the emergence of organizations such as Generations United (see Part II Web Book Butts), Generations of Hope, and the National Research Center on Grandparents Raising Grandchildren and its associated new journal *Grandfamilies* (Annie E. Casey Foundation 2014–2016; Hayslip and Musil 2017).

We have already noted in Weibel-Orlando's study of Lakota Native American elders (Part II Web Book) how the reemergence of their ancestral identity in old age served as a bridge to a key custodial childcare role. Importantly, unexpected reparenting in late life is one of those pivotal issues cross-cutting landscapes of ethnicity, class, and national boundaries (for international perspectives see Di Gessa et al. 2016; Timonen 2018).

The chapter by Marta Rodríguez-Galán takes readers into the lives of Puerto Rican grandfamilies through the eyes of grandmothers in Boston, Massachusetts, and Rochester, New York. We see both the strength of Puerto Rican heritage in two locales and the difficult context in which grandparents must take over childcare responsibilities their adult children are unable to assume. Rodríguez-Galán explores the role of *familismo* as a cultural trait in helping these women in their struggle to bring up grandchildren while dealing with a wide variety of difficulties plaguing many immigrant communities in the United States (see Angel and Angel 2014 for broad discussion of Latino elders).

WEB SPECIAL:

J. Peterson Lent and A. Otto, "Grandparents, Grandchildren, and Caregiving: The Impacts of America's Substance Use Crisis," *Generations*, Fall 2018. https://www.asaging.org/blog/grandparents-grandchildren-and-caregiving-impacts-americas-substance-use-crisis.

LEGISLATION TO FOLLOW:

This issue now cross-cuts all segments of American families. In 2018, the federal government passed the Supporting Grandparents Raising Grandchildren Act, coordinating resources for the grandparents and other kin raising children not their own (see www.congress.gov/bill/115th-congress/senate-bill/1091). Readers can check out the arguments pro/con for this legislation at: https://www.countable.us/bills/s1091-115-supporting-grandparents-raising-grandchildren-act.

Refugee Status, Cultural Context, and Cultural Spaces

Over the last several decades, with the ending of old colonial regimes and the collapse of the Soviet Union, numerous tragic civil wars have raged and still continue in parts of the world. At the beginning of 2018 the United Nations estimated that worldwide there were about 68 million refugees being forced from their home areas through wars and other disasters. The next two chapters in the section deal with two such refugee groups, from very different regions of the world.

The Web Chapter by Mary Hegland gives us a very dynamic picture of Iranians fleeing the Islamic revolution in their home country and ending up highly dispersed in the San Francisco Bay area. Having largely come from the educated and secular Muslim community affiliated with the former government of the shah of Iran, they and especially their children were able to take advantage of the booming high-tech economy of the Silicon Valley. However, these Iranian-American elders suffer a double lamentation. They have lost access to their own country as well as the Persian cultural fabric of easy engagement within socially enmeshed neighborhoods, in which one could build a lasting connection to an intergenerational body of meaningful relationships.

Yet, as some ethnic Iranian elders experienced loss—in widowhood, the death of lifelong friends, or being distanced from their central kin network—they may also turn to a broader civic engagement and new cultural scripts. Sometimes this transpires as a personal quest, such the example of Mr. Sahed, who after his wife's death took a spiritual turn and directed his energies toward helping others in homes, hospitals, and nursing facilities (for a Canadian context see Dossa 2018). This issue of activating and inspiring civic engagement of ethnic elders is being recognized as a vital, untapped community resource. It is also the focus of a national project, Project SHINE, at Temple University, linking college students and older immigrants in 18 cities in a common effort to promote service to their surrounding community (www.programsforelderly.com/awareness-project-shine.php).

In the Web Chapter by Martinez on Cuban expatriates in Miami, we see quite a different local context for elders. Unlike the highly dispersed Iranians studied by Hegland, her sample is physically centered in a distinct ethnic community. However, the context of migration and the great reduction of immediate family have created a strong degree of social isolation and aging "*out* of place." For many, this state of aging in exile has produced a social space fraught with anxiety and, for some, even the latent manifestations of post-traumatic stress syndrome. As with the Iranians in California, these elders have sought refuge in senior centers, but also in parks where the social drama of domino play is a bittersweet connection to their Caribbean cultural roots.[4]

Ethnic Elders as Community Assets

One historical response of African American peoples has been to establish community-based mechanisms of support that could buffer the shock of long-term discrimination on the individual (Coke and Twaite 1995). In this section we have two chapters that look at that process in the U.S. urban areas of Detroit and Seattle. These chapters focus on the way social and cultural spaces generated through an African American version of middle-class values and hard work become a bedrock and literal pillar of community spaces that are both physically and economically challenged. Community-based networks provided the core of stability, for not only younger kin, but the broader neighborhood. We see this clearly in Mark Luborsky and Andrea Sankar's chapter set in Detroit, Michigan. Here, set against long-term industrial pollution of waterways, they document the conjunction of African American fishing traditions and cultural knowledge to protect both health and heritage. The chapter highlights an activist approach that involves multigenerational "River Walkers" African American teams, and a project linking university students, community members, government, and public stakeholders. These efforts focus on continuing fishing activities while reducing consumption of fish with toxic residue.

In another urban setting Jane Peterson employs her dual background as professional nurse and medical anthropologist to explore the participation of older women in two key institutions in an African American community in Seattle. Despite the ever-present specter of multiple jeopardy—being black, aged, and female—a family-based role combined with the more public arena of the Pentecostal Church provide a valued context in which successful aging can take place (see also Nguyen 2018).

Through the case of Mrs. Lottie Waters, we see that mature women in their grandparenting capacity fulfill a classic "kin-keeping role": nurturing and disciplining children, being the repository of family history, and serving as key decision makers and conveners of family ritual. Such women add to the typical characteristics of wise women, a devotion to spiritual needs, and some, in the role of "nurses," apply a holistic system of healing based on herbs and faith. Peterson's ethnographic work corresponds nicely with other research showing a powerful relationship in African American churches, between religious participation and positive perceptions of well-being (Black 1999; Ruiz 2004; King et al. 2005).[5] Her chapter provides an important connection to classic studies such as Stack and Burton's exploration of "kinscripts" (1993), and books like *All Our Kin* (Stack 1974) and *A Different Shade of Gray* (Newman 2003), which all document the dynamic contribution of African American elders to kin and community.

Notes

1. An edited collection of Myerhoff's talks and final writings are found in Kaminsky and Weiss 2007. There is also a new Web site (https://jwa.org/women ofvalor/myerhoff) devoted to the life and work of Barbara Myerhoff featuring documentation of her achievements, along with audio and video clips, and a comprehensive bibliography.

2. The word *shtetl* is Yiddish, and it means "little town." Shtetls were small market towns largely in Russia and Poland.

3. See also http://www.hopkinsmedicine.org/human_resources/education _programs/employees/job_training_project_reach/retrospective/.

4. See Treas and Mazumdar 2002 for a good discussion of the general dilemma of integration versus isolation in ethnic families.

5. Important recent qualitative works on health care within African American communities include Ball et al. 2005 and Harley 2006.

Bibliography

Aguirre, A., and J. Turner. 2006. *American Ethnicity: The Dynamics and Consequences of Discrimination*, 5th edition. New York: McGraw-Hill.

Angel, R., and J. Angel. 2014. *Latinos in an Aging World: Social, Psychological, and Economic Perspectives*. New York: Routledge.

Annie E. Casey Foundation, Kids Count Data Center. 2014–2016. *Current Population Survey Annual Social and Economic Supplement (CPS ASEC)*. https://www.aecf.org/m/databook/aecf-2014kidscountdatabook-embargoed-2014.pdf.

Baker, T. A., D. K. Atakere, J. A. Minahan, A. A. Kuofie, and T. Dirth. 2018. "Diversity in the Aging Community." In *The Praeger Handbook of Mental Health and the Aging Community*, edited by D. Maller and K. Langsam. Santa Barbara, CA: ABC-CLIO.

Ball, M. M., M. M. Perkins, F. J. Whittington, C. Hollingsworth, S. V. King, and B. L. Combs. 2005. *Communities of Care: Assisted Living for African American Elders*. Baltimore, MD: Johns Hopkins University Press.

Barbour-Payne, Y. 2014. "African American Women in Appalachia: Personal Expressions of Race, Place and Gender." Master's thesis, Texas A&M University. https://oaktrust.library.tamu.edu/bitstream/handle/1969.1/153292/BARBOUR-PAYNE-THESIS-2014.pdf?sequence=1&isAllowed=y.

Basso, K. H. 1996. *Wisdom Sits in Places: Language and Landscape among the Western Apache*. Albuquerque: University of New Mexico Press.

Black, H. 1999. "Life as Gift: Spiritual Narratives of Elderly African-American Women Living in Poverty." *Journal of Aging Studies* 13(4): 441–55.

Browne, C. V., L. S. Ka'opua, L. L. Jervis, R. Alboroto, and M. L. Trockman. 2017. "United States Indigenous Populations and Dementia: Is There a Case for Culture-Based Psychosocial Interventions?" *Gerontologist* 57(6): 1011–19.

Buch, E. 2018. *Inequalities of Aging*. New York: New York University Press.

Burholt, V., C. Dobbs, and C. Victor. 2018. "Social Support Networks of Older Migrants in England and Wales: The Role of Collectivist Culture." *Ageing and Society* 38(7): 1453–77.

Centers for Disease Control and Prevention. 2007. *The State of Aging and Health in America*. Whitehouse Station, NJ: Merck Company Foundation.

Chappell, N. 2006. "Ethnicity and Quality of Life." In *Quality of Life in Old Age—International and Multi-Disciplinary Perspectives*, edited by H. Mollenkopf and A. Walker. New York: Springer.

Coe, C. 2019. *The New American Servitude: Political Belonging among African Immigrant Home Care Workers*. New York: New York University Press.

Coke, M., and J. Twaite. 1995. *The Black Elderly: Satisfaction and Quality of Life*. Binghamton, NY: Haworth.

Crist, J., J. Armer, and M. Radina. 2002. "A Study in Cultural Diversity: Caregiving for the Old Order Amish Elder with Alzheimer's Disease." *Journal of Multicultural Nursing & Health* 8(3): 78–85.

Crystal, S., D. Shea, and A. Reyes 2017. "Cumulative Advantage, Cumulative Disadvantage, and Evolving Patterns of Late-Life Inequality." *Gerontologist* 57(5): 910–20.

Cummings-Vaughn, L., and D. M. Cruz-Oliver, eds. 2016. *Ethnogeriatrics: Healthcare Needs of Diverse Populations*. Cham, Switzerland: Springer.

Czaja, S. J., C. C. Lee, D. Perdomo, D. Lowenstein, M. Bravo, J. H. Moxley, and R. Schulz. 2018. "Community REACH: An Implementation of an Evidence-Based Caregiver Program." *Gerontologist* 58(2): e130–e137.

Diaz, L., M. Y. Savundranayagam, M. Klosek, and D. Fitzsimmons. 2019. "The Role of Cultural and Family Values on Social Connectedness and Loneliness among Ethnic Minority Elders." *Clinical Gerontologist* 42(1): 114–26. https://www.tandfonline.com/doi/abs/10.1080/07317115.2017.1395377.

Di Gessa, G., K. Glaser, D. Price, E. Ribe, and A. Tinker. 2016. "What Drives National Differences in Intensive Grandparental Childcare in Europe?"

         Journal of Gerontology Series B 71(1): 141–53. https://doi.org/10.1093 /geronb/gbv007.

Dossa, P. 2018. "From Displaced Care to Social Care: Narrative Interventions of Canadian Muslims." *American Anthropologist* 120(3): 558–60.

Federal Interagency Forum. 2016. *Older Americans 2016: Key Indicators of Well-Being.* https://agingstats.gov/.

Ferraro, K., B. Kemp, and M. Williams. 2017. "Diverse Aging and Health Inequality by Race and Ethnicity," *Innovation in Aging* 1(1): igx002, https://doi .org/10.1093/geroni/igx002.

Gallardo-Peralta, L. 2018 "Family and Community Support among Older Chilean Adults: The Importance of Heterogeneous Social Support Sources for Quality of Life." *Journal of Gerontological Social Work* 61(6): 584–604.

Generations United. 2018. *Raising the Children of the Opioid Epidemic: Solutions and Support for Grandfamilies.* https://www.gu.org/app/uploads/2018/09 /Grandfamilies-Report-SOGF-Updated.pdf.

Goodkind, J. 2006. "Promoting Hmong Refugees' Well-Being through Mutual Learning: Valuing Knowledge, Culture, and Experience." *American Journal of Community Psychology* 37(1): 77–93.

Harley, D. 2006. "Indigenous Healing Practices among Rural Elderly African Americans." *International Journal of Disability, Development and Education* 53(4): 433–52.

Hayes-Bautista, D., P. Hsu, A. Perez, and C. Gamboa. 2002. "The 'Browning' of the Graying of America: Diversity in the Elderly Population and Policy Implications." *Generations* 26(3): 15–24.

Hayslip, B., and J. Hicks-Patrick, eds. 2006. *Custodial Grandparenting: Individual, Cultural, and Ethnic Diversity.* New York: Springer.

Hayslip, B., and C. Musil, eds. 2017. "The Global Phenomenon of GrandFamilies." Special issue, *Grandfamilies* 4(1). https://scholarworks.wmich.edu /grandfamilies/vol4/iss1/.

Hurston, Z. N. 1937 [1998]. *Their Eyes Were Watching God.* New York: HarperCollins.

Johnson, C. 1995. "Cultural Diversity in Late-Life Families." In *Handbook of Aging and the Family,* edited by R. Blieszner and V. Bedford. Westport, CT: Greenwood.

Kaminsky, M., and M. Weiss, eds. 2007. *Stories as Equipment for Living: Last Talks and Tales of Barbara Myerhoff.* Ann Arbor: University of Michigan Press.

Kelley, H., and K. Betsalel. 2017. "Teaching Galicia in Appalachia: Lessons from Anthropology, Ethnographic Poetry, Documentary Photography, and Political Theory." In *Rerouting Galician Studies. Multidisciplinary Perspectives,* edited by B. Sampedro and J. Losada. Cham, Switzerland: Palgrave McMillan.

Kim, B., S. Park, and T. Antonucci. 2016. "Longitudinal Changes in Social Networks, Health and Wellbeing among Older Koreans." *Ageing & Society* 36(9): 1915–36.

King, S., E. Burgess, M. Akinyela, M. Counts-Spriggs, and N. Parker. 2005. "'Your Body Is God's Temple': The Spiritualization of Health Beliefs in

Multigenerational African American Families." *Research on Aging* 27(4): 420–46.

Lincoln, K. 2018. "Economic Inequality in Later Life." *Generations* 42(2): 6–12.

Mehrotra, C., and L. Wagner. 2018. *Aging and Diversity. An Active Learning Experience*, 3rd edition. New York: Routledge.

Monterescu, D., and H. Hazan. 2018. *Twilight Nationalism: Politics of Existence at Life's End*. Stanford, CA: Stanford University Press.

Newman, K. 2003. *A Different Shade of Gray: Midlife and Beyond in the Inner City.* New York: New Press.

Nguyen, A. 2018. "African American Elders, Mental Health, and the Role of the Church." *Generations* 42(2): 61–67(7).

Noguchi, T., I. Nojima, T. Inoue-Hirakawa, and H. Sugiura. 2019. "The Association between Social Support Sources and Cognitive Function among Community-Dwelling Older Adults: A One-Year Prospective Study." *International Journal of Environmental Research and Public Health* 16(21): 4228. https://doi.org/10.3390/ijerph16214228.

North Carolina Humanities Council. 2010. *Crossroads* 14(1). http://www.nchuma nities.org/sites/default/files/documents/Crossroads%20Summer%20 2010%20for%20web.pdf.

OECD. 2017. *Preventing Ageing Unequality*. Paris: OECD. https://read.oecd-ili brary.org/employment/preventing-ageing-unequally_9789264279087 -en#page1.

Polanco, M. B. 2014. *Historically Black: Imagining Community in a Black Historical District.* New York: New York University Press.

Purewal, N., and R. Jasani 2017. "South Asian Women Elders and Everyday Lives of 'Care in the Community' in Britain: The Neoliberal Turn in Social Care and the Myth of the Family." *South Asian Diaspora* 9(2): 111–27.

Ruiz, D. 2004. *Amazing Grace: African American Grandmothers as Caregivers and Conveyers of Traditional Values.* Westport, CT: Praeger.

Sanjek, R. 1998. *The Future of Us All: Race and Neighborhood Politics in New York City.* Ithaca, NY: Cornell University Press.

Schulz, R., and J. Eden, eds. 2016. *Families Caring for an Aging America.* Washington: DC: National Academies.

Span, P. 2018. "If Immigrants Are Pushed Out, Who Will Care for the Elderly?" *New York Times*, February 2, www.nytimes.com/2018/02/02/health/ille gal-immigrants-caregivers.html.

Stack, C. 1974. *All Our Kin: Strategies for Survival in a Black Community.* New York: Harper & Row.

Stack, C., and L. Burton. 1993. "Kinscripts: Reflections of Family, Generation, and Culture." *Journal of Comparative Family Studies* 24(1): 157–70.

Timonen, V. 2018. *Grandparenting Practices around the World: Reshaping Family.* Chicago: University of Chicago Press.

Treas, J., and S. Mazumdar. 2002. "Older People in America's Immigrant Families: Dilemmas of Dependence Integration and Isolation." *Journal of Aging Studies* 16(3): 243–58.

Vesperi, M. 1998. *City of Green Benches: Growing Old in a New Downtown.* Ithaca, NY: Cornell University Press.

von Dem Knesebeck, O., M. Wahrendorf, M. Hyde, and J. Siegrist. 2007. "Socio-Economic Position and Quality of Life among Older People in 10 European Countries: Results of the SHARE Study." *Ageing and Society* 27: 269–84.

Walker, F. X. 2000. *Affrilachia.* Lexington, KY: Old Cove.

Waters, D. J., G. Hyde, and K. Betsalel. 2017 "Between the Color Lines with a Spy Camera: The Appalachian Urban Folk Photography of Isaiah Rice." *Southern Cultures* 23(1): 92–113.

Weibel-Orlando, J. 1987. *Final Report: Ethnicity, Continuity and Successful Aging.* Bethesda, MD: National Institute on Aging.

Wenger, C. 1997. "Review of Findings on Social Support Networks of Older Europeans." *Journal of Cross-Cultural Gerontology* 12(1): 1–21.

Zubair, M., and M. Norris. 2015. "Perspectives on Ageing, Later Life and Ethnicity: Ageing Research in Ethnic Minority Contexts." Special issue, *Ageing and Society* 35(5).

CHAPTER TWENTY-SIX

Migrant Elders and the Limits of Family Support in a Globalizing World

Jay Sokolovsky

The Globalization of Ethnic Elder Lives

In walking through New York City's Chinatown in 2018, it was easy enough to see examples of younger kin helping highly disabled elders struggling through the crowded streets, and one can be deceived in believing that filial devotion in such places is a panacea for late life (Photo 26.1). It might also produce an assumption of a context where most such ethnic elders lead highly satisfied and mentally secure late lives. Yet, we will see that the complex nature of how families can translate varied cultural notions of filial piety or familism (see Part IV Rodríguez-Galán) in the varied ethnic contexts in which they find themselves can sometimes result in high levels of social and emotional distress for both adult caregivers and their elderly family members.

A Dawning Reality to an Old Story

The movement of immigrant elders from family-focused cultures coming into very different national and social settings can have great challenges in maintaining kin networks that support their older kin. For example, a 2005

Photo 26.1   Helping an elder
in New York City's crowded
Chinatown, December 2018.
(Photo by Jay Sokolovsky)

PROJECTS TO FOLLOW: CHINESE HEALTH, AGING, AND POLICY PROGRAM

Improving the quality of life of the Chinese population through education, research, and sustainable community engagement in the greater
Chicago area and beyond: http://www.chinesehealthyaging.org/mission
.html.

British TV news program ran a story titled "Asian Elderly in Crisis—Care
Lacking for Asian Elderly."[1] The story reflected a deep concern stemming
from a three-year study in England showing the intersection of rapid changes
in ethnic Asian family structure with a presumption by local authorities who
believe that such families can readily handle the needs of their older members. As we shall see, this situation is *not* unique and is reflected in recent
studies in Canada, the United States, and Asian cities themselves (Kim, Park,
and Antonucci 2016; Rhee 2017; Diaz 2019). The news report came on the

heels of initiating the Minority Elderly Care Project (MEC), Europe's largest study to date focusing on older adults from ethnic minority communities in 10 EU nations (www.priae.org/projects/mec.htm).[2] This focus of concern in Europe matches what is also happening in North American with the recasting of diversity in cities and towns alike (Warnes et al. 2004).

Whether in St. Petersburg, Florida; San Jose, California; or Minneapolis, Minnesota, it is hard to ignore the dramatic rise of immigrant ethnic families drawn increasingly to North America from non-Western cultures around the globe. For example, over the past two decades, in the Tampa Bay area of Florida, groups of Somalis, Southeast Asians, and about 15,000 indigenous people from Hidalgo, Mexico, have moved into the area. While the demographic picture of these and other such emerging ethnic communities is still quite young, it is important to understand the capacity of their family systems to support their older population. This chapter will address such issues by looking at the place of older adults in ethnic communities the United States and other postindustrial nations.

Ethnicity and Aging

The broadest-based view of the link between ethnicity and aging centers on the premise that varying ethnic lifestyles will alter the way old age is encountered, perceived, and acted out. Describing precisely how much ethnic subcultures alter the conditions of aging is, to say the very least, controversial. I will address this point by asking the basic question: Do ethnic distinctions make real differences in the experience of aging? More specifically, I will concentrate on the extent to which an idealized view of ethnic subcultures has led to a policy error that places too much emphasis on the ethnic family and informal supports as the savior of the ethnic elderly. Much is at stake as the U.S. government in the first decades of the 21st century has striven to "remake America" by dismantling public sector support systems and most recently to substitute "privatization" and "faith-based initiatives" as a panacea for our nation's ills (Part VI Polivka). This is often justified by the misguided premise that government programs automatically reduce the incentives for families to care for their aged along with their other responsibilities (Cheung and Yuihuen 2006; Landers 2016).

Culture, Ethnicity, and Aging

To a cultural anthropologist such as myself, seeking the answer to these questions requires examining the general relationship between cultural variation and aging. The consideration of ethnicity as a factor affecting old age brings the question of sociocultural variation back home to our own doorstep. Ethnicity is commonly understood as social differentiation derived from cultural criteria such as a shared history, a common place of origin, language, dress, food preferences, and values that engender a sense of exclusiveness and self-awareness of membership in a distinct social group. Viewing the variations of aging in our country within the context of ethnicity seems mandated by the continuing cultural pluralism of our nation. While at the beginning of the 1990s only about 5 percent of the elderly were foreign born, by 2017 that figure had more than doubled to 13.7 percent, with a majority of these persons now claiming heritage from either Asia or Latin America.

Culture Versus Context

When dealing in general with ethnic segments of the United States we are almost never confronting "culture in the raw," unburnished from Old World or other indigenous origins. Especially in cities one can easily encounter such designations as "Moscow on the boardwalk" of Brighton Beach, Brooklyn; "Little Havana" in Miami; or the "Chinatowns" and "Little Asias" clinging to numerous downtown districts. However, there are precious few ethnic groups whose traditional lifestyles and values have not been altered by the reality of special immigration histories and the continuing social, economic, and political constraints imposed by American class stratification and ideology. However, one cannot presume, as a given, the impact of transnational migration on growing old in a new societal setting. For example a recent cross-national study of the black diaspora in the United States and England shows that especially for the Caribbean migrant, the place of migration and how they arrived provided advantages to Afro-Caribbeans in the United States compared with counterparts in England (Nazroo et al. 2007). While migration is often assumed to be a negative and disorienting experience, such changed circumstances, as Sandra Torres points out, can become the touchstone to "successful aging" (2006; Part I Lamb). In examining transplanted Asiatic ethnic groups, each with a strong "ideal" emphasis on filial devotion, one can see the impact of context on culture. For Chinese American elderly, migration to the United States in the early 20th century was largely a movement of young, single males who planned to return to China. Despite their living in well-defined ethnic communities, studies of these males in old age have found them to have the smallest family networks of any Asian American group, and relatively few express high satisfaction with life (Yu 1992). Although Yu's 1992 research showed considerable "ideal" expressions of filial support by Chinese American young adults in a Midwestern university town, actual support lagged well behind good intentions. While in the last two decades new immigration patterns have evened out the gender ratio of elder Chinese Americans, continuing insecurity focuses on linguistic and isolation, coupled with social distancing through what Lan refers to as "subcontracted filial piety." In such cases sons engage caregivers from similar ethnic backgrounds to care for their frail older kin (2002).

Just recording the young as saying "We have strong family and filial devotion" does not really help one understand how such ideas translate into the lives of ethnic families. In a study of Chinese immigrants to Canadian cities, it was found that while the younger generation did their best to live up to the principles of filial devotion, their elder relatives, due to their lack of resources, could not adequately fulfill their end of the cultural bargain by materially supporting the success of their children (Mackinnon, Gien, and Durst 2001). In this context, to prevent others perceiving them as being a burden, they avoided making demands on their children for even the simplest things such as rides to the doctor or help with buying medicine. Paralleling the findings of Zhang (Part III) for China's own cities, the authors found, "Many elderly Chinese immigrants, rather than face escalating cultural conflicts and intergenerational difficulties, are showing a growing preference for independent living" (11). Studying this emerging problem among Chinese immigrant families in urban Australia, Ip, Lui, and Hui refer to the situation there as a "veiled entrapment" (2007). Here, while the younger Chinese adult migrants have been clear economic beneficiaries of globalization, the older parents of these new capitalists "have been trapped in dependent and isolated social situations by their lack of appropriate cultural and social capital for life in the new societal setting, and have little control of their everyday lives" (734).

In the United States the most important long-term analyses of Chinese ethnic families are encompassed in the "Pine" and "Piety" studies, which have followed 3,000 Chinese older adults in the greater Chicago area (www.chinese healthyaging.org). One of the key findings of this work is that for Chinese older adults, unmet filial expectations resulted in high levels of depression for elders, and for adult children this was associated with increased hopelessness, depression, stress, and loneliness (see Web Special below).

In contrast, older Japanese Americans, while they came to this country a few decades after the Chinese, immigrated primarily in family groups and expected to become U.S. citizens. These elders not only are more likely to be

WEB SPECIAL:

You can read a special issue of the *Journal of Gerontology* (2017) focusing on the Pine Study and its focus on health and well-being: https://academic.oup.com/biomedgerontology/issue/72/suppl_1.

more deeply imbedded in kinship networks than the Chinese, but also exhibit higher levels of social and psychological success (Kanamoto 2006). While a majority (54 percent) of Japanese American elders in a San Diego study (Cuellar and Weeks 1980) said they were very satisfied with their lives, only 18 percent of older Chinese claimed this level of contentment. We will see later on, however, that being surrounded by relatives in an ethnic enclave does not ensure passage to a geriatric Nirvana.

Multiple Jeopardy or Ethnic Compensation

Understanding the context of ethnic aging also requires study of the minority aged, those who have been singled out for differential and inferior treatment (American Society on Aging 2018). In this particular clash of culture and context, there has emerged in the ethnicity and aging literature two key themes that on the surface seem contradictory. One theme stresses how minority group membership creates "multiple jeopardies" and "cumulative disadvantage" in the context of structured inequality and thereby intensifies the problems of growing old (Part IV Web Book Carson). From this first perspective Ron Manuel noted that "the distinction of the minority aged is not so much a function of the novel conditions of their aging as it is the dire circumstances of their existence" (1982: xv). Numerous studies have repeatedly demonstrated that in terms of income, housing quality, education, and rates of chronic illness, the minority aged encounter harsher conditions than the majority of older Americans. Not only are these problems more severe, but the "aging network" set up to provide services according to uniform bureaucratic standards often creates barriers preventing the minority ethnic aged from obtaining resources to which they are entitled (Burton and Whitfield 2006; Zubair and Norris 2015).

The other theme underscores the benefits or resources accruing to those elderly who remain attached to an ethnic identity and subculture (Moriarty and Butt 2004; Victor et al. 2019). Recently this notion has focused on the resilience and the ability to endure and overcome high levels of deprivation and discrimination (Yee-Melichar, Takagi, and Lui 2018). For example, it is suggested that particular cultures, if they promote community-shared positive attitudes to older adults, promote a community-level resiliency to provide resources to help its older residents survive their hardships (Wild, Wiles, and Allen 2013). This second perspective, which I will refer to as "ethnic compensation," often creeps into the discussion of minority aging in an ambivalent fashion. Manuel, after making the statement quoted above, goes on to state, "while relatively more disadvantaged because of the minority experience, the aged have often adopted distinguishable strategies for successfully coping with their problems" (1982: xv). This sentiment corresponds to the prevailing anthropological writings on aging and ethnicity, which largely echo Linda Cool's statement that, "rather than providing yet one more obstacle to be overcome in the aging process, ethnicity can furnish the elderly with a source of identity and prestige which they can manipulate to make a place for themselves in society" (1981: 185).

The two themes do not logically exclude each other, and in impoverished urban and rural communities, dense and locally situated ethnic networks may still provide the real balance of survival. Yet, putting an undue emphasis on one or the other construct shifts policy implications toward dramatically opposed viewpoints. Ethnicity as deprivation calls for social and economic justice and strengthening federal/state resources to overcome lifelong deficits. Ethnicity as compensation or resource could be construed as a rationale to decrease or at least to not shift material resources toward the ethnic minority aged (Torres 2018).

However, a major point I hope to make here is that much of the literature on ethnicity as a resource has been overly optimistic, especially in the area of informal social supports and family networks of exchange (Johnson 1995). I concentrate on the theme of ethnic compensation, not because I think it is more important, but because it has been relatively ignored. By stressing this approach, one can also ask significant questions about the nonminority ethnic elderly. Moreover, it is often in this area of aging research that the ways of testing whether the "differences make a difference" have not been up to the questions asked. All too often, ethnic distinctions are measured by mass survey questionnaires, appropriate perhaps for numerically measuring variations in health complaints, the frequency of contact with friends, or the proximity of children to an elderly parent's house. However, such measures tell us little about how ethnic differences influence the way illnesses are dealt with, how they affect the perception of old age, if they lead to premature institutionalization, or how the action of social networks actually contributes to or diminishes the successful functioning of the elderly in the family and the community.

The Ethnic Colors of "White"

This is especially the case in classic studies of the aged of European background, where statistical documentation can potentially mask subtle ethnic differences (Hayes, Kalish, and Guttmann 1986). Quite instructive is the work by Cohler, Lieberman, and Welch (1977) studying Irish, Italian, and Polish Americans in Chicago. Despite statistical similarity in levels of social contact, the authors showed how subtle differences in value orientations between the Italian and Polish communities related to the nature of support systems affecting the elderly.

In this study, the Polish were found to perceive a greater sense of isolation, and they were more likely to feel no one was available to them for aid in problematic situations. This greater degree of perceived social isolation was related to traditional Polish concerns for privacy, self-containment, and for-mality in social relations. The authors suggest that what appears to be greater social isolation among the Polish American respondents may be a reflection of their preference for formal rather than informal relationships and a ten-dency to look to the community rather than to the family for support. They argue that there is a tendency here to undervalue informal relations of the family as a source of support in deference to resources through formal ties to the community.

The Italians, on the other hand, emphasized a traditional value of "family centeredness," used chain migration to link up with fellow townspeople in the same urban neighborhood, and put an inordinate stress on family rela-tionships. In contrast to Polish respondents, the Italian aged were more will-ing to seek out family and close friends in crisis situations. Italian women were noted as gaining higher status with age, as they were much in demand to mediate problems in the family network. As we shall see, however, there are costs attached to this "mediating Madonna" role (see also Part II Web Book Weibel-Orlando).

While ethnic differences are apparent, the ultimate question remains: Do the differences make a significant difference? In fact, Cohler, Lieberman, and Welch suggest that for the groups just mentioned, ethnic saliency for explain-ing variant patterns of behavior decreases in old age, with middle-aged cohorts more distinct than aged ones (1977). Nonetheless, this does not mean that general cultural differences among the nonaged ethnics will not have an impact on the elderly. This can be especially important in socially patterned decisions about caring for one's aged parent. An indication of this is provided by a Baltimore study comparing Italians and Poles on attitudes toward institutionalization of the elderly (Fandetti and Gelfand 1976). As one might predict from the previous discussion, the authors found that a signifi-cantly stronger preference for using family arrangements was expressed by Italians than by the Polish counterparts. Here is an ethnic difference that not only directly affects differential treatment of the aged but also argues for awareness of such differences at some level of policy making.

Cross-Ethnic Comparison: Data and Its Dilemmas

The general problem of understanding the implications of statistical sur-vey variables often occurs in the discussion of informal social interaction and exchange in family and neighborhood contexts (Sokolovsky 2006). Numer-ous studies now exist purporting to compare subculturally variant family caregiving and its associated "network" behavior (Pinquart and Sorenson 2005; Wilmoth and Silverstein 2017). With the predominant use of so-called sociometric techniques for gathering data, one is hard pressed to know if statistically significant differences (or lack of variation) mean anything. A case in point is the well-known "Social and Cultural Contexts of Aging" study conducted in Los Angeles (Bengtson and Morgan 1987). Here whites were compared with blacks and Mexican Americans in terms of social inter-action with children, grandchildren, other relatives, and friends. Mexican Americans were considerably more likely than white elderly to see children and grandchildren on a weekly basis, although no difference was found for contact with other relatives. The Mexican Americans were much less likely to see friends and neighbors frequently. Older blacks and whites were shown to have almost identical frequency of contact with grandchildren or other relatives, although smaller percentages of blacks reported seeing children and neighborhood friends frequently.

What use can be made of these facts with regard to the function of the aged in familial and community networks? Just because approximately 40 percent of both whites and blacks in Los Angeles see "grandchildren" and "other relatives" weekly does not mean the aged in each ethnic group fit into kinship networks and use such resources in the same way (Jett 2002; Dil-worth-Anderson et al. 2005).

Various other studies, such as the classic research by Nellie Tate (1983), have given us clues to some of the significant differences. One of these dis-tinctions is a greater flexibility in kinship boundaries among African Ameri-can families, which results in the absorption of young grandchildren and "other relatives" into households headed by the elderly (see also Part IV Web Book Peterson). It is particularly pronounced for older black women, who are four times more likely than older white females to live with young dependent relatives under 18 years of age. In her study of Philadelphia's black elderly, Tate has suggested how this difference makes a difference: "It appears that absorbed non-independent younger blacks are more likely to accept their aged who become functionally impaired as a result of chronic conditions" (1983: 99). This is dramatically seen in the case of families caring for elders suffering from dementia. My own research on this issue in Tampa, Florida,[3] corroborates what other studies have implied, that the structure of African American families significantly reduces the perceived consequences of Alzheimer's disease on the kin caregiving unit even though the actual dis-ease stressors or patient functional capacity are likely worse than in Euro-American background families (Dilworth-Anderson, Gibson, and Burke 2006; Bonds and Lyons 2018).

An interesting parallel to this kind of analysis in North America was found in a multiethnic study of elder support in England (Moriarty and Butt 2004). The initial survey research found that not only did Asian immigrant elders have the largest density of family and coethnics in their local environ-ment, but they described a regular pattern of practical help in exchange for childcare. In contrast, European-heritage aged initially reported they only asked for help in a crisis. However, observing the actual functioning of elders in the community produced a different picture. The Anglo elders provided a great deal of voluntary help to kin and neighbors, while in the case of the Asian elders "the presence of other household members or relatives nearby was no guarantee that Asian carers would receive additional help from their families" (742). In other words, the Asian sample had the highest expectation, but the narrowest range of anticipated helpers to ask for practical support. The authors note that from the perspective of service providers, the "on the ground" situation for these seniors could be a barrier to support if help from the expected source did not materialize. The same study noted that black Caribbeans had a more flexible construct of their ideal support system and incorporated non-kin friends and church members into a mutual long-term network of emotional and practical support.

Other studies have documented substantial ethnic-based variation in familial and nonfamilial support systems. One of the most comprehensive is the research of John Weeks and Jose Cuellar in San Diego comparing the elderly in nine ethnic groups to an "Anglo," nonminority sample. Variance from "Anglo-White" norms was most prominent among "filiocentric" Asian and Pacific Island groups: Korean, Chinese, Japanese, Filipino, Samoan, and Guamanian. To cite the most dramatic case, 91 percent of elderly Korean parents were found to be living with their children, and over 80 percent said they would first turn to family members to satisfy all eight categories of need. By comparison, only 10 percent of the white aged surveyed were dwelling with their children, and fewer than one in 10 expected their family network to deal with all of their basic needs (Weeks and Cuellar 1981: 391; Weeks 1984: 101). Furthermore, important and substantial differences were noted in comparing the Asian groups among themselves. I could proceed with other examples showing the impact of the ethnic family in the life of the elderly, but I have already painted myself into a corner, if my intent was to argue against policy makers putting too much stress on ethnic support systems and the family.

The Limits of Ethnic Compensation

From where does my pessimism spring? As I interpret studies now available, the evidence indicates that the capacity of the ethnic family in dealing with the most difficult problems of its elderly members is limited. In the context of massive globalization and the rapid shift to a postindustrial economy, rural ethnic ideals such as in China (see Part III Zhang) are rapidly giving way to urban realities. For the United States even by the early 1980s, a majority of black elderly and 84 percent of Hispanic American elderly resided in urban areas. A case in point is the Hispanic American aged (see Part IV Rodríguez-Galán). Many writers have described the ideal value structure of this group as involving (1) profound family loyalty, (2) dominance of males, and (3) subordination of younger to older persons (Cuellar, Bastida, and Braccio 2004). Some late 20th-century survey studies did appear to confirm some elements of this ideal. Marjorie Cantor's triethnic elderly study (whites, Hispanics, and blacks) in New York showed that Hispanic elderly received the highest levels of assistance in terms of tasks of everyday living and the receiving of gifts (1979). Similarly, Vern Bengtson's Los Angeles study (mentioned earlier) showed considerably greater levels of family interactions for Mexican Americans than among whites and blacks (Bengtson and Morgan 1987).

However, other authors such as Gratton argue that much of the literature on the Chicano elderly is of limited utility due to a tendency to romanticize, distort, and stereotype critical elements of the Hispanic life experience (1987). Various studies, especially in the Southern California area, describe situations where, despite the continuing ideal of intense intergenerational family concern and the actual availability of a large kin network in the respective urban environment, obligations and expectations of kin support were radically declining (Hurtado et al. 1992). In San Diego, even though Hispanics who lived alone had four times more extended kin in the local area than whites, they were found to be less likely to turn to family members in times of need (Weeks and Cuellar 1981: 392). They preferred to "suffer in silence." The consequences of this, documented in a number of subsequent studies, can be high levels of alienation, low life satisfaction, and other psychological problems (Losada et al. 2006; Zlatar 2018).[4]

Part of the difficulty stems from unmet expectations of family interaction. In San Antonio, Texas, results from the largest longitudinal study of Mexican Americans have shown that those aged with greatest need for a caregiver are the most likely to report that one is not available. Number of children was not associated with reported caregiver availability among barrio Mexican Americans; many identify family other than spouse or children, or nonfamily, as perceived caregivers (see Angel and Angel 1998; Angel and Whitfield 2007).[5] Even in the previously mentioned studies in Los Angeles and New York, which showed high levels of family interaction and support for elderly Hispanic Americans, these aged were more likely to display symptoms of mental stress than either whites or blacks (see also Cuellar, Bastida, and Braccio 2004). In both locales, the main sources of concern were children and family as is also noted by Martinez for Cuban aged in Miami (Part IV Web Book). Some have even argued that the intense Hispanic pattern of female adult children giving care through extremes of self-sacrifice increases in a negative way the dependence and disability of elder kin, especially women (Losada et al. 2006).

This should be particularly disturbing to policy makers, as some studies have shown Hispanic American families to use community-based services at a very low rate, even compared to other ethnic groups surveyed (Torres 1999).

The Gender Dimension of Ethnic Kin Support

An interesting facet of research on Hispanic elderly is that the negative consequences of needs unmet through the kinship network more likely touch the lives of women than of men (Facio 1996). A study in San Antonio by Markides and Vernon (1984) corroborates this by showing that, of those elder Mexican Americans who maintained a very ethnically traditional sex role identity, only among women were there significant signs of psychological distress. They were found to have higher levels of depression than those older women who were more flexible in their gender role and less traditionally ethnic. This work, and another I will now discuss, suggest the unsettling proposition that "although it has been assumed that social relations are inherently satisfying and reduce the impact of life stress it appears that, at least in some instances, such social ties may enhance rather than reduce feelings of distress" (Cohler and Lieberman 1980: 462; see also Antonucci, Akiyama, and Lansford 1998). Bert Cohler and Morton Lieberman base this statement on their previously mentioned study of Irish, Polish, and Italian families in Chicago. These findings parallel those for the Hispanic elderly but are even more dramatic with regard to gender, ethnicity, and psychological stress. They state that among women "living in communities characterized by particularly dense social networks and complex patterns of reciprocity and obligations with adult offspring and other close relatives, there is a significant negative relationship between extent of social contact and both self-reported life satisfaction and psychological impairment" (Cohler 1983: 118). This relationship among a kin-keeping role, ethnic embeddedness, and personal maladjustment is strongest for Italian and Polish American elderly but did not hold in the Irish American case. Interestingly enough, for older men of Italian and Polish descent, the effect of ethnic embeddedness is opposite to that found for the women—they seem to benefit greatly in terms of adjustment to old age.

In the case of the Italian American aged, where this bipolar gender effect is most notable, one sees structural, gender-based differences in the nature of the social networks by which persons are linked to the local environment. Compared to females, older adult males, even after retirement, are active in a more diverse array of community-wide social contexts outside of the family unit (see also Part II Web Book Weibel-Orlando). In this case, men's social clubs have been a long-existing traditional arena where older Italian males could gain public status, recognition, and support. This opportunity to enter old age with vital connections both to lifelong friends in ethnic neighborhood associations and to relatives was seldom obtained by women in the Chicago study. Most of the ethnic elderly women here appeared very much encapsulated within the sphere of kin. As one might predict, it was found that older women who exhibited the lowest levels of psychological stress were those actively involved with friends as well as family (Cohler and Lieberman 1980: 454). That is, they had networks more like men in maintaining important social relations both inside and outside the realm of domestic/kin ties.

At a time when younger married women are entering the labor force, the traditional "kin-keeping" role of older women is often nervously mocked by the refrain, "How is it that one girl can bring up 10 kids, but 10 grown-up kids cannot care for one little old lady?" Analytically, I think the evidence is quite convincing that in terms of material and emotional exchange, women are most often left holding the short end of the stick—giving considerably more through informal kin support networks than they ever receive. The implications for policy makers are clear. Emphasizing reliance on certain ethnic family support networks as a primary service mechanism would be of benefit to aged males but may be a disaster for females, who make up the majority of older ethnic citizens.

The Limitations of Family Dependence

Recall the previously mentioned Korean aged in San Diego, where 9 in 10 lived with children and almost that number expected to depend on their families to provide for all of their needs. Yet one is surprised to read in John Weeks's analysis of his qualitative data that "among all the groups interviewed the Korean elders were least satisfied with their lives" (Weeks 1984: 190). Being poor, primarily female, lacking strong English language skills, and having been followers of their earlier migrating children, they were isolated and lonely within a small, exclusive, family life arena. Sadly, the vast majority found life hard, and one-quarter reported having contemplated suicide. In the transplanted context, generational relations ideally predicated on *hyo*, a Confucian word that means taking care of one's parents and ancestors, have become more a source of tension than a moral precept for successful aging. Studies in other urban areas have continued to corroborate the difficulties of older Korean immigrants, especially women, in terms of depression (Han et al. 2007).

Importantly, as the strength of filial piety declines in this immigrant population, recent research has indicated that elders having solid friendship networks and a daughter living nearby, rather than a son, are key factors in positive mental health (Roh et al. 2015; Oh, Ardelt, and Koropeckyj-Cox 2017). This observation is reinforced by broad studies of Asian Americans. For example, data from the 2015 Asian American Quality of Life Survey in Central Texas showed that those elders enmeshed in broad "diverse-integrated" networks, connecting family to friendship and organizational links, had the lowest levels of mental distress and the highest perception of being satisfied with their lives (Park et al. 2018).

Conclusion

My inspiration for writing this chapter was sparked many years ago and developed from a dramatic reaction to a coauthored paper I presented at an early national conference on ethnicity and aging in 1978. As the last speaker of the conference, I was supposed to present a survey of cultural variation and growing old in the United States. Toward the end of the talk, I told the audience that after reviewing the available data, I felt it would be a grave mistake for voluntary agencies to put too much pressure on ethnic families to take care of all of the needs of the elderly. At hearing this, the conference organizer, who also directed one of the types of agencies I was referring to, began to gag and actually stopped my presentation, claiming that time had run out. I knew I was on to something.

In this analysis, I am trying to be realistic about the capacity of ethnic family support systems to deal with problems of the aged (Pinquart and Sorensen 2005). My negative attitude may seem unusual given my previously published work in the areas of gerontology and mental health (Sokolovsky and Cohen 1987; Cohen and Sokolovsky 1989). In these writings, I often sought to demonstrate the benefits derived by poor inner-city elderly and released mental patients from the social networks in which their lives were enmeshed. After completing the longitudinal and applied extensions of these studies, I am certainly more pessimistic than I was in the late 1970s, when some of my publications helped feed "informal support systems" euphoria.

By following, over time, the lives of poor elderly residing in urban hotels and in analyzing an experimental intervention program, my colleagues and I readily noted the limits of informal supports. In the case of black women residents whose social networks were comparatively interconnected and contained complex exchanges, these informal structures were adequate for handling many acute health and resource problems. But longer-term difficulties could not be handled well by these intense networks. Especially in the case of alcoholism, attempts by intertwined social network members to provide support could lead to such levels of conflict that these tightly bound social matrices often disintegrated. An experimental project in one hotel to test the efficacy of interventions using informal support found that only about 20 percent of the attempts to use social networks to solve problems (such as obtaining food or getting to a hospital) were successful (Cohen, Adler, and Mintz 1983).

Admittedly, single-room occupancy environments are characterized by low levels of material resources, high personal alienation, and a lack of a sense of ethnic community affiliation. One should expect greater levels of success when applying network intervention techniques in strong ethnic communities. Examples include the *servidor* (community service broker) system in Southern California (Valle and Mendoza 1978) or the *Promotores de Salud* (lay health educators) system used in Texas (see Box IV.2). In these programs Hispanic American community members informally function as a catalyst for the utilization of services by Mexican American elders.

Most studies indicate that it is those services that John Colen (1979) calls nonmechanism specific—services that can be provided in diverse settings (such as counseling, information, and referral)—that are most appropriately handled through the social organization of the ethnic community (Colen 1982). Informal coping mechanisms, which are proportionally more evident in ethnic communities, can and should be creatively used as structures in which the fulfillment of human needs in late life are realizable (see Part IV Web Book Walton). These forms of ethnic compensation can be quite effective when coupled with nonfamilial systems of support such as respite and day-care programs and health promotion efforts. Such formal systems of care have been found to greatly enhance the capacity of families who seek to care personally for their elderly (Barresi and Stull 1993; Schulz and Eden 2016).

Perhaps the best example of this is On Lok Senior Health Services, a model of community-based long-term care developed during the 1970s in San Francisco to serve the poor and frail elderly, especially Chinese Americans. Drawing on the "day hospitals" developed in England, On Lok (Chinese for "peaceful, happy abode") created one of the nation's first adult day health centers and later expanded to develop a complete system of medical care, social support, and housing for nursing-home-eligible elderly (Kornblatt, Eng, and Hansen 2003). The On Lok model, although not initially designed to be focused on ethnic groups, uses multidisciplinary teams to assess how the culture and context of the elderly's circumstances can be used to actively integrate family resources with a broad range of formal services (Ikels 2007). This system has been quite successful in assisting ethnic families in their effort to keep even quite frail aged from spending their last years in an institutional setting. Many states are now using private foundation and federal funds in attempting to replicate the On Lok model through a program called PACE, Program of All-Inclusive Care for the Elderly (Waikar, Cappel and Meguess 2018).

The success of On Lok in San Francisco's Chinatown indicates that when generally dealing with such needs as long-term care, too much emphasis on the ethnic family would be a grave policy mistake. As was seen in the wake of the deinstitutionalization of mental health services, unrealistic or sentimental views of the strength of informal social resources can have the most unfortunate effects. More than three decades ago, gerontologists Marjorie Cantor and Virginia Little urged the development of a single system of social care incorporating informal and formal mechanisms of support for the elderly (1985). Although national political policy is not presently headed in that direction, it would be well worth the effort to harken to their plea. However, the assumption that public benefits for the needy aged merely supplement or displace family help continues to be used by political interest groups whose primary concern is minimizing social welfare costs and cutting programs that constitute the basis for economic well-being and care for the aged (see Part VI Polivka). I urge gerontologists interested in the issue of ethnicity not to become unwitting contributors to this destructive trend.

Notes

This chapter is adapted from "Ethnic Elders and the Limits of Family Support in a Globalizing World," in *The Cultural Context of Aging*, 3rd ed., edited by J. Sokolovsky (Santa Barbara, CA: ABC-CLIO, 2009).

1. Information about the show can be found at http://web.archive.org /web/20050305100957/http://www.channel4.com/news/2005/02/week_4/22 _asian.html.

2. The research objectives of this project are to draw attention to the needs of minority ethnic elders and thereby improve the provision of services for them. It will take place in the United Kingdom, Finland, France, Netherlands, Spain, Germany, Hungary, Bosnia-Herzegovina, Croatia, and Switzerland.

3. This research project, "Social Support of Caregivers for Dementia Patients," was supported by a National Institute on Aging Senior Research Service Award, IF33G05654-01.

4. It should be noted that other studies such as by Shurgot and Knight (2004) have not found the same kind of relation between acculturation and mental distress.

5. See the Hispanic EPESE (Established Populations for Epidemiologic Studies of the Elderly), which is the largest epidemiologic study of the health of Mexican American elderly: https://www.icpsr.umich.edu/icpsrweb/NACDA/studies /25041.

Bibliography

American Society on Aging. 2018. *Generations: Land of the Unequal? Economic, Social Inequality in an Aging America* 42(2).

Angel, J., and R. J. Angel. 1998. "Aging Trends—Mexican Americans in the Southwestern United States." *Journal of Cross-Cultural Gerontology* 13: 281–90.

Angel, J., and K. Whitfield, eds. 2007. *The Health of Aging Hispanics The Mexican-Origin Population*. New York: Springer.

Antonucci, T., H. Akiyama, and J. Lansford. 1998. "Negative Effects of Close Social Relations." *Family Relations* 47: 379–84.

Barresi, C. M., and D. Stull, eds. 1993. *Ethnic Elderly and Long-Term Care*. New York: Springer.

Bengtson, V., and L. Morgan. 1987. "Ethnicity and Aging: A Comparison of Three Ethnic Groups." In *Growing Old in Different Societies: Cross-Cultural Perspectives*, edited by J. Sokolovsky. Acton, MA: Copley.

Bonds, K., and K. Lyons. 2018. "Formal Service Use by African American Individuals with Dementia and Their Caregivers: An Integrative Review." *Journal of Gerontological Nursing* 44(6): 33–39.

Burton, L., and K. Whitfield. 2006. "Health, Aging, and America's Poor: Ethnographic Insights on Family Co-morbidity and Cumulative Disadvantage." In *Aging, Globalization and Inequality: The New Critical Gerontology*, edited by J. Baars, D. Dannefer, C. Phillipson and A. Walker. Amityville, NY: Baywood.

Cantor, M. 1979. "The Informal Support System of New York's Inner City Elderly: Is Ethnicity a Factor?" In *Ethnicity and Aging*, edited by D. Gelfand and A. Kutzik. New York: Springer.

Cantor, M., and V. Little. 1985. "Aging and Social Care." In *Handbook of Aging and the Social Sciences*, edited by R. Binstock and E. Shanas. New York: Van Nostrand Reinhold.

Cheung, C., and A. Yuihuen. 2006. "Impacts of Filial Piety on Preference for Kinship versus Public Care." *Journal of Community Psychology* 34(5): 617–34.

Cohen, C., A. Adler, and J. Mintz. 1983. "Assessing Social Network Interventions—Results of an Experimental Service Program Conducted in a Single-Room Occupancy Hotel." In *Rediscovering Self-Help: Professionals and Informal Care*, edited by E. Parker and D. Pancoast. Beverly Hills, CA: Sage.

Cohen, C., and J. Sokolovsky. 1989. *Old Men of the Bowery: Survival Strategies of the Homeless*. New York: Guilford.

Cohler, B. 1983. "Stress or Support: Relations between Older Women from Three European Ethnic Groups and Their Relatives." In *Minority Aging: Sociological and Social Psychological Issues*, edited by R. Manuel. Westport, CT: Greenwood.

Cohler, B., and M. Lieberman. 1980. "Social Relations and Mental Health." *Research on Aging* 2(4): 445–69.

Cohler, B., M. Lieberman, and L. Welch. 1977. *Social Relations and Interpersonal Resources among Middle-aged and Older Irish, Italian and Polish-American Men and Women*. Chicago: University of Chicago, Committee on Human Development.

Colen, J. 1979. "Critical Issues in the Development of Environmental Support Systems for the Aged." *Allied Health and Behavioral Sciences* 2(1): 74–90.

Colen, J. 1982. "Using Natural Helping Networks in Social Service Delivery Systems." In *Minority Aging*, edited by R. Manuel. Westport, CT: Greenwood.

Cool, L. 1981. "Ethnic Identity: A Source of Community Esteem for the Elderly." *Anthropological Quarterly* 54: 179–89.

Cuellar, I., E. Bastida, and S. Braccio. 2004. "Residency in the United States, Subjective Well-Being, and Depression in an Older Mexican-Origin Sample." *Journal of Aging and Health* 16: 447–66.

Cuellar, J., and J. Weeks. 1980. "Minority Elderly Americans: A Prototype for Area Agencies on Aging." Executive Summary. San Diego, CA: Allied Health Association.

Diaz, L. 2019. "The Role of Cultural and Family Values on Social Connectedness and Loneliness among Ethnic Minority Elders." *Clinical Gerontologist* 42(1): 114–26.

Dilworth-Anderson, P., B. Brummett, P. Goodwin, S. Williams, R. Wallace, R. Williams, and I. Siegler. 2005. "Effect of Race on Cultural Justifications for Caregiving." *Journal of Gerontology: Social Sciences* 60B(5): S257–S262.

Dilworth-Anderson, P., B. Gibson, and J. Burke. 2006. "Working with African American Families." In *Ethnicity and the Dementias*, 2nd ed., edited by G. Yeo and D. Gallagher-Thompson. New York: Routledge.

Facio, E. 1996. *Understanding Older Chicanas*. Thousand Oaks, CA: Sage.

Fandetti, D., and D. Gelfand. 1976. "Care of the Aged: Attitudes of White Ethnic Families." *Gerontologist* 16(6): 544–49.

Gratton, B. 1987. "Familism among the Black and Mexican-American Elderly: Myth or Reality." *Journal of Aging Studies* 1(1): 19–32.

Han, H-R. 2007. "Correlates of Depression in the Korean American Elderly: Focusing on Personal Resources of Social Support." *Journal of Cross-Cultural Gerontology* 22: 115–27.

Hayes, C., R. Kalish, and D. Guttmann, eds. 1986. *European-American Elderly: A Guide For Practice*. New York: Springer.

Hurtado, A-D., D. Hayes-Bautista, R. Valdez, and A. Hernandez. 1992. *Redefining California: Latino Social Engagement in a Multicultural Society*. Los Angeles: University of California, Chicano Studies Research Center.

Ikels, C. 2007. "Older Immigrants: Cultural Issues in Access to Health Care (Commentary)." In *Social Structures: Demographic Changes and the Well-being of Older Person*, edited by K. W. Schaie and P. Uhlenberg. New York: Springer.

Ip, D., C. Lui, and W. Chui. 2007. "Veiled Entrapment: A Study of Social Isolation of Older Chinese Migrants in Brisbane." *Ageing & Society* 27: 719–38.

Jett, K. 2002. "Making the Connection: Seeking and Receiving Help by Elderly African Americans." *Qualitative Health Research* 12(3): 373–87.

Johnson, C. 1995. "Cultural Diversity in Late-Life Families." In *Handbook of Aging and the Family*, edited by R. Blieszner and V. Bedford. Westport, CT: Greenwood.

Kanamoto, I. 2006. *Aging among Japanese American Immigrants*. New York: Routledge.

Kim, B., S. Park, and T. Antonucci. 2016. "Longitudinal Changes in Social Networks, Health and Wellbeing among Older Koreans." *Ageing & Society* 36: 9: 1915–36.

Kornblatt, S., C. Eng, and J. Hansen. 2003. "Cultural Awareness in Health and Social Services: The Experience of On Lok." *Generations* 26(3): 46–53.

Lan, P.-C. 2002. "Subcontracting Filial Piety: Elder Care in Ethnic Chinese Immigrant Families in California." *Journal of Family Issues* 23(7): 812–35.

Landers, S., E. Madigan, B. Leff, F. J. Rosati, B. A. McCann, R. Hornbake, R. MacMillan, et al. 2016. "The Future of Home Health Care: A Strategic

Framework for Optimizing Value." *Home Health Care Management and Practice* 28(4): 262–78.

Losada, A., G. Robinson, B. Shurgot, G. Knight, M. Marquez, I. Montorio, M. Izal, and M. Ruiz. 2006. "Cross-Cultural Study Comparing the Association of Familism with Burden and Depressive Symptoms in Two Samples of Hispanic Dementia Caregivers." *Aging and Mental Health* 10(1): 69–76.

Mackinnon, M., L. Gien, and D. Durst. 2001. "Silent Pain: Social Isolation and the Elderly Chinese in Canada." In *Elderly Chinese in Pacific Rim Countries*, edited by I. Chi, N. Chappell, and J. Lubben. Hong Kong: Hong Kong University Press.

Manuel, R., ed. 1982. *Minority Aging: Sociological and Social Psychological Issues.* Westport, CT: Greenwood.

Markides, K., and S. Vernon. 1984. "Aging, Sex-Role Orientation and Adjustment: A Three-Generations Study of Mexican Americans." *Journal of Gerontology* 39(5): 586–91.

Moriarty, J., and J. Butt. 2004. "Inequalities in Quality of Life among Older People from Different Ethnic Groups." *Ageing and Society* 24: 729–53.

Nazroo, J, J. Jackson, S. Karlsen, and M. Torres. 2007. "The Black Diaspora and Health Inequalities in the US and England: Does Where You Go and How You Get There Make a Difference?" *Sociology of Health & Illness* 29(6): 811–30.

Oh, H., M. Ardelt, and T. Koropeckyj-Cox. 2017. "Daughters' Generation: The Importance of Having Daughters Living Nearby for Older Korean Immigrants' Mental Health." *Journal of Family Issues* 38(16): 2329–45.

Park, N., Y. Jang, D. A. Chiriboga, and S. Chung. 2018. "Social Network Types, Health, and Well-Being of Older Asian Americans." *Aging and Mental Health* 23(11): 1569–77. https://www.tandfonline.com/doi/full/10.1080 /13607863.2018.1506751

Pinquart, M., and S. Sorensen. 2005. "Ethnic Differences in Stressors, Resources, and Psychological Outcomes of Family Caregiving: A Meta-analysis. *Gerontologist* 45: 99–106.

Rhee, S. 2017. "Acculturative Stress and Depressive Symptoms Among Korean Immigrant Elders Residing in Non-Korean Ethnic Enclaves." *Journal of Ethnic & Cultural Diversity in Social Work* 26(4): 347–65.

Roh, S., Y. S. Lee, K. H. Lee, T. Shibusawa, and G. J. Yoo. 2015. "Friends, Depressive Symptoms, and Life Satisfaction Among Older Korean Americans." *Journal of Immigrant and Minority Health* 17(4): 1091–97.

Schulz, R., and J. Eden. 2016. *Families Caring for an Aging America.* Washington, DC: National Academies.

Shurgot, G., and B. Knight. 2004. "Preliminary Study Investigating Acculturation, Cultural Values, and Psychological Distress in Latino Caregivers of Dementia Patients." *Journal of Mental Health and Aging* 10: 183–94.

Sokolovsky, J. 2006. "If Not Why Not: Synchronizing Qualitative and Quantitative Research in Studying the Elderly." In *Qualitative and Mixed Methods*

Research: Improving the Quality of Science and Addressing Health Disparities,* edited by L. Curry, R. Shield, and T. Wetle. Washington, DC: American Public Health Association.

Sokolovsky, J., and C. Cohen. 1987. "Networks as Adaptation: The Cultural Meaning of Being a 'Loner' Among the Inner City Elderly." In *Growing Old in Different Societies: Cross-Cultural Perspectives,* edited by J. Sokolovsky. Acton, MA: Copley.

Tate, N. 1983. "The Black Aging Experience." In *Aging in Minority Groups,* edited by R. McNeely and J. Colen. Beverly Hills, CA: Sage.

Torres, S. 1999. "Barriers to Mental-Health-Care Access Faced by Hispanic Elderly." In *Serving Minority Elders in the 21st Century,* edited by M. Wykle and A. Ford. New York: Springer.

Torres, S. 2006. "Making Sense of the Constructs of Successful Ageing: The Migrant Experience." In *Ageing and Diversity: Multiple Pathways and Cultural Migrations,* edited by S. Daatland and S. Biggs. Bristol, UK: Policy.

Torres, S. 2018. "Ethnicity, Race and Care in Older Age: What Can a Social Justice Framework Offer?" In *Ageing, Diversity and Equality: Social Justice Perspectives,* edited by S. Westwood. Abingdon, UK: Routledge.

Valle, R., and L. Mendoza. 1978. *The Elder Latino.* San Diego, CA: Campanile.

Victor, C, C. Dobbs, K. Gilhooly, and V. Burholt. 2019. "Exploring Intergenerational, Intra-generational and Transnational Patterns of Family Caring in Minority Ethnic Communities: The Example of England and Wales." *International Journal of Care and Caring* 3(1): 75–96.

Waikar, A., S. Cappel, and K. Meguess. 2018. "The Future of PACE Programs in the United States." *Frontiers in Management Research* 2(1): 14–19.

Warnes, A., K. Friedrich, L. Kelleher, and S. Torres, S. 2004. "The Diversity and Welfare of Older Migrants in Europe." *Ageing and Society* 24(3): 307–27.

Weeks, J. 1984. *Aging: Concepts and Social Issues.* Belmont, CA: Wadsworth.

Weeks, J., and J. Cuellar. 1981. "The Role of Family Members in the Helping Networks of Older People." *Gerontologist* 21: 338–94.

Wild, K., J. Wiles, and R. Allen. 2013. "Resilience: Thoughts on the Value of the Concept for Critical Gerontology." *Ageing & Society* 33: 137–58.

Wilmoth, J., and M. Silverstein, eds. 2017. *Later-Life Social Support and Service Provision in Diverse and Vulnerable Populations.* New York: Routledge.

Yee-Melichar, D., E. Takagi, and K. Lui. 2018. "Cultural and Ethnic Perspectives on Enhancing Resilience in Aging." In *Resilience in Aging,* edited by B. Resnick, L. Gwyther, and K. Roberto. New York: Springer.

Yu, L. 1992. "Intergenerational Transfer of Resources within Policy and Cultural Contexts." In *Caregiving Systems: Informal and Formal Helpers,* edited by S. Zarit, K. Perlin, and K. W. Schaie. Hillsdale, NJ: L. Erlbaum.

Zlatar, Z. 2018. "Subjective Cognitive Decline, Objective Cognition, and Depression in Older Hispanics Screened for Memory Impairment." *Journal of Alzheimer's Disease* 63(3): 949–56.

Zubair, M., and Norris, M. (2015). "Perspectives on Ageing, Later Life and Ethnicity: Ageing Research in Ethnic Minority Contexts." *Ageing and Society* 35(5): 897–916.

CHAPTER TWENTY-SEVEN

Detroit African Americans Fishing for Food and Heritage

Threats from Factory Toxins

Mark Luborsky and Andrea Sankar

Man is a complex being: he makes deserts bloom—and lakes die.
—Gil Scott-Heron, composer

We won't have a society if we destroy the environment.
—Margaret Mead

In distressed Detroit communities, catching and eating river fish supports both basic nutrition and cherished fishing traditions that serve to transmit historical family values for older African Americans. But these are threatened by toxic auto industry chemicals accumulating in the bodies of the fish and those who eat them. The chemicals have no taste, odor, or smell, yet are harmful. How can we protect lives by limiting exposure to toxins from eating fish without stifling a valuable cultural heritage? Anthropology offers pathways for confronting this complex public challenge by contributing insights into culture, the life course, and community.

Justine, Derrick, Keisha—Learning Life from Older African American Detroit Anglers

Justine, Derrick, and Keisha are anglers in the community of people who fish from the shoreline of the Detroit River because they lack the resources to use boats to catch fish out in deeper waters in the river or Lake St. Claire. For

Photo 27.1   Grandmother fishing patiently from the riverbank. (Hunter Photography)

them becoming and being an angler helps meet needs for survival, social participation, and life success. They share this situation with economically disadvantaged people in distressed urban settings across the United States such as Oakland, California; the Gulf Coast; and others around the globe. Readers should ask themselves how their own community is progressing to meet the 2030 United Nations targets for safe, sustainable water and food (United Nations 2015).

Teaching her granddaughter the deft cast needed to send her silvery line off the rocky shore to fish the river, Justine lectured to her: "My mom didn't

Photo 27.2   Older African American showing off the catfish she landed. (Robert Johnson Photography)

play that 'It's just men around the water.' No, no. She made sure I knew how to fish too."

For Derrick, a 62-year-old African American man, a wealth of wisdom was instilled through the shared angling community life. "Fishing was a place for my stepfather to tell me and my brothers and my cousins about the important things in life: how to handle different situations and how to take care of yourself and your family. You could talk about things you couldn't talk about with other people."

Keisha aged 60, perched on the rugged shore at Ford's legendary River Rouge factory, explained critical life lessons that learning the facts and art of fishing serves to instill:

> You got to bait your hook, and you got to throw it out there to catch what you want to catch. They use all kind of tackle here. They use minnows because they say the bass bite the minnows. Some don't bite worms. And my Daddy says, "You going to catch this and you going to catch that." How do he know? Because he been fishing. He knows what type of fish bites what hook. You take that lesson to use as a scenario to give my son. You bait your hook. Just like if you want a job, you gotta bait your hook. You gotta go out there and sell yourself, you'll get a job. It's what bait you will use. It can go past fishing. You can use fishing to teach kids a lesson.

Jasmine, Derrick, and Keisha rely on river fish as a lifeline of free food and a way to meet a spectrum of other needs for living in a distressed urban locale. Today fishing is a medium for instilling life lessons and family values, and valued as a place of respite in quiet, green nature and water away from impoverished neighborhoods. Deeply meaningful, each lure cast in the water links them to centuries of lifeways and experiences from Africa to a long history of enslavement, displacements, and freedoms, and rising and ebbing political-economic fortunes.

Today's minority anglers live in the strong current of these multiple traditions within the arc of modern industrialization in Detroit. Industrialization drew African Americans from a life of slavery and disadvantage in the U.S. South to work the new factories in the North that offered good pay. These factories required massive extractions and transportation of faraway natural resources including crude oil, minerals, and power to produce automobiles and other objects. The innovation of assembly-line manufacturing enabled the factories to disgorge massive quantities of consumer goods, but hazardous by-products were also created and cast into the environment. Circulating throughout the water, air, and soil were long-lasting poisons including mercury, PCBs, dioxins, and other wastes. Such harmful materials are a tangible heritage circulating through the bodies of Detroiters and their environment. Ultimately, industrialization created both the great benefits and the harms of our modern way of life; neither are shared equally across society.

These intertwining processes weave through the bodies of the Detroit River, its fish, and the people who eat them, and have pivotal roles and vulnerability of older persons. Detroit's case is instructive: these intertwined processes are the target of the UN 2030 Agenda for Sustainable Development Goals because they afflict many of the poorest communities along waterways in the United States and globally, spanning the Danube River in Germany, the Nile in Egypt, and the Yangtze in China (United Nations

General Assembly 2015). Similarly, a study among Alaska natives in a food-scarce environment with increasing toxic chemicals in salmon illustrated how officials were confronted with the need to set safety standards that limit salmon consumption in order to preserve the individual's health, yet this threatened the survival of tribal fishing traditions central to Inuit culture (Cassady 2010).

This chapter starts by sketching our research and discussing the anthropological lenses for conceptualizing aging, culture, and ethnicity needed for this work. Then we describe the two converging life cycles: the cycle leading to these older African American anglers coming to be angling along the Detroit River and its meaningfulness, and the historical cycle of modern industrial economic development that formerly enhanced and now erodes life. Finally, the chapter shows models for social actions, from grassroots groups to national programs, to address the dilemmas of promoting cultural survival and health for disadvantaged minority anglers.

Two Anthropology Studies: Fishing, Culture, and Action to Protect Health and Heritage

These stories are drawn from two projects designed to promote urban health in Detroit. The first study, "Bio-Monitoring of Persistent Toxic Substances in Michigan Urban Fish-Eaters," engaged university researchers, students, community members, and government and public stakeholders. It documented fish consumption practices and consequences among urban shoreline anglers along the Detroit River. Ethnographic methods were used to discover locally defined fishing spots, "venues" along the entire 28 miles of riverbank including the few official city piers, abandoned factory sites, abandoned parks, and street ends. Systematic observations were used to create a random sample (by fishing site, days, and times) of 774 anglers to learn why and how they fished and its meaningfulness. Next, randomly selected shoreline anglers were recruited who were willing to provide blood and urine samples to assess the toxic industrial chemical levels in their bodies. Results showed minorities burdened by disproportionately high levels of harmful mercury, PCBs, and dioxins, heightening the risk for physical and cognitive harm to the anglers, children, and families who shared the catch (Krabbenhoft, Manenete, and Kashian 2018).

A second project, "Improving Community Awareness of Detroit River Fish Consumption Guidelines," was a community action study to examine awareness of fish-eating advisories and evaluate a new strategy for communicating risks and encouraging behavior change. This included a novel "River Walkers" program (Photo 27.3) using two-person teams of African Americans, each with a retiree and a high school student, to walk the riverside venues and stop to discuss safe fish catching and eating practices (Erb Family Foundation 2019). "Not only do we hand out pamphlets, but we talk to the people.

I have been fishing out there for 60 years. I feel good to come back here and inform people about . . . the nice fish to catch and eat and which is not good for the health of their family" (retired city worker).

Surveys we conducted showed these in-person River Walker teams greatly improved anglers' knowledge and practices in how to safely choose, clean and cook fish compared to the posted public signs or media ads (Krabben-hoft, Manenete and Kashian 2018). Ethnographic shoreline-to-table case study interviews were done in-home to observe actual practices in cooking and cleaning of fish and how these did or did not conform to the safe fish-eating advisory signs posted along the shoreline. They also looked at the role of fish in the diet, the sharing of fish through social networks, and cultural preferences for types of fish and cooking. Such data on community values helped identify misunderstandings and guide more effective health programs to promote safer fish eating.

Anthropological Lens into Culture and Ethnicity for Studying Aging

Anthropologists seek to provide a life course view of aging as a life lived through time in specific places (Hareven 1994; Luborsky and McMullen 1999). A life course perspective illuminates the process of discovering cre-ativity and change to one's self, local community, and society in contrast to a narrow view of aging as a predetermined fixed chronological and social path (Sokolovsky 2009, Part V).

Culture is not a static homogenous set of values, identities, and preferred foods. Rather, following Renato Rosaldo (1993) we argue it is more produc-tively understood as a busy intersection of multiple heritages, histories, social forces, and value systems that emerge on the ground in social life and are in hierarchical relationship to one another. This view is not to suggest there are no shared core values. Rather, this view provides a rich understanding of lives lived in a setting as an assemblage of "cultures, peoples, places, objects, ideas, dreams, and desires [that] intersect and create dialogues, encounters, fusions, and identities" (Behar 2012).

Using this lens for culture, the river connects anglers in oceans of contested and several valued sites of life. It starts in Africa, then carries through struggles of peoples enslaved and their descendants in the Americas, to the hopes and harms of migrant lives in Detroit, and today's aftermath of that city's sociopo-litical upheavals and urban decay now relegated to the margins by gentrifica-tion. Some argue that lifetimes and water intertwine as one. We might see the life of the older anglers and the water itself of the Detroit River as a movement of "disturbance" in water, "life in the wake as living the history and present of terror, from slavery to the present . . . including the afterlife of colonization in the Americas and contemporary iterations of racial capitalism" (Sharpe 2016).

Photo 27.3   Our project "River Walkers" intergenerational outreach teams visit riverside fishing venues to promote the "3Cs": what to catch and how to clean and cook fish for safe eating. (Robert Johnson Photography)

Ethnicity is conceptualized in two modes. First, as a public social category, ethnicity is not a historically frozen, predefined social trait or identity having the same fixed meaning and relevance in every situation or at differing times in life. Instead, ethnicity is something fluid, historical, and contingent according to how that trait or identity situates the person in a particular community or era (Luborsky and Rubinstein 1987; Part IV Sokolovsky). For example, during World War II US citizens with Japanese origins faced harsh public attention, while today very different attitudes exist. Second, at the individual level, from a life course perspective ethnicity is malleable in the sense that individuals make their own choice of how salient it is to deploy, interpret, and present it to others in different situations. At an early adult life stage, it may be downplayed to help fit into a social group, yet later in life in widowhood ethnicity may become a highly desired source of group identity. So too, depending on historical period, one may seek to submerge and hide one's ethnicity. For example, today's older African Americans have experienced major shifts in public attitudes, self-defined labels and salience, and meanings over their lifetimes.

How Did Older African Americans Become Detroit Shoreline Anglers?

We next describe the less recognized origins and meanings of fishing for African Americans across time and places, and then note how anglers today find it a source for creativity and resilience in the face of hardships in a changing urban environment.

Circulation of Life Histories and Experiences of a People through Times and Places

Justine, Derrick, and Keisha were drawn to Detroit's riverbanks by a shared history of tortuous passages during two global streams of peoples. In the first great passage were millions of ancestors enslaved from Africa's west coast roughly 250 years ago in the slave trade, taken to the southern United States to work plantations. Those who survived, among the millions taken, brought a strong heritage of fishing.

Second, people in the Great Migration north from the southern United States from the early 1900s to 1970s sought opportunities and work that fed the labor needs of urban industrialization, including the rise of Detroit's auto plants. This African American population movement drew over 6 million persons to relocate from the rural South to urban northern United States, arguably our nation's largest internal population movement for a better social and economic life (Lemann 2011). Layers of significance to the fishing heritage developed in the move north. Wilkerson poignantly traces the diverse family and personal successes and tragedies of those attempting the transition from south to north (2010). A protracted journey of uncertainty and deprivation, it left profound multigenerational effects adding to the hard-ships of life for minorities today.

Fishing has an almost iconic place in African American life stemming from preslavery and enslaved times. Blount recounts the history of how African slaves' traditional expertise in fishing was critical to ensuring the survival of the first white colonialists in Georgia and South Carolina, who arrived with minimal knowledge about farming and none about fishing (2000). Fishing was one of the only sources of individual agency permitted for male slaves in the antebellum South (Giltner 2008). Enslaved people were permitted to keep the fish they caught to feed their families. In contrast, the slave owners took half of the food they grew in their personal kitchen gardens as a tithe. Expertise in fishing and hunting helped sustain freed slaves after the Civil War. Fishing remained a key resource after access to guns, and hence hunting, was forbidden under Jim Crow laws (Giltner 2008).

Circulation of Life Histories of Toxic Chemicals and Urban Industrial Development

Detroit, labeled the "Arsenal of Democracy" in World War II for its major role in producing war-related materials, was a major center of industrial innovation and production for much of the 20th century. A landing spot in the Great Migration from the South, in Detroit, African Americans helped account for a 110 percent population surge from 1910 to 1920. In Detroit, African Americans who moved to participate in the wartime economy comprised more than half of the new hires and found jobs for both men and women (Foote, Whatley, and Wright 2003). The freedoms and benefits of these well-paying industrial jobs were considerable (Becker 1971). These benefits diminished when the productivity and economic success of Detroit faltered as it failed to adapt to the challenges posed by the Japanese and European auto industries in the 1970s (Sugrue 2014). Its decline continued as Detroit became the first major American city to declare bankruptcy in 2013. Along with a collapse of city services, economy, and morale, the lengthy river shoreline became littered with abandoned sites, unwelcoming trash-strewn zones, and sites of crime.

Detroit's industries, in line with other early industrial cities, left legacies of pollutants in the environment. Today's recycling ethos misses the big picture. These toxins came from the entire cycle of production, from trucks and trains transporting raw materials, complex demands of generating energy for manufacturing, and movement of finished products. The by-products included heavy metals and toxic chemicals that not only persist in the soil, water, and buildings but also accumulate and become more concentrated as they move up the food chain from microorganisms and plants into larger and larger fish (Figure 27.1). Despite successful efforts made possible by the Clean Water Act 1972 to clean up the Detroit River, river sediment remains the

Figure 27.1   Toxic chemicals circulate from factories into air and water, enter the food chain accumulating in plants and insects eaten by small fish, moving into bigger fish, and then into anglers and families.

repository of dangerous toxic chemicals: mercury, PCBs, and dioxin.[1] The water that flows above the bottom has become significantly cleaner, to the point that swimming beaches and water recreation are encouraged. Yet, physical and mental health problems may result from ingesting these contaminants. People who eat fish caught from the shoreline typically have limited means to deal with these hazards.

While the material and social legacies of Detroit's industrial toxins are distributed across the city, unequal harms flow along social structural patterns. Inequalities are manifest in residential patterns, food availability, access to employment, and community resources and conditions. Those older minority anglers who eat fish caught along the river shoreline are most at risk for ingesting the toxic chemicals contained in the bodies of fish. The species of fish that were most highly polluted, bottom feeders such as catfish and drum, are most readily available along the shoreline. Shoreline anglers tended to be those who lacked funds to purchase or rent a boat to fish offshore, and in many cases were subsistence anglers. People most harmed by the economic downturn, the subsistence anglers, were also those most exposed to the toxic legacies of industrial pollution. Devastatingly, the most popular fish such as walleye, catfish, bass, and northern pike carry the highest levels of toxins. Mercury can harm the brain, nervous system, and kidneys; PCBs and dioxin are known carcinogens. Fetuses, children, older adults, and those with preexisting health conditions are the most at risk.

Public health and cultural heritage preservation goals can often conflict. Citizens and officials seeking to help must find ways not to discourage and stigmatize people who depend on the fish and cherish the cultural fishing traditions, but to act positively to promote a just, equitable life of well-being and health in the community.

Continuity of Creating Life Meanings, Traditions, Family, and Community

Fishing in Detroit provides more than just food. It builds life skills, family, and community. Detroiters learn fishing from parents and neighbors and then teach their children, thus weaving together lives across generations. The storylines of individual lifetimes, the collective African American story, and the city's industrial development shape ways of life and health.

In our study moral themes of creation and stewardship emerged as central meanings for being and becoming an angler. The meanings for fishing among participants include that it builds life skills and character, connects the generations, nourishes community and environment, and provides wisdom about life and aging. The voices of older African Americans fishing the Detroit River express these thematic guiding moral dimensions in their own words, as follows.

Fishing Builds Character and Life Skills

Fundamental skills and attitudes are instilled by learning to become and continuing to be a "good" fisherman. It uniquely offers important capabilities for surviving and thriving, particularly as a minority person in disadvantaged social settings and resource-poor environments. Participants expressed this theme in several ways.

> Fishing gives you a certain determination not to give up. Just because the fishing is bad, it doesn't mean that in an hour it won't improve. (66-year-old widower)
>
> My kids have used the inspiration from fishing on school projects and job interviews. . . . My kids teach their friends. It's something that, you know, the simplest thing and it's funny. How to tie a knot. I would sit here with a piece of line when I was a kid, and it would keep me busy for hours. And I wouldn't give up until I got that knot just right. Now, any of those knots, I can tie them in five seconds, and I teach other people. If the fishing is boring, bring a book. Now I am encouraging them to fish, but I am also encouraging them to read. (44-year-old man)

Fishing teaches kids that sometimes you have to hurry up and wait. Kids have to learn that you don't get everything you want right when you want it. (56-year-old man)

Fishing helps you learn to be resourceful. When I was in Iraq out in the field, I would take a paper clip to make a hook, dig for worms in the ground, and use some of my radio cables to drop a line in and catch some fish if we were near a river. (56-year-old man)

Fishing teaches patience, which is important in life because you have to understand that everyone is different. You can't push your views on other people. If you and I disagree, I have to have the patience to better understand where you're coming from. (38-year-old man)

Fishing Connects Lives across Generations

Beyond everyday life and current situations, fishing is a rich resource for creating continuity and sustainability across family and community time.

I learned to fish from my father and uncle. When I got older, my father would have me sitting in the rain and thunder to fish with him to fish with his pole. (60-year-old man)

I give about 90 percent of what I catch away. When I am downtown at the river, I give my fish away to the tourists. I gave a bass to a Ukrainian. He went back home and probably said, "I went to Detroit, and they gave me a fish!" (38-year-old man)

My kids know most of the fishermen by name and face. They fish right next to grown men, and it gives them a sense of manhood. And, they're catching fish. Last week I was fishing with my 17-year-old; he was right along next to me fishing with me, and we had our sidebar conversations going on. And talking about how the fish were biting, and how he rigged his line up to be able to catch more fish. It's been one of those experiences for him where the memories will stay long after I'm gone. He'll have the memories, "Oh, I miss my dad. I'm glad I inherited his fishing stuff, but I didn't want it this way." He has that sense of this is something that was passed on to me by my dad. And what is he gonna do? He's gonna pass it on to his kids. And his kids to their kids. It's a good thing to pass down. (44-year-old man)

Nourishing Community and Environment

The net cast by fishing spreads beyond the anglers and their families. It provides resources that integrate them more widely in the city. The sharing of fish provides them an opportunity to give and be valued as providers, rather than only receivers of a benefit.

I keep any fish I catch. But sometimes I will give fish to other people if they didn't catch anything, or I give fish to someone at church if I know they are struggling. (54-year-old man)

We always give people fish if they need it. However, we try to focus on teaching people how to fish. We teach everyone who wants to learn, even women and children. When we teach people how to fish, we are teaching the next generation. (60-year-old man)

We always give people fish if they need it: to neighbors, to my family, to people who come down here looking for something to eat. (60-year-old man)

Wisdom of Life and Aging

Philosophies about how to get along with others, how to endure hardships in order to succeed in life, and how to wisely adapt to your changing circumstances are fostered and shared through fishing on the river shoreline.

When you fish with other people, especially in close proximity, you have to consider other people. You have to know where to cast your line and to avoid getting tangled. (59-year-old man)

We all have competition down here, a friendly competition. So we can leave the fishing hole and say today I am the top dog—but tomorrow it might be someone else. (38-year-old man)

You got to bait your hook, and you got to throw it out there to catch what you want to catch. They use all kind of tackle here. They use minnows because they say the bass bite the minnows. Some don't bite worms. I might put a worm on my hook. And my daddy say, "You going to catch this and you going to catch that." How do he know? Because he been fishing. He know what type of fish bites what hook. You take that lesson if you want to use it as a scenario to give my son an example. You bait your hook. Just like if you want a job, you gotta bait your hook. You gotta go out there and sell yourself, you'll get a job. It's what bait you will use. It can go past fishing. You can use fishing to teach kids a lesson. (45-year-old woman)

Fishing has helped me teach my son a lot. He's 16. I told him that he must have a lot of trust and patience with his coach—if the coach is wrong or his philosophy is wrong, he must still go out and do it. At the same time, I have told him you can't believe everything everyone tells you in life. Just like he has learned down here fishing. He is real big on listening. He knows he doesn't know everything. (38-year-old man)

Creative and Resilient Aging

Grassroots Action: The "River Rats" Fishing Association

You can pray until you faint, but if you don't get up and try to do something, God is not going to put it in your lap.

—Fannie Lou Hamer, Indianola, Mississippi, 1964

Photo 27.4 Grassroots community groups, such as the "Detroit River Rats," host annual fish roasts sharing their catch freely, repairing and enlivening formerly abandoned and decrepit river banks. (Robert Johnson Photography)

Grassroots community groups emerged to take responsibility for maintaining some Detroit River fishing venues when the city ended services in the midst of budget crises in the 1990s. Older anglers took on key activist roles.

The local fishing association, also known by their self-chosen name, the Detroit River Rats, is a good example of such a group (Photo 27.4). This informal association of expert anglers dates to 1990 when a group of friends who grew up near the park returned and adopted the neglected park strewn with litter and drug paraphernalia. They dug in to reclaim it as their spot to share a passion for fishing and relaxing together. Today, there are over 30 members. The positive impact they have had along the riverside in this park is visible. Bringing their own tools, they mow grass, pick up trash, and haul it away to keep the park clean. Working together, they improve safety and order in the park so that people of all ages can enjoy it.

The River Rats, renowned as experts at filleting fish according to the health guidelines, do this for a small fee and freely teach others (Photo 27.5). They share the fish readily with those who are hungry.

By persistently lobbying City Hall and other agencies, they were eventually able to gain needed improvements for Mariner's Park, which included such things as guardrails with fishing pole holders, benches, and picnic tables. Today, the struggle continues, and lack of bathrooms and drinking water is the next target.

These activities keep food, life skills, and positive values circulating in the community and encourage new generations to appreciate the power of the river to improve their own lives and those of their communities. At the same

Photo 27.5   Old anglers fillet fish for free and teach how to clean fish to reduce the level of harmful chemicals. (Robert Johnson Photography)

Photo 27.6   Annual memorial services celebrate past friends and family and reaffirm community ties today. (Robert Johnson Photography)

time, local histories are re-created and kept alive over the years. Photo 27.6 shows the annual remembrance day to celebrate the lives and deaths of community members, reaffirm their continuity in the heart and soul of the group, and ensure the values and memories of their life are passed on to younger generations.

Discussion and Future Directions

In closing, we would like to indicate how our data and anthropological approach to ethnicity, aging, and culture may be relevant to other groups. The approach presented here provides a contextualized life course approach to ethnicity and aging, one that calls for attention to groups as embedded in unfolding multiple timeliness, places, and shifting social positions with other groups. It is not a static, fixed trait with the same meaning in all contexts. This approach offers a robust framework for socially engaged scholars seeking to engage with communities who face threats to a meaningful and healthy life. Context does matter. Our approach can reveal new avenues for change that are consonant with community beliefs, practices, and experiences. The neglect of these by traditional social policy and health programs tends to blunt their effectiveness by being overly decontextualized and simplistic. For example, it helps to surface and clarify the otherwise submerged conundrum posed at the start—human-made industrial toxins disproportionately harm older minority ethnic anglers in distressed communities and pose the value dilemma of preserving individual physical health versus collective cultural heritage.

Our approach using an anthropological life course perspective situated in multiple social and historical contexts suggests that these dimensions may be common to many minority and ethnic groups. This was illustrated by today's older African American anglers fishing in the Detroit River. They are also part of a larger body of interwoven rivers of peoples and heritages—valued and imposed—starting from enslavement with the flow of peoples out from Africa into new ways of plantation life and subjugation the rural U.S. South. The river continued later in the Great Migration when they shifted from rural spaces and places in search of new opportunities offered by industrialization in northern cities. This flow carried with it deep family traditions and shared experiences. These currents infused more recent life changes due to industrial decline and disadvantage into lives lived on the margins of distressed urban areas. Today's older African American anglers stand on the shoreline of a historical transformation due to gentrification that yet again threatens the lands and ways of life of their community. Further, the case of Detroit riverside African American anglers can be good to think with, when you study other questions. For example, elders invest in creating urban gardens similarly to reshape often abandoned and hazardous regions into green spaces fostering community life and needed produce in distressed and disenfranchised neighborhoods (Part V Sokolovsky). The angler's case exemplifies our argument that culture is most powerfully conceptualized, following Renato Rosaldo (1993), like a busy intersection of multiple heritages, histories, and value systems in a specific place and with differing power relationships to each other.

At the same time, we caution that the lens for conceptualizing ethnicity may have limits when applied to African Americans. In comparison to some other ethnic identities, such as elderly Italian, Irish, and Jewish widowers, African Americans' societal position, symbolic meanings, and opportunities remain less fluid across time as has the experience and meaning of being African American (Luborsky and Rubinstein 1987). The slow pace of acceptance in America for some ethnic groups serves to limit social receptivity for creative identity reworking and transformations that other groups achieved by working to destigmatize and revitalize traditional values, meanings, and practices. In brief, we need to raise our alertness to the particulars of each group, how it exists in specific times, places, and wider community power structures, to grasp the relevance and experience of aging as an ethnic person. To conclude, in light of the approach and data discussed here, we argue that studies of aging and ethnicity need to envision ethnicity as both a powerful, stable feature and as a fluid resource by which individuals and groups creatively reinvent and transform social and personal identity, self, and community. The approach here offers a richer understanding of aging and ethnicity building from a culturally contextualized and life course perspective, which is needed to guide efforts to improve the life of older persons in distressed urban environments.

Acknowledgments

Fred A. and Barbara M. Erb Family Foundation, Donna Kashian, Sherylyn Briller, Ken Stilwell, Robert Johnson. This study was conducted under IRB #058012B3E.

Note

1. This toxic legacy resides in the river mud where the plants on which fish feed grow.

Bibliography

Becker, G. 1971. *The Economics of Discrimination*. Chicago: University of Chicago Press.

Behar, R. 2012. "What Renato Rosaldo Gave Us." *Aztlán: A Journal of Chicano Studies* 37(1): 205–11.

Blount, B. 2000. "Coastal Refugees: Marginalization of African-Americans in Marine Fisheries of Georgia." *Urban Anthropology and Studies of Cultural Systems and World Economic Development* 29(3): 285–313.

Cassady, J. 2010. "State Calculations of Cultural Survival in Environmental Risk Assessment: Consequences for Alaska Natives." *Medical Anthropology Quarterly* 24(4): 451–71.

Erb Family Foundation, Fred A. and Barbara M. 2019. "Eat Safe Fish From the Detroit River—Wayne State University River Walkers Program." www.erbff.org/grants/wayne-state-university-riverwalkers-progam/.

Foote, C., W. Whatley, and G. Wright. 2003. "Arbitraging a Discriminatory Labor Market: Black Workers at the Ford Motor Company, 1918–1947." *Journal of Labor Economics* 21(3): 493–532.

Giltner, S. 2008. *Hunting and Fishing in the New South: Black Labor and White Leisure after the Civil War.* Baltimore, MD: Johns Hopkins University Press.

Hareven, T. 1994. "Aging and Generational Relations: A Historical and Life Course Perspective." *Annual Review of Sociology* 20: 437–61.

Krabbenhoft, C., S. Manenete, and S. D. Kashian. 2018. "Improving the Conscious Consumption of Fish Through an Educational Campaign on the Detroit River (Michigan, USA)." Preprints 2018120230. doi: 10.20944/preprints201812.0230.v1.

Lemann, N. 2011. *The Promised Land: The Great Black Migration and How It Changed America.* New York: Random House.

Luborsky, M., and C. McMullen. 1999. "Culture and Aging," In *Gerontology: An Interdisciplinary Perspective*, edited by J. Cavanaugh and S. Whitebourne. New York: Oxford University Press.

Luborsky, M., and R. Rubinstein. 1987. "Ethnicity and Lifetimes: Self Concepts and Situational Contexts of Ethnic Identity in Late Life." In *Ethnic Dimensions of Aging*, edited by D. Gelfand and D. Barresi. New York: Springer.

Rosaldo, R. 1993. *Culture & Truth: The Remaking of Social Analysis.* Boston: Beacon.

Sharpe, C. 2016. *In the Wake: On Blackness and Being.* Durham, NC: Duke University Press.

Sokolovsky, J. 2009. "Introduction: Human Maturity and Global Aging in Cultural Context." In *The Cultural Context of Aging: Worldwide Perspectives*, 3rd ed., edited by J. Sokolovsky, xv–xxxv. Westport, CT: Praeger.

Sugrue, T. 2014. *The Origins of the Urban Crisis: Race and Inequality in Postwar Detroit.* Princeton, NJ: Princeton University Press.

United Nations General Assembly. 2015. *Transforming Our World: The 2030 Agenda for Sustainable Development.* UN Doc. A/70/L.1. https://sustainabledevelopment.un.org/.

Wilkerson, I. 2010. *The Warmth of Other Suns: The Epic Story of America's Great Migration.* New York: Random House.

CHAPTER TWENTY-EIGHT

Web Book: *Fare insieme*

Making and Doing Things Together in Milan

Shireen Walton

Available at: http://www.culturalcontextofaging.com/webbook-walton

This chapter is adapted from a blog submitted by a researcher in the global ASSA project (see Box 01.1) focusing on how older Italian women in Milan use the cultural space of a multicultural center to connect Middle Eastern migrants to their new migrant lives.

CHAPTER TWENTY-NINE

"Demasiado fuerte" (Too Tough)

Puerto Rican Great-Grandmothers Discuss Familismo and Grandmothering in the U.S. Mainland

Marta Rodríguez-Galán

There was sometimes quite a bit of traffic when I visited grandmothers at their homes. Adult children were dropping off or picking up grandchildren and great-grandchildren; neighbors visited with errands or messages, and other family and friends were calling on their cell phones. At times, grandmothers would have to cut a conversation short to continue the interview, stating for example, "I am doing an interview," or "I will call you later." To be sure, my presence did not seem much out of the ordinary; in fact, like the other visitors, I too felt welcomed by the grandmothers' hospitality. Almost invariably, when adult children came into the house they asked for their mother's benediction or *bendición*, a show of respect towards elders in the family that is commonly observed among Puerto Ricans and other Spanish-speaking communities. Doña Marisol describes for me what a beautiful thing it is to be asked and be able to send your blessings to the younger generations in the family. She then paused and, with a heartfelt chuckle, recalled her attempts at teaching all her grandchildren to do the same, as well as their clumsy attempts at Spanish pronunciation. Very often some of the grandchildren do not know enough Spanish; however, teaching them *bendición* and its meaning is probably the most important lesson grandmothers can impart about their heritage. According to this Puerto Rican tradition, a younger family member must always greet older family members by asking them for their blessings, both at the beginning of the encounter and before leaving. For example, a grandchild would say "Bendición, abuela" (Your blessings, grandmother), to which the grandmother would respond "Que Dios te bendiga" (May God bless you). Failure to observe this ritual might be seen as a serious affront to the honor and authority of elders in the family, signaling the loss of one's cultural roots.

In this chapter, I examine how the ideology of *familismo*[1] (a strong sense of family) influences Puerto Rican great-grandmothers' child-rearing experiences on the U.S. mainland within the sociocultural context of low-income neighborhoods. A significant number of studies frame the health of Latina grandmothers within a medical paradigm to examine the health impact of the custodial role on the caregiver (Goodman and Silverstein 2002, 2005, 2006). Some studies, on the other hand, provide a more general profile of various Hispanic subgroups (Fuller-Thomson and Minkler 2007; Fuller-Thompson, Minkler, and Driver 2007; Goodman and Rao 2007). However, to my knowledge, no study to date has explored the ideology of *familismo* in relation to the child-rearing practices employed by custodial Latina grandmothers. Moreover, two larger unexplored questions remain: What cultural scripts do Latina women invoke in their decision to care for grandchildren and great-grandchildren? How do these scripts intersect with the social and cultural context of low-income U.S. urban neighborhoods? Finally, a life course approach is also conspicuously absent in the literature, a gap that further hinders our understanding of how the custodial grandmother role fits within these women's own life histories.

Against this backdrop, for this chapter, I analyze the *familismo* ideology expressed within the life course narratives of grandmothers and great grandmothers raising children. I ground my discussion primarily in two ethnographic vignettes from my research on Puerto Rican grandmothers raising grandchildren, one in Boston, Massachusetts, and the second in Rochester, New York. The aim of my larger study is to present an in-depth qualitative portrait of Puerto Rican custodial grandmothers, such as how they define and negotiate this role, its reported psychosocial effect, and the physical and social context of caregiving. To date, I have completed 14 life-history interviews with grandmothers in Boston and five in Rochester. I used semistructured ethnographic interviews, field notes, and observed and recorded details about the availability and quality of services, use of public spaces, and characteristics and type of housing where grandmothers live. In the following sections, I discuss my probing of *familismo* and child-rearing experiences.

For custodial Puerto Rican grandmothers, a strong orientation towards *la familia* is undeniable, as in feeling obligations for caregiving towards children, grandchildren, parents, and other family members; knowing one's relatives; and keeping in contact with them. These women firmly believe that their grandchildren benefit from *familismo*, and they attempt to instill in them this ideology. Consistent with findings in other studies on Latina grandmothers (Goodman and Silverstein 2002), the majority of the women with whom I spoke were primary caregivers for grandchildren and even great-grandchildren, but they often received some form of support from various family members—although it was not uncommon to find grandmothers who reported feeling unsupported. Moreover, these women did not know formal support services for grandmothers or skip-generation families were available in Boston. However, practically all of them were aware of Latino advocacy nonprofit organizations. Some reported having taken part in a support group for depression, but only one bilingual woman had participated in an English language support group for custodial grandmothers. On the other hand, family support was common, and it normally included a daughter, son, or niece whom they described as being responsible, very involved, and a good role model for their grandchildren; sometimes *comadres* (co-mothers) and other relatives offered help. Among other services, these family members (particularly daughters) helped with money or gifts; selecting more fashionable clothing for their children; providing rides to movies, parks, or other outings; helping them to obtain the services they needed; and giving them some respite during weekends and vacations. Sometimes, the mother or father of the grandchild also helped financially or otherwise, but co-parental support from their children was less reliable because they were usually still struggling with the personal problems that forced them to relinquish primary responsibility for their children in the first place.

In these women's view though, grandmothers are not all made equal. In fact they are quick to point out that many people they know refuse to accept responsibility for their grandchildren as a family obligation or to provide childcare, and if they do, they demand a fee for their services—something that is seen as a foreign concept to many Puerto Rican grandmothers. Several of my interviewees described these other women as just wanting to enjoy their own lives and adhering to the motto "Si tú pares, tú crías" (if you give birth, you give care). In other words, they view these other women as espousing a more nuclear and less familistic version of the family, where the biological parents are seen as exclusively responsible for child-rearing.

Puerto Rican grandmothers who are custodial or primary caregivers for grandchildren and great-grandchildren often describe themselves as more familistic and domestically oriented in comparison to others. In their narratives, they often allude to a dichotomous and highly gendered distinction of social life as split between *la casa* (the home) and *la calle* (the street). Typically, men and women who acquire vices are drawn to the streets; they regularly socialize and party with friends outside the home and are less responsible and family oriented. To illustrate this point, one of my interviewees noted that adolescents are very trusting of people and warns her granddaughter about the perils of the streets, telling her, "There are many good people, but you are not going to find them in the streets."

In order to teach children right from wrong, many women admit to being very strict or *fuerte* when raising their own children and even resorting to the use of physical punishment, something that in their view is also a more traditional aspect of child-rearing. In this regard, the research literature on parenting styles and child discipline in Latino families is scarce and the results somewhat contradictory. For example, it is not clear whether Hispanics use corporal punishment more often than Anglos, and there may be significant differences across various Hispanic subgroups (Cardona, Nicholson, and Fox 2000; Calzada and Eyberg 2002). Therefore, it would be unfair to paint a picture of grandmothers or Latina mothers in general as more prone to use spanking or other corporal disciplinary methods based on my small sample. However, community members and scholars agree that use of discipline is often misconstrued as child abuse in the United States (Fontes 2002). This, in fact, was a common fear expressed by several of the women whom I interviewed. Some of them now expressed regrets over their use of corporal punishment but justified such action, acknowledging that they were raised in much the same way and that it helped them to grow into respectful and responsible adults. Nonetheless, as young mothers they struggled with commanding the same *respeto* (respect) from their children, as well as with keeping them off the streets in the low-income neighborhoods where they resided. It is worth noting that the concept of respect used here, closely connected to *familismo*, has a very different connotation in Hispanic cultures compared to Anglo U.S. cultures. For family members in Spanish-based cultures, the notion of *respeto* implies submission to the higher authority of elders in the family, as in accepting instructions given by a mother or grandmother without questioning or challenging them (Falicov 2014). Grandmothers explain that in hindsight they realize the downside of being too strict; as a result, they apply a softer form of discipline to their grandchildren, by dedicating more time to talk and reason with them. Here is how Amarylis (age 44) described the difference between the older image of the mother or grandmother and her own experiences:

> *Marta*: Do you see yourself as a traditional grandmother or do you think that this role has changed in this generation?
>
> *Amarylis*: Well, in comparison with my grandparents. . . . I did not get the chance to meet them. . . . Uh, I got to know my *abuelito* only on my mother's side, but that's it, but it is more . . . How is it? How do I explain this? The behavior that I have with my grandson is not old fashioned [smiles] it is more moderate, because of course things change, uh, . . .

> Yes, I am a bit strict with him, in the sense that I tell him clearly about [my disapproval of] vices, uh, I teach him that smoking is not a good thing. Because I went through that with my daughters, I do not want to have the same problems that I had with my daughter, and the bad times I had with her to be transferred on to him. Because he is a male, men are almost always in the streets, they look for the streets and . . . they must have the same responsibilities that women have, because if one day he gets married and has a family, well, then I would like him to keep a good home and family. I always talk very straight to him, and I tell him that you should not hit a woman, because one cannot hit a mother, and I explain to him that a mother gave birth to him and that you must respect women.

For Amarylis the streets are primarily the domain of men, and it is also where bad habits are learned. Moreover, she associates the traditional family with machismo and male abusive behavior. In fact, many women shared, in gory detail, the horrific abuse their husbands subjected them to. Often, the escalation of marital conflict to violence was associated with alcohol abuse and promiscuous behavior on the part of the men. Therefore, it is possible that some of these children had been exposed to violence in the home. Although research in this area is scarce, some studies suggest that in comparison to other ethnic groups, Puerto Rican youth are at the highest risk of being affected by family violence (Estrada-Martínez et al. 2013). In Amarylis's view, it is crucial to teach her grandson the importance of respect for mothers and women in general in order to counteract the male-oriented and destructive influence garnered from the streets.

Although machismo is said to be a traditional feature of Hispanic families, scholars have also described a high level of *respeto* for the mother figure in Hispanic cultures, typically in association with the premium that Catholicism places on the Virgin Mary (*marianismo*) (Stevens 1973; Gil and Inoa Vazquez 2014). Grandmothers wholeheartedly adhered to this notion and explained that the importance of respect for the biological mother remains, in spite of the faults of the grandchildren's mothers. Paquita (age 63), explains this idea: "Well, I raised him [her grandson] since he was a baby, and for me he is just my grandson, and I have never hidden the fact that she [her daughter] is his mother . . . my daughter, that no matter what she is, he owes her *respeto*."

Similarly, Maria teaches her adopted grandson and granddaughter to respect and care for their biological mother, even though she is an alcoholic and has been physically abusive of them, a situation that caused her to lose custody and receive a restraining order:

> *Maria:* The child is now 12, he is going to be 13 soon, and I send him to check on her [her daughter and the mother of the children], and I tell

him "If you see that something is wrong, because she drinks (otherwise she is fine), if she starts drinking, then you come back here, if you see anything that seems wrong, because otherwise you would not be able to see her again, and whatever has happened [with your mom] this is just her own ignorance, but she is your mother. You two [siblings] must respect her and care for her, and you should not feel hate towards her, because she was not herself when she did that."

Teaching and maintaining *respeto* may be very difficult for grandmothers, especially when the grandchildren reach adolescence and become unruly. In the context of poor and distressed neighborhoods, disobedience to authority may translate into cutting school, joining a gang, and/or experimenting with drugs. Because many of these women do not possess the resources to provide productive social alternatives to "the streets" for their children (such as sports, after-school programs, or summer camps) managing teenagers is particularly challenging. Some of the grandmothers enroll their grandchildren in church functions, such a choir or Bible study, but these children may be interested in different types of activities not available to them. In this regard, several grandmothers complained that they had themselves been raised by either grandparents or godparents, but they respected their caregivers and accepted whatever they were able to offer them. On the contrary, their adolescent grandchildren wish to emulate the consumerism, individualism, and freedom that they observe in their peers and which their grandmother cannot give them. The biological mothers may also serve as a negative influence that may "derail" them. Although grandmothering is experienced as meaningful and rewarding, sometimes these women also feel overruled by the grandchildren's biological mothers and lament the fact that they are not accorded the *respeto* that they so rightly deserve. Moreover, children can also extort grandmothers, threatening to call or indeed calling child protective services if their guardians attempt to restrain or discipline them. Therefore, the power these women have over their grandchildren, and the resources they possess to correct them when needed, are very limited.

Though *familismo* is commonly observed among Puerto Rican grandmothers raising grandchildren, their own view of this traditional pattern is significantly more nuanced and less idealized than what the earlier literature has described (Applewhite 1988; Valle and Cook Gait 1998). The role of grandparent, especially the grandmother, raising a grandchild represents a special form of family relationship that is strongly informed by the sense of family obligation that *familismo* denotes. However, the mothering and grandmothering that these women seek to provide is frequently seen as a softer or improved version of the old family dynamics, which they view as being "demasiado fuerte" (too tough), even as they themselves must deal with very tough children.

In the pages that follow, I offer the case studies of two great-grandmothers, one from Boston and one from Rochester, which allow for a deeper examination of the constellation of factors that can make mothering and grandmothering in the U.S. mainland particularly challenging. As a prelude to my cases, I also offer a brief description of relevant information about the two communities.

The Urban Context: Puerto Ricans in Boston and Rochester

Puerto Rican communities have developed primarily in the U.S. Northeast since the passage of the Jones Act in 1917, which granted citizenship to the islanders. The most significant settlements of Puerto Ricans date back to the 1950s, during the period now known as "Operation Bootstrap," when many U.S. companies made a concerted effort to lure Puerto Ricans to go to work in industrial areas of the Northeast or, as in the case of Rochester, on the upstate New York farms. Today, the Puerto Rican population living in these areas shares disproportionally higher rates of unemployment and poverty compared to the overall population, as well as a higher number of women living alone (Collazo, Ryan, and Bauman, 2010). A larger and wealthier city than Rochester, Boston has maintained a strong Puerto Rican ethnic enclave in Villa Victoria at the heart of Boston's highly gentrified South End neighborhood. This feat was made possible thanks to grassroots organizing by the neighborhood association Inquilinos Boricuas en acción (Puerto Rican Tenants in Action). Most of the interviewees in my Boston study lived in public housing in Boston and the surrounding communities, including some residents of Villa Victoria itself. However, several interviewees still expressed issues with obtaining adequate housing for themselves and their grandchildren (Rodríguez-Galán 2013). Spanish language social services and referrals are also available through the nonprofit Latino advocacy organization La Alianza Hispana (The Hispanic Alliance), including family, elder and education services.

Proportionally, a much larger percentage of Puerto Ricans live in Rochester, where Puerto Ricans comprise 13.2 percent of the population compared to Boston where they comprise only 4.9 percent of the population (U.S. Census Bureau 2015). The Rochester Latino community emerged in the 1940s when many Puerto Ricans moved to work in the surrounding farms. Subsequently, cultural, religious, and political institutions flourished during the 1960s (Saenz 2011). Although there is no Puerto Rican enclave in Rochester per se, a significant number of Puerto Ricans live on or near Clinton Avenue and St. Joseph Street. Established over 50 years ago, the Ibero American Action League is a nonprofit advocacy organization that provides bilingual services and programs for families, youth, seniors, and people with disabilities, along with entrepreneurial services. Another important institution in the Rochester Puerto Rican/Latino community is the main Catholic Church of St. Michael's, which was for many years charismatically led by Father Tracy, a bilingual Irish American priest who grew up around the Puerto Rican community. Churches, in general, played a crucial supportive role among the women I interviewed, and this church is a case in point.

Although specific services for skip-generation families exist in both Rochester and Boston, for the most part the women that I interviewed were not aware of them, which suggests a need for greater outreach to the Latino community.

Boston Exemplary Case: Doña Gloria, Age 63

Doña Gloria, a sincere, 63-year-old, dark-skinned woman with an affable and attractive face, has lived in the same Boston neighborhood for almost 40 years. My conversation with her was particularly instructive in demonstrating the cumulative and interlocking effects of social class, gender, family violence, minority status, and their repercussions in the lives of these women as daughters, wives, mothers, grandmothers, and great-grandmothers. Doña Gloria's earnest recount of her experiences as a young woman and a mother also offers a unique glimpse into the challenges that first-generation, low-income Puerto Rican women face while raising and disciplining their own biological children in the context of poor and distressed U.S. urban neighborhoods.

Doña Gloria grew up in Mayaguez, Puerto Rico, with her mother, stepfather, and 11 siblings. From the start of the interview it became apparent that Doña Gloria, even now at age 63, was still haunted by the ghost of her own difficult childhood, a major theme throughout our discussion. Doña Gloria, who was raised by her mother and stepfather, became emotional as she recounted that she was treated "like a savage," viciously punished with the use of various objects and beaten by both him and her mother, who simply submitted to her violent husband's wishes. Doña Gloria's stepfather refused to continue to pay for her schooling when she turned 13 and demanded that she start working to provide for herself. She then went to work taking care of the children of middle-class, professional couples. Maybe because of her own difficult childhood and her work as a nanny, she has dedicated most of her life to lovingly taking care of children.

At age 18, Doña Gloria married her first husband, but this marriage did not turn out to be as good as she had hoped for and expected. Her husband was a heavy drinker and, though he never physically abused her, mistreated and disrespected her constantly. By age 26, she had two children, and after eight years in an abusive marriage, her sister-in-law helped Doña Gloria to escape by inviting Gloria to join her in Boston.

She obtained a divorce and then met her current partner, whom she characterizes as a good man who does not abuse alcohol. Though they never married, she had four children by him and reports that she began experiencing depression after this other set of children was born. Doña Gloria believes that perhaps her depression stems from the trauma she experienced earlier in her life. But, as our conversation continued, I would also learn about Gloria's struggles with raising her six children by herself—as she put it—in one of Boston's most distressed housing projects during the 1980s and 1990s, particularly as these children moved from childhood and into adolescence.

Gloria's experience raising grandchildren began when her teenage daughter had her first child and "dumped her" in Doña Gloria's house, when she was a young mother and still recovering from childbirth. This informal childcare arrangement was supposed to be temporary; however, it lasted until the girl was nine. The two grandchildren for whom she now has full custody are yet from another daughter who was infected with HIV at age 15.

Doña Gloria's family has also been touched by the deadly scourge of drug addiction. One of her sons was a drug user, and though he was not involved in selling drugs or robbery, he obtained money for his own consumption in exchange for informing the police about traffickers in the neighborhood. Doña Gloria believes that one of these dealers found out and decided to give him his last and deadly dose. He was only 22 years old.

Perhaps even more painful for Gloria than losing a son to drugs was losing custody of another son to the Department of Children and Families (DCF). When her eldest son was 13 years old, he began to misbehave in school, and one day she was called in because her son had assaulted a teacher. Doña Gloria was incensed by her son's inexcusable behavior and afraid of the possible consequences it may bring for him. When they returned home, she forcefully scolded him and, for the first time in her life, she struck him on the back of his head, not to hurt him, but to teach him a lesson. However, her son learned a different lesson. The next day he went to school and informed a teacher as to what had happened, and he eventually reported her to the DCF through the school. As a result, Doña Gloria eventually lost custody of her child. With tears coming down her eyes, Doña Gloria informed me that her son, now a 36-year old man, is still addicted to drugs. She blames the school officials and the DCF for her child's life having gone awry, a situation that continues to cause her immense pain. She believes that a great injustice was done to them, especially because she knows all too well what real child abuse is— having experienced this as a child herself—and that she had promised herself to never do this to her own children.

When Doña Gloria first came to the United States, she had not experienced a good childhood and did not know much about life. After all of these years, and having seen for herself the difficulties of parenting, she believes that she is better positioned to offer a helping hand to her family by caring for her grandchildren and great-grandchild. Her custodial granddaughter, who is now 15, has just had a baby of her own, so Doña Gloria is responsible for him as well. Although, in her experience, male children are at higher risk of getting in trouble because they are more street-oriented than girls, her grand-daughter was also *fuerte* (a tough child) during her early teenage years, and she is still learning to become a responsible mother.

Although Gloria's family of origin was also very strict with her growing up, she believes that her parents taught her right from wrong, so that she would lead a good life. Even though she describes herself today as Catholic and likes to pray at home, she grew up going to her family's Seventh-Day Adventist Church, which gave her a strict and sound moral foundation. When her parents became older, she brought them to Boston to be near her. At the time of the interview, her mother had passed away a few years earlier, and Gloria took this particularly hard. Although she felt that at times she had been complicit in the abuse she had endured, Doña Gloria forgives her mother and says she was still always a very supportive and loving mother. What may be even more surprising to learn is that she still watches over her stepfather, who is alive and living across from her house. This is the ultimate statement to her unwavering commitment to family.

There is nothing Doña Gloria values more than teaching her children and grandchildren the importance of being a close-knit, loving family, to forgive each other, to communicate and avoid acrimonious language, and to support one another. In fact, she feels that she is the strongest pillar of her family, and though she wishes her daughters would help her more and give her some respite, she enjoys the feeling of being useful and always having a full house. Furthermore, she is proud to say that in spite of all the difficulties, her children have always accorded her *respeto* as the ultimate authority figure and the matriarch in her family.

Rochester Exemplary Case: Doña Marisol, Age 75

I was able to meet Doña Marisol through a connection within the Rochester school district. She is a spirited 75-year-old woman, with medium brown skin, bright eyes, and a contagious laugh. Even though she never finished high school, Doña Marisol managed to obtain a job with the school system, which afforded her not just some financial security but also the opportunity to continue to learn and to improve her social and cultural capital through school activities and networking with teachers and administrators within the school. Given her positive experiences at work, it is not surprising that she feels very proud to see her youngest daughter now working as a school administrator. Currently in her retirement, Doña Marisol is able to live comfortably and help her children, grandchildren, and great-grandchildren while trying to maintain her involvement in the Catholic Church and volunteer work in the community. Her story sheds light on the difficulties of raising "tough children," and the precariousness of informal care arrangements. It also highlights women's challenges with maintaining domestic and community involvement, and the hope of receiving psychosocial rewards as they age through their children's ultimate redemption, love, and reciprocity.

Doña Marisol was born in Guayama, Puerto Rico, where she lived for most of her childhood. Doña Marisol moved to New York City with her parents when she was 11 years old and soon after arriving enrolled in a trade school. Her education, however, was interrupted when her parents decided to move once again to Rochester, where they found work on the farms. Around that same time, a boyfriend from New York City followed her, and the two were married when Doña Marisol was just 18. The couple had three children together. Sadly, because her husband was a heavy drinker, he died prematurely at the age of 37. A devout Catholic, Marisol never married again, but suggested that she was not a traditional or sad widow, instead describing herself as a "viuda alegre" (a merry widow), who found love again and had another daughter with a new partner; however, the two separated after a few years. Unlike Doña Gloria, Doña Marisol was always able to count on the love and support of both of her parents who lived nearby. For the past 29 years, she has lived in a subsidized housing community and has no plans of moving because there is where most of her friends and *comadres* live.

One gets the impression that, like Doña Gloria, Doña Marisol often understates the negative effect that the drug scene in the neighborhood has had on her ability to protect her own children. This context is crucial to understanding the troubles that they experienced and one of the main reasons for grandmothers becoming the caregivers of grandchildren and great-grandchildren in the first place. On the other hand, within Doña Marisol's narrative, her oldest son offers a different and enlightening point of view. When he fathered her granddaughter, he was—in his mother's own words—wandering through life's dark paths ("no estaba en buenos caminos"). By this she means that her son was using illegal drugs and socializing with addicts in the neighborhood, though he was never a hard-core user. However, after being arrested and spending one week in jail for a misdemeanor, he began to radically change his life. Doña Marisol believes that witnessing the reality of what prison life is like led him on his path towards redemption. In the quote below, she relays how her son communicated to her what he had learned:

> One day he invited me to the beach at night, and it was to show me that in the city there are no stars; you cannot see the stars; so that is why he brought me there to the dark, and he said "Ma, you know that when I was doing drugs I could not see any of this, I could not see the stars and the moon, but NOW! What a good thing it was for me to go to jail, because now I can appreciate all of this."

This lyrical and somewhat metaphorical account seems to suggest that the neighborhood environment where Doña Marisol's son grew up clouded his judgment and made it difficult for him to envision a different kind of life. In his view, one needed to move beyond the confines of the city to truly appreciate what the world has to offer, perhaps the value of life itself. From that point on, he lost contact with old friends, began attending an evangelical church, met his current wife, and moved with her to a wealthy suburb of Rochester (thanks to an affordable housing program) to live and raise his children away from the city.

In some ways, Marisol's granddaughter followed in her father's footsteps in her teenage years and as a young adult, but she ultimately also settled into a quieter life. Doña Marisol describes her granddaughter as a smart and very attractive woman—and as someone with a very quick temper—*fuerte*. She proved to be a resourceful young woman when she managed to graduate from high school and then looked for formal services and programs that would help her deal with her problems. She eventually had to leave a residential program when she got pregnant and gave birth to a child who was born with a rare disease. Doña Marisol laments that after that, the family lost her granddaughter for a while. After breaking up with the father of her child, she married a man who had troubles with the law. Their relationship was volatile and ended after she harmed him during a serious domestic violence altercation. This was a major turning point in her life. After this, she found a stable job, remarried, and had two more children. Doña Marisol currently provides free child care for two great-grandchildren, as well as for a great-granddaughter from another granddaughter who had also lived with her for a year. Her first grandson who is now a teenager is practically cured of his condition and recently has come to live with his mother. Doña Marisol is proud of her granddaughter because she recognizes that the odds were stacked against her, given how she was brought into this world with two lost teenage parents, and because, in spite of her problems as a youth, she has now created a stable life.

Doña Marisol's case is particularly notable because, in addition to her deep commitment to family, she is also active in her community. Throughout the years, she has combined her caregiving duties with paid work, church involvement, participation in various cultural events, and volunteerism. These activities included volunteer work at a Catholic shelter for homeless women and children, fundraising events for her church, baseball games, and Latin music concerts. However, currently as a caregiver for three of her great-grandbabies, she feels more confined to her home than during the earlier part of her retirement. Though she wishes she could continue her active civic and social life, she also realizes that family must come first, as long as this helps the younger generations to surge ahead and establish a better life for themselves. Finally, family care also offers the opportunity for reciprocity;

her granddaughter is now more attentive to her health care needs, such as taking her to doctor's appointments and physical therapy sessions, a role she took upon herself as a show of gratitude for her grandmother's sacrifices. In the end, all Doña Marisol wishes for is that her children and grandchildren show her love and continue to watch over her as she reaches the senescence of her life.

Conclusions: The Power and limitations of *Familismo*

Without a doubt, *familismo* is an underlying ideology that informs these women's decisions to continue to take care of children and become custodial grandmothers for as long as they are capable of doing so. While several of these women admit to being strict in their attempts to instill *respeto*, they are also loving and committed mothers. The life courses of the two women presented here offer important points of convergence and divergence. For example, both women were born on the island (Puerto Rico), did not complete high school, and married and had children when they were 18 or 19 years old. They also share the experience of having been married to husbands who were alcoholics and, at least in one of the cases, abusive. Each lost or separated from her husband when she was young and had other children with a new partner but did not remarry. Then, as single mothers, living in low-income urban neighborhoods, they struggled to protect their children from *la calle* (the streets). In both cases, at least some of their sons were involved with the drug scene in the neighborhood, and several of their children and grandchildren had children of their own when they were young. Moreover, several of their sons and daughters had run-ins with the law. These situations caused the grandmothers to step in and take care of grandchildren and great-grandchildren. They also share the fact that some of their family members, including their children, are *fuertes* (tough), a term that suggests a strong personality, quick temper, aggressiveness, rebelliousness, or a combination of these traits. In addition, many of the women whom I interviewed were taking care of children who had health and developmental problems, a finding that is consistent with quantitative research in this area (Smith and Palmieri 2007). One possible explanation is that drugs or other risky behaviors by their young biological parents may have impacted the health of these children. While poverty and drug use have been identified in the research literature as major culprits in the increased numbers of grandmothers raising grandchildren, what is not so clear are the underlying factors that explain why children are so *fuerte*, and what kinds of resources these women possess to manage these difficult children. Perhaps an analogous medicalized term often applied to adolescents is "oppositional defiant disorder," which has attracted some attention in mental health literature on Latino/a children (Arcia and Fernández 2003). It seems that the term *fuerte* is used more broadly by these women than is commonly understood by this particular medicalized definition.

Doña Gloria's case further instructs us that her abuse as a child placed her in a vulnerable predicament throughout her lifetime, and this vulnerability carried over as she migrated alone when she was a young adult, having a low level of education, acculturation, and limited support available to raise her family. On the other hand, a combination of earlier migration, support from parents, church and civic engagement, her ability to speak English, and networks with more educated friends (or more social capital) enhanced Doña Marisol's ability to provide better opportunities for her children and grandchildren and to receive sound advice during hard times.

Many grandmothers like Doña Marisol accept an informal or nonpermanent custodial arrangement in order to protect their own biological children, but this situation may be detrimental to their own caregiver role and to their grandchildren's well-being in the long run. Furthermore, it was also apparent in my conversations with Puerto Rican grandmothers, especially Doña Gloria, that many do not trust the Department of Children and Families to support them and to understand their child-rearing experiences. More efforts should be made to provide culturally sensitive services and reach out to Latina grandmothers to provide them with the same quality formal supports available to their English-speaking counterparts. These may include legal services, support groups, and conferences and workshops delivered in Spanish. Finally, more qualitative studies are needed to examine grandmothering from a life course perspective.

Some scholars have begun to problematize the notion of *familismo* as a desirable coping strategy, especially when examining this issue from a gender or feminist lens. Hispanic women provide the bulk of these caregiving services for family members, which may lead to added burden and stress (Falcón, Todorova, and Tucker 2009). Moreover, aging Hispanics in the United States commonly find themselves in the position of providing a vast amount of social support and caregiving to younger generations within their families.

Women such as those featured here are rarely given the opportunity to tell their stories and to be given a voice in the literature, but their experience as

---

WEB SPECIALS:

The Commission on the Status of Grandparents Raising Grandchildren, http://massgrg.com/web/index.html.
The New York State Kinship Navigator, http://www.nysnavigator.org/.

told to me is the best testament to what *familismo* really is. In the midst of almost unfathomable circumstances, their will to survive and their unstated but clearly strong commitment to family have carried them forward. In spite of the sacrifices, challenges, lost opportunities, and their worries about the future, the caregiver role is central to these women's own sense of identity. Moreover, it continues to offer psychological rewards, purpose, and meaning to their lives in the context of a robust allegiance to *familismo*.

Note

1. The scholarship on Hispanic/Latino families and aging has often high-lighted the centrality of family values or *familismo* as an ideology that is often invoked to explain the observed tendency among Hispanics to take care of their own elders as well as other family members. It is assumed that this strong family orientation or *familismo* is a distinctive ethnic trait that is beneficial to elders (Ruiz 2007; Shwartz 2007; Valle and Cook-Gait 1998).

Bibliography

Applewhite, S. R. 1988. *Hispanic Elderly in Transition: Theory, Research, Policy, and Practice.* Westport, CT: Greenwood.

Arcia, E., and M. C. Fernández. 2003. "Presenting Problems and Assigned Diagnoses among Young Latino Children with Disruptive Behavior." *Journal of Attention Disorders* 6(4): 177–85.

Calzada, E., and S. Eyberg. 2002. "Self-Reported Parenting Practices in Dominican and Puerto Rican Mothers of Young Children." *Journal of Clinical Child and Adolescent Psychology* 31(3): 354–63.

Cardona, P., B. Nicholson, and R. Fox. 2000. "Parenting among Hispanic and Anglo-American Mothers with Young Children." *Journal of Social Psychology* 140(3): 357–65.

Collazo, S. G., C. L. Ryan, and K. J. Bauman. 2010. "Profile of the Puerto Rican Population in the United States and Puerto Rico: 2008. U.S. Census Bureau, Housing and Household Economic Statistics Division." Paper presented at the Population Association of America annual meeting, Dallas, TX, April 15–17.

Estrada-Martínez, L. M., C. H. Caldwell, A. J. Schulz, A. V. Diez-Roux, and S. Pedraza. 2013. "Families, Neighborhood Socio-demographic Factors, and Violent Behaviors among Latino, White, and Black Adolescents." *Youth & Society* 45(2): 221–42.

Falcón, L. M., I. Todorova, and K. Tucker. 2009. "Social Support, Life Events, and Psychological Distress among the Puerto Rican Population in the Boston Area of the United States." *Aging and Mental Health* 13(6): 863–73.

Falicov, C. J. 2014. *Latino Families in Therapy.* New York: Guilford.

Fontes, L. A. 2002. "Child Discipline and Physical Abuse in Immigrant Latino Families: Reducing Violence and Misunderstandings." *Journal of Counseling & Development* 80(1): 31-40.

Fuller-Thomson, E., and M. Minkler. 2007. "Mexican American Grandparents Raising Grandchildren: Findings from the Census 2000 American Community Survey." *Families in Society: The Journal of Contemporary Social Services* 88(4): 567–74.

Fuller-Thomson, E., M. Minkler, and D. Driver. 1997. "A Profile of Grandparents Raising Grandchildren in the United States." *Gerontologist* 37(3): 406–11.

Gil, R-M., and C. Inoa Vazquez. 2014. *The Maria Paradox: How Latinas Can Merge Old World Traditions with New World Self-Esteem.* New York: Open Road Media.

Goodman, C., and M. Silverstein. 2002. "Grandmothers Raising Grandchildren: Family Structure and Well-Being in Culturally Diverse Families." *Gerontologist* 42(5): 676–89.

Goodman, C. C., and M. Silverstein. 2005. "Latina Grandmothers Raising Grandchildren: Acculturation and Psychological Well-Being." *International Journal of Aging and Human Development* 60(4): 305–16.

Goodman, C. C., and M. Silverstein. 2006. "Grandmothers Raising Grandchildren: Ethnic and Racial Differences in Well-Being among Custodial and Coparenting Families." *Journal of Family Issues* 27(11): 1605–26.

Goodman, M. R., and S. P. Rao. 2007. "Grandparents Raising Grandchildren in a US-Mexico Border Community." *Qualitative Health Research* 17(8): 1117–36.

Rodríguez-Galán, M. B. 2013. "Grandmothering in Life-Course Perspective: A Study of Puerto Rican Grandmothers Raising Grandchildren in the United States." In *Transitions and Transformations: Cultural Perspectives on Aging and the Life Course*, edited by C. Lynch and J. Danely. New York: Berghahn.

Ruiz, M. E. 2007. "Familismo and Filial Piety among Latino and Asian Elders: Reevaluating Family and Social Support." *Hispanic Health Care International* 5(2): 81–89.

Saenz, J. 2011. *Rochester's Latino Community: Bilingual Edition.* Charleston, SC: Arcadia.

Schwartz, S. J. 2007. "The Applicability of Familism to Diverse Ethnic Groups: A Preliminary Study." *Journal of Social Psychology* 147(2): 101–18.

Smith, G. C., and P. A. Palmieri. 2007. "Risk of Psychological Difficulties among Children Raised by Custodial Grandparents." *Psychiatric Services* 58(10): 1303–10.

Stevens, E. P. 1973. "Machismo and Marianismo." *Society* 10(6): 57–63.

U.S. Census Bureau. 2015. American Community Survey B03001 1-Year Estimates, Hispanic or Latino Origin by Specific Origin.

Valle, R., and H. Cook-Gait. 1998. *Caregiving across Cultures.* Oxford: Routledge.

CHAPTER THIRTY

Ancestral Landscapes of Culture

Ethnicity and Cemeteries in England

Doris Francis

Introduction—Anthropology and Biography Interrelated

My interest in cemeteries began in the late 1990s when, as an anthropologist on a course at the Royal Botanic Gardens, Kew, I was asked to design a planting plan for an older burial ground in the English Midlands. I realized that as anthropologists we knew quite a bit about the mortuary rituals of far distant cultures, but that contemporary cemetery behavior was a relatively uncharted realm in the industrialized West (Robben 2004: 1–16). Fortunately, at the same time as my interest in Western death practices was piqued, the British government was considering authorizing the reuse of old graves—those where the contents would have disintegrated over time or others that had been purchased but never used—to extend the burial capacity of its overcrowded cemeteries. To pass legislation permitting reuse, Parliament required more research data on the experiences of those populations that favor earth burial over cremation: Orthodox Jews, Greek Orthodox, Muslims, some Anglicans (churched and unchurched), and Irish Catholics. My application for funding from the Economic and Social Science Research Council on the cross-cultural meaning of cemeteries from the viewpoint of the bereaved was approved. For the next 20 years, the unique culture that exists behind cemetery gates has come to occupy much of my time.

To study cemetery behavior, innovative research methodologies were needed to augment more usual participant-observation and interviews with key informants. Having obtained the permission of cemetery managers to speak with visitors (it was agreed that I not speak with the newly bereaved), I cautiously approached people directly at the gravesite and asked if they would take part in this first study of what visitors do when they come to the cemetery. Most agreed to talk "for just a few minutes" about why they had come to the cemetery that day, but conversations often continued for an hour or more as I took notes. On occasion, interviews continued over time both at the cemetery and at the home of the study participant.

Drawing on this data, this chapter pays special attention to the elderly bereaved who have lost partners and how they use the cemetery to continue a relationship with the departed, to prepare for their own deaths, and to teach the value of family ties with the deceased to the next generation. In the sequestered setting of two London cemeteries, I was able to observe how the cemetery provides the context in which elders confront some of the most difficult tasks of late adulthood: coping with the loss of a beloved partner; maintaining health and opportunities for growth while dealing with grief; creating a kinship legacy linking present, past, and descendent generations; and consolidating their role as parent of the family unit. This research data provide understandings of how the elderly use the cemetery as a resource for dealing with death as a natural event without bereavement counseling and how they assess their progress in coping with loss.

Writing this chapter allowed me to reconsider my earlier publications on this topic such as *The Secret Cemetery* (2005) and, in some ways, helped me when I recently experienced the sudden, unexpected death of my husband of 40 years. I realize that what I previously wrote has guided me for the last two years and that, in reworking the material, which was often emotionally challenging, I found it rang true to my experiences and validated the grief process I was experiencing. It was a double source of empowerment and a difficult road to revisit and review.

Cemeteries as Landscapes of Culture—Two Contrasting Case Studies

As this chapter describes, cemeteries are sacred spaces, funerary landscapes of ritual, memory, and memorialization, where the living remember the dead and construct meaning through their grave-tending behavior and the materiality of the stone marker. The same essential components of the memorial landscape—interred bodies, stone markers and their epitaphs, the postures and gestures of the bereaved, the individual grave gardens, and the surrounding landscape of trees, shrubs, and flowers—work together at each site. However, they are configured differently to create unique environments specific to each cultural group. The appearance of each burial ground reflects the different religious beliefs, cultural ideals, and burial customs of their respective users and provides different visual and experiential clues for those who use the cemetery. These clues frame, constrain, and guide mourners' private feelings of grief and disorder and help to direct their expression through acceptable idioms. The two research sites for this chapter include the City of London Cemetery, a municipal cemetery that is favored by the Anglican (churched and unchurched) population of the East End and surrounding boroughs of London, and Bushey United Jewish Cemetery, the burial ground of the United Synagogue, a union of British centrist Orthodox Jewish synagogues. Mourning rituals at each site are shaped by the existing cemetery landscape, itself a product of the cemetery's history; the practices of previous and present generations of mourners; and current management policies. Each uses different cultural practices and meanings to maintain a continuing relationship with the deceased. This chapter looks within the cemetery as a public site for the cultural performance of rites of mourning and commemoration to see how the cemetery also offers intimate, private spaces for the ongoing construction, reconstruction, and renegotiation of personal memory and meaning. Comparative cemetery research provides unique insights into the experiences of late life mourning and bereavement and thereby increases our understanding of the complexities and dynamics of the aging process within different cultural arenas.

City of London Cemetery

Within a large area of neatly mown grass, straight rows of similar size back-to-back monuments, each fronted by an individual grave garden, characterize the Lawn Section at the City of London Cemetery (Photo 30.1). In this landscape, both individualized gravestones and carefully maintained grave gardens allow the expression of grief and memory. From the 8th to the 19th century, most people in England were buried in the churchyard. But with heavy migration to industrial cities in the 19th century, urban churchyards proved inadequate: their overcrowded conditions were perceived as a cause of epidemic diseases and as unsympathetic to the expression of grief. The City of London Cemetery, established in the mid-19th century, was developed to overcome such concerns. Its intact historic landscape reveals how images from nature convey evolving ideals and attitudes about grief and commemoration. The Victorian section, for example, was renowned for its rich and abundant plantings of purple-leaf beeches and elaborate memorials, appropriate for the wealthier classes' cult of romantic mourning. London's poor, however, were interred in deep common graves with limited opportunity for commemoration: a small memorial plaque and a jam jar filled with flowers were the only allowed expression of bereavement.

In the 1950s, a new lawn design of ordered simplicity was introduced, symbolizing a more rational control of both emotion and nature. Here

Photo 30.1　An elderly widower plants at the grave of his deceased wife. Lawn Section, City of London Cemetery. (Photo by Doris Francis)

"unresolved grief" like "unbridled" Victorian monuments was no longer acceptable. In this new open funerary aesthetic of neatly mown grass and bright flowers, death, like illness, was a loss from which one should recover and move on to form new relationships. In the postwar years, many East End families, whose parents and grandparents had been buried in common graves, could now afford a private grave with its own memorial stone. They won the right from management to plant their own small, distinctive gardens in front of each homogeneous stone and to replace the shrubs planted by the cemetery gardeners with their own individually chosen standard rosebushes. With these concessions, the newly empowered mourners took personal possession of the funerary space to convey how their form of grieving—maintaining a continuing connection with the departed—might be expressed by these new planting rituals. Their newly created funerary aesthetic does not express "moving on" but rather an older paradigm of continuing bonds with the deceased, keeping the memory of the departed as a significant and ongoing part of their lives (Klass, Silvermann, and Nickman 1996).

Bushey United Jewish Cemetery

English Jews rejected Church of England rites for burial in consecrated soil and so leased their own separate burial grounds. In contrast to the garden-like City of London Cemetery, at Bushey the burial ground is a huge expanse of closely placed white marble stones of regulated size (Photo 30.2). Amenity plantings are limited; gravel covers the ground, which is kept grass and weed free; and few graves are covered with flowers. This landscape reflects land constraints and changes in the ethnic composition of London's Jewish community. In 1873, for example, when the first United Synagogue cemetery was founded, its design emulated a Victorian garden cemetery with an elaborate landscape and graves planted with flowers. But at the turn of the century, an influx of Eastern European immigrants, many of whom maintained their standards of religious observance, led to a strengthening of orthodox tenets and a pulling back from assimilation. The design of Bushey, consecrated in 1947, thus reflects this reaffirmation of traditional religious practices with an emphasis on the immortality of the soul and equality in death. Bushey is the standard of what an Anglo-Jewish cemetery looks like. As one cemetery visitor observed, "Jewish cemeteries are functional and austere, not decorative." Visitors interpret the sacred landscape as reflecting Jewish spiritual beliefs about the separation of the soul from the body. "It's clean and neat. . . . There's just bones here now." "Only the body is in the ground, the soul goes back to the Creator." Unlike the newly created practices linking nature and death at the municipal cemetery, prescribed Orthodox Jewish rituals do not draw on the resources of nature to aid the individual grieving process. Visitors focus on the individual stone rather than the ornamental features. The ordered landscape and silent stillness of Bushey, with its restrained, reverential atmosphere, works to encourage an interiorized disposition and pensive mood that invite the processes of commemoration and memory. As one mourner elaborated: "Cemetery visits evoke emotions, melancholy, which evokes contemplation. The cemetery is a place where you get your emotions together, rather than your thoughts; you just do it, it is nonthinking, it is not intellectual thinking."

The Anglo-Jewish community marks the first year of bereavement with a series of ritual practices. This entails the funeral in the cemetery hall, the shiva week of intensive mourning following the funeral, the son's daily attendance at synagogue to recite kaddish for a year, and the setting of the memorial stone. During this time, mourners are guided and supported by the burial society, which oversees the ritual preparation and internment of the body, in addition to their synagogue rabbis and their fellow congregants, family, and friends in acknowledging and accepting loss and expressing grief. The ideal is for the memory of the departed to be held in a positive and helpful way—to remember and not forget.

Jewish custom does not advocate frequent cemetery visits during the first year of bereavement. The family is encouraged to restrict their visiting to once after the first week, again at the end of the first month, and when the memorial stone is installed approximately 11 months after the burial, which marks the end of the formal mourning period. Thus, one of the tasks of the

Photo 30.2   Bushey United Jewish Cemetery. (Photo by Doris Francis)

first year is to select the memorial stone. The tombstone names and honors the deceased and designates a particular grave where family members may visit to remember. It permanently fixes the burial site of the bodily remains of the deceased and gives concrete form to the remembered image and significance of the deceased.

The wording inscribed on the stone is strictly determined and must be approved by the office of the chief rabbi, the head of the United Synagogue community. The Hebrew name of the deceased must appear together with his or her father's name, date of death, and then the Hebrew words "May his/her soul be bound up in the bonds of eternal life," repeating in script the words of the memorial prayer recited annually at the cemetery and in the synagogue. The next of kin and names of all children alive at the time of burial may be included. Such naming links the generations and demonstrates a collective family identity in which the deceased is the central pivot. With the addition of a scriptural quotation and the choice of a religious symbol, a generic stone is transformed into a personalized monument. The stone comes to embody the personhood and meaning of the deceased. This tombstone expresses the family's interpretation of the virtues, accomplishments, and personal qualities of the departed, as well as the nature of their shared relationship. It gives material substance to the reconstructed image and meaning of the deceased. It also acts as an agent of inscribed memory for many cemetery visitors.

Custom and religious tradition encourage people to visit the cemetery annually on the Hebrew anniversary of death, to attend funerals and stone settings, when they "feel the need," and in the month of the Jewish New Year. This yearly autumn pilgrimage is a significant part of the annual ritual cycle and an important way to remember the dead. It gives behavioral form to the Jewish sense of a social relationship with the deceased: "It keeps the memory fresher." Given the sacred aspect of the yearly cemetery visit, the memorial stone takes on added meaning as the focus of ritual performance and engagement, the symbolic place where the world of the living and the dead may come into contact. During their visit, most people stand in front of the monument and meditatively read the written text and recite the appropriate memorial prayers, followed by a few moments of intimate contemplation of the deceased or a more lengthy conversation.

One important concrete memorializing practice of this annual autumn visit is the careful inspection and care of the stone monument, a metaphor for ongoing regard of the deceased and the maintenance of memory. The significance of the stone as a site of memory seems contingent upon sustained engagement: from selection and inscription, installation, visitation, and continued upkeep. Although marble may appear hard and enduring, its permanence depends upon constant human attention. In the code of cemetery culture, the stone should remain whole, clean, and white, symbolic of the upkeep of the name and memory of the deceased, of continued family devotion and respect. It serves as a metaphor for the remembrance of the deceased. Grey, weathered, or broken stones are seen as the material enactment of forgetting, that the person buried there has been forgotten. Both the stone and memory require care, diligence, and sustained engagement. Some visitors hire a stonemason or cemetery staff; others wash the memorial themselves. Small stones left on the memorial further show that the grave has been visited and respect paid.

City of London Cemetery

Following the funeral, mourners at the City of London Cemetery, in contrast to those at Bushey, are on their own without the guidance of established rituals backed by religious ideology. In today's more secular and individual society, grief is personal and private. Their attenuated religious affiliations have left many as "unguided" and open to creating new practices of cemetery mourning. Many have turned to the resources of nature to mark their grief process and have innovated new secular funerary rituals. These culturally shaped, but personal, rituals revolve around investing the memorial stone with the deceased's identity and creating a garden at the gravesite.

Initiation into this innovative culture begins with the clearing of the funeral flowers, the bringing of potted plants to create an immediate headstone, or planting the grave with flowers. In the first weeks following burial, mourners learn from one another that regular cemetery visits to tend the grave are a way to express grief and survive loss. Such innovative rituals linking nature and death are creating a new culture of commemoration where grieving behavior, often marginalized by society, is evoked and shaped, assisting in maintaining an enduring tie with the deceased.

Sometime during the first six months, mourners at the City of London usually erect a permanent memorial. As at Bushey, the stone marks the final resting place of the deceased and provides a focus for grief. Unlike the Anglo-Jewish community, however, there is no customary set of ritual practices surrounding the installation of the memorial. The cemetery determines the allowable materials and specific dimensions of the monument and approves the drawing of the proposed inscription. Most stones give the name, date of death, kinship status ("Beloved Husband, Dad and Granddad") and a short verse or epitaph ("To Meet Again in Heaven"), and sometimes a more private inscription or image. As at Bushey, mourners see an analogy between the upkeep of the stone and their ongoing devotion to the memory of the deceased. People make an annual trip to bleach the memorial, and in winter some stones are wrapped in plastic to protect them from the elements.

Mourners at the City of London have innovatively linked this maintenance of the "enduring" stone memorial with the seasonal redesign of the transitory grave garden. The "permanent" stone marker, with its written epitaph, communicates a fixed, abbreviated meaning of the deceased composed a few months after death. In contrast, the garden, created with ephemeral flowers requiring frequent attention and seasonal renewal, allows a more dynamic and expansive meaning of the departed that is shaped and reshaped over time—an evolving memorial.

The garden historian John Dixon Hunt (Hunt, 1994) has suggested that the transience of the garden makes it a particularly appropriate form of memorialization. Created with short-lived flowers requiring frequent renewal, this transitory garden encourages mourners to shape and reshape the meaning of the departed over time. A grave garden provides an opportunity for greater involvement and more time to reflect, encouraging a type of ongoing life-review. As mourners dig and fork the soil, they may gain greater understanding, acceptance, and healing of self and the unresolved conflicts and misunderstandings of a shared relationship through these parallel cognitive and material "excavations." Although many cemetery visitors select the same types of flowering plants, each plot is the unique creation of its designer and reveals agency and purposeful forethought to express the identities of the survivor and the departed, as well as their ongoing relationship. Like the personalized icons inscribed on the marker, the small grave garden publicly re-creates and makes materially manifest the remembered personhood of the deceased. In addition, tending the memorial garden makes the consoling cycles of seasonal renewal and regeneration available to mourners and allows the survivor to sustain his/her role as a caring, devoted spouse. A decorated grave, like the small stones left on the memorials at Bushey, publicly confirms the mourners' commitment to the memory of the deceased.

Coping with the Loss of a Lifelong Partner

The death of a spouse is likely to be a painful rupture. For widowed elders, a visit to the cemetery and grave-tending activities provide a place and a way for continued contact with a lifelong partner. For many spouses, the trip to the cemetery may also be a search for a part of the self that had been lost with the death of the other. As one widower in his eighties remarked: "You grow alike; after 55 years, what I like she likes. You have lost a part of your life." My research at the municipal cemetery shows that 38 percent of cemetery visitors are over the age of 65 (the group most likely to be widowed), and in that age group, 46 percent are men. Nonetheless, there is a common assumption that women primarily tend graves.

For older widows and widowers, visiting the grave frames strategies for coping with the years spent alone. The first strategy is to maintain an ongoing connection with the deceased through intimate conversation, often facilitated by grave-tending activities. As one widow explained: "You feel as though you're with them. We stand and talk, like they are right beside us talking." The cemetery offers a different type of solace from the memory-filled home, with its photographs and objects acquired over a lifetime together. As many bereaved men in their seventies and eighties explained: "There is someone here to come to." "It's a comfort to come up here to talk; we were married 53 years." Conversations involve the sharing of everyday news, the recounting of family and neighborhood events, and the reporting of one's schedule of activities—all in the manner of chatting to an old friend. Such conversations suggest that the cemetery is a place where a continuing relationship with the deceased can be maintained, despite death, through chats and by being "near" the other. Couples still grow old together and acknowledge birthdays and anniversaries by a visit to the grave. For some, the cemetery is a second space, complementary to the couple's formerly shared residence, in which to visit and talk with the departed. As one widow observed: "Because I can't see my husband at home, I come here to see him."

For many surviving spouses, it is also the deceased partner with whom they talk about the pain of loss. As one 72-year-old widow whose husband died nine years before and who visits every two weeks explained: "If I'm depressed, I come, I sit and talk and I feel better. When I'm here, I'm near him. . . . I see him as I knew him. I love to come to the cemetery, it's a day out. . . . When you're on your own, it's nice to talk to people. . . . It takes you a long time to come to terms." Thus, as a strategy, the acceptance of the reality of death and the maintenance of an ongoing relationship with the departed coexist and help with coping.

The second coping strategy shared by many elderly Anglican mourners is to embrace the Church's idea of an afterlife and the belief that the deceased was already in heaven, so that a reunion of some unspecified kind is possible. "I've always believed there's a life thereafter and we will meet, but I don't know where," remarked one widow. Connected to the idea of a heavenly reunion is an ongoing sense of the presence of the spouse. As another widow commented, "His presence is wherever I am, really, that's how you learn to cope; you mustn't think they're not here with you."

Maintaining a regular pattern of visiting the cemetery constitutes a third coping strategy. During the week, bereaved spouses generally visit alone, but on weekends many are accompanied by a son or daughter. City of London men who visit alone on weekends see Sunday as a special, sacred time, appropriate for the cemetery visit. Men tend to visit on a regular schedule, and in both the municipal and Jewish cemeteries, long-term widowers visit every month or so. Women describe daily visits after the spouse first died, then gradually reduce their visits to a few times a week, and later to weekly or once a fortnight. Men, however, tend to follow a regular schedule from the beginning and usually visit on the same one or two days every week, making this visit a part of a full schedule of activities involving home maintenance.[1]

In taking over domestic tasks and routines associated with women, working-class widowers acknowledge not only their deceased wives and their shared lives but also their own proficiency in accomplishing gender-specific duties. The purposeful assumption or continuation of domestic routines may also permit a consolidation of the living self and the deceased other. It reveals continued personal growth and pride in the development and achievements of a necessarily expanded self as the transition to the role of widower takes place. In contrast with common negative evaluations of old age and bereavement, late-life mourning can be experienced and interpreted as a time for new roles and responsibilities, for maintenance, if not expansion of physical abilities, and for increased independence. Some describe their visits to the cemetery in the context of previous caregiving efforts and as a continuation of those activities. They often have a need to review this experience and find others in the cemetery with whom they can share experiences.

Visits to the cemetery and the simple exchange of information with others at the water tap provide affirmation, support, and social contact with "the other regulars" who tend graves, an activity often disparaged outside the cemetery gates. As one widower noted: "I've met people who say, 'What do you go over there for? You can't do anything.' But for me this cemetery is the right place to express feelings. Everyone comes, you're in the same situation. . . . It makes you realize you're not the only one; there are so many others like you." Here the cemetery provides an important resource of support and validation for mourners who did not seek or receive bereavement counseling. Significantly, for those with no prior experience of death, the cemetery experience can be a resource offering suggestions of how others cope. It is a place where conversations with and observations of other mourners provide a level of understanding, instruction, affirmation, and integration not found in everyday social interactions.

Many bereaved widowers have internalized a view of the life course in which widowhood is a determinant of their later years and remarriage is not considered an option. They dedicate this later phase of life to the memory of the other and to taking care of themselves. Most adopt wellness as a goal and make their physical and psychological health a priority. For women, too, the emphasis is on health and attitude, but with a different slant: "Be cheerful, look after yourself. If you're miserable, no one wants to know you, do they?"

Thus, the cemetery is a resource for spouses coping with loss. It is a place where private emotions can be freely expressed, but it also offers ready distraction in the tasks of caring for the stone and/or tending the grave garden. It is this ability to acknowledge death while maintaining an ongoing relationship with the deceased—to accept that the dead are truly dead while continuing to converse with them—that gives many mourners the resources to deal with the powerful, often contradictory, and conflicting emotions that accompany the death of a lifelong partner.

My cemetery research suggests, however, that for those, often younger persons who do find a new partner, a connection with the deceased is still maintained while being committed to the new relationship. The surviving spouse often brings the news of a new partner to the grave of his or her deceased spouse. Sometimes the surviving spouse brings the new partner. Such occasions reveal the survivor's ongoing regard for the former spouse, acknowledgment of the new relationship, and possibly a sense of guilt and discomfort if "permission" had not be given for the bereaved to remarry, "not to be alone."

For widowed spouses, one of the keys to a successful remarriage is the inclusion of both partners. As one widower at Bushey summed up remarriage: "Now we two are four, we're like a load of old friends. With the original partner you brought your children into the world and sacrificed together. With a new relationship, it is mutual respect and love." Many decisions concerning second marriages and the shifts between ongoing ties to the first partner and attachment to the second relationship are registered on the cemetery landscape. For example, in the Orthodox Jewish community, decisions must be made within the first six months following the funeral about whether to reserve a burial space next to one's former spouse and whether to purchase a single or a double stone. Cemeteries are filled with reserved plots and never-used grave spaces as partners from second marriages are sometimes buried together.

Creating a Kinship Legacy—The Role of the Senior Generation

Just as there is a ritual timetable for visiting the cemetery at Bushey, there is an accepted calendar of cultural, religious, and secular occasions—Christmas, Easter, birthdays, Mothering Sunday, and Father's Day—at the City of London Cemetery, when mourners customarily bring wreaths, flowers, and carefully chosen cards to decorate the graves. At these two cemetery sites, Christmas and the Jewish New Year are the significant ritual occasions when family members of different age groups come together to visit the graves of ancestral kin who are not visited throughout the year. Family elders, who may also be grieving the loss of a spouse, purposely use such occasions to impart family history, traditional cultural ideals, and the reinforcement of kinship ideology and its responsibilities. These pilgrimages endorse the pivotal position of the senior generation as those who link past and future generations and who are the repositories and transmitters of family history and the teachers of remembrance through cemetery rituals. Over the years, such annual visits help preserve and revitalize the memories of grandparents and great-grandparents who might not have been known personally by their descendants. When the spouse/parent who kept these graves dies, the established route and the maintaining of the memorials—now also including the grave of the recently deceased spouse/parent—are sometimes continued as a tribute to him or her. Thus, on such annual cemetery pilgrimages, past, present, and future generations are brought together. Older adults, who bring their children and grandchildren to the cemetery in order to encourage kin relationships, are also anticipating being honored when they pass away. The journey is repeated annually as a show of respect and acknowledgment of their pivotal position.

In other cases, such as the purposeful cemetery visits of middle-aged children, deceased family members also retain their status as the family matriarch/patriarch even after death. Many adult children in their fifties and sixties bring family concerns to the graves of their parents and use the visit to seek wisdom, moral authority, advocacy, approval, and support. Here the visit is not delayed reciprocity for services rendered in childhood but a request for continuation, even after death, of the support and guidance parents formerly provided. Often the deceased mother retains status as moral arbiter and matriarch, as when two widowed cousins came to tell their mothers that each had found a new partner and would remarry. Although they had visited the graves of their dead husbands, it was at the graves of their mothers that they hoped to gain acceptance. Other middle-aged adults purposely use the commemorative cemetery visit and the quiet, meditative space of the burial grounds to reflect on family issues from the perspective of their parents and to gain guidance on family matters. Here the role of the parent as supportive confidante and trusted ally is reconfirmed, and the adult child, now him- or herself at the top of the family tree and strengthened by the cemetery "conversation," assumes this same representation within his/her own immediate family. Other adult children perceive deceased parents as having power and agency in the affairs of the living and seek their intercession and advocacy for health, work, or family crises. For others, visits to the cemetery give resolution through confrontation of complex and often contradictory emotions not fully addressed when the parent was still living—forgiveness and understanding can continue after death.

My research into the content of the ritual visit in exploring what people actually do and say suggests that differences in the meaning of cemetery visits are age related and vary with the type of loss. For example, people 75 and over still visit the graves of their parent as memories, respect, and affection endure over time, as well as continuing feelings of grief. Cemetery visits for these elderly recall life shared in the past when parents were still alive and provide continuity between older and younger selves by linking past activities with present lives.

For the very old, frail, and chronically ill, trips to the cemetery are often accompanied by an awareness of their own impending mortality. In the senior generation, the wish to put both worldly and otherworldly affairs in order is often the meaning attributed to the cemetery visit. For example, a 73-year-old man who had had four heart attacks in the previous 18 months came to the City of London Cemetery specifically to plant the family grave. He explained that he had chosen to expend his limited energy on activities that signified a tying up of loose ends, an acknowledgment of his ongoing duty as caretaker of the dead, and a preparation for his own demise. Such visits suggest that some older people come to place themselves between the domains of this world and the next. Those elderly people who come on public transportation postpone visits when the weather is bad and cut back on plot maintenance. For these individuals, the visit signals an acknowledgment, acceptance, and expectation of their own mortality and stands as a significant accomplishment that demonstrates their ongoing participation in meaningful activities.

Application of Research

Having analyzed the importance of English cemeteries as sacred, meditative spaces where private emotions are expressed publicly within the protective cloak of ritual, where grief is articulated through the language of stones and flowers, and where meaning is made and memory constructed, I felt the need to improve my local Santa Fe cemetery to create an atmosphere more conducive to healing and memorialization. At the time I returned to the United States, the dedicated Jewish section of this privately owned burial ground was a flat, unappealing, and unwelcoming field with flat, horizontal monuments and few amenity plantings. When possible, people chose to have

Photo 30.3 A woman in her eighties places a stone to mark her visit and tells the family history of the individual named on the memorial plaque. Rivera Family Funerals and Memorial Gardens Cemetery, Santa Fe, New Mexico. (Photo by Gay Block with permission)

close relatives buried in family plots back east. The cemetery was a place of disposal, not a sacred site.

The one redeeming feature of this Jewish section, however, was a beautiful corner wall built of rough-hewn Jerusalem-colored stone. People who chose to purchase a plot in this cemetery expressed a desire to be buried "within the wall," but space was limited. When I joined the Jewish Community Council of Northern New Mexico and created a cemetery committee to improve the Jewish section, the cemetery owner, wishing to work with our organization, generously doubled the amount of land available for Jewish burial. After interviewing cemetery visitors about their needs, I proposed the first landscape improvement: to extend the beautiful wall to shelter this expanded space, creating a feeling of inclusion and enclosure within the Jewish community. Two supportive rabbis recommended the sale of memorial plaques to finance the wall extension and suggested using the Jewish concept of *bimkom kever*, "in place of the grave." Through this concept, visitors can memorialize loved ones buried in other cemeteries or for whom there is no grave with a name plaque mounted on our cemetery wall (Photo 30.3). In our mobile American society, many people live in places different from where their parents and close relatives and friends are buried. These plaques "resituate" the named individual(s) to our local cemetery and permit mourners to say their memorial prayers in our Santa Fe Jewish burial ground, thus providing the ritual context and opportunity for ongoing remembrance, memorialization, and conversations with the deceased.

A skilled architect volunteered his time and worked with the cemetery committee to model the memorial plaques after the design of the Holocaust Memorial Wall in Frankfurt. However, unlike the German steel blocks on a concrete wall, the Santa Fe plaques are made from regionally sourced stones that resemble the rich, warm colors of Jerusalem. These stone plaques are engraved with the name of the deceased, which, like the gravestone memorial, becomes a powerful emblem, an evocation of the departed, of his/her memory. Each plaque has space on top to leave a stone replicating the custom of leaving a pebble on the grave to register a visit. Through new technology such as the Qeepr app,[2] these plaques can also connect to an easily accessible digital archive of the biography and family history of the deceased, with the potential to make the cemetery a living archive, a place of community history and heritage. At the annual unveiling of new plaques on the Sunday between Rosh Hashanah and Yom Kippur, family members publicly tell their feelings and memories of the departed, a process that resembles the determination of what to put on the memorial stone, or their remarks about the meaning of the deceased made at the stone setting. People report that having these plaques in our local cemetery is like bringing their relatives and friends "home," to be with them in Santa Fe, thereby creating a powerful new anchor for their identity, presence, and memory.

Over the past three years, the committee has constructed a seating area that looks over the Jewish burial ground and the memorial wall; it is a place for contemplation and reflection. With these improvements, the Jewish cemetery in Santa Fe has become a source of community pride and ownership. More and more people wish to be buried in our local cemetery and are purchasing plots. The cemetery owner has again increased the amount of land available for Jewish burial, and the third phase of the wall is planned. With Santa Fe's large elderly population, the cemetery is becoming an important and valued resource with its own developing culture and customs. In my next research project I will concentrate on understanding the developing meaning and importance of the memorial plaques honoring the parents and grandparents of Santa Fe's present older population. Like all cemeteries, it has much to tell us about how death is an important part of age and life.

Notes

1. My cemetery research suggests that people who follow a set household routine are better able to cope with the devastating loss of a lifelong partner than those who instead "take each day as it comes," without an established schedule.

The former survivors feel it is their responsibility to "take care of themselves" rather than become overwhelmed with grief. The regular and routine nature of housework offers the opportunity to keep busy with distracting tasks: "When I feel down, I get to work," explained one bereaved widower.

2. Today computer technology is available through Qeepr to digitally store the historically valuable legacy of community ancestors. This program enables relatives and friends to create a type of "face-book page" containing memories, the newspaper obituary, school and work history, prerecorded videos, photographs, and the family tree of the deceased. The Qeepr mobile app uses GPS coordinates to "geotag" the grave marker, and family members construct an online interactive memorial that can be accessed and augmented using a mobile phone or tablet.

Bibliography

Francis, D., L. Kellaher, and G. Neophytou. 2005. *The Secret Cemetery.* Oxford: Berg.

Hunt, J. D. 1994. "'Come into the Garden, Maud': Garden Art as a Privileged Mode of Commemoration and Identity." Unpublished paper, *Dumbarton Oaks Colloquium: Places of Commemoration. The Search for Identity and Landscape Design.* Washington, DC, May 19–20.

Klass, D., P. R. Silverman, and S. L. Nickman, eds. 1996. *Continuing Bonds: New Understanding of Grief.* London: Taylor & Francis.

Robben, A.C.G.M., ed. 2004. "Death and Anthropology: An Introduction." In *Death, Mourning, and Burial: A Cross-Cultural Reader,* edited by A.C.G.M. Robben. Oxford: Blackwell.

CHAPTER THIRTY-ONE

Web Book: Battling a New Epidemic

American Indian Elders and Diabetes

Linda Carson

Available at: http://www.culturalcontextofaging.com/webbook-carson

This chapter focuses on the rise of diabetes among ethnic elders of Native American communities. It draws on Carson's training in public health and gerontology to explore the devastating impact of soaring diabetes rates among older Native Americans in Oklahoma. See also: https://www.cdc.gov/vitalsigns/aian-diabetes/index.html.

CHAPTER THIRTY-TWO

Web Book: Losing, Using, and Crafting Spaces for Aging

Muslim Iranian Americans in California's Santa Clara Valley

Mary Hegland

Available at: https://www.culturalcontextofaging.com/webbook-hegland/

This chapter gives us a very dynamic picture of Iranians fleeing the Islamic revolution in their home country and ending up highly dispersed in the San Francisco Bay area.

See also: P. Dossa, "From Displaced Care to Social Care: Narrative Interventions of Canadian Muslims," *American Anthropologist* 120, no. 3 (2018): 558–60.

CHAPTER THIRTY-THREE

Web Book: Aging in Exile

Family Support and Emotional Well-Being among Older Cuban Immigrants in the United States

Iveris Martinez

Available at: http://www.culturalcontextofaging.com/webbook-martinez

This chapter examines Cuban expatriates in Miami. Unlike the highly dispersed Iranians studied by Hegland (Ch. 32), her sample is physically centered in a distinct ethnic community. However, the context of migration and the great reduction of immediate family have created a strong degree of social isolation and aging "out of place."

CHAPTER THIRTY-FOUR

Web Book: Age of Wisdom

Elderly Black Women in Family and Church

Jane W. Peterson

Available at: http://www.culturalcontextofaging.com/webbook-peterson

One historical response of African American peoples has been to establish community-based mechanisms of support that could buffer the shock of long-term discrimination on the individual. Medical anthropologist Jane Peterson draws upon her experience as a professional nurse and explores the participation of older women in both extended family and church-based care systems in an African American community in Seattle, Washington.

See also: A. Nguyen, "African American Elders, Mental Health, and the Role of the Church," *Generations* 42, no. 2 (2018): 61–67.

PART V

Age-Friendly Communities, Kinscripts, Families, and Elderscapes: Transforming Cultural Spaces for Aging

It is not enough to talk about the bind of tradition and it's not enough to talk about its disintegration. We must find ways and means of transforming it into a modern form that will make multigenerational relationships much more viable.

—Nana Apt

Introduction

Jay Sokolovsky

Ghanaian sociologist and specialist on aging Nana Apt made the remarks that open this section in a 1998 keynote address at the United Nations discussing how living arrangements and cultural traditions might be adapted to continue sustaining elders amid the multitude of changes faced by families in industrializing nations. As regional wars, genocide, and massive economic dislocation spark the largest global migration movements since World War II that afflict many parts of that world, reliance on 20th-century models of family support are dangerously misplaced in Africa or Asia, as they are among migrants in North America and Europe (Näre, Walsh, and Baldazar 2017; Hromadžic´ and Palmberger 2018). In looking at such issues, this section's chapters traverse Indonesian villages within a woman-centered society; the global, elder-friendly community movement; Ibasho cafés; neighborhoods in four world cities; community gardens creating civic ecology; and elderscapes ranging from urban India, RV communities, senior centers, and the most senior-dense county in the United States.

One approach to understanding the kinds of variation you will be reading about is to frame the information within two universal sets of social relations—the kinship systems generated by rules and practices of descent and marriage and the broader social networks that bind people within and often across communities. This applies as much to the married couple recently retired to The Villages in central Florida, the nation's largest retirement community (Photo V.1), as it does to the older homeless woman resting with her possessions in midtown Manhattan (Photo V.2) (Murphy and Eghaneyan 2018).

We can begin by considering the information seen in Figure V.1. On the surface at least, the vast majority of older adults in the industrializing ("developing") world appear securely situated in multigenerational living arrangements with family and less than 10 percent are living alone. A stark contrast is seen in the so-called developed world, where a little under a third of those

Photo V.1   A retired couple in front of their house in the Villages, an active living older adult community in Florida, 2007. (Photo by Jay Sokolovsky)

WEB SPECIALS:

1. C. Leins, "The Villages Retirement Community: 'Disney World for Adults.'" *US News and World Report*, October 11, 2017, https://www.usnews.com/news/best-states/articles/2017-10-11/the-villages-retirement-community-disney-world-for-adults.

2. A broader discussion of these types of age-focused communities is found in a November 14, 2018, *New York Times* article about a Jimmy Buffett branded community in Florida: K. Tingley, "The Future of Aging Just Might Be in Margaritaville," https://www.nytimes.com/interactive/2018/11/14/magazine/tech-design-longevity-margaritaville.html.

Photo V.2   Homeless woman resting, Midtown Manhattan, 2018. (Photo by Jay Sokolovsky)

past age 60 live with a relative other than their spouse, and close to that percent live by themselves. Within this survey data there is a great deal of variation. For instance, while only 4 percent of Denmark's older citizens live with a child or grandchild, in Bangladesh the figure is 90 percent, and while the proportion living alone is less than 1 percent in Bahrain, it reaches 40 percent in Denmark (United Nations Population Fund 2007; for recent data see United Nations Population Division 2019). In some developing nations such as Ghana we see dramatic exceptions in that during the last two decades of the 20th century there was an almost doubling of elders residing alone, from 12 to 22 percent (see Aboderin 2006 for the implication of this change).[1] We have seen in Coe's chapter in Part II how age inscriptions in Ghana are helping people begin to question on the ground the basis of family support of elder family members. As already seen in Cattell's discussion of widowhood

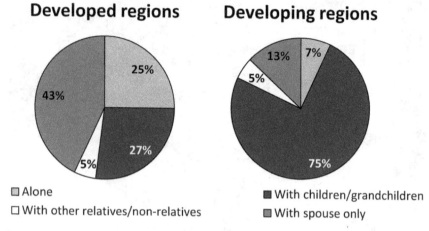

Developed regions   **Developing regions**

☐ Alone
☐ With other relatives/non-relatives
■ With children/grandchildren
■ With spouse only

Figure V.1   Living Arrangements of Persons over Age 60 in Developed and Developing Regions (Adapted from United Nations 2007, p. 33).

(Part II Web Book), gender is also a key factor here, as in all world regions, women over age 60 live by themselves two to three times more often than older males.

Such numbers, however, mask not only the inner workings of family systems but what Stack and Burton call "kinscripts" (1994), the family-centered cultural scripts that connect elders and their kin networks to the broader cultural setting in which they live (see also Sokolovsky 2002). In regions like Asia, the general filial focus is impacted by variant kinscripts. In East Asia and the northern sector of South Asia, cultures based on either Confucian, Hindu, or Muslim philosophies and an authoritarian, patrilineal system stress coresidence and care by sons and their spouses. In Southeast Asia and the southern zone of South Asia, Buddhist spiritual orders within a less rigid, bilateral kin system push adult daughters to play equal and sometimes more important support roles in eldercare than sons (Mason 1992). An important variant of this second pattern occurs in Thailand where there is a decided preference for elder parents residing with daughters. This example is particularly important in showing that despite steep drops in family size during the 1990s, the number of children in a family network has only a very modest impact on an elder's chances for coresidence and support. In fact, those elders with only one or two children reported that they felt as well cared for as those with five or six offspring (Knodel and Saegtienchai 2007; Part III Aulino).

The impact of kinscripts often comes into sharpest focus when things begin to change. A dramatic example is the Gwembe people of Gambia, studied over a 10-year period by anthropologist Lisa Cliggett (2005). The aboriginal culture was matrilineal, with the well-being of the community dependent on women's hoe-cultivation of land. The people were relocated by the building of a dam in their region, and their lands thus became more suitable for tending cattle and cattle-ploughed agriculture, which was controlled by men, especially older men. This shifted social power to patrilineal groups (men and their sons), and during periodic severe droughts old women could no longer draw on the power of their matri-kin and were reduced to surviving only on grains from grass.

In looking at another matrilineal people, the Minangkabu of Indonesia, this section's Web Chapter by Indrizal, Kreager, and Schröder-Butterfill brings to the forefront how a women-centered kin descent system structures the life course and frames late-life cultural spaces and scripts (see Van Eeuwijk 2020 for a broader discussion of Indonesian eldercare). Through a series of expertly drawn case studies we see a delicate interweaving of culture and context. Here ancient matrilineal customs called *Adat* place women at the center of economic, ritual, and family life but are situated within a local, devout version of Islam. Men as they age sit at the edge of most of these realms, but in a more complementary manner than experienced by women in male-centered societies. Particularly interesting contrasts are to be found in comparing the Minangkabu scripts and spaces for aging to those described for Mexico and China in Part III and in Part V's chapter on India. One sees in the lives examined differing impacts of late-life vulnerabilities such as childlessness, having only sons, or loss of a spouse in the context of globalizing forces (Schröder-Butterfill 2009: Fanany and Fanany 2019).

Vulnerability and Building Resilience

The vulnerability of older citizens has recently emerged as a powerful issue. This is set against both the globalizing changes discussed in Part III and the ability of family and community systems to protect elders in the context of demographic shifts or disasters such as the recent civil wars in the Middle East and Africa, the 2005 Hurricane Katrina in New Orleans, or the 2003 heat wave that struck Europe and precipitated the unanticipated deaths of numerous older Parisians (Wallace et al. 2015). The large number of deaths, especially of older residents, related to the 2018 Hurricane Irma in Puerto Rico highlighted the need to build resilience in the face of disaster in all communities.

In Box V.1 we see one response to this issue in Japan. It documents the creation of Ibasho cafes in Eastern Japan, following the dual disaster there of a massive earthquake and ensuing tsunami in 2011. Here elders led the way in developing community-based "inclusive resilience," which has become a model being developed in other parts of the world. The Japanese word *Ibasho* means a place where you can feel at home and be yourself. You can follow these developments of the Ibasho movement at: http://www.ibasho.org/web/.

Box V.1   Ibasho Cafés: Elders Take the Lead
in Building Inclusive Resilience

Led by Dr. Emi Kiyota, research has analyzed and evaluated the impact of an elder-centric, community-driven project on levels of social capital among the community members of Ofunato, Japan, a disaster-affected city. This employed a mixed-method research approach with both quantitative and qualitative data to examine (1) relationships between the Ibasho café and the level of social capital and (2) Ibasho café's influence on the well-being of community members.

Background:

Elders leading the way to inclusive community resilience

Our approach to disaster risk management emphasizes socially inclusive community resilience. Marginalized groups such as children, disabled people, displaced people, elders, indigenous peoples, migrants, youth, and women suffer disproportionately from disasters and should have equal access to necessary resources and services to manage risk. Moreover, marginalized groups are typically considered vulnerable and in need of protection. Nevertheless, their capacities and skills often go unrecognized and can be overlooked or undermined in disaster response and recovery.

This report focuses on elder issues. With the simultaneous rise in the number of elders and in climate-related natural disasters, societies worldwide are facing two critical challenges: caring for an unprecedented number of elderly people and reducing the vulnerability of elderly populations affected by disasters. Aging is typically viewed as decline, with elders often marginalized both socially and physically.

During our time in Japan after the Great Eastern Japan Earthquake (GEJE), the Ibasho team often heard people say how important it was for them to be surrounded by familiar faces after the tsunami. We also heard, "Elders knew how to manage without electricity and water." These reactions suggest that younger people could benefit from elders' skills and perspective as much as elders need the support of the younger generation in order to create a resilient community.

What Is Ibasho Café?

The first Ibasho café was developed in Ofunato, a part of Japan that had been devastated by the GEJE and tsunami of 2011. After the GEJE, the leadership of Ibasho, a nongovernmental organization, talked to community members and found that older people wanted to do something useful to help the community recover. The Ibasho approach recognizes elders as valuable assets to their community and seeks to empower them to be active participants. Doing so challenges society's negative perceptions and expectations of the elderly, which include social isolation, a loss of dignity and respect, and a sense of uselessness and irrelevance. This approach improves the community's resilience and its ability to withstand shocks such as disaster and aging, by creating a strong informal support system in which elders serve as the catalyst to strengthen bonds among community members of all ages. Since the café was completed in June 2013, all generations have connected in the space, with children coming to read books in the English library, older people teaching young people how to make traditional foods, younger people helping elders navigate computer software, and so on. Elders organized approximately 330 events and welcomed more than 11,000 visitors in the first two years.

Key Findings:

1. The frequency of Ibasho café visits has a strong relationship with sense of belonging to their neighborhood, number of friends, and sense of efficacy.

Efficacy:

Regular Ibasho attendees have a higher level of belief in their ability to control their environment. Also, older individuals, men, and wealthier individuals all felt more efficacious. The elders who manage Ibasho have organized various events to educate children about local culture, such as cooking, holiday decorations, and traditional festivals. To prepare for future disasters, elders also organize activities where younger generations learn how to live in an environmentally sustainable manner and survive without electricity and water.

Social Networks:

More regular attendance at Ibasho made it more likely that people would report having more friends. The Ibasho café facilitated the friendships more than simply by the increasing number of people to talk to. This result suggests that Ibasho serves as a place where deep relationships are formed. Attendees reported, "Now we are friends because we had conversations here." The Ibasho café has provided a comfortable, informal place where outsiders can find and get to know people from the community, and many long-distance friendships were also formed there.

Sense of Belonging:

Regular attendance at Ibasho was significantly associated with a deeper sense of belonging. There may be two reasons behind this finding. First, most of the Ibasho café users are from Massaki area, where many residents have lived for an extended period. Second, Ibasho café users may already have been inclined to participate in community activities, such as sports events or the local festival, before the GEJE, thus forming stronger relationships with members of their community.

2. Perception of Recovery.

Comparing 2013 and 2014, the quantitative data suggest that Massaki (Ibasho's neighborhood) saw a sharp change in the level of perceived neighborhood recovery over time. While we cannot be sure of the cause, two possibilities seem likely. First, the Ibasho café was built in Massaki, giving residents a permanent structure they are proud of and can use in place of temporary structures provided by the city. Second, Massaki was chosen for the Ibasho café because of its leaders' strong commitment to creating a social space for its residents. That high level of commitment may have resulted in other improvements that also influence local residents' perceptions regarding the level of neighborhood recovery.

3. Elders Have Stronger Sense of Belonging to Their Community.

The duration of residency had a positive connection to the sense of belonging to their neighborhood. Since elders reside in their community for a long period of time, they have a stronger sense of belonging to their communities than younger generations. Hence, they are more likely to invest their time and effort to improve their community to be more resilient.

4. Walkability Is a Critical Point to Determine Whether or Not Users Would Engage with This Type of Service—Especially Older Users.

Most of the regular users live within walking distance of the café. This result is especially critical to allow elders to be engaged in the Ibasho program since most of them do not drive. Moreover, the costs incurred for using public transportation may challenge individuals with fixed income, such as pensioners.

Policymakers and NGOs Should:

1. Include infrastructure development as a part of community development to provide people with a tangible way to measure their progress. It also makes it easier for them to develop a sense of ownership in a project, and to invest the effort needed to ensure long-term sustainability.

2. Empower elders to sustain the place and its programs. It is crucial to truly trust elders to run the program while providing the support they

need to develop those skills, particularly during the early stages of development and operation. As one elder told us, "Please fully trust us to operate this place, if you would like us (elders) to be in charge."

3. Rethink the role of elders in the community, and give them opportunities to be useful to others and help realize that they still can be active participants in the social web.

4. Encourage a strong solidarity and support system among elders. One individual may not be strong enough to stand up to voice an opinion, but a group of individuals who are the part of the organization can better withstand challenges and pressure from external forces such as regulators and other government officials.

5. Involve local government. To achieve stable operation of an Ibasho café or similar project, it is crucial to find ways to involve local government without compromising the initiative's community-driven nature.

6. Make sure donors understand the need for flexibility during the development process. Funders would normally like to see a project completed in a short period of time, but community members may not feel the same sense of urgency.

7. Be sensitive to cultural differences. While the fundamental needs of human beings don't change across cultures, lifestyles, community capacities, financial resources, existing knowledge and skills, and social interactions may differ greatly.

8. Provide accessible transportation. Since many elders rely on public transportation to move about, it is important to think about how people will get there when planning where to create a place, ideally selecting a site that is convenient to affordable public transportation. Otherwise, many elders and children cannot come unless someone gives them a ride.

9. Focus not only on the capacity building within their community, but also bridge and link their efforts to people who are dissimilar and other communities, so that they will gain the higher sense of efficacy and motivation to make their project to be more inclusive and sustain it for a long time.

Related Video: Elders Leading Resilience: https://www.youtube.com /watch?v=0oON18Mdb9M.

See also "Co-creating Environments: Empowering Elders and Strengthening Communities through Design," contributed by Dr. Emi Kiyota, founder of the Ibasho: https://onlinelibrary.wiley.com/doi/epdf /10.1002/hast.913; https://ibasho.org/resources.

This information is adapted with permission from "Elders Leading the Way to Resilience: Impact of Ibasho Cafe on the Level of Social Capital," http://www.ibasho.org /researches.

Social Networks, Support Systems, and Rethinking Community

Despite the proliferation of formal caregiving organizations and special-ized personnel oriented toward senior citizens, growing attention has focused on the existence of "natural" support systems, or what Antonucci calls social "convoys" *generated by the elderly themselves* (Antonucci, Ajrouch, and Birditt 2014). In seeking to understand the importance of informal social ties in meeting the needs of the elderly, one level of analysis has concentrated on the study of "social networks"—ego-centered sets of personal links and their interconnections generated among friends, kin, and neighbors (Sokolovsky 2006). Network analysis has been particularly useful for studying urban set-tings where social action is not readily understood within the context of tra-ditional social structures such as the totemic clans of the Tiwi or East African age sets (see Liu 2019 for Hong Kong).

Ironically, while measures of informal social interaction have been viewed as crucial in gerontological theory and research, too many studies have failed to examine the qualitative characteristics and cultural meaning that social networks hold for the elderly. For example, survey studies of aged living in single-room occupancy (SRO) hotels in the central core of older U.S. cities often depicted these individuals as totally isolated and incapable of replen-ishing an impoverished repertoire of social ties (Sokolovsky 2006). However, my own research with community psychiatrist Carl Cohen in New York City SROs showed that elderly living there were far from true isolates—only about 5 percent fit this description. Rather, we showed that the cultural con-struction of their networks was different from middle-class elderly patterns and was generated through three network features: structural dispersion, highly selective intimacy, and variable activation of social ties. It was found that many of these elderly identified themselves as "loners." However, this was typically a stance that enhanced local perception of their independence. It combined with their small but active social networks to connect them to their urban environment in a culturally meaningful way (Sokolovsky and Cohen 1987).[2]

In a very different cultural setting during the early 1980s, when I first developed an interest in the issue of nonfamilial environments for the elderly in Croatia's capital, Zagreb, scholars in the United States advised me not to bother. I was told that there was so little interest in homes for the aged that most of the rooms had to be rented out to students or tourists. Barely two years later, this was no longer the case, when I found that each of the nine *Dom Umirovljeni* (home for retired persons) in the city was filled to capacity with local elders, and some had waiting lists of over one year (Sokolovsky, Sosic, and Pavlekovic 1991). I found that, in general, the public was horrified at the thought of such places. Ironically, however, most of the residents them-selves thought such residences situated in the heart of their lifelong neighborhoods were wonderful places where their needs were met and they felt fortunate to be living. My research showed that the elders in these facilities typically had very few living close kin: they saw the *Dom* as a vital resource for their survival in late life.

A central issue related to social support systems among the elderly is the degree to which the development and expansion of formal supports and the built environments expands upon existing caring behaviors of kin, friends, and others (Davey et al. 2005; Duppen et al. 2019). To understand this, any student of contemporary community development for older adults has to learn a set of acronyms, blooming almost as fast as the growing crop of North American seniors. There are ACLFs, CCRCs, LCCs, LORCs, and perhaps most intriguing of all, NORCs or Naturally Occurring Retirement Communities—long-standing residential areas where a high density of elders are living in the community (Stone 2017).[3] Over the past three decades cities like Chicago and New York were in fact developing some of the world's highest concentrations of NORCs. In the 1990s New York City became one of the first U.S. urban areas to develop specific programs directing social services, including case managers and nurses, to where the elder concentration in apartment buildings went beyond 60 percent (Vladeck 2004). It eventually added to this program a few elder-dense neighborhoods or "horizontal NORCs," as they are called in suburban areas.

The Global Age-Friendly Community Movement

Beyond aging in place and personal social networks, the study of neighborhood dimensions—community design and facilitation of social engagement—has come to be seen as crucial in creating healthy environments along the life course (Ahn, Kang, and Kwon 2019). Despite the public emphasis on building totally new and separate physical environments for older adults, oriented to their changing needs, we learn in the chapter by Phil Stafford that the vast majority of older Americans consistently claim they want to stay in place. This desire is connecting with not only a growing international emphasis on promoting an active view of late life, but of conceptualizing how

---

WEB SPECIAL:

K. Capps, "What Have We Learned from 30 Years of 'Aging in Place'?" Citylab, March 31, 2015, https://www.citylab.com/equity/2015/03/what-have-we-learned-from-30-years-of-aging-in-place/389201/.

WEB SPECIAL:

M. Mather and P. Scommegna, "How Neighborhoods Affect the Health and Well-Being of Older Americans," Population Reference Bureau, February 13, 2017, https://www.prb.org/todays-research-aging -neighborhoods-health/.

---

to construct elder-friendly and life span communities and neighborhoods (Stafford 2018). The growth and development of this global age friendly movement is captured in Phil Stafford's chapter in Part V, which explores the multidisciplinary nature of these efforts to build communities of the future that unite the idea of sustainability with what we are learning about local environments persons can successfully age into (see also Stafford 2018).

In thinking about how older adults could be engaged everywhere, Phillip Stafford's chapter centers upon a discussion of the elder-friendly community movement in Bloomington, Indiana, drawing upon the principles developed through "AdvantAge" (www.vnsny.org/advantage) and the World Health Organization (WHO 2018). WHO launched its international plan in 2006 to certify age-friendly communities, and now this encompasses 300 communities in 33 countries. In the United States with the help of AARP there are now over 77 localities that impact more than 41 million U.S. residents (Turner and Morken 2016).

Stafford uses his ethnographic study to explore internationally how the local cultural construction of home and community can be directed to address elders' basic needs; optimizing well-being, maximizing autonomy for those with disabilities, and promoting civic engagement (Rowles and

---

WEB SPECIALS:

1. Moving toward age-friendly communities and environments.
AARP, "The 8 Domains of Livability: Case Studies," https://www .aarp.org/livable-communities/network-age-friendly-communities/info -2015/8-domains-of-livability-case-studies.html.

2. N. Turner and L. Morken, *Better Together: A Comparative Analysis of Age-Friendly and Dementia Friendly Communities*, AARP, 2016, https://extranet.who.int/agefriendlyworld/wp-content/uploads/2016/03 /IAReport_BetterTogether_v4.pdf.[4]

Chaudhury 2008). There are a growing number of resources that readers can use to apply the ideas in Stafford's chapter to their own communities, and some of them are indicated in the Web Special below.

An important way to see some of the ideas in Stafford's chapter put in action is to read the Part V Web Book Photo Essay by anthropologist Iveris Martinez and architect Ebru Ozer. It details in words and images the process of incorporating age-friendly design into a proposed initiative to develop the area under "The Underline," an area below the Miami Metrorail. The authors developed a collaboration between students from Florida International University and local elders who would likely use the proposed park, urban trail, and living art destination.

Global Cities and Late Life

As the majority of the globe's citizens now live in urban areas, attention has been increasingly directed to the implications for older city residents (OECD 2015). Those who are not city dwellers will still feel the effects of urban cultural desires, witness the outflow of those seeking city-based jobs, and experience the impact of huge portions of national resources being gobbled up by their mega-metropolises. Incredibly, by 2020, *none* of the top 20 largest cities in the world are found in Europe or the United States. They are dispersed throughout the nations of Japan, China, Mexico, India, and Brazil.

In some of these countries there have developed unexpected rapid changes in the age-related demography and social fabric of cities, which are mandating shifts in planning. An example comes from the country of India discussed in Part V by Sarah Lamb. For example, within the urban area of Chennai, by 2005 fertility had dropped so rapidly that the city found itself closing 10 maternity wards and retraining staff to work in new geriatric units (United Nations Population Fund 2007). In the United States "The Maturing of America" national surveys (2005 and 2010) initially found that less than half of the 1,790 communities surveyed had begun preparing to deal with an aging population (https://icma.org/documents/maturing-america). The Part V Web Chapter by Michael Gusmano brings this issue into focus by presenting some of the core data from the ongoing World Cities Project, examining aging and environment in New York City, London, Paris, and Tokyo (Rodwin and Gusmano 2006; https://wagner.nyu.edu/community/faculty/victor-g -rodwin/world-cities-project). As major global urban centers, these locales offer excellent public transportation, world-class medical facilities, and concentrations of social and cultural amenities. He finds a key dividing point between the "hard" cities of London and New York with greater risks for social isolation, inequality, and concentrated poverty than their "softer" counterparts of Tokyo and Paris (Buffel and Phillipson 2016). A critical aspect of the chapter is the differential mechanisms by which the four cities

---

PROJECT TO FOLLOW:

The Aging Readiness & Competitiveness Report: http://arc2018
.aarpinternational.org/index.html. This project is focusing on the state
of global aging policies, with an initial focus on small, innovative economies that are in 10 geographically, culturally, and socioeconomically
diverse nations.

---

developed support systems to deal with the very high percentages of those
past age 85, especially woman, who are living alone. Tokyo is the exception
here with a much lower proportion of very elderly women living by themselves, but as we learned in Part III, living alone in old age is increasing substantially in that country as well.

Ironically, we will also see in Sarah Lamb's highly nuanced chapter, centered in urban Kolkata (Calcutta) India, that aloneness does not necessarily
mean living by yourself (see also Sadler et al. 2006; Van Der Geest 2016). Here,
set among a newly emerging middle class she explores the transformation of
Sannyasa, the Hindu traditional cultural script of aging, which is ideally set in
the cultural space of the patrilineal joint family. It is to be enacted through
Dharma (duty) and *Seva* (service), the mechanisms of care by young kin, and
reciprocal blessings they should receive in return. This ideally creates a multigenerational, kin-bounded social landscape, which is elder-male dominated
and elder-female mediated. As Lamb shows, globalizing "outsourced sons" and
educated young women are transforming the meaning and enactment of the
scripts by which older adults connect with their younger generations (see also
Lamb 2009, Lamb 2018; Ahlin 2020). Aging outside of this script is culturally
interpreted as "being alone" though the person might reside in an extended
family setting. Older women moving out of the traditional family setting have
found refuge in a variety of cultural spaces such as in laughing clubs (see Box
V.2), Hindu temples, and newly forming elder residences. These latter elderscapes, although initially modeled after Western nursing facilities, are being
transformed to correspond more with cultural notions of supportive spaces for
elders. Still, for many this is perceived as a failure of their societal system,
while for others it is a logical passage into the modern, globalized world.

Another very recent pattern by some Indian middle-class urban families is
emulating a Western pattern of moving to luxury senior apartments and
enjoying "active leisure" involving regular vacation travel (Samanta 2019).
For a vivid picture of the contemporary life of elders in both in New Delhi,
India, and Kathmandu, Nepal, explore the amazing Web-based ethnography
situated in this Web Special.

Playing at Any Age

Driven by my penchant for creative playfulness, while doing research in Croatia during the 1980s I became fascinated with the Croatian word *ludost*. It translates as "playful silliness" from the Latin noun *ludus*, referring to a wide range of fun, playful things including games, shows, or sports. And just as unadulterated play for the young, which seems crucial for psychological development, was becoming hypercontrolled and watched by "helicopter" parents, the ludic turn was emerging in late adulthood. Here we have the declaration of a Gerontoludic Manifesto (De Schutter and Abeele 2015), formation of the Gerontoludic Society (http://www.gerontoludicsociety.com/), and development of the Laugh Project focused on older persons with dementia (Treadaway et al. 2018). Hopefully, you already realized the importance of play, detailed in the introduction to Part II with a focus on the intergenerational contact created by integrated preschool and senior living environments. In Box V.2 on page 438 we encounter another example in which a seemingly simple creation related to cultural ideas of health in India has reverberated in many other parts of the world.

Elders Green the Urban World

An impact of urbanization and globalization that has emerged over the last two decades has been loss of farm communities, public green space, and the broad concern over climate change (Christensen 2018). This is often coupled with a discussion of environmental justice countering the dumping of foul refuse in poor urban neighborhoods. Such acts not only dramatically alter the landscapes in which elders and their families live but increase exposure to toxic substances (see Part IV Luborsky). One response to this that unites such disparate places as Quito, Ecuador; Kampala, Uganda; and New York City is the grassroots development of urban community gardens to not only feed poor families but reclaim and restore ruined landscapes. Just as grandmothers took to the streets to protest the genocide of their disappeared children and grandchildren in Argentina, other countries have witnessed

BOX V.2   LAUGHTER YOGA REVISITED: AYURVEDIC LAUGHTER MEDICINE
GOES MAINSTREAM

A decade ago in this book's previous edition, when I wrote about Laughter Yoga, few people I talked to in North America or Europe knew what this was about. Times have changed. This became clear to me as over the past several years when I have lectured about the cultural context of aging in Denmark, Spain, and at small Ithaca College in a bucolic area of upstate New York. At all these settings I was somewhat shocked that a good number in the audience not only had heard of Laughter Yoga, but in each location there were more than a few individuals who had participated in that activity.

In India where the bonds of extended family life are often considered the only culturally accepted place to experience a satisfying old age, Sarah Lamb in Part V mentions the beginning of alternative cultural spaces harnessing age-peer power. One of these new creations is delightfully documented in the 2001 film *The Laughing Club of India*. It explores the work of Dr. Madan Kataria, who in 1995 instigated a group of mostly elderly patients and neighbors to meet daily in Mumbai's Priyadarshini Park to just laugh. Drawing on yoga postures and a breathing technique called Kapalabhati—"cleaning out your brain"— he developed various mirth-inducing techniques, with club members learning how to produce a repertoire of different styles of laughing. Dr. Kataria found that participants experienced improved health and decreased levels of stress and he claims such behavior can alleviate hypertension, arthritis, and migraine.

Subsequently Dr. Kataria set up the School of Laughter Yoga after creating World Laughter Day on May 6, 1998, where at the Mumbai racetrack 10,000 people turned out to laugh their heads off. This movement spread across India and now boasts over 50,000 clubs in 50 other nations (www.laughteryoga.org). In the United States the biggest such center for passing on Dr. Kataria's ideas is the Laughter Yoga Institute of Laguna Beach, California, where structured merriment is performed each day on sands facing the Pacific Ocean (www.joyfulb.com/laught eryoga.htm#Classes). By 2020 this Indian doctor's 20th-century invention has become a truly global phenomenon, used in an amazing array of health, recreational, and work settings and even penal institutions (http://laughteryoga.org/). It is now quite easy to find videos extolling the benefits of this practice by such luminaries as Oprah or John Cleese, of Monty Python fame (see related resources below). Dr. Kataria is also mounting a campaign for One Minute Laughter for World Peace at the Opening of the 2020 Tokyo Olympics.

Health in Old Age Is a Laughing Matter:

Dr. Kataria's creation provides a wonderful example of cultural convergence with the prior work of Dr. Norman Cousins in the United States, who stimulated research on laughter and positive immune system responses, and the efforts of Dr. Patch Adams, who sought to improve hospital medical treatment through acts of clowning. Serious medical work is showing some of the health connections Dr. Kataria initially found (Bennett and Lengacher 2008). Releasing emotions with laughter is seen as one method to boost the immune response, by reducing stress hormones while producing endorphins. Merriment healing to promote psychological well-being has now come to be practiced in senior centers and long-term care facilities (Westburg 2003; Schreiner, Yamamoto, and Shiotani 2005). After all, "A clown is like an aspirin," remarked Groucho Marx, "only he works twice as fast."

Applying Groucho's Prescription:

Laughter's stress-reducing effects is where most benefits manifest themselves. With time, the cumulative negative impact of everyday stresses piles up and breaks bodies down. The U.S. National Institute of Mental Health says that routine stress can lead to serious problems like heart disease, high blood pressure, diabetes, depression, and anxiety disorder, among others. In Japan, healthy elderly people have shown significantly increased bone mineral density and improved moods after once-weekly therapeutic laughter exercise sessions of 30 minutes for three months. And research on U.S. cancer patients has linked induced laughter to increased natural killer (NK) cell activity. These cells are instrumental in fighting disease, and that same boost was seen in NK cell activity when laughter was induced in healthy patients, too. In 2015, a Belgian nurse named Isabel Fernandez instituted a therapeutic humor practice in the cardiac and orthopedic rehabilitation departments of CHU Brugmann Hospital in Brussels. Hospital reviewers found laughter aided physical healing and general well-being, reducing stress in patients and caregivers, and her practice was quickly extended to the neurology and psychology clinics as well.

Related Resources:

The Dr. Patch Adams Gesundheit Institute—www.patchadams.org.
Video: "Benefits of Laughter Yoga with John Cleese," https://www
.youtube.com/watch?v=0N60nBD-_Mc.

WEB SPECIAL:

S. Barnes, "Revolutionary "Homefarm" Combines Retirement Homes with Eco-Friendly Vertical Farming," discusses an exciting new design for older adults in the island nation of Singapore. https://mymodernmet .com/spark-homefarm/?fbclid=IwAR3lMXLbi5oUTjIZ358YaBPUq mff_uf_15QRiXT2DM7sTqO-eOo9QE0oS9E.

---

elders at the forefront of reclaiming communities devastated by some of the impacts of globalization. The discussion of community gardens in the United States can be profitably compared to the more individualistic Allotment Garden movement in Europe that emerged in the late 19th century (Martens, Nordh, and Gonzalez 2018).

Jay Sokolovsky's chapter in Part V draws upon the concept of "civic ecology." It documents elders' roles in a dramatic battle throughout New York City to create neighborhood-based sites of civic greening and community building, forging ties across class, ethnicity, and age. The model of civic greening can have many applications, uniting generations within dangerous urban neighborhoods, improving the nutritional and health profiles of poor communities, and even serving as a central part of new therapeutic environments for extremely frail elders.

This issue of civic engagement and social capital is one of the most widely written about topics in recent literature about aging (AARP 2012; Kruse and Schmitt 2015; Nyqvist and Forsman 2015).[5] Much of the early impetus for this was a collaboration between the Harvard School of Public Health and MetLife Foundation, which established the Initiative on Retirement and Civic Engagement. As an outgrowth of a 2004 report, *Reinventing Aging: Baby Boomers and Civic Engagement*, a national campaign was launched to change public attitudes toward aging and motivate boomers to engage in community service. Some of this concern was driven by sociologist Robert Putnam's famous book *Bowling Alone: The Collapse and Revival of American Community* (2000), which foretold of a dramatic decline in civic life and social capital developing in the boomer and succeeding generations (Achenbaum 2006: Jones 2019). Much of the debate on this issue has been based on survey research and largely overlooked qualitative information on the life of community elders, especially in poorer communities (Newman 2003; Chambré and Netting 2016). In ignoring these issues, civic engagement discussions may miss much of what is emerging in elder-dense communities, especially as multimedia interaction becomes more common among older populations (Chan 2018).

WEB SPECIAL:

A. Mackenzie, "Beyond Food: Community Gardens as Places of Connection and Empowerment," Project for Public Spaces, March 1, 2016. A great blog article listing many more benefits of urban gardens. https://www.pps.org/article/beyond-food-community-gardens-as-places-of-connection-and-empowerment.

Elderscapes and Elders as Pioneers

One of the salient issues emerging from the discussion of social capital organization is how the variable nature of community organization relates to well-being in old age. A good example is provided in Maria Vesperi's book, *City of Green Benches* (1998), about St. Petersburg, Florida. Local leaders, in an attempt to change their city's image from "God's Waiting Room," undertook a revitalization plan that included the removal of the numerous green benches on commercial streets and the tearing down of old residential hotels and small stores along downtown side streets. These were the key sites where elderly residents had generated their own very active and supportive social life. However, in partial compensation, as housing and amenities declined and the remaining population continued to age in place, congregate dining sites, adult day care, and a variety of other community-based opportunities for social integration began to increase (Iwarsson et al. 2016).[6] By 2019, the couple of remaining green benches are hidden away in the Sunshine Senior Center while the rest of the downtown has become a playground for prospering millennials.

One of most powerful things now happening across the North American landscape is the rapid creation of alternative social spaces to accommodate the changing perception of aging itself. Sociologist Stephen Katz in his Part V Web Book chapter innovatively pulls together three perspectives in aging studies: institutional ethnographies, "aging in place" debates, and community network research. He unites these streams to discuss communities based on mobility in the context of a postmodern construct of late life within the nation's oldest local zone, Charlotte County, Florida. Far from the depiction of 1960s St. Petersburg as "God's Waiting Room" or "the home of the newly wed and the soon to be dead," he creatively maps the emerging new topography of cultural spaces of retired populations, with entirely new elderscapes. One of the most important parts of the chapter is situating the "Snowbird" phenomena, especially the large group of Canadian seasonal migrants to Florida, within the frame of globalization and the new flows of bicultural elders. This is literally redefining notions of home and community as these transnational migrants create rituals for double homecomings in both parts of North America.

The range of community spaces for experiencing aging reveals the great diversity encountered when trying to understand late adulthood in the 21st century. In the last two Web Book chapters, readers are provided entrée into the inner working of a small-town senior center and comparison of community formation in North American RV encampments, and a Papua New Guinea village.

Notes

1. This survey data has been complemented by more qualitatively focused sociological and anthropological research that has begun to detail how family structures are adapting to dramatic global changes in Africa (Aboderin 2006); Asia (Knodel and Saengtienchai 2007; Schröder-Butterfill 2009); and Latin America (Lloyd-Sherlock 1998; Gomes and Montes de Oca 2004). Many of these same issues are also dealt by authors in this volume, particularly in Part II, III, and IV.

2. For an ethnographic perspective on older SRO dwellers in San Diego see Eckert 1980.

3. ACLF stands for adult care living facility; CCRCs are continuing care retirement communities; LCCs are lifecare/continuing care retirement communities; and LORCs are leisure-oriented retirement communities.

4. For Europe see AGE Platform Europe, *Age-Friendly Environments in Europe. A Handbook of Domains for Policy Action*, https://extranet.who.int/agefriendly world/wp-content/uploads/2018/01/AFEE-handbook-FINAL.pdf.

5. The Gerontological Society of America has an excellent Web site with links to civic engagement: http://www.agingsociety.org/agingsociety/Civic%20Engage ment/about_civic_engagement.htm.

6. For an analysis of a more disastrous impact of urban change, see Teski et al. 1983. This is a study of how the building of casinos in Atlantic City, New Jersey, affected the community life of the elderly. A more positive perspective on planned urban change can be seen in Hornum's (1987) study of the elderly in planned cities in England.

Bibliography

AARP. 2012. "Civic Engagement among Mid-Life and Older Adults: Findings from the 2012 Survey on Civic Engagement." https://www.aarp.org/con tent/dam/aarp/research/surveys_statistics/general/2012/Civic-Engage ment-Among-Mid-Life-and-Older-Adults-Findings-from-the-2012-Sur vey-on-Civic-Engagement-AARP.pdf.

Aboderin, I. 2006. *Intergenerational Support and Old Age in Africa.* New Brunswick, NJ: Transaction.

Achenbaum, W. 2006. "A History of Civic Engagement of Older People." *Generations: Journal of the American Society on Aging* 30(4): 18–23.

Ahlin, T. 2020. "Frequent Callers: "Good Care" with ICTs in Indian Transnational Families." *Medical Anthropology* 39(1): 69-82.

Ahn, M., J. Kang, and H. Kwon. 2019. "The Concept of Aging in Place as Intention." *Gerontologist.* https://doi.org/10.1093/geront/gny167.

Antonucci, T., K. Ajrouch, and K. Birditt. 2014. "The Convoy Model: Explaining Social Relations from a Multidisciplinary Perspective." *Gerontologist* 54: 82–92.

Bennett, M., and C. Lengacher. 2008. "Humor and Laughter May Influence Health: III. Laughter and Health Outcomes." *Evidenced Based Complementary and Alternative Medicine* 5(1): 37–40.

Buffel, T., and C. Phillipson. 2016. "Can Global Cities Be 'Age-Friendly Cities'? Urban Development and Ageing Populations." *Cities* 55: 94–100.

Chambré, S., and F. Netting. 2016. "Baby Boomers and the Long-Term Transformation of Retirement and Volunteering: Evidence for a Policy Paradigm Shift." *Journal of Applied Gerontology* 37(10): 1295–320.

Chan, M. 2018. "Digital Communications and Psychological Well-Being across the Life Span: Examining the Intervening Roles of Social Capital and Civic Engagement." *Telematics and Informatics* 35(6): 1744–54.

Christensen, J. 2018. *Eldercare, Health, and Ecosyndemics in a Perilous World.* New York: Rowman & Littlefield.

Cliggett, L. 2005 *Grains from Grass: Aging, Gender and Famine in Rural Africa.* Ithaca, NY: Cornell University Press.

Davey, A., E. Femia, S. Zarit, D. Shea, G. Sundström, S. Berg, M. Smyer, and J. Savla. 2005. "Life on the Edge: Patterns of Formal and Informal Help to Older Adults in the United States and Sweden." *Journal of Gerontology* 60(5): S281–S288.

De Schutter, B., and V. Abeele. 2015. "Towards a Gerontoludic Manifesto." *Anthropology and Aging* 36(2): 112–20.

Duppen, D., M. C. J. Van der Elst, S. Dury, D. Lambotte, L. De Donder, and D-SCOPE. 2019. "The Social Environment's Relationship With Frailty: Evidence From Existing Studies." *Journal of Applied Gerontology* 3(1): 3–26.

Eckert, K. 1980. *The Unseen Elderly: A Study of Marginally Subsistent Hotel Dwellers.* San Diego, CA: Campanile.

Fanany, R., and I. Fanany. 2019. *The Elderly Must Endure: Ageing in the Minangkabau Community in Modern Indonesia.* Singapore: ISEAS—Yusof Ishak Institute.

Gomes, C., and V. Montes de Oca. 2004. "Ageing in Mexico: Families, Informal Care and Reciprocity." In *Living Longer: Aging, Development and Social Protection*, edited by P. Lloyd-Sherlock. London: Zed.

Hornum, B. 1987. "The Elderly in British New Towns: New Roles, New Networks." In *Growing Old in Difference Societies: Cross-Cultural Perspectives*, edited by J. Sokolovsky. Acton, MA: Copley.

Hromadžić, A., and M. Palmberger. 2018. *Care across Distance: Ethnographic Explorations of Aging and Migration*. New York: Berghahn.

Iwarsson, S., et al. 2016. "Synthesizing ENABLE-AGE Research Findings to Suggest Evidence-Based Home and Health Interventions." *Journal of Housing For the Elderly* 30(3). https://www.tandfonline.com/doi/full/10.1080/02763893.2016.1198742.

Jones, B. 2019. *Social Capital in American Life*. Cham, Switzerland: Palgrave Pivot.

Knodel, J., and C. Saegtienchai. 2007. "Thailand: Rural Parents with Urban Children: Social and Economic Implications of Migration on the Rural Elderly in Thailand." *Population, Space and Place* 13(3): 193–210.

Kruse, A., and E. Schmitt. 2015. "Shared Responsibility and Civic Engagement in Very Old Age." *Research in Human Development* 2(1–2): 133–48.

Lamb, S. 2009. *Aging in India and Abroad: Old Age Homes, Modern Seniors and Transnational Lives*. Bloomington: Indiana University Press.

Lamb, S. 2018. "Aging, Ambivalent Modernities, and Social Value in India." *Contributions to Indian Sociology*. 50th Anniversary Special Issue.

Liu, S. 2019. *Social Support Networks, Coping and Positive Aging Among the Community-Dwelling Elderly in Hong Kong*. Singapore: Huazhong University of Science and Technology Press.

Lloyd-Sherlock, P. 1998. "Old Age, Migration, and Poverty in the Shantytowns of Sao Paulo, Brazil." *Journal of Developing Areas* 32(4): 491–514.

Martens, N., H. Nordh, and M. Gonzalez. 2018. "Visiting the Allotment Garden—A Complete Experience." *Journal of Housing For the Elderly* 32(2): 121–34. https://doi.org/10.1080/02763893.2018.1431580.

Mason, K. 1992. "Family Change and Support for the Elderly in Thailand: What Do We Know?" *Asia Pacific Population Journal* 7(3): 13–32.

Murphy, E., and B. Eghaneyan. 2018. "Understanding the Phenomenon of Older Adult Homelessness in North America: A Qualitative Interpretive Meta-Synthesis." *British Journal of Social Work* 48(8): 2361–80. https://doi.org/10.1093/bjsw/bcx163.

Nåre, L., K. Walsh, and L. Baldazar. 2017. "Ageing in Transnational Contexts: Transforming Everyday Practices and Identities in Later Life." *Identities* 24(5): 515–23. doi: 10.1080/1070289X.2017.1346986.

Newman, K. 2003. *A Different Shade of Gray: Midlife and Beyond in the Inner City*. New York: New Press.

Nyqvist, F., and A. Forsman. 2015. eds. *Social Capital as a Health Resource in Later Life: The Relevance of Context*. New York: Springer.

OECD. 2015. *Ageing in Cities Policy Highlights*. https://www.oecd.org/cfe/regional-policy/Policy-Brief-Ageing-in-Cities.pdf. Paris: OECD.

Putnam, R. 2000. *Bowling Alone: The Collapse and Revival of American Community*. New York: Simon and Schuster.

Rodwin, V., and M. Gusmano, eds. 2006. *Growing Older in World Cities: New York, London, Paris and Tokyo.* Nashville, TN: Vanderbilt University Press.

Rowles, G., and H. Chaudhury, eds. 2008. *Home and Identity in Late Life: International Perspectives.* New York: Springer.

Sadler, E. A., A. W. Braam, M. I. Broese van Groenou, D. J. H. Deeg, and S. van der Geest. 2006. "Cosmic Transcendence, Loneliness, and Exchange of Emotional Support with Adult Children: A Study among Older Parents in The Netherlands." *European Journal of Ageing* 3(3): 146–54.

Samanta, T. 2018. "The Good Life: Anthropology and Aging. Third Age, Brand Modi and the Cultural Demise of Old Age in India." *Anthropology and Aging* 39(1): 94–104.

Schreiner, A., E. Yamamoto, and H. Shiotani. 2005. "Positive Affect among Nursing Home Residents with Alzheimer's Dementia: The Effect of Recreational Activity." *Aging and Mental Health* 9(2): 129–34.

Schröder-Butterfill, E. 2009. *Ageing, Networks and Exchange: Old-Age Support Dynamics in Indonesia.* Oxford: Oxford University Press,

Sokolovsky, J. 2002. "Living Arrangements of Older Persons and Family Support in Less Developed Countries" *Population Bulletin of the United Nations* nos. 42/43: 162–92.

Sokolovsky, J. 2006. "If Not, Why Not: Synchronizing Qualitative and Quantitative Research in Studying the Elderly." In *Qualitative and Mixed Methods Research: Improving the Quality of Science and Addressing Health Disparities,* edited by R. Shield. Washington, DC: American Public Health Association.

Sokolovsky, J., and C. Cohen. 1987. "Networks as Adaptation: The Cultural Meaning of Being a 'Loner' Among the Inner City Elderly." In *Growing Old in Different Societies: Cross-Cultural Perspectives,* edited by J. Sokolovsky. Acton, MA: Copley.

Sokolovsky, J., S. Sosic, and G. Pavlekovic. 1991. "Self-Help Groups for the Aged in Yugoslavia: How Effective Are They?" *Journal of Cross-Cultural Gerontology* 6(3): 319–30.

Stack, C., and L. Burton. 1994. "Kinscripts: Reflections of Family, Generation, and Culture." In *Mothering: Ideology, Experience and Agency,* edited by E. Glenn, G. Chang, and L. Forcey. London: Routledge.

Stafford, P. 2018. *The Global Age-Friendly Community Movement.* New York: Berghahn.

Stone, R. 2017. "Successful Aging in Community: The Role of Housing, Services, and Community Integration." *Generations* 40(4): 67–73.

Teski, M., F. Smith, R. Helsabeck, and C. Yeager. 1983. *A City Revitalized: The Elderly Lose at Monopoly.* Lanham, MD: University Press of America.

Treadaway, C., J. Fennell, D. Prytherch, G. Kenning, and A. Walters, 2018. "Designing for Well-Being in Late Stage Dementia." In *Pathways to Well-Being in Design: Examples from the Arts, Humanities and the Built Environment,* edited by R. Coles, S. Costa, and S. Watson. London: Routledge.

Turner, N., and L. Morken. 2016. *Better Together: A Comparative Analysis of Age-Friendly and Dementia Friendly Communities*. AARP. https://extranet.who .int/agefriendlyworld/wp-content/uploads/2016/03/IAReport_Better Together_v4.pdf.

United Nations Population Division. 2019. "Living Arrangements of Older Persons around the World." April. POPFACTS, No. 2019/2. https://www .un.org/en/development/desa/population/publications/pdf/popfacts /PopFacts_2019-2.pdf.

United Nations Population Fund. 2007. *Growing Up Urban: State of the World 2007: Youth Supplement*. http://www.unfpa.org/swp/2007/presskit/pdf /sowp2007_eng.pdf.

Van der Geest, S. 2016. "Will Families in Ghana Continue to Care for Older People? Logic and Contradiction in Policy." In *Ageing in Sub-Saharan Africa: Spaces and Practices of Care*, edited by J. Hoffman and K. Pype. London: Policy.

Van Eeuwijk, P. 2020. "Precarity, Assemblages, and Indonesian Elder Care." *Medical Anthropology* 39(1): 41–54.

Vesperi, M. 1998. *City of Green Benches*, rev. ed. Ithaca, NY: Cornell University Press.

Vladeck, F. 2004. *A Good Place to Grow Old: New York's Model for NORC Supportive Service Programs*. New York: United Hospital Fund. www.uhfnyc.org/usr _doc/goodplace.pdf.

Wallace, L. M., O. Theou, F. Pena, K. Rockwood, and M. K. Andrew 2015. "Social Vulnerability as a Predictor of Mortality and Disability: Cross-country Differences in the Survey of Health, Aging, and Retirement in Europe (SHARE)." *Aging Clinical and Experimental Research* 27(3): 365–72.

Westburg, N. 2003. "Hope, Laughter, and Humor in Residents and Staff at an Assisted Living Facility." *Journal of Mental Health Counseling* 25(1): 16–32.

WHO. 2018. *The Global Network for Age-Friendly Cities and Communities*. https:// www.who.int/ageing/gnafcc-report-2018.pdf.

CHAPTER THIRTY-FIVE

Web Book: The Structural Vulnerability of Older People in a Matrilineal Society

The Minangkabau of West Sumatra, Indonesia

Edi Indrizal, Philip Kreager, and Elisabeth Schröder-Butterfill

Available at: http://www.culturalcontextofaging.com/webbook-indrizal

Through a series of expertly drawn case studies Indrizal, Kreager, and Schröder-Butterfill discuss how a women-centered kin descent system structures the life course and frames late-life cultural spaces and scripts. Here women at the center of economy, ritual, and family life are situated within a local, devout version of Islam.

CHAPTER THIRTY-SIX

Old People Everywhere

The Future of Age-Friendly Communities

Philip B. Stafford

A Fieldnote: Bloomington, Indiana Ethnography of Aging in Place

Milton takes great pleasure in shopping. He spends hours in the grocery store, stopping to greet children along the way who, when riding in the grocery cart, are at eye level with him from the electric cart in which he rides. He enjoys making faces at the children who try to mimic his facial tricks and expressions. He explains "I feel babies are the closest friends I have. Everyone smiles back at me. It's a heavenly thing."

He explains that he never used to have time to talk with people and clerks in the store when he was a young parent. He says, however, that "Now it's part of my social life. Everybody knows me and I make myself known. Without relationships I'm a dead man."

Milton was one of the more interesting and insightful elders we met in conducting an ethnography of "home" in our small midwestern city.[1] He represented a new wave of older people moving into the community to enjoy its cultural assets and, as is often the case, join their children as a safety valve in old age. He was a unique individual, seen by many as eccentric, and immersed himself quickly in the everyday life of his neighborhood and the nearby downtown coffee shops. In late life he flowered creatively, taking up the study of Jewish mysticism as well as Buddhism, and began to paint in an unusual form, producing enough work to transform his little bungalow house into the "Barefoot Museum" (harking back to a hostel he operated in Bali, with his wife).

Aside from long and interesting interviews and conversations, we learned our best lessons through accompanying Milton on his daily rounds, from breakfast at the nearby hospital cafeteria, to lunch in the window of his favorite coffee shop, to shopping at the nearby Kroger grocery. This provided us the insights into some of the day-to-day difficulties of being a somewhat frail elder out in the world, as well as into his strategies and methods for navigating successfully within it. His primary goal in life? To stay socially connected. The little challenges he typically overcame were echoed again and again in our interactions and surveys with community-residing elders. We discovered just how "age-friendly"[2] (or not) our community was at the time. Many of the challenges faced by older adults concerned their confrontations with commerce and with public spaces. For example:

- Too often basic goods and services were seen as incompatible with the life-styles of older households:

  "We'd buy half a loaf of bread if somebody offered it to us."

- Salespeople were seen as insensitive to the needs of older shoppers. Twenty-five percent of our respondents reported that salesclerks were often unfriendly in the stores where they shopped.

- The physical environments created for shoppers targeted only the robust:

  "Well, many of the stores don't have enough seats or benches either, to sit down. One of the pluses for Morgenstern's Books is that they have numerous comfortable chairs and there are other stores, however, like Lazarus [sic], for instance, that have . . . the last time I was in there . . . have not a single bench in their changing rooms for men. So I stopped buying men's clothes at Lazarus. It's the only way to get across. You know, I'm one person out of a thousand. That's the kind of message they need to receive."

- Retail establishments, among other institutions, routinely underestimated the importance of the casual and friendly public encounter in the lives of older people (among others):

  "You know why I like to come to the bank (and never use the ATM?). It's one more human contact."

- "Right turn on red light" regulations convenience cars but not older pedestrians:

  "If a car is turning behind me at the intersection, I walk around all three corners of the intersection to cross my street."

These brief vignettes may seem unimportant, but they speak to a much broader societal challenge. In a rapidly changing society, it's fair to ask whether there is really a place for older adults in the flux of everyday life. A dark reading of the popularity of seniors-only spaces—senior centers, retirement communities, assisted living—might suggest that, as a society, we would prefer that older people take up with each other and not bother us with their presence. This is to ask whether we live in an age-friendly world. And, to ask whether we create a world in which we can reasonably expect to find "old people everywhere" (Alexander, Ishikawa, and Silverstein 1977). It's a debatable question, and this chapter adds to the discussion.

Anthropology and the Age-Friendly Community Movement

As an *applied* undertaking, anthropology has served as a check on interventions in the world of the elderly by so-called experts—medical professionals, housing developers, service providers, case managers, and so on. These are well-meaning people trying to improve the lives of others without always knowing elders' lives from the inside. Where gerontological (and medical) science can sometimes only see older people as individual, atomized, even replicable units, a new movement (called *age-friendly communities*) sees older people as embedded in their surroundings, attached to place. In this model, aging is not simply about the body but about the body in its environment. A similar shift in thinking about the nature of disability and dependency has occurred since a seminal article by Verbrugge and Jette (1994) and more recently reflected in the research of Jette (2006), Adams and Morse (2009), and Berridge and Martinson (2018).

Cultural anthropologists can play a vital role in helping communities plan around the lived experiences—the lifeworld—of older adults. This helps avoid the practice of homogenizing the population—creating bureaucracies that deliver uniform services in easily measured units that are predicted to produce desired outcomes in X percent of "cases." Instead, the age-friendly community movement represents an alternative approach to change, one that is placed within a cultural and environmental framework, less obsessed with individual bodies, personal responsibility, and blame.

Wendell Berry (1995) offers a useful way of rethinking the notion of health in such fundamental terms: "To be healthy is literally to be whole. . . . Our sense of wholeness is not just the completeness in ourselves but also is the sense of belonging to others and to our place. . . . I believe that the community, in the fullest sense: a place and all its creatures . . . is the smallest unit of health and that to speak of the health of an isolated individual is a contradiction in terms." As Milton stated in the epigraph, "Without relationships, I'm a dead man."

In suggesting that community is the smallest unit of health, we are drawn to an entirely new model of health in old age, one organized around the notion of the age-friendly community (Buffel, Handler, and Phillipson 2018).

In short, aging (and disability) is seen to be less about the body and the passing of time and more about the meaning of place and relationships. As such, this chapter will provide an overview of current age-friendly community change models and discuss how they differ from a medical model of aging based in a capitalist economy. Three specific age-friendly community initiatives will be reviewed in depth, and the chapter will close with a summary of some of the lessons learned across these varied approaches to change.

The Age-Friendly Community Movement

Shifting focus from the individual to the matrix of community, the age-friendly community movement is growing throughout the world under such rubrics as elder-friendly communities, communities for all ages, and, here, age-friendly communities, the phrase employed by the World Health Organization (Stafford 2019). While the elements of an age-friendly community are enumerated in various ways, the first comprehensive model was the AdvantAge Initiative, a nationwide community planning and development project of the Center for Home Care Policy and Research (Feldman and Oberlink 2003). The AdvantAge Initiative organizes the elements of an "age-friendly" community into four domains.

An age-friendly community

1. Addresses elders' basic needs,
2. Optimizes physical and mental health and well-being,
3. Maximizes independence for the frail and those with disability, and
4. Promotes social and civic engagement.

The domains themselves were derived from a series of focus group discussions with elders and community leaders in four diverse U.S. communities. Focus group participants were asked to bring homemade collages representing their idea of an elder-friendly community. These illustrations, with an example seen in Figure 36.1, provided the perfect springboard for lively and enjoyable conversations.

The domains derived from these focus groups were articulated through the identification of 33 measurable indicators. These indicators were then incorporated into a 28-minute telephone survey reaching random samples of older adults in 10 U.S. communities. The 10 pilot communities used the data from the surveys to inform citizen participation planning efforts. As of 2018, the survey had been conducted in over 63 communities and neighborhoods, providing a wealth of comparative data that enable these communities to "benchmark" themselves against others as they establish their own plans to become age-friendly (see Feldman and Oberlink 2003 for the planning

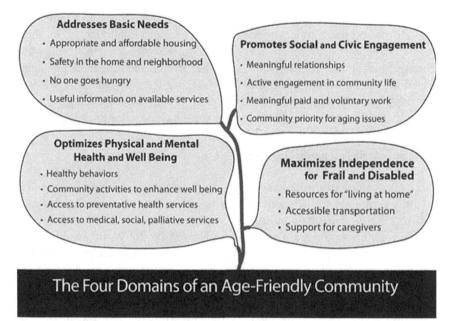

Addresses Basic Needs

- Appropriate and affordable housing
- Safety in the home and neighborhood
- No one goes hungry
- Useful information on available services

Promotes Social and Civic Engagement

- Meaningful relationships
- Active engagement in community life
- Meaningful paid and voluntary work
- Community priority for aging issues

Optimizes Physical and Mental Health and Well Being

- Healthy behaviors
- Community activities to enhance well being
- Access to preventative health services
- Access to medical, social, palliative services

Maximizes Independence for Frail and Disabled

- Resources for "living at home"
- Accessible transportation
- Support for caregivers

The Four Domains of an Age-Friendly Community

Figure 36.1   The Four Domains of an Age-Friendly Community within the AdvantAge Initiative Planning Model (Center for Home Care Policy and Research, Visiting Nurse Service of New York City. Used by permission.).

model). The domains derived from these focus groups include several subsidiary "dimensions," and these elements further connect with 33 "indicators" of an age-friendly community that are measured through random telephone surveys and employed as data for citizen-participation planning efforts.

On a more global basis, the United Nations has also shifted focus to the environmental aspects of aging. Its Madrid International Action Plan on Aging 2002 recommended "creating enabling and supportive environments" as a key focus area, and this is currently being implemented through the World Health Organization Age Friendly Cities Project (https://www.who.int/ageing/projects/age_friendly_cities/en/). A framework similar to the Advantage Initiative, titled A Blueprint for Aging, identifies eight domains around which participating communities can assess their needs and implement change (Figure 36.2).

The WHO uses this framework to develop a "certification" program that incentivizes communities around the world to plan age-friendly development. In 2017, the WHO reported 500 certified members of its Global Network on Age-Friendly Communities in 37 countries (WHO 2018). In 2013 the WHO program arrived on the shores of the United States as Portland,

Figure 36.2   WHO Dimensions of an Age-Friendly Community (Global Age-Friendly Cities: A Guide. World Health Organization (c) 2007. Available online at http://www.who.int/ageing/publications/Global_age_friendly_cities_Guide_English.pdf. Used by permission of the World Health Organization.).

Oregon, became the first major city to seek certification and develop a comprehensive age-friendly community plan (DeLaTorre 2018). Subsequent to the acceptance of the WHO program in Portland and New York City (Finkelstein et al. 2008), AARP, the largest organization of and for older adults in the world, adopted the WHO framework and offered support to U.S. communities seeking to participate in the certification process. In Portland, the age-friendly community initiative resulted in a major policy change to incentivize the development of accessory dwelling units, which are secondary structures on city lots designed for elder family members or used by elders who wish to increase their equity and income by renting to others. In New York City, a program designed to build age-friendly neighborhoods has resulted in safety improvements and benches in public spaces, and revisions in recreation program policies to benefit older citizens. By 2018, 231 U.S. towns and cities formally certified their commitment to age-friendly development. This AARP initiative aligned well with the organization's major commitment to broader issues of livability. The AARP Web site has become a rich resource of research publications, planning guidelines, policy recommendations, and links to funding sources sponsored by the organization. In a major livable communities project, AARP spent several years developing the Livability Index, a massive database on selected indicators that enables communities (down to the level of the household address) to score themselves across a set of key factors (https://livabilityindex.aarp.org/). An overall score can be provided, as can scores in specific areas of focus, including housing, neighborhood, transportation, environment, health, engagement, and opportunity—areas that have a major, impact on the quality of life for older adults (any age, actually). You can enter any address in the United States and receive a score that indicates how livable the neighborhood is.

In the United States, other major national organizations have taken up this age-friendly community approach with enthusiasm. The National Association of Area Agencies on Aging (with partners) produced the *Blueprint for Action: Developing a Livable Community for All Ages* (2007) and piloted age-friendly work in six towns and cities from 2013 through 2014. The Centers for Disease Control has developed a focus on healthy environments for aging, with special emphasis on the built environment and public health, tying research, policy, and practice recommendations to the National Prevention Strategy— the surgeon general's major commitment to health for all ages and groups. Grantmakers in Aging developed the multiyear Community AGEnda project to innovate new approaches to age-friendliness in five U.S. cities and regions (https://www.giaging.org/initiatives/age-friendly/community-agenda/).

Age-Friendly Challenges the Medical Model of Aging

While the age-friendly model aligns well with "healthy communities" thinking, it is important to understand that a healthy community is not merely an aggregate of healthy individuals. Too often, the field of public health itself is overly concerned with behavioral change in the individual and the importance of making "healthy choices." A more comprehensive framework would acknowledge that individuals can't make healthy choices if the choices are not available to them. This is the essence of a place-based approach to health and aging.

Focusing on environments for aging, however, presents its own set of challenges. The dominant discourse on healthy aging, modeled after Western biomedicine, is about individual aging bodies with lifestyle, personal responsibility, and consumerism being offered as the ticket to health and "successful aging" (see Gullette 2004 and Part I Lamb). Sickness comes to be seen as a consequence of behavioral actions—potentially blaming the victim. As noted by Eisenhauer (2001):

> By medicalizing the effects of poverty, oppression, abandonment, segregation, and ghettoization, the behavioral/medical approach both reflects and reproduces the existing social order by endorsing an interpretation of health and disease which places responsibility for the pathological effects of these conditions on individuals.

However, behavior as well as health care itself have been demonstrated to play only a moderate but not dominant role in population health. While not much can be done to modify the genetic component of health, clearly environmental and social determinants play a major role in community health. Investing in environmental and societal interventions should be at least on par with the huge investments made in medical care and personal wellness.

If, as is argued here, aging is a place-based and relationship-based experience, is there a way to identify the assets embedded in place and in relationships to the benefit of elders, seen not as individual bodies but as members of communities?

In other words, what if we were to position the older person not as an individual body but as a member of a commons? This is the challenge addressed by the global age-friendly community movement. Seeing the older person as a member of a community provides an alternative paradigm for thinking about solutions to the so-called problem of age. In fact, there are two economies available to older persons. The dominant economy, mass market capitalism, where the elder is a consumer, meets the needs of the individual through the distribution of goods and services from the outside, through the medium of money. An alternative economy, where the elder is a producer, would meet the needs of the individual through providing access to shared goods and services, through the currency of mutuality and reciprocity. In short, through membership in a community.

The Future of the Age-Friendly Community Movement

While the age-friendly movement itself has been criticized for its focus on more affluent communities, it is possible to employ the framework to address the underlying structural disparities faced by lower income older adults (Manchester, England), to reframe the position of older adults as producers rather than consumers (Kamikatsu, Japan), and to develop new policy approaches to aging and environment (Bloomington, Indiana).

Age-Friendly Manchester

One of the earliest and most successful age-friendly community initiatives can be found in Manchester, England. While the admission of Manchester to the WHO Network of Age-Friendly Communities occurred in 2010, the broad attempt to promote positive change began in the early 1990s, which no doubt helps account for the city's success (McGarry 2018). While most age-friendly initiatives are outwardly premised on the notion of the "age wave"—the rapidly growing elder population—it is ironic, perhaps, that Manchester exhibited a smaller than average older population compared to other municipalities and regions in the United Kingdom. Unlike other areas in the country, due to out-migration and natural losses, by the 2000s the cohort of late-middle-aged people grew smaller. The diminishing influence and ghettoization of older adults produced a population challenged by low resources and social exclusion. Local officials and advocates originally turned their attention to the significant level of need and associated problems. Manchester elders experienced longer periods of disability and poor health and higher mortality rates than most of their peers in other parts of the United Kingdom.

The city took advantage of new nationally scaled efforts to improve the lives of elders in need. Many new programs emerged, and the formal system of supports grew over time. Unfortunately the right-swinging trend in national government and rapidly diminishing funding provided a significant challenge to the sustainability of social, housing, and health programs. However, the city of Manchester had, early on, formulated an alternative paradigm for thinking about aging in the city. It focused on an asset-based, not a needs-based, model of aging—called the Valuing Older People Programme. Importantly, while the national government was withdrawing support for so-called soft programs (socialization, the arts, recreation, and continuing education), the city of Manchester was prepared with the experience to take up the slack for these programs at the local level. With leadership from city government, cultural programs in particular provided a useful platform to experiment with new forms of networking and organizational integration in the community. A video clip shows how this came about: https://www.you tube.com/watch?v=wmPDlF-ckq0.

When the WHO Network for the Age-Friendly Community project emerged, it provided yet another opportunity to frame the aging narrative within an exciting, integrated, and global context, leveraging the asset-based perspective of Valuing Older People onto the mainstream agenda. In October 2014, the VOP program relaunched itself as Age-Friendly Manchester. While the new paradigm provided a fresh global legitimacy for the project, the funding challenges remained, and even grew. In response to these challenges, Age-Friendly Manchester provided leadership for catalyzing action across the entire Greater Manchester region. Project leaders created the Greater Manchester Ageing Hub, a powerful new organization that could operate effectively in the context of competition among economic development interests, employment advocates, and transportation health and housing interests. This has been done by asserting that the issues of aging infuse all of these competing interests. While demonstrating the economic and social contributions of older adults to the region, the Hub has stayed loyal to its original charge to serve the most vulnerable elders. In short, citizenship-based, social justice operating principles have been incorporated into current government frameworks and branded within popular trends, layered over and branded, so to speak, within broader current trends. The successful attempt to raise awareness about the contributions of older people as well as their previous exclusion has spurred neighborhood, municipal, regional, and national attention resulting in a €10 million allocation of lottery funds to the region for "aging-better" programs, including aging well initiatives, housing and neighborhood improvement, small grant programs, and an "aging in everything" approach to public policy in the areas of employment, culture, and housing.

The strategic partnerships created outside of the traditional aging services realm have served to bring in both governmental and private funding from new sources. Partnerships with university-based programs, moreover, have enabled this age-friendly approach to develop an evidence base that demonstrates its worth and, in line with original principles of citizen participation, innovate products and services that emerge from codesign with elders themselves—thus continuing to elevate and expand the voices of older adults within civil society (Buffel 2015, 2018).

Kamikatsu: A Community Remakes Itself as Age-Friendly

Nobel Prize–winning political scientist Elinor Ostrom is credited with the now-acknowledged capacity of local groups and communities to solve their own problems of governance in the creation of sustainable economic and social systems. Going against the grain of mainstream microeconomics, she debunked the concept of the Tragedy of the Commons, a theory that argued that common properties will always be exhausted when individuals maximize their own interests (1990). It would argue that a common oceanic fishery would ultimately be depleted due to the (assumed) fact that every fishing boat will attempt to maximize its own profit at the expense of others. Over her career she demonstrated over and over again that, to the contrary, common properties are and can be sustainably governed by users themselves without the imposition of formal systems designed to negotiate across differing interests.

Many of the principles espoused in a theory of the commons are manifested in the remarkable story of the comeback of a distressed community in the mountains of Japan, well documented by Nanami Suzuki (2012) and others (Coleman 2015). While Japan is the country with the oldest population in the world, the village of Kamikatsu is "super-aged" (see Part III Kavedžija) . It falls within the category of *Genkai Shuraku* (super-aged), with over 50 percent of the population of Kamikatsu being older than age 65.

When an agricultural agent arrived in Kamikatsu about 20 years ago, he found a community nearly devoid of young people, struggling to survive in the face of major declines in the forest industry amd mandarin orange groves. In 1950 the population had peaked at 6,356, and in 1955 began to decrease due to the dramatic out-migration of adults to surrounding cities. In 2010, according to Suzuki, the population had diminished to 1,783, with 52.4 percent above the age of 65. The agent was charged with developing experimental agricultural products but was having little success.

While on a visit to Kyoto, the agent happened to overhear a group of young women at a nearby restaurant table. They were ecstatic about the leaves that the chef had used to decorate and garnish their *kaiseki*, a traditional multi-course Japanese dinner. The agent experienced an epiphany, realizing that the mountain communities he worked with were replete with these products. While he encountered resistance—"Leaves are not products"—he persevered and supported a small group of elderly entrepreneurial women to collect and prepare leaves and branches for shipping to Kyoto. It seemed that this was an industry eminently suited to employ older women, so knowledgeable about local and seasonal flora.

By 2005, according to Suzuki, 300 kinds of leaves were being shipped from Kamikatsu Town, with annual revenue exceeding ¥250 million (US$3.35 million), accounting for more than 80 percent of the product being sold at the Osaka Central Wholesale Market. Twenty percent of all Kamikatsu households participate in the industry, and the average age of the people engaged in collecting, washing, and packing leaves is 68 years. The monthly household income ranges from ¥200,000 to 300,000 (US$2,500 to $3,750), with exceptional households earning as much as US$23,500 monthly.

What is even more remarkable is the cascading accomplishments achieved by this resilient community. A wireless fax system, originally designed for natural disasters, was repurposed as a tool for communicating news of current market preferences and specific orders of leaves to the elderly agriculturalists. A volunteer taxi service, serving the many elders who are isolated in outlying areas, was repurposed as a product delivery system, getting leaves to the town center for distribution to Kyoto. A work-related newsletter expanded to become a popular vehicle for news of social events and opportunities. An existing structure of neighborhood councils became energized as elders offered ideas for improving the town and creating a "clean community." This spawned a recycling program that increased the town's recycling rate to 80 percent, compared to 19 percent in Japan overall. Kamikatsu became a leading exponent of zero waste for the entire country, attracting young people to visit, study, and, occasionally, take up permanent residence in the town. The town recycling center evolved into a collaborative production space where elders gathered to repurpose used items and enjoy the sociality of common work. A small grocery expanded its offerings of homemade foods, accompanied by recipes and instructions for using leaves as garnish. Perhaps the most significant accomplishment was reflected in elders' comments that they came to "exist with visible faces." All this was accomplished without reference to any concepts of age-friendliness but, rather, through recognition that old people have valuable knowledge and significant physical capacity.

Bloomington, Indiana, as a Lifetime Community

A small university city in south-central Indiana, Bloomington is not unlike Manchester in having a younger population that overshadows the issues and presence of older adults. The author's ethnographic work on aging in this community began in the late 1990s and provided an opportunity to foreground the experiences of aging for the broader community (Stafford 2009). While it has been a very long journey, my ethnographic work on aging cited in the epigraph has evolved into a community development approach being undertaken within a framework called the Lifetime Community. One of the most important lessons learned from the research was that older people do indeed want to live, work, and play within the heart of a community designed for all ages and abilities. Hence, the community has shied away from a singular age-friendly model. The Lifetime Community initiative strives to move towards a less age-segregated society by concentrating development efforts in a new planning mechanism referred to as the Lifetime Community District. While many rightfully see the concept as applicable to any neighborhood, the concept of a district or planning overlay enables the creation and utilization of associated urban policies and practices that can support and incentivize the kind of development we seek, as illustrated in Figure 36.3.

The Bloomington Commission on Aging has adopted the Lifetime Community framework and successfully advocated for its inclusion in the new 2040 Comprehensive Plan for the city. The plan adopts the definition and includes multiple specific recommendations for implementation of Lifetime Community elements, including expanding housing options, promoting universal design, and incentivizing downtown senior housing opportunities. A specific ordinance approving the construction of accessory dwelling units, in neighborhoods where they were formerly prohibited, has already been approved by the City Council. As noted earlier, accessory dwelling units are small attached or secondary living units set aside to provide new options for older adult caregivers, older relatives, returning adult children, and others. The commission has also partnered with the new Dementia Friendly Community initiative to

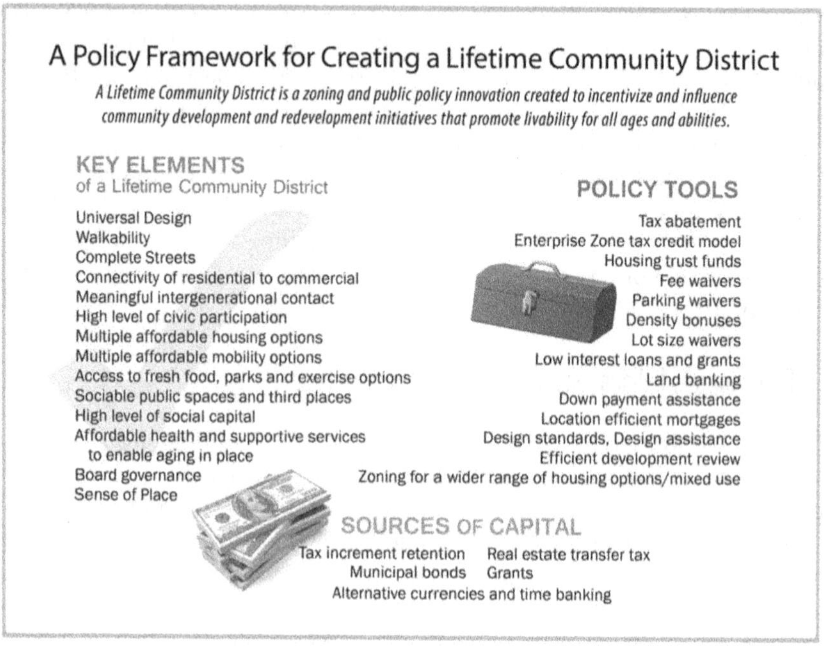

A Policy Framework for Creating a Lifetime Community District

A Lifetime Community District is a zoning and public policy innovation created to incentivize and influence community development and redevelopment initiatives that promote livability for all ages and abilities.

KEY ELEMENTS
of a Lifetime Community District

Universal Design
Walkability
Complete Streets
Connectivity of residential to commercial
Meaningful intergenerational contact
High level of civic participation
Multiple affordable housing options
Multiple affordable mobility options
Access to fresh food, parks and exercise options
Sociable public spaces and third places
High level of social capital
Affordable health and supportive services
    to enable aging in place
Board governance
Sense of Place

POLICY TOOLS

Tax abatement
Enterprise Zone tax credit model
Housing trust funds
Fee waivers
Parking waivers
Density bonuses
Lot size waivers
Low interest loans and grants
Land banking
Down payment assistance
Location efficient mortgages
Design standards, Design assistance
Efficient development review
Zoning for a wider range of housing options/mixed use

SOURCES OF CAPITAL

Tax increment retention   Real estate transfer tax
Municipal bonds   Grants
Alternative currencies and time banking

Figure 36.3 An illustrative framework was created to educate policy makers and advocates about the concept of a lifetime community and how it could be achieved (Courtesy of the author).

advocate for the incorporation of the lifetime community concept within the newly proposed zoning ordinance, which follows from the comprehensive plan. The partnership suggests that a Lifetime District zoning overlay be used in the redevelopment of a 24-acre downtown site being made available to the city by the relocation of our community hospital to a new site on the Indiana University campus. The commission is entering into a community education and outreach phase to assure that the concept is understood and supported by those citizens and stakeholders who plan to be involved in many upcoming public participation planning and design events concerning the site in the coming two years.

Lessons Learned

From the examples highlighted above, some interesting assertions can be made about the process and potential for creating and sustaining age-friendly communities around the world.

- Late life does not need to be organized around leisure (Blechman 2009) or vacuous recreation and exercise "for its own sake."

- Work—doing meaningful things together—provides a commons, a cultural space in which everyone can contribute and an interdependence that supports social welfare, while contradicting the typical portrait of elders as vulnerable and needy.

- Creativity in late life is more than the work of individual stars whom we admire and about whom we say "I wish I could do that." Rather, creativity is a social production, a kind of codesign, engendered through the development of environments that foster the identification of common challenges, needs, strengths, and solutions.

- While the age-friendly community model is often oriented to elders of all income levels, communities do not need to abandon a commitment to social justice for those at the lower end of the scale.

- Attention to what is meaningful and pragmatic at the local level helps communities adapt the generic age-friendly model to local circumstances. This is necessary for success.

- Cultural anthropology, with its fundamental attachment to the social, the community, the geography, can help the age-friendly movement avoid seeing the older population as an aggregate of individuals and, instead, as a universal family of age.

- What is the best indicator of an age-friendly community? It's simple: Old people everywhere.

Notes

1. This is a basic community design principle offered by Alexander, Ishikawa, and Silverstein in their pathbreaking work *A Pattern Language*. They suggest that, in a good community, one finds old people everywhere, in opposition to the rampant age segregation so characteristic of contemporary American cities and towns.

2. In the late 1990s, the author and colleagues conducted a multiyear ethnography of old age and the meaning of home in Bloomington, Indiana. Published works citing this effort include Stafford 2001, Stafford 2003, Stafford 2009.

Bibliography

Adams, C. E., and L. W. Morse. 2009. "Dependency Stereotypes and Aging: Implications for Getting and Giving Help in Later Life." *Journal of Applied Social Psychology* 39(12): 2967–84.

Alexander, C., Ishikawa, S., and Silverstein, M. 1977. *A Pattern Language*. New York: Oxford.

Berridge, C. W., and M. Martinson. 2018. "Valuing Old Age without Leveraging Ableism." *Generations* 41(4): 83–91(9).

Berry, W. 1995. *Another Turn of the Crank*. Berkeley, CA: Counterpoint.

Blechman, A. D. 2009. *Leisureville: Adventures in a World Without Children*. New York: Atlantic Monthly.

Buffel, T. 2015. *Researching Age-Friendly Communities. Stories from Older People as Co-investigators*. Manchester, UK: University of Manchester.

Buffel, T. 2018. "Social Research and Co-production with Older People: Developing Age-Friendly Communities." *Journal of Aging Studies* 44: 52–60.

Buffel, T., S. Handler, and C. Phillipson, eds. 2018. *Age-Friendly Cities and Communities. A Global Perspective*. Bristol, UK: Policy.

Coleman, J. 2015. *Unfinished Work: The Struggle to Build an Aging American Workforce*. New York: Oxford.

DeLaTorre, A. 2019. "The Intersection between Sustainable and Age-Friendly Development." In *The Global Age-Friendly Community Movement: A Critical Appraisal*, edited by P. Stafford. London: Berghahn.

Eisenhauer, E. 2001. "In Poor Health: SuperMarket Redlining and Urban Nutrition." *GeoJournal* 53: 125–33.

Feldman, P., and M. Oberlink. 2003. "The AdvantAge Initiative: Developing Community Indicators to Promote the Health and Well-Being of Older People." *Family & Community Health. Community-Based Innovations in Older Populations* 26(4): 268–74.

Finkelstein, R., A. Garcia, J. Netherland, and J. Walker. 2008. *Toward an Age-Friendly New York City: A Findings Report*. New York: New York Academy of Medicine.

Gullette, M. M. 2004. *Aged by Culture*. Chicago: University of Chicago.

Jette, A. M. 2006. "Toward a Common Language for Function, Disability and Health." *Physical Therapy* 86(5): 1–9.

McGarry, P. 2018. "Developing Age-Friendly Policies for Cities: Strategies, Challenges, and Reflections." In *Age-Friendly Cities and Communities: A Global Perspective*, edited by T. Buffel, S. Handler, and C. Phillipson. Bristol, UK: Policy.

National Association of Area Agencies on Aging. 2007. *Blueprint for Action: Developing a Livable Community for All Ages*. http://www.livable.org/storage /documents/reports/AIP/blueprint4actionsinglepages.pdf

Ostrom, E. 1990. *Governing the Commons: The Evolution of Institutions for Collective Action*. Cambridge: Cambridge University Press.

Stafford, P. 2001. "When Community Planning Becomes Community Building: Place Based Activism and the Creation of Good Places to Grow Old." In *Empowering Frail Elderly People: Opportunities and Impediments in Housing, Health and Support Service Delivery*, edited by L. Heumann, M. McCall, and D. Boldy. Westport, CT: Praeger.

Stafford, P. 2003. "Homebodies: Voices of Place in a North American Community." In *Gray Areas: Ethnographic Encounters with Nursing Home Culture*, edited by P. Stafford. Santa Fe: SAR.

Stafford, P. 2009. *Elderburbia: Aging with a Sense of Place in America*. Santa Barbara, CA: ABC-CLIO.

Stafford, P. 2019. *The Global Age-Friendly Community Movement: A Critical Appraisal.* London: Berghahn.

Suzuki, N. 2012. "Creating a Community of Resilience: New Meanings of Technologies for Greater Well-Being in a Depopulated Town." *Anthropology and Aging Quarterly* 33(3).

Verbrugge, L., and A. Jette. 1994. "The Disablement Process." *Social Science and Medicine* 38(1): 1–14.

WHO. 2018. Age-Friendly World. https://extranet.who.int/agefriendlyworld/who-network/.

CHAPTER THIRTY-SEVEN

Web Book Photo Essay: Working Together across Generations

An Experiment in Open Space Design

Iveris L. Martinez and Ebru Ozer

Available at: http://www.culturalcontextofaging.com/webbook-martinezozer

This photo essay by anthropologist Iveris Martinez and architect Ebru Ozer presents in words and images the process of incorporating age-friendly design into a proposed initiative to develop the area under "The Underline," an area below the Miami Metrorail. The authors developed a collaboration between students from Florida International University and local elders who would likely use the proposed park, urban trail, and living art destination.

CHAPTER THIRTY-EIGHT

Web Book: Growing Older in World Cities

Benefits and Burdens

Michael Gusmano

Available at: http://www.culturalcontextofaging.com/webbook-gusmano

This chapter brings into focus issues of aging in major urban places by presenting some of the core data from the ongoing World Cities Project, examining aging and environment in New York City, London, Paris, and Tokyo. See also: https://wagner.nyu.edu/community/faculty/victor-g-rodwin/world-cities-project.

CHAPTER THIRTY-NINE

Old Age Homes, Love, and Other New Cultures of Aging in Middle-Class India

Sarah Lamb

One sun-drenched winter morning, I stood up to take leave from three ladies living in a modest home for elders situated amid quiet, two-story homes in a middle-class neighborhood on the southern outskirts of Kolkata, India.[1] I bent down to brush the ladies' feet in the familiar gesture of *pranam* practiced by many Indians, where a junior touches an elder's feet in a sign of respect, and in turn the elder places his or her hands affectionately on the junior's head and offers blessings, such as "May you live well," "May your children be well." The first two ladies, Uma-di and Kavika-di, received the gesture and offered me blessings, but the third woman, Kalyani-di, stepped back.[2] She was the most elegant of the three, at age 81 standing tall with her long, thick silvery hair tied into an attractive knot, dressed in a fresh white and taupe sari, with thin gold bangles adorning her wrists. She asked, her voice laced with chagrin, "Why are you offering so much *pranam* to us—we, who are so full of sadness, who can't give you proper blessings?"

It was as if living in an old age home had stripped Kalyani-di of the capacity to be a fruitful, potent elder. She had just been telling me of how she imagines over and over begging her son and daughter-in-law, with whom she almost never actually speaks, to give her "release" from the old age home.

She reflected, "If we had grown up with the idea that we might live separately from our children, then it might not be so hard to get used to now. But with our own eyes we had never seen or known anything like this. We never could have even dreamed that a *briddhabas* (abode for elders) existed, that we would be here, in a place like this!" Residences for elders are a new phenomenon emerging rapidly in India's middle-class cosmopolitan centers, providing an alternative for the more traditional multigenerational, coresidential family that many have long viewed as central to proper aging and society in India.

Yet some elders are feeling optimistic about alternative spaces of aging and eldercare materializing beyond the family. Viraj Ghosh, age 72, whose only son, an economist, has settled in the United States, proclaimed: "At this age, it's better to live separate. . . . If an old man says that he needs to have his son live with him, then the son won't advance, and the country won't advance." Ghosh resides with his wife in a flat their son purchased in one of the new modern high-rises springing up in south Kolkata, and Viraj-da spends hours each day socializing with peers, exercising at the apartment complex's gym, taking vigorous walks outdoors, meditating, reading, and playing music. A founding member of the Laughing Club of Udita, a senior citizens' group that practices daily laughter yoga, Viraj-da leads the group in hearty laughter each dawn followed by tea and conversation. Ghosh receives regular video calls, money, and love from his son, remarking, "Out of sight is not out of mind!" but affirms, "I am the happiest man in the world, living in heaven! I won't live anywhere other than here, surrounded by my circle of friends."

Others who have no children to even contemplate living with—such as never-married Manu, a 58-year-old professor at a provincial college—also often appreciate new forms of intimacy and support surfacing in India, along with the more malleable gender and sexuality scripts seen in some quarters. A developing consumerist leisure culture in India is promoting travel packages, upscale retirement living, and dating sites to middle-class and affluent senior citizens (Samanta 2018; Samanta and Varghese 2018), and Manu found herself signing up for an organized trip abroad for older Bengalis. Also on the trip was 68-year-old Safal, a retired banker long estranged from his wife and whose only son lives across the nation for work. Manu and Safal developed a relationship on the trip that they retained after returning home. "I had been so lonely—tremendously alone! Who could have ever thought that at this old age, I could find this kind of love? . . . He was also very alone," Manu explained. They didn't see the benefit of marrying at this age, "but we have started to 'live in'!" Manu reported.[3] She inserted the English phrasing "live in" to refer to the locally still quite alien practice of cohabitating as an unmarried couple. Manu animatedly read to me from a Bengali essay she had found on the Facebook page for Thikana Shimla, a new organization aimed at helping Kolkata's elderly singles "find soulmates." The essay begins, "We invite elderly men and women to dispel their loneliness and fall in love [*prem korun*]," and then moves on: "Old people's marriage or 'live in' is not very new. Abroad, it's been happening for quite a long time. . . . A lot of dating sites have been established for old people abroad. . . . Just keep in mind, you are not committing any offense or sin. You are just wanting to live in joy for another few days."[4]

These brief vignettes reveal India at a culturally critical juncture marked by a gradual, yet significant, expansion of imaginaries and possibilities for aging—where not only the multigenerational family but also the market, peers, and individual can be potential sites of elder living and eldercare. Such emerging novel forms of aging are taken by many Indians to represent a profound social transformation involving not only aging per se, but also core cultural and moral visions of family, gender, the life course, and even the nation.

I focus in this chapter on diverse modes of engagement with new aging cultures among cosmopolitan middle-class Indians, those most involved with the sociocultural changes of aging explored here. In rural settings—where near 70 percent of India's population still lives[5]—emerging aging trends such as old age homes and senior dating platforms remain highly rare. However, most village communities are witnessing rural-to-urban labor migration among the younger generations. This process leaves many elders largely alone for much of the year, sometimes with daughters-in-law and grandchildren, as their sons return for visits and send remittances. Meanwhile, India's urban poor elderly tend to blame any lack of care from their children more on timeless poverty than on anything to do with social change or modernity.

Fieldwork related to this project was conducted primarily in West Bengal, India, largely in Kolkata (with two shorter fieldwork trips to New Delhi), from 1989 through the present.[6] Kolkata is the capital of the eastern Indian state of West Bengal, a city with an extended metropolitan population of near 15 million, making it the third most populous urban area in India and one of the largest in the world.[7] My research participants are primarily Hindu, with smaller numbers of Muslim interlocutors. Hindus and Muslims are India's two largest religious groups, making up about 80 percent and 13 percent of the population respectively.[8] In this chapter, as the number of non-Hindu research participants is small, persons' religious identities are Hindu unless otherwise noted.

Visions of Conventional Aging: Intergenerational Ties and the Transient Body

To understand the social changes surrounding aging and families in India, one must first consider people's sense of a more traditional past. Many Indians have conventionally recognized two salient life aims in old age: (1) kinship and being served within an intergenerational family and (2) spiritual awareness. The theme of the family figures most prominently in contemporary discourses of aging and social change, so let us begin there.

Caring for aged parents in a multigenerational family has long been upheld in India as the most natural and appropriate way of managing aging. It is viewed as a way of living that ideally not only provides material and emotional care for elders but also fosters family intimacy, practical frugality as members pool resources, and the cultural reproduction of newer generations, as elder grandparents help care for and impart core social values to their grandchildren.[9] Often referred to as a "joint family," the multigenerational household is often idealized as a quintessentially Indian way of life, morality, and tradition. Technically, a joint family refers to a household composed of related married couples linked either through patrilineal descent or collaterally as brothers, although in popular usage any household containing a grandparent or grandparents and married children—usually a son or sons—is commonly referred to as "joint." Although joint families are sometimes labeled Hindu (as in "the Hindu joint family"), the notion that adult children are naturally obligated to care for and live with their elder parents is spoken of regularly by Hindus and Muslims alike.

The workings of a joint family system rest on a notion of the value and appropriateness, even naturalness, of relations of long-term intergenerational reciprocity, as well as an acceptance of interdependence as a normal part of the human condition. Just as parents naturally care for their children when they are young and need help, so naturally do adult children care for their parents in their older years (Photo 39.1). Bengalis in both rural and urban settings speak of lifelong bonds of reciprocal indebtedness and love: Adult children—especially sons and daughters-in-law—live with and care for their aging parents, out of love, a deep respect for elders, and a profound sense of moral, even spiritual, duty to attempt to repay the inerasable debts (*rin*) they owe their parents for all the effort, expense, and affection the parents expended to produce and raise them (Lamb 2000, 2009).

Although the common discourse is that "children" provide for and co-reside with their senior parents, in practice usually sons and daughters-in-law fill this role. India remains mostly a patrilineal society—in which sons are expected to live with their parents after marriage and care for them in old age. This tradition is bolstered by the fact that despite legal reforms, sons continue to inherit a much larger share of parental property than daughters (Barik, Agrawal, and Desai 2015: 111). Upon marriage in such patrilineal settings, daughters formally relinquish obligations to their own parents, taking on responsibility for their in-laws. Ironically, though, Indians commonly describe daughters as more "loving" than sons. One Muslim man, a taxi driver with five sons and two daughters, described the difference between daughters and sons: "If I ask a daughter for a glass of water, she'll give it right away. But if I ask a son? He will say, 'Wait, I'm coming' [i.e., soon, or later]." The taxi driver

Photo 39.1   A joint family: senior parents, two sons, their wives, and children coresiding in a three-bedroom Kolkata flat. (Photo by Sarah Lamb)

laughed and repeated this scenario a few times, concluding: "Compared to a daughter's love, a son loves his parent, but not as much." Many married daughters—especially if employed and earning their own income—also offer their parents visits, gifts, and practical assistance throughout life.

The providing of care for one's seniors is often termed *seva*, respectful service or care. *Seva*, a key component of perceived traditional Indian and especially Hindu ways of aging, can be offered to deities as well as elders. When provided to elders, *seva* entails acts such as serving food and tea, massaging tired limbs, combing hair, bringing warm bathwater, and offering loving respect.[10] As part of intergenerational reciprocity, juniors perform *seva* not simply as a gift in the present, but in exchange for the elders' earlier tremendous labors in giving birth to and fostering them.

The moral imperative to serve one's elders through *seva* figures importantly in everyday talk and perceptions. In a casual conversation about how much he loves his dog, for instance, one middle-aged man who worked as a driver in New Delhi described: "If you did not take good care of your parent or grandparent," the ancestor's spirit can come back in the form of a pet dog, "to give you the opportunity to offer *seva* again." He went on to describe how caring for a dog is hard work but of immense moral and spiritual value: "Not only feeding, but also taking out for walks. No matter how tired or sleepy I am, the dog wakes me up at 5:30 a.m., and I have to take him out. Then he is

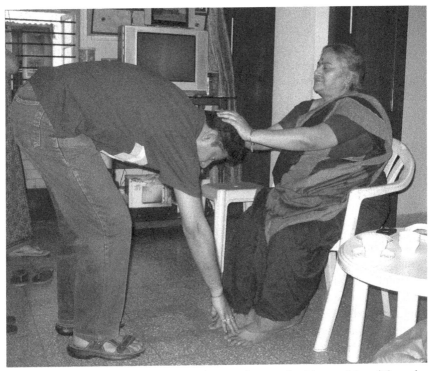

Photo 39.2   A son offers *pranam* to his mother as she blesses him. (Photo by Sarah Lamb)

at peace, and I am at peace."[11] Another man reflected to me while cleaning his mother's sheets on the shores of a pond in the village where he lived with his widowed mother, wife, and children:

> Caring for parents is the children's duty; it is *dharma* [moral-religious order; right way of living]. As parents raised their children, children will also care for their parents during their sick years, when they get old. For example, if I am old and I have a bowel movement, my son will clean it, and he won't ask, "Why did you do it there?" This is what we did for him when he was young. When I am old and dying, who will take me to go pee and defecate? My children will have to do it.

Pranam, which I tried to offer old-age-home resident Kalyani-di but was refused, is also part of serving Hindu elders properly, as well as a reciprocal action: Juniors bow down to touch their elders' feet in an act of respectful devotion and in turn receive from their elders affectionate blessings (Photo 39.2).

On their part, daughters-in-law speak of caring for parents-in-law less in terms of reciprocity than in terms of a social-moral duty, paired often with real affection and respect that can develop over years of living together, along with a not uncommon sense of tedious burden. Pratima, a Kolkata teacher in her midforties, says she cannot imagine *not* living with and caring for her widowed mother-in-law, although with her own two children settled in the United States, she does not expect the same from them. Pratima speaks of her unwavering commitment to, among other duties, sit with her mother-in-law for at least one hour each evening after she returns from work, hearing the details of the older woman's day. "It is so boring sometimes, I almost fall asleep. But I can't imagine not doing it."

Despite the centrality of family in Indian visions of normal and good aging, people realize that the family is not a flawless institution. An overriding concern in Indian gerontology, public media, and everyday talk over recent decades has been the decline of joint family living, supposedly in the face of the intersecting forces of urbanization, modernization, and globalization.[12] Ethnographies of sociocultural life in India have also long portrayed generational tensions, such as the coexistence of conflict and affection in intergenerational relationships (Gangopadhyay and Samanta 2017).[13] Nonetheless, recent studies have indicated that coresidence with adult children continues to be the most dominant living arrangement in India, with approximately 80 percent of Indian seniors aged 60 and above living with adult children, in both rural and urban contexts.[14] Further, even when the two generations do not coreside, adult children commonly provide financial and emotional support from a distance for their elderly parents (Barik, Agrawal, and Desai 2015: 111, Ahlin 2017).

Such a widely practiced system of intergenerational reciprocity contrasts with prevalent stances in the United States, where among white families in particular, the dominant expectation is that gifts will flow down from parent to child lifelong. It is proper for parents to give to children (even through gifts of money or inheritances, when their children are adults); but if an adult child gives to an aged parent, then the parent is seen as childlike.[15] Although many U.S. children spend much time and effort caring for senior parents—escorting to the doctor, preparing meals, offering love and companionship—most U.S. parents and children would be equally uncomfortable if the child were called upon to provide intimate bodily care or full material support for a parent. Further, it is common for both older Americans and their adult children to desire independence. Andrei Simic observes, "What the American elderly seem to fear most is 'demeaning dependence' on their children or other kin. Rather, the ideal is to remain 'one's own person'" (1990: 94). Noting the central role independence plays in dominant American conceptions of personhood, Elana Buch similarly finds that older adults "fear being unmade as adult persons and treated like children if they are less self-sufficient" (2018: 36). For these reasons, many older Americans prefer care from paid workers rather than descendants, as a means to sustain a sense of independence and autonomy through reciprocal market exchange (Buch 2018: 34–44).

Spiritual Strivings and the Transient Body

Another traditional narrative of aging in India presents old age as a meaningful time to attain inner peace through spiritual practice, while coming to realize the transience of all living things. Many Indians across religious traditions, including Hindu, Muslim, Jain, and Sikh, find older age to be an appropriate and welcome period to focus more on God, while spending time engrossed in religious activities—visiting temples or mosques, going on pilgrimages, reading religious texts, meditating, and singing or listening to religious music.[16]

For Hindus, one well-known model of the life course, the *ashrama* system, informs many people's perspectives on late life. Classical Hindu ethical-legal texts, the Dharmasastras, outline this model and are familiar to most Hindus, especially among the higher castes, even those who do not study the actual texts themselves. According to the *ashrama* system, the human lifespan is divided into four life stages or shelters (*ashramas*)—that of the student (*brahmacharya*), adult householder (*grihasta*), forest-dweller (*vanaprastha*), and renouncer (*sannyasa*).[17] In this schema, the two latter life phases constitute older age. When a person's hair begins to gray and children marry and bear their own children, it is time to enter the forest-dweller or *vanaprastha* phase—departing from home to live as a hermit (the literal prescription for men in the Hindu texts) or remaining in the household but focused increasingly on God. The final life stage of *sannyasa* as a wandering ascetic entails complete renunciation of the phenomenal world and its pleasures and ties. Few Hindus literally move to the forest or become wandering renouncers in old age, but many do find compelling a life course model in which one concentrates during one's adult householder years on worldly matters—marriage, reproduction, and material gains and pleasures—while turning in later life toward spiritual awareness and the loosening of worldly ties.

Not all feel that they have the luxury or economic security to think of old age as a period of economic or spiritual retirement, however; and economist Debasis Barik and colleagues report that the majority of Indian seniors must continue to work in one capacity or another (2015: 109–10). Older Bengalis in my fieldwork also commonly discuss continuing to feel deeply attached to their lives and loved ones, even or especially during old age when they realize they will soon need to cut their worldly ties of love, affection, and attachment (*maya*) when they die.

Nonetheless, almost all older Bengalis I know speak matter-of-factly in daily conversations of being ready to die, as an expected cultural discourse. When I tell older people that I look forward to seeing them next year when I return, a common cheerful reply is: "Who knows if I will still be here or not the next time you come back?" or "I may go to the cremation ground by then!" Purnima-di, a retired English professor in good health in her early seventies, peppered her conversations with comments like these:

"I am not afraid of death, because it is inevitable. Because I am born, I know I have to die. No one born can escape death."

"When clothes are worn out, you just take them off and wear new ones. The body is also like that."

"The body will die, but the soul will not die. Wherever I go, I will go *somewhere* else. Those dear ones who have died, why should I cry for them? There is no use crying for a departed soul. God is a giver and a taker. Today is mine; tomorrow I will go, and the day will be someone else's. I should not be sorry for that."

"We have to accept decay. I have accepted."

The widespread focus on spirituality and cultivating a readiness for death among older Indians may be one reason we find less emphasis on active aging and medically prolonging life in India than we find in the United States (Lamb 2014, 2019). However, as we will see below, globally circulating ideologies of active, healthy aging are beginning to take hold in India along with other new elderscapes.

Seva for Hire: Old Age Homes and Care on the Market

Perhaps the single most striking new mode of aging to emerge in India is the old age home. Until around the turn of the 21st century, old age homes scarcely existed in India, save for a handful established by Christian missionaries catering to the Anglo-Indian community and the very poor. Now there are hundreds across India's major cities, primarily for the middle and upper-middle classes.[18] People commonly refer to the homes in English as "old age homes," viewing them as predominantly Western-style institutions. Bengali alternatives include *briddhasram*—"shelter" (or ashram) for the aged or "increased" (*briddha*), and *briddhabas*—"abode" (*abas*) for the aged.

As chiefly middle-class institutions, India's elder residences are mostly available to those with retirement pensions, considerable savings, and/or professional salaried children who pay the bills. Run by both philanthropic nongovernmental organizations and private entrepreneurs, monthly fees at a modest home tend to be roughly equivalent to the salary for a full-time domestic worker. Many homes also require a sizeable security deposit of anywhere from about 5,000 to 1,000,000 rupees (or about US$70 to $14,000), afforded by selling a home, dipping into savings, or drawing on a successful child's earnings. At the high end, a few luxury retirement resorts are being established for the elite elderly, an expanding class of high-spending consumers in large cosmopolitan cities like Mumbai and Bangalore—with plush interiors and luxurious surroundings including hobby clubs, swimming pools, health spas, walking paths, and libraries. At the low end are a gradually rising number of eldercare homes partially subsidized by the government to serve those with fewer resources, following the 2007 Maintenance and Welfare of Parents and Senior Citizens Act articulating the government's obligation to support the establishment of more old age homes across the nation (A. Datta 2017: 81–82).[19] The true poor cannot consider staying in even the subsidized "pay-and-stay" homes, and to the extent they are aware of the existence of old age homes, speak of such homes as distinctly rich people's institutions.

Most old age homes to date in India require that residents be in good physical and mental health, able to walk, talk, and perform activities of daily living. Directors generally decide whom to admit based on an interview and at times a doctor's examination. Weekly or biweekly doctor visits are provided, but in the event that a resident becomes seriously ill or incapacitated, the policy of many institutions is that the resident must be sent "home." A group who had gathered at their Kolkata senior citizens club to discuss the new trend of old age homes in their nation commented on this incongruous policy: "You are given an umbrella, and then just when it starts to rain, the umbrella is taken away!" Increasingly, some homes are beginning to harbor physically or mentally disabled elders who must pay additionally for a private nurse's care.

The homes in the Kolkata region range in size from about 5 to 50 residents,[20] and accommodations can come in the form of single, double, or dormitory-style rooms or mini apartments. In some a husband and wife (or mother and daughter, or two siblings) can opt to live together. The residents come from a range of family situations: some are childless, others have only daughters, others' children are all abroad, and others (among the 100 I formally interviewed, the largest number) have sons and daughters-in-law living right nearby.[21]

The homes, which are mostly unregulated, are often arranged like the middle-class households that the residents tend to come from, with similar living, eating, sleeping, bathing, and cooking arrangements. Some of the larger homes have been established in apartment-type complexes built especially for the purpose, while others have been set up within ordinary houses and flats. All meals are provided, along with another essential ingredient of Indian social and culinary life: tea—served at dawn ("bed tea"), with breakfast, and with a few biscuits or other small snack in the late afternoon. Residents' clothes are washed and rooms cleaned; and in fact, one of the distinct advantages of old-age-home living, many say, is that older people no longer have to manage their own servants. Even most ordinary middle-class households in India maintain servants to help with household chores; yet peppering newspapers over recent years are stories of aged persons being tricked, robbed, and even murdered by domestic workers—contributing to a widespread sense that it is inappropriate and even dangerous for elders to live on their own.

Minimal formal activities are planned except in the most upscale facilities, and residents tend to spend their time reading, chatting, simply sitting, playing cards, knitting, writing journals and letters, having tea, watching television, listening to the radio, going on morning walks, or taking a stroll to a nearby market. Female residents might also help with some light cooking, such as peeling vegetables, cleaning small stones from dried lentils, or tasting a dish to see if it has turned out right. The larger homes generally house a temple, where residents can pray, make offerings to deities, and sing hymns. Most women residents and some men maintain their own small shrines in their rooms, where they perform daily *pujas*, ritual offerings of water, flowers, and sweets honoring deities as well as deceased kin such as husbands and parents. The larger, posher homes have established one or two common areas for congregating, watching television, computer use, yoga classes, or a library. Some more elaborate homes in Kolkata and its outskirts maintain gardens with flowers, fruit trees, vegetable patches, sometimes a cow or dog or two, walkways, benches, and perhaps a small fish and lily pond.

How do people make sense of the emergence of such residences for elders in India? One dominant position is that old age homes represent a radically new and alien—in fact, distinctly Western—way of life, impacting not only aging but also core principles central to Indian society and culture. Daily talk and public discourse often characterize the old age home as an institution complicit in the abandoning or "throwing away" of not only old individuals but also an idealized moral culture of care and duty. "Old Age Homes Against Our Culture" reads one representative newspaper headline, with the article moving on to report a government official in the southern state of Tamil Nadu proclaiming to a group of students that "the concept of old age homes reflects the impact of western culture" and asking the students to "take a vow that they would not leave their parents in old age homes" (*The Hindu* Staff Reporter 2004). The *Times of India* (2018) reports on "the bitter trend of aged people being deserted by their children" into the growing numbers of old age homes in India's "dark underbelly." Soumil Chowdhury, a retired engineer who had just made plans, with mixed feelings, to move into an old age home with his wife, similarly narrated:

> We are experiencing a clash between the "Indian" era and the "Western" era. We [Indians] want to live jointly, amidst our relatives, not alone. . . . In "European culture," everyone does want to live separately. . . . We like to have everyone living together. We don't want "old age homes." We want

"joint families"—sisters and brothers, daughters and sons, granddaughters and grandsons, all together. . . . This is "Indian culture."

Yet more optimistic assessments profess that old age homes offer a valuable, welcome alternative to family-based living, sustain those who have no kin readily to depend on, liberate both older and younger generations to live independently and freely, foster gendered and aged egalitarianism, and are perhaps not so radically "new" or fundamentally "Western" after all.

For instance, some expressly perceive old-age-home living as akin to the "forest-dwelling" or *vanaprastha* life phase long presented in Hindu texts as appropriate for older age, where one purposefully loosens ties to family and the world in order to pursue spiritual realization (Photo 39.3). Ashok Bose, a bachelor who had long been devoted to a spiritual life, viewed his residence in the Ramakrishna Mission Home for the Aged as a wonderful opportunity not only to be served and cared for in his later years but also to pursue *vanaprastha*, in keeping with the home's mission (as described by one of its directors), to provide "a life away from the din of family, spent in solitary religious practice." Amrit Burman, a 10-year resident of one of the larger and more upscale old age homes in Kolkata, Milan Tirtha (Place of Pilgrimage), and also a retired bachelor, explained: "Now, you must know that the 'Indian conception' of earlier times was that of *vanaprastha* [forest-dwelling]. When they grew old, people would leave their families and go to the forest, to focus on a spiritual life. This [old age home] is a modern version of that ancient practice."

Shilpa Roychowdhury, a vibrant and thoughtful resident and cofounder of the Sraddhanjali (Offering of Respect) old age home of north Kolkata, had long planned to leave family life after she retired as an engineer. Widowed when she was only 40, she finished raising her son, brought a daughter-in-law into the family apartment, and slept in the same room with her beloved granddaughter for the first 10 years of the girl's life. However, she viewed establishing and moving into an old age home for women as an opportunity to pursue spirituality in her later years. "First one lives with family and society," she reflected, "and then it is time to turn to God." She described how living in the old age home helped her pursue the goal of detachment:

Everything of mine I left in [our home]. I didn't take anything from there. Aside from God, we don't have anyone or anything. I came alone and will have to leave alone. . . . I don't want to reenter *samsar* [family-worldly life]. If I enter it, with my son and wife, then they will become my own, and I would become accustomed to that closeness. Instead, I am living very independently. . . . No one is anyone's [*keu karur nae*]. Without abandoning, one can receive nothing. Only upon God am I dependent.

Photo 39.3   Lady residents gathered at the temple of an elder ashram organized around the notions of "forest-dwelling" and spirituality, Hindu values appropriately pursued in late life. (Photo by Sarah Lamb)

Further, elders in old age homes are often the recipients of sustained *seva*, or service to and respect for the aged. Although offered by hired staff and proprietors rather than one's own junior kin (a not insignificant distinction), the residents of most homes enjoy and praise the receipt of *seva*—in the form of the faithful arrival of daily 5 a.m. bed tea, meals served, oil massaged into hair, mosquito nets tied, bathwater warmed and delivered. Several of the homes I encountered centrally figure the concept of *seva* in both their names and mission statements. Quite a few, in fact, are named Seva. Other similarly evocative names include Sraddhanjali (Offering of Respect) and Gurujan Kunja (Garden Abode for Respected Elders). The manager of Gurujan Kunja explained the home's name: "It indicates the home's purpose: to serve and honor the old people living here. You see, they are all revered people living here." In fact, for some founders, the motivation to establish an elder residence was precisely to provide *seva*—to elders who (simply by virtue of being elder) deserve to receive it but who are not able to find it within their families.

A few proprietors also established old age homes in their own deceased parents' names, as if continuing to honor their parents by serving other living elders now. In such cases, grand framed and flower-garlanded photographs of the parents grace the home's front halls. Resident Ashok Bose praised the *seva* he received at the Ramakrishna Mission old age home: "There's something you should know: We are living here *completely* without worry! *Everything* we need, we receive: the giving of food, tea, warm bath water—*whatever* we need, we receive. Truly, there are no worries! At *precisely* the right time, the tea comes, the food comes!" In representing the old age home as an appropriate locus of *seva*, such frameworks serve in part to legitimate a disassociation of the old person from the family in a newer institutional era (Cohen 1998: 115; Lamb 2009: 142–61).

Living Independently and Home-Based Care on the Market

In addition to moving into old age homes, a growing number of elders among India's urban middle classes are now living alone, in an arrangement many describe as unnatural or impossible (*asambhab*), modern, and Western. Those living singly form still only a small proportion of the population—in 2014, just 4.4 percent of rural and 3.5 percent of urban persons aged 60 and older lived alone. At the same time, 14.7 percent of rural and 15.1 percent of urban elderly lived with a spouse only and no adult children (Rajan and Balagopal 2017a: 10, Table 1.4), a condition that many in India think of as living "alone." For instance, Kolkata elders frequently refer to themselves as living "alone" (*eka*) when living without adult children, even if residing with a spouse, such as "I live alone with only my wife." A Kolkata seniors' organization, the Dignity Foundation, offers loneliness mitigation services to older "people who live alone either single or as a couple."[22] In public and media perceptions, the situation of elders living alone in India is a growing and uniquely modern phenomenon, as portrayed in the July 16, 2007, cover story of *India Today*, "Ageing Parents Home Alone" (D. Datta 2007).

Taking advantage of the rising trend of independent living, a new industry of home-based care is emerging to offer social, emotional, and practical support for elders living apart from junior kin. Nonprofit nongovernmental organizations (NGOs) as well as private businesses provide services such as medical assistance, around-the-clock telephone help lines, visits to chat over tea, meal delivery, help with household chores, escorts to late-night wedding receptions and doctor appointments, care and affection, and the promise of presence at the time of death. It is often NRI or "nonresident Indian" children, or children living and working in other Indian cities, who arrange for and fund the care services for their parents—able to supply money but not time or proximity. The director of one Delhi-based NGO, Agewell Foundation, compared their hired eldercare counselors to "surrogate sons," commenting:

ber 1, 2004   **BEYOND POLITICS**   The Times of India, Kolkata

Busy yuppies outsource errands to new chore bazaar

From Looking After Old Parents To Walking The Dog, These Corporate Jeeveses Do It All

Photo 39.4   S. I. Kamdar, "Busy Yuppies Outsource Errands to New Chore Bazaar," *Times of India*, September 13, 2004, p. 12.

"A sad situation indeed when children cannot gift their parents time. But this is a contemporary reality that has to be faced."[23] YourManInIndia (YMI) began as an enterprise offering health care for the aged parents of busy and distant NRIs and has now expanded to offer a full range of concierge services. The *Times of India* reports: "Busy yuppies outsource errands to new chore bazaar: From Looking after Old Parents to Walking the Dog, These Corporate Jeeveses Do It All" (Photo 39.4) (Kamdar 2004).

Invoking familiar themes of family and intergenerational reciprocity to frame care on the market, home-based care organizations present their counselors and care managers as kin—visiting "sons," "nephews," "grandsons," and "granddaughters" who step in for real (busy or geographically distant) family members to offer similar forms of care and *seva*. A home-based eldercare company in Ahmedabad titles itself literally The Family Member, with its motto: "To Care for Those Who Cared for Us!"[24] Kolkata-based TriBeCare offers a choice of monthly packages—Aador (love and affection), Jotno (tender, effortful care), and Suraksha (protection)—while care managers keep the elders' adult children informed through regular WhatsApp messaging. The kin-like quality of the care relationships is fostered through class parity: Both the eldercare receivers and the hired caregivers tend to share similar middle-class or higher class backgrounds.

As with old age homes, both positive and negative assessments abound regarding the outsourcing of care tasks from junior kin to private organizations. Hearing of the emergence of hired eldercare, my research assistant Hena's mother and grandmother begged her and other junior kin to please never let the private crevices of their bodies be touched or cared for by the hired hands of strangers or non-kin. "*Seva* (service to and respect for the aged) is *not* something that can be bought or sold," fervently remarked Papri

Chowdhury, founder of a neighborhood-based group for elders living alone, one that she prefers to call a "joint family" rather than an "NGO," a term that to her connotes the "modern" and "impersonal." In Papri's "joint family" organization, elders themselves or their junior kin (often from abroad) can request such services as visits over tea, reading aloud, or escorting to the doctor or a spiritual program. But, Papri is firm that she cannot charge for these services, this *seva*: Instead, people who voluntarily wish to make donations to the organization may do so at any time—but not at the same time that services are being rendered.

Papri herself, now in her fifties, grew up in a large joint family, with her father and his five brothers, their parents and children—all living together. "That was the old Indian culture," she commented in English. "It wasn't so easy to go abroad then. No one was ever lonely. . . . Now families have all become nuclear and small. Among my friends, *no one* lives with their kids. Everyone is husband-wife, husband-wife." I interjected, "It's becoming like America?" "No!—it is not *becoming* like America: It has *become* like America. It is *just* like America now!" According to Papri and many others with whom I have spoken, the most serious problem facing India's middle-class elderly—those with enough money but who are short on coresident kin—is loneliness. For those experiencing or contemplating their own potential future loneliness in old age—like Manu, who never married and so has no children who could possibly provide *seva*—the expanding market of care resources beyond the literal family offers a welcome sense of security.

Enhancing the Self: Clubs, Love, and Active Aging

Another culturally emergent phenomenon in India among the cosmopolitan middle classes is an ethos of self-focused active aging. Many elders are joining the flurry of new clubs in cosmopolitan centers for senior citizens, clubs that emphasize the cultivation of peer friendships, active volunteerism, fit bodies, and lifelong hobbies—pursuits especially appropriate for an individualist, rather than family-oriented, sense of self. Exploring the developing leisure culture for upper-middle-class older adults in India—including luxury senior retirement ventures, travel/holiday packages, and dating platforms—Tannistha Samanta sees a new "celebration of a project on the self where the responsibility to 'age well' rests with the individual" (2018: 94; see also Samanta and Varghese 2018).

Founded in 2013, Delhi-based Healthy Aging India has picked up global discourse on healthy, active aging, which emphasizes individual responsibility to make one's own aging successful by maintaining an active lifestyle, exercising, eating well, and cultivating a youthful, ageless attitude (Lamb 2014, 2019). Among Healthy Aging India's vision statements is this bold, Western-sounding aspiration: "We are striving to create a unique self-sustaining model for the elder generation so that they don't need to ever depend upon others for their survival."[25] The organization's strategies include health education and promoting physical exercise through activities such as walk-a-thons. Lots of older cosmopolitan Indians are also taking up healthy-active aging projects in their daily lives, as elders are seen increasingly in urban parks enjoying vigorous morning walks in their sneakers while socializing with peers.

In the modern apartment complex, Udita, where I resided in Kolkata doing fieldwork for five months in early 2006, an active group of senior citizens, including Viraj Ghosh of this chapter's opening, formed a Laughing Club, a group promoting laughter yoga as a means to improve health, reduce stress, and increase happiness (see Box V.2). The Laughing Club in my apartment complex was a mixed-gender group of about 30, ranging in age from their fifties to eighties (Photo 39.5). They met daily at 6 a.m. for laughter yoga, exercises, chatting, and (for those who wished to attend) Bhagavad Gita[26] reading. In the afternoon, groups of men and women gathered separately for tea, snacks, and conversation, rotating among each other's flats. I was welcomed into the club and became privy to conversations and stories. About half of the members lived in multigenerational families with a married son and grandchildren, and about half lived alone or with a spouse. Most who lived alone had children working abroad. Although those who lived right with married sons and grandchildren were generally the ones considered the most fortunate in terms of living arrangements, the general consensus was that those who lived apart from children did enjoy several advantages. One of their most energetic and convivial members was Viraj-da, who lived alone with his wife in the flat their son purchased for them, and Viraj's flat was known to be the place where friends could spontaneously congregate. Another active member of this group, Sumant Roychowdhury, a retired engineer, highly gregarious and with a perpetual witty twinkle in his eyes, lived in a more traditional arrangement with his son, daughter-in-law, and granddaughter. Although he was close to his grandchild, he had to tiptoe around his daughter-in-law and could not readily invite friends over.

Manu, who had started "living in" at age 58 with her 68-year-old "boyfriend" (as she called him), whom she had met on the overseas tour for Bengali seniors, spoke one evening over tea with a few other older never-married women we had known for several years who lived in a Government of West Bengal hostel for working women. Without precisely mentioning her new boyfriend to them, Manu tried to persuade them to attend an upcoming gathering of Thikana Shimla, the group aimed at helping elderly singles "find soulmates." Manu remarked, "It's so important to be loved and touched. Even just a small stroke of the arm feels so nice, if you haven't had that for many years." The ladies agreed. To grow old with neither a partner nor children or grandchildren—the condition of those like them who had never

Photo 39.5   The Laughing Club of Udita. (Photo by Sarah Lamb)

married—means no touch or physical affection. *Maybe* they would attend? The women laughed together.

"That Was a Very Sweet Relationship": The Work of Changing Expectations

Despite expanding imaginaries and possibilities for aging in contemporary India, the project of crafting ways of life in old age beyond the family is not one that most older Indians I have grown to know find easy or natural. Rather, it is a project they engage in with critical reflection, self-consciousness, effort, and generally some ambivalence.

I was invited to give a talk comparing ways of aging in India and the United States to a gathering of the Dignity Foundation senior citizens club in Kolkata. A lively and provocative discussion ensued on competing cultural models surrounding aging and intergenerational relationships. The gathering consisted almost entirely of comfortably well-off persons who were living separately from their children. Conversations were in English, signifying the elite and diverse regional backgrounds of the participants. Referring to the joint family system in which children and parents in turn reciprocally provide care for each other, one gentleman commented, "That was a very sweet relationship, but it is dying now." "We can't get rid of that expectation level, though," another member objected. "The problem is that we have grown up *expecting* our children to care for us. If you," he addressed this next comment to me, presumably as an American, or perhaps as a social scientist, "can show us how to *get rid* of this—our expectations—then there would be no problem." People smiled and nodded. A graceful dark-haired woman in about her seventies spoke up with an air of gentle, self-assured wisdom, "The main issue is: We should not demand money and love at the same time. We have to settle for one or the other. If we mistake one for the other, we will be disappointed." She went on:

> We invest in our children for years. But, we should *not* do so for the interest in the bank. We should not do so expecting anything in return. From the [Bhagavad] Gita, you should know—that *disinterested* action is best. If your child gives back to you, that is a blessing. But, you should not give to the child *thinking* of the interest. *That* is the problem. It will *liberate* us to think of acting with *disinterest*!

The secretary of the group, Mr. Swaminathan, then stood up to offer a tale of an Indian doctor's experiences in Canada that served to illustrate how the independent aging and individualism of the West can be *too* extreme, for an Indian's taste: An Indian doctor had settled in and was practicing medicine in Canada. He had an ailing elderly patient, a Canadian, residing in a nursing home. One night, shortly after midnight, the man died. The doctor phoned the man's son. After the phone rang many times, the son picked up. The doctor told him, "I'm calling from the nursing home." The son asked, "Is there a problem?" The doctor: "Yes, I'm very sorry to say: Your father has passed away." The son replied (Mr. Swaminathan mimicked an irritated, angry voice), "Why did you have to wake me up and call me in the dead of night to tell me this? I have given the name of the undertaker. They will take the dead body away, and then you could reach me in the morning—I will go over then." The doctor was so disturbed by this interchange that he decided to leave Canada and return to India.

Murmurs came from around the audience, "Could this be true? Is this really a true story?" "Yes!" Mr. Swaminathan insisted, "I met the doctor myself, who told me this story." "Surely this must be an extreme case, though." "Indeed, this would *never* happen in India." But, an elegant woman dressed in an ash-grey *salwar kameez* suit, offered softly, "In fact, it was a very practical reaction. True, the doctor could have simply called the undertaker, and then notified the son in the morning." This led to a conversation about the merits and demerits of individualism versus collectivism, as Western and Eastern or Indian ways of being.

As we departed into the darkening summer evening, the elegant, thoughtful woman in the ash-colored *salwar* came up to me and said, "See, if you weren't an individual, then you couldn't be going out like this, pursuing your work, giving talks, writing books. You would have to be home with your children and family." I said, "Yes, that's true. Though, still, I am *worried* about them." The meeting had gone on longer than I had expected, and I had just turned on my mobile phone showing eight missed calls from my two daughters waiting for me at our rented Kolkata flat.[27] The woman replied resolutely, "True—you can worry about them. But, still—you were able to come."

Conclusion

As new cultural imaginaries of aging well in India emerge in the contemporary moment, many or, I would say, most people continue to find dependence on the family for social-emotional care and economic support normal and welcome. Many also pursue familiar spiritual or religious goals as meaningful pathways in later life. At the same time, people sense more options at play—more flexible gender and generation systems, new forms of eldercare on the market, clubs for congregating with peers, globally circulating ideologies of self-focused active aging—creating a sense that old age may offer new opportunities for sociality, care, and growth beyond the family, potentially worth trying.

In its own way, the state is also interweaving newer and more conventional modes of aging within its eldercare policies. In 2007, the Government of India passed a Maintenance and Welfare of Parents and Senior Citizens Act making adult children—and anyone standing to inherit property from a senior citizen—not only morally but now also legally obligated to provide care (Brijnath 2012; Lamb 2013: 74–76). Under this law, implemented as of October 2009, children may be fined 5,000 rupees and jailed for up to three months if found guilty of neglecting parents. Under "Need for the Legislation," the bill's preface declares: "It is an established fact that the family is the most desired environment for senior citizens/parents to lead a life of security, care, and dignity." The legislators continue: "The traditional norms and values of the Indian society laid stress on showing respect and providing care for the aged. . . . Unfortunately, the time has come when the moral obligation of children to look after their parents in their old age has to be backed by a legal obligation."[28] At the same time, the Government of India recognizes a need for some support beyond the family, offering limited old-age pensions targeted at the poor, and modest government subsidies for old age homes and other nongovernmental organizations serving the elderly (Vera-Sanso 2015; Rajan and Balagopal 2017a: 20–24). S. Irudaya Rajan and Gayathri Balagopal analyze the Government of India's approach to old-age security: The Indian state "desperately seeks to contain social welfare expenditure. . . . Consequently, while making the pitch for targeted social security, the state simultaneously exhorts the family to care for the elderly, invoking Indian tradition, culture, and filial piety" (2017a: 1).

Moreover, some policy makers, social workers, and gerontologists in India also argue that Indian policies must promote ideologies of individual self-sufficiency as the only means to deal with the concurrent realities of population aging, decline in family support, and meager state welfare coffers. India's 1999 OASIS (Old Age Social and Income Security) Report, for instance, opens by declaring that both family and state support are inadequate in India: "In a world where the joint family is breaking down, and children are unable to take care of their parents, millions of elderly face destitution." At the same time, a true poverty-alleviation state welfare program for the elderly "would require a staggering expenditure much beyond the capacity of the government." Therefore, the solution to old-age security must lie in the individual:

> The problem will have to be addressed through thrift and self-help, where people prepare for old age by savings accumulating through their decades in the labor force. . . . We must educate people that old age is inescapable and that saving for old age could be a painless process if started early in life. . . . The government should encourage fully funded old age income security systems that emphasize the values of thrift and self-help.[29]

The assemblage of values, aspirations, policies, and lifeways making up elderscapes in India today—involving both familial and nonfamilial modes of care and identity—constitute new cultural spaces of aging, taking hold especially among the cosmopolitan middle classes. These new elderscapes form vehicles through which people are living and debating not only aging, but also gender, generation, visions of the life course, and moral ideals at the heart of India as a nation, society, and culture. Most older people approach such a project of reenvisioning aging with a thoughtful resourcefulness and complex ambivalence, borrowing from both perceived old and new lifeways, grappling with the changes and demands of the present.

Notes

1. This chapter is revised and updated from Lamb 2008 in the 3rd edition of *The Cultural Context of Aging*, "Elder Residences and Outsourced Sons: Remaking Aging in Cosmopolitan India."

2. All names of those from my own fieldwork are pseudonyms. "*Di*" is short for *didi*, "older sister" in Bengali, the primary language spoken in the Indian state of West Bengal and the neighboring nation of Bangladesh. Along with *da* for *dada* (older brother), *di* is used commonly as a sign of respect and warmth when addressing a senior person. Like other South Asians, Bengalis generally find it disrespectful to address a senior person by the first name only, so epithets such as "older sister," "older brother," "uncle," "aunt," and "grandmother" are regularly used.

3. I use single quotation marks to indicate English words used in an otherwise Bengali conversation.

4. Essay posted November 1, 2018: https://www.facebook.com/thikana shimla/. Here and elsewhere, translations from the Bengali are mine. See also R. Datta 2017.

5. https://www.business-standard.com/article/economy-policy/70-indians-live -in-rural-areas-census-111071500171_1.html; https://tradingeconomics.com/india /rural-population-percent-of-total-population-wb-data.html.

6. In 1989–1990, I spent 18 months in West Bengal studying aging, gender, and families, residing for most of the time in a large village in the Birbhum District, while spending shorter periods in Kolkata researching two of the city's first old-age homes. Since 2003, I have made nearly annual research trips to Kolkata and rural West Bengal, as I focused on new modes of aging among the urban middle classes while also exploring the rising trend of single women who never marry, including how single women envision and prepare for their own aging. From 1993 to 2008 I also researched aging and families among Indian immigrant communities in the United States (e.g., Lamb 1997, 2000, 2005, 2009, 2013, 2018).

7. http://worldpopulationreview.com/world-cities/kolkata-population/.

8. See the Religion section from the 2011 Census of India data: http://census india.gov.in/Census_And_You/religion.aspx.

9. For more on values and expectations surrounding multigenerational family living in India, see Brijnath 2014: 5–6; Lamb 2000, 2009, 2013; Rajan and Balagopal 2017b; Samanta, Chen, and Vanneman 2014; and van Willigen and Chadha 1999.

10. For more on *seva* and elders, see Brijnath 2014: 5–6; Cohen 1998; and Lamb 2000: 59–66.

11. This conversation was translated from Hindi by my colleague Ira Raja.

12. See Cohen 1998; Lamb 2009; Rajan and Balagopal 2017a: 8–9; and Samanta 2018: 103, note i, for analyses of these arguments.

13. See also Bengali villagers' perspectives on the multiple forces interfering with successful joint-family living (Lamb 2000: 70–111) and Lawrence Cohen's (1998) exploration of narratives of modern "bad families" from the colonial era to contemporary times.

14. Barik, Agrawal, and Desai examine two rounds of the India Human Development Survey, conducted by the National Council of Applied Economic Research and the University of Maryland in 2004–2005 and 2011–2012, and find a 5 percent decrease in coresidence with children over the eight-year period, but with still 84 percent of women and 81 percent of men aged 60 and over residing with children in 2011–2012, with most of the rest living either alone (in small numbers) or with only their spouse (2015: 110, Table 2). Study participants included about 72 percent from rural areas and 38 percent from urban areas (p. 109). Sathyanarayana, Kumar, and James (2012: 13, Table 6, p. 13) present similar data from the National Family Health Survey (NFHS) of

2005–2006, finding 77.5 percent of women and 79.3 percent of men aged 60 and over residing in multigenerational households with children. S. Irudaya Rajan and Gayathri Balagopal compile data from the National Sample Survey Office from 1995 to 2014, finding that in 2014, 78 percent of rural participants and 78.6 percent of urban participants lived with adult children, either with or without their spouse (2017: 10, Table 1.4), figures that represent a slight increase in the proportion of elderly living with their spouse and adult children between 2004 and 2014 (9).

15. For discussions of cultural values surrounding aging, independence, and intergenerational relationships in the United States, see, for example, Buch 2018; Clark 1972; Simic 1990; Kalish 1967; Lamb 2000: 52–53, 2014.

16. Texts exploring religion and aging in India include Gangopadhyay and Samanta 2017: 344–45, 347–49; Lamb 2000: 115–43, 2009: 141, 161–71; Tilak 1989; Vatuk 1980; and van Willigen and Chadha 1999: 18–22, 67, 72–76, 81–87.

17. This *ashrama* schema is outlined in *The Laws of Manu* (Kane 1968–75: vol. 2; Manu 1886, 1991). See also Gangopadhyay and Samanta 2017: 344–45, 347–49; Lamb 2009: 39–40, 161–71; van Willigen and Chadha 1999: 18–22; and Vatuk 1980 for more on how persons incorporate the *ashrama* schema into their everyday lives. In the Hindu texts, this schema applies specifically to upper-caste males, while little attention is devoted to defining a woman's life stages, which are determined by her relationships to the men upon which she depends for support and guidance: her father in youth, her husband in marriage, and her sons in old age (*The Laws of Manu* V.148—Manu 1886: 195, 1991: 115). In my fieldwork, however, both women and men, especially among the higher castes, commonly invoke a model of the four Hindu life stages when discussing experiences of aging.

18. From 2004–2006, I was able to locate 71 old age homes in the Kolkata area (visiting 29 of these personally and contacting the others by phone and letters) (Lamb 2009). HelpAge India's 2009 guide to old age homes lists 1,280 across India's urban centers (HelpAge India 2009; see also A. Datta 2017; Samanta and Gangopadhyay 2017).

19. The text of this act (implemented as law in 2009) can be found here: http://legislative.gov.in/actsofparliamentfromtheyear/maintenance-and-welfare-parents-and-senior-citizens-act-2007.

20. The few older, free homes for the aged around India tend to be even larger. For instance, Kolkata's Little Sisters of the Poor Old Age Home currently houses 150 elders, and the West Bengal Government home for "old and infirm political sufferers" and destitute women houses 68 (Lamb 2009). See also Liebig 2003: 170–71.

21. From 2003 to 2006, I interviewed 100 old-age-home residents in the Kolkata environs. Of these, 33 had sons and daughters-in-law living right in the Kolkata region, 30 had no children at all (21 of these had never married), 21 had children all living abroad (elsewhere in India or overseas), 18 had only daughters, and one had just a single unmarried son.

22. The Dignity Foundation is a "Senior Citizens Life Enrichment Organization," founded in 1995, with chapters now in Ahmedabad, Chennai, Delhi, Jamshedpur, Kolkata, and Mumbai (http://www.dignityfoundation.com/).

23. Founded by Himanshu Rath in 1999 in New Delhi, Agewell Foundation's mission is to "work for the welfare and empowerment of older persons of India." See https://www.agewellfoundation.org/.

24. https://www.thefamilymember.com/ (accessed December 10, 2018). See also Matta 2017.

25. http://www.healthyagingindia.in/ and http://www.healthyagingindia.in/?page_id=1576.

26. The Bhagavad Gita is an ancient Sanskrit text that many view as a classic summary of the core beliefs of Hinduism.

27. I had taken my daughters, ages 13 and 10, to the field with me, while they attended an international school in Kolkata. It turns out they were hoping simply that I would pick up some pizza on my way home!

28. The text of the 2007 bill is available at http://www.prsindia.org/uploads/media/1182337322/scr1193026940_Senior_Citizen.pdf.

29. "OASIS (Old Age Social and Income Security): A Report," http://www.seniorindian.com/oasis__.htm, February 1, 1999. See also Sivaramakrishnan 2018 for an enlightening intellectual history of aging policy in India and abroad.

Bibliography

Ahlin, T. 2017. "Only Near Is Dear? Doing Elderly Care with Everyday ICTs in Indian Transnational Families." *Medical Anthropology Quarterly* 32(1): 85–102.

Barik, D., T. Agrawal, and S. Desai. 2015. "After the Dividend: Caring for a Greying India." *Economic and Political Weekly* 50(24): 108–12.

Brijnath, B. 2012. "Why Does Institutionalised Care Not Appeal to Indian Families? Legislative and Social Answers." *Ageing and Society* 32(4): 696–717.

Brijnath, B. 2014. *Unforgotten: Love and the Culture of Dementia Care in India.* New York: Berghahn.

Buch, E. 2018. *Inequalities of Aging: Paradoxes of Independence in American Home Care.* New York: New York University Press.

Clark, M. 1972. "Cultural Values and Dependency in Later Life." In *Aging and Modernization*, edited by D. O. Cowgill and L. D. Holmes. New York: Appleton Century Crofts.

Cohen, L. 1998. *No Aging in India: Alzheimer's, the Bad Family, and Other Modern Things.* Berkeley: University of California Press.

Datta, A. 2017. "Old Age Homes in India: Sharing the Burden of Elderly Care with the Family." In *Elderly Care in India: Societal and State Responses*, edited by S. Irudaya Rajan and G. Balagopal, 77–93. New York: Springer.

Datta, D. 2007. "Ageing Parents Home Alone." *India Today*, July 16 (updated April 8, 2011).

Datta, R. 2017. "Kolkata's Senior Citizens Find Love and Marry, Thanks to Thikana Shimla." *India Today* Magazine Section, July 24.

Gangopadhyay, J., and T. Samanta. 2017. "'Family Matters': Ageing and the Inter-generational Social Contract in Urban Ahmedabad." *Contributions to Indian Sociology* 51(3): 338–60.

HelpAge India. 2009. *Directory of Old Age Homes in India.* New Delhi: HelpAge India.

The Hindu Staff Reporter. 2004. "Old Age Homes against Our Culture." *The Hindu*, September 14.

Kalish, R. A. 1967. "Of Children and Grandfathers: A Speculative Essay on Dependency." *Gerontologist* 7: 65–69.

Kamdar, S. I. 2004. "Busy Yuppies Outsource Errands to New Chore Bazaar: From Looking After Old Parents to Walking the Dog, These Corporate Jeeveses Do It All." *Times of India, Kolkata*, Wednesday, September 1:12.

Kane, P. V. 1968–1975. *History of Dharmasastra*, 2d ed. 5 vols. Poona Bhandarkar: Oriental Research Institute.

Lamb, S. 1997. "The Making and Unmaking of Persons: Notes on Aging and Gender in North India." *Ethos* 25(3): 279–302.

Lamb, S. 2000. *White Saris and Sweet Mangoes: Aging, Gender and Body in North India.* Berkeley: University of California Press.

Lamb, S. 2005. "Cultural and Moral Values Surrounding Care and (In)Dependence in Late Life: Reflections from India in an Era of Global Modernity." *Journal of Long Term Home Health Care* 6(2): 80–89.

Lamb, S. 2008. "Elder Residences and Outsourced Sons: Remaking Aging in Cosmopolitan India." In *The Cultural Context of Aging: Worldwide Perspectives*, edited by J. Sokolovsky, 418–40. Westport, CT: Praeger.

Lamb, S. 2009. *Aging and the Indian Diaspora: Cosmopolitan Families in India and Abroad.* Bloomington: Indiana University Press.

Lamb, S. 2013. "In/dependence, Intergenerational Uncertainty, and the Ambiva-lent State: Perceptions of Old Age Security in India." *South Asia: Journal of South Asian Studies* n.s., 36(1): 65–78.

Lamb, S. 2014. "Permanent Personhood or Meaningful Decline? Toward a Criti-cal Anthropology of Successful Aging." *Journal of Aging Studies* 29: 41–52.

Lamb, S. 2018. "Being Single in India: Gendered Identities, Class Mobilities, and Personhoods in Flux." *Ethos* 46(1): 49–69.

Lamb, S. 2019. "On Being (Not) Old: Agency, Self-Care, and Life-Course Aspira-tions in the United States." *Medical Anthropology Quarterly* 33(2): 263–81.

Liebig, P. S. 2003. "Old-Age Homes and Services: Old and New Approaches to Aged Care." In *An Aging India: Perspectives, Prospects and Policies*, edited by P. S. Liebig and S. Irudaya Rajan, 159–78. New York: Haworth.

Manu. 1886. *The Laws of Manu.* Vol. 25, *Sacred Books of the East.* Translated by G. Buhler. Oxford: Clarendon.

Manu. 1991. *The Laws of Manu.* Translated by W. Doniger with B. K. Smith. New York: Penguin.

Matta, A. 2017. "Family for Hire: Old and Lonely? Here's Company, and Help, You Can Get for a Fee." *Hindustan Times*, March 19.

Rajan, S. I., and G. Balagopal. 2017a. "Caring India: An Introduction." In *Elderly Care in India: Societal and State Responses*, edited by S. I. Rajan and G. Balagopal, 1–36. New York: Springer.

Rajan, S. I., and G. Balagopal, eds. 2017b. *Elderly Care in India: Societal and State Responses*. New York: Springer.

Samanta, T. 2018. "The 'Good Life': Third Age, Brand Modi and the Cultural Demise of Old Age in Urban India." *Anthropology & Aging* 39(1): 94–104.

Samanta, T., and J. Gangopadhyay. 2017. "Social Capital, Interrupted: Sociological Reflections from Old Age Homes in Ahmedabad, India." In *Cross-Cultural and Cross-Disciplinary Perspectives in Social Gerontology*, edited by T. Samanta, 109–24. New York: Springer.

Samanta, T., F. Chen, and R. Vanneman. 2014. "Living Arrangements and Health of Older Adults in India." *Journals of Gerontology: Series B Psychological and Social Sciences* 70(6): 937–47.

Samanta, T., and S. Varghese. 2018. "Love in the Time of Aging: Sociological Reflections on Marriage, Gender and Intimacy in India." *Ageing International*, September 28. https://doi.org/10.1007/s12126-018-9332-z.

Sathyanarayana, K. M., S. Kumar, and K. S. James. 2012. "Living Arrangements of Elderly in India: Policy and Programmatic Implications." BKPAI Working Paper No. 7. New Delhi: United Nations Population Fund.

Simic, A. 1990. "Aging, World View, and Intergenerational Relations in America and Yugoslavia." In *The Cultural Context of Aging: Worldwide Perspectives*, edited by J. Sokolovsky. New York: Bergin and Garvey.

Sivaramakrishnan, K. 2018. *As the World Ages: Rethinking a Demographic Crisis*. Cambridge, MA: Harvard University Press.

Tilak, S. 1989. *Religion and Aging in the Indian Tradition*. Albany: State University of New York.

Times of India. 2018. "Growing Numbers in Old Age Homes Underline Trichy's Dark Underbelly." October 31.

Van Willigen, J., and N. K. Chadha. 1999. *Social Aging in a Delhi Neighborhood*. Westport, CT: Bergin & Garvey.

Vatuk, S. 1980. "Withdrawal and Disengagement as a Cultural Response to Aging in India." In *Aging in Culture and Society*, edited by Christine Fry, 126–48. New York: Praeger.

Vera-Sanso, P. 2015. "What Is Preventing India from Developing an Inclusive National Framework for Older People?" *Population Horizons* 12(2): 77–87.

CHAPTER FORTY

Gray as Green

Civic Ecology, Community Gardens, and Elders Seeking Healing and Community

Jay Sokolovsky

Back to the Future: West 89th St. Westside Community Garden, April 17, 2016

I could not believe our luck. My wife and I had flown to Manhattan for a long weekend in mid-April 2016 to celebrate our wedding anniversary, held previously 25 years before in New York City's small Gramercy Park. Unlike the weekend of our nuptials, which was cool and rainy, we encountered a sunny 70-degree day. It was almost 20 years since I happened upon a wonderful community garden in New York's Upper West Side and decided almost instantly that I had to do a visual documentary about such places in the city of my birth (Photo 40.1). On a glorious Sunday afternoon of our most recent

---

WEB SPECIAL:

Tulip Festival at the Westside Community Garden, April 17, 2016, https://www.youtube.com/watch?v=gQy0qJchmZA.

Photo 40.1 Westside Community Garden, New York City. Tulip Festival, April 17, 2016. (Photo by Jay Sokolovsky)

visit, we returned to this garden, and it just happened to be their annual tulip festival. We strolled among the hundreds of tulips in full bloom, listened to birds singing and delighted bees buzzing from flower to flower. As we viewed small children dancing with abandon to piano music in a now prosperous urban area, I thought back to an encounter more than 16 years prior in the heart of Harlem, New York.

East 125th St. Harlem, NY, Jackie Robinson Garden

It was a vision from god. . . . He spoke to me, one day I was walking down the street and I look over there and saw all this garbage and stuff . . . and I saw they were using it for prostitution and they were shooting up over there, and I said to myself, Lord I sure would like to make a big garden over there. And the voice said "You can do that, just step out on my word." But today if you see it you wouldn't believe it. We got peach trees, grape trees . . . apple trees . . . , you wouldn't believe it to see this dump come to paradise! (Field notes, June 14, 2002)

As I sat with 72-year-old Betty Gaither, munching on one of the apples from this garden in Harlem, I indeed felt like I was in a certain version of paradise. Even though this uptown green space was wedged between elevated subway tracks, apartment buildings, and a space with junked cars, spend an afternoon there with its garden members and you might believe that *urban community greening*, linking the hands of energetic urban elders with those of younger generations, might just save the world. This perspective has been reinforced by talking to older adults involved with urban greening through North America and in Europe and seeing the florescence of this interest in places like Mumbai, India (Rademacher 2018) or Lisbon, Portugal (Harper and Afonso 2016).

Gray and Green and the Making of Civic Ecology

Betty is just one person in a score of elders who have been part of a national and even international movement to create socially enabling green spaces and community gardens in what were once abandoned urban sites left to decay, fester, and help erode a sense of neighborhood and local well-being (Linn 2007; Harper and Afonso 2016). In a broader sense what Betty and her friends were creating in Harlem was part of healthy, "place-making" efforts emerging globally in cities (Mackenzie 2016). This was also part of what has come to be discussed in gerontological literature as a "Gray and Green" focus, connecting older adults in a deep manner to "the natural environment, well-being, legacy, sense of meaning, and interpersonal connections to community and larger social structures" (Wright and Wadsworth 2014: 1–2).

There was a clear link of these ideas to what I experienced in the Jackie Robinson Garden and saw repeated in various forms, as over two decades I sought to document through ethnographic video and research the history of New York City's community garden movement and similar developments around North America (Sokolovsky 2008). It is an amazing story of how a city's poorest neighborhoods transformed otherwise barren and often criminally hazardous zones with plants, trees, simple structures, and locally inspired art, performance, and political activism. In documenting this effort I began to see a pattern in the role of active elders. Seniors helping to establish these green oases created alliances across generational, economic, and ethnic lines in powerful acts of what has come to be called "civic ecology," during one of the most troubled times in the city's turbulent history.

Here I am following the lead of Krasny and Tidball in viewing such urban community greening as acts of "civic ecology" whereby local citizens by collective action reorder a physical space into an enabling green environment, promoting and enhancing community involvement and social inclusion (2015; Krasny 2018). This idea is related to what Klinenberg calls "social infrastructure," the physical conditions that determine if social capital is generated, that is, the creation of personal relationships and interpersonal networks (2018).[1]

When community elders could not obtain adequate city help or they thought the situation required instant action, they either started these projects on their own or strong-armed a small cadre of younger kin and immediate neighbors to get things under way or protect what they had done from those who had other ideas for the space. The impact of civic ecology is especially powerful when undertaken in the face of the great social and economic inequities and rapid environmental degradation that New York City endured in the 1980s (von Hassell 2002).

This chapter will look at gray and green and civic ecology from two angles. First I will examine the rise of the community gardening movement in New York City, focusing on the involvement of seniors who used the creation of such places to enhance social capital and promote a neighborhood's "collective efficacy." I will also briefly discuss the connection to health and healing and the use of civic greening to create therapeutic spaces in public venues and care settings where the frail aged may one day reside. This latter perspective seeks to explore how enabling green spaces enhances social engagement of even the most disabled older adults and is tied into a growing perspective of eco-elders who see their successful graying tied to civic ecology through community greening.

Urban Decline and the Flowering of Civic Greening and Community Gardens

Few people would associate 21st-century New York City with gardening and urban agriculture, yet this most archetypical of reborn world cities is now home to one of the largest such urban community greening efforts in North America. Its five boroughs now contain over 600 locally developed and maintained community gardens and even small farms, and this does not include gardens created within public housing developments (Krisel 2017).[2]

From Coney Island, Brooklyn, to Manhattan's Lower East Side and the once-devastated South Bronx, poor and often minority aged such as Miss Betty and their neighbors have created seeming miracles that have been a major but unheralded part of New York City's renaissance over the past 30 years. In some senses, New York City faced what some have called an "eco tipping point" when a community's response to profound urban decay and decline pushed residents to take control of abandoned spaces through various greening projects (Brooks and Marten 2005). It has never been easy, and the reality of sustaining these green spaces as civically enabling places sometimes fails and they are often under threat especially from an expanding population and need for residential and business urban landscapes (Reynolds 2014; Rademacher 2018).

WEB SPECIAL:

See the blog of GROWNYC to check on the latest efforts at civic greening in some of the most economically challenged areas of New York City: https://www.grownyc.org/blog/programs/community-gardens.

The successful gardens would become not only civic but in some senses sacred public spaces, where (unlike a vacant lot) it was "taboo" to dump trash. The community solidarity and social cohesion that developed around them allowed residents to defend their gardens and to take action on other issues affecting their neighborhoods such as crime and trash. A positive feedback loop developed in which better neighborhood quality led to more community pride and commitment, and attracted more residents. More people on the streets reinforced control of crime and illegal dumping and stimulated more shops to open, which in turn improved neighborhood quality. As some of the neighborhoods evolved from low-income to higher-income districts, the gardens evolved to include low-maintenance plants as a place to relax rather than grow food. When the city government started to sell off garden lots to developers, the older gardeners had the experience, neighborhood pride, organization, and confidence to engage successfully in the public opinion and legal battles that saved most of the gardens.

Citizens creating urban gardens on vacant public land has a long history in the United States dating back to the late 19th century. For example, during the 1893–1897 depression, in cities like Detroit, "potato patch farms" enabled masses of the unemployed to survive by growing food in vacant lots. Since that time a multitude of related efforts have sporadically emerged on a short-lived basis in relation to economic hard times or world wars (Lawson 2005).[3] As will be noted below, Detroit in the 21st century has begun using community garden models to reinvent a livable city.

However, when most people think of green space in New York City, they conjure up "manicured" landscapes such as monumental public parks like Central Park or the magnificent botanical gardens in Brooklyn and the Bronx. When Central Park was opened by city government in 1859, it was thought of as green oasis to "civilize" the newly arrived masses of immigrants and ease the stress of urban life. Today's community gardens represent a totally different relation to place, space, and power. Here, citizens from poor and neglected neighborhoods have reversed this process by reclaiming abandoned public lands to tame city-owned spaces that they saw as totally out of control. What were once open sores on the urban landscape have become places of transcendent beauty, cultural meaning, and often social and political activism. In this regard, the latest civic greening movement appears more long-lasting. It is connected to an emerging new vision of urban possibilities, whereby citizens create by their own actions and sometimes in concert with local government and other entities more livable, more sustainable, and healthier communities (Reynolds and Cohen 2016).

In New York City, if there was not such good documentation on community gardens, which arose during one of its darkest periods, they might have been written off as pure urban myth. During the early 1970s housing stock and infrastructure were crumbling, violent crime skyrocketed, and the treasury was bare. As banks redlined neighborhoods and landlords abandoned their properties, the city acquired upwards of 20,000 lots. In the Lower East Side of Manhattan 70 percent of the population was displaced as 3,400 living units were demolished and almost daily fires and a lively drug trade moved in. Uptown in the South Bronx alone, 500 acres of former housing were burned down and reverted to the city for back taxes. Many such spaces came to be used as illegal garbage dumps, drug-shooting galleries, and places to abandon cars.

The emergence of movements to counter these acts of what could be called spacial terrorism is not a story about rich kids or bored elders in white gloves who form garden clubs to indulge their passion for hybrid roses or organic tomatoes. Here is a gut-wrenching, often lonely and continuing struggle for community control of neighborhoods, public space, and the very lives and well-being of neighborhood children (Von Hassell 2002; Chan, DuBois, and Tidball 2015). As the late, greening activist Adam Honigman frequently reminded people, "Land use is a blood sport!" Tellingly, the importance of community voice and initiative in creating and sustaining common green space is illustrated by the early efforts of city government. In 1976 New York City spent $3.6 million to design and build gardens on vacant land awaiting housing development throughout the city, but with little or no community input. Neighborhood residents who were expected to maintain them were not given tools or technical assistance, and, as might have been expected, in short order these gardens were vandalized and abandoned. The residents knew full well that they had no real say in the construction and use of these sites and that they would be sold to developers in the future to build whatever they wished.

Green Guerillas, Urban Anarchism, and the Art of Imaginative Greening

In 1973, an artist named Liz Christie got some friends together and began to reclaim as garden space a small abandoned lot on Manhattan's Lower East Side. In a dream she envisioned repeating this, even in fenced lots, by tossing over balloons armed with water and seeds. Her dream also revealed a name, "Green Guerillas" (spelled incorrectly in her vision), which became a group

---

WEB SPECIAL:

See a short video here about Adam Purple and his remarkable Garden of Eden: https://vimeo.com/29275235.

---

she formed to teach others how to repeat her success. Two years later she went on to develop the Open Space Greening Program for the city's Council on the Environment.

Around the same time many large apartment buildings in the Lower East Side of the city were being abandoned by landlords and some were taken over by squatters and artists. In one such place where an old tenement building had been torn down across from his apartment building, a middle-aged artist, who came to be known as Adam Purple, along with his partner "Eve" set out to create the Garden of Eden. The large garden/farm emerged from meticulous hand labor with simple tools and the help of local residents and anarchists. It radiated out from a centrally located yin/yang symbol to counter the pervasive hard grid of the city and produced a wide array of edible vegetables to feed the neighborhood (Brost and Wang 2013).

While the city would eventually bulldoze the garden in 1986 after a long court battle, such acts of grassroots activism were but some of the sparks that ignited New York City's current community garden movement (Photo 40.2). By late 1970s there were so many gardens being started on public lands, the city established Operation Green Thumb, which initially leased plots for $1 and provided technical support to sustain greening activities (www.green thumbnyc.org).[4] Over the ensuing three decades additional support from the Trust for Public Land and the New York Restoration Project has facilitated the purchase of more than 100 garden properties to prevent them from being sold to developers.[5]

Elders and the Community Garden Movement

It should be made clear whether looking at cities like New York, Seattle, or Philadelphia, where strong civic greening movements emerged as part of the process of community reclamation in the late 1960s and 1970s, that persons of all ages were involved with both initiating and continuing these projects. However, I have seldom encountered a well-functioning community garden in New York City where older adults were not active participants, if not involved in leadership within that space. In many cases they were instrumental in creating such places. Visit the Clinton Garden, not far from Times Square, and you might encounter a retired teacher who tends to and educates

Photo 40.2   Children's Education Day at Belmont Little Farmers Garden, in the Bronx, New York, 2002. (Photo by Pedro Diez)

all visitors about their beehives; most any summer day join Cynthia and Haja in Harlem's Daniel Wilson Memorial Garden to participate in a children's environmental learning program this elder husband-wife team developed; or stop into almost any Casita garden after work hours and listen to Puerto Rican *plena* music being played by expert older adult hands.[6]

There are some obvious reasons for the strong participation of older adults in civic greening, such as their having more free time to devote to such activities or being more likely to have been exposed to gardening in their youth. Some of the elders who became active in sustaining community gardens had spent their youth in more rural zones of South Carolina, Puerto Rico, or throughout the Caribbean region where growing food, medicinal plants, and even gourds for musical instruments was part of their early experiences. They were instrumental in providing the knowledge base to combine with the energy of younger residents or older neighbors who had no idea it was possible to grow tomatoes or collard greens in the middle of Manhattan.

From another perspective, in previously devastated zones like Manhattan's Lower East Side or the South Bronx, it was only the long-term residents who had experienced more intact, functioning communities in these areas during the 1950s and 1960s. Persons of this older generation were the ones most likely to even hope that this might again be possible (see Kweon, Sullivan, and Riley 1998). This was brought home to me very powerfully when I showed my documentary *Urban Garden* in a university class in Florida. As it was ending with an upbeat message, I heard a 30-year-old male student softly sobbing in the back of the room. I asked him what was wrong, and he told the class that he had lived the first eight years of his life in the Bronx, close to one of the beautiful gardens shown in the video, the Garden of Happiness. "Much of the area was a pile of rubble and burned-out buildings, full of violent crime and junkies. I never imaged that in my lifetime, the residents themselves could create such a thing of beauty and live across from such a garden in nice town houses, this is beyond my comprehension."

As I spent more time in a wide variety of gardens, I came to realize that while nurturing organic beauty via neighborhood hands was one of the functions of such places, it usually became secondary to the social plantings and harvests occurring within. What I began to see were community-created public spaces that beckoned those who entered to readily transcend the barriers of wealth, ethnicity, and age. I have seldom encountered urban spaces in New York City where people of differing ages and backgrounds so readily mingle for common efforts. Here in the early mid-1970s when the gardens were being established, elderly African American residents from the rural South could be seen teaching lifelong white urbanites how to plant tomatoes and greens (Photo 40.3), or Caribbean elders would grow huge squash plants and teach local kids how to turn their dried husks into musical instruments. In 2003 in a well-established garden, I observed a 12-year-old boy who sought refuge there from a difficult foster care setting being nurtured by a small group of older garden members and tutored in math by a retired 78-year-old teacher.

Studies of community gardens have produced an impressive list of benefits such as an increased sense of community ownership and stewardship; affording a neutral space for neighborhood activities; providing inexpensive access to nutritious fruits and vegetables; exposing inner-city youth to nature; connecting people across boundaries of culture, class, and generation; and even reducing crime (van den Berg et al. 2015; Egerer 2018).[7]

Some of the best documented impacts have been shown in the realm of neighborhood crime reduction. Large-scale studies in Chicago have found a strong association of safer environments and civic greening (Kuo and Sullivan 2001). The largest study of crime and community ever completed in that city, in fact, found that the surest indicator of impending neighborhood crime reduction was an area's ability to create and sustain a community garden (Sampson, Raudenbush, and Earls 1997). Such actions, if they were successful, invariably increased the level of what the authors call "social efficacy," a measure of residents' ability to act together especially for the interest of local children. In doing so, they build stronger relationships among themselves

Photo 40.3   A former resident of the rural south (on the right) helps a lifelong urban dweller get the most from his planting in an Upper West Side of Manhattan garden, being developed in the early 1980s. (Photo by Lynn Law)

and create a neighborhood support system that provides alternatives to violence (Bogar and Beyer 2016).

This idea was tested in a 2011–2014 study about the transformation of vacant lots in resource-limited Philadelphia neighborhoods by the Philadelphia Horticultural Society and University of Pennsylvania Medical School. Among 110 vacant lots there were three categories: a control set where nothing was done, a second grouping where the space was kept clear of trash, and a third where simple lawns, a fence, and some trees were planted. By 2014 the research found that crime had reduced in groups two and three, with the biggest impact on group three where people in the neighborhood reported the strongest reduction in feelings of helplessness and depression (South et al. 2018).

Health, Healing, and Therapeutic Green Spaces

I am spending the day in the Bronx at a small farm and community garden with a man of Afro-Caribbean heritage in his late sixties. He was one of several key older residents who worked to reclaim this space about a decade ago with the help of their grandkids, some neighbors, and the city's support organization, "Green Thumb." After helping him dig out an old bed of some spiny plants, he noticed a quickly developing rash on the back of my hand, which began to intensely itch. He led me into another part of the garden and bent down to show me a plant with green shiny leaves. He said, "My grandson sometimes get that," and winking his eye, tells me, "I just tell the little one to crush those leaves in his palm and put the juice on the rash." Catching on, I follow these indirect instructions and almost immediately feel relief. Over the course of a next several hours he proceeds to describe in detail the use of dozens of medicinal herbs interspersed with the food crops of corn, several varieties of tomatoes and squashes, egg-plants, greens, peaches, apples and plums. "You see, I was brought up in the Caribbean by my grandfather who was a roots medicine healer and I know everything about these plants for making people better . . . but I have to be careful about claiming to be a doctor, so when people ask, I just say well, I don't know about that, but when my wife or cousin has a prob-lem like that I just pick the so and so plant and put it in a tea for them." (Field notes, July 15, 2002)

Having such an elder with this level of folk health knowledge was not com-mon, but most gardens in ethnic minority communities maintained an assortment of medicinal plants that were regularly used for minor bodily complaints and it was the older members who people relied on for their proper use. In the broader sense of such spaces as healing places, one of the most important environmental aspects of the current community garden movement is that it rose up in marginalized, minority neighborhoods that typically had the lowest access to both public green space and fresh vegeta-bles in the city. Studies have consistently shown the ameliorative effects of civic greening in mitigating chronic urban stress among poor communities and moderating its link to negative health conditions such as hypertension, depression, asthma, or heart problems (van den Berg et al. 2015; Alaimo et al. 2016; Egerer 2018; van de Jerrett and van den Bosch 2018).[8]

Among the most frequently uttered and spontaneously offered statements people made to me about their experience in community gardens were about enhanced positive psychological moods, perceptions of stress relief, and spe-cific references to being in a peaceful, healing environment.[9] For example, in 1998, barely 15 minutes into my first encounter with a community garden, I learned of the personal impact these spaces can have. "I came to this garden in the late 1970s. I had just gotten a divorced and did not realize I was bipolar and very depressed. This garden saved me, it healed me" (Field notes, 64-year-old female, April 28, 1998). The idea of healing gardens is an old one, dating at least to the Middle Ages, and is still being employed in many kinds of formal rehabilitative settings including hospitals, hospices, and prisons (Winterbot-tom 2005; van de Jerrett and van den Bosch 2018).[10] For example at Manhat-tan's famous Bellevue Hospital, a psychiatrist has established an art-focused "sobriety garden" where patients in addictive services can help construct and interact with this "participatory landscape" as part of their treatment (https://ephemeralnewyork.wordpress.com/tag/bellevue-sobriety-garden/).

Over the past decade especially, the notion of therapeutic landscapes has come to be applied to the frail elderly, taking the premises of civic greening into highly restrictive long-term care environments (Detweiler et al. 2012). In fact, the notion of "elder gardens" has been at the center of revolutionizing and humanizing treatment of dementia, especially in developing the "Eden Alternative" and "Green House" models of care and "farm care" environments (Noone and Jenkins 2017; see Part VI Introduction; Part VI Web Book McLean). These new visions of elder-inhabited space seek to reengage the social beings hidden behind medically constructed masks of failed personhood and reduce negative impacts on cognitive health (see Thomas 1998; Cherrie 2018; Part VI Web Book McLean). As Silverman and McAllister found in their study of a specialized Alzheimer's unit:

> While activities such as gardening may be important in maintaining or reactivating certain practical skills, they are equally important in the maintenance or reactivation of a sense of self and self-worth. Such activities and the practice of specialized skills also provide a context for remembering and recounting important aspects of residents' personal history. (1995: 207)

Yet, Silverman and McAllister also found that without the specialized design skills of therapeutic horticultural experts, engaging elders with diverse sets of impairments through civic greening was not easily achieved (see Hughes 2014). One of the important advances in this area is the work of people like Ye Jen Lin, a Taiwanese physician who was trained in horticultural therapy in the United States. She has developed a training program for medical students that teaches them to help create and implement interactive therapeutic gardens, especially designed for highly impaired nursing home residents with a wide variety of severe physical and cognitive limitations (Lin et al. 2007; see also Senes et al. 2012). Importantly, a study across countries in Scandinavia showed that using such green spaces was generally effective in supporting cognitive disability, but that special care was necessary for persons with advanced dementia and required the need to develop safe green spaces such as "wander gardens" with only organically grown edible greenery (Spring 2016). In the Netherlands, which has been a leader in designing innovative environments for persons with dementia, that nation has been developing a variety of green care environments, especially in farms, as a way of rethinking approaches to dealing with severe cognitive decline (Bruin et al. 2017; see Part VI Introduction).

Conclusions: Civic Greening, Eco-Elders, and Its Many Connections

While today's urban community gardens began under dire circumstances that sparked greening efforts in earlier eras, they have not only persisted much longer but for the most part have morphed into vital community-building nodes of social inclusion.[11] This stands in sharp contrast to the exclusionary impact of all too many "urban renewal" projects that may end up destroying the only kinds of housing that elder long-term residents and their interconnected kin and friends can afford. The dramatic rise of inequality and the continuing economic crisis in a number of U.S. and European cities have again stimulated the growth of urban agriculture in places like Seville, Spain, and Paris, France (Pourias 2016). Moreover, with increased threats from global warming, in the form of devastating storms hitting New York City or Houston, Texas, there is a growing movement to implement green infrastructure into plans for building healthier cities for the future (ARUP 2014; Brown 2017).

Unfortunately, community gardens can also become the victims of their own success. As the book *Green Gentrification* notes, the very attraction of thriving spaces, in certain cases, has accelerated intense gentrification and worked to price out a diverse population from some urban neighborhoods (Gould and Lewis 2017). Importantly this very issue has stimulated a growth in research and public awareness of the need for environmental justice and the need to deal with food deserts in poor neighborhoods (Wolch, Byrne, and Newell 2014; Horst, McClintock and Hoey 2017).

Millennials and Eco-Elders Unite

Many neighborhoods in cities like New York, Vancouver, and Seattle have become dominated by millennials, some of whom think deeply about sustainability and a place for young families to engage with some local green spaces. At the same time 21st-century eco-elders, like those who worked to stabilize collapsing urban places in the last century, have sought to think big and tie local civic greening with the grander efforts to stabilize the rising potential of climate and environmental disasters (Moody 2009/2010; Summerhays 2014).

It should be noted, however, that using grassroots civic greening to center sustainable communities or care contexts often requires specialized knowledge about the environment and the means of making it accessible, usable, and meaningful to persons of varied ages, backgrounds, and physical competence. That is why in North America the most thriving and long-lasting civic greening endeavors are actively supported by experts from urban governments. They also forge partnerships with universities, NGOs, and socially responsibly corporations (see especially www.communitygarden.org).

One of the most interesting green infrastructure innovations supporting older citizens is happening in the small, exceptionally dense republic of Singapore, where its 5 million inhabitants are largely crammed into high-rise apartments. Over 90 percent of its food is imported, and there is precious little land to build traditional farms. Since the 1990s the city has used traditional one-layer rooftop gardens, but more recently, engineer Jack Ng developed what he calls the first "world's first low-carbon, water-driven, rotating, vertical farm." Importantly, it was designed with seniors and other housebound persons in mind who could maintain the vertical gardens, which rotate in aluminum beds and currently focus on a few popular, fast-growing greens that can be harvested in a month's time (Seneviratne 2012).

It is rather amazing to see the varied impact of applying civic ecology to not only restoring connections with marginalized citizens, reaching across generations, or working to repair communities blown asunder by natural disaster such as Hurricane Sandy in the New York City area (Chan, DuBois, and Tidball 2015) or unnatural wars such as that which tore apart Yugoslavia in the 1990s (Tidball and Krasny 2013). What is crucial here is that creating or restoring existing community gardens by working across generations is one of the keys to building community resilience before and after disaster does strike (Hanley 2017).

For example, beginning in 2015, a team composed of social scientists from the U.S. Forest Service, researchers from Cornell University, community members, and landscape designers developed Hurricane Healing Gardens, which helped a New York City neighborhood rebuild resilience through civic ecology after a devastating storm (see Web Special below). Elsewhere, by 2017, Detroit was developing an ambitious movement creating what it was calling America's first AgriHood, which sets "agriculture as the centerpiece of a mixed use urban development" (Malandra 2017).

In the United States these efforts can reverberate powerfully across the life course in programs such as Seattle's Tilth Alliance (http://www.seattletilth .org/about) or Brooklyn's Added Value programs (www.added-value.org). Such programs seek to empower homeless and disadvantaged youth through creating their own urban community organic farms and eventually, in the

---

WEB SPECIALS:

See video about the Hurricane Healing Gardens at https://vimeo. com/236248212; and see a video about Detroit's AgriHood at https:// youtu.be/PH6oWee5DcU.

case of Added Value, build leadership skills directed at community improvement. Moving beyond this to the somewhat obvious strategy of using such spaces to forge strong intergenerational community ties in reality is rather hard to achieve (Krasny and Doyle 2002; Larson and Meyer 2006). One of the most promising models for such a goal is Garden Mosaics, which connects youth and elders through understanding the interdependence of plants, people, and culture in gardens. These programs combine science learning with intergenerational mentoring, multicultural understanding, and community action (http://www2.dnr.cornell.edu/ext/youth/garden/index.htm). There are a number of pilot projects using this model now operating throughout the United States and in South Africa, but to be really effective in a long-term manner, such efforts should be connected to broad actions to enhance elder-friendly and life span-enabling communities (see Part V Stafford).

This chapter has suggested ways to think about late life in employing civic ecology and urban greening to address the unfolding century's most looming challenges (Hudson 2017; Skar et al. 2019). In all this, it is important to realize that no matter how beautiful and peaceful any garden may be, it is the connection established between social beings nurturing it and the sense of inclusion and community created by their actions that have the most consequence.

Notes

There are many people to thank for helping me in my research on community gardens, especially for the materials discussed in this chapter. These persons include: Edie Stone, Adam Honigman, Sid Glasser, Annie Chadwick, Betty Gaither, Gerard Lordahl, Dee Parisi, Jane Grundy, Donald Loggins, Abu Talib, Carolyn Radcliffe, Jackie Beach, Jane Weisman, Kate Chura, Lynn Law, and Daniel Winterbottom. I would also like to thank Mari Gillogli for applying her sharp editorial eye to this chapter. This chapter is adapted from "Elders, Urban Community Gardens, Civic Ecology, and the Quest for Community," published in *Urban Life*, 6th edition, 2018.

1. See K. Miller, *Social Capital and Community Gardens: A Literature Review.* NPCR Report # 1348, CURA Center for Urban and Regional Affairs, University of Minnesota, 2012. http://www.cura.umn.edu/sites/cura.advantagelabs.com/files/publications/NPCR-1348.pdf.

2. This figure does not include the 650 gardens being maintained, often by seniors, in the city's extensive public housing system, which housed 125,000 seniors in 2008.

3. Many people know about the "victory gardens," which were encouraged during World War I and World War II, but most have forgotten about the varied attempts of cities of help poor citizens grow food on vacant urban land during bad economic times. In Europe a more long-lasting system called the allotment

system developed in the 18th and 19th century with plots of land, usually on the outskirts of cities, given to poor families to cultivate and grow food (Crouch 2000; see http://en.wikipedia.org/wiki/Allotment_(gardening).

4. Operation Green Thumb was funded by federal Community Development Block Grants and continues as simply GreenThumb and has been a program of the New York City Parks Department since 1995.

5. The New York Restoration Project (NYRP) is a nonprofit begun by actress Bette Midler in 1995 to reclaim and restore underresourced parks, community gardens, and open space in New York City (see www.nyrp.org). In 1999, under the administration of Mayor Rudy Guliani, 114 gardens were set to be auctioned off to developers. Greening activist groups such as More Gardens and Reclaim the Streets mounted strong street protests, and four lawsuits were developed to prevent the sale. A day before the auction, the Brooklyn State Supreme Court issued an injunction to stop the sale. That same day the city agreed to sell the plots to NYRP and the Trust for Public Land. In 2000 the state attorney general secured a temporary restraining order that prevented the city not only from conveying land to a developer but also from entering the garden to perform test borings. After Mayor Giuliani left office in 2002, the city negotiated a settlement agreement that preserves an additional 200 community gardens (they will either be transferred to parks or sold to a land trust), establishes a review process for 115 gardens that the city wishes to develop, and allows the city to proceed immediately with the development of an additional 38 gardens.

6. For a good discussion of the cultural aspects of Casita gardens see, Saldivar-Tanaka and Krasny 2004.

7. A study in St. Louis also looked at the functions of community gardens in stabalizing neighborhoods. See the "Whitmire Study: Gateway Greening Community Garden Areas, Reversing Urban Decline," at www.gatewaygreening.org/WhitmireStudy.asp.

8. For a general discussion of health and urban greening see A. Bellows, "Health Benefits of Urban Agriculture," www.foodsecurity.org/UAHealthArticle.pdf. Also, as an interesting connection for Carson's chapter in Part VI, among Native Americans, where diabetes is reaching epidemic proportions, culturally appropriate community gardens are being explored as a means of at least partially restoring traditional diets under which this disease was much less common (see Lombard et al. 2006).

9. I should also note that the community garden experience also involved continuing struggle and sometimes significant conflict in maintaining and managing these spaces.

10. For an excellent new study of horticultural therapy and prisons, see Jiler 2006.

11. However, some of the intensely ethnic gardens can sometimes act counter to the notion of social inclusion and discourage persons from other backgrounds in taking advantage of the space.

Bibliography

Alaimo, K., A. W. Beavers, C. Crawford, E. H. Snyder, and J. S. Litt. 2016. "Amplifying Health through Community Gardens: A Framework for Advancing Multicomponent, Behaviorally Based Neighborhood Interventions." *Current Environmental Health Reports* 3(3): 302–12.

ARUP. 2014. "Cities Alive: Rethinking Green Infrastructure." https://www.arup.com/perspectives/publications/research/section/cities-alive-rethinking-green-infrastructure.

Bogar, S., and K. Beyer. 2016. "Green Space, Violence, and Crime: A Systematic Review." *Trauma Violence Abuse* 17(2): 160–71.

Brooks, S., and G. Marten. 2005. *Green Guerillas: Revitalizing Urban Neighborhoods with Community Gardens (New York City, USA)*. http://www.ecotippingpoints.org/our-stories/indepth/usa-new-york-community-garden-urban-renewal.html#Ingredients.

Brost, A., and H. Wang 2013. *Adam Purple & The Garden of Eden*. New York: Traveling Light Books.

Brown, H. 2017. "Green Infrastructure: Best Practices for Cities." U.S. Green Building Council. https://www.usgbc.org/articles/green-infrastructure-best-practices-cities.

Bruin, S., B. de Boer, H. Beerens, Y. Buist, and H. Verbeek. 2017. "Rethinking Dementia Care: The Value of Green Care Farming." *Journal of Post-Acute and Long-Term Care Medicine* 18(3): 200–203.

Chan, J., B. DuBois, and K. G. Tidball. 2015. "Refuges of Local Resilience: Community Gardens in Post-Sandy New York City." *Urban Forestry & Urban Greening* 14(3): 625–35.

Cherrie, M. 2018. "Green Space and Cognitive Ageing: A Retrospective Life Course Analysis in the Lothian Birth Cohort 1936." *Social Science & Medicine* 196: 56–65.

Crouch, D. 2000. "Reinventing Allotments for the Twenty-First Century: The UK Experience." *Acta Horticulturae* 523: 135–42.

Curran, W., and T. Hamilton, eds. 2017. *Just Green Enough: Urban Development and Environmental Gentrification*. New York: Routledge.

Detweiler, M., T. Sharma, J. G. Detweiler, P. F. Murphy, S. Lane, J. Carman. A. S. Chudhary, et al. 2012. "What Is the Evidence to Support the Use of Therapeutic Gardens for the Elderly?" *Psychiatry Investigation* 9(2): 100–110.

Egerer, M. 2018. "Gardener Well-Being along Social and Biophysical Landscape Gradients." *Sustainability* 10(96): 1–14.

Gould, K., and T. Lewis. 2016. *Green Gentrification: Urban Sustainability and the Struggle for Environmental Justice*. New York: Routledge.

Hanley, S. 2017. "Beach 41st Street Garden Healing from Hurricane Sandy in 2012: Community Gardens Help To Heal Broken Neighborhoods." CleanTechnica, October 27. https://cleantechnica.com/2017/10/27/community-gardens-help-heal-broken-neighborhoods/.

Harper, K., and A. I. Afonso. 2016. "Cultivating Civic Ecology: A Photovoice Study with Urban Gardeners in Lisbon, Portugal." *Anthropology in Action* 23(1): 6–13.

Horst, M., N. McClintock, and L. Hoey. 2017. "The Intersection of Planning, Urban Agriculture, and Food Justice: A Review of the Literature." *Journal of the American Planning Association* 83(3): 277–95.

Hudson, R. 2017. "Gray and Green Together: Climate Change in an Aging World." *Public Policy & Aging Report* 27(1): 1–3.

Hughes, J. 2014. *How We Think About Dementia: Personhood, Rights, Ethics, the Arts and What They Mean for Care.* London: Jessica Kingsley.

Jiler, J. 2006. *Doing Time in the Garden.* Oakland, CA: New Village.

Klinenberg, E. 2018. *Palaces for the People: How Social Infrastructure Can Help Fight Inequality, Polarization, and the Decline of Civic Life.* New York: Random House.

Krasny, E., ed. 2018. *Grassroots to Global Broader Impacts of Civic Ecology.* Ithaca, NY: Cornell University Press.

Krasny, K., and R. Doyle. 2002. "Participatory Approaches to Program Development and Engaging Youth in Research: The Case of an Inter-Generational Urban Community Gardening Program." *Journal of Extension* 40(5). Also available at www.joe.org/joe/2002october/a3.shtml.

Krasny, M., and K. Tidball. 2015. "Preface: Civic Ecology: What and Why." In *Civic Ecology: Adaptation and Transformation from the Ground Up.* Cambridge, MA: MIT Press.

Krisel, B. 2017. "NYC to Expand Urban Farm Program at Public Housing Developments." Patch, October 2. https://patch.com/new-york/harlem/nyc-expand-urban-farm-program-public-housing-developments.

Kuo, F., and W. Sullivan 2001. "Environment and Crime in the Inner City: Does Vegetation Reduce Crime?" *Environment and Behavior* 33(3): 343–67.

Kweon, B., W. Sullivan, and A. Riley. 1998. "Green Common Spaces and the Social Integration of Inner-City Older Adults." *Environment and Behavior* 30(6): 832–58.

Larson, J., and M. Meyer. 2006. *Generations Gardening Together: A Sourcebook for Intergenerational Therapeutic Horticulture.* Binghamton, NY: Haworth.

Lawson, L. 2005. *City Bountiful: A Century of Community Gardening in America.* San Francisco: University of California Press.

Lin, Y. J., et al. 2007. "Connecting Elders with Stroke History, Medical Students and the Community through A 'Gardening for Health' Course in Taiwan." Presented at the 28th Annual Conference of the American Community Gardening Association, Boston.

Linn, K. 2007. *Building Commons and Community.* Oakland, CA: New Village.

Lombard, K. A., S. Forser-Cox, D. Smeal, and M. K. O'Neill. 2006. "Diabetes on the Navajo Nation: What Role Can Gardening and Agriculture Extension Play to Reduce It?" *Rural Remote Health* 6(4): 640.

Mackenzie, A. 2016. "Beyond Food: Community Gardens as Places of Connection and Empowerment." Project for Public Spaces, March 1. http://www.pps.org/blog/beyond-food-community-gardens-as-places-of-connection-and-empowerment/.

Malandra, O. 2017. "EarthRx: Detroit's New 'AgriHood' Is the Future of Urban Planning." *Paste Magazine.* https://www.pastemagazine.com/articles/2017/01/detroits-new-agrihood-is-the-future-of-urban-plann.html.

Moody, H. 2009/2010. "Eco-Elders: Legacy and Environmental Advocacy." *Generations* 33(4): 70–74.

Noone, S., and N. Jenkins. 2017. "Digging for Dementia: Exploring the Experience of Community Gardening from the Perspectives of People with Dementia." *Aging and Mental Health* 22(7): 881–88.

Pourias, J. 2016. *Urban Allotment Gardens: Example of a Joint Project between Sevilla (Spain) and Paris (France).* http://www.jardins-familiaux.org/pdf/news/office/2016-03_research_project_France-Spain.pdf.

Rademacher, A. 2018. *Building Green: Environmental Architects and the Struggle for Sustainability in Mumbai.* Oakland: University of California Press.

Reynolds, K. 2014. "Disparity Despite Diversity: Social Injustice in New York City's Urban Agriculture System." *Antipode* 47(1): 240–59.

Reynolds, K., and N. Cohen. 2016. *Beyond the Kale: Urban Agriculture and Social Justice Activism in New York City.* Athens: University of Georgia Press.

Saldivar-Tanaka, L., and M. Krasny. 2004. "Culturing Community Development, Neighborhood Open Space, and Civic Agriculture: The Case of Latino Community Gardens in New York City." *Agriculture and Human Values* 21(4): 399–412. Also available at: www.gardenmosaics.cornell.edu/pgs/aboutus/materials/Culturing_Community_Development.PDF.

Sampson, R., S. Raudenbush, and F. Earls. 1997. "Neighborhoods and Violent Crime: A Multilevel Study of Collective Efficacy." *Science* 277: 918–24.

Senes, G., N. Fumagalli, R. Crippa, and F. Bolchini. 2012. "Nursing Homes: Engaging Patients and Staff in Healing Garden Design through Focus Group Interviews." *Neuropsychological Trends* 12(1): 135–46.

Seneviratne, K. 2012. "Farming in the Sky in Singapore." *Inter Press Service,* December 12. https://ourworld.unu.edu/en/farming-in-the-sky-in-singapore.

Silverman, M., and C. McAllister. 1995. "Continuities and Discontinuities in the Life Course: Experiences of Demented Persons in a Residential Alzheimer's Facility." In *The Culture of Long Term Care: Nursing Home Ethnography,* edited by J. N. Henderson and M. D. Vesperi. Westport, CT: Bergin & Garvey.

Skar, S., et al. 2019. "Urban Agriculture as a Keystone Contribution towards Securing Sustainable and Healthy Development for Cities in the Future." *Blue-Green Systems* 1: 1145. doi: 10.2166/bgs.2019.931.

Sokolovsky, J. 2008. *Urban Garden: Fighting for Life and Beauty.* Video Documentary, St. Petersburg, FL: Ljudost Productions, http://www.youtube.com/watch?v=EheWIrv9pvo.

South, E., B. C. Hohl, M. C. Kondo, J. M. MacDonald, and C. C. Branas. 2018. "Effect of Greening Vacant Land on Mental Health of Community-Dwelling

Adults: A Cluster Randomized Trial." *JAMA Network Open* 1(3): e180298. https://jamanetwork.com/journals/jamanetworkopen/fullarticle/2688343.

Spring, J. 2016. "Design of Evidence-Based Gardens and Garden Therapy for Neurodisability in Scandinavia: Data from 14 Sites." *Neurodegenerative Disease Management* 6(2): 87–98.

Summerhays, K. 2014. "The Intercultural Journey of the Chinese Eco Elders and the Civil Servant." *Knowledge Cultures* 2(5): 29–46.

Thomas, W. H. 1998. "Long-Term Care Design: Cultural Expectations and Locale Creating the Eldergarden." *Journal of Healthcare Design* 10: 64.

Tidball, K., and M. Krasny. 2007. "From Risk to Resilience: What Role for Community Greening and Civic Ecology in Cities?" In *Social Learning Towards a More Sustainable World*, edited by A. Wals. Wageningen, Netherlands: Academic Publishers. http://krasny.dnr.cornell.edu/file/Tidball_Krasny_Urban_Resilience.pdf.

Tidball, K., and M. Krasny. 2013. *Greening the Red Zone: Disaster, Resilience and Community Greening.* New York: Springer.

van de Jerrett, M., and M. van den Bosch. 2018. "Nature Exposure Gets a Boost From a Cluster Randomized Trial on the Mental Health Benefits of Greening Vacant Lots." *JAMA Network Open* 1(3): e180299. https://jamanetwork.com/journals/jamanetworkopen/fullarticle/2688340.

van den Berg, M., W. Wendel-Vos, M. van Poppel, H. Kemper, W. van Mechelen, and J. Maas. 2015. "Health Benefits of Green Spaces in the Living Environment: A Systematic Review of Epidemiological Studies." *Urban Forestry and Urban Greening* 14(4): 806–16.

Von Hassell, M. 2002. *The Struggle for Eden: Community Gardens in New York City.* Westport, CT: Bergin & Garvey.

Winterbottom, D. 2005. "The Healing Nature of Landscapes." *Northwest Public Health* Spring/Summer: 18–20.

Wolcha, J., J. Byrne, and J. P. Newell. 2014. "Urban Green Space, Public Health, and Environmental Justice: The Challenge of Making Cities 'Just Green Enough.'" *Landscape and Urban Planning* 125: 234–44.

Wright, S., and M. Wadsworth. 2014. "Gray and Green Revisited: A Multidisciplinary Perspective of Gardens, Gardening, and the Aging Process." *Journal of Aging Research* (1): 283682. doi: 10.1155/2014/283682.

CHAPTER FORTY-ONE

Web Book: Spaces of Age— About the Elderscapes of Charlotte County, Florida

Stephen Katz

Available at: http://www.culturalcontextofaging.com/webbook-katz

This chapter pulls together three perspectives in aging studies: institutional ethnographies, "aging in place" debates, and community network research. It uses the framework of elderscapes to unite these ideas to discuss communities based on mobility in the context of a postmodern construct of late life within the nation's oldest local zone, Charlotte County, Florida.

CHAPTER FORTY-TWO

Web Book: An Organization for the Elderly, by the Elderly

A Senior Center in the United States

Yohko Tsuji

Available at: http://www.culturalcontextofaging.com/webbook-tsuji

This chapter provides entrée into the inner workings of a small-town senior center. It gives a unique perspective through the eyes of a Japanese American anthropologist. For the author's broader discussion of aging in America see Y. Tsuji, *Through Japanese Eyes: Thirty Years of Studying Aging in America* (Cornell University Press, 2020).

CHAPTER FORTY-THREE

Web Book Photo Essay: "Where Are the Bones in Their Noses?"

Community Aged in North American RV Camps and in Papua New Guinea

Dorothy Counts and David Counts

Available at: http://www.culturalcontextofaging.com/webbook-countscounts

This photo essay chapter explores, through the author's ethnographic encounters, community formation within RV encampments in North America and a village in Papua New Guinea.

PART VI

The Quest for Gerontopia: Culture and Health in Late Life

The art of living consists of dying young, but as late as possible.

—Anon.

Introduction

Jay Sokolovsky

In Part I of this book we looked globally at the general issue of population aging and its implications for human communities. Policy planners who are concerned with such things often focus on promoting the physical, mental, and even social health of our eldest adults to minimize impairments, positively impact their quality of life, and support those who care about them (Butler 2008; Jönson 2018). All of the chapters in this section revolve around such issues. Dr. Seuss writes in his lyrical verse *You're Only Old Once* (1986):

> In those green-pastured mountains of Fotta-fa-Zee
> everybody feels fine at a hundred and three

He mocks the ancient and diverse myths of finding a fountain of youth in some distant land, but also the more recent false claims of extraordinary long life in places like Abkhasia and the incessant commercials about youth-restoring pharmaceuticals or longevity-enhancing medical procedures (Magalhães, Stevens, and Thornton 2017). As seen in the 16th-century painting by Lucas Cranach the Elder (Photo VI.1), this questing for an eternal young life is nothing new. Looking at the image you see another continuing gender-based pattern depicting women as being more concerned about the embodiment of aging—only elderly females enter the water on the left and come out of the pool as much younger persons, who after dressing move on to join older men at a feast.

Such gender biases are still reflected in the strong antiaging cosmetics and medical industry largely focused on helping women hide their real age. Ironically, while the number of geriatricians in the United States lags woefully behind other postindustrial nations, the last two decades have witnessed the rapid growth of the American Academy of Anti-Aging Medicine, claiming 26,000 global members in 2018. There has also been growth of numerous small chains of longevity clinics such as the Center for Healthy Living and

Photo VI.1   Lucas Cranach the Elder, *The Fountain of Youth*, panel painting, 1546. ((c) Foto: Gemäldegalerie der Staatlichen Museen zu Berlin-Preußischer Kulturbesitz. Fotograf/in: Jörg P. Anders)

Longevity. More scientifically credible endeavors have been marked by the establishment of the Stanford Center on Longevity (http://longevity3.stan ford.edu/) and investments by Google and other Silicon Valley companies to literally "hack" aging.

The Quest for Geriatric Utopias

Perhaps it is our species' envy of animals like the Greenland shark, which can survive five centuries, or the tasty quahog clam, of chowder fame, which can live just as long if not plucked from the sea. Not far from where I live in downtown St. Petersburg, Florida, is a hokey "fountain of youth," which belies tales of long-sought liquid sources of long life. It is hard to talk about aging in non-Western, "exotic" settings without inappropriately getting people's hopes up. For example, in the 1970s, print and TV media, as well as Dannon yogurt commercials, widely touted various studies of supposed "geriatric utopias"—places where the aged existed but the hard facts of aging did not. During the 1960s and 1970s exciting reports filtered into the gerontological literature and popular press about a small number of mountain peoples, especially in Abkhasia, who possessed *extraordinary* longevity. In this case, ages were claimed ranging from 120 to almost 168, with health profiles said to be like that of spry 60- and 70-year-olds. Similar assertions were made for a peasant village in Vilacabamba, Ecuador; the Hunzakut of the Karakoram mountains in Pakistan; and the inhabitants of Paros Island, Greece. It is very disquieting, then, to learn that *none* of these claims for a modern fountain of youth and hyperlongevity appear to be true (Leaf 1982; Palmore 1984; Beall 1987).

Yet, the last decade has seen some tantalizing movement inching toward immortality. For example, Elizabeth Blackburn earned the Nobel Prize in 2009 for her work on telomeres, showing how maintaining these protein caps on chromosomes may be a key to understanding aging. Since 2013 Google's $1.5 billion Calico project has pulled together an impressive research team to create a new singularity where longevity appears open-ended (www.calicolabs .com). At the same time a related effort was launched by a company called Human Longevity to find the genes that lead to long life. As noted in the Web Special below, a growing body of Silicon Valley billionaires are making a heavy bet that death is just a "technical matter," rather than a biological mandate.

Despite false claims for breaching the normal limits of the human life span, we seem to have been dealing, at least in Abkhasia, with an exceptionally healthy group of 90- and 100-year-olds. Interestingly, the details of their lifestyles, when compared with that of healthy centenarians in the United States and other countries, point to a number of common factors in promoting long life. Such persons tend to have low-fat, low-calorie diets; refrain from much caffeine, tobacco, and alcohol; and have been physically active throughout their lives (Perls and Terry 2007; Caprara 2018). Importantly, a 1996 report by the MacArthur Foundation Consortium on Successful Aging noted that only about 30 percent of the features of aging are genetically based and that by age 80 there is little genetic influence on determining what happens after that point of time. This project identified several nongenetic factors influencing successful aging: regular physical activity and social connectedness; the ability to bounce back after suffering a loss; and having a feeling of control over one's life.

On the other hand, most everyone seems to have an ancient relative who exhibits the "Uncle Irving Phenomenon"—who like my own uncle smoked

---

WEB SPECIAL:

D. Horn, "The Men Who Want to Live Forever," *New York Times*, January 25, 2018, www.nytimes.com/2018/01/25/opinion/sunday/silicon -valley-immortality.html.

and imbibed, and said "Oy" when the word exercise was mentioned. Such persons are rare exceptions to what global data teach us about general longevity and aging. However, as is detailed in the first chapter of Part VI, lifestyle has the biggest general impact on how long most people will live, but a genetic link to longevity is most associated with those who achieve exceptional long life.

The Centenarians Are Coming!

Humans are certainly not longevity record breakers among earth's life forms. Certain giant trees live for 4,000 years, some Icelandic clam species last 400 years, and when Harriet, a Galapagos tortoise, died in 2006, she was thought to be 176 years old.[1] In 2018, scientists studied another centenarian tortoise from the same region and found a genetic variant associated with a robust immune system, resistance to cancer, and enhanced DNA repair (Quesada et al. 2019).

In the United States, by 2014, despite our comparatively poor showing in terms of average longevity, our Census Bureau counted 73,000 centenarians (14,000 men and 59,000 women) and by 2040 over half a million in their 10th decade of life are expected to be around. Such predictions have spurred research on healthy longevity and show the impact self-care and lifestyle changes can have in delaying the level of frailty in late life (Tanimura et al. 2017).

Mapping the Blue Zones of Healthy Longevity

Shortly after the last edition of this book went to press, journalist Dan Buettner published an enormously popular book that documented five places in the world where residents not only lived longer on average than elsewhere but appeared to have a better chance of good health in their eighth and ninth decades of life. This book, *The Blue Zones* (2009), and subsequent editions entranced readers with personal stories from Sardinia, Italy; Seventh-Day Adventists in Loma Linda, California; Nicoya, Costa Rica; the Greek island of Ikaria; and Okinawa, Japan (https://www.bluezones.com/). The Blue Zone idea has indeed become a trademarked industry unto itself. It markets an expensive self-help plan, linked entities such as the AARP/Blue Zones Vitality Project, and a continuing book series (the latest on happiness in 2017). The Vitality Project, set in the city of Albert Lea, Minnesota, seeks the laudable goal of adding 10,000 years to the lives of residents by encouraging lifestyle changes related to what Buetner found in the five key Blue Zones. Research related to the ideas linked to the Blue Zone areas found that five lifestyle changes in our society could potentially extend life expectancy at 50 by more than a decade. These behaviors—eating a healthy diet, not

WEB SPECIAL:

M. Wildhood, "5 Ways to a Long, Healthy Life," *YES!* https://issues .yesmagazine.org/issue/decolonize/solutions.html.

smoking, getting regular physical activity, moderate alcohol consumption, and maintaining a normal weight—could boost longevity without any new single new drug discoveries or medical treatments (Li et al. 2018).

The Okinawan Centenarian Study

Among the most important research related to understanding why people reach 100 years of age or more is the Okinawan Centenarian Study, which for the past 25 years has been following the longest lived population on our planet (https://orcls.org/ocs). The chapter by Willcox and associates details the data on "extraordinary longevity" (living 110 years or more) and the connection to the growing number of international longevity projects that are now underway. Importantly, they show that older Okinawans have among the lowest mortality rates in the world from a multitude of chronic diseases. As a result they, and the Japanese in general, enjoy the world's longest health expectancy. The growing knowledge about healthy longevity is of particular interest for women, who are considerably more likely than men to survive into very late life (Zarulli et al. 2018). It is important to note that as Okinawans have become more adapted to a Western diet and lifestyle, their healthy longevity has declined. However, learning about traditional patterns of life in Okinawa and other Blue Zones has some powerful clues to improve health in late life in the United States.

PROJECT TO FOLLOW:

The Longevity Genes Project at Albert Einstein College of Medicine is a study of more than 500 healthy centenarians, near-centenarians, and their children. Follow the project at https://www.einstein.yu.edu/centers /aging/longevity-genes-project/.

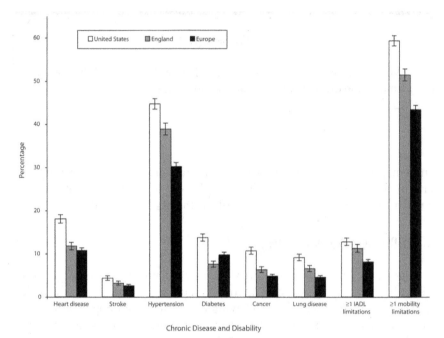

Chronic Disease and Disability

Figure VI.1   Prevalence of Chronic Disease and Disability among Those Aged 50–74 in the United States, England, and Europe, 2004 (Adapted from M. Avendano, M. M. Glymour, J. Banks, and J. Mackenbach. 2009. "Health Disadvantage in U.S. Adults Aged 50 to 74 Years: A Comparison of the Health of Rich and Poor Americans with That of Europeans." *American Journal of Public Health* 99(3): 540–48.).

This is critical to consider because the health care system in the United States does not compare favorably with other advanced nations in providing desirable health results, despite having the highest level of health care spending in the world. A 2017 report of the Health and Retirement Study notes that, compared to other high-income nations, the United States ranks among the lowest for life expectancy. As an example, in middle age at every socioeconomic level, studies of the health of U.S. citizens and those in England show that Americans are much less healthy than their English counterparts (HRS Staff 2017: 66). This is dramatically seen in Figure VI.1, showing that compared to Europeans, older Americans have consistently greater prevalence of chronic disease and disability.

It is little wonder then that globally, the United States ranks 24th on healthy longevity and 42nd in overall longevity, compared to nations like Japan. Much of this difference can be accounted for in realizing that over the past 30 years Japan has substantially surpassed the level of economic equality found in the United States, while it also dramatically expanded access to

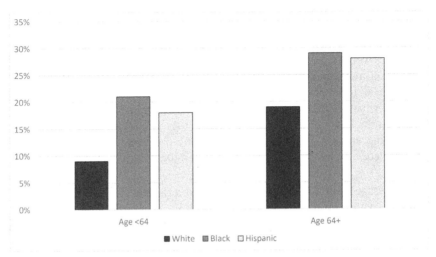

Figure VI.2   Percent with One or More ADL or IADL by Race and Age, 2014 (*Aging in the 21st Century. Health and Retirement Study.* Available online at http://hrsonline.isr.umich.edu/sitedocs/databook/?page=82.).

health care. At the same time, in the United States, its percent of middle-class families has decreased and by 2017, not only were 28.5 million without health insurance, but the medical bills remained the number one reason for personal bankruptcy (U.S. Census 2018).

Unfortunately, as documented in a new book, *Golden Years? Social Inequality in Later Life*, Deborah Carr shows that despite the expansion to an average two-decade span of postretirement years in the United States, expecting a mostly healthy late life is increasingly attached to those more privileged (2019; see also Zaninotto et al. 2020 for comparison with England). This is indicated in Figure VI.2 where the measures of functional disability (IDL or IADL) show how as disadvantages accumulate across the life course, they have a comparatively more negative impact upon older minority populations (see also Gotta 2019).

WEB SPECIAL:

T. Ghilarducci, "Inequality in Retirement Is Getting Worse," *Forbes*, March 17, 2019, https://www.forbes.com/sites/teresaghilarducci/2019/03/17/inequality-in-retirement-is-getting-worse/#18bdadca218a.

Who Will Care for Grandma? The Millennium's Growing Dilemma

Facebook Message from a former female student: 9/11/18. Hi, Jay! Hope you are well! I am very grateful for all the teaching you have done on aging and culture because the topic becomes more pressing and less academic in my life all the time. We just moved my 95-year-old mother-in-law in with us for what we are thinking is actually hospice, end-of-life care following her stroke last year and two broken hips this year. Some days I care for both her and my granddaughters. So many dimensions involved in this experience. At least it is helpful to think ethnographically about all this.

This message from a student who graduated a decade ago reflects an all-too-common pattern in many parts of the world. In the global arena, greater average life spans, a narrowing of localized kin networks, increased work of women outside of households, and international migration have created great challenges for those families seeking to care for elders. As seen for the United States in Figure VI.3—from 2010 until midcentury—there is expected to be a substantial reduction, from 7 to 3, of the Caregiver Support Ratio, the number of potential caregivers (mostly adult children) per persons age 80 and older.

In the past decade a series of national studies in the United States has documented what many already know from personal experience (see especially AARP 2018; Stringfellow 2018). Much of eldercare falls on the heads of midlife and older women who on average may have spent 17 years caring for a child and now may spend 18 years or more helping to care for a parent. The typical family caregiver is a 46-year-old female who has at least some college experience, provides more than 20 hours of care each week to a widowed woman aged 50 or older, usually her mother. By 2014 a Congressional Budget Committee found that 80 million Americans were providing care for older relatives, 81 percent were the primary carers, and two-thirds have no paid help. The typical out-of-pocket expense of eldercare for an aging parent or spouse averages about $5,500 a year, more than the average American household spends annually on health care and entertainment combined (Project Catalyst 2018).[2]

WEB SPECIAL:

AgeWell Global is a new model of eldercare coordination combining peer-based social engagement and mobile technology to improve health outcomes and drive down medical costs. Follow their work at https://www.agewellglobal.com/ and see the Innovation@50+ sales pitch by its director, https://youtu.be/TKBwDOQ9vYk.

You Take Care of Mom, But Who Will Take Care of You?

Family caregivers provide the majority of long-term services and supports (LTSS). But the supply of family caregivers is unlikely to keep pace with future demand. The Caregiver Support Ratio is defined as the number of potential family caregivers (mostly adult children) aged 45-64 for each person aged 80 and older—those most likely to need LTSS. The caregiver support ratio is used to estimate the availability of family caregivers during the next few decades.

Caregiver Support Ratio

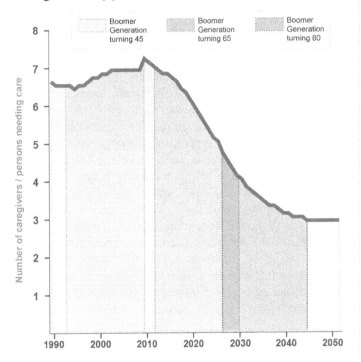

In **2010**, the caregiver support ratio was more than **7** potential caregivers for every person in the high-risk years of 80-plus.

In **2030**, the ratio is projected to decline sharply to **4 to 1**; and it is expected to further fall to less than **3 to 1** in **2050**.

POLICY ACTION: Rising demand and shrinking families to provide LTSS call for new solutions to the financing and delivery of LTSS and family support.

Figure VI.3 Caregiver Support Ratio, 1990–2050 (D. Redfoot, L. Feinberg, and A. Houser, *The Aging of the Baby Boom and the Growing Care Gap: A Look at Future Declines in the Availability of Family Caregivers*. Public Policy Institute, August, 2013. Reproduced by permission of the AARP Public Policy Institute).

Are the Robots Coming to the Rescue?

This book began with the image of an emotional support robot IPAL being produced and tested for use in a variety of new care environments in China. With the stresses emerging on family-based care, nations of the West and rapidly aging East Asia are on a quest to see if robots and related AI technology can take on some of the burden. We have already encountered discussion of robots in chapters by Prendergast on technology (Part II) and Kavedžija's dealing with Japan's culture of care (Part III). With the chapter by James Wright he plumbs the depth of this topic, initially focusing on Japan. His work shows the importance of ethnographic research and cultural context in exploring how, despite the media and government narratives of an emerging "techno-utopian" future, the reality and massive use of eldercare robots is far from assured. As the demographically oldest nation with exceptionally low fertility and limited immigration, Japan's government has invested in new medical technologies, including experimental regenerative medicine and cell therapy. Wright shows that the cultural acceptance of robots in Japan is connected to both pop cultural images of robots helpful to humanity and traditional religious animistic beliefs. Importantly, he also shows how the strong promotion by the current conservative government of eldercare robots is perceived as reinforcing traditional ideas of family, disability, and race, instead of recasting them as technological problems requiring robotic solutions (see Robertson 2017). In his chapter Wright contrasts the Japan case with integration of robots into eldercare in Denmark. Here a universal health care system is managed by well-trained service professionals versus the poorly paid, often migrant care workers in Japan.

Managing Eldercare in the "Happiest" Nation

As Amy Clotworthy notes in her contribution to Part VI, health care in Denmark became a point of great debate in the 2016 U.S. presidential campaign with Bernie Sanders positively touting the benefits of the health care systems

---

WEB SPECIAL:

G. Nejat, "Can I Help You? The Future of Socially Assistive Robots in Healthcare." A video-assisted talk about the ongoing robotics work at the University of Toronto: https://www.youtube.com/watch?v=VPv4A GuuvC4&t=4s.

Web Special:

D. P. Paul III, C. K. Schaeffer, and A. Coustasse, "Long-Term Care Policy: What the United States Can Learn from Denmark, Sweden, and the Netherlands," *Business & Health Administration Proceedings* (2017): 223–36. https://mds.marshall.edu/cgi/viewcontent.cgi?article=1177&con text=mgmt_faculty.

in Denmark and other Scandinavian nations. As if anticipating connecting this chapter to the 2020 elections, the word *socialist* has already come up as a political talking point for some politicians, designating an evil that will not be tolerated.

Here Amy Clotworthy looks at the day-to-day reality of Denmark's eldercare policy, which fosters a flexible but integrated system for home- and community-based services across its 98 municipalities. This approach to serving the needs of older citizens is often called "flexicurity" by the Danes and is part of a larger framework of health care, education, and labor policy serving persons across the life course (Bekker and Mailand 2018). Importantly, she details the recent transition from a "traditional" European welfare nation to a "competition" state focusing on a "free choice," encouraging "help to self-help" and potentially empowering elderly citizens to age in place at home. This chapter provides an important bridge to Larry Polivka's Web Chapter in this section. That reading builds upon earlier work that explored the model of community-based care, initially pioneered in Florida but eventually adopted in Denmark and other postindustrial nations (Polivka and Longino. 2006).

A Little Help from Friends

It is important to realize that when thinking about care systems involving any part of the life course, there is need to look beyond formal organizations and personnel. In this section's short Web Photo Essay from the ASSA Project blog, Charlotte Hawkins and Laura Haapio-Kirk explore in Kyoto, Japan, and Kampala, Uganda, the powerful contribution of female mutual support. In both cases "meet-ups," whether face-to-face or virtual, provide a medium of emotional and psychological support for difficult medical issues such as AIDS or cancer that are sometimes difficult to discuss with family. This chapter can provide a thoughtful comparison to Shea's chapter on China's Senior Companions Program (Part V), which takes a more directive approach in organizing volunteers to assist needy elders.

Globalization of Eldercare

Walking through my hometown of New York City, it is very common to see both young children and frail elders being looked after by women of color, often first-generation females from the Caribbean or Africa. This is just part of a massive movement of care workers from the global south to nations being impacted by the disruptive demographics, mentioned in Part I, that are just beginning to impact the United States. Despite a bump upward of female fertility just before the great recession of 2008, the U.S. pattern since then has dropped below a marker of how many births are necessary to prevent a natural decrease in population, that is, birthing 2.1 babies per woman. Virtually all other postindustrial societies and many industrializing countries are dramatically going in the same direction.

One result is the dearth of available kin for social, emotional, and physical care of elder family members. As we learned in the introduction to this book, in the United States the chances of reaching age 90 and beyond has significantly increased over the past 50 years, especially for females. A recent report using the long-running Health and Retirement Study shows that this has significantly increased the span of years needed for caregiving and stretched the capacity to provide adequate care by family caregivers who themselves are aging and in need of various supports (Wettstein and Zulkarnain 2017).

As we saw in previous chapters on Ghana (Part II Coe), China (Part III Zhang) and India (Part V Lamb), this sometimes involves caring across distant national and international borders and the production of hybrid aging scripts and imaginaries of care (Oxlund 2018). These patterns have emerged on the world stage, stimulated by both the formation of transnational communities and the greatest global refugee dislocation since World War II. In books like *Transnational Aging and Reconfigurations of Kin-Work* (Dossa and Coe 2017), *Care across Generations* (Yaris 2017), and *Care across Distance* (Hromadžić and Palmberger 2018), authors consider the dilemmas of transforming intergenerational connection and care separated sometimes by thousands of miles and political boundaries.

WEB SPECIAL:

Kaiser Health News, "The Toll of Caring for Aging Parents," *U.S. News & World Report*, August 23, 2018, https://www.usnews.com /news/healthiest-communities/articles/2018-08-23/the-toll-of-caring -for-frail-aging-parents.

This topic is explored in Part VI by Sandra Staudacher and Andrea Kaiser-Grolimund, who study how transnational spaces of aging are mediated by "triangles of care." Here the authors track the dynamic process of support for elders in urban Tanzania, involving migrating family members working in the Middle East or the United States. They find that care triangles are formed with collaboration of "observing eyes," local younger kin in Africa. Forming a leg of the triangle, they mediate the circulation of emotional and practical care, often with the help of various communication apps, the incoming flow of money, or even medicines not easily available in Tanzania (see Sadruddin 2020).

Of course, available kin and even strong cultural dictates are not the only factors in understanding family-based eldercare (see Buch 2015). We have already seen the dilemma of social context overwhelming cultural expectations and desires among Islamic Iranian immigrants in California (Part IV Web Book Hegland). Just north of where that research took place, a complex study of Chinese immigrant families with both spouses working found adult children subcontracting filial piety by engaging female caregivers from similar ethnic backgrounds to care for their frail older kin (Lan 2002; see also Ho and Chiang 2016). This in fact paralleled many dual-earner households working in Taiwan, Hong Kong and Singapore who hire low-wage migrant women from Southeast and South Asia to not only fulfill duties to serve parents but also expand autonomy from aged mothers-in-law. As we were reminded in Zhang's chapter in Part III on the transformation of filial devotion in China, we once again see the play of culture and context shaping reality (see also Gao 2018).

Social Viagra and the Family-Based Dynamics of Care

Such transnational care schemes have accelerated in the 21st century and come to be known as the circulation of care migrants (Baldassar, Ferrero, and Portis 2017). More than a decade ago journalist Thomas Friedman quipped in comparing the demographic futures of Europe and India, that next to a youthful India, Western Europe looks like an assisted-living facility with Turkish nurses (2005). This has become a global issue especially in demographically old nations such as Japan and Italy that also have a strong cultural emphasis on elders being cared for within the bosom of their family matrix. Yet, in Japan it is often Pilipino or Indonesian carers who provide what Beata Switek calls the "reluctant intimacies" of care within the evolving Japanese eldercare system (2016).

In Europe, one of the most interesting challenges for kin-based care of elders is emerging in the southern region, among traditionally family-focused cultures (Bahna and Sekulova 2019). In Italy, the research location for Gabriela Nicolescu's Part VI Web Chapter, we encounter one of the globe's highest levels of agedness and lowest fertility rates. Various attempts at what Krause calls "Social Viagra" (2007)—economic and other government incentives to produce more babies—have basically been ignored by young families, even after the nation created "Fertility Day" celebrated each year on September 22.

The issue of eldercare is highly problematic for countries like Italy, which are very reluctant to erect any serious support infrastructure for elder residences and care, fearing its negative impact on their strong ideology of kin support. Here, increasingly over the past two decades young female immigrant carers called *badantes,* often from Romania, have become a vital cog in "family"-centered care. The Web Chapter by Gabriela Nicolescu connects to a distinction of "caring for" and "caring about" developed by anthropologist Elana Buch (2013, 2015). Care means a practical action (caring for) and an affective concern (caring about) at the same time. In her research, "caring for" is directed towards the Italian elderly, while "caring about" connects to an investment by *badanti* toward their kin back in Romania. It will be instructive to connect this to Weber's chapter on Romania (Part III) to understand the economic and social pressures driving this circulation of care across Europe.

"Bioupgradability," Disability, and the Shifting Nature of Health in Late Life

A decade ago I underwent cataract operations on both eyes to help me return to playing tennis tournaments and driving safely at night. I was joining the wave of baby boomers challenging the "body inevitable" with the mindset of endless possibilities and yet another type of makeover. In two 15-minute operations this "bioupgrading" of my eyes not only eliminated my cataracts but also gave me clear, unaided vision for the first time in my life. It is interesting to note that even at the stage when the cataracts were just causing mild visual impairments, I was universally encouraged by friends and family to actively undertake this frontal assault on a sure sign of aging.

Disability, Aging, and Culture

The cross-cultural study of health and disability has been a focus of the World Health Organization since the early 1980s (Robinson et al. 2007). It has developed a useful framework for distinguishing between impairment, disability, and handicap. Here "impairment" means diminishment/loss of physical function, "disability" refers to a diminishment/loss of activity, and "handicap" constitutes a diminishment/loss of role performance (World Health Organization 1991).[3] As Albert and Cattell note, "while impairment involves clear physical properties, its expression as disability and handicap depends on cultural factors" (1994: 208).[4] An excellent example is found in Albert's own work among the Lak people of Melanesia. He found that perceptions of certain impairments such as cataracts did not translate into the Western view of disability or handicap (1987). Despite a high incidence of cataracts among the Lak elderly, this condition did not become a disabling feature of late life. Their impaired vision seldom interfered with participation in gardening, household assistance, or ritual activities. Contrastingly, North American elders like myself with similar levels of impairment typically experience cataracts as a disabling condition, which limits valued activities because of the cultural emphasis on reading, driving, and other tasks requiring acute vision.

The cultural parameters of disability in late life have received increasing attention by qualitative researchers such as in Gay Becker's classic ethnography of deaf elders (1980), Sharon Kaufman's study of stroke victims and the U.S. care system (1986, 2005; Kaufman and Fjord 2011), Luisa Margolies's (2004) book about her mother's broken hip, or Solimeo's work on coping with Parkinson's disease (2009).[5] This body of work has also included the interplay of ethnicity with disability, such as Parin Dossa's research among Muslim Canadians (2009, 2018) or the impact of the AIDS epidemic on cultural traditions in Swaziland (Golomski 2018).

In line with David Prendergast's chapter in Part II about technology, there has been an effort to employ the transformative ideas about disability initially liberating younger persons with impairments to the rest of the life course. Here in Part VI Joel Reynolds provides a road map for recasting age-associated bodily variations and abilities, not in terms of individual capacity but in terms of what he calls "the extended body." His work is part of a very broad and powerful effort to transcend a view of disability framed by constructs of pathology or impairment, sometimes referred to as "ableism"—the privileging of the "normal" able body (Warren and Manderson 2013; Aubrecht and Krawchenko 2016; Addlakha 2020). Reynolds focuses on the idea of ability transitions and the need to think critically about creating flexible social and physical environments to accommodate different abilities (Block et al. 2015).

In the Web Chapter by Barbara Pieta, we see the problem of a medicalized "ableist" narrative playing out in an Italian town. Here the medical establishment has created dichotomous terms of *autosufficiente* (self-sufficient), and *non autosufficiente* (not self-sufficient) for bureaucratic purposes. Pieta explores how this is enacted in the Golden Age Center as a group of dementia patients seeks to find a place in that elderscape. The discourse of autonomy leads to a stigmatization of those not so abled in contrast to the self-sufficient, enterprising, and model elder citizens occupying a central place in the center.

WEB SPECIALS:

1. Office of the Assistant Secretary for Planning and Evaluation, *A Profile of Older Adults with Dementia and Their Caregivers Issue Brief,* January 24, 2019. https://aspe.hhs.gov/basic-report/profile-older-adults-dementia-and-their-caregivers-issue-brief.
2. Alzheimer's Association, *Alzheimer's Disease Facts and Figures,* 2018. https://www.alz.org/media/homeoffice/facts%20and%20figures/facts-and-figures.pdf.
3. CDC Alzheimer's Disease and Healthy Aging Data Portal. https://www.cdc.gov/aging/agingdata/data-portal/healthy-people.html.

About That Senior Moment

The year 2020 will mark the 113th anniversary of the naming and clinical description, by Alois Alzheimer, of a dreaded brain disorder that struck a 50-year-old woman, severely impairing her memory and other cognitive functions. Upon autopsy, her brain was found to be shrunken and filled with strange deposits of plaques between and tangled within nerve cells. Ironically, until the 1970s Alzheimer's Disease (AD), named after the doctor who analyzed this woman's brain, was thought to be a rare, rapidly progressing disorder of midadulthood and different from "senile" dementia caused by just plain aging. This was partly due to the fact that the person after whom the affliction was named suffered from the rare version of early onset dementia, which can hit in midlife and acts relatively quickly to rob its victim of memory and life itself. There was also a lack of serious community-based research until the 1990s when the disruptive demographics of global aging were starting to be felt and acknowledged in the Western world.

According to Alzheimer's Disease International, between 2018 and 2050, dementia worldwide will triple, going from 50 million cases to an estimate of impacting more than 152 million people (2018). This is certainly one of the major health challenges for the near future. The World Health Organization has begun a major global initiative on this issue with both its new Global Dementia Observatory (GDO) providing a data and knowledge exchange platform and a Global Action Plan 2017–2025 (https://www.who.int/mental_health/neurology/dementia/Global_Observatory/en/).

Dementia as a Biomedical Space of Uncertainty

There has been found an hereditary factor in the expression of Alzheimer's disease, associated with the Apoe-E gene. Yet, some patients with full expression of this gene and excessive brain protein deposits, called beta amyloid, never have dementia symptoms, just as those lacking the gene and having little protein deposits are diagnosed with the disease. This kind of biomedical space of uncertainty has stimulated research into both the brain's capacity for adaptation and the varied cultural response to Alzheimer's disease and other dementias (Warren and Sakellariou 2020).

Bulking up the Brain with Neurobics

In the first instance, intense studies over the past two decades indicate that some people develop "cognitive reserve," a capacity of brains to compensate for cognitive impairment related to dementia (Pettigrew and Soldan 2019). As with healthy longevity, lifestyle habits can lower the risk of getting dementia. During the first decade of the 21st century, these findings stimulated the creation of a lucrative brain-health market hawking vitamin supplements like coenzyme Q10, varieties of fit-brain "neurosoftware," games like MindFit, and a series of structured physical and mental activities, called variously Memaerobics and Neurobics (see Winningham et al. 2004).

Yet this past decade has found little real-life cognitive impact of the self-improvement neurobics software programs, countering the glowing claims of companies such as Lumosity. In fact in 2016 Lumos Labs, the company behind Lumosity, was fined $2 million for false advertising by the Federal Trade Commission (Simons et al. 2016). To date only one type of computer training involving enhancing speed of cognitive processing has shown promise in lowering risk of dementia (Edwards et al. 2017).

Dementia in Cultural Context

A second approach to studying the variable response to forms of dementia in late life is to look at the impact of culture (see Box VI.2). Over the past two decades a rapidly enlarging international and cross-cultural literature has emerged that explores both the prevalence of dementia and the cultural response to this condition (Cohen 1995; Leibing and Cohen 2006; Lock 2014; Hillman and Latimer 2017; Hulkow, Wilson, and Balestry 2019; Yahalom 2019). Medical specialists now recognize over 70 different causes of

---

PROJECT TO FOLLOW:

PACT—Preventing Alzheimer's with Cognitive Training, being done at the University of South Florida and Michigan State University, https://pactstudy.org/.

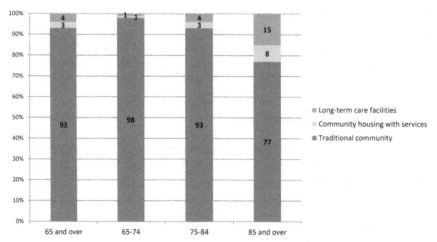

Figure VI.4   Percentage Distribution of Medicare Beneficiaries Aged 65 and over Residing in Selected Residential Settings, by Age Group, 2013 (Centers for Medicare & Medicaid Services, Medicare Current Beneficiary Survey, Access to Care).

dementia; but in most populations, Alzheimer's disease is the most common type and evokes great fears among old and young alike. In the United States the prevalence of dementia among older adults increases with age, from only 2 percent among adults aged 65–69 to 33 percent among adults aged 90 and older (ASPE 2019).

One of the important aspects of the cultural construction of any kind of dementia is the narrative that is constructed about this kind of cognitive impairment and the societal response of care it generates. This is the focus of the Web Chapter by Annette Leibing, who has looked at this issue in the country of Brazil and focuses here on heroic tales of grandchildren acting as caregivers. In this work she uses these stories to provide a critical perspective on the "personhood" approach to dementia as applied to this country and asserts that the stories may in fact reflect fallacies of care (see also Bitenc 2019).

Nursing Homes and the Promise of the Culture Change Movement

Although about 80 percent of the aged in the United States report that they can get around by themselves, it is the rapidly growing numbers of the "oldest old," those past age 85, which are creating the greatest challenge for our system of long-term care. Only about 4 percent of the 65+ population occupy nursing homes; however, for those over age 85, triple that proportion of the U.S. population resides in such care settings (Figure VI.4).

**Box VI.1   Changing Response to Dementia
in Rapidly Changing East Asia**

The nations of Japan and Korea are among the most rapidly aging nations in global context and both share extremely low fertility. These countries have embarked on preparing for large increases in dementia cases with cultural and practical changes. In Japan up to the early part of this century, this kind of cognitive impairment was considered more of a moral than a biomedical one. Differing from the Western ideas about mind-body connections, Japanese are viewed through a mind/body complex critically developed through social and moral engagement over the life course (Traphagan 2009). The traditional word for dementia in Japanese, *chihō*, has a negative association. *Chi* means "foolishness," and *hō* means "dumb or disoriented." It contributes to stigma and fails to show dignity and respect for people with dementia. By the end of 2004, the Japanese government changed the official word for dementia from *chihō* to *ninchishō*, which means "disease of cognition." The government has changed all administrative terms to the new word, and the media and academic groups have also accepted the new term. At the same time, the government launched a 10-year nationwide campaign to raise public awareness and understanding of dementia. At the heart of the campaign is the Nationwide Caravan to Train One Million Ninchishō (Dementia) Supporters. In this campaign, specialized seminars for the general public are held all around the country. With greater understanding of the disease and its impact, attendees are expected to become Ninchishō Supporters and advocates for people living with dementia. By March 2011, over 2.4 million people in Japan had attended the seminars and had become Ninchishō Supporters. They include young people, police officers, and people from all backgrounds. After seven years, the new term *ninchishō* is used widely in Japan and people understand the disease better, resulting in less stigma.

South Korea as of yet has less than 10 percent of its population under age 65. Yet as a global leader in the speed of demographic aging, by 2010 it declared a national "war on dementia." This involves training of children in dementia care, undertaking the building of hundreds of neighborhood dementia diagnostic centers, and creating a long-term-care insurance system to help defray the costs of treatment and nursing homes.

Adapted from World Health Organization and Alzheimer's Disease International, *Dementia: A Public Health Priority*, 2012, https://www.who.int/mental_health/publications/dementia_report_2012/en/. Used by permission of the World Health Organization.

Importantly, over the past three decades, the rate of nursing home use has declined in the United States. This has corresponded with a steady and substantial decrease in the overall disability rate of older adults intersecting with more options in residential care and in some states better access to home care. Counterposed with the ongoing attempt to privatize long-term care in the United States is a search for "eldertopia" and the emergence of a powerful culture change movement that seeks to physically and socially transform such environments into humane and therapeutic spaces in which to encounter frail late adulthood (Shier et al. 2014).

The Search for Eldertopia

Ruth Brent proposed a remaking of long-term care environments into "Gerontopias" that foster maintenance of autonomy, choice, and control of the nature of one's last days (1999; see also Charness 2005). Visionary physician William Thomas builds upon the writings of Brent and lays out his related idea of "Eldertopia," offering a fundamentally different way of looking at elderhood. The practical application of these ideas were first seen in Thomas's development of the "Eden Alternative," which proposed transforming traditional nursing facilities into socially engineered small "home"-like environments (Thomas and Johansson 2003; www.edenalt. org). More recently, Thomas has developed a "Green Houses" model that is designed to create a sense of a nurturing and interdependent community, what he calls "convivium." His work is a touchstone to the discussion of a long-term care culture change movement analyzed in Part VI by Athena Mclean.

The Web Chapter by Athena McLean considers such transformations in light of her ethnographic research focusing on early attempts to create new kinds of Alzheimer's units within long-term care settings.[6] Her work draws from the long tradition of qualitative research in nursing homes and expands upon her book *The Person in Dementia* (2006) to consider the possibilities of dissolving the stifling institutional structure of such places (Gillick 2017).[7] In such settings the boundary between living "in the community" and living in an "institution" is marked by two core perceptions: the medical symbolism "You are chronically sick" and the detention symbolism "You are being supervised" (Robinson 1985). McLean's chapter shows that breaking the bonds of "institutions" cannot be accomplished by physical changes alone, but must be accompanied by addressing the issue of personhood and how it exists within the cultural space of a long-term care environment. By focusing on this issue she is able to examine the reality of the liberating dream suggested by the Green House model and William Thomas's conception of Gerontopia.

Bringing Personhood and "Normalcy" to Dementia

The Netherlands seems to have taken the ideas embodied in considering dementia within the context of personhood more seriously than most other nations. This has included innovative ideas such as memory cafés created in 1997, "Dementia Villages," and the use of variety of technologies to humanize the perception of dementia-related brain changes for the people around them and the individual themselves. Some of the cutting-edge memory care communities around the world include The Netherland's Dementiaville, England's Grove Care, Scotland's dementia-friendly Stirling, and Glenner Town Square dementia village day center being built in San Diego.

Forget Memory—Remember Imagination: Genius at Work

One of the most interesting pathways to rethinking the brain changes associated with the various kinds of dementias has been through the arts and performance. A powerful voice in these efforts is Anne Basting. As a professor of theatre and a world-famous gerontologist, she has used her passion for the arts and theatre to go beyond normal ideas of memory in developing storytelling and performance techniques embodied in her "Timeslips," "Penelope," and "Peter Pan" projects to engage the altered brains of cognitively impaired

---

WEB SPECIALS:

1. D. Larsen, "How Do Different Cultures Take Care of Seniors?" *Senior Living Blog*, A Place for Mom. www.aplaceformom.com/blog/dementia-care-around-the-world-4-2-2013/.
2. C. F. Schuetze, "Take a Look at These Unusual Strategies for Fighting Dementia," *New York Times*, August 22, 2018. www.nytimes.com/2018/08/22/world/europe/dementia-care-treatment-symptoms-signs.html.

PROJECT TO FOLLOW:

The Dementia Enabling Environment Project (DEEP) Virtual Information Centre in Australia provides practical tips, guides, and resources to help make the places where we live more dementia enabling. https://www.enablingenvironments.com.au/.

elders. Her work earned Basting a 2016 MacArthur "genius" award. In Box VI.2 she lays out the argument of embedding the arts in long-term care environments and reintegrating meaning making and health. Her work intersects with efforts in other nations to explore the variety of arts in supporting persons with dementia and their families (Fancourt and Steptoe 2018; Jones, Windle, and Edwards 2019).

Death Doulas and the Darker Side of Aging

In 1983 at a gathering for his 94th birthday in Fort Lauderdale, Florida, my grandfather Max told a story I had heard before. It was being directed to my 12-year-old daughter and her same-aged cousin I had brought to the event:

> Back in my little village in Poland, when I was about eight years old, I was having fun playing outside with a wooden hoop. All of a sudden an older relative came to find me and said my aunt Sadie is dying and you must come and witness it. I tried to run away, but he caught me and dragged me to her bedside, forcing me to watch. I was angry and confused at being forced to endure this situation, but as I stood surrounded by all my relatives, I saw a brief smile on Sadie's face, but then she died, slowly seeming to fold inside herself like a beautiful rose closing for the last time. I was happy to have been forced to do this.

The kids paid respectful attention to Max's story, but my efforts to try to talk to them about it were rebuffed as something too difficult to broach.

As Western medicine has mounted an amazing attack on death, the issues of how we should think about this end of the physical life course has become particularly complex and fraught with the great nuances of cultural context. The emerging response to creating a different context for the end of life in North America has seen the development of the hospice movement and the

---

WEB SPECIALS:

1. G. Muthara, "Learning to Serve the Dying," AARP, October 8, 2019. www.aarp.org/caregiving/home-care/info-2018/end-of-life-dou las.html.

2. A. Wright, "The Death Disrupters: These Six People Are Trying to Make Dying in America Better—for Both the Living and the Dead." topic, December 2018. https://www.topic.com/the-death-disrupters.

Box VI.2   A. Basting, "How We Underestimate the Arts in Long-Term Care"

We need an ongoing focus on nonpharmacological approaches for effective interdisciplinary care in the postacute and long-term care setting. From Parkinson's disease to dementia care, a mere focus on medications cannot lead to the results we seek. Research has shown that interdisciplinary strategies based on the arts may provide an innovative answer to the need for high-quality care. The ability of the arts to connect individuals of all ages, professional and ethnic backgrounds, and diverse cultures make them a natural approach for revolutionizing care in various geriatric settings.

The last decade has seen an increase in research on and the use of the arts in long-term care. Music, movement, painting, and storytelling are increasingly used to improve quality of life for people with dementia in particular. But even with these increases, the arts are often viewed as perfunctory. This is a vast underestimation of their potential.

The arts are a mode of expression and an avenue toward meaningfulness. They bring us into connection across our differences—an emotional and symbolic language that enables us to connect across myriad differences and equalize the power hierarchies in our work and care settings. As we formalized and institutionalized medicine in the 19th century, we separated it from cultural expression. Museums and performing arts organizations were formalized and institutionalized at the same time. Inadvertently, perhaps, we severed the inherent links between meaning making and health.

We are in the first few steps of a long journey to reintegrate health and meaning. Museums are developing accessibility programming for people with a range of disabilities, such as those with low vision, hearing loss, physical challenges, or cognitive challenges like dementia. Theater companies in the United Kingdom and the United States are beginning to create performances especially for people with dementia and their care partners.

Yet bingo and balloon-toss still dominate care settings. Activities are still designed to distract, and they are still commonly offered as "one-offs"—with an implicit assumption that learning over time is not possible or important to residents and participants. The residents' families often do not consider activities something they would be interested in or welcome to participate in, and the staff commonly use activities as a time to get other things done. Activities and clinical tasks are separated in job descriptions, and the activities staff feel powerless and disrespected compared with the clinical staff.

But *what if?* What if programming in care settings provided avenues for meaning making that were designed to foster learning over time? What if the programming were so interesting that families wanted to join in and participate with their loved ones? What if it were so compelling that staff participated as equals alongside people with dementia? What if volunteers competed to partner on projects with nursing homes? What if exhibits and performances weren't considered quaint but sought-after tickets?

In other words, what if stigmatized health centers became vibrant cultural centers? Places in which meaning was made and communities built out of rigorous art-making projects?

From 2009 to 2011 I collaborated on an experiment toward this end. University students, a professional theater company, and an entire continuing care retirement community (independent living, assisted living, skilled nursing, and adult day services) collaborated on a three-year effort to retell the story of Homer's *Odyssey* from the perspective of Penelope. We called it *The Penelope Project*, and it culminated in the creation of an original, professionally produced play that we staged in scenes that moved through the care community, for an outside, paying audience. *The Penelope Project* invited families, staff, elders, artists, and volunteers to enter this challenging process of cocreation together. In the final scene of the play, anyone who wanted to was invited to join a chorus to play Penelope. Hand movements and dialogue were done in call-and-response, enabling people with dementia to participate as equals. On stage were residents with dementia, stroke, blindness, and hearing loss seated next to family, staff, and elders from independent living with no visible disabilities at all.

Qualitative and quantitative research on the project suggested that those who participated felt like they were part of something meaningful, and they felt a sense of connectedness with others. They built belonging and community. "What did you think of participating in Penelope?" asked the evaluator. "It's the last important thing I will do in my life," said a woman who lived in the nursing home.

The experiment with *The Penelope Project* has continued and grown in scale, focusing on the potential of the arts to connect us and help us form meaningful relationships and a sense of belonging to a larger community. In 2017, TimeSlips, a nonprofit organization that facilitates storytelling and creativity in eldercare, trained staff in 50 nursing homes across the state of Wisconsin in creative engagement and community-building techniques as part of its Creative Community of Care program. Of the hundreds of stories that emerged from those nursing homes, we collaborated with elders and artists to create an interactive performance complete with karaoke-style animations of the stories told in the voices of the elders.

We recently embarked on a three-year project in collaboration with Signature HealthCARE to reimagine the story of Peter Pan across 12 rural Kentucky nursing homes. A team of national and regional artists will invite staff, family, and volunteers to learn creative engagement techniques that open expression to elders of all abilities. The project culminated in three Creative Festivals with interactive exhibits and performances at the 12 nursing homes in the spring of 2019. We completed training in six VA centers across Pennsylvania, and in 2019 trained another 25 nursing homes in Wisconsin, culminating in 2020 in five Creative Festivals across the state in collaboration with student artists-in-residence at Wisconsin colleges and universities.

Is this another form of art therapy? In some ways, yes. And although researchers have struggled for funding and for large enough sample sizes, we can clearly identify health benefits in the work. In the Kentucky project, we are looking at the impact on depression and mood.

But in some ways, this approach to reintegrating meaning making and health is much bigger than therapy. We hypothesize that we will see improvements in staff job satisfaction, in family engagement, in the number of volunteers and the quality of the volunteer experience—all by making the nursing home a place of meaning making and rich cultural expression. The arts enable us to reknit community where disease and care systems fracture it.

By opening the care settings to meaningful cultural expression and partnership with cultural organizations, the system opens itself to creativity and innovation. We are inviting long-term care to see its role differently, and for its community to understand it differently as well. The transformative power of the arts goes well beyond the individual to the system of care itself, and the public's perception of that system.

Follow along as the I Won't Grow Up project unfolds in Kentucky at www.timeslips.org.

Source: Adapted from A. Basting, "How We Underestimate the Arts in Long-Term Care," *Caring for the Ages* 19, no. 7 (2018): 10, 11. https://doi.org/10.1016/j.carage.2018 .06.005. Used by permission of Elsevier.

training of death doulas to provide end-of-life support for patients and their families often in a home environment.

As Glascock pointed out in this book's first section, small-scale community environments are no guarantee that "death hastening" actions will not be directed toward frail elders. The complex dimensions of this issue require the kind of holistic qualitative approach that are found in this book's final chapter. In the United States as of 2019, physician-assisted death or "aid in dying" statutes exist in California, Colorado, District of Columbia, Hawaii, Montana, Maine (starting January 1, 2020), New Jersey, Oregon, Vermont, and Washington. Active human euthanasia is legal in the Netherlands, Belgium, Colombia, Luxembourg, and Canada.

Having worked as a medical anthropologist on the Polynesian island of Niue, Judith Barker explores the paradox of how a society known for its beneficent treatment of the healthy aged and disabled young could show seemingly heartless disregard of the unfit elderly. Barker in her Web Chapter shows that understanding the neglect directed at "decrepit" older folks does not yield to simple mechanical explanations. Such disregard is neither part of a uniform way of treating all disabled persons nor an ecological expedient dictated by low surplus production. Rather, it is crucial to view how the label of "decrepit" itself is negotiated and constructed within Niuean conceptions of the life cycle, death, and ancestral states. Her work provides an important link to the complex understanding of elder abuse in "traditional societies" (WHO 2002; Holkup et al. 2007; Pillemer et al. 2016).

Notes

1. This animal was reportedly brought back to England from Darwin's 19th-century voyage on the HMS *Bounty*.

2. Other important resources include the National Alliance for Care Giving (www.caregiving.org); the Caregiving Project for Older Americans (http://www .ilcusa.org/pages/projects/the-caregiving-project.php); a 2004 report, *Caregiving in Rural America*: www.easterseals.com/site/DocServer/Caregiving_in_Rural -compressed.pdf?docID=50643; and Reinhard et al. 2019.

3. For an excellent discussion of health aging and disability see Albert and Cattell 1994: 191–220.

4. They also suggest that the role of culture in the disablement process is likely to increase as people age, as the definition of disability becomes less tied to one's ability to remain fully economically active.

5. For a discussion of using qualitative methods along with other research approaches to study health and aging see Curry, Sheild, and Wetle 2006.

6. See also Crews and Zavotka 2006.

7. For some classic works see Diamond 1986; Shield 1988; Savishinsky 1991; Henderson and Vesperi 1995; Stafford 2003; Eschenbruch 2006; Tinney 2008.

Bibliography

AARP. 2018. *Millennials: The Emerging Generation of Family Caregivers*. https:// www.aarp.org/content/dam/aarp/ppi/2018/05/millennial-family-care givers.pdf.

Addlakha, R. 2020. "Kinship Destabilized!: Disability and the Micropolitics of Care in Urban India." *Current Anthropology* 61(Supplement 21). https://www.journals.uchicago.edu/doi/pdfplus/10.1086/705390.

Albert, S. 1987. "The Work of Marriage and of Death: Ritual and Political Process among the Lak." PhD diss., University of Chicago.

Albert, S., and M. Cattell. 1994. *Old Age in Global Perspective: Cross-Cultural and Cross-National Views*. New York: G. K. Hall.

Alzheimer's Disease International. 2018. *World Alzheimer Report 2018*. https://www.alz.co.uk/research/WorldAlzheimerReport2018.pdf.

ASPE. 2019. "National Plan to Pddress Alzheimer's Disease: 2019 Update." https://aspe.hhs.gov/report/national-plan-address-alzheimers-disease-2019-update.

Aubrecht, K., and T. Krawchenko. 2016. "Disability & Aging: International Perspectives." Special issue, *Review of Disability Studies* 12(2 & 3).

Bahna, M., and M. Sekulova. 2019. *Cross Border Care Lessons from Central Europe*. Cham, Switzerland: Palgrave.

Baldassar, L., L. Ferrero, and L. Portis 2017. "'More Like a Daughter Than an Employee': The Kinning Process between Migrant Care Workers, Elderly Care Receivers and Their Extended Families." *Identities* 24(5): 524–54.

Beall, C. 1987. "Studies of Longevity." In *The Elderly as Modern Pioneers*, edited by P. Silverman. Bloomington: Indiana University Press.

Becker, G. 1980. *Growing Old in Silence*. Berkeley: University of California Press.

Bekker, S., and M. Mailand. 2018. "The European Flexicurity Concept and the Dutch and Danish Flexicurity Models: How Have They Managed the Great Recession?" *Social & Policy and Administration* 53(1): 142–55.

Bitenc, R. A. 2019. *Reconsidering Dementia Narratives: Empathy, Identity and Care*. New York: Routledge.

Block, P., D. Kasnitz, A. Nishida, and N. Pollard, eds. 2015. *Occupying Disability: Critical Approaches to Community, Justice, and Decolonizing Disability*. New York: Springer

Brent, R. 1999. "Gerontopia: A Place to Grow Old and Die." In *Aging, Autonomy, and Architecture: Advances in Assisted Living*, edited by B. Schwartz and R. Brent. Baltimore, MD: Johns Hopkins University Press.

Buch, E. 2013. "Senses of Care: Embodying Inequality and Sustaining Personhood in the Home Care of Older Adults in Chicago." *American Ethnologist* 40(4): 637–50.

Buch, E. 2015. "Anthropology of Aging and Care." *Annual Review of Anthropology* 44: 277–93.

Butler, R. 2008. *The Longevity Revolution: The Benefits and Challenges of Living a Long Life*. New York: Public Affairs.

Caprara, G. 2018. "Diet and Longevity: The Effects of Traditional Eating Habits on Human Lifespan Extension." *Mediterranean Journal of Nutrition and Metabolism* 11(3): 261–94.

Carr, D. 2019. *Golden Years? Social Inequality in Later Life*. New York: Russell Sage.

Charness, N. 2005. "Age, Technology, and Culture: Gerontopia or Dystopia?" *Public Policy and Aging Report* 15(4): 20–23.

Cohen, L. 1995. "Toward an Anthropology of Senility: Anger, Weakness, and Alzhimer's in Banares, India." *Medical Anthropology Quarterly* 9(3): 317–334.

Crews, D., and S. Zavotka. 2006. "Aging, Disability, and Frailty: Implications for Universal Design." *Journal of Physiological Anthropology* 25(1): 113–18.

Curry, L., R. Sheild, and T. Wetle, eds. 2006. *Improving Aging and Public Health Research: Qualitative and Mixed Methods*. Washington, DC: American Public Health Association.

Diamond, T. 1986. "Social Policy and Everyday Life in Nursing Homes: A Critical Ethnography." *Social Science and Medicine* 23(12): 1287–95.

Dossa, P. 2009. *Racialized Bodies, Disabling Worlds: Storied Lives of Immigrant Muslim Women*. Toronto: University of Toronto Press.

Dossa, P. 2018. "From Displaced Care to Social Care: Narrative Interventions of Canadian Muslims." *American Anthropologist* 120(3): 558–60.

Dossa, P., and C. Coe, eds. 2017. *Transnational Aging and Reconfigurations of Kin-Work*. New Brunswick, NJ: Rutgers University Press.

Edwards, J. D., H. Xu, D. O. Clark, L. T. Guey, L. A. Ross, and F. W. Unverzagt. 2017. "Speed of Processing Training Results in Lower Risk of Dementia." *Alzheimer's & Dementia: Translational Research & Clinical Interventions* 3(4): 603–11.

Eschenbruch, N. 2006. *Nursing Stories: Life and Death in a German Hospice*. New York: Berghahn.

Fancourt, F., and A. Steptoe. 2018. "Cultural Engagement Predicts Changes in Cognitive Function in Older Adults over a 10 Year Period: Findings from the English Longitudinal Study of Ageing." *Scientific Reports* 8: 10226. doi:10.1038/s41598-018-28591-8.

Friedman, T. 2005. "A Race to the Top." *New York Times*, June 3.

Gao, Z. 2018. "The Emergence of an Elder-Blaming Discourse in Twenty-First Century China." *Journal of Cross-Cultural Gerontology* 33(2): 197–215.

Gillick, M. 2017. *Old and Sick in America: The Journey through the Health Care System*. Charlotte: University of North Carolina Press.

Golomski, C. 2018. *Funeral Culture: AIDS, Work, and Cultural Change in an African Kingdom*. Bloomington: Indiana University Press.

Gotta, M. 2019. *Waiting on Retirement: Aging and Economic Insecurity in Low-Wage Work*. Stanford, CA: Stanford University Press.

Henderson, J., and M. Vesperi, eds. 1995. *The Culture of Long Term Care: Nursing Home Ethnography*. New York: Bergin & Garvey.

Hillman, A., and J. Latimer. 2017. "Cultural Representations of Dementia." *PLoS Medicine* 14(3): e1002274. doi:10.1371/journal.pmed.1002274.

Ho, E., and L.-H. Chiang. 2016. "Translocal Families: The Challenges of Practicing Filial Piety through Transnational Parental Care." *Translocal Chinese: East Asian Perspectives* 9: 232–58.

Holkup, P., E. Salois, T. Tripp-Reimer, and C. Weinert. 2007. "Drawing on Wisdom from the Past: An Elder Abuse Intervention with Tribal Communities." *Gerontologist* 47: 248–54.

Hromadžić, A., and M. Palmberger. 2018. *Care across Distance: Ethnographic Explorations of Aging and Migration.* New York: Berghahn.

HRS Staff. 2017. *Aging in the 21st Century: Challenges and Opportunities for Americans.* Ann Arbor, MI: Health and Retirement Study. https://hrs.isr.umich .edu/about/data-book.

Hulkow, W., D. Wilson, and J. Balestry. 2019. *Indigenous Peoples and Dementia.* Seattle: University of Washington Press.

Jones, C., G. Windle, and R. Edwards. 2019. "Dementia and Imagination: A Social Return on Investment Analysis Framework for Art Activities for People Living with Dementia." *Gerontologist,* https://doi.org/10.1093 /geront/gny147.

Jönson, H. 2018. "Taking a Dubious Route—At the Nexus of Ageing and Disability Policy." Blog of the International Network of Critical Gerontology. https://criticalgerontology.com/ageing-and-disability-policy/.

Kaufman, S. 1986. *The Ageless Self: Sources of Meaning in Late Life.* New York: Meridian.

Kaufman, S. 2005. *And a Time to Die: How American Hospitals Shape the End of Life.* New York: Simon and Schuster.

Kaufman, S., and L. Fjord. 2011. "Medicare, Ethics, and Reflexive Longevity: Governing Time and Treatment in an Aging Society." *Medical Anthropology Quarterly* 25(2): 209–31.

Krause, K. 2007. "Fertility Politics as 'Social Viagra': Reproducing Boundaries, Social Cohesion, and Modernity in Italy." *American Anthropologist* 109(2): 350–62.

Lan, P. 2002. "Subcontracting Filial Piety: Elder Care in Ethnic Chinese Immigrant Families in California." *Journal of Family Issues* 23(7): 812–35. http://pclan.social.ntu.edu.tw/html/word/Filialpiety.pdf.

Leaf, A. 1982. "Long-Lived Populations: Extreme Old Age." *Journal of the American Geriatrics Society* 38: 485–87.

Leibing, A., and L. Cohen. 2006. *Thinking About Dementia: Culture, Loss, and the Anthropology of Senility.* New Brunswick, NJ: Rutgers University Press.

Li, Y., A. Pan, D. D. Wang, X. Liu, K. Dhana, O. H. Franco, S. Kaptoge, et al. 2018. "Impact of Healthy Lifestyle Factors on Life Expectancies in the US Population." *Circulation* 137(23): 345–55.

Lock, M. 2014. *The Alzheimer's Conundrum: Entanglements of Aging and Dementia.* Princeton, NJ: Princeton University Press.

Magalhães, J., M. Stevens, and D. Thornton. 2017. "The Business of Anti-Aging Science." *Trends in Biotechnology* 35(11): 1062–73.

Margolies, L. 2004. *My Mother's Hip: Lessons from the World of Eldercare.* Philadelphia: Temple University Press.

McLean, A. 2006. *The Person in Dementia: A Study of Nursing Home Care in the US.* Orchard Park, NY: Broadview.

Oxlund, B. 2018. "The Life Course in a Migrating World: Hybrid Scripts of Ageing and Imaginaries of Care." *Advances in Life Course Research* 38: 72–79.

Palmore, E. 1984. "Longevity in Abkhazia: A Reevaluation." *Gerontologist* 24: 95–96.

Parreñas, R. S. 2015. *Servants of Globalization: Migration and Domestic Work*, 2nd ed. Stanford, CA: Stanford University Press.

Perls, T., and D. Terry. 2007. "Exceptional Longevity." In *Global Health and Global Aging*, edited by M. Robinson, W. Novelli, C. Pearson, and L Norris. San Francisco: Jossey-Bass.

Pettigrew, C., and A. Soldan. 2019. "Defining Cognitive Reserve and Implications for Cognitive Aging." *Current Neurology and Neuroscience Reports* 19(1). https://doi.org/10.1007/s11910-019-0917-z.

Pillemer, K., D. Burnes, C. Riffin, and M. S. Lachs. 2016. "Elder Abuse: Global Situation, Risk Factors, and Prevention Strategies." *Gerontologist* 56(Suppl 2): S194–S205.

Polivka, L., and C. Longino. 2006. "The Emerging Postmodern Culture of Aging and Retirement Security." In *Aging, Globalization and Inequality: The New Critical Gerontology*, edited by J. Baars, D. Dannefe, C. Phillipson, and A. Walker. Amityville, NY: Baywood.

Project Catalyst. 2018. *Designing Technology for Caregivers: Understanding What Works and Doesn't.* https://www.aarp.org/content/dam/aarp/research/sur veys_statistics/ltc/2018/designing-tech-caregiving.doi.10.26419%252 Fres.00191.001.pdf.

Quesada, V., S. Freitas-Rodríguez, J. Miller, J. G. Pérez-Silva, Z. F. Jiang, W. Tapia, O. Santiago-Fernández, et al. 2019. "Giant Tortoise Genomes Provide Insights into Longevity and Age-Related Disease." *Nature Ecology & Evolution* 3: 87–95.

Reinhard, S., L. Friss Feinberg, A. Houser, R. Choula, and M. Evans. 2019. *Valuing the Invaluable: A New Look at the Economic Value of Family Caregiving.* AARP Public Policy Institute, https://www.aarp.org/content/dam/aarp /ppi/2019/11/valuing-the-invaluable-2019-update-charting-a-path-for ward.doi.10.26419-2Fppi.00082.001.pdf.

Robertson, J. 2017. *Robo Sapiens Japanicus: Robots, Gender, Family, and the Japanese Nation.* Berkeley: University of California Press.

Robinson, J. 1985. "Architectural Settings and the Housing of Older Developmentally Disabled Persons." In *Aging and Developmental Disabilities: Issues and Approaches*, edited by M. Jaricki and H. Wisniewski. New York: Van Nostrand Reinhold.

Robinson, M., W. Novelli, C. Pearson, and L. Norris. 2007. *Global Health and Global Aging.* San Francisco: Jossey-Bass.

Sadruddin, A. F. A. 2020. "The Care of 'Small Things': Aging and Dignity in Rwanda." *Medical Anthropology* 39(1): 83–95.

Savishinsky, J. 1991. *The Ends of Time: Life and Work in a Nursing Home.* New York: Bergin & Garvey.

Shield, R. 1988. *Uneasy Endings: Daily Life in an American Nursing Home.* Ithaca, NY: Cornell University Press.

Shier, V., D. Khodyakov, L. W. Cohen, S. Zimmerman, and D. Saliba. 2014. "What Does the Evidence Really Say About Culture Change in Nursing Homes?" *Gerontologist* 54(S1): S6–S16.

Simons, D. J., W. R. Boot, N. Charness, S. E. Gathercole, C. F. Chabris, D. Z. Hambrick, and E. A. Stine-Morrow. 2016. "Do 'Brain-Training' Programs Work?" *Psychological Science in the Public Interest* 17(3): 103–86. https://journals.sagepub.com/doi/full/10.1177/1529100616661983.

Solimeo, S. 2009. *With Shaking Hands: Aging with Parkinson's Disease in America's Heartland.* Piscataway, NJ: Rutgers University Press.

Stafford, P., ed. 2003. *Gray Matters. Ethnographic Encounters with Nursing Home Culture.* Sante Fe, NM: School for American Research.

Stringfellow, A. 2018. *The State of Caregiving 2018.* https://blog.caregiverhomes.com/stateofcaregiving.

Switek, B. 2016. *Reluctant Intimacies: Japanese Eldercare in Indonesian Hands.* New York: Berghahn.

Tanimura, C., J. Matsumoto, Y. Tokushima, J. Yoshimura, S. Tanishima, and H. Hagino. 2017. "Self-Care Agency, Lifestyle, and Physical Condition Predict Future Frailty in Community-Dwelling Older People." *Nursing & Health Sciences* 20(1). https://doi.org/10.1111/nhs.12376.

Thomas, W., and C. Johansson. 2003. "Elderhood in Eden: Geriatric Rehabilitation for the Soul." *Topics in Geriatric Rehabilitation* 19(4): 282–90.

Tinney, J. 2008. "Negotiating Boundaries and Roles: Challenges Faced by the Nursing Home Ethnographer." *Journal of Contemporary Ethnography* 37(2): 202–25.

Traphagan, J. 2009. "Brain Failure, Late Life and Culture in Japan." In *The Cultural Context of Aging*, 3rd ed., edited by J. Sokolovsky. Westport, CT: Praeger.

U.S. Census Bureau. 2007. *American Community Survey.* Washington, DC: U.S. Census Bureau.

U.S. Census Bureau. 2018. *Health Insurance Coverage in the United States: 2017.* September 12, Report P60-264. Washington, DC: U.S. Census Bureau.

Warren, N., and L. Manderson, eds. 2013. *Reframing Disability and Quality of Life: A Global Perspective.* New York: Springer.

Warren, N., and D. Sakellariou. 2020. "Neurodegeneration and the Intersubjectivities of Care." *Medical Anthropology* 39(1): 1–15.

Wettstein, G., and A. Zulkarnain. 2017. *How Much Long-Term Care Do Adult Children Provide?* Report 17-11, Center for Retirement Research, Boston College. https://crr.bc.edu/wp-content/uploads/2017/06/IB_17-11.pdf.

Winningham, R., R. Anunsen, L. M. Hanson, L. Laux, K. D. Kaus, and A. Reifers. 2004. "MemAerobics: A Cognitive Intervention to Improve Memory Ability and Reduce Depression in Older Adults." *Journal of Mental Health and Aging* 9(3): 183–92. https://digitalcommons.wou.edu/cgi/viewcontent.cgi?article=1013&context=fac_pubs.

World Health Organization. 1991. *World Health Statistics Annual 1990.* Geneva: World Health Organization.

World Health Organization. 2002. *Missing Voices: Views of Older Persons on Elder Abuse, A Study from Eight Countries: Argentina, Austria, Brazil, Canada, India, Kenya, Lebanon and Sweden.* Geneva: World Health Organization.

Yahalom, J. 2019. *Caring for the People of the Clouds: Aging and Dementia in Oaxaca.* Norman: University of Oklahoma Press.

Yaris, K. 2017. *Care across Generations: Solidarity and Sacrifice in Transnational Families.* Stanford, CA: Stanford University Press.

Zaninotto, P., G. Batty, S. Stenholm, I. Kawachi, M. Hyde, M. Goldberg, H. Westerlund, J. Vahtera, and J. Head. 2020. "Socioeconomic Inequalities in Disability-Free Life Expectancy in Older People from England and the United States: A Cross-national Population-Based Study." *Journals of Gerontology,* Series A, glz266: 1–8.

Zarulli, V., J. A. Barthold Jones, A. Oksuzyan, R. Lindahl-Jacobsen, K. Christensen, and J. W. Vaupel. 2018. "Women Live Longer Than Men Even during Severe Famines and Epidemics." *PNAS* 115(4): E832–E840.

CHAPTER FORTY-FOUR

Beyond the Blue Zones

Insights from the Okinawa Centenarian Study

*D. Craig Willcox, Bradley J. Willcox, Jordan Kondo,
Matthew Rosenbaum, Jay Sokolovsky,
and Makoto Suzuki*

Introduction

My first impression of Tsuru when I met her at the venerable age of 104 was that of a regal older woman who was the center of her large, extended family. Standing no more than 5 feet tall and weighing less than 70 pounds, she was a thin wisp of a woman. Yet she also appeared lithe and energetic, sporting a cane that she leaned on when she walked through her neighborhood or tended to her garden and carp pond (Photo 44.1). Six years later she greeted me after turning 110 years old, joining the ranks of an elite group that gerontologists have termed "supercentenarians" (those who have achieved the extreme age of 110 years or more). Tsuru had become the oldest living person in Okinawa. She was born the youngest of five children in a small village where she had lived her whole life. Well educated for her cohort, she passed an exam that qualified her to enter college and fulfill her dream to become a teacher, one of the few professions available to women during the early 20th century.

Unfortunately, she was not able to attend college due to objection from her parents, who insisted that she find a husband as soon as possible. She married at age 21, but her husband divorced her because she was unable to conceive a child. Tsuru remarried at 28 years of age with a man 17 years her senior, but she did not bear a child with him either. However, she brought up the child of her second husband, a likable young boy whom she loved and raised as her own. By the time Tsuru had turned 110, the second husband was long deceased, as were her adopted son and his wife. With these losses, her household had shrunk to three members. Tsuru's grandson and his wife, now in their sixties, attended to Tsuru's daily needs for home care. A great-grandson and his wife, in their thirties, were living next door and had yet to have a child. The support of her grandchildren was supplemented by a home helper who visited five times per week and a visiting nurse who came twice a week. This was mostly paid for by Japan's long-term care insurance system, first implemented in 2002 (see Part III Kavedžija). Noticeably thinner and frailer since I had last seen her at age 104, I thought back on the life of this typical (as representative of her times) yet remarkable (supercentenarian) woman. Tsuru had led the life of a woman of her generation, keeping house, raising her child, working the fields of sugar cane, growing vegetables for home consumption, making her own tofu, and when time permitted, making straw hats and selling them in the marketplace.

She had been healthy throughout her incredibly long life and, other than cataract surgery in her eighties, never experienced a major illness until she came down with pneumonia at age 105. This illness left her practically bedbound and in need of intensive daily support in order to carry out normal activities of daily living. What was the secret of her remarkable longevity? Was it just good fortune? Perhaps she just had a great set of genes. Maybe it was her good health habits. Her only unhealthy habit seemed to be that she had smoked a pack of cigarettes a day for 40 years, a practice that she gave up in her early seventies. She drank alcohol in the form of medicinal herb liquor (garlic or plum sake) but only on social occasions. She practiced ancestor worship and looked after the family altar with care. Her grandson and his wife reported her character as forward looking, someone who refused to dwell on negative thoughts. She seemed to have been conscientious about her health and exercised regularly, being an active walker. She was also careful about her meals and considered the nutritional content of the food. (from D. C. Willcox field notes, August 8, 2001, Yomitan Village, Okinawa, Japan)

Tsuru's case is remarkable in several ways, not only for her exceptional age, but also for the fact that she reached her 110th year and hence became a "supercentenarian" in relatively good health. As a participant in the Okinawa Centenarian Study (OCS), she had geriatric health assessments at various points from the time that she became a centenarian. Even at the incredible age of 110 years, Tsuru was not taking any prescription medications and these exams revealed no major diseases throughout this period (other than

Photo 44.1   Tsuru with Okinawa Centenarian Study investigators Craig Will-cox and Makoto Suzuki, 2001. (Photo by Koari Higa)

pneumonia). To put her aging achievement in perspective, when Tsuru was born toward the end of the 19th century, average life expectancy in Japan for men and women was only slightly more than 40 years of age. That she lived decades longer surviving through a century fraught with tuberculosis, gastroenteritis, malaria, measles, flu epidemics, earthquakes, fires, and World War II, which ravaged Okinawa in 1945, seems miraculous. In Japan, only a handful of people of her generation achieved "exceptional longevity" (EL) and survived to the age of 100 years, and less than one in a thousand of these centenarian elite lived to reach "supercentenarian" status of age 110 years or older (Japan Ministry of Health, Labour and Welfare 2007). Although the centenarian population in Japan continues to grow rapidly, in 2015, almost a decade after Tsuru died, only about two in a thousand centenarians became "supercentenarians" (Statistics Bureau of Japan 2016).[1]

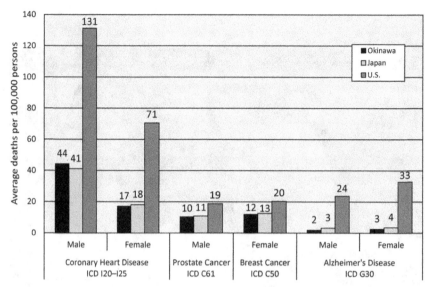

Figure 44.1 Age-Adjusted Mortality Rate per 100,000 Persons for 2015 for Age-Associated Diseases in Okinawans, Japanese, and Americans. Coding was according to ICD-10 codes; populations were age-adjusted to 2000 U.S. Standard Population (Japan Ministry of Health Labor Welfare 2017; Centers for Disease Control and Prevention 2017a).

In Ogimi village, a little farther north from Tsuru's home, a stone welcome marker stands near the beach. The marker displays the declaration of Ogimi village elders that reads "At 80 you are merely a youth, at 90 if the ancestors invite you into heaven, ask them to wait until you are 100 . . . and then you might consider it." When this stone marker was erected in the early 1990s, it could easily have been the region's motto. Older people in this area tend to be quite healthy and active, typically appearing youthful beyond their years. They are among the longest lived of the Japanese, who in turn are among the longest lived people in the world (Suzuki, Willcox, and Willcox 2007; Willcox et al. 2017).

To understand the significance of this health phenomenon, it is helpful to consider a typical disease and its impact upon a typical city of 100,000 inhabitants in both Okinawa and the United States (Figure 44.1). Consider coronary heart disease—the leading cause of death in the United States. If the city were located in Okinawa, nearly three times fewer males and more than four times fewer females would have died from this ailment in a typical year compared to the same city in the United States (Japan Ministry of Health, Labour and Welfare 2017a; Centers for Disease Control and Prevention 2017a). This is a profound difference.

Okinawa as a "Blue Zone"

Appropriately, Okinawa has been characterized as a "Blue Zone," a concept that refers to a demographic and/or geographic area with high population longevity and originating from the blue color on demographic maps (Poulain, Herm, and Pes 2013; Buettner 2017). Despite continuing disparities in healthy longevity between Okinawa and the United States, the rise of individuals attaining exceptional longevity in all postindustrial societies is dramatic. The global growth of centenarians, primarily in middle- and high-income countries, has been accelerated rapidly over time and it is estimated to exceed 21 million by 2100 (Robine and Cubaynes 2017; United Nations 2017).[2] In the United States, the number of persons aged 100 years or over in 2016 was estimated to be 81,896, and this number doubles about every 10 years (U.S. Census Bureau 2017).[3] In Japan, the centenarian population was doubling at *twice* the rate found in the United States in the 2000s—about every five years (Willcox et al. 2008a). Recently, the rate of doubling has slowed to about every 10 years, similar to that of the United States (Japan Ministry of Health, Labour and Welfare 2017a; U.S. Census Bureau 2017).[4]

How far can we go from here? What can help us to get the most out of our increased years? And what can we learn from research into the lives of people like Tsuru—who achieve longevity in relatively good health?

The Okinawa Centenarian Study

One of the research efforts to understand these issues is the Okinawa Centenarian Study (OCS), now in its 45th year, longer than any other such projects (www.orcls.org/ocs). Using an integrated approach combining researchers from many different fields, the OCS has sought to evaluate and investigate the exceptionally long-lived population found in the Ryukyu archipelago in southern Japan (Okinawa Prefecture). As of 2020, the study includes interviews and examinations of more than 1,000 Okinawan centenarians and thousands of younger elders in their seventies, eighties, and nineties, looking for commonalities in their diets, exercise habits, genetics, psychological and spiritual practices, and social and behavioral patterns that could possibly explain their long-term vitality and healthy longevity. That is, to gain insight into processes promoting healthy life extension and disease prevention by studying exceptionally aged individuals in social and cultural contexts.

Despite being the poorest prefecture in Japan, Okinawa Prefecture has historically been well known throughout Japan for its extraordinary health and longevity advantage, very low rates of cardiovascular diseases and cancers, and the highest proportion of centenarians among the 47 prefectures (although recent changes that will be discussed later have seen its advantages in longevity diminish). These "healthy-agers" are often characterized by a slow rate of physiological decline and less vulnerability to age-associated disease. Throughout this chapter, we will refer to "healthy aging" as chronological aging with minimal loss of function and low prevalence rates of the diseases that usually accompany the aging process.[5]

This chapter will draw upon insights gained through over four decades of study in Okinawa and connect this work with the growing number of centenarian and longitudinal healthy aging projects now going on around the world. First, we will examine the demography and epidemiology of healthy life expectancy, including some of the numerous false claims of extraordinary longevity.

Demography and Epidemiology of Healthy Life Expectancy

Exceptional Longevity Myths and the Importance of an Evidence-Based Approach

Although the absolute potential for human aging is unknown, the oldest age-verified human being is Jeanne Louise Calment of France, who died aged 122 years and 5 1/2 months (Robine and Allard 1999). No one in recorded history has ever been verified as living longer than this; in fact, only about 12 people in human history have been documented as having reached the age of 117 years or more (Los Angeles Gerontology Research Group 2018).[6] With increasing numbers of healthy elderly and advancing preventive medical care, we expect that this record will be broken within the coming decades, although some gerontologists doubt that this record will ever be broken (Dong, Milholland, and Vijg 2016).

Myths of exceptional longevity have been around for more than two millennia and are found in many different cultures both geographically and temporally separated (Willcox, Willcox, and Ferrucci 2008b).[7] The German painter Lucas Cranach the Elder (1472–1553), painted at age 74 his famous *Fons Juventutis* (the fountain of youth), depicting a miraculous spring with withered ancient women getting in and nubile, rejuvenated youths emerging from the waters. Of course, this was also the age of trying to turn lead into gold (See Part VI Introduction).

In the 1970s there appeared reports and a story in National Geographic from several different remote parts of the world that claimed to document a number of individuals between the ages of 120 and 168! These all provided fascinating and hopeful media stories, but on closer examination the facts and figures just did not add up (Mazess and Forman 1979; Leaf 1982; Bennett and Garson 1983). The case of the unfounded claims in the Caucasus (located in the former Soviet republics of Georgia, Azerbaijan, and Armenia) is typical of false claims of exceptional long life in many locales.

The problem with the Soviet data was that few of the so-called centenarians actually possessed birth certificates because no central birth registration system existed until after the Soviet Union was formed in 1917.[8] Some men had exaggerated their age to escape military service by assuming the identity of an older, deceased relative, others in order to gain the respect that came with being the most senior elder in the village. Shirali Mislimov, the oldest such claimant, was said to be 168 years old, and his picture even appeared on a Soviet postage stamp.

In this area's Muslim villages the link of status to elevated age was particularly important for men, and this probably explains why there were more men recorded as supercentenarians than women. If nothing else, this gender differential, dramatically opposite of any other place in the world, should have made researchers much more skeptical. For example, in February 2020, an international list of 29 validated living supercentenarians indicated that 28 were female and just *one* was male (Los Angeles Gerontology Research Group 2020).[9] Clearly, in studies of exceptionally long-lived individuals, or populations that claim to have high numbers of centenarians, careful scrutiny of birth records, death records, and other age-related documents is necessary in order to support longevity claims.

Japan has long been considered to have among the highest quality data for the oldest old (Kannisto 1994). In Japan (and Okinawa), the household registry (*koseki*) dates back to the 1870s so age verification (equivalent of a birth certificate) is possible for all citizens, including centenarians. The *koseki* is supplemented by a regular census undertaken every five years. While its accuracy has been debated, life tables calculated from these data for Okinawa show one of the world's longest life expectancies, and prevalence data show one of the world's highest known concentrations of centenarians for any country or state (Willcox et al. 2008a; Willcox, Willcox, and Suzuki 2017; Japan Ministry of Health, Labour and Welfare 2017b).[10]

Centenarian Studies around the World

In the early 1970s, the first comprehensive attempt to scientifically study centenarians took place in Hungary (Beregi 1990) and was followed soon after by the Okinawa Centenarian Study, established in 1975 when Dr. Makoto Suzuki arrived in Okinawa to establish a Department of Community Medicine at the new medical school in University of the Ryukyus (Suzuki 1985; Willcox, Willcox, and Suzuki 2001). One important finding from these and subsequent studies with rigorous age validation methodology is that there do seem to be areas in the world with particularly high prevalence of centenarians. These global "Blue Zones" include the Mediterranean island of Sardinia, Italy; the island archipelago of Okinawa, Japan; the community of Seventh-day Adventists in Loma Linda, California; the Nicoya Peninsula region in Costa Rica; and the island of Ikaria, Greece. Each "Blue Zone" offers a unique opportunity to assess healthy aging patterns from a different perspective as well as look for underlying common elements (Davinelli, Willcox, and Scapagnini 2012; Buettner 2017).

Over the past several decades, the breadth of centenarian studies have made important contributions to understanding the aging process and longevity (Willcox, Willcox, and Poon 2010). From this work it soon became clear that common stories of cigar-smoking, whiskey-swilling centenarians who could effortlessly hike mountain ranges were a myth. When truly population-based research was conducted, and all centenarians were identified, it was clear that there was wide heterogeneity in the centenarian population. Some centenarians were remarkably well preserved, while others had high levels of disease and disability—in Okinawa about one-third were found to be functionally independent, about one-third needed major assistance with activities of daily living (ADL), and about one-third were very ill and disabled (Sanabe, Ashitomi, and Suzuki 1977; Suzuki et al. 1995).[11]

Not surprisingly, only a minority could be characterized as "independent" in their activities of daily living (Andersen-Ranberg, Schroll, and Jeune 2001). Importantly, while high levels of disability are present in these exceptional survivors, an important caveat is that most centenarians seem to be healthier than the average person throughout their lives and remain functionally independent until their mid-nineties (Willcox et al. 2008c; Andersen et al. 2012).

Trajectories of Health and Decline

Although studies have yet to adequately characterize the prevalence and timing of age-associated illness among exceptionally long-lived persons, the New England Centenarian Study (NEC) suggests that there may be multiple routes to achieving longevity and that there are gender differences regarding which route is taken (www.bumc.bu.edu/centenarian). Initially a small population-based study of centenarians in New England, the NEC has become national in its scope by locating long-lived families and supercentenarians throughout the United States and concentrating mainly on genetic aspects (Perls et al. 1999; Perls and Terry 2007). Researchers there found that centenarians fall into three morbidity profiles—survivors, delayers, or escapers.[12] The survivor profile fit those who had an age-associated disease prior to the age of 80 years. Delayers were those who delayed the onset of age-associated illness until at least the age of 80 years. Escapers were those who made it to 100 without age-associated illness. However, when examining only the most lethal diseases of aging (heart disease, cancer, stroke), 87 percent of males and 83 percent of female subjects escaped or delayed these diseases until the time they had reached centenarian status (Evert et al. 2003). This healthy aging phenomenon becomes even more evident among supercentenarians (110 years). It was found that the majority of Okinawan supercentenarians had minimal clinically apparent disease until late in life, were functionally independent at age 100 years, and few were institutionalized before the age of 105 years (Willcox et al. 2008c).[13]

Typically, as found in New England, Okinawa, and almost all other areas of the world, approximately 80 to 90 percent of centenarians are female. One unique exception is a longevity Blue Zone in Sardinia, Italy, that demonstrates a noticeable gender equality due in part to a lifestyle of high energy expenditure by male centenarians during the first half of the 20th century as shepherds in the mountainous geography (Poulain et al. 2004; Pes et al. 2013). As noted above, despite the fact that male centenarians are generally fewer in number, they tend to have lower levels of disability and disease than their female counterparts. The reasons are as of yet unclear; however, women may be physiologically and behaviorally more adaptable than men when it comes to living with age-associated illness. The risk of dying for men seems to rise quickly relative to similarly aged women, and therefore it appears that men must be relatively disease-free to make it to 100 (Ballard et al. 2011).[14]

By the 21st century there was a proliferation of centenarian studies. For example, a project by the Albert Einstein Medical School on ethnic and religious populations, rather than persons within a geographic area, is taking place in the United States with Ashkenazi Jews and a religious community of Seventh-day Adventists (Fraser and Shavlik 2001; Barzilai et al. 2003). There are now over a dozen active centenarian studies using various study models, and increasing collaboration is occurring between centenarian researchers and other longevity researchers.[15] For example, OCS is part of the 5-Country Oldest Old Project (5-COOP) evaluating mortality among centenarians and the functional health status of those over age 85 years in Denmark, France, Japan, Switzerland, and Sweden (Robine et al. 2010).[16] Figure 44.2. summarizes 2015 data for six locations from several studies of centenarians.

There are a few problems with providing updated *Centenarian Prevalence* (CP) data:

- In 2015, Okinawa was ranked 10th out of 47 prefectures for CP.
- Oligastra, Sardinia, is a rather small region of Sardinia, which is where many centenarians are found. The CP for total Sardinia is only 28 per 100,000.
- As outlined by Poulain, Herm, and Pes (2013), CP is sensitive to migration and changes in fertility, which may alter the relative proportion of elders.

A combination of these factors has likely contributed to Okinawa's lower relative rank for CP. Current rural prefectures with high CP (e.g., Shimane)

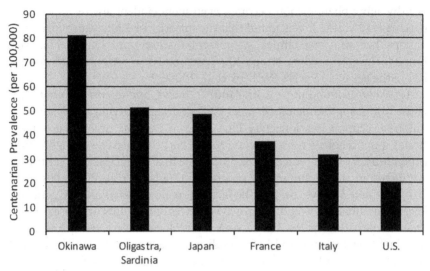

Figure 44.2   Prevalence of Centenarians in Selected Countries for 2015 (Number of centenarians per hundred thousand persons). (Human Mortality Database 2017; Istituto Nazionale di Statistica (ISTAT) 2017; Japan Ministry of Health, Labour and Welfare 2017a).

may be artificially inflated due to low birth rates and migration. In contrast, Okinawans continue to have the highest birth rates nationwide.

Living Longer in Japan

In order to put the Okinawan longevity phenomenon in proper context, it is helpful to examine the dramatic increase in postwar Japanese life expectancy as a whole. In the four decades following World War II (1950–1990), two separate demographic and epidemiological transitions occurred, one affecting mainly younger age groups, the second affecting mainly older age groups. The combined effect of these two transitions accounts for the rapid gains in average life expectancy that resulted in Japan, a longevity laggard until then, catching up and usurping Sweden as the longest-lived country in the world in the mid- to late 1970s (Yanagishita and Guralnik 1988).

From 1950 to 1965, the decrease in death rates under five years of age from communicable and vaccine-preventable diseases accounted for over half of the increase in average life expectancy.[17] Sustained extension of longevity after the mid-1960s was attributable to declines in mortality for non-communicable diseases among older groups (over 50 years). For example, between 1985 and 1990, mortality decreases in people aged 75 years or older accounted for nearly a third of life expectancy gains, and this trend has only strengthened in years since.

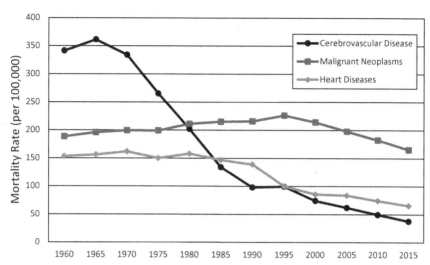

Figure 44.3   Age-Standardized Mortality Rates in Japanese Males: 1960–2015. (Japan Ministry of Health, Labour and Welfare 2017a).

One of the most important factors promoting life expectancy gains in Japan was the government's strong stewardship of public health by investing in key interventions. A major accomplishment of Japan's public health system was the decrease in stroke mortality, which came about in large part due to mass screening of the population for hypertension, government-mandated salt reductions in commonly consumed foods such as soy sauce, and increased use of cost-effective antihypertensive drugs (Ikeda et al. 2011; Figure 44.3). These practices have resulted in Japan's dramatic decrease in (age-standardized) stroke mortality––from over 350 per 100,000 in the early 1960s to 18 per 100,000 in the year 2015 for men and 9 per 100,000 in 2015 for women (Japan Ministry of Health, Labour and Welfare 2017a). There was already an extremely low death rate from the number one cause of death in the West, coronary heart disease (CHD), which in Japan is only one-fourth of U.S. or Swedish levels.[18] These factors helped to create improvements and the context for Japan's incredible rise in life expectancy and the emergence of a large centenarian population, which grew from 153 persons in 1963 to over 67,000 in 2017 (Japan Ministry of Health, Labour and Welfare 2017a).

The Socioeconomic Context for a Longevity Boom

Postwar social and economic changes contributed to reduced mortality from the various causes discussed in the previous section. First, the introduction of new antibiotics, immunizations, and mass preventive screening processes under universal health insurance coverage dramatically reduced mortality from infectious diseases. Second, technological innovations contributed to the decrease in mortality from particular causes. For instance, near-universal access to refrigerators in the mid-1960s contributed to an increased consumption of fresh food, which is richer in vitamins, minerals, and other antioxidants and helps lower risk for stomach cancer and other age-associated diseases. Refrigeration also decreases prevalence of *Helicobacter pylori*, a bacterium that exists in poorly sanitized locales and is a common cause of stomach cancer. In addition, refrigeration also led to a reduced consumption of sodium-rich preserved foods, likely contributing to a major decrease in mortality due to stroke, stomach cancer, and other diseases (Kobayashi et al. 2004; Nagata et al. 2004). Thus, many synergistic forces, particularly important for public health, helped drive mortality rates lower in postwar Japan.

The health professions in Japan also underwent major change in the 1960s, resulting in a dramatic increase in both number and quality of health care facilities and health care professionals. After the establishment of a national health insurance system in 1961, screening campaigns aimed at reducing the burden of common chronic illnesses have helped in prevention and early detection of many lifestyle-related diseases. Studies have shown that subpopulations in Japan with high participation in these screening exams suffer lower levels of mortality, and lower associated medical costs (Iwasa et al. 2007).

The economic boom that followed the war resulted in a large increase in average income and greater access to education, the effects of which were felt relatively evenly across the population, resulting in less income disparity than is seen in most Western countries, especially when compared to the United States. The dramatic increase in economic equality and in access to preventative health care has been a key factor in the decline of mortality rates and the nation's soaring longevity figures (Fukuda, Nakamura, and Takano 2005).[19] In the 1990s, Japan experienced a prolonged economic recession. Income inequality has since increased, which has coincided with reports suggesting widening health disparities and less impressive gains in life expectancy in recent years (Ikeda et al. 2011).

The Cultural Context of Healthy Aging in Okinawa

Despite more than a century of cultural oppression and assimilation, major cultural differences remain between Okinawa and mainland Japan, including key differences in identity, language, social organization, religion, art, music, and dietary habits (Willcox, Willcox, and Suzuki 2001). Franklin poetically described Okinawa as

Japan with salsa—a hybrid culture where formal kimonos are streaked with bold geometrics, breezy palm trees grow alongside fluttering cherry, and Japanese precision and punctuality are tempered by an easygoing cadence known locally as "Okinawa time." (1996: 56)

Champuru: The Food Culture of Okinawa

During the prewar period (before 1945) the traditional food culture of Okinawa was a fusion of Chinese, Japanese, and Southeast Asian influences. Often referred to as *champuru* or *chample* in the Okinawan language, which means "mixture," it was truly a mixed plate of Asian influences. The staple food of traditional Okinawan cuisine was neither polished white rice nor other grains, but many varieties of colorful sweet potatoes.[20] Almost every meal included steamed sweet potatoes, a large variety of simmered or steamed green leafy and/or yellow root vegetables, and soy products such as miso soup, tofu, and miso flavorings. Smaller servings of fish or lean meats and tropical fruits often accompanied these staples. For seasoning, Okinawans had a taste for bonito-flavored broths and used herbs and spices such as turmeric or mugwort liberally in place of salt, leading to lower sodium consumption and lower risk for stroke and stomach cancer (Willcox and Willcox 2014). Festival days (which provide an opportunity to eat ceremonial dishes) seem to have taken place often enough to ensure regular supplementation of a variety of other food sources such as rice, kombu seaweed, various meats, and other seafoods. Noodles, from wheat or buckwheat, bread, and eggs were also consumed on rare occasion.

In the postwar period, rice completely replaced the sweet potato as the staple food, and the volume of food products imported into Okinawa increased rapidly in line with the progress of globalization. In modern Okinawa, people enjoy a widely varied diet, although large generational differences now stand out, with elders sticking closer to the traditional diet.[21] In addition, in the traditional dietary habits, there was a focus on small portion sizes and not eating until completely full. Even now a common saying among Okinawan elderly is *hara hachi bu* (Eat until only 80 percent full).

Biocultural Benefits of the Okinawan Lifestyle

How might culture and biology have intertwined to decrease the risk of disease in Okinawa? First, research suggests that dietary patterns associated with a reduced risk of chronic disease are similar to the traditional Okinawan diet, which is characterized by its high consumption of vegetables (therefore phytonutrient-rich) but reduced in meat, refined grains, saturated fat, sugar, and salt (Willcox et al. 2009).[22] Many characteristics of the traditional Okinawan diet are shared with other healthy dietary patterns such as the Mediterranean diet (both vegetable heavy) and the researcher-designed dietary approaches to stop hypertension (DASH) and portfolio (cholesterol-lowering) diets (Willcox and Willcox 2014).[23]

Second, the low-calorie, phytonutrient-rich, and nutritionally dense food choices, the healthy eating habits, and the high levels of physical activity resulted in a population that had consumed a nutrient-rich but calorie-poor diet. We estimate that Okinawans prior to the 1960s consumed 10–15 percent fewer calories than would normally be required per caloric guidelines. When faced with a persistent energy deficit, mammals adapt by becoming more energy efficient, producing less heat and converting a higher proportion of food into usable energy. A host of other metabolic adaptations occur that may confer longevity.[24] These changes are commonly observed in animal studies of "caloric restriction" (CR), and this is the only consistently reproducible manner of increasing mean and maximum lifespan in animal experiments, other than select genetic manipulations. (Fontana, Partridge, and Longo 2010).[25]

Additionally, the traditional Okinawan diet appears to be a rich source of foods that may mimic the biological effects of CR, acting as caloric restriction "mimetics." CR-mimetics are compounds that provide the physiological benefit of CR without the need for restriction of calories through multiple mechanisms, including reduced oxidative stress. In the Okinawan language, a common saying is *nuchi gusui*, which can best be translated as "Let food be your medicine." This reflects the cultural context wherein the distinction between food and medicine blurs in Okinawa, and deeper analyses reveal that many of the traditional foods, herbs, and spices in the Okinawan diet have medicinal properties, which are under investigation (Willcox and Willcox 2014).[26]

The longevity benefits from a combination of plant-based nutrition, caloric restriction, and CR-mimetics can be appreciated in the reduced mortality risk for key diseases like stroke in Okinawa. While the leading killer in North America and Northern Europe has long been heart disease, in Japan the major problem was cerebrovascular disease (stroke). It is hypothesized that the stroke risk was exacerbated by high salt intake and elevated due in part to an insufficient intake of fat and animal protein, which weakened arterial walls (Matsuzaki 1992). A combination of low blood cholesterol levels, amino acid deficiency, and high salt intake dramatically increases risk of stroke and was typical of the mainland Japanese dietary pattern before the 1960s (Kagan et al. 1985). The better balanced traditional Okinawan diet (lower salt intake, more varied sources of protein and fat from soy and lean pork) has likely been contributing to the lower stroke mortality rates in Okinawa, which were about half that of the mainland from 1973 to 1992 (Okinawa Prefecture 1995).[27]

Comparative Studies of the Elderly in Okinawa and Japan

Long-standing differences in a complex mix of culture, social organization, and health practices persist between Okinawa and the rest of Japan that seem to have given the current generation of Okinawan elders a longevity edge.

One of the best ways to see this is by comparing the long-lived Ogimi village in northern Okinawa with a demographically similar village in Akita Prefecture with the shortest life expectancy in Japan (Shibata et al. 1994). There was a much higher death rate from stroke in Akita, situated in the northeastern part of Japan. An examination of the diets of elderly persons in both villages revealed some major differences in the foods consumed. The Okinawan elderly consumed higher levels of meat, green/yellow vegetables, and tofu, whereas the Akita elderly consumed more white rice, fish, shellfish, seaweed, and fruit. Okinawan villagers consumed higher levels of protein, calcium, and mono- and polyunsaturated fats, whereas those in Akita had higher salt intake.[28] Okinawan dietary factors and possibly genetic factors (which may affect cholesterol levels) have contributed to population-wide low LDL ("bad" cholesterol) and high HDL ("good" cholesterol), a combination often seen in healthy centenarians (Suzuki, Willcox, and Willcox 2001). The abundance of antioxidant-rich vegetables (mainly sweet potatoes) and soy foods containing high levels of flavonoids may also provide protective effects against certain cancers, osteoporosis, and hypertension (Willcox, Scapagnini, and Willcox 2014).[29]

Compared to the elderly in Akita, the Okinawan elders were more active with higher levels of activities of daily living (ADL),[30] had more social contact, were employed longer, and had lower rates of hospitalization (Shibata et al. 1994). Interestingly, nearly 40 percent of elderly women in the Okinawan sample lived alone, compared with less than 10 percent of women in the Akita sample (where most lived with children). Support networks were also different between the two villages, Akita's being mainly family-centered whereas Okinawa's was centered around friends and neighbors (Shibata et al. 1994). The tight settlement pattern in Okinawan villages and high rates of autonomy of Okinawan elders may encourage them to stay employed longer and have greater levels of social contact.

In more recent times, maintaining social support networks has become even more important for older people in depopulated rural villages because reliable support from younger family members can no longer be taken for granted. The Okinawan elderly have found ways to enhance interdependence among intimate age peers by relying on mutual supportive practices based on two forms of institutionalized social relationships: friendships and associations. Practices such as informal visiting behavior, fictive kin-keeping, sharing of work tasks, and exchanges of gifts, information, and other items are based upon a norm of reciprocity and help to create informal community organizations. These and other types of association form strong social ties and supportive relationships between the elderly (Willcox 2009).[31]

Okinawa's Healthy Older Women

Women almost everywhere outlive men (see Part I Wan He and Kinsella). In Okinawa, the gender gap in life expectancy is particularly large (over seven years). Part of the longer life expectancies for women in general seems to be based in biology, but differences in this gap between societies lends weight to the importance of social and behavioral factors. Women in most postindustrialized societies are generally more health conscious than men. Women tend to have better eating habits, lower rates of smoking and drinking, more regular medical check-ups, stronger social networks, and less risk-taking behavior (lower rates of accidents, suicide, and homicide). Okinawan women are no exception to the above; however, they also seem to possess a few other aces up their sleeves—particularly older women.

Compared to older women in Western nations, women in Okinawa tend to experience menopause with fewer physiological complaints and fewer medical complications (Willcox, Willcox, and Suzuki 2001; Part II Shea). There is a markedly lower reported incidence of hot flashes, depression, and mood changes. Medical complications such as hip fractures and coronary heart disease are also much lower. Lifestyle determinants include diet, avoidance of smoking, and exercise in the form of dance, soft martial arts, walking, and gardening. Diet is particularly interesting. Okinawan women have a very high intake of natural estrogens through their diet, mainly from the large quantities of soy-enriched products that they consume. Legumes such as soybeans are rich in phytoestrogens, or plant estrogens, called flavonoids.[32] Although the jury is still out, high soy consumption has been associated with reduced menopause problems in Japanese women (Willcox et al. 2009).[33]

Okinawan women also have extremely low risk for hormone-dependent cancers including cancers of the breast, ovaries, and colon. Compared to North Americans, they have approximately 50 percent less breast cancer, and less than half the ovarian and colon cancers. Some of the most important factors that may protect against these cancers include low caloric intake, high vegetable/fruit consumption, higher intake of good fats (omega-3, monounsaturated fat), high-fiber diet, high flavonoid intake, low body fat level, and high level of physical activity.

Other unique factors may be operating within this particular cultural context that have yet to be adequately explored. One such factor includes the interconnected role of religion, spirituality, aging, and health in the lives of older Okinawan women. A key factor is the high level of social integration of women, especially older women, in various aspects of daily life. A good example of this is the *Basho-fu* weaving of Ogimi village in northern Okinawa (Photo 44.2). In this unique style of weaving, the time- and labor-intensive process of cleaning the fibers and spooling the thread is performed mainly by groups of older women. In addition to providing social opportunities, it allows these women to be respected and active members of the local economy as well as supplements their income (Willcox et al. 2007c).

Religion and spirituality may be particularly important for women throughout the Ryukyu Island archipelago as Okinawa remains the only contemporary society in which women actually lead the mainstream,

Photo 44.2   Collective production of *Basho-fu*. (Photo by Jay Sokolovsky)

publicly funded religion (Matayoshi and Trafton 2000). Numerous studies have shown benefits of positive spirituality on aging and health (Zimmer et al. 2016; Part IV Web Book Peterson). Some researchers have questioned the current paradigm of successful aging for not explicitly including spirituality in the model (Part I Lamb; Part I Web Book Moody). In Okinawa, elderly women's active engagement in religious roles may be playing a part in reducing depression and associated rates of suicide (Photo 44.3) (Willcox and Katata 2000). Rates of suicide for elderly Okinawan women have, for many years, been among the lowest in East Asia, a region known for high rates of suicide among older women (Pritchard and Baldwin 2002).[34]

What Is the Potential for Healthy Human Aging?

Achieving Healthy Aging

Until the 1970s, the common perception was that a person's genes ultimately determine an individual's predisposition to disease and their potential to live a long and healthy life. One of the first and most important studies that changed this view and gave support to the position that lifestyle (not genes) was the major determinant of healthy longevity was the

Photo 44.3   Okinawan sacred priestesses leading the community ritual (men in background). (Photo by Craig Wilcox)

Ni-Hon-San study (which later gave rise to the Honolulu Heart Program).[35] This international collaborative project compared Japanese immigrants and their offspring in Honolulu (Hon) and San Francisco (San) to Japanese remaining in Japan (Nippon). Because the study population did not marry into other ethnic groups, the gene pool was similar to the Japanese population, forming a genetic control; and the variables of concern were environment and lifestyle (Willcox et al. 2004). One of the important findings from the study was that the longer the Japanese Americans lived in their adopted country, the more their life expectancy and diseases resembled those of the host country. In other words, since there was little genetic variation between the Japanese and Japanese American populations studied, the difference in disease risk was due primarily to lifestyle factors (Trombold, Moellering Jr, and Kagan 1966; Willcox et al. 2007b). Indeed, growing evidence suggests that most variation in overall human lifespan—and perhaps more importantly, health span—is environmental (Rattan 2012; Giuliani, Garagnani, and Franceschi 2018).

Many of the scientifically based recommendations for healthy aging are the most obvious, including not smoking, avoiding excessive drinking, maintaining a healthy weight, and minimizing risk for accidents. In a large number of developed countries, many of the main causes of death—including coronary heart disease (CHD), cancer, and stroke—are greatly influenced by lifestyle. In fact, in the United States it is estimated that 80 percent of CHD and type 2 diabetes and 40 percent of cancers may be prevented by improving dietary habits, engaging in regular physical activity, and avoiding tobacco use (Centers for Disease Control and Prevention 2009). Nutrition is among the most important means of mitigating age-associated chronic diseases, and a recent 20-year landmark study found that dietary factors accounted for the majority (26 percent) of the risk for early death and the most disability-adjusted life years lost in the United States (U.S. Burden of Disease Collaborators 2013; Mokdad et al. 2018).[36] When optimal health habits are followed, the average life expectancy can increase dramatically, as exhibited by Seventh-day Adventists living in the Loma Linda Blue Zone. Because of religious beliefs they do not smoke or drink alcohol, are more active, tend to be leaner, and follow a largely vegetarian dietary regime. Not surprisingly, they live an average of 10 years longer than the typical American (Fraser and Shavlik 2001).

Contrastingly, Japanese who immigrate to Brazil are also a good example of what can happen when long-lived persons are removed from their health-promoting environment. In these immigrants we see a major change in eating habits, with Japanese Brazilians consuming less fish and vegetables, while consuming more than three times the amount of sugar and a staggering 18 times the amount of meat as Japanese remaining in their homeland (Moriguchi 1999). These numbers are especially pronounced when we look at Okinawan Brazilians, whose rates of obesity and hypertension are 1.6 and 2 times higher than those of Japan. Moreover, average longevity is 17 years shorter, and the proportion of centenarians less than one-fifth that of those remaining in Okinawa.

What About Those Genes?

Genetics has long been a focus of the Okinawan Centenarian Study. Longevity is a complex trait, and to survive another 15 or more years beyond the average, people may need a relatively rare or exceptional combination of environmental, behavioral, and genetic factors—and many of these factors run in families. Okinawans have traditionally married within their own villages, and geographic isolation has limited gene inflow, resulting in less genetic variability in Okinawans than in other Japanese (Bendjilali et al. 2014). These factors can favor clustering of genetic variants, leading to extreme phenotypes, such as longevity (Willcox et al. 2006a).[37]

Regarding genetic factors and longevity, in 1985, OCS investigators performed the first extensive study of centenarian pedigrees, finding more longevity among siblings in centenarian families than control families (Suzuki et al. 1995). Two decades later, with a larger data set, OCS investigators found that cumulative survival advantages for the centenarian sibling cohort increased over the life span such that female centenarian siblings had a 2.58-fold likelihood and male siblings a 5.43-fold likelihood, of reaching their 90s versus their birth cohorts (Photo 44.4) (Willcox et al. 2006b).[38]

Photo 44.4   Twin OCS investigators Craig and Bradley Willcox with Kin and Gin—Japan's oldest twins at 105 years. (Photo by Makoto Suzuki)

Historically, genetic research in this area relied upon studies utilizing identical and fraternal twins. Findings from twin studies have suggested that environment/lifestyle accounts for about two-thirds of lifespan, while genetics accounts for one-third (Ljungquist et al. 1998). Other twin studies have also come up with estimates in the 25–30 percent range (McGue et al. 1993; Herskind et al. 1996; Pili and Petretto 2017).[39]

The Future of Healthy Aging

What can we realistically achieve in terms of healthy human aging? There is ongoing debate that seems to swing between two poles. Some optimistically argue that technological breakthroughs may soon extend human lifespan to a thousand or more years (Helland 2011; Part VI Introduction). However, there is a heavy burden of proof before most gerontologists will agree. Others argue that we have already "hit the wall" in terms of the potential for growth in human life expectancy and we might even witness declines in the 21st century due to obesity and the reemergence of infectious disease threats (Olshansky et al. 2005).

Compressing Morbidity and Maximizing Healthy Years

Rather than an old age plagued by disease and disability, one scenario would be maintaining a level of reasonable functionality followed by a quick decline towards death (Willcox et al. 2007b). This is best described by the "compression of morbidity" paradigm as first postulated by Fries in 1980. As mentioned earlier, we can see that many centenarians have markedly delayed or avoided clinical expression of many major diseases that have killed younger elderly people and the majority also remain functionally independent (as defined by ability to perform basic activities of daily living) for most of their lives (Ismail et al. 2016).

Improved medical advances in end-of-life care have resulted in "life extension," which may delay mortality from various chronic diseases but not necessarily decrease their prevalence. This may result in a prolongation of the duration of chronic disease and possibly disability. For example, better treatment of hypertension results in longer survival with this particular "disease" and thus increases the prevalence of this disease in the population of older individuals. However, there is evidence that major diseases, such as cardiovascular disease and cancer, can be delayed or avoided until late in life. Olshansky et al. (2007) estimated that delaying typical age-related morbidity in Americans by just seven years would decrease the age-specific risk of disability and death by 50 percent, allowing a substantial population-wide improvement in both health span and life span. These authors label this as the "longevity dividend" and suggest better health habits might improve the length of life and might result in the "compression of morbidity" (at least for major chronic diseases), resulting in longer, healthier, and more functional lives (Olshansky 2013).

One oft-presumed implication of extended longevity is a rising cost of medical care for the elderly.[40] Perhaps we should rethink this issue. It may seem counterintuitive, but living longer through promoting *healthy* longevity may actually help reduce medical costs. For example, Nakajoh et al. (1999) studied the medical records of older people who died in a small village in Japan and discovered that the medical costs incurred for those dying at an older age (average 82.2 years old) were more than a third less than those dying at a younger age (average 76.7 years old). Similarly in America, the cost for caring for centenarians during the last five years of their life has been estimated to be only $1,800 per year, significantly less than the approximately $6,500 per year for those dying at age 70 (Hazzard 1997). Authors of the "longevity dividend" estimate the economic value of delayed aging to be $7.1 trillion over 50 years (Goldman et al. 2013).[41] A study of cumulative Medicare costs in the United States for those living until 100 years of age were approximately equal to those living to 65 years of age, suggesting that those who survived to older ages were healthier over the course of their lives and had less need for acute care (Spillman and Lubitz 2000). However, lifetime costs of long-term care (not covered by Medicare) were markedly higher due mainly to the high cost of nursing home care (see Section VI Polivka).

Measuring Healthy Life Expectancy

In line with these global trends, the World Health Organization (WHO) uses a measurement of healthy life expectancy referred to as HALE (health adjusted life expectancy) in order to better assess the quality of population health. HALE is calculated from life expectancy and adjusted for morbidity of debilitating conditions/illnesses. HALE is best thought of as a measure of disability-free life span.[42] Although there is a correlation between life expectancy and HALE, there is still a significant amount of variation in HALE between countries with similar life expectancies. For example, within the 89 countries WHO lists with a life expectancy fewer than 70 years for males, HALE varies from 44 to 63 years (World Health Organization 2018).

Using HALE provides deeper insight into the overall health of a population than just considering life expectancy (see Figures 44.4a and 44.4b below). This is particularly true in countries such as Oman and Iraq, where the life expectancy is reasonably high but healthy life expectancy is comparatively low. In these countries, people succumb to disease or debilitating conditions relatively early and spend a disproportionate number of years in a state of disability.

As of 2016, Japan trails Singapore with the second-highest HALE at birth in the world at 72.6 years for men and 77.6 years for women (WHO 2018). However, the longevity advantage experienced by Okinawa Prefecture has been gradually eroding over the past couple of decades with the growth rate of life expectancy (at birth) being among the slowest in Japan (Willcox et al. 2007b; Japan Ministry of Health, Labour and Welfare 2017b).[43]

Healthy Aging in Peril

Within the past few decades, Okinawan lifestyle changes have included diets higher in calories with more fat intakes and lower vegetable consumption, less physical activity, as well as increased tobacco and alcohol consumption and socioeconomic challenges (such as high unemployment rates). These factors are likely contributing to emerging problems of obesity, diabetes, increased cardiovascular risk factors, and higher rates of lung cancer, liver disease, and suicide for large subsets of the population—especially younger and middle-aged men (Willcox et al. 2012). In reflection of increased health risks, Okinawan men are now ranked 36th place and Okinawan women are ranked seventh place for life expectancy (at birth) among 47 prefectures in 2015 (Japan Ministry of Health, Labour and Welfare 2017b).[44] Looking at

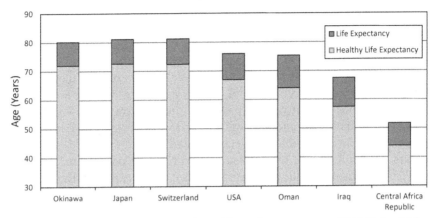

Figure 44.4a   Life Expectancy and Healthy Life Expectancy (HALE) for Males in Selected Countries for 2016 (WHO 2018; Japan Ministry of Health, Labour and Welfare 2018).

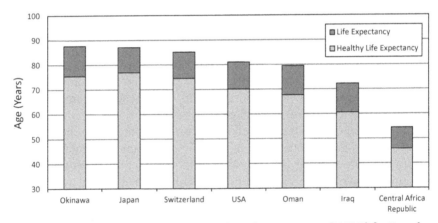

Figure 44.4b   Life Expectancy and Healthy Life Expectancy (HALE) for Females in Selected Countries for 2016 (WHO 2018; Japan Ministry of Health, Labour and Welfare 2018).

specific causes of death that contributed to recent slowing of life expectancy for Okinawans, we can see that lifestyle-related diseases such as diabetes, liver disease, chronic obstructive pulmonary disease, and suicide (particularly for middle-aged Okinawan males) are all playing a role (Japan Ministry of Health, Labour and Welfare 2017a). This is in contrast to older generations, who are still among the highest nationwide in health profiles and lifespan.[45]

Expanding the Blue Zones: Lessons from Okinawa

What we may see in the future is two distinct groups of oldest old emerging. One marked by those who lived a healthy lifestyle—they will possess a history of eating a healthy diet, avoiding smoking and excessive alcohol consumption, exercising regularly and taking good care of their bodies and minds, and engaging in regular preventive health care. These individuals will live unusually long and vibrant lives, and we see evidence of their emergence already in active Blue Zone communities around the world. The other group, who will be frail or disabled for much longer periods and, without medical advances, would otherwise have died much earlier, will instead be pushed into uncharted regions of survival through medical technology.

It is not too late to reverse these concerning trends. As advocated by Appel (2008), adopting healthy lifestyle changes have the potential to "expand the Blue Zones." Remarkable results are emerging from communities of health-conscientious Americans who have pledged to create healthier environments. For example, leaders in Albert Lea, Minnesota, teamed up with the Blue Zones Project (www.bluezonesproject.com) in 2009 to transform the city's troubled health by applying principles from Blue Zone areas such as Okinawa. As a result of community design improvements that included healthy initiatives for workplace, food, and tobacco cessation, Albert Lea has reported that participants' lifespan increased by a projected 2.9 years. Within its first year, Albert Lea moved up to 23 places in the Minnesota County Health Rankings, all while saving $7.5 million in annual health care costs for employers due to a decline in smokers.[46]

In Okinawa, current research efforts are aimed at improving dietary habits in younger generations in primary school. The famous Chample Study, begun in 2005 originally to study the functionality of Okinawa vegetables, has since evolved to educating children and families about balanced nutrition. Early results show that higher nutrition knowledge in children and guardians is associated with higher vegetable intake (Asakura, Todoriki, and Sasaki 2017). To turn the tide on the concerning and rapid rise in obesity in Okinawa and around the world, focusing efforts to establish wholesome dietary habits at a young age is promising and has been shown to continue into adulthood (Mikkilä et al. 2005).

Healthy aging is achievable, and Okinawa provides ample evidence (and lessons) for exceptional longevity. Whether future generations of elderly continue the trend toward reduced disability and an extended health expectancy may well depend upon the lifestyle choices that individuals make in midlife or earlier. These gains will be coupled with the investments in preventive medicine, public health infrastructure, and long-term care that societies make in the coming decades in order to determine the longevity of generations to come.

Notes

1. According to the 2015 Japan Census, there were an estimated 146 super-centenarians among 61,743 centenarians. Thus, the odds of reaching supercentenarian status was about two in a thousand centenarians (Statistics Bureau of Japan 2016). These odds are calculated from census data, as the Japan Ministry of Health, Labour and Welfare no longer reports the number of supercentenarians in its annual centenarian report.

2. The estimates of the Population Division of the United Nations (UNDP) are assembled from model life table data. It should be noted, however, that since few countries are able to provide high-quality, quantitative, longitudinal data about its oldest old population, it is difficult to assess the accuracy of forecasted numbers (Robine and Cubaynes 2017).

3. In actuality, this number is likely lower than 81,896, as this number is estimated from census data, which routinely overestimate centenarian prevalence (Krach and Velkoff 1999; Humes and Velkoff 2007). While data quality remains an issue, there is evidence of improved centenarian age data in the 2010 census (U.S. Census Bureau 2012). For a more accurate centenarian count, a prevalence study is necessary. See Perls et al. (1999) for a prevalence study of centenarians in the New England area.

4. Globally, the forecasted pace of growth of centenarians is expected to slow down based on 10-year increase ratios (United Nations 2017). Given the observations that quality of life declines after age 100 and no increase in maximum human lifespan has been observed in recent times, some researchers argue that this scenario may reflect a natural "limit" of human longevity (Dong, Milholland, and Vijg 2016).

5. A particular challenge in these investigations is that there is no universally accepted definition of biological (or social) aging, or easily quantifiable methods for measuring it (Gems and Partridge 2013; Martin et al. 2015). Biological aging may perhaps be best defined as "the accumulation of damage to the body's building blocks of life (DNA)." This damage is in contrast to age-related disease such as cardiovascular disease, cancer, or Alzheimer's disease. Until recently, most aging research had been directed towards "curing" age-associated disease rather than dealing with the aging process itself, which is a much more daunting endeavor (Hayflick 2000). Recent work has sought to understand the biology of aging and has identified a range of interventions and pathways that control aging rate. The emerging signaling network underlying the aging process appears to be sensitive to nutritional status and controls growth, stress resistance, and senescence. Yet the underlying biological processes with which these pathways act to control life span remain unclear. Furthermore, conflicting evidence has led researchers to question long-held assumptions about aging such as the oxidative damage theory, which postulates that aging is caused by "wear and tear" damage, particularly at the molecular level from reactive oxygen species (ROS). As fundamental aging assumptions are reexamined, new theories and

concepts are emerging (Gems and Partridge 2013). One theory that has gained wide currency is "inflamm-aging," first articulated by Franceschi et al. (2000a), which holds that a low-grade chronic proinflammatory status is a main feature of the aging process. Many age-associated diseases are associated with inflammation; recent findings suggest that inflammation is an important malleable driver of aging and, as a biomarker, predicts mortality at extreme old age in Japanese centenarians (Franceschi and Campisi 2014; Arai et al. 2015).

6. The Guinness Book of World Records stated: "No single subject is more obscured by vanity, deceit, falsehood, and deliberate fraud than the extremes of human longevity" (Guinness World Records 2005). Case in point, in the 1980s, the age of 114 years was the maximum age at death that had obtained a modicum of credibility by Guinness standards. In subsequent years, the first three people to be acknowledged by Guinness as having reached age 114 have all had their claims disputed.

7. One of the earliest recorded myths of exceptional longevity came from the Chinese who so believed in immortality that they invested significant financial resources searching for it. In the 2nd century BCE, the first Chinese emperor Ch'in sent out a mission of some 2,000 individuals in search of the mythical "Eastern Sea Islands" where it was thought the "immortals" dwelled.

8. Church or baptismal records were the most valued documents for confirming actual ages, but unfortunately, most churches in the region were destroyed in the early days of the Soviet Union.

9. In addition, other factors such as illiteracy within a population, differing calendar systems, lack of emphasis on dates of birth or age, or not having a longstanding age registration system can all contribute to age exaggeration (Willcox et al. 2008a). In hindsight it should come as no surprise that claims of exceptional longevity from societies with low average life expectancy that also lack longstanding age registration systems will be less credible than claims from areas where average life expectancy is long and a good birth registration system exists. An important example of why validation of age is critical to the study of EL comes from the United States, where record keeping is generally good for most aspects of public health. Despite generally high-quality demographic data, the U.S. Social Security Administration possesses public death records for more than a hundred citizens that list age at death between 160 and 190 years, none of them thoroughly validated (Alter 1990; Hill and Rosenwaike 2001). Distinguishing genuine supercentenarians from alleged supercentenarians requires thorough documentation of life events and rigorous proof of birth and is a painstaking process. It has only been within the past century or so that most countries have had age registration systems for their citizens, and in many nations around the world they still lack good data, particularly for older citizens (Kannisto 1994; Robine and Cubaynes 2017).

10. The accuracy of the reported centenarian rate in Okinawa has been debated regarding possible age misreporting by U.S. staff during the reconstruction of the *koseki* following the widespread destruction during World War II

(Poulain 2011; Le Bourg 2012). While the specific details of reconstruction are limited, historical records indicate that U.S. staff were not directly involved in the age validation process, but were instead recipients of the data collected at the municipal level by local authorities (Kugai 1970; Robine et al. 2013). Although sensationalized media interpretations of the so-called missing centenarian raise questions regarding the accuracy of centenarian reports in Japan, these rare, isolated cases account for less than 0.5% on official centenarian counts (Saito, Yong, and Robine 2012). Furthermore, rigorous validation has revealed no systematic age exaggeration in Okinawa (Willcox et al. 2008a; Poulain 2011).

11. In terms of measuring autonomy of centenarians elsewhere, Andersen-Ranberg, Schroll, and Jeune (2001) defined autonomy as living at home, being relatively ADL-independent, and cognitively intact, and found 12 percent of Danish centenarians to be autonomous.

12. It was found that 24 percent of male subjects and 43 percent of female subjects fit the survivor profile; 44 percent of male and 42 percent of female subjects fit the delayer profile; and 32 percent of male and 15 percent of female centenarians belonged to the escaper profile.

13. It is becoming clearer that centenarians who are able to delay or escape morbidity and maintain functional independence at age 100 years are highly likely to reach the age of 105 years (semi-supercentenarians) or even age 110 years (supercentenarian). This has led some to suggest that semi-supercentarians who have achieved EL in relatively good health provide an ideal model for the study of human longevity (Arai et al. 2017).

14. Interestingly, many studies indicate that an association between genetic variants and longevity are more present in males and not females; however, underlying reasons for this striking gender difference are unclear (Franceschi et al. 2000b; Bonafè et al. 2001; Bao et al. 2014).

15. We are at a unique point in gerontology. Several cohorts that were originally recruited for the study of limited diseases, such as cardiovascular diseases or cancer, have now been followed for several decades. Some of these very old cohorts now have National Institute on Aging (NIA)–funded studies of aging and longevity, such as the Framingham Study and Honolulu Heart Program (HHP), both funded by the National Heart, Lung, and Blood Institute for many years. Additionally, a few rare cohorts that were originally created to study aging, such as the Baltimore Longitudinal Study of Aging, are still in existence. These studies are among a select few that have decades of prospectively collected data and contain a significant number of nonagenarians and centenarians (Willcox, Willcox, and Ferrucci 2008b).

16. In growing recognition of the need for a global effort, leading researchers are beginning to call for the formation of a Worldwide Centenarian Consortium (WWC100+) to better unite efforts to address the complexity of aging (Franceschi et al. 2017).

17. In 1950, the probability of death for children under five years of age in Japan was over 80 per 1,000 live births and was very high compared to other developed countries. By 1965, this mortality rate had decreased to about 20 per

1,000 live births. During this time, life expectancy at birth increased by 10.1 years in males and 11.9 years in females (Ikeda et al. 2011).

18. All studies using death certificate data are dependent on the quality of those data. The results of the above analysis thus depend upon the uniform reporting of the causes of death and coding of death certificates in different countries. Secular changes in diagnostic, reporting, and coding practices could influence some of the trends reported above. Quality of information depends in turn upon the extent to which the person had been examined prior to death, the physicians' knowledge of the disease history of the deceased, and whether an autopsy was performed. Hasuo et al. (1989) maintain that differences in cerebro-vascular mortality between Japan and the United States have been confirmed by many specialized studies in which no marked differences in accuracy of diagnosis with regards to stroke were found.

19. By contrast, the high level of income disparity in the United States results in differential (better) care for the wealthy and leaves the less fortunate with limited, if any, access to medical care (Weinick, Byron, and Bierman 2005). These discrepancies in the United States are thought to be contributing to the significant differences in life expectancy by ethnicity (Banks et al. 2006). For example, a white male born in 2003 has an average life expectancy of about 75 years, compared with 69 years for a black male born in the same year (U.S. Census 2007). In recent years, this gap has slightly narrowed, and a white male born in 2015 has an average life expectancy of 76.6 years, compared with 72.2 years for a black male born in the same year (Centers for Disease Control and Prevention 2017b). However, differences continue to persist.

20. Once derisively known as a "poor farmer food," sweet potatoes now are highly recommended for their health-enhancing properties with endorsements from the American Cancer Society, the American Heart Association, and the Center for Science in the Public Interest (CSPI), among others. In fact, the CSPI has ranked the sweet potato as the "healthiest all vegetables," mainly for its content of dietary fiber, naturally occurring sugars, protein content, vitamins A and C, potassium, iron, and calcium as well as its low amounts of fat (especially saturated fat), sodium, and cholesterol. Interestingly, what the typical American diet lacks in nutrients (particularly potassium, magnesium, vitamin C, and carotenoids) and fiber seems to be what the sweet potato contains in abundance (Willcox et al. 2009; Shao et al. 2017). Furthermore, Okinawan sweet potatoes, like many other commonly consumed items in the Okinawan diet, have several interesting nutritional characteristics that may have antiaging effects by reducing oxidative stress and inflammation. For example, sporamin is the main protein of the sweet potato and demonstrates strong free-radical inhibitory and scavenging activity (Senthilkumar and Yeh 2013). The sweet potato also has significant anti-inflammatory properties from multiple phytonutrients that include phenolic acids, flavonols, anthocyanins, and carotenoids (Willcox and Willcox 2014).

21. A recent dietary survey of Okinawan centenarians revealed the most frequently consumed food was white rice. However, there was a striking abundance

and variety of low-caloric density vegetables and legumes (including soy-products or tofu), indicative of traditional dietary habits (unpublished data).

22. Ten characteristics of the traditional Okinawa diet:

1. low-caloric intake
2. high-vegetable consumption (particularly yellow root and green leafy vegetables and seaweeds)
3. high consumption of legumes (mostly soybean)
4. moderate consumption of seafood (more in coastal areas)
5. low consumption of meat (mostly lean pork)
6. little to no dairy products
7. low-fat intake (high mono- and polyunsaturated/saturated fat ratio)
8. low glycemic load
9. high fiber intake
10. moderate alcohol consumption (Willcox et al. 2009)

23. Overall, the important shared features of these healthy dietary patterns include high intake of unrefined carbohydrates, moderate protein intake with emphasis on vegetables and legumes, fish and lean meats as sources, and a healthy fat profile (higher in mono/polyunsaturated fats, lower in saturated fat, rich in omega-3 fatty acids). Additionally, the lower caloric density and higher amounts of fiber from such plant-based diets result in lower caloric intake, a lower glycemic load, and a higher intake of phytonutrients. Combined, these factors are important for minimizing risk for age-associated disease (cardiovascular disease in particular) and maximizing conditions for healthy aging and longevity (Suzuki, Willcox, and Willcox 2001; Fung et al. 2008; Appel 2008; Sofi et al. 2010).

24. This includes less oxidative damage, increased DNA repair, increased resistance to stress, improved cholesterol profile, and increased insulin sensitivity.

25. The process by which CR works is not yet fully known, but may be linked to nutrient-sensing biological pathways, which modulate growth and biological systems responsible for stress resistance and, ultimately, aging. A growing consensus favors the hypothesis that this low nutrient intake induces a low-level stress called "hormesis" that triggers the upregulation of stress-resistance biological pathways, which include genes encoding for *FOXO3* and mammalian or mechanistic target of rapamycin (*mTOR*) (Gems and Partridge 2013; Willcox and Willcox 2014). Yet the question of whether caloric restriction can delay incident age-associated diseases and extend the human life span is still debated; the growing evidence is encouraging. While the benefits of CR in nonhuman primates have been debated, studies seem to suggest benefits consistent with model organism data (Mattison et al. 2017). Human studies, by nature, have been limited and mainly short term. Nonetheless short- and longer-term (3 to 15 years) studies have also demonstrated adaptations consistent with model organism data, that is, lower risk for cardiovascular disease and cancer, and biomarker

changes suggestive of slower aging (Willcox et al. 2004, 2006c; Weiss and Fontana 2011; Anderson and Weindruch 2012; Redman et al. 2018). Moreover, the benefits from current caloric restriction intervention trials seem to corroborate the findings from OCS.

26. Commonly consumed items that play dual roles as both traditional medicines and foods include sweet potatoes (pulp, skin, and leaves), bitter melon, multiple green leafy vegetables, ginger, turmeric, mugwort (*Artemisia vulgaris*), peppers (*Piper hancei*), and carotenoid-rich marine foods (such as seaweeds), among others (Willcox et al. 2014). Many of these foods have antiaging properties by reducing oxidative stress and inflammation, two key factors that underlie the development of most age-related diseases.

Why does Okinawa appear to have so many food items with medicinal properties? Climate may offer a scientific basis for this phenomenon. Compounds that have potential CR-mimetic properties, such as carotenoids, flavonoids, and other phytochemicals, are synthesized by plants to help scavenge free radicals formed due to stress from extremes of heat, insects, UV light, or other threats that are common to subtropical Okinawa. Interestingly, when typical food items were compared between Okinawa and mainland Japan, it was found that Okinawan foods have, on average, stronger free radical scavenging properties (Murakami et al. 2005; Willcox and Willcox 2014). Clinical laboratory studies on the Okinawan centenarians have found healthier blood chemistry and hematology, younger hormonal patterns, and lower oxidative stress (Suzuki et al. 2010).

27. Interestingly, studies on laboratory animals have found that the optimum protein-to-carbohydrate ratio is consistently about 1:10 or less, with about 10 percent or a little less of total calories coming from protein. Remarkably, this is almost identical to the ratio in the traditional Okinawan diet (i.e., 9 percent protein and 85 percent carbohydrates) (Le Couteur et al. 2016). In fact, this reduced stroke mortality accounts for much of the difference in life expectancy between Okinawa and mainland Japan, with most of the remaining difference due to lower rates of heart disease and certain cancers, particularly hormone-dependent cancers, such as breast and prostate cancer, as well as stomach cancer (Willcox, Willcox, and Suzuki 2001). These diseases have strong connections to diet and lifestyle (Willcox et al. 2007a, 2007b).

28. Akita is located in the northern region of Honshu where fresh vegetables were very limited in the cold winters. Whereas fresh vegetables were available year-round in Okinawa, mainland Japanese ate mostly pickled vegetables in winter, contributing to a very high intake of sodium and a related high incidence of cardiovascular diseases (particularly stroke) and stomach cancer (Nagata et al. 2004; Tsugane and Sasazuki 2007). Additionally, hypertensive effects of high sodium consumption were partly attenuated in Okinawa through consumption of vegetables containing antihypertensive minerals such as potassium, magnesium, and calcium, as well as profuse sweating in a hot and humid subtropical climate (Willcox et al. 2009). Among all the prefectures, Okinawans continue to

have low or the lowest sodium consumption (9.1 g/d male; 8.0 g/d female) (Japan Ministry of Health, Labour and Welfare 2017c). However, this trend is inconsistent across age groups such that younger Okinawans have higher than national average sodium consumption while older Okinawans still have lower than national average sodium consumption. This further reflects changing dietary habits that greatly affects younger generations (Okinawa Prefecture 2013).

29. The protective mechanisms are not entirely clear, but lower oxidative stress, reduced insulin signaling, and stimulation of protective nutrient-sensing pathways are among the common findings (Willcox et al. 2007a; Davinelli, Willcox, and Scapagnini 2012). While its health effects are still debated, the Okinawan elders have a naturally nutrient-rich calorically poor diet, which is thought to be a major contributing factor to their longevity and good health. (Willcox et al. 2014). Although historical data on nutritional intake, recent nutritional surveys, and biochemical testing data support caloric restriction as a nutritional factor that influenced healthy aging and longevity in Okinawa, there is still ongoing debate in the scientific community with regard to both the CR phenomenon and its purported health effects in Okinawans and other humans (Le Bourg 2012; Gavrilova and Gavrilov 2012; Robine et al. 2013). One argument is that restricted caloric consumption in prior generations has caused an epigenetic response and led to the disappearance of health advantages in younger Okinawans (Le Bourg 2012, 2013). However, lifestyle risk behaviors and changes that have resulted in higher caloric intake, less physical activity, and an overall positive shift in energy balance (which has led to among the highest obesity rates in Japan) suggest the loss of the life expectancy advantage in younger Okinawans compared to their mainland Japanese counterparts is due to elevated risk factor profiles (Willcox et al. 2012; Gavrilova and Gavrilov 2012; Robine et al. 2013). Some researchers have argued that the Okinawans achieved a long life expectancy for genetic (or other) reasons, but the rapid disappearance of the CR phenotype, as well as the longevity disadvantage in younger Okinawans who did not experience CR, suggests otherwise (Willcox and Willcox 2014). Population-wide CR was over by the 1960s, and generations thereafter have had a higher BMI across all age strata, as well as more metabolic syndrome and worse cardiovascular risk factors than other Japanese. The life expectancy advantage for Okinawans, which used to be the highest in Japan for all ages, is now seen only in older ages, consistent with a residual CR-related cohort effect in older Okinawans (Willcox et al. 2007a; Willcox, Willcox, and Suzuki 2017)

30. The ADL scale rates a subject's ability to perform basic daily tasks such as dressing, toileting, and range of movement, among others.

31. A similar study comparing the range of mobility of Okinawan elders to elderly in rural and urban Alabama showed that Okinawan elderly had significantly better walking speed and greater range of mobility than age-matched Alabamians (Schell et al. 2005).

32. The other important major phytoestrogens are lignans, which are derived from flax and other grains. All plants, especially legumes (beans, peas), onions,

and broccoli, contain these natural estrogens, but not nearly in the same quantity as soy and flax.

33. The China Study provides an interesting hypothesis for soy and reduced menopause symptoms (Campbell and Campbell 2016). The China Study says soy protein doesn't raise estrogen levels in females as much as it does from animal protein–based diets (i.e., Western). Thus, when women reach menopause, the "estrogen crash" in women on plant-based diets is much less severe than that of animal protein–based diets, and that it is this crash that is responsible for much of the menopause symptoms.

34. It is noteworthy that although women outlive men in all postindustrial countries with an average 6 more years of life expectancy, the gap in Okinawa is particularly great at 7.17 years in 2000 (compared with Japan's 6.23 years). In addition, Okinawa has a high ratio of female centenarians to male centenarians in Japan with 7.74 women for each man (Japan Ministry of Health, Labour and Welfare 2017a). The reason for this huge gap is that men have double the mortality rate from cancer/heart disease, stroke, and pneumonia and about four times the mortality from suicide and accidents. Aside from possible biological factors for this difference, women in Okinawa also have a much lower rate of risk-taking behaviors such as smoking, alcohol consumption, accidents, and suicide (Willcox et al. 2012).

35. The Honolulu Heart Program (formally the Honolulu branch of the Ni-Hon-San study), has become one of the longest running prospective studies with over 40 years of consistent follow-up on the same cohort of Japanese American men. Although it began as a study on cardiovascular disease in 1965, the focus has gradually shifted towards aging, as members of the cohort are now in their eighties, nineties, or over a hundred (see Honolulu Asia Aging Study, Hawaii Lifespan Study, and Hawaii Healthspan Study at https://www.kuakini.org/wps /portal/kuakini-research/research-home/kuakini-research-programs/kuakini -honolulu-asia-aging-study). The study has been collecting data on genetics, blood biochemistry, medical history, diet, smoking, alcohol consumption, BMI, socio-demographic and psychological factors, among other characteristics, and has been the source for many scientific breakthroughs, including the effects of genes and lifestyle on longevity, and various diseases (Willcox et al. 2004; 2008d; 2013; Bell et al. 2014).

36. This is not surprising when one considers that more than two in three Americans are overweight with more than one in three being obese, and far too many people still smoke while far too few exercise regularly.

37. A pilot genome-wide association study (GWAS) investigated characteristics of the Okinawan genome. When compared to other ethnic populations in human genetic databases, analysis showed that Okinawans cluster strongly with East Asians with little outside mixture (Bendjilali et al. 2014). These data support the hypothesis that Okinawans, while related to Japanese and Chinese, are also genetically distinct.

38. The original pedigree study was followed by the first study of candidate human longevity genes and found that Okinawans in their nineties and centenarians

had higher prevalence of anti-inflammatory type-2 human leukocyte antigen (HLA) alleles and a lower prevalence of pro-inflammatory alleles (Takata et al. 1987). Several of these findings have been replicated in other populations, and inflammation has since become a major focus of studies in cardiovascular disease, cancer, and other age-related diseases (Franceschi and Campisi 2014). The aforementioned studies do not address whether Okinawans have population-wide genetic advantages; rather, they suggest that human longevity is influenced by particular genes.

39. Where the line is drawn may depend on which age group one is examining, as the power of genes seems to become more apparent at advanced ages. Ljungquist et al. (1998) provided empirical support for this hypothesis when they found a larger effect from genetics in a sample population of long-lived twins than compared with a sample of twins who only lived to an average life expectancy. Other scientists, using multiple methods, have argued that the contribution from genetics for predicting very long life is closer to one half (Perls, Kunkel, and Puca 2002).

40. Especially as of late, national health expenditure is an urgent problem that increasingly concerns more and more Americans as baby boomers reach Medicare eligibility. Medicare spending alone is projected to nearly double as a share of gross domestic product (GDP), from 3.1 percent in 2017 to 6.1 percent in 2047, and account for more than three-quarters of the increase in spending for major health care programs over the next 30 years (U.S. Congressional Budget Office 2017).

41. In contrast, addressing heart disease and cancer separately would yield diminishing improvements in health and longevity by 2060—primarily due to competing risk factors such as high blood pressure. The hypothetical "delayed aging" scenario could increase life expectancy by an additional 2.2 years (Goldman et al. 2013).

42. Measurements of disability-free or disability-adjusted life expectancy are still in their infancy and differ between countries. One commonly used scale from the Japan Ministry of Health, Labour and Welfare calculates disability-free life expectancy through calculating the term that one remains "self-reliant," that is, without the need for long-term nursing care (*kaigo*). The need for care or support in activities for daily living such as bathing, going to the toilet, dressing, standing, etc. is assessed at five levels ranging from a low level of care (level 1) to a completely bed-ridden condition (level 5).

43. Men in particular have been experiencing slower increases in life expectancy (LE) at birth. In 2000, this led to what is called the "26 shock" in Okinawa reflecting the fact that Okinawan men dropped from among the top 5 long-lived prefectures within Japan to 26th place among 47 prefectures for LE. In addition to slow LE (at birth) growth rates, Okinawa is further struggling to improve its HALE (at birth). For Okinawan women, the gap between average HALE and LE was 12.16 years in 2016 (Japan Ministry of Health, Labour and Welfare 2018). This gap is comparable to the 12-year discrepancy for women in Bahrain, which has the largest HALE and LE gap among all WHO countries (World Health Organization 2018).

44. Okinawa no longer has the highest centenarian prevalence in Japan. In 2017, Okinawa was ranked 10th of 47 prefectures and had a centenarian prevalence of 80.75 per 100,000 persons. However, it has been noted that centenarian prevalence is sensitive to migration and changes in fertility, which will artificially alter the proportion of elders (Poulain et al. 2013). A combination of these factors has likely contributed to Okinawa's lower relative rank for centenarian prevalence. Current rural prefectures with high centenarian prevalence, such as Shimane, may be artificially inflated due to low birth rates and migration. In contrast, Okinawans continue to have the highest birth rates nationwide.

45. For Okinawan men, the life expectancy rank relative to other prefectures climbs with each older generation, such that by age 75 years they are second place in Japanese life tables with 12.62 remaining years of life expectancy versus 12.06 for the all-Japan male average—over half a year advantage. Similarly, the life expectancy advantage seen in Okinawan women tends to increase by generation too. They lead the female life tables from age 65 years onward. By age 75 years, Okinawan women have 16.51 remaining years of life expectancy versus 15.68 for the all-Japan female average—an impressive almost one year advantage (Japan Ministry of Health, Labour and Welfare 2017b).

46. For more information on Blue Zones Projects, visit www.bluezones project.com to view other designated cities in the United States and the extraordinary health benefits emerging in each community.

Bibliography

Alter, G. 1990. "Old Age Mortality and Age Misreporting in the United States 1900–1940." Working paper number 24. Population Institute for Research and Training, Indiana University, Indiana.

Andersen, S., P. Sebastiani, D. Dworkis, L. Feldman, and T. Perls. 2012. "Health Span Approximates Life Span among Many Supercentenarians: Compression of Morbidity at the Approximate Limit of Life Span." *Journals of Gerontology. Series A, Biological Sciences and Medical Sciences* 67A(4): 395–405.

Andersen-Ranberg, K., M. Schroll, and B. Jeune. 2001. "Healthy Centenarians Do Not Exist, but Autonomous Centenarians Do: A Population-Based Study of Morbidity among Danish Centenarians." *Journal of American Geriatric Society* 49(7): 900–908.

Anderson, R., and R. Weindruch. 2012. "The Caloric Restriction Paradigm: Implications for Healthy Human Aging." *American Journal of Human Biology* 24(2): 101–6.

Appel, L. 2008. "Dietary Patterns and Longevity: Expanding the Blue Zones." *Circulation* 118(3): 214.

Arai, Y., C. Martin-Ruiz, M. Takayama, Y. Abe, T. Takebayashi, S. Koyasu, M. Suematsu, N. Hirose, and T. von Zglinicki. 2015. "Inflammation, But Not Telomere Length, Predicts Successful Ageing at Extreme Old Age:

A Longitudinal Study of Semi-supercentenarians." *EBioMedicine* 2(10): 1549–58.

Arai, Y., T. Sasaki, and N. Hirose. 2017. "Demographic, Phenotypic, and Genetic Characteristics of centenarians in Okinawa and Honshu, Japan: Part 2 Honshu, Japan." *Mechanisms of Ageing and Development* 165: 80–85.

Asakura, K., H. Todoriki, and S. Sasaki. 2017. "Relationship between Nutrition Knowledge and Dietary Intake among Primary School Children in Japan: Combined Effect of Children's and Their Guardians' Knowledge." *Journal of Epidemiology* 27(10): 483–91.

Ballard, F., I. Beluche, I. Romieu, D. Willcox, and J. Robine. 2011. "Are Men Aging as Oaks and Women as Reeds? A Behavioral Hypothesis to Explain the Gender Paradox of French Centenarians." *Journal of Aging Research* 2011: 371039.

Banks, J., M. Marmot, Z. Oldfield, and J. Smith. 2006. "Disease and Disadvantage in the United States and in England." *Journal of the American Medical Association* 295(17): 2037–45.

Bao, J., X. Song, Y. Hong, H. Zhu, C. Li, T. Zhang, W. Chen, S. Zhao, and Q. Chen. 2014. "Association between FOXO3A Gene Polymorphisms and Human Longevity: A Meta-analysis." *Asian Journal of Andrology* 16(3): 446–52.

Barzilai, N., G. Atzmon, C. Schecher, E. Schaefer, A. Cupples, R. Lipton, S. Cheng, and A. Shuldiner. 2003. "Unique Lipoprotein Phenotype and Genotype Associated with Exceptional Longevity." *Journal of the American Medical Association* 290(15): 2030–40.

Bell, C., R. Chen, K. Masaki, P. Yee, Q. He, J. Grove, T. Donlon, J. Curb, D. Willcox, L. Poon, and B. Willcox. 2014. "Late-Life Factors Associated with Healthy Aging in Older Men." *Journals of Gerontology. Series A, Biological Sciences and Medical Sciences* 62(5): 880–88.

Bendjilali, N., W. Hsueh, Q. He, D. Willcox, C. Nievergelt, T. Donlon, P. Kwok, M. Suzuki, and B. Willcox. 2014. "Who Are the Okinawans? Ancestry, Genome Diversity, and Implications for the Genetic Study of Human Longevity from a Geographically Isolated Population." *Journals of Gerontology. Series A, Biological Sciences and Medical Sciences* 69(12): 1474–84.

Bennett, N., and L. Garson. 1983. "The Centenarian Question and Old-Age Mortality in the Soviet Union, 1959–1970." *Demography* 20(4): 587–606.

Beregi, E. 1990. "Centenarians in Hungary. A Social and Demographic Study." *Interdisciplinary Topics in Gerontology* 27: 331–39.

Bonafè, M., F. Olivieri, L. Cavallone, S. Giovagnetti, F. Mayegiani, M. Cardelli, C. Pieri, M. Marra, R. Antonicelli, R. Lisa, M. Rizzo, G. Paolisso, D. Monti, and C. Franceschi. 2001. "A Gender-Dependent Genetic Predisposition to Produce High Levels of IL-6 Is Detrimental for Longevity." *European Journal of Immunology* 31(8): 2357–61.

Buettner, D. 2012. *The Blue Zones: 9 Lessons for Living Longer from the People Who've Lived the Longest*, 2nd ed. Washington, DC: National Geographic Books.

Buettner, D. 2017. *The Blue Zones of Happiness: Lessons from the World's Happiest People.* Washington, DC: National Geographic Books.

Campbell, T. C., and T. M. Campbell. 2016. *The China Study*, ref. and expanded ed. Dallas, TX: BenBela.

Centers for Disease Control and Prevention. 2009. *The Power of Prevention: Chronic Disease, the Public Health Challenge of the 21st Century.* National Center for Chronic Disease Prevention and Health Promotion, Department of Health and Human Services.

Centers for Disease Control and Prevention. 2017a. "Compressed Mortality File 1999–2016 on CDC WONDER Online Database." National Center for Health Statistics. Data are from the Compressed Mortality File 1999–2016 Series 20 No. 2U, 2016, as compiled from data provided by the 57 vital statistics jurisdictions through the Vital Statistics Cooperative Program.

Centers for Disease Control and Prevention. 2017b. "Health, United States, 2016: With Chartbook on Long-term Trends in Health." National Center for Health Statistics, Department of Health and Human Services. Hyattsville: MD.

Davinelli, S., D. Willcox, and G. Scapagnini. 2012. "Extending Healthy Ageing: Nutrient Sensitive Pathway and Centenarian Population." *Immunity & Ageing* 9: 9.

Dong, X., B. Milholland, and J. Vijg. 2016. "Evidence for a Limit to Human Lifespan." *Nature* 538(7624): 257–59.

Evert, J., E. Lawler, H. Bogan, and T. Perls. 2003. "Morbidity Profiles of Centenarians: Survivors, Delayers, and Escapers." *Journals of Gerontology. Series A, Biological Sciences and Medical Sciences* 58(3): 232–37.

Fontana, L., L. Partridge, and V. Longo. 2010. "Extending Healthy Life Span— From Yeast to Humans." *Science* 328(5976): 321–26.

Franceschi, C., M. Bonafè, S. Valensin, F. Olivieri, M. De Luca, E. Ottaviani, and G. De Benedictis. 2000a. "Inflamm-aging. An Evolutionary Perspective on Immunosenescence." *Annals of the New York Academy of Sciences* 98: 244–54.

Franceschi, C., and J. Campisi. 2014. "Chronic Inflammation (Inflammaging) and Its Potential Contribution to Age-Associated Diseases." *Journals of Gerontology. Series A, Biological Sciences and Medical Sciences* 69(Supplement 1): S4–S9.

Franceschi, C., L. Motta, S. Valensin, et al. 2000b. "Do Men and Women Follow Different Trajectories to Reach Extreme Longevity? Italian Multicenter Study on Centenarians (IMUSCE)." *Aging (Milano)* 12(2): 77–84.

Franceschi, C., G Passarino, D. Mari, and D. Monti. 2017. "Centenarians as a 21st Century Healthy Aging Model: A Legacy of Humanity and the Need for a World-Wide Consortium (WWC100+)." *Mechanisms of Ageing and Development* 165: 55–58.

Franklin, D. 1996. "The Healthiest Women in the World." *Health* 9: 56–64.

Fraser, G., and D. Shavlik. 2001. "Ten Years of Life: Is It a Matter of Choice?" *Archives of Internal Medicine* 161(13): 1645–52.

Fries, J. 1980. "Aging, Natural Death and the Compression of Morbidity." *New England Journal of Medicine* 303(3): 130–35.

Fukuda, Y., K. Nakamura, and T. Takano. 2005. "Municipal Health Expectancy in Japan: Decreased Healthy Longevity of Older People in Socioeconomically Disadvantaged Areas." *BMC Public Health* 5: 65.

Fung, T., S. Chiuve, M. McCullough, K. Rexrode, G. Logroscino, and F. Hu. 2008. "Adherence to a DASH-Style Diet and Risk of Coronary Heart Disease and Stroke in Women." *Archives of Internal Medicine* 168(7): 713–20.

Gavrilova, N., and L. Gavrilov. 2012. "Comments on Dietary Restriction, Okinawa Diet and Longevity." *Gerontology* 58(3): 221–23.

Gems, D., and L. Partridge. 2013. "Genetics of Longevity in Model Organisms: Debates and Paradigm Shifts." *Annual Review of Physiology* 75: 621–44.

Giuliani, C., P. Garagnani, and C. Franceschi. 2018. "Genetics of Human Longevity Within an Eco-Evolutionary Nature-Nurture Framework." *Circulation Research* 123(7): 745–72.

Goldman, D., D. Cutler, J. Rowe, P. Michaud, J. Sullivan, D. Peneva, and S. Olshansky. 2013. "Substantial Health and Economic Returns from Delayed Aging May Warrant a New Focus for Medical Research." *Health Affairs (Project Hope)* 32(10): 1698–705.

Guinness World Records. 2005. *The Guinness Book of World Records*. New York: Time, Incorporated Home Entertainment.

Hasuo, Y., K. Ueda, Y. Kiyohara, J. Wada, H. Kawano, I. Kato, T. Yanai, I. Fujii, T. Omae, and M. Fujishima. 1989. "Accuracy of Diagnosis on Death Certificates for Underlying Causes of Death in a Long-Term Autopsy-Based Population Study in Hisayama, Japan; with Special Reference to Cardiovascular Diseases." *Journal of Clinical Epidemiology* 42(6): 577–84.

Hayflick, L. 2000. "The Future of Ageing." *Nature* 408(6809): 267–69.

Hazzard, W. 1997. "Ways to Make 'Usual' and 'Successful' Aging Synonymous." *Western Journal of Medicine* 167(4): 206–15.

Helland, K. 2011. *Who Wants to Live Forever? Scientist Sees Aging Cured*. London: Reuters.

Herskind, A., M. McGue, N. Holm, T. Sørensen, B. Harvald and J. Vaupel. 1996. "The Heritability of Human Longevity: A Population-Based Study of 2872 Danish Twin Pairs Born 1870–1900. *Human Genetics* 97(3): 319–23.

Hill, M., and I. Rosenwaike. 2001. "The Social Security Administration's Death Master File: The Completeness of Death Reporting at Older Ages." *Social Security Bulletin* 64(1): 45–51.

Human Mortality Database. 2017. *Period Life Tables*. University of California, Berkeley (USA), and Max Planck Institute for Demographic Research (Germany). www.mortality.org.

Humes, K., and V. Velkoff. 2007. "Centenarians in the United States: 2000." Poster presented at the 2007 Annual Meeting of the Population Association of America. New York.

Ikeda, N., E. Saito, N. Kondo, M. Inoue, S. Ikeda, T. Satoh, K. Wada, et al. 2011. "What Has Made the Population of Japan Healthy?" *Lancet* 378: 1094–105.

Ismail, K., L. Nussbaum, P. Sebastiani, S. Andersen, T. Perls, N. Barzilai, and S. Milman. 2016. "Compression of Morbidity Is Observed Across Cohorts with Exceptional Longevity." *Journal of the American Geriatrics Society* 64(8): 1583–91.

Istituto Nazionale di Statistica (ISTAT). 2017. *Resident Population on 1 January 2015 by Age, Sex and Marital Status*. dati.istat.it.

Iwasa, H., H. Yoshida, H. Kim, Y. Yoshida, J. Kwon, M. Sugiura, T. Furuna, and T. Suzuki. 2007. "A Mortality Comparison of Participants and Non-participants in a Comprehensive Health Examination among Elderly People Living in an Urban Japanese Community." *Aging Clinical and Experimental Research* 19(3): 240–45.

Japan Ministry of Health, Labour and Welfare, Health Bureau for the Elderly. 2007. *Annual Centenarian Report*. Tokyo: Statistics and Information Department.

Japan Ministry of Health, Labour and Welfare, Health Bureau for the Elderly. 2017a. *Annual Centenarian Report*. Tokyo: Statistics and Information Division (In Japanese).

Japan Ministry of Health, Labour and Welfare. 2017b. "Overview of Age-Adjusted Death Rate by Prefecture in 2015." *Demographic Statistics Special Report*. Tokyo: Statistics and Information Division (In Japanese).

Japan Ministry of Health, Labour and Welfare. 2017c. *Results of the 2016 National Health and Nutrition Survey*. Tokyo: Statistics and Information Division (In Japanese).

Japan Ministry of Health, Labour and Welfare. 2017d. *Overview of Japan's Life Table by Prefecture in 2015*. Tokyo: Statistics and Information Division (In Japanese).

Japan Ministry of Health, Labour and Welfare. 2018. *Extension of Healthy Life Span and Reduction of Health Disparity*. 11th Health Japan 21 Promotion Special Committee Document. Tokyo: Statistics and Information Division (In Japanese).

Kagan, A., J. Popper, G. Rhoads, and K. Yano. 1985. "Dietary and Other Risk Factors for Stroke in Hawaiian Japanese Men." *Stroke* 16(3): 390–96.

Kannisto, V. 1994. "Development of Oldest-Old Mortality, 1950–1990: Evidence from 28 Developed Countries." *Monographs on Population Aging No 1*. Odense, Denmark: Odense University Press.

Kobayashi, T., S. Kikuchi, Y. Lin, K. Yagyu, Y. Obata, A. Ogihara, A. Hasegawa, et al. 2004. "Trends in the Incidence of Gastric Cancer in Japan and Their Associations with *Helicobacter pylori* Infection and Gastric Mucosal Atrophy." *Gastric Cancer* 7(4): 233–39.

Krach, C., and V. Velkoff. 1999. *Centenarians in the United States*. U.S. Bureau of the Census, Current Population Reports, Series P23-199RV. Washington, DC: U.S. Government Printing Office.

Kugai, R. 1970. "The Reconstruction of the Family Register in Okinawa." *Jurist* 457: 16–44 (In Japanese).

Leaf, A. 1982. "Long-Lived Populations: Extreme Old Age." *Journal of the American Geriatric Society* 30(8): 485–87.

Le Bourg, E. 2012. "Dietary Restriction Studies in Humans: Focusing on Obesity, Forgetting Longevity." *Gerontology* 58: 126–28.

Le Bourg, E. 2013. "About the Article 'Exploring the Impact of Climate on Human Longevity,' (*Exp. Geront.* 47, 660–671, 2012)." *Experimental Gerontology* 48(8): 839.

Le Couteur, D., S. Solon-Biet, D. Wahl, V. Cogger, B. Willcox, D. Willcox, D. Raubenheimer, and S. Simpson. 2016. "New Horizons: Dietary Protein, Ageing and the Okinawan Ratio." *Age and Ageing* 45(4): 443–47.

Ljungquist, B., S. Berg, J. Lanke, G. McClearn, and N. Pedersen. 1998. "The Effect of Genetic Factors for Longevity: A Comparison of Identical and Fraternal Twins in the Swedish Twin Registry." *Journals of Gerontology. Series A, Biological Sciences and Medical Sciences* 53(6): M441–46.

Los Angeles Gerontology Research Group. 2020. Supercentenarian Research and Database Division. www.grg.org.

Martin, P., N. Kelly, B. Kahana, E. Kahana, B. J. Willcox, D. C. Willcox, and L. W. Poon. 2015. "Defining Successful Aging: A Tangible or Elusive Concept?" *Gerontologist* 55(1): 14–25.

Matayoshi, M., and J. Trafton. 2000. *Ancestors Worship: Okinawa's Indigenous Belief System*. Toronto: University of Toronto Press.

Matsuzaki, T. 1992. "Longevity, Diet, and Nutrition in Japan: Epidemiological Studies." *Nutrition Reviews* 50(12): 355–39.

Mattison, J., R. Colman, T. Beasley, D. Allison, J. Kemnitz, G. Roth, D. Ingram, R. Weindruch, R. de Cabo, and R. Anderson. 2017. "Caloric Restriction Improves Health and Survival of Rhesus Monkeys." *Nature Communications* 8: 14063.

Mazess, R., and S. Forman. 1979. "Longevity and Age Exaggeration in Vilcabamba, Ecuador." *Journal of Gerontology* 34(1): 94–98.

McGue, M., J. Vaupel, N. Holm, and B. Harvald. 1993. "Longevity Is Moderately Heritable in a Sample of Danish Twins Born 1870–1880." *Journals of Gerontology* 48(6): R237–44.

Mikkilä, V., L. Räsänen, O. Raitakari, P. Pietinen, and J. Viikari. 2005. "Consistent Dietary Patterns Identified from Childhood to Adulthood: The Cardiovascular Risk in Young Finns Study." *British Journal of Nutrition* 93(6): 923–31.

Mokdad, A. H., K. Ballesteros, M. Echiko, S. Glenn, H. E. Olsen, E. Mullany, A. Lee, et al. 2018. "The State of US Health, 1990–2016: Burden of Diseases, Injuries, and Risk Factors among US States." *JAMA* 319(14): 1444–72.

Moriguchi, Y. 1999. "Japanese Centenarians Living Outside Japan." In *Japanese Centenarians*, edited by H. Tauchi, 185–94. Aichi: Institute for Medical Science of Aging.

Murakami, A., H. Ishida, K. Kobo, I. Furukawa, Y. Ikeda, M. Yonaha, Y. Aniya, and H. Ohigashi. 2005. "Suppressive Effects of Okinawan Food Items on Free Radical Generation from Stimulated Leukocytes and Identification of Some Active Constituents: Implications for the Prevention of Inflammation-Associated Carcinogenesis." *Asian Pacific Journal of Cancer Prevention* 6(4): 437–48.

Nagata, C., N. Takatsuka, N. Shimizu, and H. Shimizu. 2004. "Sodium Intake and Risk of Death from Stroke in Japanese Men and Women." *Stroke* 35(7): 1543–47.

Nakajoh, K., T. Satoh-Nakagawa, H. Arai, M. Yanai, M. Yamaya, and H. Sasaki. 1999. "Longevity May Decrease Medical Costs." *Journal of the American Geriatrics Society* 47(9): 1161–62.

Okinawa Prefecture Department of Health and Welfare. 1995. "Okinawa-ken ni okeru seijinbyou sibou no ekigakuchousa" [Epidemiological research on age-associated diseases in Okinawa Prefecture]. Naha, Japan: Okinawa Prefecture Department of Health and Welfare (in Japanese).

Okinawa Prefecture Department of Health and Welfare. 2013. *Outline of 2011 Prefecture Health Nutrition Survey.* Naha, Okinawa. (In Japanese).

Olshansky, S. 2013. "Reinventing Aging: An Update on the Longevity Dividend." American Society on Aging, *Aging Today*, March/April. http://www.asaging .org/blog/reinventing-aging-update-longevity-dividend.

Olshansky, S., D. Passaro, R. Hershow, J. Layden, B. Carnes, J. Brody, L. Hayflick, R. Butler, D. Allison, and D. Ludwig. 2005. "A Potential Decline in Life Expectancy in the United States in the 21st Century." *New England Journal of Medicine* 352(11): 1138–45.

Olshansky, S., D. Perry, R. Miller, and R. Butler. 2007. "Pursuing the Longevity Dividend: Scientific Goals for an Aging World." *Annals of the New York Academy of Sciences* 1114: 11–13.

Perls, T., K. Bochen, M. Freeman, L. Alpert, and M. Silver. 1999. "Validity of Reported Age and Centenarian Prevalence in New England." *Age and Ageing* 28(2): 193–97.

Perls, T., L. Kunkel, and A. Puca. 2002. "The Genetics of Exceptional Human Longevity." *Journal of the American Geriatric Society* 50: 359–68.

Perls, T., and D. Terry. 2007. "Exceptional Longevity." In *Global Health and Global Aging*, edited by M. Robinson, W. Novelli, C. Pearson, and L. Norris. San Francisco: Jossey-Bass.

Pes, G., F. Tolu, M. Poulain, A. Errigo, S. Masala, A. Pietrobelli, N. Battistini, and M. Maioli. 2013. "Lifestyle and Nutrition Related to Male Longevity in Sardinia: An Ecological Study." *Nutrition, Metabolism and Cardiovascular Diseases* 23(3): 212–19.

Pili, R., and D. Petretto. 2017. "Genetics, Lifestyles, Environment and Longevity: A Look in a Complex Phenomenon." *Gerontology and Geriatric Medicine* 2(1): 555576.

Poulain, M. 2011. "Exceptional Longevity in Okinawa: A Plea for In-Depth Validation." *Demographic Research* 25: 245–84.

Poulain, M., A. Herm, and G. Pes. 2013. "The Blue Zones: Areas of Exceptional Longevity around the World." *Vienna Yearbook of Population Research* 11: 87–108.

Poulain, M., G. Pes, C. Grasland, C. Carru, L. Ferrucci, G. Baggio, C. Franceschi, and L. Deiana. 2004. "Identification of a Geographic Area Characterized by Extreme Longevity in the Sardinia Island: The AKEA Study." *Experimental Gerontology* 39(9): 1423–29.

Pritchard, C., and D. Baldwin. 2002. "Elderly Suicide Rates in Asian and English-Speaking Countries." *Acta Psychiatrica Scandinavica* 105(4): 271–75.

Rattan, S. 2012. "Rationale and Methods of Discovering Hormetins as Drugs for Healthy Ageing." *Expert Opinion on Drug Discovery* 7(5): 439–48.

Redman, L., S. Smith, J. Burton, C. Martin, D. Il'yasova, and E. Ravussin. 2018. "Metabolic Slowing and Reduced Oxidative Damage with Sustained Caloric Restriction Support the Rate of Living and Oxidative Damage Theories of Aging." *Cell Metabolism* 27(4): 805–14.e4.

Robine, J., and M. Allard. 1999. "Jeanne Calment: Validation of the Duration of her Life." In *Validation of Exceptional Longevity*, edited by B. Jeune, 145–72. Odense: Odense University Press.

Robine, J., S. Cheung, Y. Saito, B. Jeune, M. Parker, and F. Herrmann. 2010. "Centenarians Today: New Insights on Selection from the 5-COOP Study." *Current Gerontology and Geriatrics Research* 2010: 120345.

Robine, J., and S. Cubaynes. 2017. "Worldwide Demography of Centenarians." *Mechanisms of Ageing and Development* 165: 59–67.

Robine, J., F. Herrmann, Y. Arai, D. Willcox, Y. Gondo, N. Hirose, M. Suzuki, and Y. Saito. 2013. "Accuracy of the Centenarian Numbers in Okinawa and the Role of the Okinawan Diet on Longevity: Responses to Le Bourg about the Article 'Exploring the Impact of Climate on Human Longevity.'" *Experimental Gerontology* 48(8): 840–42.

Saito, Y., V. Yong, and J. Robine. 2012. "The Mystery of Japan's Missing Centenarians Explained." *Demographic Research* 26: 239–52.

Sanabe, E., I. Ashitomi, and M. Suzuki. 1977. "Social and Medical Survey of Centenarians." *Okinawa Journal of Public Health* 9: 98–106.

Schell, J., P. Sawyer, B. Willcox, D. Willcox, E. Bodner, and R. Allman. 2005. "Multi-ethnic Comparisons of Life-Space Mobility." *Gerontologist*, Special issue II, 447–48.

Senthilkumar, R., and K. W. Yeh. 2013. "Multiple Biological Functions of Sporamin Related to Stress Tolerance in Sweet Potato (*Ipomoea batatas Lam*)." *Biotechnology Advances* 30(6): 1309–17.

Shao, A., A. Drewnowski, D. Willcox, L. Krämer, C. Lausted, M. Eggersdorfer, J. Mathers, J. Bell, R. Randolph, R. Witkamp, and J. Griffiths. 2017. "Optimal Nutrition and the Ever-Changing Dietary Landscape: A Conference Report." *European Journal of Nutrition* 56(Supplement 1): 1–21.

Shibata, H., H. Haga, S. Yasumura, T. Suzuki, and W. Koyano. 1994. "Possible Factors Influencing Difference in Rate of Aging in Japan." In *Facts and*

Research in Gerontology: Epidemiology and Aging, edited by B. Vellas, J. Albarede, and P. Garry, 51–59. New York: Springer.

Sofi, F., R. Abbate, G. Gensini, and A. Casini. 2010. "Accruing Evidence on Benefits of Adherence to the Mediterranean Diet on Health: An Updated Systematic Review and Meta-Analysis." *American Journal of Clinical Nutrition* 92(5): 1189–96.

Spillman, B., and J. Lubitz. 2000. "The Effect of Longevity on Spending for Acute and Long-Term Care." *New England Journal of Medicine* 342(19): 1409–15.

Statistics Bureau of Japan, Ministry of Internal Affairs and Communication. 2016. "Table 3–1. Population (Total and Japanese Population, by Age (Single Years) and Sex, Percentage by Age, Average Age and Median Age—Japan and Prefectures)." *Data Set: 2015 Census.* www.stat.go.jp/english/.

Suzuki, M. 1985. *The Science of Centenarians.* Tokyo: Shinchosha (in Japanese).

Suzuki, M., M. Akisaka, I. Ashitomi, K. Higa, and H. Nozaki. 1995. "Chronological Study Concerning ADL among Okinawan Centenarians." *Nippon Ronen Igakkai Zasshi* [Japanese Journal of Geriatrics] 32(6): 416–23 (In Japanese).

Suzuki, M., B. Willcox, and D. Willcox. 2001. "Implications from and for Food Cultures for Cardiovascular Disease: Longevity." *Asia Pacific Journal of Clinical Nutrition* 10(2): 165–71.

Suzuki, M., D. Willcox, M. Rosenbaum, and B. Willcox. 2010. "Oxidative Stress and Longevity in Okinawa: An Investigation of Blood Lipid Peroxidation and Tocopherol in Okinawan Centenarians." *Current Gerontology and Geriatrics Research* 2010: 380460.

Suzuki, M., D. Willcox, and B. Willcox. 2007. "The Historical Context of Okinawan Longevity: Influence of the United States and Mainland Japan." *Okinawan Journal of American Studies* 4: 46–61.

Takata, H., M. Suzuki, T. Ishii, S. Sekiguchi, and H. Iri. 1987. "Influence of Major Histocompatibility Complex Region Genes on Human Longevity among Okinawan-Japanese Centenarians and Nonagenarians." *Lancet* 2(8563): 824–26.

Trombold, J., R. Moellering Jr., and A. Kagan. 1966. "Epidemiological Aspects of Coronary Heart Disease and Cerebrovascular Disease: The Honolulu Heart Program." *Hawaii Medical Journal* 25(3): 231–34.

Tsugane, S., and S. Sasazuki. 2007. "Diet and the Risk of Gastric Cancer: Review of Epidemiological Evidence." *Gastric Cancer* 10(2): 75–83.

United Nations, Department of Economic and Social Affairs, Population Division. 2017. *World Population Prospects: The 2017 Revision.* New York: United Nations.

U.S. Burden of Disease Collaborators. 2013. "The State of U.S. Health, 1990–2010: Burden of Diseases, Injuries, and Risk Factors." *Journal of the American Medical Association* 310(6): 591–608.

U.S. Census Bureau. 2007. *Expectation of Life and Expected Deaths by Race, Sex and Age: 2003*. Washington, DC: U.S. Government Printing Office.

U.S. Census Bureau. 2012. "Centenarians: 2010." *2010 Census Special Reports*. C2010SR-03. Washington, DC: U.S. Government Printing Office.

U.S. Census Bureau. 2017. "International Population Statistics: Life Expectancy at Birth—Male and Female, 2015." *Data-Planet™ Statistical Datasets by Conquest Systems, Inc.* [Data-file]. Dataset-ID: 001-036-011.

U.S. Congressional Budget Office. 2017. *The 2017 Long-Term Budget Outlook*. Washington, DC: Congress of the United States.

Weinick, R., S. Byron, and A. Bierman. 2005. "Who Can't Pay for Health Care?" *Journal of General Internal Medicine* 20(6): 504–9.

Weiss, E., and L. Fontana. 2011. "Caloric Restriction: Powerful Protection for the Aging Heart and Vasculature." *American Journal of Physiology—Heart and Circulatory Physiology* 301(4): H205–19.

Willcox, B., T. Donlon, Q. He, R. Chen, J. Grove, K. Yano, K. Masaki, D. Willcox, B. Rodriguez, and J. Curb. 2008d. "FOXO3A Genotype Is Strongly Associated with Human Longevity." *Proceedings of the National Academy of Sciences of the United States of America* 105(37): 13987–92.

Willcox, B., M. Suzuki, T. Donlon, Q. He, J. Grove, K. Masaki and D. Willcox. 2013. "Optimizing Human Health Span and Life Span: Insights from Okinawa and Hawaii." *Annual Review of Gerontology and Geriatrics* 33:135–70.

Willcox, B., and D. Willcox. 2014. "Caloric Restriction, the Traditional Okinawan Diet, and Healthy Aging in Okinawa: Controversies and Clinical Implications." *Current Opinion in Clinical Nutrition and Metabolic Care* 17(1): 51–58.

Willcox, B., D. Willcox, Q. He, J. Curb, and M. Suzuki. 2006b. "Siblings of Okinawan Centenarians Share Lifelong Mortality Advantages." *Journals of Gerontology. Series A, Biological Sciences and Medical Sciences* 61(4): 345–54.

Willcox, B., D. Willcox, and L. Ferrucci. 2008b. "Secrets of Healthy Aging and Longevity from Exceptional Survivors Around the Globe: Lessons from Octogenarians to Supercentenarians." *Journals of Gerontology. Series A, Biological Sciences and Medical Sciences* 63(11): 1181–85.

Willcox, B., D. Willcox, and M. Suzuki. 2001. *The Okinawa Program*. New York: Random House.

Willcox, B., D. Willcox, and M. Suzuki. 2017. "Demographic, Phenotypic, and Genetic Characteristics of Centenarians in Okinawa and Japan: Part 1—Centenarians in Okinawa." *Mechanisms of Ageing and Development* 165(Part B): 75–79.

Willcox, B., D. Willcox, H. Todoriki, A. Fujiyoshi, K. Yano, Q. He, J. Curb, and M. Suzuki. 2007a. "Caloric Restriction, the Traditional Okinawan Diet, and Healthy Aging: The Diet of the World's Longest-Lived People and Its Potential Impact on Morbidity and Life Span." *Annals of the New York Academy of Sciences* 1114: 434–55.

Willcox, B., K. Yano, R. Chen, D. Willcox, B. Rodriguez, K. Masaki, T. Donlon, B. Tanaka, and J. Curb. 2004. "How Much Should We Eat? The Association between Energy Intake and Mortality in a 36-Year Follow-Up Study of Japanese-American Men." *Journals of Gerontology. Series A, Biological Sciences and Medical Sciences* 59(8): 789–95.

Willcox, D. 2009. "Aging, Reciprocal Dependency and Changing Social Support Systems in a Rural Okinawan Village." *Okinawa International University Journal of Social Welfare and Psychology* 7(1): 13–56.

Willcox, D., and J. Katata. 2000. "Kenko Chouju to shinkoshin, shukyou, girei no kakawari" [Psycho-physiology of ritual in aging and health in Okinawa]. *Ronen Igaku* [Geriatric Medicine] 389: 1357–64 (In Japanese).

Willcox, D., G. Scapagnini, and B. Willcox. 2014. "Healthy Aging Diets Other Than the Mediterranean: A Focus on the Okinawan Diet." *Mechanisms of Ageing and Development* 136: 148–62.

Willcox, D., B. Willcox, Q. He, N. C. Wang, and M. Suzuki. 2008a. "They Really Are That Old: A Validation Study of Centenarian Prevalence in Okinawa." *Journals of Gerontology. Series A, Biological Sciences and Medical Sciences* 63(4): 338–49.

Willcox, D., B. Willcox, W. Hsueh, and M. Suzuki. 2006a. "Genetic Determinants of Exceptional Human Longevity: Insights from the Okinawa Centenarian Study." *Age (Dordrecht, Netherlands)* 28(4): 313–32.

Willcox, D., B. Willcox, and L. Poon. 2010. "Centenarian Studies: Important Contributors to Our Understanding of the Aging Process and Longevity." *Current Gerontology and Geriatrics Research* 2010: 484529.

Willcox, D., B. Willcox, S. Shimajiri, S. Kurechi, and M. Suzuki. 2007b. "Aging Gracefully: A Retrospective Analysis of Functional Status in Okinawan Centenarians." *American Journal of Geriatric Psychiatry* 15(3): 252–56.

Willcox, D., B. Willcox, J. Sokolovsky, and S. Sakihara. 2007c. "The Cultural Context of 'Successful Aging' among Older Women Weavers in a Northern Okinawan Village: The Role of Productive Activity." *Journal of Cross-Cultural Gerontology* 22(2): 137–65.

Willcox, D., B. Willcox, H. Todoriki, J. Curb, and M. Suzuki. 2006c. "Caloric Restriction and Human Longevity: What Can We learn from the Okinawans?" *Biogerontology* 7(3): 173–77.

Willcox, D., B. Willcox, H. Todoriki, and M. Suzuki. 2009. "The Okinawan Diet: Health Implications of a Low-Calorie, Nutrient-Dense, Anti-oxidant Rich Dietary Pattern Low in Glycemic Load." *Journal of the American College of Nutrition* 28 (Supplement 4): 500S–516S.

Willcox, D., B. Willcox, N. Wang, Q. He, M. Rosenbaum, and M. Suzuki. 2008c. "Life at the Extreme Limit: Phenotypic Characteristics of Supercentenarians in Okinawa." *Journals of Gerontology. Series A, Biological Sciences and Medical Sciences* 63(11): 1201–8.

Willcox, D., B. Willcox, S. Yasura, I. Ashitomi, and M. Suzuki. 2012. "Gender Gap in Health Span and Life Expectancy in Okinawa: Health Behaviours." *Asian Journal Gerontology* 7(1): 49–58.

World Health Organization. 2018. "Life Expectancy and Healthy Life Expectancy, Data by Country." *Global Health Observatory Data Repository.* Geneva: World Health Organization. http://apps.who.int/gho/data/node .main.688?lang=en.

Yanagishita, M., and J. Guralnik. 1988. "Changing Mortality Patterns That Led Life Expectancy in Japan to Surpass Sweden's: 1972–1982." *Demography* 25(4): 611–24.

Zimmer, Z., C. Jagger, C. Chiu, M. Ofstedal, F. Roio, and Y. Saito. 2016. "Spirituality, Religiosity, Aging and Health in Global Perspective: A Review." *Population Health* 2: 373–81.

CHAPTER FORTY-FIVE

The New Frontier of Robotics in the Lives of Elders

Perspectives from Japan and Europe

James Wright

Introduction

As I wheeled Pepper, a four-foot-high, white plastic-and-metal humanoid robot (see Photo 45.1), along the corridor of an elderly nursing home in Kanagawa Prefecture, Japan, my curiosity about how it would be received was tempered by a feeling of slight trepidation. Pepper was the sleek US$25,000 service robot launched in 2015 that had started appearing in retail stores across Japan and promised to revolutionize many aspects of the service industry—including eldercare. A range of apps for Pepper was being marketed for a variety of uses in care homes. It was a spring day in 2017, and I was in the middle of a seven-month stint of fieldwork at Sakura[1] public eldercare home where several types of care robots—including Pepper—were being tested. Over this time, I had become familiar with the elderly residents and care staff and with the daily rhythm of life in the institution. Now, Pepper was being introduced for the first time, and I wondered what they would make of it. Was this the future of care?

I pushed Pepper towards the communal living room area at the end of the corridor, where members of staff had gathered together around 20 residents and explained that a robot was coming to visit. Most residents—the majority women in their eighties and nineties suffering from some degree of dementia—looked

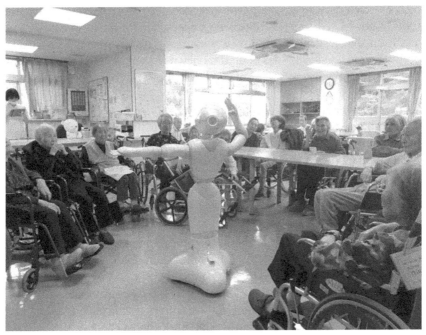

Photo 45.1   Pepper performing a song and dance. (Photo by James Wright)

on with interest at the new device, and I overheard several favorable comments: "That's amazing . . . Wow, that's great!" An older man, Takahashi-san, who wore a beanie hat and often played with a large plush teddy bear, asked admiringly: "How did they make that?" One of the male carers, Maeda, used a touchscreen tablet on Pepper's chest to access an app and select a preprogrammed routine. Pepper started to dance energetically and sing a pop song ("Fortune Cookie in Love," a 2013 single by the popular Japanese girl band AKB48) with a mixture of Japanese and English lyrics: "C'mon c'mon c'mon c'mon baby, read my fortune" (see photo above). I waited, somewhat tensely, for the reaction of the residents.

Pepper was on a six-week loan from its company, SoftBank Robotics. Although this initial demonstration was a one-sided performance, Pepper was also intended to lead more interactive recreational activities involving singing and gentle exercises. Two other robots were also being trialed at the care home: Intelligent System's Paro, a communication therapy device shaped like a cute harp seal pup, and Fuji Machine Manufacturing's Hug, a lifting robot (see Wright 2018a for a discussion of Hug).

Scenes like the one at Sakura described above were being repeated across Japan, as thousands of care homes around the country trial tested robotic devices, such as Pepper, that were designed (or repurposed) for eldercare tasks. Care-related robotics[2] has been experiencing a boom in investment and in media, academic, and industry interest. The Japanese government—both national and local—has poured money into their development and promotion, and media coverage of such devices has been predominantly positive.

The rationale driving this commitment to robot care is explained in state and media discourse primarily with reference to Japan's aging population (see Part III Kavedžija). As the country struggles to confront what is cast as a demographic crisis, many politicians and technocrats see robots as a panacea. The Ministry of Health, Labour and Welfare estimates that the percentage of people aged over 65 in Japan reached 27.7 percent of the overall population in 2017 and that this figure will rise to 30.0 percent by 2025 and 37.7 percent by 2050—percentages that climb far higher in many rural areas due to outmigration of younger people to cities (Cabinet Office 2018). As the population continues to age, social benefit spending for the elderly is at an all-time high—in 2012 it reached ¥74.1 trillion, or approximately US$741 billion, representing 21 percent of national income (Cabinet Office 2015).[3]

In spite of government support and incentives, the eldercare industry is unable to train, recruit, and retain enough professional caregivers to keep up with the increasing numbers of elderly people requiring formal care services. According to nationwide figures provided by the Association for Technical Aids, the shortage of care staff will reach 377,000 by 2025.[4] This shortfall has been exacerbated by the introduction of the Long Term Care Insurance (LTCI) system in 2000. This nationwide scheme used revenue partly derived from a new tax for over-forties to fund most of the cost of long-term care for those aged over 65. This in turn has led to substantial growth in the market for eldercare goods and services, as much care that was previously done informally by family members has been transferred to the formal care sector.

One might conclude that Japan would be the ideal place to introduce care robots. Yet despite the enthusiasm of Sakura's manager about the potential of applying new technologies such as robots to care, and despite the broadly pro-robot political and media climate, by the end of the trial period he decided not to purchase or lease any of the robots. As we will see, he was not alone: care robots have yet to take off in Japan in the way envisaged by many of their proponents. Why would this be the case, in a country famous for its positive attitudes towards robots, in the midst of a severe and worsening care labor shortage—not least at Sakura itself?

This chapter explores attitudes towards care robots among carers and elderly people in Japan beyond techno-utopian narratives constructed by government and media, from the perspective of actual use. This approach demonstrates the salience of qualitative ethnographic fieldwork and the critical role it plays as a research methodology in enabling us to identify and deconstruct fantasy, stereotypes, and hype. We will also look at how attitudes in Japan compare with those in Denmark, another country that has also demonstrated a great deal of interest in care robots. The differences in the approaches taken by these two countries tell us much about how different cultural contexts engender variable attitudes towards eldercare and technology. Finally, we will look at what the future may hold for robotic care devices in an aging world (see also Part II Prendergast).

Care Robots in Japan: Development and "Acceptance"

In recent years, there has been an explosion in international efforts to develop care robots. Japan has taken the lead in this wave of development, with the Japanese government spending tens of billions of yen over the past decade on collaborative projects between public research institutes and private robotics companies. This interest was sparked by a growing conviction in the late 1990s that robots would be used in the near future for a wide variety of medical and care-related tasks, as part of a broader expansion in the application of robotics from manufacturing into the service industry. An influential 2001 joint report from the Japan Robot Association and Japan Machinery Federation (JARA/JMF 2001) provided one of the first forecasts of a large service robotics industry in the near future and estimated that by 2025 the global market for medical and welfare robots alone would reach ¥1.1 trillion (~US$11 billion).[5] This report and others over the past few years predicted that service robots would become in the 21st century what automobiles had been in the latter half of the 20th century—one of the most important drivers of the Japanese economy, both domestically and for the export market (Robertson 2018).

Government-funded projects have endeavored to make these forecasts a reality. A 2009–2013 Project for the Practical Utilization of Personal Care Robots aimed to build the basic infrastructure necessary to support future care robot development, establishing a key international standard for "personal care robots" and resulting in the construction of a large robot safety testing center in Tsukuba, Japan (ISO 13482). This was followed by an even more substantial "Project for the Development and Promotion of the Introduction of Robot Care Devices," from 2013 to 2017, which provided financial and technical support for the actual development of various types of care robots by private companies. These development projects have been accompanied by a glut of subsidies from both the national and local governments to support the purchase or lease of these robots by care institutions. In Japan, this strategy has been characterized by a phased top-down approach, with the state carefully directing industry efforts and linking parameters for the functionality of robot care devices to the provision of public funds for development.

In Europe and the United States, the approach to developing care robots has not been driven by such a strong strategic central government vision as in Japan. Instead, technological institutes, universities, and businesses have worked on such devices rather more independently. Sources of funding also differ: in the United States, branches of the military often fund robot research institutes, while in Japan this has been expressly prohibited under the pacifist constitution.[6] Meanwhile, the biggest technology companies in the United States and Europe have been focused on different engineering megaprojects, such as self-driving vehicles. For example, Google's parent company, Alphabet, had toyed with the idea of developing robots and in 2013 acquired nine of the world's leading robot research companies including Boston Dynamics (a spin-off from MIT) and Schaft (a spin-off from the JSK Robotics Laboratory at the University of Tokyo), before abandoning their plan to build a robot division and selling these companies to Japan's SoftBank in 2017. In 2015, SoftBank also purchased Aldebaran, the French company that developed Pepper. In this sense, SoftBank is something of an outlier: most nonindustrial robotics companies in Japan, as elsewhere in the world, are relatively small spin-offs either from universities, research institutes, or larger technology companies.

Overall, the Japanese government and industry have invested far more in the development of eldercare robots than other countries, and this is reflected in the greater number, range, and sophistication of care robot prototypes and products developed and marketed in Japan. Exhibition halls are filled with robots from small university research labs right up to giants like SoftBank or Panasonic. What explains the level of state-driven as well as grassroots interest in robot development in Japan? Is it simply down to the potential economic benefits of creating a domestic and international market in care robots that also addresses spiraling eldercare costs and the care labor shortage?

A common narrative about Japan and care robots runs something like this. Japanese people have a liking—even a love—for robots and other high technologies. This is partly due to the fact that Japanese pop culture (particularly manga and anime) is replete with positive representations of robots. Astro Boy (a boy robot with super powers) is perhaps the most famous robotic character of the postwar era; Doraemon (a blue robot cat sent from the future) is also extremely popular. Unlike portrayals of robots in Europe and North America, which have tended to be far more negative and pessimistic with regard to the future (think Terminator, Westworld, and so on), robot characters in Japan are typically depicted as helpers of humans.[7]

Moreover, according to uniquely Japanese Shintō and Buddhist animistic beliefs, all things (including robots) are imbued with spirit and can therefore be more easily understood and respected as valued entities with agency and personhood. In accordance with these "techno-animist" values, Japanese people "accept" robots more easily than their "Western" counterparts, giving them names, talking to them as if they were people or pets, and even providing them with formal burial ceremonies (Canepari and Cooper 2015). At the same time, the narrative continues, older Japanese people dislike foreigners and prefer robots as carers rather than immigrants. Add to this the demographic crisis and ever-worsening care labor shortages in Japan, and it thus becomes *inevitable* that robots will be developed and adopted, becoming vital to the future of eldercare.

The narrative I present here is, of course, slightly exaggerated, yet it does capture something of the often deterministic tone adopted in state and media rhetoric and even in some scholarly treatments of robot care in Japan. Non-Japanese accounts are rarely based on any substantive research conducted in Japanese on the ground, relying instead on Japanese government reports or media coverage, which in turn are often based on brief, carefully controlled visits to eldercare institutions or desk-based research. Yet when we look at work based on actual ethnographic fieldwork, and combine it with various secondary sources such as figures of care robots sales, a more nuanced account emerges.

Recent research has indicated that animist attitudes towards machines are not the sole preserve of Japanese people. Studies increasingly indicate that people from other cultures similarly anthropomorphize machines and share ways of thinking about and responding emotionally to robots, which could equally be described as techno-animist (Jensen and Blok 2013; Leeson 2017). At the same time, there is a growing acceptance that assumptions about the universally positive reception of robots in Japan are just as skewed a perspective as the opposite idea that non-Japanese people universally reject them. Despite ubiquitous positive cultural representations of robots in Japan, several recent studies have shown similar rates of "acceptance" of care robots between Japan and other countries, and some surveys conducted in Japan have shown negative reactions such as anxiety about the future use of robots (Broadbent, Stafford, and MacDonald 2009; Kato 2009). During my own research, I found that carers often had complex and even contradictory feelings about robots (Wright 2018a).

In fact, robotic devices are far from common in Japanese care homes or indeed private households, and their actual *use* in the context of everyday care is even rarer. According to my own research, based on analysis of care robot sales figures and national surveys of professional care workers, only around 5–10 percent of publicly funded care homes (between 2,500 and 5,000 out of a national total of around 50,000) had some type of care robot as of 2016 (Wright 2018b). This amounts to only a few thousand devices in use across Japan. To put this in perspective, the latest generation of Sony's popular robot dog toy, AIBO, sold over 11,000 units in just the first three months of its relaunch in January 2018. Even in institutions that had one or more devices on hand, it is highly likely that many were not actively being used—a problem acknowledged by several of my interlocutors, including both robot engineers and care home managers.

Similarly, assumptions about supposedly xenophobic older people, and their preference for robots rather than foreigners, are rarely based on solid data. Surveys that are aimed at measuring the level of support among elderly people for using care robots can be misleading, particularly when the elderly respondent has never actually used or even seen such a device, and when the term "care robot" itself is not clearly defined. As anthropologist Jennifer Robertson reminds us, "one must take into account the 'bandwagon effect' of such government-administered public opinion polls. Such surveys can serve to reinforce and compel conformity to official views" (2018: 19).

Beata Świtek, an anthropologist who has conducted ethnographic research into the experience of Indonesian carers working in Japan, has analyzed their resolutely positive portrayal in the Japanese press, suggesting that some moves are being made to reimagine the future of Japan in terms of diversity and multicultural coexistence (Świtek 2014). She also found that these carers often formed social bonds with elderly residents based on a shared experience of social marginalization (Świtek 2016). Although carers at Sakura were split on the effectiveness of foreign carers, as one carer at Sakura told me firmly, "Nationality totally doesn't matter to users."

Why does the government in Japan specifically have such a strong interest in developing care robots? Robertson, who has researched humanoid and other service robots in Japan for over a decade, argues that despite their futuristic branding, such robots are in fact seen by the conservative Japanese government led by Prime Minister Shinzō Abe as a way of embodying and reinforcing traditionalist and ethnonationalist views on gender, the family, race, and disability in Japan: in other words, as "retro-robotics and retro-tech" (Robertson 2018: 23). As she argues, this strategy enables conservative politicians such as Abe to avoid addressing the complex social, political, and economic factors behind the current demographic changes in Japanese society, instead recasting them as technological problems requiring robotic solutions.

This narrative of "acceptance" of care robots in Japan can thus serve to obscure and preclude the pursuit of alternative (and perhaps less politically palatable) options: for example, raising taxes to increase pay and improve working conditions for professional carers or relaxing immigration laws to increase the number of foreign carers allowed to work in the country. The term "acceptance" (*ukeireru* in Japanese) is common in various literatures about care robots, and about robots more generally. But use of this term obscures the questions of which "robots" are supposedly being accepted, by whom, in what ways, and to what extent.

Care Technologies in Denmark

If care robots are not yet widespread or readily accepted in Japan—at least, among many carers and residents who are their target users—what is the situation in Europe, where a very different cultural context of eldercare and care technologies pertains?

While Japanese attitudes have tended towards techno-utopian imaginaries of robots, Euro-American representations in media and academic work in recent years have tended to depict robotics and automation as a threat to jobs, to intimacy (in the case of sex robots), and even to life (in the case of killer robots). Some scholars have warned that care homes could become dehumanized "eldercare factories" (Sharkey and Sharkey 2012), and indeed various ethical issues have been identified by researchers and highlighted in the media well in advance of the development of devices whose use could actually create these issues.

Nevertheless, care robots and related technologies have been and continue to be developed, tested, and implemented in eldercare homes, particularly in Northern Europe. Denmark has been a pioneer in the introduction of such devices since the launch of a nationwide initiative for welfare technology in nursing care in 2007, led by the Danish Ministry of Science and Ministry of Finance (Hasse 2013). This nation also has a rapidly aging population and expects a growing labor shortage in care to develop in the coming years, albeit at a slower rate than in Japan. In 2013, Danish prime minister Helle Thorning-Schmidt introduced a "Digital Welfare" strategy, promoting further widespread implementation of new technologies across the public sector to raise the quality of service provision while cutting costs. This strategy involved the development of close international collaborations, particularly with Japan, to develop new welfare robots—and especially those intended for eldercare (Leeson 2017).

These initiatives mirrored Japanese government-led investments, but with a somewhat different emphasis. Whereas the government and industry in Japan were aiming to make institutional care more efficient and therefore to mitigate a significant existing—and rapidly growing—care labor shortage, in Denmark the emphasis has been more heavily focused on using care robots to maximize independence among older people and improve the quality of institutional and home care services (Leeson 2017).

In 2017, I visited the Danish Technological Institute (DTI) in Odense, Denmark, to interview Troels Pedersen, the chief program officer in charge of care robot research. He told me that, shortly after joining the institute in 2007, "One of the very first things I did was to go to Japan to find Japanese care technologies to bring to Denmark." Whereas Japan was aiming to develop a wide range of robotic care products domestically, in Denmark the strategy primarily involved sourcing already-developed technologies (particularly from Japan) and then testing their effectiveness and adapting them for the social and cultural context of the Danish market. For example, the seal-shaped social robot Paro was introduced into care homes across the country from 2007 following studies at the DTI. Other robots, such as a tele-operated humanoid robot called Telenoid, were also given a trial. Both Paro and Telenoid were tested in collaboration with the Japanese engineers who had developed them (Hasse 2013; Leeson 2017).

At the same time, such devices were being debated in the public arena in Denmark—indeed, 2007 also saw the release of *Mechanical Love*, a documentary by Danish filmmaker Phie Ambo which took a critical approach towards the use of Paro at one eldercare home. In response to these efforts to try out care robots, newspaper articles announced that Denmark was becoming a "guinea pig" (or in the government's language, a "test-market") for new welfare and particularly eldercare technologies such as Paro. The public debate about the pros and cons of care robots continued, and a key landmark came in 2010, with the release of a report on the use of social robots by the Danish Council of Ethics, which highlighted the potential for such technologies while calling for ongoing ethical scrutiny.

Pedersen told me that during his visits to Japanese care homes he had found significant differences in terms of attitude and use compared with Denmark:

> I visited Japanese care homes. They have none—no [robot care] devices. In Denmark, there's a much higher proliferation of actual care-related technologies in care homes and private homes, and they're well accepted. We're at a place now where it's not discussed basically if that's something we can do or not do—it's accepted to do it. The discussions are more related to: is this specific tech working well, or is this one actually saving money, or is this one actually increasing the quality of care. So we've passed the "Will we do it?" discussion and are in the "How can we do it?" discussion. (Interview, September 27, 2017)

Structural factors in the care profession played an important role in the ways in which care robots were adopted. In Japan, care jobs are often seen as temporary forms of employment, and the industry turnover rate is high; this in turn is linked to the low salaries of carers and different expectations about long-term employment particularly among the female staff who make up the bulk of professional carers. Pedersen pointed out that in Denmark care is seen as a long-term profession and that carers tend to stay in their jobs for decades. Staff turnover is lower, and pay is relatively higher than in Japan. Carers can therefore be trained over a significant amount of time in new technologies of care—and this investment is worthwhile because there is less risk that the carer will leave the job and move elsewhere or quit the care profession after a year or two. This was significant for attempts to implement care robots. As Pedersen put it, "the actual set up of the care home in Japan—of the economy, turnover of staff—actually does not open itself up very easily towards implementation of technology."

Nevertheless, these factors were not entirely reflected in the case of Sakura: for example, staff turnover was lower than the industry average. To understand why the robots implemented there failed to be adopted, it is necessary to look at how they were actually used.

Pepper in Use

At around 2 p.m., a female carer, Kubo, spends a few minutes starting up Pepper and making sure that it is working correctly. Just before 2:30 p.m., she wheels it from the cluttered staff room where it is stored to the front of the dining hall, where most of the residents are sitting quietly or chatting. Kubo asks if residents remember Pepper's name, but they don't, so she reintroduces it and tells everyone that it will be leading a recreational exercise session. "Definitely please try to mimic it!" she adds. Kubo selects a 30-minute exercise program from the menu using the touchscreen tablet on Pepper's chest. Pepper starts by playing some rhythmic and whimsically upbeat marching music and modeling some gentle stretches that gradually become slightly more demanding, involving residents holding out their hands and clapping. As each stretch starts, Pepper calls it out in a high-pitched voice and Kubo, who stands next to Pepper, echoes it while herself modelling Pepper's stretch.

At the end of the first part of the routine, Pepper thanks everyone for taking part, and asks someone to pat its head. Kubo and several of the residents clap, and Kubo asks everyone, "How was it?" She leads a female resident, Saito, by the hand to come up and pat Pepper's head to move on to the next part of the routine. The residents seem to enjoy going up to touch Pepper, and Saito takes its rubbery hand and laughs. As she pats its head, Pepper says sheepishly, "I'm a bit ticklish," sparking further laughter. The next part of the routine involves singing a song with accompanying exercises. Pepper says, "Please sing with a loud voice!" Kubo repeats, "Sing out with a loud voice, yeah?" Pepper starts playing background music and singing a song, moving its arms, and some of the residents sing along, copying the movements. Pepper simultaneously sings and asks the residents to make specific movements and do certain exercises at set points during the verse, and then repeats the song again. The song lasts for about four minutes, and now another resident is asked to come up and pat Pepper's head.

Throughout, Kubo copies and reinforces what Pepper says, while working the crowd: "Good work, keep going!" After several more exercises and another song, Pepper ends with several *banzai* cheers, the robot and residents saluting each other with 10,000 years of long life. Pepper frequently tells jokes during the routine or says cute, naïve things ("My head is smooth and shiny, isn't it!"), which elicits laughter from residents and carers. Most of the residents copy Pepper's movements as Kubo models them, and they continue to bop their heads in sync with Pepper until the end, mimicking its movements even when the exercises have finished. Finally, Pepper plays some relaxing music and asks, "How did you feel today?" One resident replies, "Good, thanks!" At the end, the residents and Kubo clap, with several residents thanking Pepper. One resident exclaims to Pepper, "You did well!" Carers used Pepper every couple of days to lead afternoon recreation sessions with residents in a similar manner to that described for the duration of the six-week trial. Carers and residents seemed to enjoy using Pepper, although there was noticeably less interest in it at times when a human carer did not stand next to Pepper and model the exercises.

Yet Pepper—as well as the other robots trialed at Sakura—also caused problems. The use of robots infringed on the meanings and values of care that gave the job meaning for carers. For example, carers were reluctant to use Hug, the lifting robot, in part because the human touch involved in lifting a resident, for example, from bed to wheelchair, formed part of a practice of joking, tactile care that helped build stronger care relationships between staff and residents. This was particularly the case for residents with dementia who sometimes struggled to communicate verbally. Many carers told me that recreation in particular was one of the most enjoyable parts of their job. Recreation each afternoon meant having a couple of hours set aside simply to communicate and have fun with the residents. They would tell jokes and stories, play games, or even sing karaoke together. This was often impossible to do at other times of the day because carers were often too busy and felt understaffed. Bringing Pepper into this routine meant giving the robot center stage, and hence led to the possibility that carers themselves might lose some of the limited opportunity to build and strengthen their social relationships with residents, which they saw as vital for good care.

Just as important was the problem of time. Care staff found themselves caring not only for the elderly residents of Sakura but also for the robots. All three types of robot required additional work duties from carers, including recharging them, rebooting them, configuring them, moving them from one room to the next, and monitoring their use. These tasks soon added up, particularly in an environment where carers were already—literally—running around at busy times of the day. Another study in a Danish care home (Leeson 2017) found that even care staff who are well disposed towards a robot, want to use it, and believe that it could improve the quality of care will stop using it if it takes up too much of their time.

Finally, Pepper and the other robots were expensive to buy. Pepper would have cost around US$25,000 over three years; the lifting robot Hug cost around $14,500, and the seal robot Paro cost about $4,000. These prices were simply unaffordable in the case of Sakura, which was a publicly funded institution facing a number of growing costs, partly as a result of new legislation that was speeding up the cycle of admissions and the intensity of care required by new residents, and partly because they were increasingly having to pay steep referral fees to find new—and increasingly elusive—human care staff.

The Future of Care Robots

Perhaps the greatest irony of care robot development in Japan is that, in a country suffering from an increasingly acute carer shortage, the technologies being developed to "solve" the problem through labor replacement in fact *exacerbate* it by taking up even more time—and themselves demanding care and attention. In Denmark, by contrast, the expectations surrounding robots seemed more realistic and less inflated by media hype: in particular, there was less expectation that robots would be able to replace human care labor in the immediate future.

Robots may seem like neutral technological devices. Yet as we have seen, both in terms of public discourses and representations of robots, as well as the politics, economics, and social aspects of the institutional care landscape, cultural context plays an integral role in how such machines are perceived, developed, and actually used. If care robots such as Pepper are to be widely adopted in Japan, it seems that a different approach is needed—one that takes into account existing practices of care and the meanings imbued in these practices. At the same time, a more open approach involving upfront debate about the pros and cons of robot care, as in Denmark, might help temper public expectations while alleviating fears about the potential impacts of their implementation.

That day at Sakura care home, residents seemed enthralled by the spectacle of Pepper's pop idol performance. Over the following weeks, as the novelty started to wear off, the limitations of the machine became clearer to staff and residents. Yet as one SoftBank representative told me, when I asked what he really thought of Pepper being used in care homes: "This is just the first—the very first—of this kind of robot. The future ones will be better." One thing is for certain: Pepper will not be the last robot that "walks" the corridors of Sakura and care homes like it, in Japan and around the world.

Notes

1. Sakura is a pseudonym, as are all names of residents and staff.

2. The term "care robot" can refer to many different types of devices used across all aspects of care, and there is no universally accepted definition (just as there is no universally accepted definition of the term "robot"). In Japan, the phrases *kaigo robotto* ("care robot") and *seikatsushien robotto* (literally, "lifestyle support robot") are most commonly used.

3. This figure includes the total cost of pension benefits, medical care, and welfare services for those whom the state defines as elderly people, as well as subsidies for companies employing them.

4. Seminar at the "Home Care and Rehabilitation" exhibition in Tokyo, given by the Association for Technical Aids (ATA), "Opening Up the Future through

the Use of Care Robots" (介護ロボットの活用で未来を拓く), October 13, 2016. Similar figures were still being used by METI in 2018 (Hurst 2018). It is important to question the accuracy of these figures, as their provenance is not disclosed by the ATA, and the claim that there was no shortfall in carers in 2013 seems to have little basis in fact—according to two public eldercare home managers I interviewed, care homes have struggled to recruit enough staff for far longer. Nevertheless, my point here is that such statements, figures, and reports form an important part of the background of the argument and justification for developing care robots.

5. More recently, a major 2015 national robotics strategy paper targeted a nursing care robot market in Japan of ¥50 billion (~US$500 million) by 2020 (Headquarters 2015).

6. It is, however, important to note that this has been changing under Prime Minister Shinzō Abe's administration, which has passed laws reinterpreting key articles of the constitution.

7. This has not always been the case. Early science fiction literature on robots in Japan, as well as some postwar portrayals, expressed anxiety and deep moral ambivalence towards robots (Gomarasca 2002; Nakamura 2007).

Bibliography

Broadbent, E., R. Stafford, and B. MacDonald. 2009. "Acceptance of Healthcare Robots for the Older Population: Review and Future Directions." *International Journal of Social Robotics* 1: 319–30.

Cabinet Office, Government of Japan. 2015. *Annual White Paper on the Aging Society*.

Cabinet Office, Government of Japan. 2018. *Annual White Paper on the Aging Society*.

Canepari, Z., and D. Cooper. 2015. "The Family Dog." *New York Times*, June 17. http://www.nytimes.com/video/technology/100000003746796/the -family-dog.html.

Gomarasca, A. 2002. "Robots, exosquelettes, armures: le mecha-corps dans l'animation japonaise." In *Poupées, Robots: La Culture Pop Japonaise*, edited by A. Gomarasca. Paris: Autrement.

Hasse, C. 2013. "Artefacts That Talk: Mediating Technologies as Multistable Signs and Tools." *Subjectivity* 6(1): 79–100.

Headquarters for Japan's Economic Revitalization. 2015. "New Robot Strategy: Japan's Robot Strategy."

Hurst, D. 2018. "Japan Lays Groundwork for Boom in Robot Carers." *Guardian*, February 6.

JARA/JMF. 2001. "Summary Report on Technology Strategy for Creating a 'Robot Society' in the 21st Century."

Jensen, C., and A. Blok. 2013. "Techno-animism in Japan: Shinto Cosmograms, Actor-Network Theory, and the Enabling Powers of Non-human Agencies." *Theory, Culture & Society* 30(2): 84–115.

Kato, K. 2009. "Age Differences and Images of Robots: Social Survey in Japan." *Interaction Studies* 10(3): 374–91.

Leeson, C. 2017. "Anthropomorphic Robots on the Move: A Transformative Trajectory from Japan to Danish Healthcare." PhD diss., Faculty of Social Sciences, University of Copenhagen.

Nakamura, M. 2007. "Marking Bodily Differences: Mechanized Bodies in Hirabayashi Hatsunosuke's 'Robot' and Early Showa Robot Literature." *Japan Forum* 19(2): 169–90.

Robertson, J. 2018. *Robo Sapiens Japanicus: Robots, Gender, Family, and the Japanese Nation.* Oakland: University of California Press.

Sharkey, N., and A. Sharkey. 2012. "The Eldercare Factory." *Gerontology* 58(3): 282–88.

Świtek, B. 2014. "Representing the Alternative: Demographic Change, Migrant Eldercare Workers, and National Imagination in Japan." *Contemporary Japan* 26(2): 263–80.

Świtek, B. 2016. *Reluctant Intimacies: Indonesian Eldercare Workers and National Imagination in Japan.* New York: Berghahn.

Wright, J. 2018a. "Tactile Care, Mechanical Hugs: Japanese Caregivers and Robotic Lifting Devices." *Asian Anthropology* 17(1): 1–16.

Wright, J. 2018b. "Technowelfare in Japan: Personal Care Robots and Temporalities of Care." PhD diss., Hong Kong Institute for the Humanities and Social Sciences, University of Hong Kong.

CHAPTER FORTY-SIX

"Train Yourself Free"

How Elderly Citizens Exercise Freedom of Choice in the Danish State

Amy Clotworthy

Introduction

Welcome to Denmark! Consistently rated one of the "happiest countries in the world" by the Organisation for Economic Co-operation and Development (OECD 2018) and the World Economic Forum (WE Forum 2018), this is the land of *hygge* ("coziness") and probably the best beer in the world. Prior to the publication of these happiness indices, most people living outside of the Nordic region primarily knew this small Scandinavian country through English playwright William Shakespeare's 16th-century tragedy, *Hamlet* ("Something is rotten in the state of Denmark": Act I, scene 4), even though the kingdom of Denmark first emerged as a prominent seafaring nation in the 10th century, and the Danish national flag (*Dannebrog*) is the oldest in the world. After many years of sitting quietly among its former strongholds in Sweden and Germany, Denmark's high rankings on the international happiness charts began to shine a spotlight on the country, sparking widespread interest in the "secret" behind Danes' satisfaction with life. The Nordic region—and particularly the Scandinavian countries of Denmark, Sweden, and Norway—has traditionally ranked high on global measures of economic freedom, which may contribute to citizens' subjective feelings of happiness, well-being, and security (Lidegaard 2009; Heritage Foundation 2017). But more significantly, the happiness reports also point to a complex set of factors that are related to the Nordic welfare model of social and economic development, which has long been characterized by "a strong emphasis on security, safety, equality, rationality, foresight, and regulation" (Gullestad 1989: 73).

The happiness rankings have also spurred a political interest in how other countries might "import" the Danish version of social cohesion, egalitarianism, and economic freedom—factors that have been instrumental in how Denmark became a modern European welfare state (Lidegaard 2009: 28, 32)—in order to boost their own productivity and improve citizens' quality of life. This was seen most clearly when Denmark's social-welfare model became a heated point of discussion in the debates leading up to the 2016 presidential election in the United States. In particular, the Democratic hopeful Senator Bernie Sanders (I-VT) was outspoken in his admiration for Scandinavian ideals and values, stating, "We should look to countries like Denmark, like Sweden and Norway, and learn from what they have accomplished for their working people" (CNBC 2015).

However, Senator Sanders's "radical" ideas about introducing universal health care and Scandinavian-inspired welfare benefits in the United States prompted criticism from his detractors, who did not appreciate his "socialist" ambitions. Former Danish prime minister Lars Løkke Rasmussen, however, decided to set the record straight, saying: "I know that some people in the US associate the Nordic model with some sort of socialism. . . . The Nordic model is an expanded welfare state which provides a high level of security to its citizens, but it is also a successful market economy with much freedom [*sic*] to pursue your dreams and live your life as you wish" (Yglesias 2015).

Framing the Danish Care System

The quote above from Senator Sanders suggests that there are certain perceptions and assumptions about *how things are in Denmark*. As an American citizen who has been living and working in Denmark since 2008, I am often asked what it is like to live here—and is it better than the United States? From both a personal perspective and my research as an ethnologist, I would say that many perceptions about life in the Danish welfare state are not wholly accurate. For example, among the *World Happiness Report*'s six major factors that contribute to happiness (income, healthy life expectancy, social support, trust, and generosity), having the freedom to make life choices is considered significant (Helliwell, Layard, and Sachs 2018). But, as I discuss in this chapter, this "freedom" is conceptualized differently in Denmark. The Danish form of freedom of choice—"to pursue your dreams and live your life as you wish"—contains a number of reciprocal exchanges and obligations, which tend to be normative and may contain certain moral judgments. A central focus of this chapter is how this plays out in the context of a new reablement or "everyday rehabilitation" program. Based on my ethnographic study of this program and other municipal health initiatives for the elderly, I discuss how the Danish social-welfare model expects its citizens—particularly older citizens—to exercise their freedom to make *certain* life choices (Clotworthy 2017). But this freedom can be complicated by the "messy subjectivity" of human actors.

My research is framed in the public-health policies being implemented by government officials. In Denmark and many other Western countries, policies are often made in collaboration with medical professionals and other experts, who are increasingly determining the parameters for the health and everyday lives of people after they retire. As other scholars have discussed, elderhood—or what some call the Third Age—is a specific stage of life that has been culturally and socially defined (e.g., Gilleard and Higgs 2000; Fung 2013; Part II Albert and Kao). I argue that it is also increasingly being *politically* defined (see Pieta Part V). Not just via pension schemes—which have arbitrarily determined that reaching age 65 or 67 signals the end of a person's work productivity—but also via policies and initiatives targeted specifically at people age 65+. I have found that, within these initiatives, the categorization of later life as "old age"—which positions older citizens over age 65 as a high-risk, potentially burdensome subgroup of society—has become entangled with the positive discourse of healthy aging to constitute what I call a "limited yet limitless ageing consumer" (Clotworthy 2017). My conceptualization of this ideal type refers to a post-retirement citizen who may suffer from certain health limitations and be in need of supportive services, but is still considered to have unlimited value and potential as a productive consumer and a contributing member of society. As such, these "elderly" citizens have been positioned as an abstract category that has to be managed in specific ways (Gilleard & Higgs 2007; Petersen 2008).

One of my aims in this chapter is to describe some of the political and cultural forces that have constituted how eldercare and aging are actually *done* in Denmark. I first begin by briefly outlining Denmark's transition from a "traditional" European welfare state to a "competition" state, with a particular focus on its *Free Choice* scheme. Then I present some examples from my ethnographic fieldwork in a Danish municipality. These illustrate what happens when the political discourse about elderly citizens' potential, productivity, and "freedom" to choose enters an older citizen's private home in the form of municipal health professionals. Specifically, I describe Denmark's focus on the concept of "help to self-help" (*hjælp til selvhjælp*) as it relates to empowering elderly citizens to age in place at home. With my analysis, I hope to provide a sociocultural perspective on how certain political expectations for aging and functional ability have developed in Denmark, and to elucidate some of the challenges that arise when these expectations are actualized in everyday life.

Denmark's Emergence as a Competition State

When I began the research for my PhD project at the University of Copenhagen, I did not know much about the cultural-historical emergence of the Danish welfare state, nor its move towards being a "neoliberal" society. This refers to "the new political, economic, and social arrangements within society that emphasize market relations, re-tasking the role of the state, and individual responsibility" (Springer, Birch, and MacLeavy 2016: 2). Despite having lived in Denmark for several years, I held many of Senator Sanders's assumptions about the Scandinavian healthcare system, the welfare state, and some of the perceptions of *how things are in Denmark*. But, as I learned when I began my ethnographic fieldwork in 2014, the Danish state as an institution did not appear out of nowhere—it was constituted and defined by a complex series of historical, socioeconomic, and cultural developments, which have affected the overall political culture as well as "the values[1] upon which the Danish community is said to rest" (Pedersen 2011: 169).

In particular, the "traditional" Danish welfare state was built upon the idea of a citizen who is an equal part of the larger social collective, actively participates in the democratic process, "owns" a share of the state, and has a nearly unrestricted right to state benefits (Petersen, Petersen, and Christiansen 2010; Lidegaard 2009). Social programs to help "needy" and "weak" citizens first began to flourish in the 1920s and 1930s. Initially, Danish municipalities offered a range of services and support to elderly citizens within local public institutions (e.g., "old age homes") until basic in-home care services were established in 1949 in connection with a postwar "housewife replacement" scheme (Blom 2014: 44). During the "golden age" of the welfare state in the 1950s and 1960s, the provision of care and supportive services was guaranteed and framed as a universal right of citizenship; for example, the National Insurance Act of 1958 allowed older citizens to receive a range of assistance in their own homes (Ringsmose and Hansen 2005: 10).

However, since the 1960s, there has been a general shift away from state-provided welfare schemes in Europe, which has resulted in more fragmented, privatized, and plural forms of governance (Twigg 2002; Jensen and Lolle 2013; Part VI Polivka). In Denmark, this was first seen in widespread public-sector reforms in 1970, which consolidated the municipalities and completely overhauled the country's social- and health-services sectors. A series of political and economic forces then propelled Denmark's turn towards neoliberalism in the 1980s, which contributed to its emergence as a "competition state" (Pedersen 2011). With this move, an emphasis was placed on each individual citizen being a productive worker and consumer in order to promote industrial growth and development. At the same time, many municipalities began to implement programs with a greater focus on standardization and efficiency; as such, the welfare state's core aim to provide "compensating" practical help to "needy" citizens shifted to a more neoliberal emphasis on individual responsibility, self-governance, and enabling "self-help."

Following a long period of high unemployment from the mid-1970s to the mid-1990s, the number of welfare recipients in Denmark dramatically increased (Henriksen 2006). As a result, the prime impetus of the government was to get citizens into (or back into) the job market as soon as possible. These workers were considered to be the economy's driving force, and the focus was on their potential for production, especially in relation to helping Denmark become more competitive in global markets (Pedersen 2011). In the political transition from a welfare state to a competition state, the citizen as an individual was also redefined—from a "moral member of the shared community" with compassion for their vulnerable and/or marginalized co-citizens to a "private opportunist" who has value as a tax-paying worker and consumer (Pedersen 2011). Thus, despite the traditional welfare state's emphasis on social cohesion and egalitarianism to benefit "the greater good," one of the distinctive features of the modern Danish state is its focus on the needs, obligations, and responsibilities of each individual citizen within the collective (Henriksen 2006).[2]

During the 1990s, the government institutionalized the work of municipal "Visitation" staff (Lønstrup 2008); this specially trained group of health professionals conducts authoritative in-home evaluations of citizens who have applied to receive state assistance. By the early 2000s, the Danish government began to focus on avoiding the "traditional top-down imposition of welfare" in relation to the provision of benefits and care services (Rostgaard 2006: 444). To further control public-sector expenditures and improve efficiency, the government also introduced a particular kind of "free choice," which primarily applied to citizens who were not healthy, fully active, and contributing members of the economic workforce (e.g., children, the disabled, the elderly) (Petersen 2008: 94).

The *Free Choice* Scheme

In 2003, the Danish Ministry of Finance implemented a policy document, *Frit valg og kvalitet—afregningsmodeller på de kommunale serviceområder* (Free choice and quality—Payment models for the municipal service areas) to help the municipalities manage citizens who requested services that were funded by the state through taxation. The scheme was intended to "strengthen citizens' freedom of choice . . . in order to increase the quality of and satisfaction with the services provided. At the same time, this freedom of choice must be weighed against the municipalities' potential to appropriately manage expenditures and control capacity" (Ministry of Finance 2003: 47). This policy outlines standardized choices for the public institutions available to citizens, such as schools and nursing homes, as well as private companies that provide in-home services. The scheme explicitly describes the type of choices available, stating:

> A freer choice weakens the possibility of referring individuals to specific suppliers or services, therefore reducing the municipalities' ability to manage capacity and service levels. This increases the significance of other management tools; i.e., Visitation, to manage the municipality's decision on the allocation of specific offers and services to the individual citizen. (Ministry of Finance 2003)

This scheme was developed as part of the ministry's efforts to control the public sector and make it more efficient, as well as to improve quality and flexibility in the municipalities. It was inspired by the rise of New Public Management (NPM) approaches[3] in the 1990s, which included ideas about outsourcing, performance management, and technology. While NPM is no longer widely used in Denmark, many of its ideas continue to influence political decisions and policies to the present day (Pedersen and Andersen 2016). Some scholars have argued that the *Free Choice* scheme was also a "regime change" that was meant to alter the relationship between the market, the state, health professionals, families, and care recipients because it reinforced the state's new definition of citizens as *consumers* of welfare services (Petersen 2008: 94–95, my emphasis) as opposed to *recipients* of care and assistance in the traditional welfare state. Thus, in the Nordic welfare model's "successful market economy" that former prime minister Rasmussen mentioned, "individuals exert their 'free choice' but are at the same time guided by those who designed the incentives to induce more or less of a certain behavior" (Larsen and Stone 2015: 5).

In other words, the political rationale behind the promotion of "free choice" in Denmark is to activate all citizens' potential to be more productive and self-governing. With regards to health services, providing individual citizens with this free choice can be understood as a form of social regulation that should guide them towards acting as "the government wishes them to act, and adopt more healthy lifestyles" (Vallgårda 2001: 387). One of the most striking examples of this approach is in-home care for the elderly, which has been "the political test case [for] the provision of the Danish notion of 'a free choice'" (Rostgaard 2006: 444). Here, some scholars believe that the state's attempt to manage complexity via free choice may be "the obvious answer to the massive future challenges of an aging society in which the elderly will be more demanding in relation to the provision of public services" (Rostgaard 2006: 452). The concept of "free choice" has thereby become increasingly important as Denmark's elderly population continues to grow.

Managing the Elderly

As of 2017, approximately 25.3 percent of Denmark's total population of 5,750,000 inhabitants are age 60 and over, and 4.4 percent are age 80 and over (United Nations 2017; Statistics Denmark 2018). This 80+ group has been rapidly expanding—from 52,000 in 1950 to 228,000 in 2010, and it will continue to grow by 150,000 people each year over the next 10 years (Statistics Denmark 2018). Based on current population-growth projections, by 2053, more than one in every 10 Danes will be over age 80. By 2057, there will be 667,000 or 2.5 times more people age 80+ than there are today (Statistics Denmark 2018). Denmark is also experiencing low national fertility rates and has been trying to promote an increase in the birth rate in order to ensure that its working population is large enough to continue to support the social-welfare system (Hansen 2015). To address these demographic trends and improve overall population health, many of Denmark's recent public health programs have focused on prevention—specifically, preventing lifestyle-related diseases in order to produce better average life-expectancy rates and thereby "improve Denmark's ranking in the global longevity competition, [which is] necessary for the common good of society" (Anderson 2011: 247). Most of the noncommunicable diseases from which Danes suffer are linked to high rates of modifiable risk factors—i.e., high blood pressure, harmful use of alcohol and tobacco, obesity, and physical inactivity (World Health Organization 2012). This has prompted the Danish government to take significant steps to implement targeted public health interventions at the national level.

However, many older people tend to suffer from one or more of these diseases simultaneously—and to live with them for longer—which has put additional strain on the Danish health and welfare sector. To manage the expected demand, Denmark has developed national health-promotion and prevention initiatives "to combat the social exclusion of older people by fostering their active participation in society" (Otto 2013: 131). Here, the political belief is that remaining physically and socially active will reduce health risks among the elderly and, most important, mitigate their potential need for (expensive) in-home care services. As such, these initiatives have become an integral part of municipal efforts to offer "citizen-oriented health promotion which aims at creating, shaping and facilitating certain ways of ageing healthy" (Otto 2013: 114).

For example, during the rise of NPM, the government established the Act on Preventive Home Visits to the Elderly in 1996; this law made it obligatory for all Danish municipalities to offer preventive home visits (PHV) twice a year to all citizens age 75 and over. The program's purpose "is to discuss the individual citizen's current life situation, and to support them in utilising their own resources, maintaining their functional ability, and achieving greater well-being" (DHMA 2015: 19). These visits are meant to help strengthen older people's resources and enable them to attain a better quality of life, and Denmark is considered a pioneer in developing such visits for the elderly (Mahler et al. 2014: 36). But, following the principles set forth in the *Free Choice* scheme, these visits are offered as an elective service, which means that citizens may choose to contact the PHV visitors in their local municipality to arrange a "health-promoting interview."

The government's "elderly package" of support, first offered in 2002, outlined the municipal service options available to older citizens. Older citizens were given a choice to receive either municipal services (free/subsidized) or private help, paid for by the citizen and meeting the same level of service quality that the municipality offers. This contributed to establishing a market for welfare services and constructed these citizens as "freely choosing elderly" consumers (Højlund 2006). As I mentioned, this form of free choice is meant to enable "needy" citizens to become more self-helping and independent, and thus to "create the self-caring self" (Rostgaard 2006: 452). In other words, postretirement citizens should *choose* to master (or remaster) certain skills in order to remain active and self-sufficient at home for as long as possible.

Here, the political ambition is framed as a market exchange—if the state provides citizens with the tools and resources they need to take responsibility for their own health, then they should choose to become more self-helping. But what actually happens when representatives from the state offer this "free choice" to elderly citizens? As an ethnologist and cultural analyst, I was interested in investigating how both municipal health professionals and elderly citizens interpret, experience, and react to this form of freedom, and how their "free" choices affect the political goals for the provision of health services to the elderly.

An Ethnographic Study

To examine how the politically defined concepts of "help to self-help" and "free choice" are *done*, I conducted 15 months of ethnographic fieldwork in Toftsby Municipality,[4] which has long held a privileged position as Denmark's wealthiest municipality. Nearly 75,000 people live in the seven districts that comprise this quiet commuter suburb that lies along the country's eastern coast, and there are a significant number of international and/or elderly residents. Historically, Toftsby has avoided much of the municipal consolidation caused by the national public-sector reforms; as such, it has been able to operate with more political autonomy than other municipalities that have struggled to ensure social equality and provide their citizens with access to a full range of welfare benefits and care services. Toftsby's socioeconomic stability and political consistency have also positioned it as a "strong" municipality with ample resources to support its increasing number of elderly residents. However, despite its economic wealth, the municipality is not an autonomous entity, and it must comply with the Danish state's imperative to manage municipal budgets and reduce health-related expenditures. Thus, the officials in Toftsby have been actively promoting the "healthy aging" paradigm, that is, that older citizens should be independent, active consumers who are "free" from the need for municipal services and can remain in their own homes and care for themselves as long as possible, even after they start to exhibit signs of age-related decline.

In the coming years, the political leadership of Toftsby expects significant growth in residents between the ages of 65 and 84: officials predict an increase of 8 percent by 2020 and 16 percent by 2025 (Toftsby Municipality 2014: 7); this is one of the highest rates in Denmark. At the time of my fieldwork, Toftsby's annual budget for 2014–2015 was approximately 14.6 million DKK (over US$2.1 million). A large portion of this money was earmarked for the maintenance of physical structures for the elderly, such as assisted-living facilities and nursing homes (especially for citizens diagnosed with dementia or Alzheimer's disease) as well as activity centers. These factors made Toftsby an ideal setting to study the effects of certain political initiatives and sociocultural changes with regards to how eldercare is done in Denmark.

During my fieldwork, I researched the everyday work practices of municipal health professionals from three departments; specifically, I followed 6 Visitation staff (who were randomly selected based on availability) on visits to evaluate the functional ability and living conditions of 9 citizens: 3 men (age 61–90) and 6 women (age 57–91) between October and December 2014. I next followed 2 professionals from Preventative Home Visits (PHV) throughout March 2015; this included home visits to 4 citizens: 1 man (age 77) and 3 women (age 74–87); the man and one of the women were a married couple. I then began fieldwork with a newly established Cross-disciplinary Training Team beginning in June 2015, shadowing a different therapist each time (who, like the Visitation staff, were randomly selected based on availability). During this period, I followed 9 members of the team (out of 12): 3 physical therapists, 4 occupational therapists, and 2 Social and Healthcare (*social- og sundhedsassistenter, SOSU*) assistants. This included participant observations in their office and evaluations of / training visits to 20 citizens: 6 men (age 54–90) and 14 women (age 54–93). Finally, I followed 1 physical therapist and 1 occupational therapist through a full course of reablement training—from initial evaluation to the end of the program—with 2 citizens each. This lasted from October 2015 to February 2016, during which I closely followed the training program of two women (age 78 and 79) and one man (age 67).[5] I then conducted semistructured interviews with select professionals and citizens. In the following sections, I provide some examples from my ethnographic fieldwork to elucidate how free choice and freedom in eldercare operate in Denmark.

"You Need to Decide for Yourself"

When older citizens apply to receive certain municipal services (i.e., assistance with ADLs),[6] they first undergo an authoritative evaluation to determine whether they need to receive "activating" help from professionals who will support them in performing these tasks for themselves.[7] For example, in their (usually) one-time evaluative visits, a member of the Visitation staff (known as a Visitator) assesses a citizen's physical body in order to determine what it is/is not capable of doing *right now*, as well as how it functions within its physical surroundings (most often in relation to the spatiality and materiality of the home environment). With the government's focus on enabling self-help, an older person's need for care and support is no longer pre-given and, due to the operating logics that inform their work, the Visitators must assume that all citizens will choose to take responsibility for managing their own health and quality of life. Their evaluations focus on "why we want [the citizen] to keep active"; in particular, the Visitator Brynja said that she wants elderly citizens "to understand why we don't just throw help at them. . . . If they just sit down and get helped, they'll only get worse" (interview; February 25, 2016). Here, "getting worse" signifies greater physical deterioration, disability, and decay, which would strain the state's economy due to a need for more supportive services, medical treatment, and possibly hospitalization.

This idea was also emphasized by the Visitator Britt, who told me, "The most important thing is for [citizens] to understand that they have to—and should have the desire to!—take responsibility for their own lives as long as they can" (interview; March 1, 2016). During their meetings with elderly citizens, the Visitators often use the phrase "for as long as possible," which implies a promise, not necessarily of immortality and infiniteness, but rather of a fulfilling life that will continue to be active with a vague, indeterminate end. This articulation reinforces the idea of the elderly citizen as a "limited yet limitless ageing consumer" who has the potential and the freedom to choose how they want to live.

I saw this play out when I accompanied the Visitator Freja to evaluate Ejvild (age 90) after he was discharged from the hospital following surgery on his lower intestine (Photo 46.1). He is almost completely deaf and has heart problems, so his physician recommended that a Visitator assess his living situation to ensure that he could take care of himself at home. He and his wife had also recently applied for a placement in an assisted-living facility subsidized by the municipality. During the assessment, Freja asked Ejvild how he was managing various ADLs, which are the specific areas she needs to assess. Ejvild could manage many of these tasks; e.g., he could bathe himself, get dressed, read the newspaper, walk with a cane, and climb the stairs unassisted. She told him:

Freja: You have the right to attend free exercise sessions and activity classes offered by the municipality. The classes are held nearby, so you can get there easily.

Ejvild: Yes.

Freja: You'll also be able to get out of the house and talk with the other participants.

Ejvild: Uh-huh.

Freja (*looking at her notes*): It might also be good for you to go out for regular walks again, especially once the weather warms up. That will help [improve] your energy and allow you to sleep better at night.

Ejvild (*pleasantly but firmly*): I'm doing fine!

Freja (*nodding*): Of course, you need to decide for yourself.

Field notes, December 3, 2014

In her expert opinion (and following the political discourse), Freja believed that Ejvild would benefit from attending exercise classes for the elderly at a local activity center, and she gave him the choice to participate. She framed the state-supported options she offered—to attend activity classes and take regular walks—as opportunities to improve his energy, engage with other citizens, and sleep better.

As such, Freja gave Ejvild the choice of how he wanted to act and the possible ways he could choose to improve his quality of life. With the free choice to "decide for [themselves]," the Visitators offer elderly citizens a moral choice to remain productive, competent social agents and self-helping citizens—to be a "limited yet limitless ageing consumer." In many of the Visitation encounters I followed, disability and death are treated like an epidemic that can be avoided (Foucault 2003: 244), especially if the citizen chooses to engage in exercise to improve or maintain their physical capacity for as long as possible. However, like many people who may not be particularly interested in exercising, Ejvild insisted that he was "doing fine!" and declined the municipal offer. By resisting the political intention that he remain an active and productive citizen, he made a choice about how he wanted to live. But Ejvild's free choice to "live your life as you wish" also complicates how the state is able to manage him. This is part of the rationale behind Denmark's newest offer to elderly citizens.

Offering a New Choice

One of the Visitator's tasks is to act as a gatekeeper to other municipal programs and services in which specially trained health workers can support citizens in making the "correct" choices. In particular, due to an addendum to the Social Services Act that went into effect in 2015, all Danish municipalities

Photo 46.1   During her authoritative evaluation, the municipal Visitator Freja interviews Ejvild (age 90) about his health and living conditions to determine if he is eligible to receive state-supported assistance at home (December 2, 2014). (Photo by Amy Clotworthy)

must now offer reablement, a short, time-limited "everyday rehabilitation" (*hverdagsrehabilitering*) program to any citizen who has been evaluated as having decreased functional abilities and could benefit from physical training. The overall purpose of these programs is almost identical in each municipality, but the organizational framework can vary (Kjellberg et al. 2013). Each municipality can also determine the length and intensity of the training offer, which may range from six weeks to an indefinite duration (Hansen 2013). The premise of the program is that training at home will reduce an older citizen's need for hospitalization, medical treatment, and especially in-home welfare services—such as meal preparation, personal care, and house cleaning. In order to follow the political logic that governs and defines their work, the reablement therapists are supposed to help citizens make the "correct" choices so they can "master" their everyday lives and achieve a better quality of life— to "train themselves free" from the need for municipal services.

However, in contrast to the work of Visitation, which requires an authoritative and standardized evaluation of the older citizen's present needs and abilities—as well as a determination of their willingness to remain a "limited yet limitless ageing consumer" to benefit the state—the Training Team's therapeutic work reveals the citizen as a complex person who cannot easily fit into an ideal type or the state's preconceived categories. Here, each person also makes an investment in the outcome: the citizen because their health is at stake, and the professional because they are concerned for the citizen's welfare (Charles, Gafni, and Whelan 1999: 656). As I discovered, the relational space of the training session contains complex forms of collaboration, interaction, and connectivity. These encounters are based on shared decision-making, wherein a citizen is given the opportunity to choose activities and actions together with the therapist. By collaboratively defining the "narrative" structure of training (i.e., its beginning, middle, end; Mattingly 1994: 817), the citizen is given the freedom to choose which activities they want to train. As the physical therapist Sofie explained to me, "Despite what the referral is about, the older person completely has the opportunity to tell us and think about what they want. And what they don't want" (interview, December 21, 2015). Moreover, in order to make progress with the training, the therapists must encourage older citizens to display their "messy subjectivity." Because of this change in subject position, the matter of free choice also transforms.

"I Need to Do It So I'm Not Dependent"

To address concerns about population aging, many Western countries have begun to implement specialized rehabilitation or reablement programs. Typically, this form of training is a "time-intensive, time-limited intervention provided in people's homes or in community settings, often multi-disciplinary in nature, focusing on supporting people to regain skills around daily activities" (Aspinal et al. 2016: 1). In Scandinavia, the Swedish version is called *hemrehabilitering* (home rehabilitation), while the term *hverdagsrehabilitering* (everyday rehabilitation) is used in both Norway and Denmark. These programs are meant to increase elderly citizens' level of physical and social activity, as well as to maintain and delay a deterioration of functional ability (Månsson 2007).

In August 2014, the municipal leadership in Toftsby formally established the Cross-disciplinary Training Team, which is comprised of both occupational and physical therapists as well as SOSU assistants. In general, the municipality offers "everyday rehabilitation" to all eligible citizens, but the program is primarily targeted at older people who have requested supportive services. Both Visitation and the Training Team in Toftsby use an internal distinction to categorize citizens in relation to their goals for participating in

Photo 46.2   Ulla (age 78) trains to put on her support stockings by herself under the watchful eye of the occupational therapist Katrine, who provides guidance (December 2, 2015). (Photo by Amy Clotworthy)

the program: "train yourself *free*" means the citizen can do much more than before and no longer needs any municipal help; "train yourself *freer*" means the citizen can do much more than before and needs less municipal help; and "train yourself *stable*" means the citizen maintains a stable functional ability but still needs some municipal help. As the occupational therapist Katrine explained to me, "train yourself stable" is mostly for citizens who live in a nursing home, while those who live in their own homes generally fall into the "train yourself freer" category (field notes, October 22, 2015).

I followed Katrine's training sessions with Ulla (age 78), who has chronic obstructive pulmonary disease (COPD), which affects her breathing and circulation. She has also undergone several surgeries to her back as well as a knee replacement. Ulla's constant pain severely limits her ability to walk unassisted; she chose to participate in the rehabilitation program because she hoped to reduce her pain and maintain her current level of functionality. In addition to improving her ability to walk, one of the training goals was for her to put on and remove her support stockings by herself[8] so that she did not need a Home Care worker to do this for her every morning and evening (Photo 46.2).[9]

During one session, after practicing with the stockings several times, Katrine noticed that Ulla was breathing heavily and getting tired; she encouraged her to take breaks if she needed to, giving her a chance to catch her breath. As they continued, Ulla repeatedly said, "This is really hard work"— and, after each rest-break, Katrine asked, "Do you have the strength to take them off and put them on again?" and "Do you have the courage to try it again?" Ulla persevered until Katrine decided to end the training:

> *Ulla*: I don't have any more strength. . . . I don't think I can do it again.
>
> *Katrine*: No, you should just keep [the stockings] on now.
>
> *Ulla*: But I thought we needed to train more.
>
> *Katrine*: No, you've done it two times—that's enough.
>
> *Ulla*: Well, I need to at least try to do it myself. . . . I need to do it so I'm not dependent.

Field notes, December 2, 2015

As I observed during many of the training sessions I followed, the therapists encounter a citizen's "messy subjectivity," which refers to the complexity of the human agent as a person. More than someone's unique identity or sense of self, this form of subjectivity encompasses the various "modes of perception, affect, thought, desire, fear . . . that animate acting subjects" (Ortner 2005: 31). These modes of affect and thought can be shaped by cultural and social formations, especially in relation to how people act on the world "even as they are acted upon" (Ortner 2005: 34). The display of these subjectivities makes social beings much more than the holders of certain subordinate identities and categorizations, such as "the elderly." Like in the example with Ejvild declining the Visitator's offer, I consider these active forms of subjectivity to be "messy" because, when they are displayed, they can complicate—and often contradict—the docile compliance or individual rationality that is expected in the political context of a home-health visit or training session (Clotworthy 2017). Humans do not always make rational choices—especially if they are sick, injured, or dying. In these situations, they may be overcome by emotions that compromise their self-control as well as their "rational agency" (Walter and Ross 2014: S18). Thus, a complex person with their messy subjectivity may not always make the "correct" choices or behave like a rational consumer that follows the political discourse or conforms to the logic of a market economy.

However, in this case, Ulla did make the "correct" choice, saying that she thought they "needed to train more." This highlights how the political discourse about being a more self-helping and "independent" citizen—or at least one who is "not dependent" on the state—has permeated Ulla's perception of why she should train. Animated by the political and cultural discourses that shape her everyday life, Ulla freely chooses to train more, even though she is in pain and exhausted. But in the context of their relational collaboration as social actors, Katrine recognized that Ulla could no longer manage the physical operation of putting on her stockings. And *she* made the choice to end the session, telling Ulla "that's enough."

In this example, Katrine made a judgment and a decision about how much activity Ulla could realistically handle that day; she acknowledged the hard work that Ulla had already done and helped her modulate her choices, which gave Ulla a sense of reassurance and security. There was no individualized moral judgment here—in particular, Katrine did not push Ulla to do *more* to become self-helping. This is because, in the social relationship that has developed between them through shared decision-making, she does not encounter Ulla as a "limited yet limitless ageing consumer." Instead, in order to make progress with the training, Katrine has acknowledged Ulla's "messy subjectivity" and recognized her as a complex person who can only achieve her goals—to "live your life as you wish"—if she sets reasonable limits for herself. Thus, Katrine defies the political discourse and expectations that frame their encounter. By making this choice, Katrine thereby frees Ulla from the state's moral obligations, which gives Ulla the freedom to resist the political forces that shape how she should grow old.

Conclusion

How and when we are considered "old" is greatly dependent on our social environment, and there are particular sociocultural systems that shape and affect how we age. There are also specific discourses that inform both the public mindset and everyday practices, and which contribute to how we become positioned as different types of subjects. More and more, certain perceptions about aging are being reinforced through advertisements, films, television programs, and social media. But, as I described in the introduction to this chapter, there are also certain perceptions of *how things are in Denmark*—in terms of happiness and *hygge*, but also with regards to healthcare and services for the elderly. For example, there was a video posted online in October 2017 titled "Denmark's Senior Care Is Much Better Than America's."

WEB SPECIAL:

"Denmark's Senior Care Is Much Better Than America's." https://archive.attn.com/stories/18945/denmarks-senior-care-much-better-americas.

The video was produced by a team of researchers and journalists at a Los Angeles–based media company called ATTN:, and it is part of a popular online series called "America Versus," which compares various U.S. policies to those in other nations. The text that accompanies the video says: "In Denmark, senior care is designed to keep elders active and independent. Everyone receives free help and medical care from professionals. In America, seniors are often neglected and abused."

The video depicts certain perceptions about the aging process and elder-care in Denmark. Specifically, that the state freely supports older citizens in being active and independent, that they can freely choose their living arrangements and care services, and that they receive free help from their local municipality. However, as I have suggested in this chapter, nothing in Denmark is really *free*. Individual freedom and free choice are tightly regulated by the government and controlled by its representatives in the municipalities. The freedom to make life choices and to "live your life as you wish" is only possible if social actors fulfil their politically determined obligations as productive, self-governing workers and citizens. But, rather than being stifling or oppressive, this tacit social contract ensures that Danes feel a sense of security and satisfaction from knowing exactly what is expected of them as citizens and exactly what they can expect from the state. In a Danish context, having unlimited liberty and the freedom to choose is not necessarily commensurate with happiness. Danish philosopher Søren Kierkegaard even suggested that the freedom to make choices produces a particular form of anxiety or dread: "Anxiety is the dizziness of freedom"—i.e., the awareness of the possibility of *being* able to make a choice (Kierkegaard 1844/1981). This means that, in addition to considering the state's secure (some might say "tight") social-welfare framework as a way to manage societal complexity and growth, the Danish notion of "free choice" may also be a way to reduce ambiguity and mitigate existential anxiety among citizens in order to stabilize society.

Thus, with regards to the "secret" of Danish happiness, I believe that one of the main reasons is that Danes have long trusted the government and their fellow co-citizens (*medborgere*; Ludvigsen 2016: 90) in the homogenous collective to take care of them "from cradle to grave," and they generally accept both the political and societal expectations for the choices they are allowed to make in life. Although many contemporary Danish health policies and programs emphasize self-governance and individual responsibility, it is important to note that defining ourselves as individuals requires us to relate to *others* in the social collective, and choices are not made by autonomous individuals in isolation from their complex social environments. During my fieldwork, both the health professionals and citizens consulted with and made decisions in collaboration with many other external actors (i.e., friends, family members, neighbors, colleagues). In this way, care for the individual citizen's welfare becomes a shared responsibility that is distributed among and between a range of actors in the collective Tronto 2017: 30). When this happens, the individual person becomes articulated as a different type of subject—a subject who is interconnected and included as part of a whole.

With the everyday-rehabilitation program and other eldercare services, the political leadership in Denmark recognizes that some citizens—especially those with certain health conditions or functional limitations—may need to receive specific forms of support, knowledge, tools, and/or assistance from municipal health professionals so that they can remain independent and self-sufficient in their own homes. Rather than excluding older citizens from the collective (e.g., by denying their personhood and agency, forcing them into nursing homes), such programs are meant to help these citizens remain socially engaged for as long as possible. The everyday-rehabilitation program also enables older citizens to be more physically mobile, which allows them to continue to care about and take a shared responsibility for others in their local community. This is reminiscent of the social values that defined the "golden age" of the Danish welfare state: there is no "individual," only the "community" of which everyone is equally a part, and to which everyone equally contributes. Fundamentally, we humans need care, human connection, recognition, security, and inclusion in a social collective much more than we need unlimited freedom and choices. Caring for and about others (and being cared for and about ourselves) is an essential part of what makes us human, social actors.

Of course, as the Danish state continues to develop and transition, the expectations for and choices available to citizens are also changing. While care and collective responsibility (and yes—happiness) are alive and well in the "rotten" state of Denmark, my research suggests that we should question the limits of neoliberal individualism, rationality, efficiency, and capitalist development—as well as the archetype of the "limited yet limitless ageing consumer." Thus, I would caution anyone (such as Bernie Sanders) who wants to import the Danish welfare model to another setting. Mostly, because this would require them to import a particular set of social actors who have been both socially and politically constituted. But also because they would have to import a shared history of cultural values, norms, and traditions—in addition to a complex range of socioeconomic developments and political expectations—that have shaped Denmark's particular cultural context. Most important, though, because they would also have to import the Danish form of care, community, and free choice.

Notes

1. This refers to the social values promoted by the Danish "enlightenment" movement of the 1880s, which encouraged free thought, an open exchange of ideas, a strong social consciousness, a lack of restrictions on economic activities,

egalitarianism, and a sense of shared community (Lidegaard 2009: 28, 32; also www.grundtvig.dk).

2. During the 1990s, national politicians also began to decentralize and reform the public sector, privatizing a number of state-owned companies (Lidegaard 2009). This development had implications for the provision of supportive health services and programs.

3. Due to a changing economic environment, many wealthy European countries—including Denmark—began "adjusting their models of welfare capitalism" (Green-Pedersen 2002: 271) during the 1980s and 1990s. These adjustments included reforms of the public sector, such as "the introduction of explicit measures of performance, decentralization, private-sector styles of management, contracting out, and privatization" (Green-Pedersen 2002: 271). These reforms generally fall under the category of New Public Management.

4. The name of the municipality and the names of all my interlocutors have been changed to preserve anonymity.

5. The fourth participant—a woman, age 95—became hospitalized after three sessions and had to stop training.

6. *Activities of daily living* (ADLs) are "basic self-care tasks . . . They include feeding, toileting, selecting proper attire, grooming, maintaining continence, putting on clothes, bathing, and walking." *Caring*, "What are ADLs and IADLs?" www.caring.com/articles/activities-of-daily-living-what-are-adls-and-iadls.

7. Much like Denmark's National Insurance Act (*Lov om Folkeforsikring*) from 1933 (Aarhus University 2017), receiving this form of state assistance is meant to be a *temporary* support that should help the citizen regain their former productivity.

8. Support stockings are used to improve circulation in the body, which is vitally important to someone with a cardiopulmonary condition such as COPD. They are typically custom-measured and fit, and are extremely tight. Putting these stockings on is an arduous process that can take several minutes for even an experienced, able-bodied professional to perform.

9. While the political rhetoric focuses on the importance of training citizens to be more self-reliant and independent, this is primarily a cost-cutting measure; an official in another municipality estimated that, by training 100 citizens to put on their own support stockings, the municipality could save 1.7 million DKK (ca. US$260,700) per year on staff expenses. TV2-Fyn 2011. "Ældre skal selv klare støttestrømpen" [Elderly must manage the support stocking themselves], May 17. http://www.tv2fyn.dk/node/38238.

Bibliography

Aarhus University. 2017. "Socialreformen af 1933" [The social reform of 1933]. http://danmarkshistorien.dk/leksikon-og-kilder/vis/materiale/socialre formen-af-1933/.

Anderson, S. 2011. "The Obligation to Participate: Micro-integrative Processes of Civil Sociality." In *The Question of Integration: Exclusion and the Danish*

Welfare State, edited by K. F. Olwig and K. Paerregaard. Cambridge: Cambridge Scholars Publishing.

Aspinal F., J. Glasby, T. Rostgaard, H. Tuntland, and R. Westendorp. 2016. "Reablement: Supporting Older People towards Independence." *Age and Ageing* 45: 574–78.

Blom, A. 2014. "Det kommunale sundhedsområde i et historisk perspektiv" [The municipal health area in a historical perspective]. In *Det kommunale sundhedsvæsenet* [The municipal healthcare sector], edited by B. M. Pedersen and S. R. Petersen. Copenhagen: Hans Reitzels Forlag.

Charles, C., A. Gafni, and T. Whelan. 1999. "Decision-Making in the Physician–Patient Encounter: Revisiting the Shared Treatment Decision-Making Model." *Social Science & Medicine* 49: 651–61.

Clotworthy, A. 2017. "Empowering the Elderly? A Qualitative Study of Municipal Home-Health Visits and Everyday Rehabilitation." PhD diss., University of Copenhagen, Faculty of Humanities. https://curis.ku.dk/ws/files/185 504536/Ph.d._afhandling_2017_Clotworthy.pdf.

CNBC. 2015. "Clinton and Sanders: Why the Big Deal about Denmark?" https://www.cnbc.com/2015/10/14/clinton-and-sanders-why-the-big-deal-about-denmark.html.

Danish Health and Medicines Authority, DHMA (*Sundhedsstyrelsen*). 2015. *Forebyggelse på ældreområdet: Håndbog til kommunerne* [Prevention for the elderly: Handbook for the municipalities]. https://www.sst.dk/da/aeldre/forebyggelse/~/media/06270654E0FD44EFB919F2112ABF794D.ashx.

Foucault, M. 2003. *"Society Must Be Defended": Lectures at the Collège de France, 1975–76*, translated by David Macey. New York: Picador.

Fung, H. H. 2013. "Aging in Culture." *Gerontologist* 53(3): 369–77.

Gilleard, C., and P. Higgs. 2000. *Cultures of Ageing: Self, Citizen, and the Body*. London: Taylor & Francis.

Gilleard, C., and P. Higgs. 2007. "The Third Age and the Baby Boomers: Two Approaches to the Social Structuring of Later Life." *International Journal of Ageing and Later Life* 2(2): 13–30.

Green-Pedersen, C. 2002. "New Public Management Reforms of the Danish and Swedish Welfare States: The Role of Different Social Democratic Responses." *Governance: An International Journal of Policy, Administration, and Institutions* 15(2): 271–94. http://blogs.helsinki.fi/nord-wel/files/2009/03/green-pedersen.pdf.

Gullestad, M. 1989. "Small Facts and Large Issues: The Anthropology of Contemporary Scandinavian Society." *Annual Review of Anthropology* 18: 71–93.

Hansen, B. R. 2013. *Hverdagsrehabilitering—et velkomment guldæg?* [Everyday rehabilitation—A welcome golden egg?] Speciale i Politik og Administration; CCWS Aalborg Universitet.

Hansen, R. 2015. "The Politics of Denmark and Germany's Low Birth Rates." *Brown Political Review*, October 23. www.brownpoliticalreview.org/2015/10/the-politics-of-denmark-and-germanys-low-birth-rates/.

Helliwell, J., R. Layard, and J. Sachs. 2018. *World Happiness Report 2018.* New York: Sustainable Development Solutions Network. http://worldhappiness .report/ed/2018.

Henriksen, I. 2006. "An Economic History of Denmark." In *Encyclopedia of Economic and Business History,* edited by R. Whaples. https://eh.net/encyclopedia/an-economic-history-of-denmark/.

Heritage Foundation 2017. *Index of Economic Freedom.* http://www.heritage.org /index/country/denmark.

Højlund, H. 2006. "Den frit vælgende ældre" [The freely choosing elderly]. *Dansk Sociologi* 1(17): 42–65.

Jensen, P. H., and H. Lolle. 2013. "The Fragmented Welfare State: Explaining Local Variations in Services for Older People." *Journal of Social Policy* 42: 349–70.

Kierkegaard, S. 1844/1981. *The Concept of Anxiety: A Simple Psychologically Orienting Deliberation on the Dogmatic Issue of Hereditary Sin,* edited by R. Thomte. Princeton, NJ: Princeton University Press.

Kjellberg, P. K., A. Hauge-Helgestad, M. H. Madsen, and S. R. Rasmussen. 2013. "Kortlægning af kommunernes erfaringer med rehabilitering på ældreområdet" [Mapping of the municipalities' experiences with rehabilitation in the elderly area]. Odense, Denmark: KORA for Socialstyrelsen.

Larsen, L. T., and D. Stone. 2015. "Governing Health Care through Free Choice: Neoliberal Reforms in Denmark and the United States." *Journal of Health Politics, Policy and Law* 40(5): 941–70.

Lidegaard, B. 2009. *A Short History of Denmark in the 20th Century.* Copenhagen: Gyldendal.

Lønstrup, L. 2008. "Samarbejdsproblemer i ældreplejen: forskerinterview med Tine Rostgaard" [Cooperation problems in eldercare: Researcher interview with Tine Rostgaard]. *Djøfbladet* 32(9): 42–45.

Ludvigsen, B. H. 2016. "Når ældre mennesker bliver gamle" [When elderly people become old]. *Tidsskriftet Antropologi* 73 (Velfærdsstaten 2): 89–110.

Mahler, M., A. Sarvimäki, A. Clancy, B. Stenbock-Holt, N. Simonsen, A. Liveng, L. Zidén, et al. 2014. "Home as a Health Promotion Setting for Older Adults." *Scandinavian Journal of Public Health* 42 (Supp. 15): 36–40.

Månsson, M. 2007. *Hemrehabilitering: vad, hur och för vem?* [Home rehabilitation: What, when and for whom?] Stockholm: Förlag Fortbildning AB.

Mattingly, C. 1994. "The Concept of Therapeutic 'Employment'." *Social Science & Medicine* 38(6): 811–22.

Ministry of Finance (*Finansministeriet*). 2003. *Frit valg og kvalitet—afregningsmodeller på de kommunale serviceområder* [Free choice and quality—Payment models for the municipal service areas]. Copenhagen: Ministry of Finance Working Group. www.fm.dk/publikationer/2003/frit-valg-og-kvalitet.

OECD. 2018. "OECD Better Life Index: Denmark." http://www.oecdbetterlifeindex.org/countries/denmark/.

Ortner, S. B. 2005. "Subjectivity and Cultural Critique." *Anthropological Theory* 5(1): 31–52.

Otto, L. 2013. "Negotiating a Healthy Body in Old Age: Preventive Home Visits and Biopolitics." *International Journal of Ageing and Later Life* 8(1): 111–35.

Pedersen, L. H., and L. B. Andersen. 2016. "Ved NPM's dødsleje—tre ting vi har lært" [At NPM's deathbed—Three things we have learned]. *KORA Publications.* November 23. http://www.kora.dk/aktuelt/temaer/resultatbaseret -styring/udgivelser/i13945/KORA-Ved-NPM's-doedsleje-tre-ting-vi -har-laert.

Pedersen, O. K. 2011. *Konkurrencestaten* [The competition state]. Copenhagen: Hans Reitzels Forlag.

Petersen, J. H. 2008. *Velfærd for ældre—holdning og handling* [Welfare for the elderly—Attitude and action]. Odense, Denmark: Syddansk Universitets- forlag.

Petersen, J. H., K. Petersen, and N. F. Christiansen, eds. 2010. *Frem mod social- hjælpsstaten: Dansk velfærdshistorie bd. 1, 1799–1898* [Towards the social- help state: Danish welfare history, part 1: 1799–1898]. Odense, Denmark: Syddansk Universitetsforlag.

Ringsmose, J., and M. B. Hansen. 2005. "Fælles sprog og ældreplejens organ- isering i et historisk perspektiv" [Common language and the organiza- tion of eldercare in a historical perspective]. *Politologiske Skrifter* 1: 1–46.

Rostgaard, T. 2006. "Constructing the Care Consumer: Free Choice of Home Care for the Elderly in Denmark." *European Societies* 8(3): 443–63.

Springer, S., K. Birch, and J. MacLeavy, eds. 2016. *The Handbook of Neoliberalism.* London: Routledge.

Statistics Denmark. 2018 *Markant flere ældre i fremtiden* [Significantly more elderly in the future]. Copenhagen: Statistics Denmark. https://www.dst .dk/da/Statistik/nyt/NytHtml?cid=26827.

Toftsby Municipality. 2014. "Borgmesterens skriftlige beretning ved 2. behan- dlingen af Toftsby Kommunes budget 2015; onsdag d. 8. oktober 2014" [The mayor's written report at the second reading of Toftsby Municipality's budget 2015; Wednesday, 8 October 2014]. In author's files.

Tronto, J. 2017. "There Is an Alternative: *Homines curans* and the Limits of Neo- liberalism." *International Journal of Care and Caring* 1(1): 27–43.

Twigg, J. 2002. "The Body in Social Policy: Mapping a Territory." *Journal of Social Policy* 31(3): 421–39.

United Nations. 2017. *World Population Ageing 2017—Highlights* (ST/ESA/ SER.A/397). New York: United Nations, Department of Economic and Social Affairs, Population Division.

Vallgårda, S. 2001. "Governing People's Lives: Strategies for Improving the Health of the Nations in England, Denmark, Norway and Sweden." *Euro- pean Journal of Public Health* 11(4): 386–92.

Walter, J. K., and L. F. Ross. 2014. "Relational Autonomy: Moving beyond the Limits of Isolated Individualism." *Pediatrics* 133(1): S16–S23.

WE Forum. 2018. "These Are the Happiest Countries in the World." https://www.weforum.org/agenda/2018/03/these-are-the-happiest-countries-in-the-world/.

World Health Organization. 2012. *Healthy Ageing in Denmark*. Copenhagen; Regional Office for Europe. www.euro.who.int/_data/assets/pdf_file/0004/161797/Denmark-Healthy-Aging-Strategy-Final-July-2012.pdf.

Yglesias, M. 2015. "Denmark's Prime Minister Says Bernie Sanders Is Wrong to Call His Country Socialist." *Vox*, October 31. http://www.vox.com/2015/10/31/9650030/denmark-prime-minister-bernie-sanders.

CHAPTER FORTY-SEVEN

Web Book Photo Essay: Female Mutual Support in Kyoto and Kampala

Charlotte Hawkins and Laura Haapio-Kirk

Available at: http://www.culturalcontextofaging.com/webbook-hawkin shaapiokirk

This photo essay chapter from the ASSA Project blog explores in Kyoto, Japan, and Kampala, Uganda, the powerful contribution of female mutual support. See also: https://www.ucl.ac.uk/anthropology/assa/.

CHAPTER FORTY-EIGHT

Web Book: Keeping the Elderly Alive

Global Entanglements and Embodied Practices in Long-Term Care in Southeast Italy

Gabriela Nicolescu

Available at: http://www.culturalcontextofaging.com/webbook-nicolescu

Nicolescu explores here the success of the "migrant in the family" model of eldercare and the controversial role of female migrant *badanti* in Italy.

CHAPTER FORTY-NINE

Triangles of Care in Transnational Spaces of Aging

Social Engagements between Urban Tanzania, Oman, and the United States

Sandra Staudacher and Andrea Kaiser-Grolimund

Bi Sharifa and Her Caring Son in Oman

As many times before, my research assistant Saada and I[1] knocked on the huge iron gate outside the compound of a new, impressive pink house in a better-off area in the city of Zanzibar (Photo 49.1). The house was surrounded by a nicely cultivated garden. It was around ten o'clock in the morning. A child came to open the gate and led us past the busy women in the inner courtyard to Bi Sharifa,[2] who was sitting on a mat. We greeted each other in the typical way between (Muslim) women, touching the palm of her hand and adumbrating to lead my hand to my heart. The frail older woman needed help to get up as she wanted to move to a more private room. Saada and I sat down in the living room, like Bi Sharifa, not on the velvety sofas but on the carpet. The living room in the spacious house was nicely decorated with artificial flowers, pictures, and curtains. It was well equipped with electronics like a hi-fi system and a big TV. This grandmother insisted that we stay even though she had a low fever, was tired, and sometimes dozed off while we were there. Bi Sharifa sat around most of the time because, she said, she does not feel like she could do anything anymore:

> My health condition is that I am old, and I am not strong anymore, and my legs are not healthy. My child [the daughter of her niece] cooks for me, I just receive the food. I can bathe myself. But I can't do the laundry. . . . I can talk and sleep. But I can't do the laundry, grate coconut, collect firewood, fetch water because of my chest. Asthma is always bothering me. Until I get an injection, I am unable to sleep.

Bi Sharifa needs help for almost everything. She is grateful about the care she receives from her family in the household. About the daughter of her niece with whom Bi Sharifa stayed, she said: "She does everything. She is my Mama. It is not one or two things that she does for me. She does everything, all the work is up to her: eating, dressing, traveling, sleeping." Besides the care she receives during the day, she sleeps in a room together with two young girls, the daughters of Mama, who assist her at night.

Apart from the support of "Mama" and the people in her household, she receives care from the son of another niece, whom she also raised in Zanzibar and who moved to Oman many years ago. Bi Sharifa brought up her niece's son Omar like a son. When I was with her, she did not talk about him often, but she gave us his phone number and some sweet and salty snacks for him when we told her that we were planning to go to Oman to meet the relatives of older people in Zanzibar. Omar, who is in his late forties, mostly lived with Bi Sharifa before he went to Oman. Omar moved to Oman with a scholarship to study Arabic 20 years ago. After he married in Muscat, Oman he sent a visa to Bi Sharifa, who came to visit him for four months. Since then he has travelled to Zanzibar once every year. He calls Bi Sharifa every day even though it is not always easy because she has lost many mobile phones. If he does not reach her, he can call his siblings who live with her in Zanzibar.

Omar said that he makes sure that he provides her with everything. Doing less would make him feel imperfect considering all that she has done for him. Omar, who is an imam and takes care of the neighboring mosque, told us that the Quran advises people to live with their parents and other older people, and to provide them with whatever they want without complaining. Additionally, he mentioned that one should help a mother three times more than a father. Omar regularly sends money from Oman to Bi Sharifa in Zanzibar. If she needs more financial means, for example, for a treatment of a health problem, he arranges for his brother in Dar es Salaam to send her the amount. Omar tried to convince Bi Sharifa to live with him in Muscat, but she told him that she does not want to do so because she could not move around independently without driving a car in Oman.

Photo 49.1   Saada, the research assistant, is knocking at the big gate of Bi Sharifa's house in a better-off area in Zanzibar City. (Photo by Sandra Staudacher)

Bibi Annette and Her Daughter in New York, United States

Bibi Annette is a retired sports teacher living in a former civil servant's area of Dar es Salaam. She was 70 years old when we[3] met for the first time. Bibi Annette has an interesting life story, that she told me with her almost accent-free English in one of our lively conversations in the courtyard in front of her house. Here we usually sat and talked, while drinking a glass of her favorite apple juice that she bought in the shop nearby. Related to her job, she had traveled to Australia, Europe, the Middle East, and elsewhere in Africa. Bibi Annette told me that when she traveled she usually observed what people did for their health, increasing her knowledge about a healthy old age. She tried to walk to places instead of taking the public transport. Although diagnosed with hypertension and back pains, she only complained about her body weight, which according to her was too high. She was also very particular about food. Bibi Annette used a vitamin powder imported from South Africa and made sure that her diet was balanced. She explained her idea of a good old age with the following words:

> Everything you have to do in small amount, for example, if you are drinking, take a little alcohol and if you eat, just take little amounts of food and

not too much, you should not overdo anything you are doing and that will
be good for you, so everything in life you have to do in good measure even
if you are learning otherwise you might get stress that's what I believe even
if you are playing basketball!

Bibi Annette shared her house with two of her sons. Her older son James
was married and came to stay with his wife and their newborn baby to get
some support from Bibi Annette and the household helper working in the
house. The younger son David suffered from depression, causing her many
sorrows. He was diagnosed and took some antidepressants, while Bibi
Annette cared for him. Bibi Annette separated from her husband when she
was in her mid-fifties, when he decided to marry a younger wife. Sometimes
she regretted being a single mom, during the time her sons would have
needed more financial support to access higher education, she explained.
That is why she always very proudly talked about her daughter Debora, the
last-born child, who was about to study and work in the United States when
we met. Bibi Annette lived from the rents that she collected from the six
shops in front of her house, and in times when everything went well, she did
not need any support from her children; rather, she sent some money for her
daughter's school fees to the United States. Debora moved to the United
States several years ago. At first, she was able to stay with a parental aunt to
save costs for living, but later she moved to New York City to make her own
living and pay off the debts that she accumulated during her studies in
upstate New York.

Debora and her mother Bibi Annette had a very close relationship and
exchanged phone calls almost daily despite the time difference between the
continents. From time to time, Debora sent shoes to her mother or other
"nice things" as well as some American dollars hidden in letters. In addition,
Debora communicated with her brother James through the instant messaging application Viber, through which they also exchanged pictures. When
Bibi Annette's husband and Debora's father became seriously sick, Debora
became involved by financially supporting his hospital visits from a distance.
Because of her good health condition, Bibi Annette became a caregiver for
her husband and took over his physical care for almost one year before his
death. He died just one day before his daughter Debora arrived in Tanzania
from New York.

Introduction

This chapter sheds light on how some older Tanzanians age in transnational contexts.[4] As the two vignettes have shown, care in old age may connect several actors within a care arrangement that spans far across national
borders, in our case from Zanzibar to Oman and from Dar es Salaam to the

United States. These care arrangements can be described as "transnational" with migrants as well as those who stay behind remaining connected in social spaces or "multi-layered, multi-sited transnational social fields" exchanging care over time (Levitt and Glick Schiller 2004: 1003). Transnational migration is thus commonly described as a process of "simultaneous embeddedness in more than one society" (Glick Schiller, Basch, and Szanton Blanc 1995: 48). Transnational migration and connected flows of people, goods and ideas can be observed all over the world (Appadurai 2003). Transnational care, however, that circulates through these channels becomes particularly crucial in contexts in which formal social protection like pension and health schemes are not accessible for all and much of the care work is relying on informal actors, such as relatives.

Although the African continent is commonly described as "the world's youngest continent,"[5] in recent years, life expectancy increased drastically in many African countries, so that the number of older people on the continent is expected to more than triple (from 46 to 165 million) by 2050 (United Nations 2017). This demographic transition in Africa is accompanied by a health transition leading to an increase in noncommunicable diseases (such as cardiovascular diseases, cancers, chronic respiratory diseases, and diabetes), which often render older people unable to perform everyday tasks on their own and consequently increase the need for long-term care (Van Eeuwijk and Obrist 2016; World Health Organization 2017). At the same time, younger people especially must be mobile to achieve higher education or make a living elsewhere and consequently, they move away from their aging parents (Grätz 2010). However, the fact that younger adults migrate to "greener pastures" does not necessarily lead to a neglect of older people, as often only few relatives move away—while many other potential caregivers remain in geographical proximity to the older person.[6] Therefore, instead of following a narrative about neglect that is based on the assumption that needy older people are left behind, in this chapter we focus on their engagements in transnational caregiving.[7]

Understanding older people as active agents, we use the constructs of "spaces of aging and caring" and "triangles of care" to better understand the simultaneous and interconnected multiperson networks of caregiving involved in local as well as transnational spaces and the engagements of older people involved in these processes. Additionally, this approach considers the active involvement and agency of older people and illustrates the diversity and dynamic of transnational aging and caregiving in urban African contexts.

In this chapter, we draw on ethnographic data from 17 months of research among a hundred randomly sampled elderly people and their social networks in eight different areas in the cities of Dar es Salaam and Zanzibar, Tanzania, conducted between 2012 and 2015. This was connected with two months of work within Tanzanian heritage communities located in cities and suburbs

Photo 49.2   The two men to the right left Zanzibar in their youth and settled in Muscat after having completed their education in different countries. They regularly travel to Zanzibar, support older relatives in Zanzibar financially, and are contacted as elders if important decisions need to be made. Saleh, the research assistant to the left, traveled with Sandra from Zanzibar to Oman, where he also has many relatives with whom he regularly interacts. (Photo by Sandra Staudacher)

of four U.S. states and Muscat, the capital of the Sultanate of Oman. Through semistructured interviews with open-ended questions, informal talks, and observations, we gathered a considerable quantity of information on elders' health, their aging process, and care arrangements in Zanzibar and Dar es Salaam. We also interviewed the relatives whom the seniors mentioned as their most important caregivers. Because the elderly people mentioned relatives abroad as important providers of their care, we traveled to the United States and Oman to follow particular flows of care (Photo 49.2). The aim was to obtain insights into the transnational spaces in which some older people are embedded and often search for help in critical health situations. We followed up on the older people's contacts and additionally used a snowball system to collect data from emigrated caregivers using their own networks in order to meet other migrants engaged in eldercare from a distance.[8]

The two Tanzanian cities, Dar es Salaam and Zanzibar City, witnessed massive increases in inhabitants in recent years, providing a particular context of aging within a continuing rapid urbanization (URT National Bureau of Statistics 2013). This population shift has been particularly rapid in Dar es Salaam, which is described as the ninth fastest-growing city in the world and home to 6,047,600 million people or 10 percent of the total population of the Tanzania Mainland. Based on the latest national census, only 3.5 percent of the city's population are aged 60 years and above (URT National Bureau of Statistics 2013). In the city of Zanzibar and its agglomeration where around 569,000 inhabitants are living, 3.6 percent of the population is over 60 years.[9] This is still a small percentage of the population, despite the spectacular rise of the life expectancy in Tanzania from 50 years to 65 years over the last 20 years.[10]

In Tanzania, as in many other countries on the African continent, only few institutional arrangements for care of older people exist. Tanzania's Aging Policy stipulates that the family is the "basic institution of care" in old age (URT Ministry of Labour 2003). An estimated 96 percent of people above 60 years in the whole of Tanzania do not have a secure income, while 73 percent of older people remain economically active (HelpAge International 2013). Most of them are not entitled to a pension in old age, and those who are cannot live from it. These elderly people are thus forced to generate an income and/or rely on relatives for (financial) care. Also, when it comes to health costs in old age, health insurance is not widespread. In Zanzibar City, health care is officially free of charge, and in Dar es Salaam the nationwide exemption for people above the age of 60 years comes into play. Nevertheless, due to additional costs incurred from transport to health facilities, medication, or further treatment, access to quality health care remains a challenge.[11]

In an environment where pension schemes and health insurance is not widespread, older people need to find other ways to receive care. Of the 50 elderly research participants in each city, 37 in Zanzibar and 12 in Dar es Salaam had relatives abroad. Many were able to draw on help from these kin and like Bi Sharifa and Bibi Annette were engaged in transnational caregiving practices.[12]

Places of Aging and Caring

Especially in the Global North, often the discourse on aging and care centers around "aging in place," which can be described as aiming at staying relatively independent in one's home and the community instead of moving to institutional caregivers (Wiles et al. 2012). We agree with Baldassar et al. who contend that policy development centered around aging in place, while important, serves to distract attention away from other possible experiences of aging. They contend it is now necessary to consider the implications of aging "out of place" and even "beyond" place, as new transnational and virtual social fields become more significant for social life (Baldassar et al. 2017: 7). Nevertheless, we argue, that place should not entirely be left out in the analysis in the study of transnational aging and caregiving, as it can work to facilitate or hinder care, as we will see below (in more detail: Staudacher 2019a). We must frame care systems within transnational engagement, which entails spaces for both older people and their social network in the country of residence, as well as for their relatives or acquaintances abroad.

We understand place in the sense of Cresswell, as "a meaningful site that combines location, locale, and sense of place" (2009: 169). Cresswell defines the element *location* as an "absolute point in space," which has a certain distance from other locations and defines where a place is. To think with the concept of location can thus be interesting when thinking, for example, how far older people live away from relatives or health facilities. *Locale* includes the material setting for social relations as the "buildings, streets, parks, and other visible and tangible aspects of a place" (Cresswell 2009: 169). For older people, it can be important whether an area has paved roads, or if they are not passable by foot during rainy season, or if their house is surrounded by a big wall, or if they can just sit in front of their house and chat with people passing by. Bi Sharifa, for example, lived in an area with planned public infrastructure, such as roads, electricity, tap water, and garbage collection but also health facilities and available pharmacies. The relatively big house of her niece and the inviting environment of the area allowed for the comfortable hosting of relatives from abroad when they came to visit her. Being able to host visitors at this place allowed her to exchange and engage extensively with relatives from abroad and not only to see them during a short visit. This differed from much smaller houses or shacks of other older people living in poor and dirty surroundings, known for being epicenters for regular cholera outbreaks, at whose places relatives did not want to stay. As a *sense of place* Cresswell understands the individual or shared "meanings associated with a place: the feelings and emotions a place evokes" (Cresswell 2009: 169). This aspect turned out to be important for some of the older research participants as well as relatives who moved out of Tanzania who had strong emotions and especially often nostalgic feelings in relation to the place they grew up or where their parents had lived. Omar, for example, raved about the fresh fruits in Zanzibar, the healthier life of moving around and chatting in one's own language, the pleasant climate, the family members, friends, and memories he has there.

Spaces of Aging and Caring

Having the concept of place in mind, we understand *social space* in contrast to place as a zone that shapes how people interact with and relate to people, commodities, and ideas *between* diverse places. Space in this sense is a social product based on values, the social production of meanings, which affects spatial practices and perceptions (Lefebvre 1974 [1996]). Even though a considerable number of urban elderly people in Tanzania have relatives abroad, this does not mean that they could automatically draw on care or support from them. We found it useful to think with three spaces of aging and caring as an analytical lens to grasp the unequal social engagements of older people: first, a localized space of aging and care; second, a cosmopolitan space of aging and care; third, a transnational space of aging and care. In these spaces, we understand the concept of space as dynamic and being socially produced (Herzig and Thieme 2007: 1079). Space is reproduced relationally in everyday practices and can be defined by the interactions between social practices and place. While we elaborate on the three aging and care spaces in detail elsewhere (Staudacher 2019a, 2019b), we briefly introduce the three spaces below and then, in this section, focus on the transnational space. It is important to understand that the engagements in these spaces are, as we will see, situationally determined.

If older urban residents engage in what we call a localized space of aging and caring, their agency is limited to a narrow local field in their social and spatial surroundings.[13] Here they typically do not have relatives abroad or are not in contact with them. In this specific urban space, access to what we call *cosmopolitan living*—the willingness and possibility to engage with cultural "others" in the urban environment—is hardly possible (Skrbis, Kendall, and Woodward 2004). Older people who can only engage in this space mostly do not have the means to maintain relationships with relatives who live elsewhere since many of these older people and their families live in socioeconomically poor places where, for example, access to means of communication and transportation is limited. In a localized space of aging and care, older people are often not able to overcome major health crises or struggle to deal well with untreated chronic conditions. The case of Bi Sharifa shows us how, even though this elderly woman is part of a transnational family, she usually only engages in a localized space. She does not have the energy or capacity to participate in urban life. The fact that she lives in an area on the outskirts of the city also constitutes an obstacle for her moving around freely.

A second space of aging and caring points to a cosmopolitan orientation of some older people. We understand this cosmopolitan space as being produced by the elderly people who engage in modes of discourse and practices that reflect international mixing and appropriation of cultural styles and symbols from multiple, geographically dispersed places (Fair 2004: 13). For certain research participants cosmopolitanism even became a lifestyle and moral position (Kleinman 2012). Levitt and Schiller argue that the literature on cosmopolitanism neglects exploring social relations and positioning, and focuses on the intersection of the individual and the global (2004: 1008).

Thinking about this space requires bringing the contexts, structures, and practices of cosmopolitanism together. Having said this, it is important to acknowledge that many of the people who live in Zanzibar and Dar es Salaam are very much connected to other parts of the world, be it through their personal history, social relations, commerce, tourism, or media. Some have ancestors from the Comoros, India, or Oman, and they still cultivate relationships with (extended) family in these places. Quite a few older Zanzibari study participants, and especially men, had spent time abroad studying or working (including as football players and actors) while several older people in Dar es Salaam traveled abroad for further education, many of them during their state employment. And there are for example many families that trade with or import goods from Dubai, India, and China (Verne and Müller-Mahn 2013). Like Bibi Annette, who was presented at the onset of this chapter, most older people who are at times involved in such a cosmopolitan space of aging and care have worked or studied abroad and live in social environments with transnational ties. They thus orient their practices toward many different cultural spaces at once. Such persons are more likely to have a higher education and are financially capable of translating their ideas into practice.

The third space to which older Tanzanians relate is a transnational space of aging and caring. Some people are only occasionally involved in this space. For example, some have acquaintances or relatives outside the country but are only sporadically in contact with them. They typically receive visitors from abroad for a short time, and they call each other on important holidays.[14] They usually can expect help from relatives abroad in case of an emergency like a health crisis. Others have one or several relatives or acquaintances abroad and exchange a lot of care in a broad sense. They may communicate with relatives abroad on a daily, weekly, or monthly basis; receive regular remittances; and regularly visit each other. Some elderly people can go for medical treatments abroad, exchange gifts, and receive medicaments and medical tools (Photo 49.3). Relatives abroad often support the older person through their networks in and outside of Zanzibar and Dar es Salaam. Bi Sharifa as well as Bibi Annette do regularly engage in such transnational spaces of aging and caring, as they have a routine of exchanging ideas on the phone or material support with their close relatives in Oman as well as the United States. Bi Sharifa becomes involved in a transnational space interacting with her niece's son who stays in Muscat, especially when she is ill or confronted with a health emergency. The example of Bi Sharifa shows how older people can be involved at times in local spaces and at other times relating to relatives abroad in transnational spaces. Zanzibari have been living for decades in Oman, but still feel responsible to care for older family members in the city of Zanzibar. The older study participants in Zanzibar mostly understood obligations to transnational caring as resulting from the education of their children and from their familial relationships, which created expectations and duties for both sides. Even though it might look at first

Photo 49.3 This active widower lives with his youngest, unmarried daughter and his older brother in Zanzibar. From his other children in the United Kingdom and Canada he regularly receives remittances as well as medical gadgets, medications, or fancy devices like electronic cigarettes. (Photo by Sandra Staudacher)

glance like older urban residents were just receiving this care over a distance, these transnational spaces result from interactions and exchanges between older Tanzanians and their relatives abroad, which often grew over decades. We argue that the engagement in such a transnational space can foster common moralities of aging and care of elderly people and their relatives abroad. Between older people in Zanzibar and their relatives in Oman, for example, we observed common narratives, formations, and practices that marked reciprocity, religious duty, and nostalgia (Staudacher 2019a).

With a comparative approach of thinking with different spaces, we aim at giving a more nuanced picture of the unequal transnational processes of aging and care. It is critical to understanding how only some elderly people in specific situations are able to participate in such transnational spaces of aging and caring, while others' access is limited to localized social spaces. Their embeddedness in and exclusion of certain dynamic spaces of aging and caring shapes older people's imaginations about their own old age, which becomes then visible in their daily aging and care practices. Additionally, elders will draw on different spaces for care depending on their health condition, location within cities, their gender, and previous experiences.

Looking at the different agents involved in the creation of a transnational space, we argue that it is also important to take into account the economic and legal situation of the caring migrant abroad (Lutz 2018: 585). In the Dar es Salaam case we observed that many Tanzanians traveled to the United States with a visitors' or students' visa and overstayed. However, for these overstayers, sending back regular support became difficult due to their non-legal status and low-paying jobs.

The social and legal position of the group of irregular, illegal, or undocumented migrants is "one of almost total exclusion from rights and entitlements" (Vertovec 2007: 1039). For Tanzanians who were supporting parents on a regular basis, it was more common among the so-called well established, those who traveled to the United States with a scholarship or green card, or who were able to turn their initially illegal status into a legal permission to stay. In addition, due to their immigration status, some also became naturalized during their stays, and with a more stable financial situation, they were (legally) able to invite their parents for health checkups to the United States, and traveled back home regularly.[15] The majority of relatives living in Oman had been there since the 1970s or 1980s, acquired citizenship of the Sultanate of Oman, and many came to be state employed and financially and educationally privileged compared to other Omani. Furthermore, other Tanzanian migrants can be described as "temporarily employed." They normally travel to the United States or Oman with a visitor's visa, for example, as nannies. Since their stay is short, they focus on accumulating money to do things like pay for their children's education or to build a house in Tanzania, rather than send home remittances on a regular basis. Migrants in the United States, but also in Oman, engaged in nursing sector employment, sometimes caring for other seniors while leaving their older relatives or parents with other siblings or relatives in Tanzania.

Triangles of Care

To analyze the involvement of different actors in a transnational care space, we focus here on the concept of triangles of transnational care.[16] In our research it became clear that transnational old age care circulates asymmetrically between different places (Baldassar and Merla 2014b). These triangles of transnational care connect older people in the Global South who did not migrate themselves, their spatially close-by caregivers, and their family members in the Global North (United States) and the Global South (Oman). The perspective of a triangle allows us to analyze transnational care from a holistic perspective including all parts of the lived experience of support flowing through translocal and transnational spaces of aging and care.[17]

The spatializing image of a triangle implies that care circulates among more than two people (i.e., younger care giver and elderly care receiver) involved. It helps to shed light on often unnoticed caregivers who live close to the older person in Tanzania. In many cases these caregivers in Tanzania are indispensable in transnational care, in communicating with the migrants in the United States and in Oman and helping organize the flows of remittances. Although neglected by literature on transnational care, these caregivers are greatly valued by Tanzanian migrants in our study. For example, Goodluck, who lived with his parents in Dar es Salaam, explained his function in the transnational care that was provided by his sister and his two brothers residing in the United States as follows: "I am the eye of my brothers in America here in Tanzania, we often communicate through phone, WhatsApp and Facebook. They are highly involved in family issues."[18]

Observing Eyes

Inspired by Goodluck's words, we refer to these local caregivers involved in transnational care as "observing eyes." The observing eyes in Tanzania were usually relatives of the older person. Like Mama, the daughter of the niece of Bi Sharifa in the vignette presented at the beginning of this chapter, these observing eyes are the ones who engage in the practical and technical elements of care. By "being there" Mama and other observing eyes can provide care and closely observe the health condition of an aging parent. The observing eye's engagement comes close to what is described with the Swahili notion of *kuangalia*—to watch the older person (Photo 49.4). In most of the cases, one person was the responsible observing eye; however, the task could also be shared among more than one sibling or relative. They provide information for those far away, which is crucial as often not all aspects are exchanged over the phone, including details withheld by the older person, such as their health condition.

In addition, observing eyes become crucial when flows of goods and money arrive in Tanzania, since the movement of financial support but also gifts or medical equipment has to be organized by somebody trustworthy on site. If Omar wants to financially support Bi Sharifa, he contacts his brother in Dar es Salaam who serves as an interlocutor. This care arrangement is typical and illustrates what we mean by the triangle of care in which the older person, a relative abroad, and an "observing eye" in Tanzania are involved.

Furthermore, observing eyes support the communication between the older person and the migrant through their knowledge of new communication technologies, such as WhatsApp, Skype, or Viber, as in the case of Debora in New York who exchanges pictures with her brother living with Bibi Annette. Also, as in the initial Zanzibar case, to facilitate the interaction of Omar with the elder Bi Sharifa, the daughter of her niece takes care of the older woman in everyday life and enables the communication by providing a mobile phone or organizing the visits of her brother to her house.

Photo 49.4   With the financial
help of their relatives abroad
and the support of someone on
site, some older Tanzanians
engaged in chicken or egg production. (Photo by Andrea
Kaiser-Grolimund)

   Due to the involvement in care provided by Tanzanian migrants to their
older relatives in Tanzania, it became evident that transnational care circulates among several family members involved, as others have noted (Baldassar and Merla 2014c). These authors argue that transnational care cannot be
seen as unidirectional, traveling only from the migrants to the home country,
but rather circulating among several family members in different locations.
Furthermore, as the case of Bibi Annette and her daughter Debora shows,
flows of transnational care within these triangles is dynamic and changes
over time. In times when Bibi Annette enjoyed relatively good health that
allowed her to engage in care for others and earn her living, she invested in
her daughter's school fees in the United States while her daughter just sent
her back shoes or other "nice things" from abroad. However, as soon as a
health problem occurs, relations and exchanges and thus flows may change
directions. In the case of Bibi Annette it was the deteriorating health of her
husband that made his daughter Debora financially support his hospital stay,
while before she was the one receiving financial support from her mother in
Tanzania.

The Shades of Transnational Care

Within the described transnational triangles, various forms of care circulate between different aging contexts. As Kleinman and van der Geest aptly note, care has "various shades of meaning" (2009: 159). This is especially found in transnational networks, where caregiving cannot be of a physical kind as when providing practical support for an older person in their house—such as preparing food or helping an elder take a shower. Through distance, other forms of care become important, for example, emotional and moral support (Baldassar and Merla 2014a: 49). Also, Tronto's distinction between *caring for* and *caring about* can be helpful here to emphasize that when care is delegated to a third person or an institution, the family member may still be "caring about" (Baldassar and Merla 2014a; Tronto 2001). Therefore, if emigrated children do not have enough means to financially care *for* their parents, they can still care *about* their parents.

ICT-Based and Other Types of Co-Presence

Over distance, relations between parents and children cannot be formed or reinforced through bodily practices of caring but have to use other practices to create closeness and cultivate relatedness. Engagements in different forms of care over distance are thus used to express solidarity and belonging (Baldassar and Merla 2014c: 11). Hence, despite the physical absence, a sense of "co-presence" within the kin network can be maintained by fostering these relationships through care (Baldassar and Merla 2014c: 6).[19] Baldassar and Merla argue for a broad definition of care that also encompasses virtual forms of "caring about" (Baldassar and Merla 2014a: 40). Information and communication technology (ICT) can facilitate virtual forms of caregiving and facilitate what can be called an "ICT-based co-presence," allowing their presence in the country of origin and in the country of migration at the same time (Baldassar et al. 2016: 134; Part II Prendergast). Through phone calls and the use of social media, Tanzanian migrants in the United States and Oman and their parents and other relatives in Tanzania remained connected. The range in the use of ICT was very wide among older people in both cities. While some older people had no mobile phone at all and few older people in Dar es Salaam and Zanzibar had access to a smartphone, others were involved in sophisticated ICT arrangements. One older bedridden woman in the city of Zanzibar, for example, had a tablet installed over her bed, by which her son in Oman could surveil and chat with her around the clock.

In addition, transnational care does not only involve the exchange of financial resources and goods but also the communication of ideas and practices "associated with other societies . . . adopted and adapted by various social actors" (Coe 2017: 543). Ideas about practices of care and health in old age circulate within transnational triangles through medical remittances[20] of medicines, medical equipment such as blood pressure monitors, walkers, or other equipment for care such as diapers. As for now, "literatures on care worker migration have tended to neglect how transnational networks act as conduits through which orientations, ideas and ideologies of care are circulated and mediated within and across 'national' terrains" (Yeates 2011: 1126). Hence, global policy concepts such as "successful aging" circulate with transnational care and can be mirrored in older people's aging practices somewhere else (Rowe and Kahn 1997; Part I Lamb).[21]

Conclusion

Tanzania as well as other African countries are currently witnessing rapid transitions related to a growing and aging population, continuous urbanization, and an increasing number of older people living with chronic illnesses. In this rapidly changing context, actors on all levels from older persons and their relatives up to national and international agents are struggling to handle the transforming and newly emerging issues of eldercare. While in some countries, government policy statements call for a return to the "virtues of the past"[22] (Geest 2018: 21), new forms of eldercare emerge. As described for Ghana, new services for older people have emerged that outsource care beyond family networks and are organized by returning migrants (Coe 2017; Part II Coe). In contrast the handful of "old age homes" in Zanzibar and Dar es Salaam were described by the research participants as a last resort. While we could not observe a tendency to build new nursing homes or care services for elderly people in Tanzania for now, some attempts to outsource care exist, such as when relatives living in Oman and the United States employ a nurse or a physiotherapist for their aging parents in Tanzania, while having a local "observing eye" supervise these services.

As we have shown, in research transnational aging and caregiving are more and more recognized as important intersections between aging and migration (Ammann and van Holten 2013; Palmberger and Hromadžic´ 2018). While a number of studies are concerned with transnational care provided for children within global care chains of workers (Hochschild 2001; Skornia 2014; Lutz 2018), only a few studies looked at aging in connection to transnational care provision so far (Mazzucato 2008; Lamb 2009; Torres and Karl 2016; Dossa and Coe 2017). If we analyze the interconnection of aging and migration, we can see at least three different categories of older people: "aging migrants," "migrant elderly" and the "left-behind elderly" (Wilding and Baldassar 2018: 227). Our studies presented in this chapter, which we conducted among urban elderly people in Dar es Salaam and Zanzibar as well as among their relatives abroad, showed that a focus on elderly "nonmigrants" is crucial to understand the complexity of this transnational phenomenon (Baldassar, Baldock, and Wilding 2007). At the same time, however, we think it is important to contrast the situation of "transnational nonmigrant elderly people" with older people who do not have access to transnational spaces at all. Only through contextualizing can we attempt to understand what transnational aging actually means to transnational nonmigrant elderly people.

The importance of the possibility to engage as an older person in informal transnational care spaces becomes especially obvious in contexts with few formal structures that offer social protection like strong pension schemes, free access to health care, or support in caregiving at large. Fostered by access to new media and travel opportunities, the role of informal support networks that go beyond the local or proximate scale are growing and need to be further acknowledged in research and policies (Wilding and Baldassar 2018: 232). Within these networks, not only money and goods travel across national borders but also ideas shaping (future) aging imaginations of transnational nonmigrant older people. In order to explore transnational aging and connected dynamics, a multisited research approach is crucial (Mazzucato 2009). In doing so researchers can take into account the changing local, national, and international contexts as well as the diverse and sophisticated ways of being connected that are at stake in eldercare over a distance within transnational social spaces.

Notes

1. The research in Zanzibar (Tanzania) and Muscat (Oman) was conducted by Sandra Staudacher with the support of the research team in Zanzibar consisting of Saada Omar Wahab and Saleh Mohammed Saleh, and the research team in Muscat consisting of Nujaida Al Maskari and Saleh Mohammed Saleh. Further reflections on the collaboration with research assistants can be found in Kaiser-Grolimund, Ammann, and Staudacher 2016.

2. All personal names are anonymized in order to protect the identity of the interlocutors.

3. The research in Dar es Salaam was conducted by Andrea Kaiser-Grolimund with the support of the local research team consisting of Neema Duma, Monica Mandao, Elisha Sibale Mwamkinga, Frank Sanga, and Judith Valerian.

4. Our PhD studies were part of the comparative research project "Aging, Agency and Health in Urbanizing Tanzania" headed by Dr. Brigit Obrist and Dr. Peter van Eeuwijk (University of Basel), Dr. Joyce Nyoni and Dr. Vendelin T. Simon (University of Dar es Salaam), in collaboration with Sara N. Seme (State University of Zanzibar). The project was funded by the Swiss National Science Foundation (no. 140425 and no. 152694). The Tanzanian National Institute for Medical Research (NIMR/HQ/R.8a/Vol.IX/1376 and NIMR/HQ/R.8a/Vol. II/266) and the Tanzania Commission for Science and Technology (COSTECH

no. 2012-386-NA-2012-125 and no. 2013-305-NA-2013-81) as well as the Zanzibar Research Committee approved the project. In Oman, Dr. Salem Said Al Touby, dean of the Oman Nursing Institute of the Ministry of Health, supervised the research in Muscat. In the United States, Prof. Sarah Lamb, Brandeis University, acted as supervisor for studies in Maryland, Massachusetts, New York, and Ohio.

5. Several Web sites point to the youth of the African continent: Gates 2018; Knowles 2018.

6. This was especially valid for the urban Tanzanian contexts, while research on aging and care in remote rural areas revealed that many older people remained in villages on their own while their children and relatives from a younger generation moved to urban areas, thus engaging in translocal care arrangements (Büsch 2014; Klerk 2011).

7. Even though not in the context of transnational migration, in the literature the fact that in Tanzania and elsewhere in Africa more people age in the urban space today leads to the assumption that a "weakening [of] what were previously imagined to be robust 'traditionally extended family structures' which used to cater to the elderly and the sick" is currently at stake (Makoni 2008: 200). The romantic picture of "African solidarity" is thus seen as threatened by urbanization processes and demographic change that overburden families and as a consequence lead to neglected older people (for a critical debate cf. Aboderin 2004).

8. We then worked with the qualitative data-analysis software MAXQDA and adapted Charmaz's (2006) interpretation of grounded theory (Glaser and Strauss 2010) to analyze our data. Using theoretical as well as emic categories, we coded over 400 audio-recorded interviews. After a period of qualitative data analysis, we again went back to Tanzania for one month of follow-up research. During this stay, we discussed our preliminary findings with each elderly study participant and with Tanzanian academics as well as state and NGO representatives during dissemination workshops at the State University of Zanzibar and the University of Dar es Salaam. Listening to their opinions and comments concerning the findings was a very fruitful process.

9. The age officially defined as "elderly" by the Tanzanian State is 60 (United Nations 2014: 346).

10. See "Tanzania: Life Expectancy at Birth," https://countryeconomy.com /demography/life-expectancy/tanzania.

11. In 2016, a universal pension was introduced in Zanzibar, but only people above 70 can draw the pension, which is a fractional amount of what an older person would need and is thus rather symbolic. In Zanzibar only around 5 percent of all people above 60 receive a pension of a contributory pension scheme (Revolutionary Government of Zanzibar 2013: 27). Those older people who do receive such a pension are mostly former state employees, and only recently the pension scheme was opened for all employees who want to contribute. However, the option is hardly used. In Dar es Salaam the number of people benefiting from a pension from a former employer after their retirement amounts at least to

8 percent, males 14.6 percent (Mboghoina and Olsberg 2010: 5). This number is higher if compared to other regions of the country (4.4 percent for all of Tanzania). While government employees profit from a pension, and those who retired after 2009 also from health insurance coverage, the majority of older people are left with very few governmental supports. The only assistance that is provided is the exemption from health costs at the age of 60 (URT Wizara ya Afya na Ustawi wa Jamii 2007: 32).

12. The older people in Dar es Salaam who were able to engage in transnational spaces tend to belong to a middle income group or "middle class" of whom some former state employees had studied abroad and came back to the country after that. The fact that only one of the four sampled subwards of Dar es Salaam belong to a middle-income area explains, therefore, the low number of emigrated relatives in the Dar es Salaam sample. Many older Zanzibari had relatives spread all over the world. Most Zanzibari, and especially those residing within the city, identify as Swahili and are a well-known example of a mercantile civilization (Middleton 2004). Founded by Arab migrants, urban Swahili communities such as Zanzibar have historically built up long-standing relations and exchange with Arab, African, and Asian societies (Caplan and Topan 2004; Mazrui and Shariff 1994), which were after the Zanzibar revolution in 1964 again tightened through the emigration or displacement of Zanzibari with "non-African" backgrounds who built up their new lives for example in Oman, the United States, or Europe. Today, building on these relations there are also many families that trade with or import goods from Dubai, India, and China (Verne and Müller-Mahn 2013).

13. In our understanding of agency, we rely largely on Emirbayer and Mische (1998).

14. Such as Eid al Fitr or Christmas.

15. Vertovec distinguishes for the United Kingdom six different possible immigration statuses: workers; students; spouses and family members; asylum-seekers and refugees; irregular, illegal, or undocumented migrants; and new citizens (Vertovec 2007: 1036–38). We simplify his enumeration by distinguishing three groups ("well-established," "overstayers," and "temporarily employed") since these three groups seem to make a difference when it comes to the care that they provided to their parents back in Tanzania (see Kaiser-Grolimund 2018a).

16. For an elaboration on transnational triangles of care see also Kaiser-Grolimund 2018b.

17. As Wilding and Baldassar state, "the image of the 'left-behind' elderly abandoned by their migrant kin is becoming increasingly anachronistic" (2018: 230).

18. Cf. Kaiser-Grolimund 2018b.

19. Similar to care relations when care receiver and caregiver are based in the same locality, not cultivating these relations over distance can lead to a process of de-kinning (Schnegg et al. 2010: 24).

20. Medicine that travels between two countries is described by Zanini et al. (2013) as "medical remittances." With the concept, the authors "indicate

the circulation of medicines within personal networks, which also rely on the disparities in income and different therapeutic options available in the respective national and social context" (15). Zanini et al. base their concept on its use by Kane (2012), who talks about remittances of medicine, and Pribilsky (2008), who uses the concept but rather as a descriptive notion without a closer definition of it.

21. Recommendations and the aforementioned medical equipment were sent with particular ideas and ideologies over national borders (Yeates 2011: 1126). The same holds true for vitamin pills, through which migrants impose a particular way of aging to an older person. The fact that healthy people take pills to remain healthy is very much attached to the American culture of "successful aging." It was therefore interesting to observe in Tanzania that some older people did not take these pills on a regular basis, as prescribed by their children or the package insert, but randomly swallowed them, when they felt weak or dizzy.

22. "Unwillingness and inability to provide tangible and effective support to its ageing citizens is camouflaged with calls for a revival of traditional values. As mentioned before, the government's policy presents a stark contradiction with its own diagnosis of the problems that care givers face but it also has political logic: by blaming families for neglecting their older relatives and calling for a return to the virtues of the past it tries to keep up the appearance of good governance" (Geest 2018: 20).

Bibliography

Aboderin, I. 2004. "Modernisation and Ageing Theory Revisited: Current Explanations of Recent Developing World and Historical Western Shifts in Material Family Support for Older People." *Ageing and Society* 24: 29–50.

Ammann, E. S., and K. van Holten. 2013. "Getting Old Here and There: Opportunities and Pitfalls of Transnational Care Arrangements." *Transnational Social Review* 3(1): 31–47. doi: 10.1080/21931674.2013.10820746.

Appadurai, A. 2003. *Modernity at Large: Cultural Dimensions of Globalization*. 6th ed., *Public Worlds*. Minneapolis: University of Minnesota Press.

Baldassar, L., C. V. Baldock, and R. Wilding. 2007. *Families Caring across Borders. Migration, Ageing and Transnational Caregiving*. New York: Palgrave MacMillan.

Baldassar, L., and L. Merla. 2014a. "Locating Transnational Care Circulation in Migration and Family Studies." In *Transnational Families, Migration and the Circulation of Care. Understanding Mobility and Absence of Family Life*, edited by L. Baldassar and L. Merla, 25–58. New York: Routledge.

Baldassar, L., and L. Merla, eds. 2014b. *Transnational Families, Migration and the Circulation of Care: Understanding Mobility and Absence in Family Life*. Vol. 29, *Routledge Research in Transnationalism*. New York: Routledge.

Baldassar, L., and L. Merla. 2014c. "Introduction: Transnational Family Caregiving Through the Lens of Circulation." In *Transnational Families, Migration and the Circulation of Care. Understanding Mobility and Absence of Family Life,* edited by L. Baldassar and L. Merla, 3–24. New York: Routledge.

Baldassar, L., M. Nedelcu, L. Merla, and R. Wilding. 2016. "ICT-Based Co-Presence in Transnational Families and Communities: Challenging the Premise of Face-to-Face Proximity in Sustaining Relationships." *Global Networks* 16(2): 133–44. doi: doi:10.1111/glob.12108.

Baldassar, L., R. Wilding, P. Boccagni, and L. Merla. 2017. "Aging in Place in a Mobile World: New Media and Older People's Support Networks." *Transnational Social Review* 7(1): 2–9. doi: 10.1080/21931674.2016.1277864.

Büsch, F. 2014. "Giving the Elderly People a Voice. Care Arrangements for and by Frail Elderly People in Rural and Remote Communities in Tanzania." Master's thesis, Swiss Tropical and Public Health Institute, University of Basel.

Caplan, P., and F. Topan, eds. 2004. *Swahili Modernities: Culture, Politics, and Identity on the East Coast of Africa.* Trenton, NJ: Africa World.

Charmaz, K. 2006. *Constructing Grounded Theory: A Practical Guide through Qualitative Analysis.* London: SAGE.

Coe, C. 2017. "Transnational Migration and the Commodification of Eldercare in Urban Ghana." *Identities* 24(5): 542–56. doi: https://doi.org/doi:10.7282 /T3VM4FG7.

Cresswell, T. 2009. "Place." In *International Encyclopedia of Human Geography,* edited by N. Thrift and R. Kitchen, 169–77. Oxford: Elsevier.

Dossa, P., and C. Coe, eds. 2017. *Transnational Aging and Reconfigurations of Kin Work.* New Brunswick, NJ: Rutgers University Press.

Emirbayer, M., and A. Mische. 1998. "What Is Agency?" *American Journal of Sociology* 103(4): 962–1023. doi: 10.1086/231294.

Fair, L. 2004. *Remaking Fashion in the Paris of the Indian Ocean: Dress, Performance, and the Cultural Construction of a Cosmopolitan Zanzibari Identity.* In *Fashioning Africa: Power and the Politics of Dress,* edited by J. M. Allman, 13–30. Bloomington: Indiana University Press.

Gates, B. 2018. "The World's Youngest Continent. Gates Notes." https://www .gatesnotes.com/Development/Africa-the-Youngest-Continent.

Geest, S. van der. 2018. "Will Families in Ghana Continue to Care for Older People? Logic and Contradiction in Policy." In *Ageing in Sub-Saharan Africa: Spaces and Practices of Care,* edited by J. Retief Hoffman and K. Pype. Bristol, UK: Policy.

Glaser, B., and A. Strauss. 2010. *Grounded Theory. Strategien qualitativer Forschung.* 3., unveränd. Aufl ed. Bern: Huber.

Glick Schiller, N., L. Basch, and C. Szanton Blanc. 1995. "From Immigrant to Transmigrant: Theorizing Transnational Migration." *Anthropological Quarterly* 68(1): 48–63.

Grätz, T. 2010. "Introduction: Mobility, Transnational Connections and Sociocultural Change in Contemporary Africa." In *Mobility, Transnationalism and Contemporary African Societies,* edited by T. Grätz, 1–15. Newcastle: Cambridge Scholars.

HelpAge International. 2013. "The State of Older People in Tanzania." https:// www.helpage.org/silo/files/helpage-tanzania-brochure.pdf.

Herzig, P., and S. Thieme. 2007. "How Geography Matters: Neglected Dimensions in Contemporary Migration Research." *Asiatische Studien: Zeitschrift der Schweizerischen Asiengesellschaft* 61(4): 1077–112. doi: http://doi.org /10.5169/seals-147765.

Hochschild, A. 2001. "The Nanny Chain." *American Prospect* 11(4): 32–36.

Kaiser-Grolimund, A. 2018a. "The New Old Urbanites. Care and Transnational Aging in Dar es Salaam, Tanzania." PhD diss., Institute of Social Anthropology, University of Basel.

Kaiser-Grolimund, A. 2018b. "Healthy Aging, Middle-classness, and Transnational Care between Tanzania and the United States." In *Caring on the Move. Ethnographic Explorations of Aging and Migration Across Societies*, edited by A. Hromadžić and M. Palmberger, 32–52. New York: Berghahn.

Kaiser-Grolimund, A., C. Ammann, and S. Staudacher. 2016. "Research Assistants: Invisible but Indispensable in Ethnographic Research." *Tsantsa. Journal of the Swiss Ethnological Society* 21: 152–56.

Kane, A. 2012. "Flows of Medicine, Healers, Health Professionals, and Patients between Home and Host Countries." In *Medicine, Mobility, and Power in Global Africa. Transnational Health and Healing*, edited by H. Dilger, A. Kane, and S. A. Langwick, 190–212. Bloomington: Indiana University Press.

Kleinman, A. 2012. "Caregiving as Moral Experience." *Lancet* 380(9853): 1550– 51. doi: http://dx.doi.org/10.1016/S0140–6736(12)61870–4.

Kleinman, A., and S. van der Geest. 2009. "'Care' in Health Care." *Medische Anthropologie* 21(1): 159–68.

Klerk, J. de. 2011. *Being Old in Times of AIDS. Aging, Caring and Relating in Northwest Tanzania*. Vol. 37. Leiden: African Studies Centre, African Studies Collection.

Knowles, D. 2018. "How Long before the World's Youngest Continent Revolts?" UnHerd, June 19. https://unherd.com/2018/06/long-worlds-youngest -continent-revolts/.

Lamb, S. 2009. *Aging and the Indian Diaspora. Cosmopolitan Families in India and Abroad*. Bloomington: Indiana University Press.

Lefebvre, H. 1974 [1996]. *The Production of Space*. [Reprint.] Oxford: Basil Blackwell.

Levitt, P., and N. Glick Schiller. 2004. "Conceptualizing Simultaneity: A Transnational Social Field Perspective on Society." *International Migration Review* 38(3): 1002–39.

Lutz, H. 2018. "Care Migration: The Connectivity between Care Chains, Care Circulation and Transnational Social Inequality." *Current Sociology* 66(4): 577–89. doi: 10.1177/0011392118765213.

Makoni, S. 2008. "Ageing in Africa: A Critical Review." *Cross Cultural Gerontology* 23: 199–209.

Mazrui, A. M., and I. N. Shariff. 1994. *The Swahili: Idiom and Identity of an African People: The Idiom and Identity of an African People*. Trenton, NJ: Africa Research & Publications.

Mazzucato, V. 2008. "Transnational Reciprocity: Ghanaian Migrants and the Care of Their Parents Back Home." In *Generations in Africa*, edited by E. Alber, S. van der Geest, and S. Reynolds Whyte, 91–112. Berlin: LIT.

Mazzucato, V. 2009. "Bridging Boundaries with a Transnational Research Approach: A Simultaneous Matched Sample Methodology." In *Multi-sited Ethnography Theory, Praxis and Locality in Contemporary Research*, edited by M.-A. Falzon, 215–32. Farnham, UK: Ashgate.

Mboghoina, T., and L. Olsberg. 2010. "Social Protection of the Elderly in Tanzania: Current Status and Future Possibilities." In *Special Paper 10/5*. Dar es Salaam: Repoa.

Middleton, J. 2004. *African Merchants of the Indian Ocean: Swahili of the East African Coast*. Long Grove, IL: Waveland.

Palmberger, M., and A. Hromadžić, eds. 2018. *Care across Distance: Ethnographic Explorations of Aging and Migration*. New York: Berghahn.

Pribilsky, J. 2008. "Sending Energías from the Andes: The Social Efficacy of Travelling Medicines." *Anthropology News* 49(5): 13–14.

Revolutionary Government of Zanzibar. 2013. *Zanzibar Social Protection Policy (3rd Draft, 27 January 2013)*.

Rowe, J., and R. Kahn. 1997. "Successful Ageing." *Gerontologist* 37(4): 433–40. doi: https://doi.org/10.1093/geront/37.4.433.

Schnegg, M., J. Pauli, B. Beer, and E. Alber. 2010. "Verwandtschaft heute: Positionen, Ergebnisse und Forschungsperspektiven." In *Verwandtschaft heute. Positionen, Ergebnisse und Perspektiven*, edited by E. Alber, B. Beer, J. Pauli, and M. Schnegg, 7–44. Berlin: Reimer.

Skornia, A. K. 2014. *Entangled Inequalities in Transnational Care Chains: Practices across the Borders of Peru and Italy*. Bielefeld: Transcript-Verlag.

Skrbis, Z., G. Kendall, and I. Woodward. 2004. "Locating Cosmopolitanism: Between Humanist Ideal and Grounded Social Category." *Theory, Culture & Society* 21(6): 115–22.

Staudacher, S. 2019a. "Cosmopolitan Aging in Zanzibar: Elderhood, Health and Transnational Care Spaces Related to Oman." PhD diss., Institute of Social Anthropology, University of Basel.

Staudacher, S. 2019b. "Shifting Urban Margins: Accessing Unequal Spaces of Ageing and Care in Zanzibar and Muscat." *Anthropological Forum* 29(1): 77–94. doi: 10.1080/00664677.2019.1586644.

Torres, S., and U. Karl. 2016. "A Migration Lens on Inquiries Into Ageing, Old Age and Elderly Care: Carving a Space While Assessing the State of Affairs." In *Ageing in Contexts of Migration*, edited by U. Karl and S. Torres, 1–12. New York: Routledge.

Tronto, J. C. 2001. "An Ethic of Care." In *Ethics in Community-Based Elder Care*, 60–68. New York: Martha B. Holstein.

United Nations, Department of Economic and Social Affairs, Population Division. 2014. *World Urbanization Prospects: The 2014 Revision, Highlights.* New York: United Nations.

United Nations, Department of Economic and Social Affairs, Population Division. 2017. *World Population Prospects: The 2017 Revision, Key Findings and Advance Tables.* New York: United Nations.

URT Ministry of Labour, Youth Development and Sports. 2003. *National Ageing Policy.* Dar es Salaam, Tanzania: Ministry of Labour, Youth Development and Sports.

URT National Bureau of Statistics. 2013. *2012 Population and Housing Census. Population Distribution by Age and Sex.* Dar es Salaam, Tanzania: National Bureau of Statistics.

URT Wizara ya Afya na Ustawi wa Jamii. 2007. *Sera ya Afya.* Dar es Salaam: Ministry of Health and Social Welfare.

Van Eeuwijk, P,, and B. Obrist. 2016. "Becoming Old and Frail in Coastal Tanzania." In *The Routledge Handbook of Medical Anthropology*, edited by L. Manderson, E. Cartwright, and A. Hardon, 186–89. New York: Routledge.

Verne, J., and D Müller-Mahn. 2013. "'We Are Part of Zanzibar'—Translocal Practices and Imaginative Geographies in Contemporary Oman-Zanzibar Relations." In *Regionalizing Oman: Political, Economic and Social Dynamics*, edited by Steffen Wippel. New York: Springer.

Vertovec, S. 2007. "Super-Diversity and Its Implications." *Ethnic and Racial Studies* 30(6): 1024–54.

Wilding, R., and L. Baldassar. 2018. "Ageing, Migration and New Media: The Significance of Transnational Care." *Journal of Sociology* 54(2): 226–35. doi: 10.1177/1440783318766168.

Wiles, J. L., A. Leibing, N. Guberman, J. Reeve, and R. E. S. Allen. 2012. "The Meaning of 'Aging in Place' to Older People." *Gerontologist* 52(3): 357–66. doi: 10.1093/geront/gnr098.

World Health Organization. 2017. *Towards Long-Term Care Systems in Sub-Saharan Africa.* Geneva: World Health Organization.

Yeates, N. 2011. "Going Global: The Transnationalization of Care." *Development and Change* 42(4): 1109–30.

Zanini, G., R. Raffaetà, K. Krause, and G. Alex. 2013. "Transnational Medical Spaces: Opportunities and Restrictions." *MMG Working Paper* 13–16.

CHAPTER FIFTY

The Extended Body

On Aging, Disability, and Well-Being

Joel Michael Reynolds

> The function of a social structure is to set up institutions to serve needs. A society that drives its members to desperate solutions is a non-viable society, a society to be replaced.
>
> —Fanon (1970: 53)[1]

Insofar as many older adults fit some definition of disability, disability studies and gerontology would seem to have common interests and goals. However, there has been little discussion between these fields.[2] The aim of this paper is to open up the insights of disability studies as well as philosophy of disability to discussions in gerontology. In doing so, I hope to contribute to thinking about the good life in late life by more critically reflecting upon the meaning of the body, ability, and the variability of each. My central argument is that we should conceptualize age-associated bodily variations and abilities not in terms of individual capacity, but in terms of what I call "the extended body." It is in light of the meaning of embodiment and ability in general that we must think differently and more capaciously about the meaning of late life in particular.

Frail or Failed—Framing Social Gerontology

If philosophy or religion is one's guide, then the good life is hard to achieve. The good life in late life appears harder still. However one conceives of it, at no age is the good life merely a question of individual will or ability—it is possible only thanks to social contexts and environments that support it. In light of this insight, scholars in social gerontology have called concepts such as "successful aging" and "frailty" into question, noting their overly individualistic framing and stigmatizing effects (Rubinstein and de Medeiros 2015; Grenier, Lloyd, and Phillipson 2017). This *deficit model* of aging is especially potent in discourses surrounding Alzheimer's and other forms of dementia and concerning the "fourth age," in which substantial age-associated impairments begin to occur. Critics argue that the deficit model exacerbates already prevalent ageism in individualistic cultural milieus such as in the United States and that it mischaracterizes the variety and complexity of lived experiences pertaining to late life.

Such criticisms sound similar in multiple respects to those found in disability studies and philosophy of disability. Scholars have long argued that philosophers and political theorists mistake and misunderstand the nature of our bodies and the range of flourishing humans' experience. This misunderstanding, critics argue, is rooted in ableism (that is, the privileging of the "normal" able body), a profound lack of knowledge about the lived experiences of disability, and the ableist conflation of disability with pain, suffering, and disadvantage (Reynolds 2017). Are these misunderstandings at the root of deficit models of aging as well? With this question in mind, I turn to a brief history of disability studies and disability theory.

A Brief History of Disability Theory

Disability studies is a multidisciplinary and interdisciplinary field that examines human experience through the lens of disability. The field involves researchers using the tools of empirical, data-driven science as well as those of reflective, critical inquiry. Since its origins in the early 1980s, disability studies has extended into numerous fields spanning the humanities and social sciences. According to most accounts, disability studies began by following the insights of disability activists in the United Kingdom and United States and by arguing against the *medical model* of disability. On the medical model, "disability" indicates a personal misfortune or tragedy due to genetic abnormality or environmental accident: disability is something bad that happens to an individual. Contrast this with the *social model*, which relies on a core distinction between disability and impairment. "Impairment" refers to an atypicality or abnormality of one's body or bodily state, whereas "disability" refers to the negative effects caused by social and political responses to impairment.

The textbook example of this distinction concerns wheelchair use: one might be impaired with respect to ambulation, but it is a world intentionally designed without curb cuts, ramps, or elevators and filled with gawkers and people continually asking, "What's wrong with you?" that make one disabled. The social model of disability profoundly affected local and global understandings of disability, informing arguments that led to the passage of the Americans with Disabilities Act of 1990 as well as those of the United Nation's 2006 Convention on the Rights of Persons with Disabilities.

However, multiple scholars have come forth in the last two to three decades to criticize its limitations, offering what I'll here group as *critical models* of disability. Philosopher Susan Wendell and sociologist Tom Shakespeare contend that the social model fails to take into consideration forms of disability concomitant with pain or significant illness, for disability is not solely a question of social conditions and responses to impairment. It is a "complex predicament" (Shakespeare 2011; Wendell 1996). For example, no amount of curb cuts will substantively benefit one with epilepsy or neuropathic pain; in cases such as those, the medical model is in many respects apt, necessary, and beneficial.

Philosopher Eva Kittay argues that, especially with respect to forms of disability that require intensive care, the social model poorly conceptualizes nested conditions of interdependence and the labor surrounding caregiving (1999). Upon giving experiences of disability their philosophic due, Kittay suggests that they should lead us to reconfigure the very foundation of dominant social and political theories, placing care alongside traditional core values such as liberty, equality, and justice. Cultural critic Lennard J. Davis asserts that disability as an identity is fundamentally unstable in ways that upset understandings of both impairment and disability on the social model. Whether one looks to technological advances or shifts in medical knowledge and practice, everything from polio to moderate visual impairment to attention deficit hyperactivity disorder have either nearly disappeared or grown as forms of disability. Recognition of this fact, Davis (2013) holds, demands a "new ethics of the body," one far more attuned to its profound variability and critical of the social and political power wielded by the concept of normality. Bioethicist and literary scholar Rosemarie Garland-Thomson (1997) argues that it is not the figure of the human primate, but that of the "normate" against which we judge bodily difference and by which we ascribe worth to a life. Across her body of work, she demonstrates how it is more the presence or absence of supportive environments and less the intrinsic value of certain abilities or "normal" ways of being that makes people fit or instead *misfits* (2011).

Philosophers Fiona Kumari Campbell (2001) and Shelly Tremain (2015) maintain that once one takes into account the history of modern medicine, jurisprudence, and the rise of public health governance, the meaning of impairment is as shot through with social and political history as is the meaning of disability. Uncritically conceptualizing impairment as a fact about bodies misses the historical forest for the political trees. Finally, bioethicist Erik Parens, building on years of work at the intersection of bioethics and disability studies, suggests that a sagacious engagement with disability studies requires one to don a "binocular" view of human well-being, one that critically fuses medical and social models together in context (2015). Echoing concerns animating scholars such as Wendell and Shakespeare, a binocular approach to the meaning of disability attempts to take into greater account the multiplicity of disability experiences across a given lifetime and across social, cultural, and historical contexts.

Although the thinkers I have discussed use the term *ableism* with varying frequency, each demonstrates the ways in which ableism is foundational to understanding what it means to be disabled. Whether one employs medical, social, or critical models of disability, the fact that the world is, on the whole, structured for the "normal" able body is an undeniable fact. And the able body, according to the curious logic of common-sense ableism, is a body that does not experience substantive ability transitions. Being able-bodied is further taken to mean that one is able to do something of one's own accord. This logic ignores the fact that no one can do anything without an environment that supports one's purposive action as well as the general conditions of purposivity itself, namely, one's body. Actions and abilities require affording environments, both social and natural.

Ageism and Ableism

For those who have not reflected on the pervasive role that ableism plays in human life, the experience of becoming disabled through aging is especially revelatory. Every institution, every community, and every practice operates by virtue of assumptions and expectations concerning the abilities of their participants. When one becomes comparatively less abled due to aging, one's world transforms. For many, this might mean an acquired inability to work, to engage in certain types of valued activities, or to think and be in the same manner. Ableism, the privileging of the "normal" able body, is at work with respect to any and every stage of human life because anything and everything can be cast under the light of normality, the light of ever-entwined assumptions about how bodies are and should be. Just as one cannot conceptualize aging without ability, one cannot conceptualize ageism without ableism.

Despite the fact that ableism is at the core of ageism, it has not been a central concern for many gerontologists, a problem exacerbated by individualistic theories of aging. In their 1998 book *Successful Aging*, John Rowe and Robert Kahn laid out arguments that would heavily influence gerontology for years to come. On their account, successful aging involves three components: overall well-being, low probability of disease and disability, and high cognitive and physical capacity and active engagement with life (see also Rubinstein and de Medeiros 2015: 34). Note, first of all, that the ableist conflation is at work here: disability is conflated with pain, suffering, disease, and illness, despite the fact that they are fundamentally different phenomena (Reynolds 2017). This is further aggravated by the fact that Rowe and Kahn appear ignorant of the social model's crucial distinction between disability and impairment. Second, and unsurprisingly from a disability studies perspective, critics argue that the successful aging paradigm renders those who don't or can't meet its requirements as failed: "frailty and decline" are in many ways a euphemism for "failure and divide" (Gilleard and Higgs 2010; Grenier, Lloyd, and Phillipson 2017; Pifer and Bronte 1986). This issue is leveraged by what I take to be the paradigm's primary, if not fatal, error: its overly individualistic understanding of the body and well-being. As I will argue below, such an understanding of the body and of ability fundamentally misunderstands the nature of each as well as the role that ableism plays in shaping human experience.

At this point, one might retort, how else than with "frailty" and "decline" should one describe and conceptualize a period of life that does, in point of fact, involve comparative impairment, loss, illness, and often various forms of pain? And especially if one is referring specifically to Alzheimer's or similarly degenerative conditions? In light of the vast body of work in disability studies surveyed above, there are many ways to describe, conceptualize, and experience such ability transitions and their resulting ability states. Let me offer one such way.

The Extended Body

Recall that debates over the meaning of disability ultimately turn on disagreements over the nature of the relationship between bodies and their social and natural environments. Each model emphasizes different nodes of this relationship, whether it be individual biology, social institutions, historical conditions, or political power. I will here suggest that a helpful way to understand this relationship is in terms of the extended body.

"The extended body" refers to the ways in which one's body always extends into its environment, just as its environment extends into it. For example, my ability to run a five-kilometer race depends on a host of natural and social conditions, from proper running gear to navigable paths to a nontoxic environment. It also depends on the conditions of my upbringing and labor: what I was or was not exposed to as a child and the types of demands my economic situation places on my lungs and immune system. It of course also involves my particular body: circulation; central nervous system functioning; joint, ligament, and muscular strength and flexibility; the presence, absence, or particular formation of lower limbs; and so forth. But the point is that my body is just one component, and my ability to run extends far beyond it.

Even if I lacked lower limbs, I might run a 5k using prosthetics. Given current technologies, I might even be faster than someone with "organic" legs. But whether I have access to such technologies—a social, political, and historical question—becomes a condition of my body, just as my body is a condition of the need or relevance of such access. And whether there is air pollution in my immediate environment also becomes a condition of my body, just as my body is a condition of my comparative ability to manage poor air quality, allergies, and the like. To drive this point home, note that my environment and my body are also conditioned by what we could call my *social body*—my class, race, place, gender, sexuality, ethnic history, and so on, and the power and networks they afford. My social body will shape my ability to mobilize larger social and political forces to meaningfully alter things like air quality or technological innovation, things that individual actors cannot change all on their own. My social body will also determine whether I get harassed while running, whether I get the police called on me or can call on them for help, and whether I am taken as a threat or spectator's object. In short, abilities neither end nor begin at the skin, but instead supervene on and extend to the world in which one lives and on which one ever depends. On the extended body view, abilities emerge through context-dependent relationships between an organism and its environment.

The Extended Mind and Body

To better understand the concept of the extended body, let us compare it to the famous philosophical argument for the "extended mind" introduced by Andy Clark and David Chalmers in 1995, an argument that uses an example of age-related disability to make its central point.[3] They contend that we should consider the many tools humans use to expand our memory and problem solving, from writing in notebooks to the innumerable abilities of computers, as extensions of our individual minds. Take their central thought experiment, which centers on just two characters: Inga and Otto. Inga wants to go to the Museum of Modern Art to see an exhibit. She recalls where MoMA is located and heads there. Otto, by contrast, has poor memory due to Alzheimer's disease and uses a notebook to remember things. Otto also wants to go to MoMA, so he refers to his notebook to determine where to go.[4] Is there a philosophically important difference between these two cases? Clark and Chalmers argue no: "There is nothing sacred about skull and skin. What makes some information count as a belief [in one's memory] is the role it plays, and there is no reason why the relevant role can be played only from inside the body." But what if one takes their arguments about belief and the mind and extends them to the body? If memory is in neither the skull nor skin, what about human abilities more generally?

In modern industrial societies, we live in highly modified and constructed environments. Water and sewer sanitation. Roads and public transportation. Investment vehicles and trust funds, including Old-Age, Survivors, and Disability Insurance, also known as Social Security. Such structures exist to facilitate and, ideally, enrich life. Just as I argued above that the ability to run includes everything from the regulation of air pollution to one's social position and body, so we should consider these structures, systems, and modified environments as part of our ability to exist. Without these extensions of the body, many, if not most, bodies end up *dis*-abled, in the sense of having an impairment, and in multiple ways. Take Inga and Otto again, but let us expand the extended-mind thought experiment to incorporate this argument. Call this "the extended body thought experiment."

It is not just the neurotypicality of Inga's brain that allows her to remember MoMA's location. It is also because Inga, as a white, cisgender, heterosexual, able-bodied, 30-something, upper-middle-class individual, has benefitted from her social position in multiple ways. For example, her stress levels have not affected her memory. To be clear, numerous factors affect cognitive functioning. While there are many types of life events that could have rebalanced the effects of her social privilege on her cognitive functioning (trauma, domestic violence and other abuse, death of a loved one, and so on), Inga has, so far, been lucky enough to avoid these.[5] Her specific social positioning currently affords her access to healthy food, regular exercise, and multiple social supports; some mitigation of sexism; and buffering from the profoundly damaging effects of systemic racism, colonialism, cissexism, heterosexism, ableism, and classism.

In the extended-body thought experiment, it is clear that Inga's body extends to all of the things that afford her extended memory in the first place. And it extends to the many more things afforded her given the type of body she has in her specific historical and sociopolitical context. In a phrase, abilities are relational (Gibson 1977). Inga's memory is not simply a matter of whether certain structures exist in her environment, but of *how* her identity, individual history, ancestral history, and the social capital leveraged by each interact with her environment. Just as her memory is not limited to her biological brain, neither are her abilities limited to her biological body. The human body, brain, and mind are extended. And this is a constitutive, not incidental fact: extension makes them what they are.

With respect to Otto, it is not just the neurodiversity of his brain that allows him to remember MoMA's location. It also because Otto adapted to memory impairment through medical resources provided by Medicaid as well as practical and emotional assistance from family members. Otto, as a Latino, bisexual, disabled, 80-something, low-income individual, already had to learn many coping mechanisms to deal with the multiple structural oppressions presented by his social position before acquiring Alzheimer's.[6] It is also the case that while Otto did not need a caregiver to go to MoMA today, he soon will. Otto's body extends to all of the paid caregiving labor from public funds and unpaid familial labor that, in part, afford him the ability to reliably use his notebook for memory, sometimes travel alone, and manage his life activities.

As this recasting of Inga and Otto makes clear, the extensions of the mind cannot be understood without the extensions of the body, and vice versa. Theorizing the good life in late life is a practice in thinking about the variability of the body, including the thoroughgoing extension of the body into one's environment. On the extended body view, the ability to age "successfully" is not a question of one's individual will or effort—to think so would be to misunderstand the nature of ability. It is a question of such will or effort in intricate concert with a vast range of social, political, economic, legal, and other such factors. On the extended body view, losing one's memory, being unable to care for oneself, or having troubles with emotional regulation are not simply and solely negative for an individual—to think so would be to misunderstand the nature of ability and the transitions in ability that all organic life undergoes. Such events mark transitions in the foci, expression, supports, and projections of one's extended body. If one lives in a just, caring society and in the presence of caring providers, family members, and friends, the meaning and lived experience of these transitions will more reliably tend toward the positive.

Ability Transitions and the Good Life

If the thesis of the extended body is right, then the good life in late life is one conditioned by personal, social, and environmental flexibility to ongoing ability transitions. Instead of ableist paradigms of success or harrowing narratives of decline, the best way to conceptualize age-associated ability transitions in particular is in terms of a shift in one's extended body more generally. As the example of Inga and Otto makes clear, this includes the flexibility of everything around one: from caregiving to medical care to accessible housing and transportation to a supportive cultural milieu.[7] There are indeed a host of obstacles to overcome: fear of the body, interdependency, and ability transitions in general; inflexibility of the built environment (massive shortages of homes built for care, accessible public spaces, meaningful public representation, and so on); and inflexibility or sheer absence of structural social supports (health care systems, living wages, retirement plans). If for no other reason than the increased need for care and support that fall outside of ableist assumptions, aging can bring one into closer contact with the many psychosocial inaccessibilities and oppressions that structure our society today, from ageism to ableism, racism to classism, to sexism, cissexism, and heterosexism.

Consider a study in the United Kingdom that followed 34 people over 70 years of age, each of whom had health issues that required varying levels of support and care. The aim of the project was "to identify factors perceived to promote or undermine a sense of dignity in older people in need of support and care," and the analysis found that "the prospect of being helped with personal care and of strangers seeing their naked bodies was unimaginable for some . . . [while] others described how they would accept help in particular circumstances for 'a proper reason' . . . highlighting the moral nature of such decisions" (Lloyd et al. 2014).

Note that the expressed concerns about aging here are tied not simply to engagement in valued activities but also to fear about interdependency. Yet it is not a fact of human nature that people are afraid to be touched by others or to be seen naked by strangers. For people such as myself, who have lived in families with people who require care, that fear appears as a pernicious effect of ableism and ageism. Our body is always and forever in contact with and supported by an infinity of things—our bodies are extended. It is our failure to better facilitate this contact and care in late life that is a primary hindrance to experiencing the potential goodness of this part of life. If ableism is indeed at the core of ageism, then critical reflection on each is necessary to more justly conceptualize and respond to the experiences of late life and to forge a communal future supportive of the good life in it for all.

Notes

1. Many thanks to Andrea Pitts for pointing me to this passage.
2. In philosophical research more generally, there has been relatively little work on aging and even less on disability and aging. With respect to the latter, see Weiss 2017. In both cases, such scholarship rarely, if ever, seriously engages gerontology.
3. Given the aims of this chapter, I focus more on memory than on beliefs embedded in memory, as do Clark and Chalmers.
4. To be clear, Clark and Chalmers do not describe Otto as going to MoMA as part of the well-known Meet Me at MoMA program for people with dementia and their caregivers.
5. I am thankful to two anonymous referees for pressing me to make this point.
6. In this thought experiment and in keeping with the obviously heuristic aim of making a strong contrast, Otto is decidedly not trans because the likelihood of survival to age 60 for trans folk and trans people of color in particular is so comparatively and appallingly low. This tragic fact itself attests to the truth and also import of the extended body. See "A Time to Act: Fatal Violence against Transgender People in America 2017," *Human Rights Campaign Foundation*, Trans People of Color Coalition, http://assets2.hrc.org/files/assets/resources/A_Time_To_Act_2017_REV3.pdf.

7. Matsudo Japan is an example of a community more open to and engaging of people with dementia.

Bibliography

Campbell, F. K. 2001. "Inciting Legal Fictions: 'Disability's' Date with Ontology and the Ableist Body of Law." *Griffith Law Review* 42: 42–62.

Clark, A., and D. Chalmers. 1998. "The Extended Mind." *Analysis* 58(1): 10–23.

Davis, L. J. 2013. "The End of Identity Politics and the Beginning of Dismodernism: On Disability as an Unstable Category." In *The Disability Studies Reader*, 4th ed., edited by L. J. Davis, 231–42. New York: Routledge.

Fanon, F. 1970. *Toward the African Revolution*. Harmondsworth, UK: Penguin.

Garland-Thomson, R. 1997. *Extraordinary Bodies: Figuring Physical Disability in American Culture and Literature*. New York: Columbia University Press.

Garland-Thomson, R. 2011. "Misfits: A Feminist Materialist Disability Concept." *Hypatia* 26(3): 591–609.

Gibson, J. J. 1977. "The Theory of Affordances." In *Perceiving, Acting, and Knowing: Toward an Ecological Psychology*, edited by R. Shaw and J. Bransford. Hillsdale, NJ: Routledge.

Gilleard, C., and P. Higgs. 2010. "Aging without Agency: Theorizing the Fourth Age." *Aging & Mental Health* 14(2): 121–28.

Grenier, A., L. Lloyd, and C. Phillipson. 2017. "Precarity in Late Life: Rethinking Dementia as a 'Frailed' Old Age." *Sociology of Health & Illness* 39(2): 318–30.

Kittay, E. 1999. *Love's Labor: Essays on Women, Equality, and Dependency*. New York: Routledge.

Lloyd, L., M. Calnan, A. Cameron, J. Seymour, and R. Smith. 2014. "Identity in the Fourth Age: Perseverance, Adaptation and Maintaining Dignity." *Ageing and Society* 34(1): 1–19.

Parens, E. 2015. *Shaping Our Selves: On Technology, Flourishing, and a Habit of Thinking*. New York: Oxford University Press.

Pifer, A. J., and L. Bronte. 1986. *Our Aging Society: Paradox and Promise*. New York: W. W. Norton.

Reynolds, J. M. 2017. "'I'd Rather Be Dead Than Disabled'—The Ableist Conflation and the Meanings of Disability." *Review of Communication* 17(3): 149–63.

Rowe, J. W., and R. L. Kahn. 1998. *Successful Aging: The MacArthur Foundation Study*. New York: Pantheon.

Rubinstein, R. L., and K. de Medeiros. 2015. "'Successful Aging,' Gerontological Theory and Neoliberalism: A Qualitative Critique." *Gerontologist* 55(1): 34–42.

Shakespeare, T. 2011. "Nasty, Brutish, and Short? On the Predicament of Disability and Embodiment." In *Disability and the Good Human Life*, edited by J. E. Bickenbach, F. Felder, and B. Schmitz. New York: Cambridge University Press.

Tremain, S., ed. 2015. *Foucault and the Government of Disability*, 2nd ed. Ann Arbor: University of Michigan Press.

Weiss, G. 2017. "The 'Normal Abnormalities' of Disability and Aging: Merleau-Ponty and Behavior." In *Feminist Phenomenology Futures*, edited by H. Fielding and D. Olkowski. Bloomington: Indiana University Press.

Wendell, S. 1996. *The Rejected Body: Feminist Philosophical Reflections on Disability*. New York: Routledge.

CHAPTER FIFTY-ONE

Web Book Photo Essay: "Differently Young" and "*Non autosufficienti*"

Managing Old-Age Stigma in a Senior Center

Barbara Pieta

Available at: http://www.culturalcontextofaging.com/webbook-pieta

This chapter explores how the medical establishment has created dichotomous terms of *autosufficiente* (self-sufficient) and *non autosufficiente* (not self-sufficient) for bureaucratic purposes in Italy. Pieta explores how this plays out in the "Golden Age" Center as a group of dementia patients seeks to find a place in that elderscape.

CHAPTER FIFTY-TWO

Web Book: Heroic Stories of Dementia Care

Grandchildren as Caregivers and Fallacies of Care

Annette Leibing

Available at: http://www.culturalcontextofaging.com/webbook-leibing

This chapter explores the cultural construction of dementia set in the country of Brazil and focuses on heroic tales of grandchildren acting as caregivers. Leibing's work uses these stories to provide a critical perspective on the "personhood" approach to dementia as applied in this country and asserts that the stories may in fact reflect fallacies of care.

CHAPTER FIFTY-THREE

Web Book:
Beyond the Institution

Dementia Care and the Promise
of the Green House Project

Athena McLean

Available at: http://www.culturalcontextofaging.com/webbook-mclean

This chapter details the ongoing transformations of long-term care often discussed as a "culture change" movement. It shows that breaking the bonds of "institutions" cannot be accomplished by physical changes alone, but must be accompanied by addressing the issue of personhood and how it exists within the cultural space of a long-term care environment.

CHAPTER FIFTY-FOUR

Web Book: The Future of Aging in Postindustrial Context

Larry Polivka

Available at: http://www.culturalcontextofaging.com/webbook-polivka

This chapter builds upon earlier work that explored the model of community-based care, initially pioneered in Florida. It explores the changing landscape of long-term care policy in European postindustrial nations.

CHAPTER FIFTY-FIVE

Web Book: Between Humans and Ghosts

The Decrepit Elderly in a Polynesian Society

Judith C. Barker

Available at: http://www.culturalcontextofaging.com/webbook-barker

Judith Barker explores here the ends of life in the Polynesian island of Niue. She details the paradox of how a society known for its beneficent treatment of the healthy aged and disabled young could show seemingly heartless disregard of the unfit elderly.

About the Editor and Contributors

Jay Sokolovsky, PhD, is professor of anthropology at the University of South Florida St. Petersburg. He is a cultural anthropologist with specialties in the anthropology of aging, psychological/medical anthropology, the globalization of indigenous Mexico, urban anthropology, and video documentation. His research has been done in a Mexican indigenous community; New York City; Baltimore; Florida's Tampa Bay region; the new town of Columbia, Maryland; Croatia; and England. This research has been funded by NIMH, NIH, NSF, UNESCO, the U.S. Census Bureau, the Reed Foundation, and the Florida Humanities Council. In 2013 he was awarded the Textor Award for Anticipatory Anthropology by the American Anthropological Association for his pioneering research and publications in the anthropology of aging and the creation of the first full multimedia-enabled ethnographic book in anthropology. He is the author of numerous articles and five books including *Old Men of the Bowery* (1989) and *Indigenous Mexico Engages the 21st Century* (2015).

Steven M. Albert is professor and chair of the Department of Behavioral and Community Health Sciences in the Graduate School of Public Health at the University of Pittsburgh. He has conducted fieldwork in Papua New Guinea, Sri Lanka, and Israel. He focuses mainly on the social determinants of health in aging, with a particular interest in interventions that address health disparities. He is currently examining ways to use the hospital electronic health record to improve community health and develop targeted interventions for vulnerable populations.

Felicity Aulino, PhD, MPH, is a five-college assistant professor based at the University of Massachusetts Amherst, Department of Anthropology. Her ethnographic work in Thailand focuses on care, morality, subjectivity, and social change. In *Rituals of Care: Karmic Politics in an Aging Thailand* (2019, Cornell

University Press), she explores habituated practices of providing for others at individual, interpersonal, and collective levels—along with the historical antecedents, political associations, and transformative potential of such acts.

Jenny-Anne Bishop, OBE, is a retired chemist, a volunteer worker for the transgender/LGBT communities, and an elder of the URC LGBT-congregation Manchester.

Amy Clotworthy received an MA in applied cultural analysis and a PhD in ethnology, both from the University of Copenhagen (Denmark). Her doctoral research focused on how the Danish state's political goals and health policies affect the real-life interactions between health professionals and aging citizens in the context of home-based programs for the elderly. Amy is interested in how health infrastructures, public health initiatives, and new technologies are entangled in the everyday practices of both health professionals and citizens.

Cati Coe is a professor of anthropology at Rutgers University. Her research focuses on transnational migration, care, and education in West Africa. She is the author of *The New American Servitude: Political Belonging among African Immigrant Home Care Workers* (2019) and *The Scattered Family: African Migrants, Parenting and Global Inequality* (2013). She was a coeditor of *Transnational Aging and Reconfigurations of Kin Work* (2017) and *Everyday Ruptures: Children, Youth, and Migration in Global Perspective* (2011).

Doris Francis holds a PhD in anthropology and social gerontology and has taught at the New School, the Cleveland Institute of Art, and the University of North London where she was a visiting professor. She is presently the chair of the Cemetery Committee of the Jewish Community Council of Northern New Mexico, where she raises funds to improve the Jewish section of her local cemetery and has turned this once-neglected site into a sacred space of community pride, ownership, and historical heritage. She is also a research associate at the Museum of International Folk Art. She has published books and scholarly articles on topics ranging from a comparison of how different ethnic groups (Greek Orthodox, Orthodox Jewish, Church of England—churched and unchurched, Muslims, and Irish Catholics) use London cemeteries as sites of memory and memorialization; to the Alexander Girard Collection of amulets and *milagros*; to how retirees make occupational folk dealing with their former world of work to ease the retirement transition; to older women, dress, and identity. Her book, *Will You Still Need Me, Will You Still Feed Me, When I'm 84?*, a comparative study of the lives of the elderly from the same towns in Eastern Europe who settled in Cleveland, Ohio, and Leeds, England, was selected by *Choice* as an "outstanding academic book." She has also earned additional advanced degrees in horticulture and botany from the Royal Botanic Gardens, Kew, and in the conservation of historic parks, gardens, and cemeteries from the Architectural Association.

Wan He is head of the Aging Research Program at the U.S. Census Bureau. Her main research focus is the U.S. and global population aging process and socio-demographic-health characteristics of the older population. She has extensive experience conducting large dataset analyses and has published numerous analytical reports on population aging, including the series of *65+ in the United States, An Aging World* and *Health and Well-being in SAGE Countries*, and reports such as *Subjective Well-being of Eldercare Providers* and *Older Americans with a Disability*. She has also contributed to the *Encyclopedia of Gerontology and Population Aging*.

Andrea Kaiser-Grolimund is a research associate and lecturer in the field of medical anthropology at the Institute of Social Anthropology, University of Basel, Switzerland and the Swiss Tropical and Public Health Institute. Her areas of interests include aging, (cancer) care, human animal health, migration, middle classes, and urban anthropology. She completed her dissertation titled "The New Old Urbanites. Care and Transnational Aging in Dar es Salaam, Tanzania" within the frame of a Swiss National Science Foundation funded research project.

Philip Y. Kao is a research associate in the Department of Anthropology at the University of Pittsburgh. He obtained his PhD from the University of St Andrews and is a lifetime member of the Association for Anthropology, Gerontology, and the Life Course (AAGE). Additionally, he served several years as an editor for the journal *Anthropology & Aging*. He is a former University of Pittsburgh Provost Postdoctoral Fellow and has taught a variety of college courses at the University of Pittsburgh and Harvard University.

Iza Kavedžija is a lecturer in anthropology at the University of Exeter. She specializes in the anthropology of Japan, particularly meaning in later life, life choices, well-being and creativity. Her monograph examining the experience of aging among older people in Osaka, entitled *Meaning in Life: Tales from Aging Japan*, is published by University of Pennsylvania Press.

Kevin Kinsella was a study director with the National Academy of Sciences Committee on Population, where he oversaw congressionally mandated examinations of the long-run macroeconomic implications of population aging in the United States. His previous career was with the U.S. federal government, most recently with the National Institute on Aging where he managed grants relating to demography and sociology. Prior to working at the

NIA, Kinsella headed the Aging Studies Branch within the Census Bureau's International Programs Center. He undertook his graduate coursework in sociology at Cornell University.

Jordan Kondo is currently a Fulbright Fellow at Okinawa International University and research associate at the Okinawa Research Center for Longevity Science and the Kuakini Honolulu Heart Program. After graduating from the University of Southern California with a BS in human biology and minor in Japanese, he has been living in Japan and researching the interaction between lifestyle, genetics, and longevity in Okinawa, Japan.

Sarah Lamb is professor of anthropology at Brandeis University. She received a BA in religious studies from Brown University and a PhD in anthropology from the University of Chicago. Her books include *White Saris and Sweet Mangoes: Aging, Gender, and Body in North India; Aging and the Indian Diaspora: Cosmopolitan Families in India and Abroad;* and (as editor) *Successful Aging as a Contemporary Obsession.* Her research has been recognized with several major awards, including a 2019 Carnegie Fellowship.

Mark Luborsky, PhD, is director of Aging & Health Disparities Research, Institute of Gerontology; professor of anthropology and gerontology at Wayne State University; and professor of gerontology, Department of Neurobiology, Care Sciences & Society, at the Karolinska Institute Medical University, Sweden. He publishes on critical theory, research design and analyses, and interventions. His work is funded by the NIH, Department of Defense, CDC, USAID, and Sweden, China, Rwanda, and Thailand. He serves on the Johns Hopkins/Harvard University Mixed Methods Research Training program and was editor of *Medical Anthropology Quarterly: International Journal for Analyses of Health.*

Caitrin Lynch, PhD, is professor of anthropology at Olin College of Engineering in Massachusetts. She is the author of *Retirement on the Line: Age, Work, and Value in An American Factory* (2012, Cornell), which has been translated into German and Japanese. She is also the author *Juki Girls, Good Girls: Gender and Cultural Politics in Sri Lanka's Global Garment Industry* (2007, Cornell). She is producer of the documentary film, *My Name Is Julius,* about a 100-year-old man who was deaf and worked until his last days to do good for others.

David Prendergast is a social anthropologist and professor of science, technology, and society at Maynooth University in Ireland where he is currently head of the Department of Design Innovation. Previously David worked at Intel where he was a principal investigator at the Technology Research for

Independent Living Centre and cofounder of the Intel Institute for Sustainable Connected Cities. He has also served as visiting professor of healthcare innovation at the School of Nursing and Midwifery at Trinity College Dublin. His latest book, *Aging and the Digital Life Course* edited with Chiara Garattini, was named a CHOICE Outstanding Academic Title by the American Library Association.

Joel Michael Reynolds is an assistant professor of philosophy at the University of Massachusetts Lowell and the 2017–2020 Rice Family Fellow in Bioethics and Humanities at the Hastings Center. His work explores the relationship between ethics, society, and embodiment. He is especially concerned with the meaning of disability and the issue of ableism, and how philosophical inquiry into each might improve the lives of people with disabilities and the justness of social institutions ranging from medicine to politics.

Marta Rodríguez-Galán is associate professor of sociology at St. John Fisher College, where she also directs the gerontology program. For over a decade, she has been conducting research on aging and health with a particular focus on Hispanic/Latino communities in the United States. She is currently researching civic engagement among low-income older Latinos and the benefits of college-based intergenerational programs for students, elders, and community agencies.

Matthew Rosenbaum, MD, is a pathologist at Beth Israel Deaconess Medical Center in Boston. His research in Okinawa was accomplished with a Fulbright Fellowship at Okinawa International University and through serving as a research associate at the Okinawa Research Center for Longevity Science.

Andrea Sankar, a medical anthropologist, is professor and chair of anthropology at Wayne State University. She is author of *Dying at Home* and, with Jaber Gubrium, editor of *The Home Care Experience* and *Qualitative Methods in Aging Research*; and cofounder of the Social Work and Anthropology (SWAN) doctoral program.

Phillip B. Stafford received his PhD from Indiana University. He is adjunct professor, Department of Anthropology, faculty affiliate at the Ostrom Workshop in Political Theory and Policy, and the retired director of the Center on Aging and Community, at Indiana University. He is a past president of the Association for Anthropology and Gerontology. His major publications include *Gray Areas: Ethnographic Encounters with Nursing Home Culture* (2003: SAR Press), *Elderburbia: Aging with a Sense of Place in America* (2009: Praeger) and *The Global Age-Friendly Community Movement: A Critical Perspective* (2018, Berghahn).

Sandra Staudacher is a medical anthropologist and lawyer with expertise in social and cultural aspects of health, aging, and care. Since 2018 she has had a postdoc position at the Institute of Nursing Science (INS) at the University of Basel (UNIBAS). Before joining the INS she was a lecturer and PhD candidate at the Institute of Social Anthropology and member of the Graduate School of Gender Studies at UNIBAS. She wrote her dissertation "Cosmopolitan Aging in Urban Zanzibar: Elderhood, Health and Transnational Care Spaces Related to Oman" in the frame of a Swiss National Science Foundation funded project. Sandra Staudacher completed her BA and MA studies in social anthropology and law at UNIBAS and the University of Lausanne. From 2015 to 2016 she was a research fellow at Harvard Medical School. At the Swiss Tropical and Public Health Institute she collaborated as scientific assistant (2016) and as consultant (2017). From 2013 to 2014 she was a visiting lecturer at the State University of Zanzibar. Besides her academic activities, she worked as a legal consultant and program manager counseling asylum seekers with the Red Cross Switzerland and HEKS (2009–2012).

Makoto Suzuki, MD, PhD, is a cardiologist and geriatrician. He is professor emeritus and former director of the Department of Community Medicine at the University of the Ryukyus in Okinawa, Japan. Currently, he is director of the Okinawa Research Center for Longevity Science. He is the founder and principal investigator of the Okinawa Centenarian Study. Dr. Suzuki has more than 700 scientific publications and was recently presented with the Nishi-Nihon News Award in recognition of his lifetime contributions to health and well-being in Japan.

Gerard A. Weber is an associate professor in the Department of Social Sciences at Bronx Community College of the City University of New York. He completed his doctorate in cultural anthropology at the Graduate Center of the City University of New York in 2009. He has conducted research on the lives of pensioners in Galați, Romania, in the aftermath of the communist period, focusing on the impact of the transformation to capitalism. His research has been published in *Human Organization: Journal of the Society for Applied Anthropology; Anthropology Now; Synergy; Transylvanian Review; Analize: Journal of Gender and Feminist Studies;* and online.

Sue Westwood is a social gerontology scholar working as a lecturer in law at York Law School, University of York. Her interests are aging, gender, sexuality and law; human rights, old age housing and care; and death rights.

Bradley J. Willcox, MD, MSc, FGSA, is professor and director of research at the Department of Geriatric Medicine, John A. Burns School of Medicine, University of Hawaii, at the Kuakini Medical Center (KMC) Campus. He also is director of the NIH-funded KMC Center of Biomedical Research Excellence for Clinical and Translational Research on Aging, principal investigator of the KMC Hawaii Lifespan Study and KMC Hawaii Healthspan Study, and co-principal investigator of the Okinawa Centenarian Study.

D. Craig Willcox, PhD, MHSc, FGSA, is professor and chair of the Department of Human Welfare at Okinawa International University in Okinawa, Japan. He has extensive research experience in cross-cultural gerontology and medical anthropology, particularly in Japan and Hawaii, specializing in biocultural and epidemiological approaches to healthy aging. Dr. Willcox has been studying genetic and lifestyle factors associated with healthy aging and longevity for over three decades and has successfully established numerous cross-national research collaborations through the U.S. National Institute on Aging and projects supported by national funding agencies in Japan, such as the Japan Society for Promotion of Sciences, among other sources. He currently serves as co-principal investigator of the Okinawa Centenarian Study as well as a co-investigator for several studies on aging from the Okinawa Research Center for Longevity Science and the Kuakini Honolulu Heart Program.

James Wright is an anthropologist of technology whose PhD project looked at the development and use of care robots in Japan. He is currently Michelin Fellow at the Centre for French-Japanese Advanced Studies in Paris, where his research focuses on public innovation policy in Japan.

Hong Zhang, PhD, is associate professor of East Asian studies at Colby College in Waterville, Maine. She completed her doctorate in anthropology from Columbia University. Her research interests include changing family life and marriage patterns, the effects of China's one-child policy, population aging, intergenerational relations and eldercare patterns, rural-urban migration, and urbanization in contemporary China.

Index

Note: Page numbers in *italic* indicate figures/photos/boxes.

Abandonment, 152; of elderly (Thailand), 239; of parents (China), 257; spaces of (Japan), 218–220, 226

Abkhasia, 518–519

Ableism, 531, 658, 660–661; definition of, 658; robots and (cyborg ableism), xviii. *See also* Disability; Impairment

Active aging, xix, 50–52, 436, 481–483. *See also* Successful aging

Activism: in Detroit, 369–370, 377–379, *378*; greening programs, 497–498, 504–506; resilience and, 377–379

Activities of daily living, 139–141, 617–618; defined, 626 n.6; Denmark, 617–618; Okinawan elderly, 563; robotic assistance, 139–140; support stockings, putting on, 621–623, *621*, 626 nn.8–9

Adat (matrilineal customary law), 427

Adult children: caregiving in Ghana, 151–152; daughters in patrilineal households, 426; eldercare anxieties of, 253, 257, 349; eldercare responsibility, 100, 213–214, 253, 257–258; filial piety, xxviii, 201, 257, 257–258, 269–270, 345, 348–349; gender equity and daughters in China, 261; Indian, 469–472, *470*, 485–486; joint family system (India), 469–470, *470*, 481, 483–484

Affrilachian Elder Club, *325–327*

Africa, xxxviii, 30; demographics, 6, 7, 27, 637; fertility rate, 36–37, *36*; Ju/'hoansi, 9–12, 20 n.3; life expectancy, 637; median age, 31, 32; Tanzania, 529, 633–656; youth of population, 7, 27, 30, 31, 637. *See also* Transnational spaces of aging

African American elderly, 339–340, 353; Detroit African Americans, fishing, 365–382; Seattle, xxx, 339; women, 339–340; women, kin-keeping role, 339–340. *See also* Detroit African Americans

African Americans: churches, 340; Detroit, Michigan, 365–382; ethnic identities, 381; families, 353; Hamer, Fannie Lou, 377; kinship boundaries, 353; migrations of, 372–373, 380; multiple jeopardy of, 339; segregation and, 324

Age: global elderly population, *4*; global median, 31–32, *33*; measures